Explaining Crime

Fourth Edition

Paul S. Maxim
Paul C. Whitehead
The University of Western Ontario

Butterworth–Heinemann
Boston   Oxford   Johannesburg   Melbourne   New Delhi   Singapore

Butterworth–Heinemann supports the efforts of American Forests and the Global
ReLeaf program in its campaign for the betterment of trees, forests, and our environment.

Explaining Crime, Fourth Edition, by Paul S. Maxim and Paul C. Whitehead, is based on
Explaining Crime (1974), by Gwynne Nettler; *Explaining Crime,* Second Edition (1978), by
Gwynne Nettler; and *Explaining Crime,* Third Edition (1984), by Gwynne Nettler.

Library of Congress Cataloging-in-Publication Data
Maxim, Paul S., 1950–
    Explaining crime / Paul S. Maxim, Paul C. Whitehead.—4th ed.
      p.   cm.
    Rev. ed. of: Explaining crime / Gwynne Nettler. 3rd ed. 1984.
    Includes bibliographical references and index.
    ISBN 0-7506-9784-9 (alk. paper)
    1. Criminology. I. Whitehead, Paul C. (Paul Charles) 1942–   .
    II. Nettler, Gwynne. Explaining crime. III. Title.
    HV6025.M372 1998   97-32804
    364—DC21   CIP

British Library Cataloguing-in-Publication Data
A catalogue record for this book is available from the British Library.

To our mentors and our students

Contents

Preface

"The seeds of every crime are in each of us," Leo Tolstoy believed. The point of Tolstoy's aphorism is to indicate a possibility common to all of us. The poverty of his statement is that it does not describe *how* the criminal seeds are germinated. We have disputes about this, and the victim in the accompanying cartoon is no more confused in his response to crime than many of us.

Quarrels about morals are common, and particularly so in mobile, heterogeneous populations. In such aggregates, and beyond some fluctuating core of consensus, people dispute which acts are wrong, and which wrongs should be considered crimes. The struggle about induced abortion is but one example.

Moral quarrel translates into ambivalence about crime, even such common law crimes as larceny and murder. Publics selectively condemn and praise thieves and killers. Big robberies, carried off with panache, are cheered. O. J. Simpson appeared on 90 magazine covers in 1995. Fraud is both decried and excused, particularly in the political arena. Concern for victims and for the maintenance of social order is countered with concern for the plight of offenders and for the oppression, alleged or demonstrable, deemed to cause their criminal activity. The citizenry argues whether the violence of conditions justifies the violence of persons, and juries debate whether crimes "understandably motivated" should be pardoned.

Intellectuals—the occupationally thoughtful—join the fray. They too can be heard condemning and recommending arson, theft, and murder, depending on their agreement with the political motives of perpetrators and their approval or disapproval of victims.

As succeeding chapters show, criminologists participate in these debates. We dispute what should be called crime and how to count it. We quarrel, too, about where to look for causes.

Biopsychologists examine differences—neurochemical and psychological—between persons who are more and less criminal. Economists who apply their vocation to the study of crime assume that many (most?) people are rational. They therefore regard stealing, dealing, and some kinds of killing as more rewarding than costly for some actors.

Psychoanalysts disagree. They tend to think of most (all?) offenders as "sick" and in need of treatment.[1]

[1.] A Stanford University professor of law and psychiatry writes, "The next step . . . is to expand the principle of limited or diminished responsibility of the mentally ill offender to include all definitions of crime. . . . The ultimate step will be the extension of the treatment principle to all prisoners—sane, insane, fully responsible, and partially responsible" (Diamond 1961–1962: 68).

Social psychologists are a mixed tribe. Some attribute behavior to particular mental activities called "believing," "valuing," or "interpreting the situation." Others attend to the processes, called *socialization,* that presumably shape behavior as persons develop. And a few social psychologists appreciate human action as generated by individual constitutions that meet, and make, social environments to which they then respond.

Anthropologists and sociologists are seldom interested in individual personalities that select and produce environments. They prefer to look to social structures as forces that mold conduct, and they identify culture as a particular kind of structure into which one is born and by which one is nurtured.

A political aspect of the sociological orientation attributes behavior to circumstance, particularly to one's position in a power structure. This explanatory attitude blames criminal activity on moral entrepreneurs who are said to have the power to define crime, to enforce their definitions through police and courts, and to label people criminal or crazy. Advocates of this perspective call for redistribution of power, and they condemn elected officials who presumably have the knowledge, ability, and obligation to remedy disapproved circumstance.

It is unfortunate for explanatory simplicity, and for neat political prescription, that all criminological theories rest on notions of causation. They do so implicitly or explicitly, and sometimes reluctantly, but, *au fond,* theories point to causes.

However, causation is itself a difficult and multifaceted idea. We shall contend that there is more than one concept of "causing," and that morals affect the location of causes.

Social inquiry is made particularly difficult by the fact that no reader of this book is an intellectual virgin, and neither were its authors, before or after writing it. The American psychologist William James assured us that temperaments select philosophies, and recent research verifies his hypothesis.[2] All of us bring ethicopolitical preferences[3] to our study of human activity. This makes dispassionate inquiry about how we are, and how we come to be that way, tough work. If, however, we strive to be scholarly, then we attempt the difficult task of controlling ourselves, and we put truth-seeking first and moral concern second. Fact trumps wish.

Some students of social affairs title themselves "scientists." Among them, theories are tested for adequacy by their contribution to the prediction and control of human action. It will be seen that most explanations of criminal conduct fail this test.[4]

It is recommended, then, that criminology be studied as a liberating exercise, one that expands awareness of what people do and of how we think about the actions of others and our own. Despite the different theoretical emphases described in following chapters, we know something about the generators of

---

[2.] James (1906: 488, 501). For research vindicating James's intuition, see Provine (1973).

[3.] *Ethicopolitical* is our neologism employed to indicate that all political positions have ethical implications and that moral concerns takepolitical form.

[4.] Bernard (1990).

behavior. But our knowledge is not sufficient to justify a technology of social engineering.

Subsequent chapters address three principal issues: *definition, measurement,* and *explanation* of criminal conduct. Throughout our exposition, the attitude is critical. Criticism rests on three standards: *clarity* of concepts, *quality* of evidence, and *utility* of theory for public policy.

All the explanations to be described say some true things. However, the prices we pay when we believe one explanation rather than another vary.

Our discourse concludes with a statement about conditions that generate more and less crime, and we add some of our own lessons derived from our excursion.

Acknowledgments

It is one of life's ironies that the preparation of a text on explanations of human conflict should itself involve conflict. Despite great aspirations and good intentions, there was a time when it appeared that this work would not see completion. Yet, as with the task of explaining crime, hope springs eternal and the book now exists.

In all that we do there are many who deserve credit and is some cases they remain in our hearts and minds rather than on the page. This is the case here. We have been exceedingly fortunate to start with an excellent work that has shaped our thinking and has been used in our teaching upon which we could build. Much like Adam Smith's *invisible hand,* the spirit of the creator of those words guided our direction despite his wish to remain anonymous. For that, we are grateful.

We also extend thanks to John Kunke, good friend and colleague, who enhanced our knowledge of learning.

Part I
What Is Crime?

1. Crimes and Other Wrongs

Defining Wrongs: Crime

Crime is one of the words used to describe the wrongs we do ourselves and others. *Wrong* is, of course, a moral term. It represents an evaluation of acts or conditions, rather than a description of them. Definitions of crime rest, then, on moral grounds, and the meaning of the word moves with moral judgment. Consequently, there is no essence of criminality to be observed in an act or situation.

The roster of conceivable wrongs is enormous, and the word crime does not encompass all the damage done. In its legal sense, crime refers only to those injuries condemned by the criminal code of a state and prosecuted by a government. Because there are so many possible wrongs and because crime denotes only a select sample of all disapproved acts, the definition of crime varies from time to time and from place to place, and there is continuing controversy about what should or should not be called crime. The laws and morals that dictate which wrongs are to be dealt with as crimes are themselves under challenge in changing societies.

How the Notion of Crime Develops

Sin

The general idea out of which the notion of crime has developed is a moral idea, the concept of sin. *Sin* is a breach of divine law, an offense against the commandment of God. Sin is not a popular word among social scientists, but the moral motive that defines some acts as sin persists in the definition of crime.

Vice

Another conception of wrong that affects the definition of crime is the notion of vice. A *vice* is the wrongful use of one's appetites. According to some observers, the harmful or degrading satisfaction of our desires is vice when we do not know we are acting badly and sin when we do (Brock 1960: 34).

Notions of sin and vice may be uncomfortable for some modern thinkers, but both concepts underlie the idea of crime. Quarrels about which wrongs should be considered crimes and about the relative gravity of crimes remain moral quarrels. The idea of crime starts with some conception of proper behavior. The conception of proper behavior may be justified by reference to divine commandments or to naturalistic ethics, but a moral conception is at the root of the idea of crime.

Shifting Morals and Changing Crimes

Morals change, whether or not we approve of this, and with the changes go variations in the content of crime. The broad boundaries of offenses against property, person, and society remain fairly steady, but the criminal content within these boundaries varies. In 1934, the American financier Samuel Insull expressed the point this way:

> If two men walked down Fifth Avenue a year ago—that would have been March 1933—and one of them had a pint of whiskey in his pocket and the other had a hundred dollars in gold coin, the one with the whiskey would have been called a criminal and the one with the gold an honest citizen. If these two men, like Rip Van Winkle, slept for a year and again walked down Fifth Avenue, the man with the whiskey would be called an honest citizen and the one with the gold coin a criminal. (Schultz 1972: 135–136)

Despite such interesting variations in the definition of crime, all societies recognize some kinds of property appropriation as theft, whether the property is deemed to belong to the gods, the state, or individuals. Similarly, all societies define some kinds of killing of its members as murder and some kinds of disloyalty to the group as treason. The particular acts and circumstances that constitute theft, murder, and treason fluctuate, however, and in changing societies the meanings of these terms are contested.

Example: The Vocabulary of Homicide.   The conflict over whose wrong should be a crime is reflected in the names we give to the killing of other people. The word we use to refer to a homicide indicates whether the killing is justified or deplored. For example, *murder* is the name for legally unjustified, intentional homicide. The word has a *legal* meaning—homicide that the criminal law calls crime. Yet it also has a *moral* meaning—homicide that is disapproved. Thus, when terrorists kill their enemies or the symbols of their enemies in the form of innocent bystanders, they absolve themselves from blame for murder by calling their killing *execution.* Elevating homicide to execution makes a claim for its justice; reducing homicide to murder denies the fairness with which death is dealt.

BIERCE ON HOMICIDE

The cynical journalist Ambrose Bierce (1842–1914?) placed in his *Devil's Dictionary* this definition of homicide: *Homicide,* n. the slaying of one human being by another. There are four kinds of homicide: felonious, excusable, justifiable, and praiseworthy, but it makes no great difference to the person slain whether he fell by one kind or another—the classification is for the purposes of the lawyers.

The quarrel in semantics is apparent also in the debate about abortion. Those who oppose the legality of induced abortion call it murder. Those who favor legal access to abortion speak of "terminating pregnancy" or "removing tissue." Those who are pro-life say that life begins with the fertilized egg. Those who are pro-choice distinguish between stages in the development of human life: they refer to a zygote (a fertilized ovum), an embryo (up to the last part of the third month of pregnancy), and a fetus (during the remainder of pregnancy). The point is that different vocabularies reflect different moralities.

No facts will resolve such a moral debate, because life and death are matters of definition, and definitions can be *chosen*, as Humpty Dumpty told Alice. In matters of right and wrong, morals, not facts, decide definitions. Being "murdered" or "executed," and being alive or dead, are more than matters of passing some observational or physiological test. They are also matters of social definition.

Every society sets boundaries to what it considers life and death, justifiable homicide and murder. Ordinarily we do not notice that we have *defined* such issues. Our daily definitions are conventional, and the meanings to which we have become accustomed are part of us. Occasions do arise, however, when a *decision rule* is required—that is, an official definition that permits action. For example, Sudnow reports that for an American hospital

> an expelled fetus is either considered "human" or not. . . . The dividing line is 550 grams, 20 centimeters, and 20 weeks of gestation. Any creature having smaller dimensions or of lesser embryonic "age" is considered non-human . . . and if "born" without signs of life, is properly flushed down the toilet, or otherwise simply disposed of. . . . Any creature having larger dimensions or of greater embryonic "age" is considered human, and if "born" without signs of life, or if born with signs of life which cease to be noticeable at some later point, cannot be permissibly flushed down the toilet, but must be accorded a proper ritual departure from the human race. (1966: 176–177)

Morality and Self-Interest.   To show that our morals define wrongs is disturbing, particularly when others challenge our morality and its preferred definitions. All contestants in moral disputes like to think that their preferences are divinely ordained, historically progressive, based on facts, or justified by some combination of these virtues. It is probable, however, that our morals, and hence our conceptions of crime, are learned preferences that define our ethnic and personal identity. Morals support self-interest, at least in the sense that a shared morality is valuable for personal identity, for knowing how to act. Apart from this grounding in self-interest, though, it is doubtful that concrete results, or other facts, affect morals as much as morals select facts to support ethical preferences.

Defining Victims

How Concepts of Victims Affect Concepts of Crime

The grounding of conceptions of crime in conceptions of wrong means that defining crime is easiest when there is an identifiable victim. Moreover, it is easiest to define crime when the identifiable victim is one of "our people" rather than an alien or an enemy. It becomes more difficult to define crime, however, when the victim is a collection of individuals—a corporation or a university, for example. It is a commentary on our honesty that even "good" people find it easy to steal if the victims are not visible persons but invisible collections of anonymous others. Not only is stealing from organizations—such as the government, insurance companies, or the phone company—a common practice, but it also does not appear to be theft to many noncriminal people. If an organization is big enough, and distant, guilt about stealing from it diminishes (Smigel and Ross 1970: 34). Modern pirates focus their energies on popular computer software and consider their gains to come at no cost to Microsoft or other large companies. Vocabularies shift, again, to express differences in our moral appreciation of such acts, and stealing is translated as "expropriation" or "ripping off." Euphemism relieves conscience, and, conversely, the words we use to describe the wrongs we do reveal whether there is a conscience to be relieved.

VICTIMLESS CRIME?

Famed country singer Johnny Cash had a popular song, *One Piece at a Time*, about an auto worker who helped himself to pieces of cars that he assembled into an unusual hybrid. Taking parts at this rate from a large company allowed him to claim that this did not constitute stealing.

There is a further anomaly in our attitude toward crime. If the crime is carried off with flair and if the prey is big government, big business, or some detested victim like the stodgy rich—and if, in addition, the thieves are people with whom we can romantically identify, like Robin Hood, Robert Redford, or Paul Newman (for example, see the film *Butch Cassidy and the Sundance Kid*)—then thuggery is less likely to be considered criminal and more likely to be thought of as belonging to another category of sin or adventure. To many citizens in Washington, DC, for example, Marion Barry is a political and social hero who breaks rules that are only thought important by prosecutors and other outsiders (Fineman 1994: 40–41).

A measure of this differential definition of some "big" crimes is that neither their perpetrators nor large segments of their audience seem to regard them as criminal. Thus the first American skyjacker to parachute with an extorted fortune immediately became a folk hero, his name emblazoned on T-shirts and his act imitated by others.

A similar attitude is witnessed in the case of a small-town banker who allegedly stole about $5 million. Many of his acquaintances said they felt, "Well, he got caught and should be punished, but he is still a good old guy" (Maxwell 1972, 1973). A comparable attitude was expressed toward a Midwestern stockbroker who misused securities in his trust and left four brokerage houses and a bank with losses of about $39 million. Despite his frauds, the broker's flamboyant life made him a folk hero. Songs were written about him, T-shirts printed, and lapel buttons flaunted. One songwriter titled his piece, "Take the Money and Run: Outlaw Ballad No. 23." The balladeer explained the local popularity of his song by saying, "America loves its outlaws, but here in Iowa we do not really get our share" (Minsky 1982).

Bandits, ancient and modern, have always had their defenders and their prosecutors. In the public eye there have been "noble robbers" as well as monsters. Much depends on who the victim is and how the bandit handles himself or herself. Thus the poet dos Santos has eulogized the modern Brazilian robber Lampeao by claiming that, although he "killed for play and out of pure perversity," he also "gave food to the hungry" (dos Santos 1959).

A MODERN DAY ROBIN HOOD

A modern day female Robin Hood rose to fame in the northern Indian province of Uttar Pradesh. Phoona Devi was born in a poor village where her family were members of the fisher caste, a group slightly above the untouchables. She was married off by her father at age 11, but soon ran away from her husband. In 1979, at age 21, she was kidnapped by dacoit bandits, who are viewed by many in India as occupying a Robin Hood role—stealing from the rich to give to the poor. She was raped by the gang leader, then rescued when the leader was shot by a fellow outlaw. Devi's benefactor was himself murdered and a three-week gang-rape followed before Devi was rescued again, this time by a priest. Seeking revenge, she organized her own band of dacoits. In February 1981, this group went after Devi's tormentors. Twenty-two upper-caste village men were executed along the banks of the Yambuna River. It is from this episode that the legend of Devi was born. Pursued by the police, she surrendered in 1983 and spent the next 11 years in jail. In 1996, while on parole, she was elected a member of Parliament, defeating a member of the ruling Congress Party. In the same year, an internationally acclaimed movie, *The Bandit Queen*, was made depicting her life story.

There is, of course, some threshold of tolerance for glamorous banditry beyond which a community rebels, depending on how many, and who, get hurt. It will be a recurring theme of this book that some crimes are rational; they achieve objectives. Consequently many citizens look upon crime with a schizoid attitude, condemning it when they or their revered institutions are damaged and praising it when the victims are despised or the predators seem heroic. In short, when wrongs are done, "victims" are variously defined. Some wrongdoers are themselves considered victims of circumstance, pressured into their wicked ways and therefore more to be understood than blamed. Yet other malefactors are deemed to be "persons," responsible for their decisions to do wrong and therefore blameworthy.

Those who are injured are also variously evaluated. Some are held to be victims, while others are not. Sometimes we believe that an injured person "deserved what she got" or "contributed to his own misfortune." A judgment like this makes such a contributory actor less innocent and hence less of a victim, as with prosperous victims of some scams (see Box 1.1).

Conclusion: Spreading the Pain Reduces the Blame

Defining a victim depends, then, on attributions of responsibility and conceptions of harm. If criminal damage is dispersed among us so that no one person seems to be injured, our sense of offense is diminished. If, in addition, everyone seems to profit in the short run, the wrong becomes difficult to discern. However, crime that lacks immediately apparent victims may still have high social costs—that is, we all pay for such crime in the end.

Example: Automobile Theft and Automobile Insurance Fraud.   Automobile theft is a prime example of crime with reduced immediate pain, high profit, and long-term costs. No one appears hurt much by the stealing and fencing of automobiles and automobile parts. The victim is inconvenienced, but is compensated for the loss by insurance. Car thieves are seldom punished. Purchasers of "laundered" vehicles get a good deal, and the insurance companies pass the costs of this crime back to the consumers of automobiles in higher premiums.

With the damage so distributed, victims are difficult to define, and automobile theft continues to be a profitable business. In 1995, 1.5 million vehicles

---

Box 1.1 Example of a "Nigerian Oil" Scam Letter

Strictly Confidential
Alhaji Abba Gana
Lagos, Nigeria

Dear Sir, REQUEST FOR URGENT BUSINESS RELATIONSHIP

I am an Executive Director with the Nigerian National Petroleum Corporation (NNPC) and a member of an ad-hoc committee set up by the Federal Government of Nigeria to review contracts awarded by the past military administration between 1985–1993. . . .

Our request is anchored on our strong desire to establish a lasting business relationship with you and your company. We hence solicit your partnership to enable us transfer into your account the said funds. You have been recommended to us in confidence and we were assured of your ability and reliability to prosecute business transactions that require maximum confidentiality.

I have therefore been mandated . . . to look for a foreign partner into whose account we could transfer the sum of US$25,320,000 . . . hence I am writing you this letter. We have agreed to share the funds thus:

(1) 65% for us (the committee members)

(2) 25% for account owner (you)

(3) 10% to be used in settling taxation and all local and foreign expenses that will be incurred in the course of this transaction.

It is from the 65% that we wish to commence the importation business. Please note that this transaction is 100% safe and guaranteed since the law under which our committee was set up has empowered us to disburse all the funds found to be floating in the Central bank of Nigeria redundant accounts from 1985 till date. . . .

Yours faithfully,

Alhaji A. Gana

NB: This letter is being sent by ordinary mail for confidentiality purposes.

---

were stolen in the United States. It is estimated that the value of vehicle theft is approximately $7.6 billion—twice that of burglary, robbery, or other high-profile crimes (Wilson 1997).

The high cost of automobile theft is not the only item that inflates automobile insurance costs. It is estimated that up to one-third of all collision-based bodily injury claims involve some element of fraud. Only a small amount consists of outright fraud (e.g., staged accidents); most consists of opportunistic padding of legitimate claims. In total, it is estimated that such activities inflate insurance premiums by 17 to 20%, for a total cost of $6.3 billion (Insurance Information Institute 1997).

Some police officers call automobile theft "happy crime" because everyone seems to profit and no one feels the sting. The point of this example is, again, that crime can have high social costs without immediately apparent individual costs.

Crimes Against Ourselves:
The Notion of Victimless Vice

Difficulties in defining crime do not end with difficulties in defining victims. If it is difficult to recognize wrong where the victim is an unknown aggregation of individuals rather than an identifiable person, it is even more difficult to define injuries that we willingly inflict upon ourselves or upon that vague entity, society. Thus we debate whether licensing or ignoring pornography, sexual aberration, violent television programs, and drugs hurt their consumers and the social order. We quarrel about the right of individuals to harm themselves, and we are not certain how much self-inflicted injury is a threat to society. We are far from clear whether people who damage themselves should be viewed as persons or victims. No matter which definition is accepted, however, it will be a moral definition rather than a purely factual one.

How Concepts of Victimless Vice Affect Concepts of Crime

Since societies differ in morals, they draw different boundaries between persons and victims. A person is one who decides; a victim is one who suffers. A person chooses to act in a certain way; a victim suffers from defective will or from what others decide. Alternatively, it is assumed that a person's choices are informed and therefore beneficial, while a victim's choices are ignorant and therefore harmful.

These definitions are provided by morals, not by facts. They are attributions, not observations. They change, therefore, with moral movements and with "the side we are on." As we will see (Chapter 11), our moral stance also affects the assignment of causation to human action.

Within this shifting boundary between rights and wrongs and between victims and persons, every society defines as criminal some acts that have no apparent individual victims. Every society condemns some violations of religious or ideological commandments, some offenses against public decency, or some threats to its welfare, although no particular person is deemed to have been damaged by such acts.

Despite the universality of laws against offenses that do not immediately harm another person, Western criminologists, but not their Eastern counterparts, have been concerned with defining categories of victimless crime that, it is believed, should be decriminalized. Thus, Schur has questioned the advisability of legal penalties against induced abortion, homosexuality, and drug use (Schur 1965). To this list, Geis adds prostitution and gambling, and urges that

> the most efficacious method of dealing with deviancy is to ignore, to the furthest point of our tolerance, those items which we find offensive. Such response is predicated upon the assumption that there exists in our society a core of values which exert enough appeal to win over the deviant ultimately, or at least to keep him within the society in terms of other aspects of his behavior, provided that he has not been irresolutely shut off from conformant living. (Geis 1972: 261)

Toward preferences for abortion, homosexuality, prostitution, the drug trade, and gambling, Geis advocates "tolerance and flexibility, combined with attitudes designed to encourage and reward desired behavior" (Geis 1972: 262).

Recommendations for decriminalization do not end here, of course. From Sweden, the Netherlands, and Great Britain come additional suggestions for reducing the inventory of crimes. For example, England and Wales removed suicide and attempted suicide from the criminal code in 1961. Canada and the United States, however, continue to condemn aiding and abetting suicide as a serious crime. Such law is now challenged by a British organization called EXIT that is concerned with "easy death." Easy death is not to be confused with euthanasia, which implies assistance of a physician or a nurse in administering a lethal agent. EXIT is interested only in making available drugs and information about them so that individuals may choose the time of their dying. EXIT has prepared a booklet describing effective means of suicide, but the British Medical Association and some lawyers object to the publication of this document (*Lancet* 1980).

Jack Kevorkian, Michigan's "Dr. Death," has fought to make physician-assisted suicide lawful. As of mid-1996, he has assisted in seven suicides, attended at least 34 others, and spent time in court and jail as a result. He has twice been found not guilty. Juries accepted Kevorkian's position that what he did was to help persons alleviate their suffering in a way that resulted in death. The prosecution's view was that he was assisting death to be caused and that the alleviation of pain was simply the consequence of the crime (Martin and Taylor 1996).

Decriminalization is also urged for categories of "sexual offenses" other than homosexuality and prostitution. The Swedish psychiatrist Lars Ullerstam not only recommends decriminalizing so-called perversions, but also advocates state subsidies of facilities for "erotic minorities" (Ullerstam 1966). In a parallel extension of "sexual rights," Tom O'Carroll, head of the Paedophile Information Exchange in England, argues that adults who prefer children as sex partners should not be the object of criminal law (O'Carroll 1980). Although PIE has folded, other organizations such as the North American Man/Boy Love Association (NAMBLA) have taken up the cause (Pascal 1992). At different times two Canadian university professors have publicly argued that sex with children can be a good thing for both parties.

Many criminologists recommend that some so-called "victimless crimes" be taken off the books for both practical and moral reasons. On practical grounds, the overloading of police and courts in Western countries urges that some acts once deemed criminal be differently defined. This has happened in several jurisdictions, for example, in the case of homosexual acts conducted in private between consenting adults.

Furthermore, laws against these behaviors are difficult to enforce, and not spending so much time and energy on them seems practical. Such laws are difficult to enforce because many of these offenses are vices, and vices are pleasures. For the glutton, overeating is a pleasure; for the addict, smoking opium; for the gambler, risk; for the masochist, an encounter with a sadist. Except for induced abortion and some pedophilic relationships, the allegedly victimless crimes involve a self-inflicted injury or a voluntary exchange between a buyer and a seller—as in the drug trade or prostitution. Even some incestuous connections, particularly between brother and sister, are voluntary and considered desirable by their participants (Canadian Press 1995; Santiago 1973; Weinberg 1955).

Since victims of vice are not likely to complain about their pleasures, the police have difficulty finding a plaintiff, and the enforcement of laws against vice requires surveillance rather than response to citizens' complaints. Such enforcement is costly.

These practical reasons for challenging the criminalization of vice are seconded by moral doubts. When individuals choose to harm themselves, philosophers in free societies are placed in a quandary about whether vice is wrong and, right or wrong, whether it deserves legal attention. By contrast, philosophers in totalitarian societies have no such doubts. Totalitarian regimes are bolstered by an ideology and managed by an elite with an unchallenged monopoly of power. The ideology includes moral conceptions of how people should behave. Modern tyrants, therefore, have no hesitation about punishing activities they define as immoral—activities ranging from homosexuality and prostitution to drunkenness, absenteeism from work, the use of narcotics, the expression of "wrong" ideas, and being "corrupters of the earth" (Pahlavi 1980). There is no freedom in Cuba (see Figure 1.1), the People's Republic of China, Iran, or Russia to be a "drag queen," a prostitute, or a dissident. Moreover, there is no public debate in these countries about whether people *should* be free to choose some forms of morally defined self-destruction or to criticize their social orders (Bassiouni 1994; Connor 1972; McColm 1981; Solzhenitsyn 1973, 1975; Tuchman 1972; Zeitlin 1967).

In contrast, the very notion of a free society requires that individuals be responsible for their conduct and, therefore, that the state leave them alone. In this tradition, the psychiatrist Thomas Szasz argues that self-damaging behavior is none of the state's business and that a person who chooses to commit suicide slowly with tobacco, alcohol, or heroin, or more quickly with a gun, should be free to do so

Figure 1.1 Fidel Castro is a revolutionary who exercises tight control over the population of Cuba. Photo courtesy of Corbis.

(Szasz 1961, 1963). Szasz and others believe that enough crimes occur of an interpersonal sort—the damage we do each other—for the state to attend to and that these wrongs are more deserving of official attention. In this liberal tradition, it is also argued that the state that begins to protect individuals from themselves will be difficult to bridle and will progressively intrude upon private lives.

Liberalism and "Victimless Crimes": Liberal Roots

Such doctrines in defense of liberty are historically rare. In modern times Western intellectuals trace their debt to John Stuart Mill (1806–1873) whose famous essay *On Liberty* (1859) attempted to set the proper limits to state power. Mill objected to the state "pushing people around."

MILL ON LIBERTY
The only freedom which deserves the name is that of pursuing our own good in our own way, so long as we do not attempt to deprive others of theirs, or impede their efforts to obtain it. We are the proper guardians of our own health, whether bodily, or mental and spiritual. People are greater gainers by suffering each other to live as seems good to themselves, than by compelling each to live as seems good to the rest. (Mill 1859: 75–76)

People who favor liberty, in this Millian sense, used to be called "liberals," but this fine label has been so stretched in the twentieth century that those who now use it have to specify which kind of liberal they are. Thus some nineteenth-century "small-*l*" liberals who live in the twentieth century have changed their political name to "individualist" or "libertarian" to distinguish themselves from other breeds of modern liberals who have less fear of state power.

The change of title suggests that believing in freedom and practicing consistently what one preaches about restricting state power is difficult. It is difficult for many reasons. One is that we cannot ask the state to do things *for* us without inviting it to do things *to* us. If the state is asked to guard our welfare, it will guard our welfare even when we have not asked it to—as when it protects our health against alcohol, fast cars, and other pleasures.

This is not the only reason why being consistently liberal is difficult. Being a true believer in freedom is also tough because we have to live together as people with different tastes. We therefore cannot help intruding upon one another, and we are constantly redefining the boundaries—called our "rights"—of this intrusion. The issue in criminology is whether the criminal law ought to be used to define and defend these boundaries. It is our thesis that no one can be consistently liberal. At some point all of us ask the state to defend our morals against others'. Saying this recommends nothing. It is a description, not a prescription.

Difficulties in Being Liberal: The Myth of Victimless Vice

The idea of victimless crime has liberal roots. It is connected to the notion of victimless vice. Mill did not call purely personal wrongs by these titles, but he did try to define personally harmful actions that ought not to be anyone's business but the actor's. However, a difficulty with the liberal notion of victimless vice is that victims, like wrongs, are defined. Depending upon the definition, then, of vice and harm, there is often a victim of what seems to be a private act. If our spouses wrong their bodies, we pay a price. If children harm themselves, their parents are victims. If parents are dissolute, their children are victims. If enough individuals harm themselves, society is the victim. In brief, the notion of victimless vice requires that no one influence anyone. As long as someone pays a price for someone else's action, that action is not victimless.

The prices paid can be offenses to one's taste or invasions of one's privacy and purse. They can vary from insults to eye, ear, and nose; to having to wend one's way on public streets through aggressive prostitutes; to having to pay taxes in support of rehabilitation centers for sick addicts. Even our teacher, John Stuart Mill, got himself into this tangle and could not preach his principle with consistency. For example, Mill believed that drunkenness and idleness were none of the state's business unless the drunk was violent or the lazy person was supported by the state, but he also believed that "there are many acts which . . . if done publicly are a violation of good manners, and coming thus within the category of offenses against others, may rightly be prohibited. Of this kind are offences against decency" (Mill 1859:153).

We can all agree with Mill when he remains general, but the minute our legislators become specific, as in their attempts to pass laws concerning obscenity, we are aware that good manners and decency are themselves up for negotiation when we live as one tribe among many under the power of a single state. For example, the psychiatrist Szasz, who (we saw) believes that the state has no right to interfere with those who want to use heroin or otherwise endanger themselves, believes the state does have the right to prevent one person from injuring another. Again, *injury* can be defined, as Mill did, to include offenses against public decency. Thus, Szasz would not allow people to copulate in public (Szasz 1963: 21). In a similar vein, Mill did not believe that allowing people to be free includes the right to sell oneself into slavery, for "by selling himself for a slave, he abdicates his liberty. . . . The principle of freedom cannot require that he should be free not to be free. It is not freedom to be allowed to alienate his freedom" (Mill 1859:158).

This argument—that freedom does not mean the freedom to choose slavery—can be extended, of course, to other ways of "abdicating our liberty." All that is required is a stretching of the word "slave." Thus, moralists have used Mill's principle to oppose the freedom to be a prostitute or an addict. They extend Mill by defining "whoring" and "doping" as forms of slavery. If, according to this liberalism, no one should be free *not* to be free, then the state has a right to intervene.

Conclusion: Lessons of Victimless Crime

We have returned full circle to the theme with which we began: conceptions of crime derive from conceptions of wrong and that the notion of wrong includes ideas of sin and vice. This means that offenses may be committed against oneself, the gods, and society, as well as offenses committed against other individuals.

Given the moral underpinning of the criminal law, all attempts to change concepts of crime encounter moral objections. Thus, while some groups proselytize for freedom for "erotic minorities," others contest this "right" and hold that incest violates "the right to a childhood . . . free of . . . sex abuse" (Muldoon 1979).

A lesson learned from this and similar debate is that words like crime, rights, wrongs, justice, and freedom have no fixed reference. They do not point to any one kind of condition or activity, permanently and universally. What they mean has to be determined each time a person uses such terms. Furthermore, there is no principle by which one can discover what should be, or must be, the content of such words.

Crime, to repeat, is a word applied to someone's conception of wrong. There-fore, if we are to be semantically accurate, there can be no such activity as a vic-timless crime. Putting these two terms together makes no sense—although we recognize the intent of those who have invented the phrase, namely, to remove some laws from criminal codes. Combining these words makes no sense because an act called "criminal" by some individuals is an injury as they conceive it. And the idea of an injury includes someone as a victim.

What is deemed to be an *injury* is another matter. Damages are not merely objectively perceived; they are also subjectively conceived. They may, then, include everything from the major wrongs dealt by fate and wicked people to an inventory of minor wrongs like breaches of etiquette to the unforeseen conse-quences of the plans of well-intentioned, but ignorant, leaders. As we will see (Chapters 12–14), some theories of crime causation direct attention to one set of wrongs rather than another.

In summary, human beings injure one another, and themselves, in countless ways. Some of these ways have been selected for codification as crimes. This fact says that not all wrongs are crimes. It also suggests that some crimes, from someone's perspective, may not be wrong.

Battling About Crime

Our discussion thus far leads to two conclusions: not only is crime rooted in a conception of wrong, but it also seems inescapable that a shifting balance will remain among the wrongs selected for nomination as crimes. It would require a heaven on earth, such as radical criminologists promise, before a society is "[cre-ated] . . . in which the facts of human diversity, whether personal, organic, or social, are not subject to the power to criminalize" (Taylor et al. 1973: 282).

Demand for New Crimes

In Western lands today, the movement to decriminalize many acts that are now illegal is met with demands that other acts that are now lawful be made criminal. It is argued that "complex societies" need more governmental regulation and that regulation is required of "noncontractual behavior that is risky and therefore potentially harmful to others," whether or not there are individual complainants (Pilon 1978).

In recent times, advocates have recommended that new categories of victims be defined and protected by the criminalization of such formerly lawful acts as driving without a seat belt, riding a bicycle without a helmet, adding preservatives to foods, or traveling to third-world countries to have sex with young people. It is also urged that polluting the environment by emitting noise, fumes, or liquid and solid waste is criminal—whether this is done by corporations, governments, or individuals and their animal pets (see Figure 1.2).

Sponsors demand, too, that the publication and distribution of "hate literature" be made a criminal offense, as it now is in some jurisdictions. For example, the Canadian law against insulting messages has been applied in the arrest of persons in Toronto who were passing out leaflets to tourists urging, "Yankee, go home" (Canadian Press 1975c). With hate literature illegal, advocates urge that the definition of hate propaganda be broadened. Thus Ludwig asks that rewriting history to deny the "Holocaust"—the Nazis' attempt to exterminate Jews and other "inferior races"—be made criminal (Ludwig 1982).

"SON OF SAM" LEGISLATION

Many people believe that it is a good idea not to allow offenders to make secondary profits from their crimes. This has led to such legislation as the 1977 "Son of Sam" law passed in New York that allows funds to be confiscated that would normally be received by offenders from telling their story in a book, movie, television show, or other medium. As originally enacted, the legislation would have redirected any monies earned by the notorious murderer David Berkowitz ("Son of Sam") and other felons to the state victim compensation fund. Since 1977, 42 other states have passed similar legislation. In 1991, however, New York's law was challenged in the case *Simon & Schuster, Inc. v. New York Crime Victims Board*. In this case, the U.S. Supreme Court held that the law was unconstitutional under the First Amendment. Essentially, the court held that the law was too broad, and as written would prevent the publication of such authors as St. Augustine, Malcom X, and

Figure 1.2 When the Exxon Valdez tanker ran aground off the coast of Alaska and its oil spill damaged wildlife, vegetation, and seashores, there were calls for new laws to deal with crimes against the environment. Photo courtesy of Corbis.

Thoreau since these authors also mentioned crimes they had committed in their books. The point here is that extending rights or prohibitions to one group invariably affects the rights of others. (*Simon and Schuster, Inc. v. New York Crime Victims Board,* 112 S.Ct 501, 1991)

Canadian law on the publication of hate literature permits expressions of opinions on religion if these are made "in good faith." This has produced debate about whether anti-Catholic comic books can or cannot be forbidden. Canada Customs claims that it can ban importation of such books under the law while the province of Alberta allows their distribution under its interpretation of the law (*Alberta Report* 1981).

Such legislation and quarrels about it show that the appropriate limit to "free speech," and the conditions under which speech and gesture constitute injury, remain in dispute. While traditional concerns with censorship surround the speech and the publication and distribution of books, recent advances in technology have broadened the scope of those concerns. Bills have been introduced in the U.S. Senate by senators Exon and Hyde, for example, to criminalize the distribution of "indecent" material on the Internet (Wallace and Mangam 1996). In Germany, a major Internet provider was threatened with revocation of its license until it "voluntarily" agreed to restrict the distribution of sexually explicit text and graphic material (Souhrada 1996).

Thus, the right of Protestant "Orangemen" to march through Catholic neighborhoods in Northern Ireland is simultaneously defended as a civil liberty and attacked as an insulting and inflammatory gesture (Clarity 1996). Similarly, the right of white residents to protest the first African-American family in their neighborhood by congregating outside their house is both defended as "legitimate expression" and condemned as "intimidating and injurious action" (Arkes 1978: 590). We are reminded that assault need not be bodily and that injuries are conceived and also perceived.

The impulse to criminalize is apparent also in the use of a consumer advocacy, which demands that the manufacture, sale, and use of "harmful" products be penalized. These harmful products range from alcoholic beverages, aspirin, and tobacco to some kinds of detergents, insecticides, cosmetics, automobiles, bicycles, and tricycles (Weaver 1975).

Concern with rapid population growth has led some people to demand the creation of yet another kind of crime—that of bearing more than two children. Willing (1971), for example, would enforce laws against "excessive fertility" by tattooing and sterilizing offenders.

Beyond these advocacies, many styles of discrimination are now criminal that once were not, and there is demand that new forms of discrimination be punished by the state. It is urged that unfair treatment in housing, education, occupation, or any public service due to age, sex, race, creed, national origin, income, physical disability, or tested traits of personality and intelligence be made criminal (Loftus 1976; Thomas 1972; Williams 1974).

✳ Demand for New Interpretations of Present Laws

Crimes are produced or reduced not merely by legislation, but also by judicial interpretation. Judicial interpretation varies with moral movement. The impact of a changing morality upon demand for criminal law can be seen in revised interpretations of the law. For example, the law of self-defense constructs an excuse against the charge of culpable homicide. In the United States such law is being reenacted, judicially but not legislatively, by some recent decisions.

Traditionally, a person who pleads self-defense in a homicide must show that there was an *immediate* danger of being killed or gravely injured by the threatening victim. The excuse has been narrowly construed and limited to the use of reasonable self-protective force, where reasonableness depends upon circumstance (*Acer v. United States,* 1896; *Addington v. United States,* 1897; *People v. McGinnis,* 1908). The excuse of self-defense has not been allowed in cases where one kills another to preserve one's own life (killing for cannibalism in a lifeboat, for example) or where one kills because of a past or future threat to one's life.

Current concern with battered wives has introduced a new claim upon the judiciary, the claim that a history of abuse, rather than an immediate danger, permits a plea of self-defense. Analyzing a number of cases, Rittenmeyer (1981) finds such broadening of the self-defense excuse to be itself sexually discriminatory and believes that such interpretation of the law will aggravate, not lessen, the problem of domestic violence.

In another recent case, a Calgary socialite shot her estranged husband six times. At the time of the attack, he posed no physical threat and was visiting his ex-wife's home at her request. Her defense included details of physical abuse to which she had been subjected by her husband. The jury found her not criminally responsible (Canadian Press 1996). Alan Dershowitz has taken the position that the "abuse excuse" has come to take a prominent and inappropriate place in the criminal justice system (Dershowitz 1994).

Conclusions

Conclusion 1: No End to Crime

The number of wrongs recommended for elevation to crimes seems endless, particularly in social environments that favor using the power of the state to improve our lives. Improving lives includes righting wrongs. Given the broad spectrum of injuries we can be deemed to inflict on ourselves and others, the tide may be running toward the invention of more crimes rather than toward a reduction in their number.

In the People's Republic of China, "party organizations at all levels have called on the masses to resolutely deal blows to . . . criminals" who violate laws against reproduction. "Couples who produce a third child will be fined ten percent of their pay or, if they are commune workers, of their work points. The docking of pay will last for 14 years, the age at which the government concludes that most children become a member of the productive work force" (Kramer 1979).

China's Communist party chairman Hu Yaobang has called for stricter enforcement of laws against "unhealthy Western music, the literature of complaints and discontent, and plays and books which show admiration for violence, murder, sex, and other disgusting and dirty activities" (*Economist* 1981a). The Republic of Ireland reinforced penalties for abortion, homosexuality, and the sale of contraceptives (*Economist* 1981b).

Meanwhile, in North America, many interest groups call for the legislation of new crimes. For example, in 1971 some Canadians made news when they urged that physicians be charged with an indictable offense if they do not report children's wounds that could represent instances of child abuse (van Stolk 1972). There are now laws for the compulsory reporting of such events in all provinces, and they extend to teachers and social workers. It is also suggested that "the federal government should establish a tribunal to test and license prospective parents with a history of violence and to enforce sterilization of unfit mothers" (van Stolk 1978). This has not yet happened, but the idea continues to have appeal among many who see few alternatives to the abuse of children and the high rates of children giving birth to children.

Other citizens, concerned with "public apathy," have recommended that failure to report a crime be made a crime (CTV 1974). The Canadian national sport, ice hockey, has been examined for its possible criminal violence. The question is whether athletic assault is part of the game or whether it should be criminally prosecuted (Canadian Press 1975a, 1975b; Matheson 1975).

The United States recently introduced the Helms-Burton Law (*Economist* 1996). It prevents foreign firms from operating in the United States if they conduct business with companies in Cuba, or operate in Cuba using properties expropriated by the communist regime from American interests before the revolution. The United States' largest trading partner is Canada, a country whose citizens are allowed to visit and engage in trade with Cuba. Canadians have found it difficult to sympathize with Helms-Burton, perceiving the law as an unjustified application of extraterritoriality.

The United States, with its passion for solving problems by passing laws, is not surpassed in its production of crime through legislation. In the 1996 presidential campaign, the President of the United States called for legislation that would restrict gun ownership for persons convicted of spouse abuse even when the abuse did not involve a weapon.

Conclusion 2: Of Social Harms We Have No Measure

In 1670 the Dutch philosopher Benedict (Baruch) Spinoza (1632–1677) wrote that

> he who seeks to regulate everything by law is more likely to arouse vices than to reform them. It is best to grant what cannot be abolished, even though it be in itself harmful.

By the beginning of the twentieth century, this sentiment was reversed. The American criminologist A. C. Hall claimed that

> the persistent enlargement of the field of crime is a necessity for all truly progressive nations. Many acts, formerly harmless, or socially beneficial, become harmful as civilization grows higher and more complex. . . . Society's conflict with its criminal members, due to the enforcement of new social prohibitions, is one of the chief means by which humanity, in every age, has risen from a lower to a higher plane of civilization. (Hall 1902)

Conflict persists between those who would enlarge the scope of government attention to wrongs with punitive power and those who would limit it. While Western scholars urge decriminalization of a select roster of "victimless crimes," they urge criminalization of currently lawful acts or conditions deemed to be socially harmful. In opposition to this movement, one may doubt that we can measure social harms and benefits. A balanced measure is difficult because there is no agreement about which consequences of human activity and public policy to count and whether the tally should be of direct, indirect, short-run, or long-run effects. There can be no bookkeeping of the good and evil of private enterprise and social policies insofar as individuals have differing hierarchies of values, insofar as ignorance masks the consequences of our actions, and insofar as responsibility is diffused and camouflaged.

On this broad topic, there is only judgment that is personal and contextual—a judgment that is not to be misled by the avowed intentions of legislators because good intentions are no guarantee of either intelligent action or beneficent result.

These comments justify a narrowed scope for criminology. Narrowing the scope of this study does not deny curiosity or concern, but it limits attention to a few questions rather than addressing the entire spectrum of injury and misery.

Limiting Wrongs: Criminology

Studies of quarrels about who should have the power to define wrongs as crimes and which wrongs should be considered crimes are interesting in their own right. They are part of what criminology is about, but they are only a part. More questions are asked of criminologists than these. As professional students of behavior, however, criminologists can no more respond to every question all at once than other thinkers can. The answers we get depend on the questions we ask, of course, but we can intelligently answer only a few questions at a time. The first maxim of a scholar is: Know your question.

SPENDING ON CRIMINAL JUSTICE
Spencer (1993) concludes that responses to crime are based on considerations that are other than rational, logical, and effective: . . . governments allocate resources to criminal justice with little, or no, attention to outcomes. . . . Criminal justice expenditures decisions are made on the basis of short-term demands, either political, ideological, or due to . . . "sentiment." . . . There are few discernible results to suggest that any of it has any significant effect on crime levels.

This maxim recognizes that there are many reasons for asking questions. Certainly many of our questions are "interested": that is, they are motivated by an interest, by a concern to attain or maintain something of value. This is not the only reason for taking thought, however, and we also ask questions merely to satisfy our curiosity.

Whatever the motive for asking questions, each style of question directs attention to different facets of life. Different consequences flow from this movement of attention. Part of the debate, then, about what criminology should address is stimulated by different desires. The revolutionary's questions are not the reformer's, and neither of these thinkers is apt to be intrigued by the conservative's questions.

Criminologists respond to these different styles of question by dividing their work. They turn their attention to three broad categories of question: (1) the sociology of law, (2) the study of social response to crime, and (3) theories of crime causation (criminogenesis).

Sociology of Law

The sociology of law tries to understand why some acts, but not others, are made the subject of the criminal law. It is concerned with how social groups come to define their expectations of behavior that shall receive formal, public attention. Among literate peoples, the sign of formal, public attention is codification in law. Within the field of criminology, the only pertinent laws are those that describe the behavior in question as an injury penalized by the state—that is, as crime. Students of the sociology of law are interested in such questions as these:

1. What are the determinants of definitions of behavior worthy of, or irrelevant to, legal notice?
   a. What factors may be correlated with changes in these definitions?
   b. What consequences may be attributed to such changes? Concern with this question raises issues about the rationality of different modes of social response to disturbing behaviors. These issues overlap with some questions asked about "social response to crime," but the attention here is to the consequences of criminal stigmatization and the possibilities of reacting in more economical ways to crime and criminals.
2. How does the social group implement its criminal law? This question promotes study of courts, judges, and juries; of the differential administration of law; of the determinants of differential sentencing practices; and of the occupations concerned with processing the law (police, lawyers, corrections officers, and others).

Study of Social Response to Crime

The study of social response to crime concerns the measures societies take against violations of their formal, public expectations. Researchers in this area are interested in the consequences of different styles of social response, in the justifications given for these differing reactions, and in the determinants of both the reactions and their consequences. Inquiries address questions of the rehabilitation of offenders and the deterrent effects of punishment. Research also considers the economy of police systems, of mechanical surveillance equipment, and of the defensive possibilities in the physical arrangement of residences and businesses.

Obviously, the research interests of students of social response overlap the interests of students of the sociology of law. The difference is one of emphasis. Under the topic of sociology of law, scholars question whether the laws are themselves rational. Under the topic of social response, scholars are less likely to question the law and more likely to consider how to carry out its intent.

Theories of Crime Causation (Criminogenesis)

Theories of crime causation are concerned with changes in crime rates and with the characteristics of individuals and groups that do or do not violate specific bundles of criminal laws. The study of crime causation deals with the methodological issues inherent in finding out the characteristics of violators, victims, and nonviolators. It attends, also, to the theories constructed to explain both individual involvement in crime and historical and comparative variations in the rates of different kinds of crime. This is the part of criminology to which the following chapters are principally addressed.

Questions and Answers in Criminology

Although a question-and-answer "division of labor" exists within criminology, the divisions are not sealed from each other. What might be the same question can be answered under different rubrics. The purposes of the inquirer have an influence on where the answer will be sought. For example, some criminologists answer the question, "What causes crime?" by replying, in effect, "The criminal law." Such an answer calls attention to the politics of lawmaking and law enforcement.

This kind of answer and its focus of attention are of interest to students of the sociology of law. If, however, we look at crime from the point of view of popular concern, this kind of response provides no answer. When the public and its representatives ask, "What causes crime?" they mean something like, "What produces variations in those acts that have been universally condemned as 'wrongs in themselves'?" With some exceptions, these wrongs are the acts defined as criminal by the laws of Western countries. The nature of such definition is the subject of Chapter 2.

2. Definition of Crime

Crime is a word, not a deed. It is a word that describes deeds, of course, but if it is used only to express moral condemnation, no one will be able to identify a criminal act with certainty. The meaning of the word varies with the morality of the user. Thus, people use "crime" variously, as when they say, "It's a crime the way he treats her," or "Private property is a crime," or "It's a crime to have to live like that." Attempts to define crime more rigorously look to the law for help. Nevertheless, laws attend to a wide range of injuries, not all of which are deemed to be crimes. With the proliferation of laws regulating a great array of personal habits and interpersonal relations, the boundary between criminal acts and other wrongs gets blurred, and so does the distinction between a *punishment* and a *penalty*. Today there is no clear line between those things regarded as crimes, those personal injuries treated as civil actions (torts), and those many violations of regulatory laws to which penalties are attached where these violations are not called "crimes" and the penalties are not called "punishment."

In short, *there is no essence of criminality*. No quality can be found in acts called "criminal" that distinguishes them from noncriminal injuries, breaches of contract, violations of regulations, and other disappointments (Williams 1955).

The question, then, is why we should bother trying to define crime. There are, of course, different reasons for clarifying our terms.

Functions of Definitions

Defining words serves several purposes. One purpose is to gain our audience's attention. When we define a term in a particular way, we are saying, "Look here. Attend to what I'm talking about."

Definition also has a personal function. Defining terms for ourselves helps us discover whether we know what we are talking about. We use many words automatically, and we often think we know what they mean until we are asked to define them. Defining a word tells us whether we are using it emotionally—to arouse a particular feeling, or denotatively—to refer to something.

A third function of definition is that of aiding communication. It derives from the second function, but here definition is an attempt to ensure that two or more people attribute the same meaning to a word. If we are interested in communicating our ideas accurately, we need clear definitions. If, on the other hand, we wish to use words merely to be persuasive, we need to be less clear about their definitions.

Legal Definition of Crime

The closest approximation to a clear definition of crime is that given by Tappan (1947): "a crime is an intentional violation of the criminal law, committed without defense or excuse, and penalized by the state."

Without further interpretation, this definition draws a circle. It says that a crime is a certain kind of breach of "criminal laws." However, we can use this unsatisfactory definition for the purposes of gaining attention and aiding communication if our questions are clear. We should keep at least the following questions separate so that we can think more calmly about their answers:

1. Why does this society treat certain acts, but not others, as crimes? This is a question for the sociology of law; it is beyond the scope of this book.
2. Why does a certain society exhibit more or less of those wrongs universally regarded as crimes—those more serious wrongs such as treason, murder, sexual assault (rape), assault, and theft? This is a question for theories of the origins of crime. It is the kind of question raised by public concern with crime, and attempts to answer it are the subject of this book.

Wrongs universally regarded as serious violations have been called *mala in se* (wrongs in themselves). Public concern with such offenses narrows our attention. Such concern means that we need not ask why people commit those minor infractions that are crimes only because a local jurisdiction has prohibited them—crimes called *mala prohibita*. Social concern about crime is not with such "delinquencies as that of a housewife who shakes her doormat in the street after 8 A.M., or a shopkeeper who fails to stamp a cash receipt, or a guest who fails to enter his name, nationality, and date of arrival in the hotel register. . . ." Few people want to spend time explaining why such ordinances are violated.

The context of the question asked about crime causation is that of public anxiety about those crimes regarded as serious. In this context, it seems most reasonable to employ a legal definition of crimes. It regards a crime as an intentional act that violates the prescriptions or proscriptions of the criminal law under conditions in which no legal excuse applies and where there is a state with the power to codify such laws and to enforce punishment in response to their breach. This definition says several things that require amplification. It holds that (1) there is no crime without law and without a state to punish the breach of law; (2) there is no crime where an act is justified by law; (3) there is no crime without intention; and (4) there is no crime where the offender is deemed *incompetent,* that is, without capacity to form intent. Each of these elements has its own history, its peculiar difficulties, and a range of implications.

No Crime Without Law

The legal idea of a crime restricts its meanings to those breaches of custom that a society has recognized in either its common or its statutory law. As it is applied in Western countries, this restriction implies four characteristics that define "good" criminal law: politicality, penal sanction, specificity, and uniformity.

Politicality refers to the idea that there can be no crime without a state to define it. *Penal sanction* refers to the power of a state to punish violations of its law. This definition says that the legal meaning of crime requires a state, an organization with a monopoly of power, to enforce the law and to attach pains to its breach. Laws that are not backed by force are less than law and more like agreements or aspirations. Laws without the possibility of punishment are hollow.

Law and Liberty

The conception of crime that places it within the boundaries of law has strong implications for civil liberties. The maxim that there can be no crime without a law means that people cannot be charged with offenses unless these have been defined. Protection of citizens against vague charges depends upon this ideal—that there must be a clear statement setting the limits of one's conduct in relation to others and defining the limits of the state's power to interfere in our lives.

This ideal has promoted other considerations concerning the formulation of "good law" as opposed to "poor law," particularly as good and poor laws are conceived in the Anglo-American tradition. These additional ideals are that the criminal law must be specific and applied uniformly.

Good laws specify actions that are criminal and specify punishment for each breach. Poor laws are omnibus condemnations, such as one from a dead German code that prohibited "behaving in a manner contrary to the common standards of right conduct." This kind of phrasing lacks the specificity that is an ideal of Western criminal jurisprudence. Similarly, it is an objective of modern jurisprudence that laws be framed and enforced to guarantee their uniform application. The ideal of uniform application does not require that each person and each crime be treated the same way. People, and their crimes and circumstances, vary. Our law therefore allows consideration of individual cases and some discretion in judicial response.

The ideal of uniform application does require, however, that extralegal characteristics of the offender not affect arrest, conviction, or sentence. Extralegal characteristics are those features of the offender *that are not related to the purposes of the law*—characteristics such as race and religion. Age and sex, however, may be deemed legal considerations, given stated purposes of the law.

As we will see, the ideal of uniform application is easier to express in general terms than it is to assess in particular instances. It is easier to express than to assess because some extralegal factors are entangled with legally relevant considerations, as happens when ethnic differences are associated with differences in patterns of criminal activity.

Not All Wrongs Are Crimes

The legal conception of crime as a breach of the criminal law has an additional implication. It narrows the definition of wrongs. Not all the injuries we inflict upon one another are recognized by law, nor are all the injuries recognized by law called crimes.

For example, American, Canadian, and European law recognize breaches of contract or trust, so that people who feel themselves thus harmed may seek a remedy from the law. Similarly, the law acknowledges other damages to person, reputation, and property, called torts, which, while not breaches of contract, may entitle one person to compensation from another.

> ### Bringing Action Against O. J.
> It is the "people of Los Angeles County" in the form of the Office of the District Attorney that brought *criminal* charges of murder against O. J. Simpson for the deaths of Ronald Goldman and Nicole Brown Simpson. It is the parents of Ronald Goldman and the estate of Nicole Brown Simpson who brought a *civil* suit for wrongful death against O. J. Simpson for the same two deaths. The criminal action exposed Simpson to jail; the civil action resulted in financial burdens.

Overlaps exist between the ideas of crime and tort. The same act can be both a crime and a tort, as in murder or assault. However, we can distinguish between the wrongs defined by contract and tort law and the wrongs defined by criminal law as to the procedures employed in response to these different categories of wrong. The procedural difference lies in "who pursues the offense." A crime is deemed an offense against the public, although it may have a particular victim and a particular complainant. It is the state that *prosecutes* crime, but it is individuals who *pursue* offenders against tort and contractual laws.

No Crime Where an Act Is Justified by Law

Defenses or excuses against the application of the criminal law can be analyzed in three categories: (1) justifiable acts, (2) unintentional acts, and (3) acts of incompetent agents. The first category consists of legally recognized justifications for committing what otherwise would be called a crime. Both literate and preliterate societies recognize the right of individuals to defend themselves and their loved ones against mortal attack. The injury or death that may be inflicted against one's assailant in self-defense is thereby excused.

Similarly, all states accord themselves the right of self-defense. As noted by the French philosopher Sorel (1908), states distinguish between *force*, the legitimate use of physical coercion constrained by law, and *violence*, its illegitimate use. The damage that occurs through the state's application of force is excused from the criminal sanction. Thus, homicide committed in the police officer's line of duty may be deemed "justifiable" and the injury defined as noncriminal.

No Crime Without Intention

How Notions of Intention Affect Ideas of Crime

Because of our moral and legal history, the criminal law tries to limit its definition of criminal conduct to intentional action. Accidents supposedly do not count as crimes. As the American jurist Oliver Wendell Holmes, Jr. put it, the law attempts to distinguish between "stumbling over a dog and kicking it." If "a dog can tell the difference between being kicked and being stumbled over," Justice Holmes believed, so too can judges and juries. This assumption seems plausible, but it gets sorely tried in practice. It gets tested and disputed because, in real life, some accidents are still defined as the actor's fault. Negligence may be criminal.

All criminal laws operate with some psychological model of the human being or the person. According to the model prevalent in Western criminal law, "reasonable persons" ought to use judgment in controlling their behavior so that some classes of accidents will not occur. For example, reckless drivers may not intend to kill pedestrians, but their accidents can be judged to have been the probable consequence of erratic driving. Persons licensed to manipulate an automobile are assumed to know the likely results of their actions. They are assumed, further, to be able to control their actions, and they are held accountable, despite lack of homicidal intent.

Western criminal law is based on this changing, and challenged, set of assumptions. It therefore qualifies its desire to restrict crime to intentional breaches of the criminal code. This qualification is accomplished by distinguishing classes of crime—the impulsive from the premeditated, the accidental from the purposive. Since the law wishes to hold able, but negligent, people to account, it includes the notion of *constructive intent,* a term that stretches "intent" to cover the unintended, harmful consequences of some of our behavior. The punishment for doing damage through negligence is usually lighter than that for being deliberately criminal; yet the term "crime" covers both classes of conduct.

A related issue concerns how much reasonable persons can be expected to control their behavior. The law allows excuses—*mitigating circumstances* such as assault or insult—that may reduce the gravity of the crime, as when a homicide is called "manslaughter" rather than "murder."

For example, *provocation* is recognized as a category of events that reduces the ability of reasonable persons to control their conduct. Yet what makes up such unbearable provocation varies, again, with morals. Thus, if a wife admits to her husband that she has been sexually unfaithful, this has been deemed to be reasonable provocation in Kentucky, Mississippi, and South Carolina, but not in California, Georgia, or Iowa (Fiora-Gormally 1978: 36–39).

Issues such as these concerning negligence and provocation and, as we shall see, insanity, repeatedly cloud the notion of intention that is part of the definition of crime.

Intention and Motivation

Motivation is sometimes used by lawyers to prove intention. The two concepts are not the same, however. An *intention* is that which we have in mind when we act. It is our purpose, the result we wish to achieve. The criminal law is particularly concerned with punishing illegal intent when it is acted upon. A *motive* is, strictly speaking, that which moves a person to act. The word may apply to an intention, but it need not. Intentions are but one of the many motors of action.

Intention is a word with narrow and specific reference; *motivation* is a term with broad and general reference. A jewel thief may intend to steal jewels; the motive is to become richer. This motive is widespread and it does not distinguish a thief from an entrepreneur. "Intention to steal jewels" describes a specific class of action, but this kind of action is only one way of satisfying the motive to gain wealth. An intention may or may not move a person. It may remain a wish, a plot, a dream. A criminal intention, without the action, is not a crime.

Motives, on the other hand, may move us haphazardly, purposelessly, without the focus of intent. A motive may be purely physiological and variously gratified. It may even be unconscious, if we believe the psychoanalysts. An intention, however, is only something conscious, and is reserved for thoughts and verbalizabled plans. It does not refer to those subterranean urges or those physiological fires that may have kindled the ideas.

Since intent is part of the definition of crime, prosecutors in Western countries must establish such purpose in the actor, and they sometimes try to do this by constructing the motive. The strategy of demonstrating intention from motivation calls for showing good reasons why a person might act as the accused is alleged to have acted. The good reasons, the alleged motives, may all have been there, however, without the actor's having formed the criminal intent that the prosecutor is attempting to establish. This is simply because good reasons are not always the causes of actions.

The prosecutor's best evidence of intention is material evidence of preparation for the crime. When such evidence is combined with what the lawyer calls "the motive"—that is, the accused's good reasons—this is as good as one can do in establishing intent.

The distinction between "movers of action" and "intentions" becomes important as criminal law takes heed of another qualification in its definition of crime, the qualification that people shall be held responsible for their actions, and therefore liable to the criminal law, only if they are mentally competent. The legal meaning of intention is embedded in the notion of competence.

No Crime Without Capacity

How Notions of Capacity Affect Ideas of Crime

The condemnation that is implicit in calling actions criminal is based on moral premises. It is part of our morality to believe that persons ought not to be blamed for actions that are beyond their control. The notion that behavior is within or beyond one's control rests on conceptions of *capacity* or competence. These conceptions, in turn, are cultural. They vary in time and with place, and they remain disputed today. The dispute concerns the criteria of competence, but the debate does not challenge the legal and moral principle that people must be somehow able before they can be judged culpable.

Selective Determinism

We will note repeatedly that explanation of human action, and particularly of disapproved conduct, become entangled in a selective determinism. The tendency is to interpret the bad acts of people with whom we sympathize as caused, while the evil deeds of people we dislike are chosen. And, of course, only chosen action is deemed to be blameworthy.

Conversely, people we like who do good deeds are believed to have decided to act that way, while people we dislike who happen to do good deeds are assumed to have been pressured into such uncharacteristic goodness. Judgments about who is caused to behave in a certain way and who prefers to behave that way are seldom influenced by any facts. Such judgments are more frequently a function of moral preferences.

Cognitive Tests

In modern countries, the tests of competence are cognitive. They look to *mens rea*, the "thing in the mind," as defining the ability to form a criminal intent and as the regulator of one's actions. *Until* the "mind" is sufficiently well formed to control the actor's behavior, and *unless* it operates in normal fashion, Western criminal law excludes the person from criminal liability. Actors are considered not responsible or less responsible for their wrongdoing if they are judged (1) to have acted under duress, (2) to be under age, or (3) to be insane.

Crime under Duress.   The first exclusion consists of criminal deeds performed "against one's will." The law recognizes circumstances in which a person may be forced into a criminal action under threat. Since intent and the capacity to act freely are diminished when this is the case, so too is legal responsibility.

Age and Capacity.   A second application of the moral principle that people must have some minimal mental capacity before they ought to be held legally accountable concerns limitations of age. Laws of modern states agree that persons below a certain age must be excluded from criminal liability. The number of years required to attain legal responsibility varies by jurisdiction, but the legal principle persists in declaring individuals who are under age to be incompetent or "legal infants." They may be protected by laws, but they are not subject to the criminal law. In most Anglo-American jurisdictions a child under the age of seven years cannot be held responsible for a crime. In Canada, the age is 12 years. The excuse is that of nonage.

   1. *Juvenile delinquency.* Above the age boundary that defines nonage and below 21 years, young people in industrialized countries are variously categorized as to their legal responsibility for crime. In the common law of English-speaking states, it was assumed that a *legal infant,* someone between the ages of 7 and 14 years, did not have the capacity to form criminal intent, although in cases of serious crimes this assumption might be refuted by showing that the actor could distinguish right from wrong. Between the ages of 14 and 21 years, the common law assumed capacity adequate for legal responsibility, but this assumption, too, was open to legal rebuttal. Beyond 21 years, age was no longer a defense against liability for one's criminal acts.

   As the common law became codified, these assumptions were carried into effect, with qualifications, in particular jurisdictions. The statutory laws of industrialized countries have come to define a special status of offender called a *juvenile delinquent* or a *young offender.* In most Western jurisdictions, the upper age limit of this category is 18 years. From 18 years on, a person is treated as an adult by the criminal law. This age boundary varies, however, with the jurisdiction and sometimes with the sex of the young person.

   In most industrialized countries, however, the tendency is to raise and narrow the age boundaries that define a special category of responsibility called delinquency or, in Canada, youthful offending. The tendency is to make the age boundaries uniform across jurisdictions, as does the Canadian Young Offenders Act passed in 1982 (Solicitor General 1981a). The United States, with its 50 state criminal codes and a federal criminal code, however, has yet to apply a uniform definition of young offending to its many statutes.

The justification of a special status for youthful offenders rests, again, on the moral premise that people ought not to feel the full force of the criminal law unless they are responsible for their conduct. This moral maxim has been bolstered by a practical concern that seeks to protect children from harmful influences, prevent their waywardness, and guide them into acceptable patterns of conduct when they have shown deviation that might become chronic.

This mixture of purposes has meant that the definition of delinquency in Anglo-American law has included the commission of crime, but it has also included as the object of legal attention some noncriminal conduct and some noxious circumstances. Among the varied jurisdictions of the United States, for example, an underage person has been treated as a delinquent for such matters as

- Being habitually truant
- Being incorrigible
- Growing up in idleness or crime
- Immoral or indecent conduct
- Habitually using vile, obscene, or vulgar language in public
- Attempting to marry without consent in violation of the law
- Being given to sexual irregularities
- Using tobacco or alcoholic beverages or being addicted to drugs
- Habitually wandering about railroad yards or tracks or wandering about the streets at night (Sussman 1959: 20)

Extending the word "delinquency" to cover more than criminal activity increases the risk that the law may be vague and that efforts to protect children may violate their civil liberties. It is notable that the laws of Asian, Middle Eastern, and Latin American countries include only criminal conduct in their attention to youthful offenders (United Nations 1953, 1960, 1965a, 1965b). This is also the case with the Canadian law with respect to young offenders. The legal responsibility of juveniles may be diminished under these statutes, but the status of a delinquent, if this term is defined at all, implies that the person has broken the criminal law.

2. *Status offenses.* Status offenses are behaviors that would not be an offense if they were committed by a person with different social characteristics. The attack on such status offenses in the United States is being led by law-reform groups whose objective is to separate child welfare services from attention to juvenile crime.

3. *Trends*

a. United States: helping versus arresting. Efforts have been made in the United States to reform the law and to separate legal attention to juvenile offenders from protection of children's welfare. Aultman and Wright term this a shift toward a "fairness" or "justice" paradigm (Aultman and Wright 1985). Because juvenile justice is a state responsibility, the effectiveness of these efforts has varied from state to state. It is interesting that the federal Office of Juvenile Justice and Delinquency Prevention now defines a delinquent act as "an act committed by a juvenile for which an adult could be prosecuted in a criminal court, but when committed by a juvenile is within the jurisdiction of the juvenile court" (Butts et al. 1994). Despite this definition, in many jurisdictions juveniles are still subject to a number of status offenses such as breaking curfews, loitering, and runaway prohibitions. Some commentators do suggest, however, that substantial reforms have been made in sentencing, release policy, and juvenile parole to bring practices in juvenile justice more in line with those in the adult system (Forest, Fisher, and Coates 1985; Ashford and LeCroy 1993). It is here, as in the debate about insanity as a defense, that the legal profession battles with the "helping" professions. Social workers, psychiatrists, and some judges would use the judicial system as part of a welfare system that tries to meet children's needs. Lawyers, on the other hand, are chary of expanding the power of state agencies to control children under the guise of helping them, unless adequate legal safeguards are built in. The attorneys' caution derives from the fact that many juvenile delinquency statutes do not satisfy the legal ideal that actions be specified before state control can be applied. "Having done something" is more readily determinable than "being something." Just as we would not want the criminal law to apply to those of us who are "in a state of criminality," lawyers are generally opposed to the idea of charging youths with being "in a state of delinquency" (Cousineau and Veevers 1972: 244).

b. Canada: Young Offenders Act. Despite continuing conflicts about the appropriate definition of young malefactors, the present climate of civil liberties and the recognition that much delinquency is serious crime is combining to produce legislation that will *separate* government attention to child welfare from legal concern with youthful crime. Thus the Canadian Young Offenders Act, which in 1983 replaced the 75-year-old Juvenile Delinquents Act, does the following:

1. Raises the age of criminal responsibility from 7 to 12 years.
2. Fixes the maximum age of juvenile status at under 18 years.
3. Allows youths charged with minor crimes to avoid court appearance. Substitute "diversion programs" include assignment to community service, to special education programs, or to counseling and restitution agreements. Appeal is permitted accused youths so that a court appearance can be arranged if it is desired.
4. Builds in legal safeguards to ensure protection of an accused youth's civil liberties, provision of defense counsel, and right to bail.
5. Allows youths who are charged with serious crimes, or whose careers suggest commitment to crime, to be dealt within adult court. This is permitted only if the offense was committed after the youth's fourteenth birthday.
6. Allows judges a wide range of disposition including absolute discharge, fine, restitution or community service orders, probation up to two years, or commitment to intermittent or continuous custody for

up to two years. However, "in no case [is] a young person subject to a greater penalty than the maximum penalty applicable to an adult committing the same offense" (Solicitor General, Canada 1981a).

7. Opens court hearings to the public except in unusual circumstances.
8. Protects the anonymity of accused youths, victims, and witnesses and applies penalties to journalists if they publish names.
9. Expunges the records of those who appear in youth court after completion of their *disposition* (for youths, a sentence is termed a disposition) and after expiration of a crime-free period following completion of disposition. The crime-free period required is two years for those convicted of lesser offenses and five years for those convicted of more serious offenses.

The intent of this law is to ensure that neglected and abused children are not confounded by those who commit crimes. This intention is stimulated by recognition that the kind of help needed by abandoned youngsters need not be the same as the attention to be directed toward young criminals.

c. Conclusion: age and crime. Conflicts about definitions of adolescent crime reflect changes both in the behavior of youths and in attitudes toward them. However, the present point is that all definitions of crime mark off some ages below which people are deemed not to have the capacity for criminal activity. In addition, industrialized countries often establish a borderland, occupied by youths, within which legal liability is acknowledged, but diminished, and in which the stigmatizing effect of the criminal sanction is avoided or attenuated by special treatment.

Duress and youth are thus two indicators of diminished capacity for forming criminal intent and controlling one's conduct. They join insanity as an additional indicator of reduced competence.

Insanity as a Defense.   A third excuse by which one may reduce or escape the application of the criminal law is *insanity,* the claim that the offender's capacity to control his or her behavior has been damaged. The locus of this incapacity, is, again, the mind.

Defects of the mind seem clear in the extremes of senility, idiocy, and the incapacitating psychoses. They are clear, too, as one can link abnormal performance to lesions of the central nervous system. However, it is in the gray area between these extremes and more normal behavior that citizens, lawyers, and their psychiatric advisers dispute the capacity of offenders.

It bears repeating that this dispute rests on moral considerations. Quarrels are stimulated by the belief that only people capable of choosing their conduct deserve punishment for their crimes, that accidents and irresistible impulses do not count, and that other classes of behavior beyond one's control should not be punished. The philosophical questions opened by this debate range beyond our present concern. These questions include, at a minimum, the ancient issues of free will and determinism, of the justice and value of praise and blame, and of the proper ends of the criminal law.

These questions intrude upon the law and ensure that attempts to define mental competence are all imperfect. They are less than perfect because moral conceptions of the "causes" of behavior color the assignment of responsibility to actors. They are less than perfect, also, because the boundaries of the defense of insanity move with the justifications of the criminal law. That is, what we want the law to do changes definitions of "incompetence." When we speak of insanity as a defense in a criminal case, insanity is a legal term; it is not a medical term. It refers to that degree of mental illness that will be enough to find the person not guilty; that is, not a free agent who willfully did wrong.

1. *Tests of insanity.* The criminal law attempts to evaluate capacity from signs of sanity. *Sanity* refers to soundness, to wholeness. These conceptions, in turn, rest on models of the human being. They rest on notions of how "fully functioning" persons ought to behave. Being less than whole, being of "unsound mind," is, therefore, a legal defense against accountability to the law. In 1723, the rule of insanity that applied in England was called the Wild Beast Rule: " . . . to avail himself of the defense of insanity a man must be totally deprived of his understanding and memory, so as not to know what he was doing any more than a wild beast."

Defining sanity is difficult, however, and it is an embarrassment to a profession which, like the law, depends so heavily on the precision of its terms. One part of the trouble lies in courts having to decide "either-or," a person is or is not sane, whereas the truth is that people are more-and-less sane. A jingle says, "Crazy people are not all crazy all the way, every day, in every way." Psychologists and psychiatrists agree and, consequently, the word "insane" has poor credentials among them. Nevertheless, the law has looked to these students of the mind for help in assessing the competence of defendants. The decision of insanity when the insanity defense is invoked, is made by a lay jury. The rule to be used serves as a "bridge, for a lay jury, between medical science and complex social objectives" (Goldstein 1967: 90). The history of rules of insanity and the regulations by which they are applied is a history of expanding and contracting definitions in response to whether it is perceived as too often used by "inappropriate" persons.

In the Netherlands, Denmark, Norway, and Sweden, the test of insanity is simply the testimony of such medical experts. In Belgium, France, Italy, and Switzerland, the test is psychiatric judgment concerning the ability of the offender to understand what he or she was doing at the time of the crime and to control that behavior.

Anglo-American law has attempted to guide judges, juries, and psychiatrists in assessing the competence of defendants by formulating more specific tests used alone or in qualified combinations. Until recently, the most popular of these guidelines have been the *McNaughton rules*, to which amendments have been made.

Under the influence of the once-dominant Freudian model of mind, some jurisdictions broadened the definition of insanity so that almost anyone who committed a bizarre crime was deemed to be of "unsound mind." Such expansion resulted in excusing some predators whose rationality contradicted the public's conception of a "mentally incompetent" person. In turn, violation of the public's sense of justice produced a reaction that has resulted in a flurry of legislative changes.

It will be seen that no principle thus far set out for judging insanity is perfectly clear. All contain ambiguities, and, therefore, the very idea of an "insanity defense" is under attack. We should expect this, of course, whenever we seek to implement moral sentiments with written regulations. Under such circumstances, the cognitive framework shifts. Moral judgments are easier to "feel" than to justify with principles. Nevertheless, Anglo-American law attempts to distinguish sane offenders from insane ones, and to do so by formulating rules for decision.

2. *The McNaughton rules.* Beginning in the fourteenth century, English common law excused from criminal responsibility persons believed to be so mentally defective as to be unable to control their conduct. Early in the nineteenth century, however, the McNaughton case resulted in the formulation of rules that were to help courts make this judgment. Daniel McNaughton was a woodturner from Glasgow who suffered from the delusion that Tories were persecuting him. He traveled to London, hung around government offices, and on January 20, 1843, thinking that he was firing at the prime minister, Sir Robert Peel, shot and killed Sir Robert's clerk, Edward Drummond.

Given the medical evidence presented to the court, the presiding judge interrupted the trial and directed the jury to declare McNaughton not guilty by reason of insanity. This decision created such a furor, including an inquiry from Queen Victoria, that the House of Lords asked the judges to give opinion on the determination of insanity. Their opinion, later called the McNaughton rules, has influenced the nature of the insanity defense in English-speaking countries for more than 150 years. These tests provide the only definition of insanity in several American states and, with some qualification, inform the insanity defense in Canada and Great Britain. The rules state that

> every man is to be presumed to be sane, and . . . that to establish a defense on the ground of insanity, it must be clearly proved that, at the time of the committing of the act, the party accused was labouring under such a defect of reason, from disease of the mind, as not to know the nature and quality of the act he was doing; or if he did know it, that he did not know he was doing what was wrong. (Goldstein 1967: 45)

Here, as elsewhere, common words become cloudy when one attempts to use them with precision, and each of the key terms in the McNaughton formula has been debated. "Disease of the mind" is vague. "Wrong" may mean morally so or legally so. The meaning of the phrase "the nature and quality of the act" has been disputed, and even the apparently simple verb "to know" is troublesome. Critics of the McNaughton rule have argued that "knowing" may refer only to intellectual awareness, and they have wanted to substitute a psychiatric sense of "knowing," one that would include "emotional appreciation" and cognitive understanding. As employed in Canada, the "knowledge test" with the McNaughton rules has been broadened so that "the act must necessarily involve more than mere knowledge that the act is being committed; there must be an appreciation of the factors involved in the act and a mental capacity to measure and foresee the consequences of the violent conduct" (Canada 1955: 12–13).

As the professions of psychology and psychiatry developed and grew in authority, their practitioners attacked the McNaughton principle for its vague language and added to this attack the claim that under its test psychotic people could be, and have been, declared sane. With the popularizing of the ideas of psychoanalysis, legislators have taken account of the possibility that "knowledge of right and wrong" is only one test of capacity. It is now recognized that some psychotic persons may be moved by beliefs that we regard as false, but they believe to be true and over which they seem to have no control. When such a delusion can be shown to have caused a crime, some jurisdictions excuse the agent as incompetent. Canada, for example, adds the defense of delusive incapacity to the McNaughton rules in defining insanity, but it qualifies this excuse by saying that "a person . . . shall not be acquitted on the ground of insanity *unless* the delusions caused him to believe in the existence of a state of things that, if it existed, would have justified or excused his act or omission" (emphasis added) (Canada 1996).

3. *The substantial capacity test.* In 1953 the American Law Institute (ALI) drew up a model penal code that proposed a different definition of "responsibility" (American Law Institute 1953). This is the test now used in American federal courts and 26 states.

> This principle holds that a person shall not be held accountable for a crime "if at the time of such conduct, as a result of mental disease or defect, he lacks substantial capacity either to appreciate the criminality of his conduct or to conform his conduct to the requirements of law." This proposal adds, however, that "the terms 'mental disease or defect' do *not* include an abnormality manifested *only* by repeated criminal or otherwise anti-social conduct." (American Law Institute 1953; sec. 4.01, emphasis added)

Those who would broaden the insanity defense and who consider all criminal activity to be "caused" rather than "chosen" are not satisfied with the ALI test, because it works like the McNaughton rule with an "irresistible impulse" test added. On the other hand, the phrase "lacks substantial capacity" appeals to some forensic psychiatrists who believe it allows them to speak of degrees of competence. Of course, what "substantial" means is debatable. At least one federal judge, Trask, in *Wade v. United States*, holds that this notion creates more difficulties than it solves. For example, he notes that, "The jury could believe that a 25% lack of capacity is 'substantial' and acquit one who is otherwise mentally responsible" (*Wade v. United States* 1970).

This possibility is illustrated by what Stuart Taylor calls "the most elaborate insanity defense case ever staged—that of John W. Hinckley, Jr., for shooting President Ronald Reagan and three other men (see Figure 2.1) (Taylor 1982). A jury found Hinckley not guilty by reason of insanity of 13 charges ranging from carrying an unlicensed gun to attempted assassination of the President of the United States. Judicial proceedings took almost 15 months at an estimated cost of $3 million. The search for justice employed three independent teams of mental health experts to try to decide the soundness of Hinckley's mind. Three psychiatrists and a psychologist worked for the prosecution and produced a 628-page report. A similar team worked for the defense, and two prison psychiatrists and a psychologist gave an additional report to the court. These examinations cost more than $500,000.

Figure 2.1   More than 100 changes to laws of insanity as a defense were made in response to John Hinckley being found not guilty in the shooting of President Ronald Reagan and his Press Secretary James Brady. Photo courtesy of Corbis.

After these hours of examination, and after weeks of hearing this, and other, evidence at trial, 12 jurors were, in Taylor's words,

> locked up with orders to decide the fate of a would-be assassin by pondering riddles about free will, determinism, and moral responsibility that have confounded the world's philosophers for millennia . . .
>   "Even though we had the doctors and the professors there, they did not prove anything either with all their knowledge and degrees," juror Maryland T. Copelin, a fifty-year-old elementary-school cafeteria worker, observed after the verdict. "They couldn't prove him insane, they couldn't prove that he was sane—how can we laymen do it?" she said on another occasion. (Taylor 1982: 57)

Stuart Taylor, who covered the trial for the *New York Times* and is himself a law school graduate, wonders whether we now have "too much justice." In the aftermath of this decision, 79% of Americans said that they disapproved of laws allowing the insanity excuse, while 83% felt that justice was not done in the Hinckley trial (ABC Survey 1982). In 1997, the question was one of whether Hinckley was sufficiently improved to be allowed away from prison for 12 hours at a time under the supervision of his parents.

Lorena Bobbitt made headlines—and many men squirm—when she cut off the penis of her abusive husband while he slept (see Figure 2.2). She was found not guilty of malicious wounding as a result of temporary insanity brought on by the behavior of her husband during years of their stormy relationship (see Box 2.1).

Figure 2.2 Lorena Bobbitt's actions being celebrated in a parade. Photo courtesy of Corbis.

BOX 2.1 LORENA BOBBITT FOUND NOT GUILTY

MANASSAS, VA—In a verdict that highlighted the plight and rights of abused women, a jury found Lorena L. Bobbitt not guilty of the criminal charges, including that she was temporarily insane when she cut off her husband's penis with a kitchen knife.

The defense argued—and the jury agreed, after slightly more than six hours of deliberation—that Mrs. Bobbitt, flooded with nightmarish images of her husband's abuse and suffering from a variety of mental illnesses, snapped psychologically after her husband raped her and yielded to an "irresistible impulse" to strike back.

In testimony, Mrs. Bobbitt said she had not realized what she had done until later, when she fled their home and was in the car. She said she then discovered the knife in one hand and her husband's penis in the other. She threw what she called his "body part" in the underbrush, from which it was retrieved, and, after nine hours of surgery, reattached.

The prosecutor in the case . . . expressed fears that the verdict could send the wrong message about deterrence and punishment.

"I have a certain amount of sympathy for Mrs. Bobbitt, but that doesn't justify what she did. . . . A whole lot of people go to the penitentiary who in some ways tug at your heart strings, but when you violate the law, you've got to be punished, in my opinion, and this is no exception. I'm happy she went out the back door rather than the front." (Margolick 1994: 1, 7)

---

4. *Debate on insanity.* Debate continues about which people should be held accountable for their actions. It is a debate that moves with the moral tides and reflects the society's sense of whether the right persons are successful in using the defense of insanity.

Most citizens believe that, if people knew what they were doing at the time of a crime, then they should not be excused as insane. The majority also objects to the use of indeterminate treatment rather than punishment in response to crimes of this nature (Isaacson et al. 1982). In fact, during the mid-1990s, three states (Idaho, Utah and Montana) passed legislation that eliminated the defense of insanity.

A sentence to treatment places responsibility on psychiatrists to judge when a person has been cured of psychiatrically defined disorders, many of which are not, as yet, *disease entities*. Saying that such disturbances of thought and action are not disease entities means that no specific etiology—no identifiable cause—has been discovered. In addition, a sentence to treatment makes psychiatrists responsible for predicting the pacification of a once violent offender upon release. However, tallies of psychiatrists' forecasts suggest that they have no such expertise (Cocozza and Steadman 1976; Ennis and Litwak 1976; Koppin 1976; Monahan 1978; Tanay 1979).

Conclusion

Our theme has been that assignment of responsibility is not dependent so much upon matters of fact as upon matters of morality. That is, blaming and punishing categories of offenders is influenced at least as much by what we want to *do* in response to their crimes as by what we want to *achieve* by our response.

If there were a harmonious, singular set of objectives in response to crime, then we might be able to assign responsibility and excuses in a practical manner—so as to achieve some empirical result. In Western societies, however, citizens and their lawmakers seek a medley of objectives in response to crime. These objectives mix moral and practical considerations. Therefore, who should or should not be held accountable will continue to be debated.

3. The Study of Crime

Scientific versus Nonscientific Questions

To use an old philosophical dichotomy, science addresses questions of fact; philosophy addresses questions of value and morality. Yet, perhaps more than most issues studied by social scientists, crime is clearly based on a set of moral or normative underpinnings. Fundamentally, crime is an *ought* phenomenon in the sense that we argue that certain behaviors either ought or ought not to be criminal. In the broader study of criminology, it is usually those with a background in philosophy and law who focus their attention on these normative components of crime. As social scientists, however, our attention is directed more to the *factual* or empirical consequences of crime.

This distinction in disciplinary approaches to the study of crime (the intellectual division of labor if you will) is clearly illustrated in the types of questions asked. Those with a bent toward legal philosophy ask questions such as: "Should abortion be considered a criminal offense?" and "Is it consistent with our political philosophy to allow companies to bribe public officials to gain contracts?" Social scientists, however, ask different, but related questions. Social scientists focus on such questions as: "Why do some societies criminalize certain behaviors and others do not?" "Why do some people obey the criminal law and others do not?" "What factors distinguish those who conform to legal norms from those who do not?" and "What social conditions or factors lead to greater or lesser compliance with the law?"

This is not to say that the practice of science is totally independent of any moral framework. Science is based on numerous value assumptions such as the following: knowledge is preferable to ignorance; objective knowledge carries more weight than subjective knowledge; and certain aspects of social life are useful objects of scientific scrutiny while others are not. That is, science cannot answer questions of morality; it can, however, tell us what people believe to be moral and what are some of the consequences of engaging or not engaging in those behaviors. Thus, asking whether Susie and Joe are good people is not a scientific question. Asking whether Susie and Joe are perceived by their peers as good people, however, is a legitimate scientific question. Sometimes the distinction between a scientific and a nonscientific question is subtle. The consequences of distinguishing between the two types of questions are crucial.

Ultimately, what distinguishes scientific questions from other forms of questions is that the validity of the propositions embedded in those questions is based on some empirical outcome. That is, science avoids the arbitrary or received wisdom underlying most religious forms of understanding; it shuns the mysticism of magic, and attempts to avoid the circular or tautological basis of knowledge that underlies some areas of philosophy. The key to scientific propositions is that they must be clear, unambiguous and above all, open to negation. In other words, scientific propositions must be stated so that they can be proven incorrect under a specified set of empirical conditions.

Some assertions are clearly not scientific propositions under these criteria. For example, the statement "criminals are people who break the law" is not a scientific proposition since it is true by definition; breaking the law is part of the definition of being criminal. Asserting that "people commit crimes because they are in league with the devil" is also not a scientific proposition since there is no empirical way of showing that criminals are *not* in league with the devil.

All "sane" people, by definition, can tell the difference between a silly question and an answerable one. We can tell the difference at some extreme, such as when someone asks, "What color is justice?" or "Why are you growing your father's hair?" There is nothing to be experienced—there are no observables—that can tell us whether answers to such questions are correct or not. These questions are not empirical.

Unfortunately, the frontier between empirical questions and silly ones is vague. Within this borderland we acknowledge that some questions may not be foolish, although they do not require empirical answers. Such utterances sound like questions. For example, there are times when we express emotion in the form of questions ("What can go wrong next?"). These questions do not require empirical answers.

At other times we want to be rational. We want to know what course of action will economically get us what we want. On such occasions, we ask empirical questions. An empirical question is one whose answer can be tested by facts, by something observable. By contrast, if an answer can be maintained as true no matter what occurs, then the question to which the answer is addressed is not empirical. If nothing that happens, or everything that happens, makes the answer correct, then the question is beyond experience.

Perhaps the greatest difficulty posed by many explanations is that they are based on circular reasoning or tautologies. A typical example may be found in many court cases where defense attorneys attempt to show that their clients are innocent due to insanity. For example, (1) Jeffrey Dahmer dismembered his victims, (2) only an insane person would kill and dismember another human being, therefore, (3) Jeffrey Dahmer must be insane. In fact, Dahmer's dismemberment of his victims might not be an indicator of legal insanity, but instead, an indication of a clearly rational act to hide evidence in response to the fear of being caught.

Collecting Observations

The ultimate test of how well an explanation of crime works is how well it corresponds to the behavior it purports to address. It is important, therefore, that the observations that we make—that is, data that we collect—are valid and reliable. Valid data measure what they are supposed to measure, while reliable data are consistent in that measurement. If reports of crimes are fabricated, or if deviant but noncriminal acts are included in the tally of observations, then those observations are considered invalid. If recorded observations of murders and manslaughters are confused through miscoding, then the data are considered unreliable.

As we will see in later chapters, two primary sources of data are used by students of crime: official statistics and unofficial statistics. Official statistics are collected by government agencies such as the police and the courts. These agencies attempt to maintain a record of all crimes reported to them; therefore, these data might be considered an attempt to generate a census. Most unofficial counts of crime are collected by researchers and are based on samples drawn from a broader population. Usually, our interest does not lie solely in the characteristics of the sample, but in the characteristics of the population from which the sample is drawn. We sample, however, because measuring an entire population may be impractical given the available resources. For example, measuring an entire population may be too expensive or too time-consuming.

Ironically, well-designed samples may produce more accurate results than attempts to measure an entire population. This situation arises because we can often expend more effort in ensuring that a few observations are valid and reliable than we can expend when collecting many observations. Furthermore, the statistical theory underlying sampling assures us that if certain rules are followed, valid estimates of population characteristics can be made from the sample characteristics, within calculable levels of certainty. The primary rules for ensuring that inferences from samples to populations are valid are the following: (1) the elements sampled from the population must have a known probability or likelihood of selection, and (2) the selection process must be based on some unbiased, random procedure. If every element in the population is selected at random and has an equal chance of selection, then the sample is known as a simple random sample.

While these dictates are easy to specify, they are often extremely difficult to meet in practice. For example, if we wish to conduct a survey of skid row alcoholics, it is difficult to know what any given individual's chances of selection might be, since we do not know beforehand the total population of skid row alcoholics. We are also likely to have a biased, or nonrandom sample, since only certain skid row alcoholics may be available to us for interviewing. If the group we observe forms a biased sample, then any attempt to generalize back to the parent population will likely be invalid. Researchers refer to the ability to generalize our knowledge from samples to the broader population as *external validity*.

Much early research in criminology was based on samples drawn from jail populations. While those samples likely allowed one to infer the characteristics of all incarcerated individuals, they were very unlikely to generate an accurate depiction of all offenders—both incarcerated and otherwise. In fact, we now know that incarcerated populations are older, are more likely to have a record, have often committed more offenses, and have often committed more serious offenses than nonincarcerated offenders.

It is the role of methodologists to study ways of improving the validity and reliability of our observations and to find ways of increasing the accuracy of inferences made from samples. Unfortunately, none of the procedures we have developed to collect and analyze data is perfect. Some techniques and procedures are better than others; some researchers are better than others in applying those techniques and procedures. It is for this reason (among others) that individual studies can generate inconsistent or even conflicting results. No one study can determine the validity of a particular explanation; scientific knowledge is cumulative over many independent tests of particular explanations.

How Are Crime Counts Manipulated?

Counting behaviors that interest us is difficult; interpreting the tallies compounds the difficulties. Statistics, as with any other information, become more or less adequate in terms of one's purposes. Much depends on what we want to do with what we know.

Absolute Numbers

For some purposes, absolute numbers—straight counts—are good enough. Learning that so many thousands of people died of lung cancer last year or that motoring fatalities on a holiday reached a certain number may be sufficient for our concern. For example, to report that the 1990 census of China estimated the population to be over 1 billion people cannot be stated more forcefully (United Nations 1997 Demographic Yearbook).

When we want to make comparisons for a population over time or comparisons between groups then absolute numbers are less satisfactory. When we are seeking a choice among hypotheses we prefer to think about ratios, proportions, or rates, rather than absolute numbers.

Comparative Numbers: Ratios, Proportions, Rates

Not all dictionaries make distinctions among these arithmetic tools of comparison, but statisticians do. A *ratio* compares one segment of a population with another where both numbers come from the same tally and usually make up the whole. For example, the ratio of men to women with respect to reported offenses can be expressed as 3.7:1, meaning that for each reported offense by a woman 3.7 offenses are committed by men or that reported offenses are 3.7 times more common among men than women.

A *proportion* describes the relation between a part and the whole of which it is part. Saying that females comprise 51% of the population of a country is to express the proportion of the whole population that is female. Similarly, in the previous example, we could state that 21.3% of all reported crimes are committed by women.

A *rate* compares events during a specified time against some base of other events, conditions, or people. An important feature of a rate is that one set of events may not come from the same records as other events or conditions. For example, the rate of homicide is expressed as the number of homicides per some unit of population such as 100,000.

Rates are frequently expressed in terms of incidence and prevalence. Each of these expresses the frequency of something happening per some unit of population, usually 100,000, per some unit of time. Each expresses a different feature about the phenomenon in question.

Incidence refers to the number of new cases of a phenomenon per 100,000 persons in the population in some period, usually a calendar year. Therefore, we might speak of the incidence of incarceration in a jurisdiction and express it as 130/100,000 in 1998. This would mean that in 1998 there were 130 persons who started a term in jail for every 100,000 persons in that jurisdiction.

In contrast, three types of *prevalence* allow us to express different features about the frequency of incarceration. *Period prevalence* refers to the number of persons per 100,000 population in the jurisdiction who experienced the situation in question at any time during the year. Whereas incidence indicates those who began a jail term in a given year, prevalence includes persons who were already incarcerated at the beginning of the year. Therefore, period prevalence would never be less than incidence and would usually be higher.

Occasionally knowing *point prevalence* is useful. Point prevalence is the number of persons per 100,000 population who were incarcerated at a specific time such as noon on December 31, 1998. Only those persons who are in jail at that time are counted. Point prevalence is usually lower than period prevalence.

The third type of prevalence that is useful in the study of crime is *lifetime prevalence*. Rather than being limited to a single year or to a single point in time, lifetime prevalence indicates the rate (number per 100,000) of those who have experienced this situation anytime in their life. This can be useful if we want to compare the experiences of different cohorts of persons and if we want to express careers of crime for some category of persons as in the number of incarcerations per 100,000 persons in a given population.

Because incidence and prevalence can result in widely differing estimates of criminality, some jurisdictions report both. Canadian juvenile statistics, for example, report both duplicate (prevalence) and nonduplicate (incidence) counts. Note that all these tools of comparison express relationships. In interpreting crime statistics, it is usually necessary to convert raw numbers into one of these relative forms. When the form is a rate, questions are often raised about its basis.

Bases of Rates

One criticism of official crime rates is that the population base is known with some certainty only for census years. For each succeeding year within a decade, the national population can only be estimated. If the estimate is low, the reported rate is inflated, so that crime rates for, say 1989, are given a spuriously high number in comparison with rates for the census year, 1980.

The question of the appropriate population base to be used in statistics does not end, however, with problems of counting people. Since not all persons are equally vulnerable to the events that interest us, the composition of a population becomes important. Under conditions of unequal risk, it is possible that changes in population composition, rather than changes in behavior, may account for variations in the incidence of events. For example, if adolescents are more frequently involved in automobile theft than people of other ages, then a difference in the number of such crimes committed in two populations may reflect a difference in their age composition rather than a real difference in behavior. Just by looking at age composition, we should expect less automobile theft in a retirement community than in a neighborhood with a large proportion of young people. Similarly, since males commit murder more frequently than do females, a comparison of homicide in two populations requires some control for differences in the proportions of males in the two groups.

The reason for the computation of rates is to express the relation between "the actual and the potential," as Petersen puts it (Peterson 1969b: 79). To increase the accuracy of forecasts, a rate should be refined so that it includes in its denominator all those persons and only those persons who are at risk of whatever kind of event is being tallied in the numerator. Birth rates can be expressed in an undefined way as the number of births per 1,000 persons in the population—known as the *crude birth rate*. Not all persons are at risk of giving birth so the expression of the rates is frequently refined by taking into account the age and sex of persons who are "at risk" of giving birth—women in their childbearing years. Therefore, for purposes of making a population forecast age and sex specific rates are used and expressed as the number of births per 1,000 women between the ages of 15 and 45 in the population in a given year.

To refine a rate in this manner means that one must know something about these relative risks. Sometimes the population at risk is obvious; sometimes it is not. For example, the chance of being killed while traveling by automobile requires that one be in such a vehicle (the hazard of being killed by an automobile is still another matter). Official figures of traffic mortality are not computed on this basis, however. In Canada and the United States the number of traffic fatalities per year is compared with the midyear population of a region or of the country. Sometimes this is refined by estimating from gasoline consumption the number of passenger miles traveled. Nevertheless, no one knows how many people travel how many miles by automobile in specific zones. This means that a jurisdiction with a small residential population, but a large transient population, such as the state of Nevada, will have an artificially inflated rate of death in automobile collisions. Traffic mortality rates are in this sense "crude."

Crime rates are similarly crude approximations of the calculated risk that individuals, groups, or localities will experience different rates of offense. At a minimum, we should expect crime rates to be refined by controlling for age and sex. Infants and the aged are not likely to be offenders. Males and females do differ in their conduct. In addition, much property crime is a function of things to be stolen. Comparisons between populations become more accurate, then, when the rates employed are age-specific, sex-specific, and, if possible, wealth-specific.

Reliability and Validity

Reliability

When social scientists speak of *reliable* measures, they are referring to observations that are consistent and accurate. Measures that are prone to error are, by definition, inconsistent and inaccurate, and consequently, unreliable. Reliability is not an all-or-nothing phenomenon; therefore, social scientists refer to measures having varying degrees of reliability. All indicators of reliability are based on some measure of correlation (discussed below) with the most popular reliability coefficients have a range of zero to one, where zero indicates complete unreliability and one indicates total reliability.

The reliability of measures of crime is affected by many factors. The reliability of official statistics, for example, is influenced by changes in recording patterns. Other things that can introduce error into our measures are attentiveness, variations in memory, and differences in the willingness to tell the truth.

Validity

Valid measures are those that measure what they are supposed to measure; there is a congruence between the measure and social reality it is meant to gauge. Valid indicators of crime reflect how much crime takes place and do not confuse crime with behaviors that are merely noxious, abhorrent, or deviant. For a measure to be valid it must be reliable, although it is possible for reliable (that is, consistent and accurate) measures to be invalid.

Assessing validity is far more difficult than reliability largely because measures can be highly precise and stable but meaningless. Among the ways validity is assessed are the following:

1. Correlating an indicator with related measures. Valid measures ought to correlate highly with other theoretically related measures; invalid measures will likely not do so.
2. Determining whether a measure is consistent with different methods of measurement. For example, do self-reports produce the same results as official indicators of crime?
3. Determining whether measures discriminate between known groups such as persons with criminal records and persons who do not have them.

Correlates and Causes

The search for the causes of conduct among the correlates of behavior requires a comment on correlation and causation. Students who have had courses in statistics will be familiar with some of the points to be made, but a review of these issues is preliminary to criticism of theories of crime causation in later chapters. *Correlation* refers simply to association, while *causation* refers to power to effect a change in events or situations. Science seeks knowledge of causes by sifting correlates suggested as possible causes. The meaning of correlation is therefore crucial.

How Correlations Are Described

There are many measures of association. Most of them express the degree of association between two variables (things that vary in measured quality or quantity) as decimals between zero (no association) and 1 (perfect correlation). The direction, degree, and shape of an association can vary.

The most commonly used correlation in social research is known as *Pearson's r,* so named after the statistician Carl Pearson. If two things are perfectly related and move in the same direction (for example, for every unit increase in the unemployment rate there is some corresponding *increase* in the crime rate), then $r = +1.0$. If absolutely no relationship occurs between the two items, $r = 0.0$. If

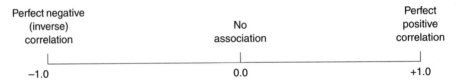

Figure 3.1   Range of the correlation coefficient.

there is a perfect relationship between the items, but they move in opposite directions (for example, for every unit increase in the unemployment rate some corresponding *decrease* in the crime rate appears), then $r = -1.0$. Clearly, the closer
we find the estimated correlation coefficient between two items to the absolute
value of one, the stronger the relationship is between the items.

It is customary to call the variable considered causal, or *independent,* x and to
call the variable considered its effect, or *dependent, y*. When measures of x and y
are plotted on a graph, called a *scattergram* or *scatterplot,* it is again a conven-
tion to draw the x variable along the horizontal axis (abscissa), with small
amounts on the left and larger amounts toward the right. The y variable is plotted
on the vertical axis (ordinate), with small amounts at the bottom and larger quantities toward the top.

Thus, a graph describing measures of income and violent crime might be
drawn like Figure 3.1. This would suggest a perfect, rectilinear (straight-line),
positive association between income and violence, and it would be read as saying
that as x increases or decreases, so does y (that is, they move in the same direction). The association could run in the opposite direction, of course, and describe
a perfect, rectilinear, negative (inverse) association between income and violence, as in Figure 3.2. Negative correlations are expressed with a minus sign to
indicate the inverse nature of the relationship; that is, that the values of the variables move in opposite directions.

In addition, there is no reason in nature why the things we are measuring must
be associated in a straight line, as they have been drawn in Figures 3.2 and 3.3.
Associations may have different shapes; they may curve in many ways. This

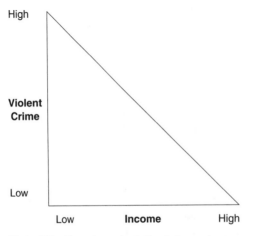

Figure 3.2   Negative association between income and violence.

means that there may be threshold effects—that associations may not be observed for x and y between values of this and that, but are observed, to such-and-such degree, after a certain threshold (value or score) has been passed.

Discussions in the social studies speak constantly of positive and negative correlations. Graphically, this is their meaning. However, it must be remembered that direction is only one quality of an association. Variables are also correlated by degree, that is, by the "closeness" of their association. This refers to the amount of change in y that accompanies a unit change in x.

Why Correlations May Not Be Causes

Various difficulties affect the interpretation of correlations as causes. These can be outlined briefly as issues: (1) temporal and spatial distance between causes and effects, (2) number of data points, (3) spurious interpretation, (4) aggregative fallacy, and (5) confusion of degree of correlation with causal power.

Spatial-Temporal Distance

One problem concerns the distance in time and space that will be allowed to separate a nominated cause from its alleged effect. Sometimes we prefer immediate (proximate) events as probable causes while at other times we look to background (historical) events as causes. Sometimes the correlates must be physically close to their effects as per the dictum, "No causation without communication." Yet at other times, researchers accept causal factors among things presumably associated over great physical, as well as temporal, distance or when one believes that the position of the sun and planets at birth influences daily conduct throughout life.

Debate about distance has an impact upon those social studies that are practical, rather than merely descriptive. In policy sciences, disputes take the form of arguing for, or against, the root causes as opposed to the immediate causes, which are regarded as merely symptoms of the more distant and basic sources of the behaviors to be changed. The conclusion of this book, to be amplified in later

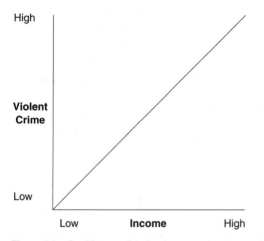

Figure 3.3   Positive association between income and violence.

chapters, is that researchers' purposes and political preferences often select causes and select the distances in time and space over which causation is considered possible (Whitehead and Hayes 1998).

Data Points

A second issue concerns the number of data points from which a correlation coefficient is calculated. It is possible to change how much association is found between two or more variables by adding or subtracting cases from one's scatterplot.

Spurious Interpretation

It has long been noted that one can find correlations among seemingly disparate events. It is this possibility that produces superstition and that makes for interesting statistical games of nonsense correlation. For example, George Marshall found a high relationship (+.86) between death rates in the state of Hyderabad, India, from 1911 to 1919, and membership in the International (solely American) Association of Machinists, from 1912 to 1920 (cited by Cohen and Nagel 1931: 92, n.4). Statisticians call such meaningless correlations "spurious," but this is a misnomer. The correlation is not false; it is actual. What is allegedly spurious is interpretation of such correlations as causal.

Many seemingly nonsensical correlations can be made meaningful by taking into account (controlling for) one or more other variables. Thus, the association in Scandinavia between the number of storks in neighborhoods and their birthrates is made sensible by noting that the association disappears when the rural-urban nature of neighborhoods is controlled—storks residing more frequently in the country. However, a troublesome question persists about which additional variables should be controlled and when. Theory is supposed to advise us on these matters, but, as we will see, judgment is required in evaluating theories.

Significant Correlation and Causal Power

A common error confuses high correlation with causal likelihood. Statisticians have contributed to this confusion by using phrases such as "variance accounted for" and "variance explained by" when interpreting the meaning of correlation coefficients. Such language leads some students to think that "variance accounted for" means causal power. It does not. In nonexperimental research, the degree of association found between two or more variables cannot logically be translated into causal power.

Causal power refers to a prediction, a bet, that if we change x this much, we shall affect y that much. However, a trouble with social scientists' causes is that one cannot infer causal efficacy from correlational significance. Closeness of association is not a measure of causal power.

This point is important because the translation of correlations into causes is probably the most common error in popular thinking and the social studies. It is an error that has affected advice given by economists and sociologists to governments, and it is an error against which we persistently struggle.

Research Designs

To draw inferences and impute causal relationships, researchers use several research designs. While many variations are illustrated in the research literature, four basic approaches dominate: the "true" experimental design, quasi-experimental designs, surveys, and longitudinal designs. While no design is ideal under all circumstances, the different approaches offer advantages and disadvantages for different applications. All research is conducted under practical constraints. These constraints include costs (including dollar costs and time costs) and moral, ethical, and political considerations.

True Experiments

True experimental designs consist of one or more *experimental* groups or conditions and one or more *control* groups or conditions. Experimental conditions identify the circumstances or factors that we believe have some influence or impact. Control conditions act as a comparison against which we compare the behavior of the experimental conditions. If the behavior of an experimental group differs significantly from that of the control group, then we have some reason to infer that the experimental conditions have some influence on behavior not otherwise seen. A comparison or control group is always needed for drawing inferences since no fact or bit of information makes sense on its own. Information only makes sense when it is compared with something else. For example, it is not very instructive to know that the average age of an offender is less than 20 years until we know that the average age in the population at large is more than 20 years. Knowing the homicide rate among white Americans is not very interesting unless we have a point of comparison, such as the homicide rate among Latinos or African Americans, or non-Americans.

Beside incorporating a control or comparison group, true experimental designs address the problem of spuriousness by incorporating the element of *random assignment*. That is to say, the researcher assigns people to either the experimental condition or the control condition on the basis of chance. Where the researcher has no control over who gets into what group, there is always the potential for selection bias. That is, people may choose, or be somehow assigned to one group or the other on some systematic basis that is related to the objective of the study. We may, for example, hypothesize that people who participate regularly in the labor force are less likely to commit crimes than those who are irregular labor force participants. If we do not randomly assign people to labor force conditions, then we cannot be sure that any differences we observe between the two groups are not a consequence of some third factor, such as self-concept, value orientation, or level of formal education.

By randomly assigning people to either the experimental or the control condition, we are reasonably safe in making the assumption that all factors that might influence the outcome, except the one being studied, will cancel themselves out. That is to say, in the previous example no systematic difference should appear between the experimental and control groups on the theoretically spurious factors of self-concept or value orientation since approximately equal numbers of people with high and low values on those factors will be assigned to each group.

While true experimental designs are often seen as the ideal to which we aspire in the social sciences, they are often difficult or impossible to carry out in practice. Besides being impractical, it is generally considered unethical to randomly assign people to labor force conditions simply to observe any potential criminal outcome. Testing the hypothesis that "broken homes cause delinquency" would involve the random assignment of children to "broken" and "nonbroken" homes—again an ethically tenuous act. Unfortunately, testing for many of the variables that we believe to be associated with criminal behavior in experimental circumstances creates these ethical conundrums. Callous experimentation on human subjects, as for example, the many experiments carried out by the Nazis in the early part of this century, makes most of us reel with horror.

Still, where true experimental conditions can be set up (as happens in much of social psychology) we can generally be assured that the control of the experimenter over the circumstances leads to high *internal validity*. That is to say, we can place a high level of credence on the results. Unfortunately, often the artificial circumstances generated by practical experiments lead to poor *external validity*. In other words, we are often not able to generalize the results much beyond the experiment to the population at large.

Quasi-Experiments

Quasi-experimental conditions are those that have many of the same characteristics of true experiments, but are missing one or more crucial components. Most often, quasi-experimental designs do not have a true control group; one that includes individuals randomly assigned to it. Most quasi-experimental designs have one or more comparison groups that *ought* to be similar to the experimental group before the application of the experimental condition. That is, we prefer to have no reason to believe that the comparison groups differ systematically from the experimental group along the study's relevant dimensions.

Quasi-experimental designs are often used to assess the impact of policy changes. For example, the effect of implementing gun control legislation in one jurisdiction may be assessed by comparing that jurisdiction to itself before the legislation was implemented or to others that seem similar except that they have not implemented the legislation (Mundt 1990).

The inferential credibility of quasi-experimental designs is much weaker than for true experimental designs, but they often have greater external validity since the experiment is most often conducted under more realistic circumstances than those found in true experiments conducted under laboratory conditions. Hence, we trade off internal validity for external validity.

Surveys

Surveys are ideal for estimating quantities within populations. For example, if we wish to know the mean income in a community, or to find rates of victimization, we turn to surveys. On the other hand, survey research is a poor device for imputing causal relationships. The difficulty of imputing causal relationships within surveys stems from two facts. First, and most importantly, surveys do not allow for the physical control of spurious variables. In survey research, the researcher has no control over who ends in what circumstances. Commonly, the groups to which people belong are self-selected. Over the years, we have developed some very sophisticated statistical techniques for addressing the problem of selection bias and spuriousness, but this approach is less than ideal. Only those factors that we can identify as likely having an impact are controlled in statistical models. Unlike experimental designs with their random assignment procedure, unthought of or unidentified factors that may affect surveys are not addressed.

A second problem with most surveys is that they are point-in-time snapshots of social processes. Most surveys do not include a *longitudinal,* or time, component. Thus, while we can easily correlate the two factors, *A* and *B*, in survey research, it is difficult to decide whether factor *A* came before factor *B* or vice versa. As you will recall, a necessary condition for imputing causality is that the cause precedes the effect. In models tested with survey data, we must make strong theoretical assumptions about what precedes what—something that has not always proved successful.

In criminology, survey research is the workhorse for generating data. Relatively speaking, large-scale surveys are easier to carry out than large-scale experiments; they have high levels of external validity, and they avoid many, but not all, of the ethical issues sometimes associated with experiments. Unfortunately, they are lower on internal validity than well-formulated experiments. It is for this reason that we so often face apparently contradictory results in the research literature.

Longitudinal Designs

In an attempt retain the strength of survey designs, but to mitigate some of their limitations, many researchers are now turning to longitudinal research. At the individual level, they employ such things as cohort models, where a group of people is followed over time. Actual dates of events are recorded so that we can see how social processes evolve in people's lives instead of relying on the single point snapshot. Sometimes this research is called life history research. Unlike with simple survey research, life history research helps us to disentangle the causal relations among factors of interest. Unfortunately, the major limitation of life history research is that it takes us a long time to collect the data (over a lifetime) and the relationships that we discover are always subject to the possibility that they are a consequence of unique historical circumstances. Much life history research is also expensive to conduct since it requires detailed data collection over long periods. A great deal of cost is associated with tracking people as they move and unless observations are made in short intervals, recall or memory decay may be a major problem. The successful analysis of life history data also requires a level of statistical expertise beyond that pursued by most social scientists.

A second form of longitudinal research involves the collection of aggregate data over time. Often, this involves the use of official statistics. A great deal of recent research into the economics of crime has focused on the impact of aggregate economic factors (e.g., the rate of unemployment, per capita expenditures on policing) on crime rates. While this research offers some technical statistical challenges, the greatest difficulty is posed by official statistics not always being collected in the same manner over time. How unemployment or crime is defined and counted, for example, does not stay the same in the long term. Who is considered unemployed is influenced by how we define those seeking jobs as opposed to those simply out of the labor force (the so-called "discouraged," for example). The pool of behavior defined as criminal changes as some behaviors are decriminalized and yet others become criminal.

Overall, research designs are the procedures we employ to help us in describing criminal behavior and in imputing likely causal relationships. No single design is ideal under all circumstances, and all have their inherent strengths and weaknesses. What we think we know in the social sciences evolves as our theoretical and methodological experience grows and we accumulate results from a variety of research. Our knowledge is certainly less than perfect, but it improves in validity as the discipline evolves.

Conclusion: Interpreting Correlation

Causation is a common idea and an indispensable one. It is not, however, a clear concept. In fact, more than one idea is embedded in the notion of causation (Collingwood 1940; Hertzberg 1975). Without becoming entangled in philosophical questions about the meaning of causation and the ways in which causes are known, it is sufficient for present purposes to note that criminologists study the social locations of various offenses as part of their effort to explain differences in conduct. The social locations of the serious crimes are the facts upon which explanations of crime are built. They are also the facts that such explanations must make comprehensible.

It is important, then, to look at the major correlates of the more serious offenses. In reviewing these associations, remember that these correlations do not in themselves describe causes and that the strength and shape of these relationships vary with what surrounds them. An exception occurs, we will see, with the shape of the age distribution of criminality. Otherwise, the connections to be described are not absolute; they do not operate in a vacuum, and they need not remain as they are now observed. The correlates of crime are themselves variables whose meaning for behavior changes with the social setting in which the association occurs. In the chapters that follow, we will consider the various sources of information used in the study of crime, the major social correlates of crime (social locations of serious crime), and a broad range of explanations of crime.

Part II

Measurement of Crime

4. Counting Crime Officially

Why Count Crime?

Tallies of crime are important for several reasons. They are required for purposes of description, risk assessment, program evaluation, and explanation.

1. *Description.* In modern times legislators and concerned citizens have been interested in the "moral health" of their communities and countries. Crime statistics represent one gauge of communal well-being, and it is usual for increases in crime to be interpreted as a sign of social decay.
2. *Risk assessment.* Measures of criminal activity among different social groups permit estimates of the relative risk of appearing on either or both sides of crime: becoming an offender or becoming a victim.
3. *Program evaluation.* Lawmakers and their constituents commonly justify responding to crime as rehabilitative, incapacitating, and deterrent. To determine how much any of these ends is achieved by different modes of prevention and control requires tallies of crime. These tallies allow us to be rational rather than emotional about the issue.
4. *Explanation.* Criminological theories address themselves principally, but not solely, to explanations of differences in crime rates from one time to another and between social groups. For most people, explanations are causal statements, and even those theorists who minimize or deny the search for causes nevertheless use implicit causal models. Identifying causes requires, at a minimum, that we can relate differences in rates of crime to differences in people and their situations. In short, the search for causes requires facts.

Later chapters describe and criticize major attempts to explain crime. For scientific purposes, the usefulness of such theories depends upon how well they fit the facts. In contrast, for political purposes theories are as good or bad as the side they support. Since our concern is with satisfying the quest for knowledge, we direct our attention to the quality of facts about crime.

Any measure of human action becomes less accurate as it is filtered through social sieves. The more the records used as measures of crime are "socially processed," the less valid they are as indicators of all criminal acts. This source of distortion affects, in various degrees, all attempts to count crime and other social events. It leads to another criminological axiom: every measure of crime for an aggregate of individuals probably underestimates its actual amount. The assumed, but unknown, quantity of criminal activity is called the *dark figure* of crime.

The dark figure would not be an obstacle to understanding crime causation if the underreporting were random or if it were systematically biased in some known manner. If the difference between crimes committed and crimes recorded is biased in some unknown way, then many competing explanations of differences in rates of crime may be plausible.

There is competition among explanations. The kind of criminogenic theory one is apt to find most satisfactory is only partly related to the facts one believes. How satisfactory an explanation seems is also affected by one's philosophy of social life and what one wants to see accomplished.

Six Counts of Crime

Six kinds of tallies have been used in counting crime: official statistics and five types of unofficial measures. The unofficial tallies, to be discussed in Chapters 5, 6, and 7, include counts made through direct observation, private policing, unobtrusive (indirect) measures, surveys of victims, and self-reports.

As might be expected of attempts to count complex activities in varied settings, none of these measures is without error. Each has its distinctive set of advantages and disadvantages. Each is insensitive to some segment of the range of all possible wrongs. We will examine whether these different measures point toward similar or different clusters of criminal conduct. The results have implications for being able to make a reasoned choice among competing explanations of crime.

The Nature of Official Statistics

Crimes Known to the Police

The most popular measure of crime is official statistics of crimes and, in particular, offenses "known to the police." This is a different measure, of course, from arrests made, prosecutions begun, and convictions obtained. There is a large loss in numbers as one moves down each of these steps in response to crime. The social processing of crime reduces the amount of crime being assessed.

Crimes known to the police are themselves a result of social processing. The majority of crimes that police departments investigate are reported to them, rather than discovered by them. Complaints to the police are subject to errors that result from mistakes and from lies. With an awareness of such errors, every modern criminal justice system has developed counting rules to be applied by the police in an effort to count only the "actual amount" of crime after discounting for mistakenly and maliciously reported injuries. Crimes known to the police are corrected by subtracting from all complaints those which, upon investigation, are judged to be *unfounded*; that is, did not happen or were not attempted.

It is obvious that some discretion is involved in the application of these, and other, counting rules. Discretion means that different police departments may interpret the same rules in different ways and thus "produce" more and less crime of a particular kind (Black 1970; Ferracuti et al. 1962; Seidman and Couzens 1974).

The proportion of unfounded crime varies with the kind of crime. The emotionally charged contexts of different criminal events seem to affect the amount of unfounding. For example, figures for the United States discount on average 4% of the allegations of "serious offenses," according to the FBI's annual Uniform Crime Reports. Such discounting usually ranges from about 2% of larceny complaints to around 15% of forcible rape complaints.

What Do Official Statistics Measure?

Statistics on crime are constantly disputed. They should be. The critical citizen's doubts about the validity of public figures have never been better summarized than by an English economist who was long accustomed to their use. Sir Josiah Stamp (1880–1941) advised us that "the government are very keen on amassing statistics. They collect them, raise them to the nth power, take the cube root, and prepare wonderful diagrams. But you must never forget that every one of these figures comes in the first instance from the village watchman, who just puts down what he damn pleases."

Stamp's warning applies today. There are errors in every tally of social events. Just counting the number of people in a country is difficult enough. A cross-check of the United States censuses for 1970, 1980, and 1990, for example, suggested that 2 to 3% of the overall population were probably missed, (Choldin 1994; Jennis 1984; Skogan 1974) and even higher percentages among selected social groups (Jennis 1984; Choldin 1994). The problem is not limited to the United States. Similar undercounts are found in both France (Coeffic 1993) and Great Britain (Simpson 1994). If recording mere numbers of people is open to error, counting what they are like and what they do is even more difficult.

All social statistics are suspect. Modern governments and large interest groups such as labor unions and manufacturers' associations all have research departments that count people, conditions, and events. Their tallies are used as arguments for their preferred policies. Yet, we are aware that all these enumerations have deficiencies.

The question every serious student asks is, "Who counted what, and how?" When this question is raised about the statistics we take for granted, the consequence is an illuminating shock. How, for example, is race or ethnicity counted? By asking people about their identity, by guessing from their appearance, or by making judgments on the basis of surnames—with the consequence that tallies of "races" in a multiethnic society can be moved about whimsically, as the demographer William Petersen has shown with Hawaiian data (Peterson 1969a).

How are suicide and other causes of death counted? Not by witnessing them, but by attributing them in a social process of definition and negotiation (Douglas 1967). How are "illegitimate" births counted? In some of the United States, not at all. In other states, "children of all married women—including separated women regardless of whether the father of the child is their husband—are considered legitimate" (Berkov and Sklar 1975: 365).

How is "unemployment" counted? Chiefly by means of a survey that asks a representative sample whether they had been working "last week" and, if not, whether they were looking for a job.

Criticism of Official Statistics

A critical attitude toward tallies of social events does not mean that one dispenses with statistics; it only makes one careful about using them. In criminology, those who take such an attitude admit that the real amount of all crime is never known. There are, however, differences across types of crime in the adequacy of official statistics.

Differences in police activity, for example, make a difference in the swelling and receding of crime rates. Thus, upon the death of the antipornography laws in Denmark in the 1960s, some "sex crimes" were reported to have declined. It would be more accurate however, to say that while human sexual behavior probably did not change much in Denmark, the law did, and with it police activity.

A difference in vigilance on the part of the police is apparent, too, in the English experience with changes in laws concerning homosexual offenses. The Wolfenden Committee on Homosexual Offenses and Prostitution was initiated in 1954. Within a year or two, it was common knowledge that this committee would recommend not using the criminal law to interfere with the private sexual behavior of consenting adults. Walker notes that by 1966 the number of recorded homosexual offenses had dropped to half the number recorded in 1955, even though no change in the law had occurred (Walker 1971: 27). Behavior had undoubtedly not changed all that much, but police activity had.

Official tallies of criminal activity are questioned, therefore, as to what counts; how the official numbers are interpreted; and who does the counting, and how.

What Counts?

Definitions and Decisions

An occurrence called a "crime" may involve one offender, or many; one victim, or many; and one breach of the criminal law, or more. A political assassin may kill the head of state and wound two bystanders. An embezzler may steal $1,000 a month for eight years before being caught and may forge some documents in the process. A father may have intercourse with his daughter several times before he is apprehended. One robber can hold up ten people in a tavern, take their money, shoot and kill the bartender, and make a getaway in a stolen car.

In each of these examples, a decision is involved about how many crimes to count. The rule in England and Wales for attacks on a person is "one victim, one crime." Canada and the United States follow a similar practice. For offenses against property, the English have as yet no clear rule for counting, while Americans and Canadians try to call "one operation, one crime." In North America, when more than one crime occurs in an "operation," as in our example of the holdup in the tavern, the most serious of the offenses is counted. The gravity of an offense is determined by the maximum legal punishment it carries.

Definitions and decisions intrude upon all these principles, and they do so in a way that makes official statistics inadequate measures of who is doing what to whom. For example, Silverman and Teevan point out that under the counting rules that apply in North America, robbery may be tallied differently depending upon where it occurs, even though the losses are identical (Silverman and Teevan 1980: 72). "If," they note, "four people live in four different apartments in the same building and each [is robbed], then four offenses are counted in official statistics. However, if those four people happen to be gathered in the lobby of that apartment building and are robbed . . . then only one offense is counted."

In this example, the robber may be charged with more than one offense whether or not the tally of offenses shows one crime or four. This possibility suggests yet another difficulty with official counts of crime. From present statistics, there is no way of knowing how many offenders commit how many crimes, of which variety, and with how many victims.

Interpreting and Using Official Figures

All social statistics are imperfect measures of whatever they are supposed to indicate. The concerned citizen does well to pay attention to what has been counted when interpreting all official figures. Such attention sometimes provides a new view of social reality. It is a healthy exercise, for example, to find out what is counted by the official recorders in one's city as they compute such "social indicators" as unemployment, suicide, income per person, mental health, and educational opportunity.

The utility of imperfect measures of social events and conditions depends on what one is trying to do with them. It will become obvious in this chapter and in Chapters 5 to 7 that neither official statistics nor unofficial tallies are sensitive measures of all the criminal damage human beings do one another. This does not, however, render them useless. If our purpose is to ascertain whether approximate quantities of the serious crimes vary among individuals in different social locations, then we can obtain a more reliable estimate by using several measures to map crime of a particular kind. As the maps drawn by a variety of estimation devices become similar, we gain confidence in our picture of reality. On the other hand, if different measures of presumably the same activity locate crime in widely different segments of the population, then criminologists are without facts. Facts are both what are to be explained and the means by which explanations are constructed. Fortunately, the major maps of criminality converge; they plot similar patterns of kinds of crime. What to count when counting crime, however, remains in contention. The issue is part of the question about who does the counting, and how.

Who Does the Counting, and How?

Statistical Problems

Official statistics on crime are imperfect not only because of what is and what is not included, but also because of imperfections in the way in which the counting is done. Those who criticize official records on this score reaffirm Sir Josiah Stamp's skepticism. If human beings are doing the counting, they themselves are a source of unreliability in the tallies. Questions must be raised about the biases of those who do the recording and the procedures by which they come to record a crime.

Official statistics on crime are generated by the police in two ways—in response to complaints made to them and through their own surveillance. In both cases, a decision is involved as to whether a crime has been committed and whether it is worth acting upon.

The vigilance with which a police department responds to complaints and records them is a variable. Vigilance varies, for example, with the organization of the police department, with the discipline of its personnel, and with the political pressures upon it. When more or less attention is paid to certain types of crime than was the case previously, this will manifest itself in changes in the officially reported rates of crime. The changed rates do not reflect changes in criminal behavior, but changes in enforcement behavior or recording behavior.

Reactive Measures

One trouble with police statistics on crime is that such measures may be reactive; that is, they may respond to considerations other than the events being counted. Statistics on crime as set down by the police are to some unknown extent manipulable for political purposes. Since these figures are used as a measure of police performance, police departments can improve their "paper performance" by misclassifying or downgrading offenses or even by failing to record citizens complaints (Ericson 1981, 1982; Seidman and Couzens 1974; Valentine 1971).

Coding Variations

Political pressures and biases are not the only possible sources of unreliability in official records. Coding practices also may differ. When a complaint is made to the police and logged as "known to the police," a clerk must classify the crime. What shall it be called? Although modern countries have rules of classification under which local departments are supposed to sort offenses, there is leeway in definition. It is conceivable, then, that even the best-intentioned, unbiased police departments may record crimes known to them under different headings. For example, Silverman finds that cities of comparable demographic characteristics, in the same geographic region, operating under one set of reporting rules, can nevertheless put the rules into practice in ways that yield different pictures of the quantity of crime. Silverman was intrigued by the fact that two large Canadian cities, Calgary and Edmonton, located only 180 miles apart in the same province, and operating with the same coding rules as set out by the Canadian Uniform Crime Reporting System (CUCR), listed consistent differences in crime rates between 1969 and 1975 (Silverman 1980).

Edmonton consistently showed $1\frac{1}{2}$ to $2\frac{1}{2}$ times the number of forcible rapes that Calgary reported, $1\frac{1}{2}$ to 2 times the number of assaults, and 2 times the number of robberies. After interviews with officers in charge of records and tests of coders' reliability, Silverman concludes that much of the variation in reported crime between these cities results from different ways of processing information.

This does not mean that a police department is doing something wrong. It means that human events are complex actions and that the title given an occurrence depends on many variables, including the subjective importance attached to elements in the happening (Bateson 1979).

In this vein, Silverman notes that sex offenses are particularly difficult to classify:

> The meanings of rape, indecent assault, and "other sex offenses" seem to baffle police, classifiers, and many other participants in the criminal justice system. This results from the concepts of sexual morality that underlie these offenses. . . . The nature of the offense and the cultural meanings we give to those offenses can make it unclear whether a rape, an indecent assault, or an act of gross indecency has taken place. (Silverman 1980: 272)

It is sometimes difficult for police and crime coders to make distinctions between "assault," "assault occasioning bodily harm," and "wounding." Furthermore, "assault with intent to steal" may be counted as an assault in one city and a robbery in another.

All of this means that, while trend lines can be drawn in crime rates for a city that does not change its coding practices, comparisons between cities and, even more, between countries using different coding rules have a questionable validity.

Suggested Remedies

Difficulties in classifying events finely can be relieved by broadening the classification. Thus, one could avoid the unreliability in coding rapes and related sexual attacks by grouping them under the broader title of "sexual assault," which is what changes to the Criminal Code of Canada have done. This procedure gains reliability at the cost of more detailed information.

Police Discretion

The fact that criminal conduct must be socially processed before it becomes part of the official record has stimulated studies of the differential selection of offenders, particularly juveniles, for arrest and referral to court.

Western Studies

In Western countries, studies of police discretion do not give evidence of any striking extralegal bias in response to the more serious offenders. Research of the past 30 years can be summarized as follows:

1. About 80 to 85% of incidents to which police attend are *calls for service* or *dispatches.* That is, police find out about crimes principally from citizen complaints. About 15% of crimes become known to the police through *on-view mobilizations,* in which officers initiate contacts in response to events that occur in their presence. About 5% of police action occurs in response to requests from "citizens in the field" (Black and Reiss 1967).

2. The majority of police contacts with juveniles are handled informally without referral to court. Gravity of a crime is the principal factor determining a police decision to proceed with judicial action. The social status and ethnicity of offenders are insignificant factors affecting police response to young people. Young people's demeanor toward police makes a difference in their response to minor offenses, but not to serious ones (Black 1970; Friedrich 1977; Goldman 1963; Hohenstein 1969; Ludman et al. 1978; McEachern and Bauzer 1967; Pilavin and Briar 1964; Shannon 1963; Terry 1967; Thornberry 1973; Weiner and Willie 1971).

3. Complainants' attitudes toward young predators affect the decisions of the police. A large-scale study of policing in Boston, Chicago, and Washington, DC, reports that "in not one instance did the police arrest a juvenile when the complainant lobbied for leniency. [However], when a complainant explicitly expresses a preference for an arrest . . . the tendency of the police to comply is also quite strong" (Black and Reiss 1967: 71).

Black and Reiss note that African Americans have a higher rate of arrest as juveniles than whites because (1) more serious crimes were charged against them and (2) African Americans were more frequently involved in encounters where there were complainants, themselves predominantly African American; and (3) African American complainants more frequently pressed for arrest than did white complainants.

4. Studies of police response to offenses by adults also indicate that gravity of the crime is the major factor affecting arrest (Lundman et al. 1978; Sykes and Clarke 1975; Sykes et al. 1976).

In Western countries, legal factors determine decisions far more than extralegal biases do at all levels of the criminal justice apparatus—from decisions to report a crime, to arrest of a suspect, to release of a suspect before trial, to decision to prosecute, and on to sentencing and the administration of offenders in institutions and on probation and parole (Friedman 1975; Gottfredson and Gottfredson 1980; Hann et al. 1973; Konechi and Elobesen 1986; Nettler 1979; Walsh 1991). This generalization does not mean that justice is perfect, but rather that, in the present context of concern with the meaning of official data, police activity is largely responsive to legally relevant considerations.

Uniform application of the criminal law does not require equal outcomes in administration of the law. Legally permissible considerations may produce unequal outcomes. Thus, a philosophy that wishes official response to juvenile offenders to be protective and reformative, rather than punitive, constrains the options of decision makers. One such option, for example, is remanding errant youths to responsible homes rather than placing them in detention. Different ideas about what justice is, also affect uses of the law. The following example from a multiethnic society illustrates the point.

Research in Israel

Israel is a multicultural society, sensitive to differences among its citizens in ethnicity and socioeconomic status. Investigators have therefore tested for possible biases in administration of the criminal law. Their research illuminates again the relationship between legally specified responses to crime and the discretion required by different peoples' senses of justice.

Rahav tested for differential response to the delinquencies of Jews of European descent (Ashkenazim), Jews of Afro-Asian ancestry (Sephardim), and Arabs (Rahav 1980). He found that punishment varied with the social status of these ethnic groups. Rahav controlled for age, number of siblings, broad categories of offenses, and number of previous arrests. He found that Afro-Asian Jews were treated more harshly than European Jews. In addition, Arab youths were more likely than Jewish youths to be incarcerated.

Rahav does not attribute these differences to bias. Arab officers handle Arab youths in Israel, and these officials "assign more weight to the social harm caused by the offense, settlement of the issue between the offender's and victim's families, and local public opinion" (Rahav 1980: 71). Arab officers, working with their conceptions of justice, recommend incarceration more frequently for their delinquents than Jewish officials do for Jewish delinquents.

The differential treatment of Ashkenazim and Sephardim by Jewish officials is a function of Sephardic families having poorer resources for controlling their children. Officials therefore assume that more Afro-Asian children are in need of supervision when they break the law.

Landau also studied police decisions in prosecuting juvenile offenders in Israel (1978). He examined the relationship between status variables and police disposition for four classes of offenders: (1) those who had no previous arrest; (2) those with a previous arrest, but no previous referral to court; (3) those with previous referral to court, but without proceedings having been taken; and (4) those with previous court appearance. He found that previous referral to court and previous court appearance were strong predictors of police decision to prosecute. In general, Landau found no bias in police processing.

These Israeli investigations remind us that a group's sense of justice affects how its laws are interpreted. Tests of fair application of police and judicial discretion must recognize the reasons that discretion is allowed in the application of the law. These purposes vary with a people's sense of justice. More accurately, such purposes constitute a people's sense of justice.

Note: On Data Processing

Landau's research points to a deficiency in much previous testing for bias in judicial functioning that deserves comment here.

Decision makers—whether they be police, judges, juries, or citizens—do not make up their minds by weighing isolated factors one at a time. Decision making derives from a patterning of data and from making sense of a number of intertwined considerations. Therefore, to be fair, statistical tests of judgment must operate more like a decision maker; it becomes inappropriate, then, to test for bias one variable at a time. Correlations that appear significant between one factor and an outcome can dissolve toward nonsignificance when many variables are simultaneously tested for their relationship with a presumed effect.

Wilbanks and Lewis (1981) provide a demonstration similar to Landau's. They do so in response to a newspaper's allegation that Florida police are disciplined in a different fashion when they allegedly use "excessive force" against Anglos, African Americans, and Latinos. The newspaper had come to its conclusion after examining correlations between disciplinary treatment of officers and legally relevant and irrelevant variables one at a time. When Wilbanks and Lewis reanalyze the data with techniques that assess the relative degree of association between one variable and an outcome with a number of variables controlled simultaneously, they find no evidence of ethnic bias in responding to complaints against officers.

Conclusion: Police Discretion

Getting arrested is an interactional process. The police force, the police officer, the victim, and the offender do make a difference—up to some limit—in determining what is recorded as crime. The question is whether this interaction systematically biases the official statistics of a particular jurisdiction or for a particular period. The best answer seems to be that official records in democracies reflect the operation of a judicial sieve.

What are counted, finally, as crimes are those offenses that are more obvious and more serious and that have complaining victims or dead ones. What counts is those crimes for which the public puts pressure on the police to make arrests. A survey of research on the uses of police discretion in Canada and the United States concludes that "police powers seem to reside, for better or worse, in the hands of the people" (Hagan 1972: 11).

For those localities in which the matter has been studied, official tallies of arrests do not seem to be strongly biased by extralegal considerations. These studies confirm common sense. They indicate that if you are apprehended committing a minor offense, being respectful to the police officer may get you off. If, on the other hand, you are apprehended for a minor violation and you talk tough to the "cop," the encounter will probably escalate into arrest. If you are caught in a more serious crime, for example, robbing a bank, being respectful to the police is not likely to keep you from being arrested.

To repeat, similar findings of fairness are reported in Western democracies for other facets of the criminal justice process than policing. As previously noted, studies of decisions to prosecute, to release suspects before trial, to sentence, and to administer offenders on parole or probation show in general that legal factors determine activities far more than do extralegal prejudices (Friedman 1975; Gottfredson and Gottfredson 1980; Hannet et al. 1973; Konechi and Ebbeson 1982).

Don and Michael Gottfredson conclude their survey of (mostly American) research on many phases of judicial work by stating that "throughout the system" three factors play "a persistent and major role" in decisions: gravity of the offense, previous criminal record of the offender, and the personal relationship between offender and victim (1980: 330).

Complaints by Victims

Official statistics of crime are reactive indicators. They respond to something other than the amount of crime. It has been noted that the official numbers may be responsive to changes in police activity—changes either in the use of police discretion or in police coding of crimes. There is, however, an additional influence on recorded statistics on crime, and that is changes in the willingness of victims to report to the police.

It has been pointed out that police work is largely responsive to citizens' complaints. It involves reaction rather than surveillance. This means that the amount of crime known to the police will fluctuate with changes in a citizenry's habits of reporting crimes. It is possible, then, that crimes known to the police may increase, not because more crime is being committed, but because more crime is being reported.

Crime Counts

Despite the great concern most citizens have for crime, few have any but the vaguest notions of how much crime is committed either in their community or country. Furthermore, when asked to provide an estimate, most will overestimate the relative proportion of serious personal offenses and underestimate the proportion of property offenses.

One of the likely reasons for this lack of knowledge concerning the amount of crime that takes place is due to the sources from which people draw their information regarding crime. For many, views of crime are molded by television series and newspaper accounts of notorious incidents. Interestingly, decent estimates of crime, especially at the national level, are relatively recent events. The first systematic attempt to collect official statistics at the national level is generally believed to be the French *Compte Générale*, originally published in 1825 (Vold 1986). Systematic reports of American crime statistics did not occur until the introduction of the FBI's (UCR) in 1930.

The UCR consisted of submissions to the FBI of crimes known to the police and arrests by local police departments throughout the United States. As the title suggests, an attempt was made to make the reporting of crime uniform through the use of a common set of recording procedures. Because of definitional and counting problems, attention was focused on a set of *index crimes* that originally included murder and nonnegligent manslaughter, forcible rape, robbery, aggravated assault, burglary, larceny-theft, and motor vehicle theft. Later, in 1979, arson was added to the index. The first four offenses are often used to index "violent personal crimes" while the latter four index "property crime." The concept of a crime index has proven to be popular over the years both among the public and law enforcement officials since it is simple, concise, represents a reasonable mix of more serious offenses and in the days before networked computers, could be generated in a timely fashion. As the national collation of official police statistics broadened, the index crimes became known as Part I offenses while other categories of recorded offenses became known as Part II offenses. While originally somewhat sparse in coverage, the FBI now claims to incorporate 98% of the nation in the annual reports.

As indicated previously, official police statistics have been the focus of significant criticism. The demand that they serve as a "true" count of how much crime exists in a community will likely never be met. At best, it may be possible for official statistics to act as a valid "indicator" of the amount of crime that exists, and at least, as an indicator of police productivity. In order to serve these purposes well, however, it is essential that the data recorded by the police are accurate, timely, and consistent. Those requirements are highly influenced by technology, particularly in a large jurisdiction such as the United States. Taking advantage of technological innovations in information processing, the National Incident Based Reporting System (NIBRS) was introduced in 1991. The NIBRS is designed to collect data on single incidents known to police and arrests within 22 crime categories. For each offense known, incident, victim, property offender, and arrestee information is to be gathered and recorded where it is available. In 1995, nine jurisdictions were submitting data based on the NIBRS with many more involved in pretests. Ultimately, it is expected that all police agencies will contribute to the NIBRS data base.

Brief definitions of the index crimes have been extracted from the UCR and are reproduced in Box 4.1.

Table 4.1 presents the number of index crimes known to police as reported in the 1995 UCR. As the table indicates, there were an estimated 23,000 criminal homicides (murder and nonnegligent manslaughter) in 1995. This turns out to be a rate of about 9 per 100,000 people. Fortunately, these acts occur far less frequently than other index offenses. The most common offenses, on the other hand, are crimes against property, with larceny/theft being recorded at a rate of 3,025 per 100,000 people (see Figure 4.1).

If we are concerned with the reliability of official statistics, it is likely that the figures for criminal homicide are a more accurate representation of the "actual" amount of crime that exists than those for the less serious property offenses. It is certainly not unreasonable to conclude that property offenses are significantly underestimated because they are underreported. The only significant exception to this is probably motor vehicle theft. Since most cars are insured against theft, a higher proportion of this type of theft is reported to the police.

Given that the index crimes likely constitute a biased index, the question immediately arises as to whether police statistics ought to be used for anything other than workload indicators. One response is that biased indicators can be useful, if the bias is consistent. Thus, while the counts for burglary or larceny may underestimate the true count by some unknown factor, that undercount may not be a problem if it is relatively consistent from year to year. Index crimes, therefore, may still provide a reasonable index of the variation in crime from year to year. Figure 4.1 shows the trend in index crimes for the past three and a half decades. For the most part, what we see is a fairly constant increase from 1960 to date. Some have suggested, however, that there has been a leveling-off in rates throughout the late 1980s and early 1990s. Several categories of property crimes such as burglary and theft appear to confirm this suspicion.

Table 4.1 Crimes Known to the Police: Part I Offenses, 1994.

Offense	Number of crimes known to police	Rate per 100,000 people	Percent cleared by arrest
Murder and nonnegligent manslaughter	23,305	9	62.7
Forcible rape	102,096	39	51.4
Robbery	618,817	238	24.0
Aggravated assault	1,119,950	430	55.1
Total violent crime	1,864,168	716	45.3
Burglary	2,712,156	1,042	12.8
Larceny / theft	7,876,254	3,025	20.5
Motor vehicle theft	1,539,097	591	13.1
Total property crime	12,127,507	4,658	18.8

Source: FBI (1995). Uniform Crime Reports, Washington, DC: USGPO.

Box 4.1   Definitions of Index Crime

1. *Murder and nonnegligent manslaughter:* The willful (nonnegligent) killing of one human being by another, committed without defense or excuse. Not included are deaths caused by negligence, suicide, or accident; justifiable homicide; and attempts to murder or assaults to murder, which are scored as aggravated assaults.
2. *Forcible rape:* The carnal knowledge of a female forcibly and against her will. Assaults or attempts to commit rape by force or threat of force are also included; however, statutory rape (without force) and other sex offenses are excluded.
3. *Robbery:* The taking or attempting to take anything of value from the care, custody, or control of a person or persons by force or threat of force or violence and/or putting the victim in fear.
4. *Aggravated assault:* An unlawful attack by one person upon another for the purpose of inflicting severe or aggravated bodily injury. This type of assault is accompanied by the use of a weapon or by means likely to produce death or great bodily harm. Attempt is included since it is not necessary that an injury result when a weapon is used which could result in serious person injury if the crime were successfully completed.
5. *Burglary:* The unlawful entry of a structure with intent to commit a felony or theft. The use of force to gain entry is not required to classify an offense as a burglary.
6. *Larceny/theft:* The unlawful taking, carrying, leading, or riding away of property from the possession or constructive possession of another. Included are shoplifting, pocket-picking, purse-snatching, thefts from motor vehicles, thefts of motor vehicle parts and accessories, bicycle thefts, etc., in which no force, violence, or fraud occurs. Excluded are embezzlement, "con" games, forgery, issuing worthless checks, and motor vehicle theft (which is treated separately).
7. *Motor vehicle theft:* The theft or attempted theft of a motor vehicle; includes stealing of automobiles, trucks, buses, motorcycles, motorscooters, snowmobiles, etc.
8. *Arson:* Any willful or malicious burning or attempt to burn, with or without intent to defraud, a dwelling, house, public building, motor vehicle or aircraft, personal property of another, etc. Fires of suspicious or unknown origin are excluded.

Source: FBI (1996). Uniform Crime Reports, Washington, DC: USGPO.

Column four of Table 4.1 indicates the percentage of crimes known to the police that are cleared by arrest. There are two aspects of these data that are of particular importance. First, only a minority of offenses appear to be cleared by arrest and second, there is considerable variability in clearance rates across categories of crime. The rates of clearance by arrest are highest for homicide or other personal offenses where the offender is most likely to be known or recognizable to the victim. Property offenses, particularly in those instances where the offender remains anonymous or unseen, are the least likely to be cleared. Thus, it is apparent that the use of arrest data to measure rates of crime would undoubtedly lead to gross undercounts.

Besides the fact that annual clearance rates tend to give substantially lower annual estimates than crimes known to police, annual rates of arrest pose another problem. That problem arises because not all crimes that end up being cleared, are cleared in the year in which they take place. Some homicides, for example, end up being cleared 20 or more years after the event takes place. The

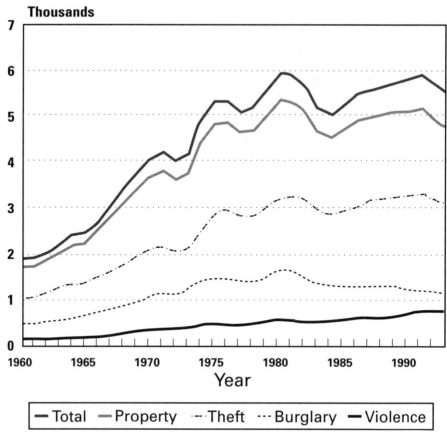

Figure 4.1   Offenses known to police (per 100,000 inhabitants), 1960–1993 (Maguire and Pastore 1993).

time lag for clearances of property crimes is probably less dramatic than for some homicides but the fact remains that there will be some "bleeding" across reporting periods.

International Comparisons

Despite the fact that most countries, particularly in the developed world, have had systematic collecting and reporting schemas for official statistics for many years, little international research based on those data has been conducted. The primary reason for this appears to be that differences in definitions of crimes and variations in the collection and reporting of data have made researchers dubious of the validity of such comparisons. Where such research does exist, however, it tends to focus primarily on crimes against the person with a particular emphasis on murder and homicide (Archer and Gartner 1984; Avison and Loring 1986; Li 1995; Pampel and Gartner 1995).

It is often interesting, however, to gauge how well one's own society stacks up to other societies. While direct comparisons are difficult since definitions of crimes and criminal justice procedures vary from one society to another, some comparisons are close enough to give us a relative perspective.

Table 4.2   Crimes Known to Police for England and Wales, 1993 (United Kingdom, 1994).

Offense	Rate per 100,000 population
Violence against the person	400
Sexual offenses	61
Robbery	113
Burglary	2,671
Theft and handling stolen goods	5,367
Fraud and forgery	318
Criminal damage	1,768
Other offenses	80
Total	10,777

Tables 4.2 and 4.3 represent summaries of crimes known to the police for England and Wales and for Canada. Both are analogous to those generated by the UCR. Both of these nations share a common law heritage with the United States; thus, one would expect there to be a reasonable similarity among the definitions of criminality. Despite the similarities in heritage, however, it is clear that perfect matching is not possible.

As indicated, one offense for which considerable effort has been made to elicit international comparisons is criminal homicide or murder. In Table 4.4, homicide rates are provided for 13 major international cities. What is of particular interest here is that most large international cities have significantly lower homicide rates than those found in comparable American cities. On the other hand, a

Table 4.3   Crimes Known to Police, Canada, 1994.

Offense	Number	Rate per 100,000 persons
Homicide	596	2
Attempted murder	918	3
Sexual assault	31,690	108
Nonsexual assault	236,364	808
Robbery	28,888	99
Other crimes of violence	4,942	17
Total crimes of violence	303,398	1,307
Breaking and entering	387,877	1,326
Motor vehicle theft	159,663	546
Theft	843,659	2,885
Possession	30,522	104
Fraud	103,210	353
Total property crimes	1,524,931	5,214
Other offenses	804,501	2,751
Total	2,632,830	9,002

Modified from: Statistics Canada. *Canadian Crime Statistics 1994,* Ottawa: Minister of Industry, table 3.3, pp.13–16, 1995.

Table 4.4   Rates of Homicide in Selected Cities.

Country and City	Homicides per 100,000 people
Austria—Vienna	5.0
Canada—Toronto	6.1
Denmark—Copenhagen	10.5
Finland—Helsinki	15.3
Germany—Berlin	6.8
Hungary—Budapest	2.7
Israel—Jerusalem	3.1
Japan—Tokyo	1.6
Netherlands—Amsterdam	38.0
Norway—Oslo	9.3
Spain—Madrid	2.7
Sweden—Stockholm	15.9
United Kingdom—London	2.5

Taken from: United Nations. *Human Development Report, 1996.*
New York: Oxford University Press, 1996, table 28.

number of international cities located in countries often assumed by Americans to have low crime rates, have rates that are comparable to America's "homicide capitals." For example, the major Scandinavian cities—Copenhagen, Stockholm, Helsinki—as well as Amsterdam in the Netherlands, all have rates of crime over 10 per 100,000 inhabitants. Those rates compare "favorably" with 1995 rates reported for New York (at 14.2 per 100,000), Detroit (at 13.0 per 100,000), and Washington, DC (at 13.4 per 100,000) (FBI 1996).

Conclusions on Criticism of Official Statistics

Are Official Counts Biased?

The major charge against the use of official statistics as data for criminological theory is that they are biased, and biased principally against poor people and against some visible minorities. This accusation is more common in Canada and the United States, with their numerous ethnic groups, than it is on the European continent. Nevertheless, the belief that rich people can get away with crimes for which poor people are hanged is universal. It is a belief substantiated by the fact that money buys legal defense (as exemplified in the O. J. Simpson criminal case) and by the fact that the kinds of theft available to trusted business and government officers are less public than strong-arm robbery (Sampson et al. 1981). The act of fraud is more clever, less readily apparent, and more difficult to discover than a burglary or a sexual assault. Apart from discovery of the crime, there is also the matter of discovery of the criminal. Here, the burglar may have an advantage over the embezzler. It is more difficult to catch an external thief than an internal one.

The question of bias in official records can be raised, therefore, but it cannot be definitively answered. It is a charge that could be verified only if there were accurate tallies by segments of societies of the proportions of people committing various offenses of ranked seriousness and known frequency.

The gravity of the prevalent offenses is one element in evaluating judicial bias. The number of offenses and the proportion of a population committing them are two additional, and different, measures of criminality. The proportion of offenses of a particular kind committed by the offenders in particular segments of society—a measure of the intensity of criminality—is yet another indicator of crime.

No measure of criminal activity that is now used, official or unofficial, is sensitive to the full range of crime and, at the same time, sensitive to variations in the perceived seriousness of these crimes while it counts how many persons in each stratum of society commit how many crimes. This allows political preference to affect the choice of measures of crime and their interpretations.

Do Different Counts Converge?

Confidence in public records increases as other types of measurement yield similar results. If each method of counting crime gave widely different results, no theories of crime causation could be well supported. One explanation would then be as good as another and no policy of intervention could be justified in preference to another. As will be seen, however, the various imperfect measures of the serious crimes point in the same general direction for their social location—with the following qualification.

Looking for convergence among different ways of counting crime assumes that each measure is counting the same thing. This assumption is questionable, but the degree to which it is questionable or acceptable varies with the instrument used, the kind of crime tallied, and the samples of people studied.

It cannot be assumed, for example, that asking people what they have done represents the same kinds of events that get counted in a police tally. Frequency, visibility, and social context (who does what to whom) affect reporting of events to the police and may affect their recording in interviews and on questionnaires (see Chapters 6 and 7).

Judgment is required in assessing convergence or divergence in the pictures drawn by different techniques of observation. Judgment rests on recognition that a law defining a "kind of crime" need not describe a homogeneous set of actions, produced by a particular class of actors, all of whom come to that crime by the same route. There may be many roads to the same legally defined category of crime, and it remains an empirical question whether there are kinds of personalities that disproportionately commit categories of crime and whether such persons travel one or several roads to that career (Nettler 1982a).

With this understanding, we can examine portraits of offenders and styles of offense provided by unofficial observations. This is done in Chapters 5, 6, and 7.

5. Observations: Direct and Indirect

Unofficial Counts of Crime

The imperfect nature of official statistics on crime has led sociologists to invent other ways of counting violations of the law. Some of these procedures are helpful in filling out the picture of crime and its causes. They give us a better sense of the variety of crime and criminals and an appreciation of the persistent inventiveness of human beings in devising ways of cheating, stealing, and attacking.

With some discrepancies, these optional methods of study do not drastically revise official tallies. Some of these observations open our eyes to new forms of criminal enterprise, but they do not change markedly the maps of criminal conduct drawn from official data.

A fair conclusion to be drawn from a comparison of different measures of crime is that, where the unofficial tallies of crime disagree with official statistics, no one knows which is the more valid. On the other hand, where the official and unofficial tabulations agree, one is more confident of the facts with which explanations of criminality are built. Fortunately for theories of criminogenesis, official and unofficial counts of crime are in general agreement in mapping the social locations of serious offenses.

Unofficial procedures for counting crime include observations of criminal activity, private-policing reports, unobtrusive measures, test situations, surveys of victims, and studies of admissions of crime. This chapter discusses some of the results of watching people, privately policing them, and recording crime through unobtrusive tallies and tests. Chapter 6 will describe studies of victims; Chapter 7, confessions of criminality.

Observations of Criminal Activity

An interesting way of counting crime is to live with a group of people and to keep a log of their criminal conduct. But such direct observation is expensive, restricted in its application, and subject to variations traceable to differences in attention and recording on the part of the observer. Direct observation has been supplemented by indirect assessment of criminal activity, as when sociologists and psychologists interview criminals and their intimates, including their pursuers, the police. In addition, test situations and other unobtrusive measures have been devised to assist us in locating crime among persons and their situations.

TYPES OF OBSERVATION

Observation takes several forms in field research. These techniques may be categorized on a continuum according to the role played by the researcher (Gold 1969; Maxfield and Babbie 1995). At one degree of involvement, the researcher observes an activity or individuals without their knowledge. A researcher watching shoplifters through a one-way mirror in a department store is an example of this technique . . . *the complete observer.* At a more involved level of interaction, the researcher is identified as a researcher and interacts with the participants in the course of their activities, but does not actually become a participant . . . *observer-as-participant.* The *participant-as-observer* . . . technique involves participating with the group under study while making clear the purpose of conducting research. (Cromwell 1996: x)

Cambridge-Somerville Youth Study

A now classic example of observational research is the Cambridge-Somerville Youth Study, based on a delinquency prevention project started in 1937 in two crowded industrial cities near Boston, Massachusetts (see Box 5.1). The project was curtailed in 1941 by entry of the United States into World War II, but the research persisted with some changes until 1945. In 1955 Joan and William McCord brought the information up-to-date and reexamined the findings. Over these years a tremendous dossier was developed for each of the 750 boys originally in the project. The McCords comment that

> seldom has so large a group of children been so carefully studied over such a long period of time. Social workers investigated the neighborhoods and recorded the school progress of each boy. Perceptive investigators visited their homes, talked with their parents, and observed their families. Psychologists and psychiatrists measured intelligence and analyzed the personalities of the children. The social and psychological observations . . . told about their boyhood homes, their families, their neighborhoods, and their personalities. (McCord and McCord 1959)

As a part of getting to know the boys, caseworkers maintained records of observed and admitted crimes, whether officially recorded or not. What is of importance for our purposes is, again, the enormous amount of "hidden delinquency" and the *relation between the persistence and gravity of offenses committed and action taken by the police.* In a special study of 101 of these youths, F. J. Murphy et al. noted that 61 of the boys had committed a variety of delinquencies without being sent to court (Murphy et al. 1946). Another 40 boys did appear in juvenile court.

Boys who commit the more serious crimes, and more of them, run a higher risk of appearing in official statistics. Only 95 (about 1.5%) of the 6,416 offenses observed resulted in court action. The boys who become "officially delinquent" committed from 5 to 323 violations each, with a median of 79 crimes. By contrast, the "unofficial delinquents" committed an average of 30 offenses each.

We may all have broken some criminal laws, but some of us have done so more frequently and more seriously than others. Frequency and gravity of offense are among the strong determinants of official notice.

A Study of Thieving Gangs

Another way of observing crime involves associating with groups allegedly at risk. Thus, under the direction of Walter B. Miller, field-workers have become intimate

---

Box 5.1   On Effects of Treatment

The Cambridge-Somerville Study is important because of its attempt to prevent delinquency by providing a panoply of social services and because it counted results. An original aggregate of 750 boys judged to be "at risk" of committing crime was randomly divided into experimental and control groups (McCord and McCord 1959). The boys in the experimental group were given individual counseling, medical care, recreational opportunities, special tutoring, and, in some cases, financial assistance. Their families were also counseled. These boys have been followed into adulthood and their careers evaluated at five-year intervals. Joan McCord reports that, among the 506 men available for study 30 years after the start of the project, those who had been treated fared worse than their matched, untreated peers (McCord 1978, 1980).

Compared with their controls, those who received services have had more trouble with alcohol and, hence, with work. They are in poorer health. They have been divorced more often and are more likely to be dissatisfied with their present marriages. More of the treated cohort have been diagnosed as psychotic and more of them have died before they reached 35 years. In addition, the treated men have been disproportionately repeaters in crime.

---

with American urban gangs of males and females and have counted three classes of their larcenous conduct: "behaviors in some way oriented to theft, arrestable acts of theft, and appearance in court" on charges of theft (Miller 1967). As happens in all comparisons between official statistics and hidden crime, Miller's workers observed that a large amount of criminal activity was going unrecorded.

A Study of Able Criminals

An interesting example of research conducted by means of indirect observation is that of John Mack in Europe (Mack 1972). By gaining the confidence of the police and some successful thieves, Mack was able to draw a portrait of practitioners of "rational-economic" crime who differ from "textbook crooks" in their success and in certain psychological attributes (Mack and Kerner 1975a, 1975b). While these able criminals differ *psychologically* from less successful thieves— in a manner, incidentally, similar to the ways in which successful dentists or accountants differ from their less able colleagues—they do *not* differ from them in social background (Mack 1972: 45). The map of criminogenesis is not greatly changed by information about this kind of adept thief. There are, of course, other avenues into rational-economic theft that qualify this picture without invalidating it (see Chapter 13).

More recently Adler published the results of a study of upper-level drug dealing where the information was collected during years of participant observation (Adler 1993). Adler and her husband became friends with members of the drug dealing community and earned their trust and confidence. This allowed them to conduct interviews, gain insights, and observe the activities of people involved in the drug trade.

Living with and interacting with drug dealers allowed Adler to understand how dealers saw themselves, how they functioned, and how they viewed the rest of society. It also allowed her the opportunity to appreciate the scope of crimes committed as part of practicing an illicit trade where the day-to-day activities are shielded from public view and do not usually appear in official statistics.

In Summary: Observing Crime

Observations of people obeying and breaking criminal laws reinforce the commonsense impression that violations are frequent, that they vary by kind and amount with different social locations, and that the policing process operates like a coarse net that is more likely to catch the repetitive, serious offender than the now-and-then, minor offender. It is also more likely to catch the impulsive and stupid thief than the more deliberate and intelligent one.

TANNER ON ETHNOGRAPHIC STUDIES

More recently, there has been something of an ethnographic revival . . . inspired by dissatisfactions with both the official statistics and self-report surveys. A partial listing of recent technographic studies would include Hagedorn's study of youth crime and youth gangs in Milwaukee (1988); Moore's examination of subcultural deviance among Mexican youth in Los Angeles (1991); Padilla's account of the "Diamonds," a Puerto Rican gang based in Chicago (1992); Sullivan's research on growing up working class in three New York City neighborhoods (1989); Paul Willis's celebrated analysis of how working-class kids in Britain get working-class jobs (1977); and Jay McLeod's replication of that study in an unnamed (Boston?) American city (1987). (Tanner 1996)

Private Policing Reports

Large retail stores, industries, and even some neighborhoods police themselves. Such private policing is done by investigators who may be full-time store detectives or members of security forces, and sometimes by auditors and management consultants whose major duty is not the detection of theft. While police employed by corporations and private citizens work to prevent theft and to apprehend thieves, the less formal "detectives," such as accountants and consultants, more often stumble upon stealing. Both kinds of private policing reports expand our conception of crime, reduce our confidence in public honesty, and confirm other measures of levels of larceny.

Shoplifting

Private policing yields most of the information we have about that largely unreported crime, shoplifting. Shoplifting is "theft from a retail store by people who pose as legitimate customers of the store" (Cameron 1964: 61). In the jargon of thieves and detectives, it is the "five-finger discount" or "inventory shrinkage."

Thieves who shoplift can be categorized as "honest crooks" and dishonest ones. Honest thieves are rare among shoplifters. They are the "boosters," the pros who know that they are thieves, who deliberately practice their art, and who come equipped with techniques for stealing. By contrast, the overwhelming majority of shoplifters are dishonest thieves. They are amateurs who do not acknowledge themselves to be thieves.

Shoplifting is a difficult crime to study in that all observation may be biased. Bias is possible because security officers, and even researchers, cannot watch everyone. They tend, therefore, to follow kinds of people selectively, in accord with their conceptions of persons considered likely to steal. Detectives' response to this allegation is that their selective observation is justified by experience. Without a total-scanning videotape of all shoppers, there is no way to resolve the dispute.

A second possible source of bias stems from the fact that most research on shoplifting does not relate the kinds of people caught to a population at risk. For example, women disproportionately shop in grocery and department stores, and they probably spend more time per visit in those stores. They are, then, differentially at risk. For the sake of accurate comparison, research should attempt to relate kinds of people apprehended to a population base of persons at risk.

N. M. Warner attempted to control for "population at risk" in his study of shoplifting in a large Edmonton department store (Warner 1979). Warner made periodic door counts of the demographic characteristics of entrants. His findings contradict a common assumption that shoplifters in such stores are disproportionately female. His enumeration at the door indicated that only one-third of shoppers were male, but males accounted for 60% of those arrested. This disproportion is produced principally by young (15- to 19-year-old) male thieves, a finding that accords with other measures of sex and age differences in petty theft.

The many studies of this common crime allow these tentative conclusions:

1. The kind of person who shoplifts varies with the kind of store and its location. People steal the kinds of things they tend to buy (Warner 1979). In sporting goods stores, young men steal the kind of equipment they use. In supermarkets women shoppers are disproportionately caught taking food (Won and Yamamoto 1968). In drugstores youngsters steal candy and cigarettes.

2. Each individual shoplifter takes little of value per theft. This is particularly true of the amateur. Warner's (1979) study finds that 85% of those apprehended had taken things totaling less than $50. Kirkwood (1977) reports that Canadian shoplifters possess on the average about $28 worth of stolen property when they are caught. Of course, many shoplifters stealing small amounts repeatedly can still account for large losses. Thus Harbin (1979) estimates that sporting goods stores lose about 5% of the value of their annual sales to shoplifters.

3. In larger stores, it can be assumed that some 5% to 7% of shoppers steal something. Hughes (1974) reports a study in which four American stores were saturated with security officers for one day. These guards tried to follow all customers. They observed 109 shoppers out of 1647 (6.6%) steal at least once.

4. Apprehended shoplifters, particularly young ones, steal again unless they are punished. Wisher (1974) finds that 85% of young men and 62% of young women "lifted" again after their first discovery. Kraut (1976) reports that the average apprehended shoplifter stole over five times after apprehension.

5. Shops in American university districts are particularly vulnerable to shoplifting. Kirkwood (1977) calculates that stores in university areas suffer about three times as much inventory shrinkage as similar shops in other neighborhoods.

6. Shoplifters are disproportionately persons of modest or low social status. This statement refers to relative distributions, not absolutes. That is, it does not say that no rich people steal. Moreover, this statement is more accurate as one controls for age.

Studies of shoplifting have difficulty assigning socioeconomic status (SES) rankings to those who are apprehended. They have done so in two principal ways: by asking offenders their occupations and by inferring their wealth from the neighborhoods in which they live.

For example, in an early study Cameron compared the residences of arrested shoplifters in Lakeside County (near Chicago) with the residential distribution of claimants in the county's lost-and-found department, a measure which Cameron believes is representative of typical shoppers in the store she studied (1953, 1964: 147). She concludes that the majority of her amateur shoplifters were "mainly 'respectable' employed persons or equally 'respectable' housewives."

By contrast, Warner's Canadian study controlled for shoplifters' ages in assessing their SES (1979). Among juvenile offenders, Warner records 80% as "students" and 14% as "unemployed." Among adult offenders, he finds 38% "unemployed," 18% "unskilled laborers," and 12% "retired." In sum, Warner comments that "56% of adult shoplifters are either without a job or are doing a job requiring no technical skill. Only . . . 5% do jobs that can be classified as professional or managerial" (1979: 94).

Warner's mapping of the residences of apprehended shoplifters coincides with earlier "ecological" studies of the distribution of crime rates in urban areas (Shaw and McKay 1942): "in general . . . shoplifters come from the older, core areas of the city, they have lower-middle income characteristics, and they are either out of work or in manual labor" (Warner 1979: 94).

Warner also reports that large downtown department stores are victimized by persons who do not live in the city. About one-third of his apprehended thieves were from out of town. Slightly more than half of these (56%) had no fixed address, and the remainder were visitors from the suburbs. Warner is careful to qualify his findings by noting that they refer to one type of large store in a central city location.

7. Apprehended adult shoplifters differ from the general population by ethnicity. The differences suggest that some "minorities," deemed to be disadvantaged, are differentially caught shoplifting. In Hawaii, Won and Yamamoto (1968) report that Hawaiians are apprehended far in excess of their numbers in the population, while Japanese, the largest ethnic group in the islands, are greatly underrepresented among shoplifters. Caucasians are arrested for this crime in proportion to their numbers in Hawaii.

In what was West Germany, Blankenburg (1976) found that foreigners were apprehended in proportions greater than their resident population. In eastern Canada, Normandeau (1971) tallies an overrepresentation of French Canadians among shoplifters in six Montreal department stores. In western Canada, Warner (1979) notes that Indian, Inuit, and métis shoppers are disproportionately caught stealing.

These reports run in parallel with information from official statistics for similar low-level theft. They should be interpreted with caution, however, because of possible differences in law enforcement between stores, within cities, and between countries (Blankenburg 1976).

8. Studies of shoplifting suggest that many people will steal if things of value are exposed (placed at risk) with little probability of thieves' apprehension and little probability of pain upon their apprehension. The probability of pain upon arrest is greater in communities where, by definition, people know one another and shame operates. In contrast, the pain of arrest is lessened when people live in civil aggregates, loosely bound by citizenship, dubiously affiliated by a common culture, and freed by their anonymity from control by shame and guilt.

Theft by Employees and Persons in Positions of Financial Trust

Shoplifters are thieves external to business and bureaucracy. Their thefts are probably exceeded in value by "internal stealing," that done by employees and by persons in positions of financial trust (see Box 5.2).

The exact proportion of employees and trusted officers who steal, in different corporate and governmental locations, is not known. However, informal observations suggest that most people can be tempted to steal—if they are exposed to enough unguarded wealth for long enough. The "enoughs" in this equation are vague, of course, and the assumed thresholds of temptation will vary with individual training and taste. But we have some estimates from unofficial tallies of the passion for other people's property. Persons who work at providing store security estimate that internal thieves steal more per thief than robbers and burglars do (Kirkwood 1977) and that the ratio of internal to external theft in the United States and Canada has remained constant over the past 20 years at about five to one (Hollinger and Dabney 1996; Parker 1977). In North America, the cost of inventory shrinkage is about $30 billion dollars per year and as is displayed in

---

Box 5.2   Does Shoplifting Add to the Cost of Shopping?

Retailers say that 1.8% of the cost of a product is due to theft and measures taken to "up security" (all that retailers do to stop theft) adds another .5% to the cost of a product. In total, 2.5% of the cost of products in stores is due to a combination of theft and the measures taken to avoid theft.

Millions are stolen every day from store shelves and storerooms. . . . Customers steal an average of $82 [in Canada; $142 in the USA] every time they rip off a retailer. . . .

Customers pay for dishonesty . . . [because] retailers are forced to pass on some of the costs of shoplifting to the consumer because they must recoup the lost revenue. . . .

In one retail survey, stores estimate they lose on average between 1% and 4.5% of their merchandise to shoplifting. (Canadian Broadcasting Corporation 1997)

Table 5.1, the sources of these losses are similar if not exactly the same in the United States, Canada, and Great Britain.

Norman Jaspan, the head of an engineering consulting firm, found that "in more than 50% of assignments involving engineering projects with no hint of dishonesty, white-collar crime was uncovered. In addition [in a single year] our staff . . . unearthed more than $60 million worth of dishonesty with more than 60% attributable to supervisory and executive personnel" (Jaspan 1960: 10). Interviewed a decade later, Jaspan said he believed that firms in Canada and the United States suffer "a better than 50% chance" of being victims of "sizable dishonesty" (Jaspan 1970).

Jaspan's opinion is supported by surveys within the construction industry. Such studies lead to the belief that on-the-job larcenies take some 1 to 6% of the net worth of a contractor's equipment each year. This low percentage is balanced by the high value of the equipment, much of it "heavy," that is stolen. Thefts range from hand tools and building materials to diesel tractors. Stolen materials are used not only for private purposes, but also in the "underground economy." Inflation has made it profitable to "moonlight" on after-hours jobs, and many such moonlighters are able to work at less than the going rate because they steal material and equipment from construction sites.

Insurance company detectives take it as an axiom that people who handle money and property will steal if the valuables are not closely guarded. They estimate that employees take about 80% of the amounts lost by Canadian and American banks. Much of this loss occurs from the rare, but lucrative, crime of embezzlement. In short, bank employees steal more money than bank robbers do.

Workers who handle baggage in airports also illustrate the detective's hypothesis. These employees are in a prime position to steal from luggage or to abscond with shipments. At London's Heathrow Airport, for example, the crime is so popular that the terminal is referred to as "Thiefrow." Moynahan estimates that Heathrow insiders steal about $15 million a year (1978). Reports of "theft rings" from other major airports such as JFK in New York surface from time to time.

Table 5.1   Inventory Shrinkage in the United States, Canada, and Great Britain.

| | *Inventory Shrinkage*[a] | | | | | |
| | *United States*[b] | | *Canada*[c] | | *Great Britain*[d] | |
Source	*Value*	*% of loss*	*Value*	*% of loss*	*Value*	*% of loss*
Shoplifting	$9.7b	35.8	$1.2b	54.2	$1.6b	43.3
Employee theft	$16.4b	38.4	$643m	29.0	$1.1b	30.2
Administrative error	$5.3b	19.4	$371m	16.8		
Vendor theft	$1.7b	6.4				
Other					$1.0b	26.5
Total	$33.1b		$2.2b		$3.7b	

a. In U.S. dollars.
b. *Source:* Hollinger and Dabney (1994).
c. *Source:* Retail Council of Canada study cited by Canadian Broadcasting Corporation (1997).
d. *Source:* Bamfield (1994).

Other Studies by Private Police

Numerous other private policing reports repeatedly confirm the vast amount of cheating and stealing that goes unrecorded. For example, the American Bankers' Association has compiled one of the longest continuous records of a specific crime, bank robbery. Its tallies, which were begun in 1931, show that bank robbery rates, calculated either by population or by the number of banks, rose during the 1960s, although the rate did not exceed that of the worst years of the depression (Mudge 1967). Furthermore, changes in the style of banks have brought a new breed of robber into this kind of theft. The more open facade of banks, with tellers less frequently behind grills and with fewer, if any, armed guards visible, results in a higher proportion of robberies by amateurs. It is interesting to note that after decades of target hardening by having more sturdy and more complex vaults as a way of preventing bank robbery that the preferred mode has turned to simply reducing the amount of cash that is available.

The business of private policing is itself a source of information about concern with crime if not about the actual level and location of kinds of crimes. There are, for example, two to three times as many private police at work in Canada and the United States as public officers (Skelly 1974: 5), and the security industry has grown over the past in terms of personnel, types of service offered, and sales volume. Burns Security Services, Inc., now has agencies in Europe and Japan and has spun off a subsidiary, Rentadog Security, Ltd., that provides guard dogs, motor patrols, and courier services. Pinkerton's, Inc., also reports increases in business (Matthewson 1980). Identicator Corporation sells an antifraud device, an imprinter, that provides businesses with protection against stolen credit cards and bad checks. Identicator's work has been increasing internationally (*U.S. News and World Report* 1973).

In response to kidnapping and terrorism, industries are using electronic tracking devices on executives' cars, installing metal detectors in mail rooms, and employing special services, such as that of Guardsmark, to train chauffeurs in "antiterrorist" driving techniques (Matthewson 1980).

Unofficial records indicate that official statistics underestimate the true amount of crime. Unfortunately, much private policing describes the amount of such unrecorded crime without telling us much about the characteristics of the criminal. This is also a limitation on many unobtrusive measures of crime and of victimization surveys, but it is a deficiency that is partially overcome by studies in test situations.

Unobtrusive Measures

An *unobtrusive measure* is one that is relatively uncontaminated by irrelevant considerations in counting the events of interest. That is, it is nonreactive. The nature of the instrument has little effect on the behavior being studied (Webb et al. 1966).

It is best to think of unobtrusive measures as more and less so, rather than as absolutely nonreactive. We note, then, that the recording tools most frequently employed by social scientists are among the most contaminated: interviews and questionnaires. These make up the instruments used in about 90% of sociological research (Brown and Gilmartin 1969). Chapter 7 discusses some of the sources of distortion when it is assumed that answers to questions are valid indicators of how people act. Here we look at some unobtrusive measures of criminal activity. Findings from employment of such measures draw maps of lawbreaking that are largely in accord with those charted from official statistics and experimental (test) data.

The simplest form of nonreactive gauge of offensive behavior is the hidden witness who counts events. Such recording is augmented today by concealed cameras and tape recorders.

The few studies in natural settings that have observed violations of some code of conduct, criminal or not, have produced a characteristic curve of conformity and deviation, a curve that is unimodal (one-humped) and that looks like a j or an l, depending on how it is drawn. F. H. Allport (1934) proposed a "j-curve hypothesis" of conforming behavior as a measure of the vitality of social norms: the steeper the curve and the shorter its tail, the more *vital* the social norm. That is, a lively social norm would have most people obeying it and few people violating it, and such violations as did occur would be less serious—"closer to the norm."

Allport tested his thesis with unobtrusive tallies of the number of observances fulfilled in a religious ritual as people participated in church services. The distribution of participants' conduct confirmed their practice of a social norm. Similarly, Farnsworth and his students recorded drivers' behavior at intersections in Palo Alto (La Piere and Farnsworth 1949). Conformity with the law and violation of it again take the shape of a j curve. This means that most people obey a traffic law and a few people break it, and the number who break the law *decreases* as the seriousness of the violation *increases*. Violations also decrease with increases in the clear threat of punishment.

A similar distribution will be seen later among self-report measures of delinquencies when they are weighted by frequency and gravity of offense. A J curve also seems approximated when one counts hotel and motel losses weighted by frequency and value of items taken by guests (Lasky 1974): many more take items of less value (e.g., a towel) than take items of greater value (e.g., a TV set).

Other unobtrusive indicators can be extracted from sales records. For example, increased use of private police has been accompanied by increased sales of protective devices, principally electronic burglar alarms. ADT Security Systems, operated almost 80,000 theft alarm installations in North America in 1975 (*U.S. News and World Report* 1975a). By 1996, when the company was sold, that number had grown to more than 1 million (*Security Sales Magazine* 1996: 12).

Industrywide, the development of the private security industry in the United States is even more impressive. According to an industry trade journal, the electronic security industry's revenue in 1995 was $10.5 billion; there were 2.19 million systems installed in 1995 alone, and approximately 16.5% of all U.S. homes had a residential alarm system (*Security Sales* 1996).

Increased sales of such defensive devices have been accompanied by an increase in private arming, particularly in the United States. Citizens have bought weapons in such numbers that one investigator has termed the phenomenon "the urban arms race" (Seidman 1975). Seidman's study shows that the tendency of citizens to purchase weapons is closely correlated with officially reported crime rates in their cities. This relationship is uniform in cities from coast to coast, and it is not associated with differences in political attitudes among the citizenry.

Other unobtrusive indicators of trends in crime are changes in the way people live, including changes in their recreational habits, modes of residential security, and work. For example, downtown businesses in North American cities report increased difficulty in hiring nighttime help. Security has become a selling point in advertisements of luxury apartments and sealed-off residential enclaves. Some towns and entire zones barricade themselves against unidentified vehicular traffic. Such activities indicate fear of crime, rather than actual amount of crime.

Test Situations

A fascinating way of studying which kinds of people are more and less honest and violent is to test tendencies to lie, cheat, steal, and attack under conditions that allow the investigator to control the circumstances and count the conduct. Most of these experiments employ unobtrusive measures, but we treat them separately because they often stimulate the crimes they observe and because, in some situations, respondents may be aware they are being tested and, hence, the measure can be somewhat reactive.

Social psychologists have used a variety of techniques on a variety of people, from schoolchildren to adults, to test their honesty and compassion. Some of these tests have merely provided opportunities to deceive or attack, but other research has actually tempted people and even ordered them to be offensive. By necessity, most, but not all, of the research on resistance to temptation has involved minor offenses, such as lying and cheating, rather than actual crimes, such as stealing and wounding. However, even these minor experimental temptations are challenged today as "entrapping" innocent subjects and leading them into unethical behavior. Nevertheless, a large library of experimental work has been accumulated that tells us whom to trust most. Here we can only sample this research for its illumination of the social locations of crime and of the many circumstances under which people deceive and injure one another.

Feldman's Studies

Roy Feldman and his coworkers tested the relative honesty of French citizens, Greeks, and Americans in a variety of situations in which there was an opportunity to cheat fellow citizens and foreigners (Feldman 1968). For example, investigators asked people in Paris, Athens, and Boston for directions. They did this in fluent French, Greek, and Boston-accented English, but they also conducted their tests as foreigners who could not speak the language of the country. Researchers also overpaid cashiers in stores and observed who kept the overcharge, and they counted tendencies of taxi drivers to cheat native and foreign customers. Another kind of test noted which people made false claims for money from a stranger.

As common travel experience would suggest, Parisian taxi drivers cheated American tourists significantly more often than their fellow citizens in an ingenious variety of ways. Similarly, cashiers who were overpaid "kept the change" in 54% of the Parisian stores, 51% of the Athenian stores, and 33% of the Boston stores. On the other hand, false claims for money were made by only 6% of Parisians, as compared with 13% of the Athenians and 17% of Bostonians sampled. A significant finding for mapping the social location of these kinds of petty larceny was the tendency for cheating to be more common among persons of lower social status.

Hartshorne and May's Research

The negative correlation of social status with honesty found by Feldman and reported by official statistics is also confirmed in a series of experiments among American schoolchildren conducted by the psychologists Hartshorne and May and their associates (1928–30). These investigators constructed a variety of opportunities for children to lie, cheat, and steal. They gave youngsters the chance to cheat on tests of reading, spelling, arithmetic, information, and grammar; on puzzles; and in parlor games. They also devised ways of tempting children to steal coins without being observed, but in a manner that allowed the theft to be recorded. Last, the researchers gave children opportunities to make false statements on questionnaires where there were two kinds of motive for lying: to win approval and to escape disapproval.

All these measures of deceit run together, but with varying degrees of closeness. There is, for example, a higher association between one kind of cheating and another, and between lying and cheating, than there is between cheating or lying and stealing. The more similar the style of deceit, the greater the consistency of conduct.

Furthermore, Hartshorne and May found what seems obvious—that the amount of cheating, for example, increased as it became easier to cheat, with less risk of being caught, and as a little cheating produced success.

Hartshorne and May thought that, while the correlations between the various tests of honesty were positive, they were too low to allow one to speak of a general trait of honesty. However, Burton recalculated Hartshorne and May's data, omitting from his analysis those tests that were unreliable (Burton 1963). Among the reliable measures of behavior, Burton found a *general tendency* for children to be more or less honest. "There is," he concludes, "an underlying trait of honesty which a person brings with him to a resistance to temptation situation" (Burton 1963: 492).

This general disposition was found to be significantly associated with the social status of the child's family. Furthermore, on Hartshorne and May's tests, honest persons tended to be more consistently honest, while dishonest persons were less consistently dishonest. In addition, these children showed more consistency in their behavior as they grew older. This meant that higher-status children became more honest, and lower-status children more dishonest, with age (Burton 1963). Furthermore, the brighter the child, the more likely he or she was to be honest and to exhibit consistent behavior, a finding that again accords with research on the personalities of more and less officially delinquent youngsters (see Chapter 12).

Note: On Hartshorne and May's Findings

These findings are based on moderate correlations. Exceptions are therefore to be expected. The proper interpretation is that these results indicate tendencies rather than absolute determination. People cannot be divided into clear categories of honest and dishonest persons without overlap. There is a continuum of deceit that approximates the bell-shaped distribution of other psychological traits (McCurdy 1961: table 31). Few people are completely honest or dishonest in all situations, and most people are of mixed tendency.

An additional finding from Hartshorne and May's study has significance for both the social location of crime and our understanding of its causes. Birds of a feather do flock together. Children who were friends were found to have more closely related scores on measures of honesty than children paired at random. Additionally, putting friends together in a classroom increased their tendencies toward honesty or dishonesty.

Two Studies on Cheating the Customer

Another way of testing people for honesty in situations where they do not think they are being observed is illustrated by a *Reader's Digest* survey taken among a sample of small businesses in the early 1940s (Riis 1941a, 1941b, 1941c). A man and a woman were employed by this magazine to tour garages and radio and watch repair shops in the United States. The automobiles, radios, and watches that they submitted for repairs had been deliberately "jimmied" to make them appear out of order. The test of honesty consisted of noting how many shops made charges for false repairs. According to this test:

- Of 347 garages visited, 63% were dishonest.
- Of 304 radio repair shops visited, 64% were dishonest.
- Of 462 watch repair shops visited, 49% were dishonest.

This seems like an inordinate amount of fraud among people we often need to trust. Critics of the *Reader's Digest* study have suggested two explanations in mitigation of its terrible statistics. One is that much of the dishonesty that Riis and his teams unearthed was induced by the poor business climate of the end of Depression years. This might explain the fact of much cheating without erasing it. Another suggestion is that what appeared to be fraud may actually have been incompetence, as when a television repairer installs a new picture tube because of not knowing what is really wrong with the set.

The possibility that incompetence sometimes looks like fraud is a real one. However, the suggestion that it was "only the Depression" that moved repair shops to cheat their customers is challenged by a more recent study of garage work in New York City. The *New York Times* tested the honesty of automobile repair shops in a manner similar to that used in the *Reader's Digest* study.

Thirteen out of twenty-four garages visited either wrongly diagnosed the test car's "defect," lending substance to the idea of incompetence, or recommended expensive and unnecessary repairs (Bacon 1976). More recently and using television technology the CBS news magazine *60 Minutes* captured on camera service station operators deliberately damaging vehicles or placing oil to make it appear that there were repairs that needed doing when they were, in fact, unnecessary.

Testing Violence

Psychologists have tempted people not only to lie, cheat, and steal, but also to aggress. Again, there is a large amount of literature on this subject that can only be sampled here to illustrate procedures for counting offensive behavior under controlled circumstances.

Injuring others, even innocent others, is commonplace. We quarrel, however, about how common violence is, about what causes it, and about whether some people really are more dangerous than others (Carr-Hill 1970; Nettler 1982b, 1982c).

Milgram's Experiments

Stanley Milgram tested one aspect of these questions in a now famous experiment that has been adopted, with modifications, by other investigators (Milgram 1963, 1974). Milgram advertised for people to help him in a "learning experiment" in which the volunteers acted as "teachers" who were to train stooges, the "learners," in a paired-associates learning task. The "learner" was connected to electrodes, and the "teacher" was to improve the learner's performance by administering an electric shock every time the learner gave a wrong response. Moreover, the teacher was told to increase the shock each time the learner made a mistake.

The shock generator bore a large identifying label, plus the information that it was "TYPE ZLB, DYSON INSTRUMENT COMPANY, WALTHAM, MASS., OUTPUT 15 VOLTS–450 VOLTS." An elaborate instrument panel, controlled by 30 switches, was marked off in 15-volt increments from 15 to 450 volts. Each group of four switches carried labels, from left to right, reading: "SLIGHT SHOCK; MODERATE SHOCK; STRONG SHOCK; VERY STRONG SHOCK; INTENSE SHOCK; EXTREME INTENSITY SHOCK; DANGER: SEVERE SHOCK." The last two switches were marked simply "XXX."

Each teacher took a shock of 45 volts in learning to use the machine. The experiment then consisted in observing how much pain the teacher would administer to the learner under a sequence of suggestions from the experimenter. No real shocks were administered in the experiment, of course, but the teachers believed that the shock generator was actually working.

Just as official statistics underestimate the true amount of crime, official students of human behavior underestimate the violent propensity of the creatures they study. A first finding from Milgram's work was how wrong psychiatrists and psychologists were when asked, in advance of the study, how others would act. There was considerable agreement among Milgram's colleagues and among other researchers that most people would refuse to do violence against an innocent person. All these scholars predicted that "only an insignificant minority would go through to the end of the shock series . . . The most 'pessimistic' member . . . predicted that three [of 100 persons] would continue through to the most potent shock available; . . . [but] upon command of the experimenter, each of the 40 subjects went beyond the breakoff point . . . and 26 obeyed the orders of the experimenter to the end" (Milgram 1963: 375–377).

Milgram's results have been replicated by other investigators (Kaufman 1968). Given the proper authority for violence, human beings are more aggressive than some scholars think they are.

Milgram's research does not adequately describe which people are more and less prone to violence under command. His principal finding is that people who resist such violent authority attribute more responsibility for their actions to themselves (Milgram 1974: app. 11). By contrast, people who accede to suggestions to injure another put the responsibility on the official who gave the orders. This finding conforms to a common justification of "normal brutality": "I was only following orders."

Other Investigations

Other investigations have used adaptations of Milgram's shocking technique as well as observations of offensive behavior under controlled conditions to ascertain which kinds of people, if any, are more likely to injure others. Such research can be summarized for the light it sheds on the kinds of people and the kinds of circumstances that are more and less violent.

1. Males are more violent than females. This fact pertains to children as well as adults, and it is universally true. Males are physically more aggressive in a variety of cultures and under a variety of conditions. The fact that males are more violent than females has been substantiated both by direct observation and in test situations. A sex difference in propensity to attack appears early in life. It is as observable in our primate cousins as it is in human beings, and it is related to sex-hormonal balance (Dobash et al. 1992; Eysenck and Nias 1978; Hutchinson 1978; Maccoby and Jacklin 1974: 242–243).

The fact that males and females differ in their tendencies toward violence does not mean that females may not be aggressive in other ways—for example, verbally, in business, or through the law (Campbell, Muncer, and Coyle 1992). Moreover, the fact of a biological sex difference does not mean that aggression cannot be learned or that cultures cannot channel the occasions on which the sexes are more and less aggressive. Chapter 8 will show that ratios of aggressive crimes committed by males and females do vary with cultures. The biological tact means only that males are more "prepared" to do violence than females. This is in keeping with what official statistics tell us about crimes against the person.

2. Aggression is contagious. Watching violence stimulates it. We are not able to specify how long the stimulation lasts or how far it spreads, but seeing others do violence encourages us to attack (Berkowitz and Macaulay 1971; Windom 1989; McCarthy et al. 1975).

3. Expressing aggression—"blowing off steam"—does not reduce it. Fantasies of violence may have a cathartic effect on some persons, but in general this is not the case. Thinking about violence and imagining it are more likely to stimulate aggression than to diminish it (Berkowitz 1965, 1967, 1970, 1973; Berkowitz and Rawlings 1963).

4. Frustration sometimes stimulates attack (Dollard et al. 1939). "Frustration" is a fuzzy word, however, and we must handle it with care. To frustrate someone is to prevent that person from getting what he or she has set out to obtain. To be frustrated is to be blocked. This usage of "frustration" (goal blocking) should not be confused with the inaccurate, popular usage of "being frustrated," meaning "feeling angry or deprived."

To be thwarted in an endeavor does not always make people angry, and attack is not a uniform response to failure to get what one wants (Morlan 1949). It is fortunate that this is so because frustration is a condition of life. We do not usually get all that we want as easily as we should like.

People respond differently to apparently similar quantities of goal blocking. Some people, on some occasions, respond to frustration with resignation; others respond with renewed effort. Some people become apathetic when frustrated; others revert to childlike behavior (Whiting 1944). And, of course, some people attack the frustrating agent or a substitute.

How we respond to frustration may be learned, and it varies also with how much we wanted what we were prevented from getting. It varies, too, with whether the frustrated actor takes the blame for a failure to get over the hurdle or puts the blame on others. Personality differences are important, therefore, and they affect how people define their frustrations and how they handle them (de Charms 1968; Feathers 1967; Rotter 1966).

A personal characteristic that reduces the likelihood of a violent response is the general trait of *willingness to defer gratification* (Cherek et al. 1997; Lessing 1968). However this trait may be produced, it has been found repeatedly to distinguish gang-running delinquents from their less delinquent peers and certain kinds of violent adults from less aggressive persons (Bixenstine and Buterbaugh 1967; Farley and Farley 1972; Ganzer and Sarason 1973; Hindeling 1973; Walsh 1987).

5. Parents who dislike their children produce violent ones. Children who are rejected by their parents are unable to identify with them. Parental rejection and a child's lack of identification with his or her parents are associated, too, with squabbling between the parents.

To compound the matter, the success of attempts by parents to control aggression through punishment depends on whether the child has been nurtured by the parents and identifies with them. Parents who neglect and reject their children are ineffective teachers. Their punishment does not reduce aggression in their children but actually stimulates it (Eron et al. 1971).

Chapter 12 illustrates in greater detail the relation between parental care and children's tendencies to steal and attack. The social location of such parents coincides with other maps of crime and delinquency.

6. Violence that is approved by others will be more frequently employed. Approval includes tacit approval, that is, being *permitted* to do violence as well as *encouraged* to do it (Berkowitz 1968; Windom 1989).

Not all aggression is violent, of course, and different styles of aggression are recommended in different social locations. Intellectual aggression and economic aggression, for example, are middle-class values. Physical attack is a lower-class value. Moreover, the physical attack that is deemed unfair by middle-class standards—"ganging up," for example—is a lower-class prescription: "Hit 'im first, before he's ready, and hit 'im hard" (Miller 1958; Thompson 1966).

These different recommendations for aggression and injury agree, again, with the social map of kinds of offender drawn by other indicators, including official measures.

7. Violent people like violence. This seemingly circular statement says that people who act violently in one arena adopt the violent style in other places. Thus physically aggressive boys like to *watch* violence as well as practice it (Bandura 1973; Lefkowitz et al. 1972; McCarthy et al. 1975).

8. Aggression that succeeds escalates. Violence is an instrument as well as an expression, and violence that gets the desired result tends to be repeated (Berkowitz 1974). Furthermore, observing the successful violence of others encourages its imitation (Windom 1989).

Points (1) through (8) describe violent people and their circumstances in ways similar to official tallies of attack. In addition, points (2) through (8) state that violence tends to reinforce violence. This reinforcement is provided differently in different social locations. Our knowledge of these differences comes from observations in real life and in test situations. It is knowledge that is supported by studies of perpetrators and their victims. These studies can be summarized as locating more assault among low-income families, families receiving public assistance ("welfare"), African-American or Hispanic families, one-parent families, families in which the mother is poorly educated, and families in which there is more reported conflict between parents and children, more delinquency, more addiction to television, and lower school achievement (Florsheim et al. 1996; Palermo 1995; Rosebaum 1989; Salts et al. 1995; Taylor et al. 1997).

Violence is only one face of crime, of course. It remains to be seen whether surveys of victims and collections of confessions provide similar results concerning offenses against property as well as attacks on persons. This is the task of Chapters 6 and 7.

6. Surveys of Victims

Why Survey Victims?

Unofficial counts of crime help clarify the meaning of official statistics. Of the unofficial tallies, criminologists most frequently use surveys of victims and measures of confessions (self-reports). This chapter looks at victims; Chapter 7 examines self-reports.

Questions have been asked of citizens in the United States, Canada, and some European countries concerning their experiences as victims of various crimes. The intention behind such surveys has been to illuminate the *dark figure* of crime, the amount of crime unreported to police. As these surveys were undertaken, it was also expected that their illumination of hidden crime might change the map of crime; that it might show us social locations of crimes different from those described by official statistics.

The summaries of studies of victimization that follow show that this research has, unsurprisingly, fulfilled the first objective but not the second. The summaries can themselves be summarized as saying the following: (1) more crime is committed than is known to the police; (2) the amount of unreported crime varies with the kind of crime; (3) the rank order of crimes in a society appears quite similar whether we use official statistics or victims' statements; but (4) the correlates of kinds of crime sometimes change with the measure of crime used.

American Studies of Victims
National Crime Victimization Survey

The United States has the longest and most extensive experience with surveys of citizens asking about their suffering from crime. Under sponsorship of the Law Enforcement Assistance Administration (LEAA) of the Department of Justice, the Bureau of the Census began interviewing people in 1972 for the National Crime Survey, after having spent several years of testing questions and survey methods. The National Crime Victimization Survey (NCVS) as it is now known, includes interviews with approximately 93,000 persons in as many as 60,000 households every six months (Bureau of Justice Statistics 1994).

The objectives of this survey are "to measure the annual change in crime incidents for a limited set of major crimes and to characterize some of the socioeconomic aspects of both the reported events and their victims" (Penick and Owens 1976: 220). It was believed that fulfilling these objectives would also satisfy other aims such as: (1) identifying segments of the population at high risk of victimization; (2) estimating rates of multiple victimization; (3) providing data with which to evaluate the efficacy of crime prevention programs; and (4) permitting comparisons of levels, trends, and locations of crime with the FBI's Uniform Crime Reports (UCR).

Originally, commercial establishments and households were surveyed, but commercial reports are no longer collected. The surveys of households interview occupants aged 12 years or older every six months for three years on a "rotating panel" basis. The entire national sample of households is divided into "rotation groups" of about 10,000 units each so that a fresh panel of households enters the sample every six months as an old panel drops out.

The NCVS samples household locations, but its reports are of victimization among both households and individuals. An individual informant is asked "basic screen" questions and questions about "crime incidents." The screen questions ask about personal characteristics of occupants and about their criminal victimization. When a criminal incident is uncovered by the screening, almost 100 questions are asked about each event.

Kinds of Crime Counted

The NCVS addresses the kinds of crime included as Part I index crimes (most severe) in the UCR, except arson and homicide. Questions are asked about victimization by assault, "personal larceny," forcible rape, and robbery—considered as crimes against *individuals*—and about automobile theft, burglary, and "household larceny"—considered as crimes against *households*.

The category "personal larceny" includes "noncontact" losses, such as theft of one's coat from a cafe or objects from a gym locker, and "contact" crimes committed without the use of force or its threat, such as purse snatching and pocket picking. "Household larceny" refers to theft by people inside a household who have a right to be there—employees, guests, and members of the household—and to theft that occurs near the domicile, such as losses of outside furniture, garden tools, and bicycles.

In addition, the survey tabulates individual events of crime and "crime series," the latter consisting of three or more similar incidents occurring to the same person during a reference period such that the victim cannot recall details specific to each event.

Limitations

Before summarizing the more interesting findings of the NCVS, recognizing the limitations of such a survey is important.

1. *Counting victims is different from counting offenders, and neither tally is a direct measure of criminal incidents.* Comparisons between the UCR and the NCVS are illegitimate to the extent that they are comparisons of different things: predators, prey, and incidents. It is true that some victims are also culprits, and this might be the case particularly when one plots the social location of victims and offenders for serious, violent attacks (Gottfredson 1981).

Asking victims about the characteristics of their attackers is possible, of course, and this has been done (Danser and Laub 1981). Nevertheless, such inquiry can address only "crimes with contact" and can ask only about broad categories of offenders defined by age, sex, race, and acquaintance. Findings of such research are reported later in this chapter.

2. *Counting persons is different from counting organizations.* Organizations and individuals are victims of crime, and, for certain kinds of crime, they are disproportionately at risk. For example, Reiss notes that

> the robbery rate reported in the NCS for . . . 1976 was 6.5 per thousand whereas the . . . rate was more than six times that at 38.5 per thousand commercial organizations. . . The 1976 burglary rate reported by NCS for households was 88.9 per thousand households, but was actually 217.3 per thousand commercial establishments. (Reiss 1981: 707)

In a 1994 Commercial Victimisation Survey of 1,259 manufacturers in England and Wales, it was determined that two-thirds of the establishments had experienced one or more of the crimes surveyed during the previous year (Mirrless–Black and Ross 1995). Twenty-four percent had been the victims of burglaries alone. A similar survey of retail establishments suggested that eight out of ten retailers had been the victimized at least once in the previous year (Mirrless–Black and Ross 1995). Forty-seven percent reported that they were aware of customer theft while 24% reported burglaries. About 8% reported experiencing employee theft.

Moreover, some studies show that this differential in victimization is reflected in differences in complaints to the police. For example, only about half the robberies of individuals are reported to the police as compared with more than 80% of robberies of businesses (Gottfredson and Hindelang 1979:13). In addition, organizations, as compared with individuals or households, suffer disproportionately from arson and vandalism, and also from robbery, burglary, and theft by employees; but the NCVS does not tally such incidents.

The NCVS ignores organizations as victims because, as Reiss puts it, "we lack a demography of organizations" that would allow adequate sampling of organizations and construction of a base from which to calculate rates. Furthermore, surveys can better collect information from individuals than they can from large organizations in which no one person can report on all victimization.

Some organizations, such as banks and insurance companies, are reticent to report victimization in order not to undermine public confidence in their institutions or encourage even more fraud.

3. *Surveys omit some important crimes.* Surveys omit important categories of crime besides arson, homicide, and crimes against organizations. They do not include kidnapping, and they omit being victimized by drunkenness, disturbances of the peace, impaired driving, drug abuse, sexual solicitation, and procuring. Furthermore, surveys are not sensitive to crimes committed against victims who may not have been aware that they were being "taken," as in an assortment of frauds. Surveys are also insensitive to crimes that damage a diffuse population through indirect or long-breeding injuries such as in tax evasion and violations of industrial safety codes.

Lastly, no attempt is made in victimization surveys to study crimes toward which the victim contributed—at some stage. This omits victimization by a variety of con games and swindles, blackmail and extortion, loan-sharking, and illegal gambling.

4. *A victim's residence may not locate the crimes he or she suffered, and transient victims may not be recorded.* Given the mobility of modern populations, persons may suffer crimes in locations distant from their residence. Thus, some portion of the crimes that the NCVS lists by cities did not occur within those localities. Estimates of victimization suffered outside the city of the victim's residence run from a low of 4% for New Orleans to a high of 20% for San Diego (National Crime Panel 1975: 3).

Comparisons between cities are made questionable when American metropolises differ in the degree to which their occupants are residents. For example, over half the labor force commutes into such cities as Boston, Miami, Newark, and Washington, DC. By contrast, Baltimore, Chicago, Houston, and San Diego are occupied by a small proportion of commuters (Skogan 1976: 115).

Facts such as these should be taken into account when interpreting citizens' vulnerability to crime in different areas. Such facts also affect the meaning of those population characteristics examined as correlates of victimization.

5. *The reliability of surveys is questionable.* Reliability is that quality of a measuring instrument that assures us that it yields the same result upon repeated application to the same thing or event. Reliability is best determined through repeated testing, although other procedures can be employed. It is an axiom of testing, however, that single observations of a performance are often unreliable. Asking only one question about an experience always produces measurement error. The amount of such error varies with the subject matter, and with respondents, interviewers, and their interactions. The reliability of answers to questions about crime victimization has not been well studied.

6. *The validity of surveys is also questionable.* Validity is similar to truthfulness. It is that quality of a measuring instrument that assures us that it is counting what we assume it to be counting. A measuring instrument can be reliable without being valid, but it cannot be valid without being reliable. Two variations of one procedure have been used to test the validity of surveys of victims: forward and reverse record checks. A *forward record check* starts with victims' reports and checks them against crimes known to the police. A *reverse record check* starts with police tallies and traces them back to victims to assess whether they were reported to interviewers. Convergence of these tallies varies with kind of crime.

Other discrepancies are revealed by reverse record checks. They suggest that only about 70% of victims known to the police report their victimization to interviewers. While some 90% of burglaries known to the police are reported to interrogators, fewer than half the assaults known to the police are revealed to interviewers (Garofolo and Hindelang 1977).

Discrepancy between tallies of attacks recorded by police and reported to interviewers is a variable function of two possibilities: shame at having been so victimized and the fact that most assaults occur between acquaintances. In such fights, particularly domestic ones, some calls to the police are not so much complaints about crime as threats against a spouse or lover. Such threats can be made, and are made, even when no actual assault has taken place. Moreover, some complaints to the police are demands for resolution of a dispute or calls to be taken to a hospital. All of this explains, incidentally, why wives who call police to arrest battering husbands sometimes turn against the police when they try to collar the alleged offender.

In brief, one portion of the discrepancy between assaults known to the police and assaults recalled for an interviewer is produced by calls to the police in cases in which the complainant does not regard the battle as a crime and therefore forgets it when the interviewer comes to question. A check of what people remember about their conflicts with direct observation of their quarrels shows that dispute between intimates that are privately settled are more readily forgotten than fights with strangers (Koch 1974: 23–24).

This source of discrepancy overlaps another: that *evaluation* of injury depends on whether the damage was done by a stranger or an intimate. A large library of research tells us that attacks by intimates are viewed as less serious than attacks by strangers (Fagen and Brown 1994; Nader and Todd 1978). Such differential appreciation results in differential reporting to police and to interviewers, particularly if the interview occurs after the heat of the fight has abated.

Yet another source of bias intrudes. It is the possibility that people of diverse culture and experience *interpret* similar events differently. Thus, a large volume of research suggests that middle-class people regard violence as more dangerous than do lower-class people. In keeping with this finding, middle-class persons more often report that they remove themselves from threatening situations, when they can, while lower-class persons are more likely to respond to a violent threat with attack. Studies in England, Scandinavia, and the United States show that middle-class respondents are more likely than lower-class respondents to mention attempted or threatened attacks and simple rather than aggravated assaults (Sparks 1976: 59).

Some Notes on Validity: Words and Memories

Our discussion of self-report measures of criminality will have more to say later about words as indicators of deeds. Here we are reminded of the gambler's maxim, "Never bet on anything that talks."

The validity of victimization studies depends on agreement between interviewers, respondents, and researchers about the meaning of words and the classification of events. Such surveys suffer, to some unknown degree, from all the limitations of any public opinion poll—doubts about how representative the respondents are, refusals of some potential subjects to participate, bias and cheating by interviewers, and the perennial difficulty of ensuring that the same question means the same thing to respondents in widely varying social positions.

In addition, asking people about the crimes they have suffered runs into the problem of how good their memories are and whether people of diverse status have equally good memories for events important to them. Then, too, there is the question of honesty or, if you will, of "openness." People do differ in their willingness to talk about themselves—whether on paper to an anonymous questionnaire or in person to a strange interviewer. For example, one researcher notes that a respondent who had been interviewed five times over a period of two years failed to report having been regularly beaten by her husband. A sixth session extracted this information. Many such intimate assaults may not be reported to interviewers or police for a variety of reasons such as fear of reprisal, embarrassment, and lack of rapport between interviewer and respondent.

Deficiencies in memory are another source of distortion. Investigators have been particularly interested in validating the memories of respondents. They have noted two sources of distortion in recall: time telescoping and forgetting. *Time telescoping* refers to placing an incident earlier or later than its actual date of occurrence. *Forgetting* refers to memory decay that may, in some part, vary with the interview situation. That is, the interview has "demand characteristics" that vary with respondents, and these "demands" can stimulate forgetting, careless remembering, or invention.

In an attempt to test the accuracy of respondents' memories, Schneider and Sumi checked patterns of survey results on burglary victimization for 18 cities against the UCR for those cities month by month (Schneider and Sumi 1981). They found that unreported burglaries were telescoped more than reported burglaries and that cities with marked seasonal variations produced an overestimation of crimes alleged to have occurred during the summer. Schneider and Sumi conclude that correcting for such biases requires knowledge of the true distribution of criminal incidents, a knowledge that is now lacking.

Attempts are continually being made to address these issues. The NCVS, for example, conducts some interviews monthly to address the problem of time compression. Recent surveys have honed questions and incorporated "cues" to improve recall (U.S. Department of Justice 1995). More complex sampling procedures, such as network or "snowball" sampling, which involve tracking people through interpersonal contacts, have been suggested for identifying victims not reached by more standard sampling procedures (Czaja and Blair 1990).

Findings of National Crime Surveys

Although victimization surveys have defects, as do all attempts to count crime, we are interested in the degree to which they draw trend lines and maps of crime similar to, or different from, the pictures given by other tallies. To this end, a summary of some of the findings from national victimization surveys follows (Ennis 1967; Hindelang et al. 1978; Maguire and Pastore 1995; Paez 1981; Bureau of Justice Statistics 1994).

1. *Much more crime is committed than is reported to the police.* An early study in Washington, DC, counted more than 9,000 criminal incidents experienced by victims of which only some 400 were known to the police—a difference on the order of 23 to 1 (Biderman et al. 1967).

National surveys also find discrepancies, but of a lower order. An example of the variability in reporting rates is presented in Table 6.1 where selected rates of victimization and the percent of crimes reported to police are shown for the 1993 NCVC. The gap between crimes known to the police and those reported by victims to interviewers varies, of course, by kind of crime and by location. As a rule, over a broad range of crimes, about twice as many offenses are committed as are reported to the police.

Table 6.1   Rates of Victimization and Percent Crimes Reported to Police, 1993.

Type of crime	Rate per 1,000 households	Percent of all victimizations	Percent reported to police
Rape/sexual assault	2.3	1.1	28.8
Robbery	6.1	3.0	56.1
Assault-aggravated	12.1	5.9	53.2
Assault-simple	30.8	14.9	35.2
Total personal crimes	53.7	26.1	40.9
Household burglary	59.9	13.7	48.9
Motor vehicle theft	19.6	4.5	77.7
Theft	242.6	55.7	25.6
Total property crimes	322.1	73.9	33.1

Source: Adapted from Maguire and Pastore (1995). "Bureau of Justice Statistics Sourcebook of Criminal Justice Statistics—1994." Washington, DC: USGPO, tables 3.1 and 3.32.

Characteristics of victims, their relations with offenders, and gravity of crime interact to determine what is reported to police. Thus only about one-fourth of "personal larcenies without contact" are reported to police although these thefts make up about 70 percent of all "personal crimes." By contrast, about half the robberies ("contact larcenies") are reported to police. As we should expect, robberies that result in injury more frequently produce calls to police than those without injury (Lentzner 1980: 12).

Age of the victim, and gravity of crime, makes a difference in reporting to police. Teenagers are least likely to make their losses and injuries known to officials. Only about one-third of young victims of robbery call police, whereas about 70% of persons aged 50 to 64 years do so. Of course, the size of the loss may make a difference here. Furthermore, only 13% of thefts from adolescents "without contact" are reported to police compared with about one-third of those committed against adults (Lentzner 1980: 12).

Block and Block (1980) traced the flow of noncommercial robberies in Chicago, 1974–1975 from victims' reports to interviewers, to their complaints to police, to police decision to record and investigate the incident, to police decision to log the crime as "founded." In short, they followed a crime from its occurrence to its transformation into an official figure. As expected, they found a decrease in events counted at each decision point. Only about half the personal robberies are reported to police. Of these, police investigated and recorded only 73% as robbery. In turn, 79% of investigated robberies became founded and thus robberies known to the police. The attrition is such that, for Chicago in the mid-1970s, only 29% of all noncommercial robberies became official statistics—crimes known to the police.

Incidentally, age, sex, and race of victims had no influence on decisions at each juncture in reporting and recording this crime, a finding that runs counter to popular charges of police bias (Block and Block 1980: 627).

2. *Reporting crimes to police depends on the gravity of the crime and the victim's conception of the utility of reporting.* Both the judged seriousness of an offense and conceptions of what good it will do to report it vary with the relationship between offender and victim. However, for crimes in general, the most common reasons given for not reporting them to police are that the incident was not sufficiently important or that calling the police provided no remedy for the loss or injury. Secondarily, some crimes are unreported because victims believe them to be private matters. By contrast, the high rate of reporting motor vehicle theft is a consequence of the necessity of filing a complaint with police as a prerequisite to making an insurance claim.

3. *The rank order of the frequency of serious offenses reported by victims closely parallels that given by official statistics.* Despite the underreporting that characterizes crimes known to the police, the amount of different kinds of crime is ranked in the same order by official tallies and surveys of victims. An exception in some surveys is vehicle theft.

4. *There are no huge surges in the amount of crime—so-called crime waves.* Crime rates, tallied from victims, usually fluctuate year by year and by kind of crime. The National Crime Victimization Surveys from the 1970s onward found annual fluctuations without any notable leap from one recording period to another (Bureau of Justice Statistics 1994; Paez 1981).

The level of criminal activity of certain kinds may increase or decrease, of course, without there being "crime waves" or "ebb tides." Some crime waves are depredations of single predators or small gangs on a rampage.

5. *Victimization surveys parallel official statistics in that it is generally males, younger people, and members of ethnic and racial minorities who are most likely to be victims of crime.* This is illustrated in Table 6.2, which shows selected demographic extracts for the 1993 NCVS.

6. *Usually, people are less likely to be victims of crime the farther they live from America's central cities.*

7. *Men are more frequently robbed by strangers than are women.*

8. *Men who live alone, and unrelated people living in households, suffer disproportionately from robbery.*

9. *Households headed by women suffer above-average victimization by burglary and larceny, and children in such households experience the highest rates of aggravated assault of all demographic categories.*

10. *At all levels of income, African Americans suffer more violent attacks than whites or members of other ethnic groups* (Boland 1976: 31–38; Ennis 1967; Lentzner 1980: 2). *However, whites suffer less from burglary as their income rises, but African Americans suffer more from burglary at higher income levels* (Ennis 1967: 30).

11. *According to victims' reports, African Americans are overrepresented as offenders in rape, robbery, assault, and personal larceny.* Hindelang notes that victims of personal larceny identified 70% of their predators as African American (1978). Sixty percent of robbers are so identified, 40% of rapists, and 30% of attackers in assaults. This finding parallels official statistics for such crimes and challenges the charge of racial discrimination in administration of the law.

Table 6.2   Rates of Victimization per 1,000 Persons by Selected Characteristics, 1993.

	Total crimes of violence	Rape/sexual assault	Robbery	Aggravated assault	Simple assault
Males					
12 to 15 years	145.7	0.0[a]	19.0	29.7	97.1
16 to 19 years	134.9	2.4[a]	15.7	41.2	75.7
20 to 24 years	101.8	0.9[a]	13.0	32.9	55.1
25 to 34 years	69.7	0.8[a]	9.5	19.1	40.3
35 to 49 years	46.2	0.1[a]	6.6	12.1	27.5
50 to 64 years	21.9	0.0[a]	4.6	5.3	12.0
65 years and over	6.0	0.0[a]	1.7[a]	0.9[a]	3.4
Females					
12 to 15 years	94.4	9.2	8.1	16.8	60.3
16 to 19 years	97.9	12.2	7.1	18.4	60.2
20 to 24 years	85.4	10.4	8.1	20.6	46.3
25 to 34 years	47.6	4.0	5.1	10.5	28.0
35 to 49 years	38.9	3.2	3.4	5.5	26.8
50 to 64 years	12.6	0.5[a]	1.5[a]	2.7	8.0
65 years and over	5.2	0.4[a]	0.8[a]	1.2[a]	2.8
Race					
African American	71.1	2.7	12.7	18.7	32.1
White	51.7	2.3	5.1	11.3	31.0
Other	41.6	0.8[a]	7.9	8.8	20.8
Ethnicity					
Hispanic	62.5	2.1	10.8	17.2	29.0
Non-Hispanic	52.9	2.3	5.7	11.7	30.9

a. Estimate is based on about 10 or fewer sample cases.

Source: Taken from Maguire and Pastore (1995). "Bureau of Justice Statistics Sourcebook of Criminal Justice Statistics—1994." Washington, DC: USGPO, tables 3.4, 3.5, and 3.6.

12. *The more time a person spends in public places, the more likely he or she is to suffer personal victimization* (Hindelang et al. 1978: 251–253). This means, among other things, that the more time one spends among strangers, the more one is likely to suffer personal larceny (Hindelang et al. 1978: 260).

13. *Victimization is not distributed randomly; some people experience "more than their share."* It has long been observed that "good things tend to go together, and bad things too" (Nettler 1982b: chapter 3). Crimes are not distributed by chance, and some persons experience more of them. The disposition to be a victim varies with the way people live and the kind of company they keep. For example, Gottfredson reports that surveys in 26 American cities show that

> regardless of the age, race, income, marital status, or sex of the respondent, the likelihood of being the victim of a personal crime was much greater for persons whose households were also victimized during the reference period. A clustering of risks was also found within households. Persons residing in households in which other household members reported a personal victimization were far more likely to report experiencing a victimization themselves than were persons in "victimizationless" house- holds. Also, repetitive victims were more likely to be victimized

by non-strangers than were nonrepetitive victims, though two-thirds of the repetitive victims were victimized by strangers. These data are important since they establish a link between personal and household victimization independent of the demographic correlates of victimization, thus implying a time and space risk dimension. (Gottfredson 1981: 718)

Conclusions about the clustering of risk of crime derive not only from American research (Hindelang et al. 1978; Nelson 1980; Reynolds et al. 1973), but also from research in Canada (Statistics Canada 1994b), England (Sparks et al. 1977), Denmark (Wolf 1972), and Finland (Aromaa 1971, 1973, 1974).

14. *The chance of being a victim of crime increases among people who share the demographic characteristics of more likely offenders.* Individual differences in age, sex, ethnicity, and residence correlated with offending are also correlated with being a victim (Hindelang et al. 1978: 257–259). A similar association is reported in Finland (Aho 1967; Aromaa 1974).

15. *Predators choose their victims from among persons who appear vulnerable and desirable, and who are convenient.* Hindelang et al. note that offenders generally commit their crimes near their own residences and that they attack people who are desirable targets in the sense that they are likely to yield a monetary return with little risk of retaliation (Hindelang et al. 1978: 264–266).

National Institute of Education Survey

Some national findings are supported by a large-scale study of crime in public schools. Reports of violence and vandalism in America's public schools moved Congress to require a survey of school crime. The National Institute of Education sent questionnaires to 4,014 school principals, 23,895 teachers, and 31,373 students. In addition, 6,283 randomly selected students were interviewed (National Institute of Education 1978).

Findings

Some of the findings of the National Institute of Education survey are given below.

1. *Crime varies with the social location of schools.* Junior high schools may be more dangerous places than senior high schools, and crime rates at both levels decline uniformly as one moves from large cities to smaller cities, suburbs, and rural areas.

Public schools in the central zones of big cities have the highest rates of reported victimization. These are schools with high proportions of minority students from low-income families. They are also schools with higher rates of recorded deficiencies in reading and arithmetic. In a review of this study, Toby notes that "schools in which a majority of students were from minority backgrounds had rates of assault and robbery against both students and teachers twice as high as schools where white students predominated" (Toby 1980: 23).

2. *School crime is real crime.* American public schools suffer from the crimes of theft, assault, vandalism, and from the "lesser" offenses of threats, foul language, and dirty gestures.

Reports of victimization are accompanied by a comparable gradient of truancy stimulated by fear of violence. In big-city junior high schools, 80% said that they had stayed home sometime during the preceding month for fear of being injured. In small-city, suburban, and rural junior high schools, 4 to 5% reported fear-induced truancy.

In metropolitan schools, about 17% of teachers reported having been victims of theft in the preceding month. About 1.5% of teachers said they had been robbed and about 2% that they had been physically attacked. The proportions of such victimizations decline steadily from big city schools to schools in smaller cities, suburbs, and rural areas. The National Institute of Education estimates the cost of replacing damaged and stolen property in schools at $200 million a year.

3. *Victims are selected.* In conformity with findings from the NCVS, predators in schools attack persons who share some of their demographic characteristics. Thus African-American teachers are disproportionately victims of attacks by African-American students because they often teach in schools with high crime rates. Males, both students and teachers, are more likely to be victims than females, and younger students and teachers suffer disproportionately.

4. *A violent few produce most of the crime.* The by-now commonplace finding that a few bad actors contribute disproportionately to serious crime is repeated by this school survey. Investigators observed behaviors in ten schools for a minimum of two weeks and interviewed teachers, counselors, school guards, and parents. They concluded that a hard-core, say, 10%, of students caused most of the damage, that these students could be identified, and that they were in trouble in school, on the street, and at home. However, during any school "crisis," this troublesome minority can stimulate violent reaction among any number of allies. They can promote violence in others and produce it themselves.

Recommendations

When principals, teachers, and students are asked what to do about school crime, the most popular response among all three groups mentions "discipline and supervision," where this includes "enforcement of rules," "suspension or expulsion," and "controlling student movement and visitors' entrance to school grounds." Victimization research outside the United States has not been as detailed, but what little there is reinforces some of the conclusions of American investigations.

International Studies

Although most victim surveys have been conducted in the United States, similar research has taken place elsewhere.

Canadian Studies

Canadian research confirms findings from other countries concerning the dark figure of crime, the rank ordering of crimes, and the kinds of conditions that increase vulnerability to crime. The two primary victim surveys conducted in Canada are the 1988 and 1993 studies incorporated into the General Social Survey (GSS) (Statistics Canada 1994). The GSS consists of a telephone survey of approximately 10,000 Canadians aged 15 years and older. Again, it was found that young males are more likely to be victimized. There are exceptions, of course, by kind of crime. Thus, women more frequently report having been molested or sexually harassed. Failure to call police is explained by the same kinds of attitudes revealed by surveys elsewhere: triviality of the offense, fear of being embarrassed by the facts of the victimization, and the belief that police could not do much about the crime.

Victimization in Greater Vancouver

In preparation for a national survey, a large schedule of questions was tested in metropolitan Vancouver (Evans et al. 1982: 26–43). The principal findings support results from other areas and can be summarized briefly:

1. Style of life affects the probability of victimization. Young men run a disproportionate risk of being victimized and particularly so if they are frequently out at night.
2. According to victims' reports, most of their attackers are young, male, and strangers. Women are substantially represented as predators (31%) only in "thefts of personal property" (Evans et al. 1982: 26).
3. In about half the personal confrontations, victims report their predators to have been under the influence of alcohol or drugs (Evans et al. 1982: 26–27).
4. Marriage and its associated way of life seem to provide immunity against victimization. The Greater Vancouver survey does not report victimization by marital status controlling for age; thus the finding that people who have never been married are disproportionately crime victims is "contaminated" by the age factor. However, age seems better controlled when one compares victimization among those who become single through divorce or separation with that among married people. Divorced and separated persons have rates of victimization that are two and a half times that of married persons.
5. In comparison with metropolitan experience in the United States, fewer guns are used in personal attacks in Vancouver. Consequently, more people in Vancouver try to defend themselves and they are more often injured. Eighty-six percent of attacks with handguns did not result in injury to victims, but almost one-third of the attacks with blunt instruments did result in injuries.
6. Intimates physically hurt their victims more than strangers do. In most fights, those between people who know each other well more often produce injuries, and the injuries are more serious than those generally received from strangers.
7. Women who fight when attacked are more likely to be injured. Of those who fought their assailants, 52% received injuries compared with 43% of those who "screamed or yelled." These proportions are about double the percentage reported by women who ran away, reasoned with their predators, or did nothing.
8. Victimization of households supports the repeated finding that unoccupied premises invite theft (Cohen and Felson 1979; Reppetto 1974).

European Studies

In England, for example, Sparks et al. (1977: 102–189) surveyed residents in three areas of London: Brixton, a heterogeneous area with a large West Indian settlement now famous for its 1981 riot; Hackney, a working-class district in East London; and Kensington, a zone of middle-class residents and tourist attractions just west and southwest of Hyde Park.

Given differences in samples and instruments, the concordance of English findings with reports from other countries is remarkable. Some of the more pertinent results are these:

1. Overall, the English citizenry ranks crimes by their gravity in the same order as does the law.
2. English people's decisions to report crimes to police are based on the same grounds as the decisions of Americans and Canadians.
3. Contrary to the radical image of lawmaking in "bourgeois society," working-class people regard crimes against property even more seriously than middle-class people do.
4. Lower-class individuals are more likely to approve of violent responses to invasions of their "rights" than are middle-class people.
5. Those who more frequently admit to violent acts are also more likely to be victims of violence.

Following the study by Sparks et al., the British Home Office began the British Crime Survey (BCS), which has been conducted intermittently since 1982 (Maxfield 1987, Mayhew and Smith 1985).

Several studies have also appeared in the Scandinavian countries of Sweden (Sveri 1966), Denmark, Norway, and Finland (Hauge and Wolf 1974). One interesting finding from these studies is that while non-Scandinavians often view these countries as culturally homogeneous, significant cleavages do exist and they are reflected in marked differences in the individual country's crime patterns. Finland, in particular, has very high rates of violence, including criminal homicide.

International Comparisons

Largely because of the success of the NCVS in the United States and the BCS in Great Britain, several other countries have embarked upon national victimization surveys. One of the largest coordinated surveys to date consists of the 1989 International Crime Survey (ICS) undertaken by 14 European countries, Australia, Canada, and the United States (van Dijk et al. 1990). This was followed by a second survey in 1991 consisting of 35 countries, excepting the United States (Block 1993).

The method underlying the surveys was similar to that used in the NCVS, with different countries using varying proportions of telephone interviews and face-to-face contacts. Excluding the American NCVS survey, sample sizes averaged 2,000 respondents and ranged from approximately 1,000 to 5,300. Response rates varied considerably across the surveys. For example, in the 1989 ICS survey, van Dijk et al. report an average response rate of 41%. The lowest response rates were found in Germany and the United States (at 30% and 37%, respectively), while the highest response rates were obtained in Norway, Finland, and Switzerland (all around 68%–71%). Block, however, reports higher response rates for the 1991 survey (Block 1993: 184).

As might be expected, overall rates and patterns of crime varied across the countries surveyed (Table 6.3). Van Dijk et al. summarize the variations in national findings in the 1989 ICS as follows (van Dijk et al. 1990: 95–98):

- The risk of having a car stolen was highest in France, Australia, the United States, and England and Wales. This is partly accounted for by high levels of car ownership.
- Burglaries were highest in Australia, the United States, and Canada. Within Europe, highest risks were found in France, the Netherlands, Finland, and Belgium. The lowest risks were in Norway, Finland, and Switzerland.
- Robberies were most common in Spain and the United States. "In 40% of incidents in Spain, the offender used a knife, compared with 20% on average. In the United States, 28% of offenders used a gun, compared with 8% on average."
- Rates for nonviolent theft were highest in Canada, Spain, and Australia.
- "Sexual assaults (rape, attempted rape, and indecent assault) were highest in the United States (2.3% of women reported an assault . . .), Canada (1.7%), Australia (1.6%), and [the former] W. Germany (1.5%)."
- The highest prevalence rate for all crimes was found in the United States (28.8%). "High rates were also found in Canada (28.1%) and Australia (27.8%). Among the participating European countries, the highest rates were in the Netherlands (26.8%), Spain, (24.6%), and W. Germany (21.9%). The lowest rates were found in Norway (16.5%), Finland (15.9%), Switzerland (15.6%), and Northern Ireland (15.0%)."

Table 6.3   Percent Reporting Victimization by Country and Offense Type, 1988.

Offense	United States	Canada	Australia	Europe	England and Wales	France	Nether- lands	Norway	Switzer- land
Theft of car	2.1	0.8	2.3	1.3	1.8	2.3	0.3	1.1	0.0
Burglary	3.8	3.0	4.4	1.8	2.1	2.4	2.4	0.8	1.0
Robbery	1.9	1.1	0.9	1.0	0.7	0.4	0.9	0.5	0.5
Personal theft	4.5	5.4	5.0	3.9	3.1	3.6	4.5	3.2	4.5
Sexual assault	2.3	1.7	1.6	0.7	0.1	0.5	0.5	0.6	0.0
Assault-threat	5.4	4.0	5.2	2.5	1.9	2.0	3.4	3.0	1.2
Assault-force	2.3	1.5	3.0	1.2	0.6	1.2	2.0	1.4	0.9
All crimes	28.8	28.1	27.8	20.9	19.4	19.4	26.8	16.5	15.6

Source: Adapted from van Dijk, Mayhew, and Killias (1990). *Experiences of Crime Across the World: Key Findings from the 1989 International Crime Survey.* Boston: Kluwer, table E.1.

The substantive findings concerning the who, what, and where of victimization, however, closely parallel what we already know. As van Dijk et al. (1990: 99–100) reported:

- For most types of crime the young tend to be more at risk than the elderly, men more than women, and city dwellers more than inhabitants of rural areas or small towns. Those who go out most often in the evening for recreational purposes have higher risks of all offenses.
- Victimization rates in general are higher among those with above-average incomes.
- Of all offenses measured, nearly half had taken place near the victim's own home, and a third elsewhere in the city or local area. Roughly one in ten offenses took place elsewhere in the country.

Many results of international surveys conducted contrast with the long-standing results obtained by the NCVS studies in the United States. In focusing on this comparison, Block (1993: 201) notes the following:

- U.S. robbery rates are probably higher than those of most other countries.
- Household burglary rates are high but so are those of several other countries.
- U.S. prevalence rates of assault and threat are relatively low in comparison to countries that have similar coverage.
- U.S. levels of weapon use, especially of guns, are much higher than that of the few other countries that asked the question.
- U.S. rates of lethal violence far exceed those of other countries.
- U.S. rates of lethal violence, whether involving a gun or not, exceeds the total rate of lethal violence for the other countries studied.

Reporting to the Police

Before considering the question about how well victimization surveys correspond to official statistics (that is, crimes reported to the police), it is worthwhile examining responses to questions on reporting behavior in the various victimization surveys. For the 1989 ICS, van Dijk et al. noted that avowed reporting patterns vary considerably by the type of offense and the social characteristics of the victim. Specifically, van Dijk et al. (1990: 101) note the following:

- The overall rate of reporting crimes to the police across all crimes and surveys was about 50%.
- Rates of reporting differ significantly by type of crime. The highest reporting rates were for car theft (93%) and burglary (77%)—two offenses for which most people had insurance. Lower rates of reporting occurred for robbery (49%), personal thefts (41%), and assaults (31%). "Sexual incidents" had the lowest reporting rate at 10%, yet rates of reporting for sexual assault (24%) and rape (48%) were much higher.
- Victims in the lowest income group were less likely to report an offense than others (38% versus 51%).

- The main reasons given by victims for not reporting were that the incident was: "not serious enough" (40%), that the "police won't do anything" (19%), and that the "police could do nothing" (10%).

Conclusion: Correlating Victimization Surveys with Official Statistics

Every measure of a social behavior has its critics, and all the criticism has some substance. If official counts of crime are held up against some criterion of perfect information, they may be accused of invalidity; so too may tallies of victims and, as will be seen, measures of confessions.

Criticism of attempts to measure crime would be important if surveys of victims revealed striking differences in the social location of major crimes from what is shown on the map drawn by official statistics and other unofficial tallies. One would not know, then, what to believe about crime, and any explanation of criminal activity would be as good as any other. An observer who cannot use the statistics of aggregates of individuals to locate the sites of different kinds of crime cannot speak reasonably of what causes crime. Nevertheless, it is notable that difficulties in finding facts about who commits which crimes, and where, do not prevent politicians, journalists, or even criminologists from advancing hypotheses about the causes and cures of crime.

Maps of the social locations of crime agree, whether they are drawn with official statistics or other tallies. However, a tendency does not mean absolute coincidence, and there are some discrepancies between the *amount* of crime reported by UCR and NCVS measures and, therefore, between the *correlates* of those crimes revealed by the two indicators with aggregated data.

For example, Cohen calculates correlations for 26 American central cities between the amount of assault, rape, larceny, burglary, robbery, and automobile theft as suggested by official statistics and by asking people about their experiences (Cohen 1981). Cohen tabulates a *negative correlation* (−.41) between the amount of assault reported to the police and that claimed to have been experienced by victims. The amount of rape suggested by these two measures shows almost no correlation (+.03), while the amount of larceny reported by these indicators correlates +.33. It is only for the amounts of burglary, robbery, and automobile theft that high correlations are found between UCR and NCVS measures—correlations, respectively, of +.79, +.80, and +.83.

Discrepancies between amounts of assault and rape reported to police and to interviewers probably result from the different *qualities* of these events that result in official complaint and recall under interrogation. The differential significance of "kinds of crime" may also explain some discrepancies found when one correlates UCR and NCVS data with some alleged criminogenic variables.

Table 6.4 provides a brief comparison of the percentage of respondents in the ICS studies reporting being victimized with estimates of crimes reported to police in the corresponding countries. The police statistics are reported in rates per 100,000. Unfortunately, they cannot be converted into readily comparable percentages with the results of the victimization surveys since the survey esti-

**Table 6.4   Ratio of 1989 International Crime Survey Results
and Crimes Reported to Police in Selected Countries
(Ratio = Survey : Police).**

Country	Assaults/ threats	Sexual offenses	Robbery
United States	8.39:1	n/a	5.00:1
Canada	13.85:1	28.58:1	6.00:1
Australia	34.29:1	33.75:1	6.25:1
England and Wales	4.79:1	14.00:1	6.67:1
France	21.43:1	22.50:1	6.00:1
Netherlands	15.84:1	18.58:1	6.67:1
Norway	56.67:1	33.34:1	15.00:1
Switzerland	16.06:1	18.34:1	16.67:1

Note: Survey results are based on the annual average over a five-year period. The ratios have been calculated by adapting the data provided by van Dijk, Mayhew, and Killias (1990). *Experiences of Crime Across the World: Key Findings from the 1989 International Crime Survey. Boston: Kluwer, table E.9.*

mates represent prevalence rates while the official statistics represent incidence rates. Still, the comparability is worthy of note.

Using the fuller range of ICS results, van Dijk et al. correlated the survey measures of victimization with offenses reported to the police for many offenses. They found the correlations between the two measures varied considerably. For example, they estimated correlations of .79 for vehicle theft, .44 for burglary, .37 for robbery, .35 for sexual offenses, and .04 for assaults (van Dijk et al. 1990: 182).

It needs to be emphasized again that surveys of victims and official statistics provide tallies of different things:

1. Surveys of victims count individuals who have been attacked or who have lost property. Official statistics of property crimes count "incidents," and incidents may have more than one victim.
2. Eligibility to be counted differs. Surveys of victims tally events among residents in an area. Police statistics record crimes occurring within an area to residents and nonresidents.
3. Victimization surveys omit crimes against organizations (commercial crimes), but police tallies record both commercial and noncommercial crimes.
4. Victimization surveys often include fewer serious offenses, but crimes known to the police are usually tallies of the more serious offenses. For example, surveys of victims reveal more attempts to commit crimes than are recorded as official statistics.

Debating which procedure gives the more accurate picture of criminal activity is therefore inappropriate. We learn something from each mode of measurement, and we form an approximate map of the social locations of crimes as different measures give converging pictures. However, some blurred pictures are produced when we ask people for confessions of their crimes, the subject of Chapter 7.

7. Self-Reports

How Self-Reports Work

The fact that surveys of victims and official crime statistics tend to produce parallel findings has not reduced skepticism about the validity of official tabulations. Doubt remains, and it has moved criminologists to attempt to find out who has committed how much of which crimes by asking people to confess. Measures based on such *self-reports* have been devised in a number of ways including:

1. Asking people to complete anonymous questionnaires
2. Asking people to complete questionnaires that identify the respondents
3. Conducting face-to-face interviews

Unfortunately, these procedures still provide imperfect measures of what people have done. Whether they are better or worse indicators of criminal activity than official records and victimization surveys is an awkward question. It is a poor question because personal admissions of crimes, like victims' reports to interviewers, to some extent measure kinds of events different from those that result in police records. It is not surprising then that studies using confessional techniques both agree and disagree among themselves, but more recent studies yield greater consensus in mapping crime and delinquency.

Background

In 1946, Austin Porterfield published the first systematic self-report study of delinquent and deviant behavior among samples of college students in Fort Worth, Texas. The samples of young women and men surveyed by Porterfield were presented with questionnaires that they were asked to complete anonymously. Although followed by a similar study by Wallerstein and Wyle (1947), it was not until Nye and Short's (1957a) study appeared in a major sociological journal that self-report studies became a significant tool for investigating delinquent and criminal behavior.

Nye and Short's sample consisted of 570 high school boys aged 16 and 17 years, and 170 boys of similar age from a state school for young offenders. From the outset, the results of this study were important. Not only did the results go against the conventional wisdom, which assumed that most people would not readily admit to socially undesirable behavior, the data also confirmed that there is much more crime than what is reported in official statistics. Although limited in the number of items investigated, the Nye and Short study produced two findings that have been reproduced many times: first, the prevalence of delinquency is much greater than official statistics would suggest; and second, a primary difference between official and nonofficial delinquents is that official delinquents commit more offenses than so-called straight kids.

Since Nye and Short's research in the mid-1950s, self-report surveys have grown to become a frequently used mechanism for studying delinquent behavior.

Findings from Self-Reports

Areas of Consensus

Many international studies employing self-report indicators agree on these rather obvious findings: (1) that almost everyone, by his or her own admission, has broken some criminal law; (2) that the amount of hidden crime is enormous; and (3) that people who commit crimes are better described as representing a continuum, as having committed more or fewer crimes, rather than being all-or-none criminal or noncriminal. As Chapter 6 indicated, behaviors guided by social norms tend to describe a unimodal (one-humped) graph that looks like a J or an L, depending on how it is drawn.

While self-report studies are still conducted of selected groups of inmates (English 1993), much of our attention is now directed toward the broader population. In many jurisdictions, self-report surveys are conducted regularly to monitor changes in rates of delinquent or deviant behavior.

One of the longest ongoing studies of self-reported delinquency is the Monitoring the Future project by Johnston, Bachman, and O'Malley (1993) at the University of Michigan's Institute for Survey Research. From 1975 onward, this project has surveyed some 130 high schools throughout the United States monitoring several concerns, including participation in selected juvenile offenses. Figure 7.1 presents some results for the years 1982–1994 inclusive for several items. Specifically, the questions asked were:

"During the last 12 months, how often have you. . .

- Gotten into a serious fight in school or at work?
- Used a knife or gun or some other thing (like a club) to get something from a person?
- Taken something not belonging to you worth under $50?
- Taken something not belonging to you worth over $50?
- Taken something from a store without paying for it?
- Taken a car that didn't belong to someone in your family without permission of the owner?
- Gone into some house or building when you weren't supposed to be there?
- Gotten into trouble with police because of something you did?"

Figures 7.1 and 7.2. display the proportion of students who indicate having committed the selected delinquent acts at least once in the previous year.

Beyond the intrinsic interest we might have in knowing the absolute rates of these self-reported behaviors, their broader importance lies in comparing them with what we have seen in reports of official statistics. For example, it is clear from these data that absolute rates of offending are higher than those reported in the

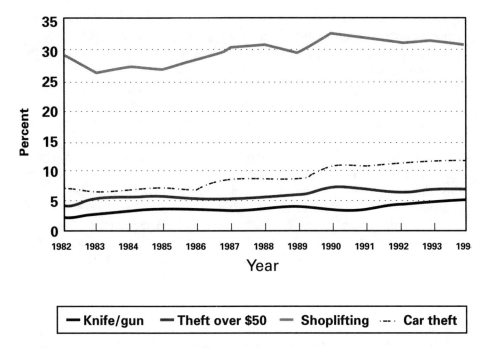

Figure 7.1   High school seniors self-reporting selected delinquencies, 1982–1994. Adapted from Maguire and Pastore (1995), table 3.41.

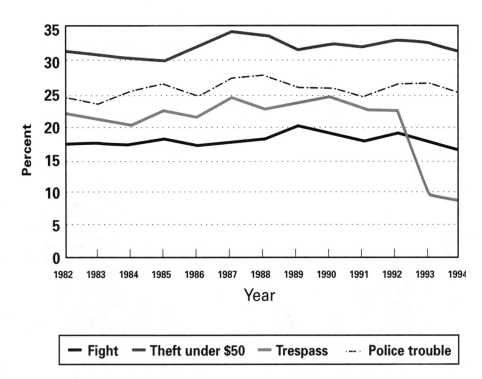

Figure 7.2   High school seniors self-reporting selected delinquencies, 1982–1994. Adapted from Maguire and Pastore (1995), table 3.41.

police statistics. It is also the case, however, that the trend for all of the offenses reported here is relatively flat. That is, only minor variations in self-reported offending are apparent from year to year. This is in stark contrast to the greater variations reported in the official arrest statistics (Chapter 4, Figure 4.1).

The relevance of these differences is not that one method of collecting information more closely approaches the truth than the other. Rather, what is relevant is that we appreciate that different methods can produce different estimates and that neither is necessarily the best indicator of the true rate of crime.

A third point to note is the extreme downturn that occurs on the question concerning getting into trouble with the police (Figure 7.2). In 1993, the wording of this question was changed from "Gotten into trouble with police because of something you did" to "Been arrested and taken into a police station." While one might view this change as simply a variation on a theme, the behaviors indicated by each question are quite different. Thus, the moral to be learned here is that one must be careful in interpreting results. Minor variations in method, such as how questions are phrased, can produce differences in apparent outcome, independent of actual behavior.

Johnston et al. have conducted a similar series of self-report surveys concerning drug use among high school seniors (Johnston, O'Malley, and Bachman 1995). Results of selected drug use are presented in Figure 7.3. Again, the graph shows those who report having used these drugs at least once in the previous 12 months. Overall, the data suggest a general decrease in drug use, especially in the consumption of alcohol and marijuana, from 1985 to 1995. For this sample, there is even a noticeable reduction in the use of cocaine—a drug that has received considerable attention over the previous years.

The number of persons who exceed these central tendencies decreases as one moves toward the extremity of committing many crimes and more serious crimes. While some criminality is common, persistent and grave violations of the law are the experiences of a minority. This holds true whether the measure is confession or official statistics.

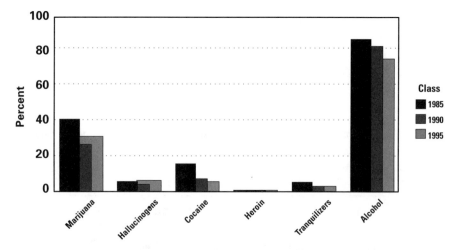

Figure 7.3 Self-reported use of selected drugs among U.S. high school seniors, classes of 1985, 1990, and 1995. Taken from Maguire and Pastore (1995), table 3.59.

Furthermore, both measures of criminality show a relationship between being persistent as an offender and being a serious offender. All observations of conduct suggest that the more often a person breaks the law, the more likely he or she is to commit more grave offenses. The finding of a skewed distribution of admitted delinquencies agrees with the distribution of criminal activity shown by court records where we find that a slim majority of repetitive, serious violators justifies the picture of incorrigible toughs or hard-core delinquents.

An example of high volume self-reporting is presented in Table 7.1. These data are taken from a study by English (1993), who surveyed a sample of 128 female and 872 male prisoners in the state of Colorado during a six-month period in 1988. The prisoners were asked if they had committed a certain

Table 7.1   Description of Crime Frequencies (English 1993: 368).

Type of crime	Women	Men
Total cases	128.0	872.0
Claimed no activity in period	29.0	261.0
Burglary		
Mean	45.7	68.5
Median	2.0	6.0
Cases	9.0	181.0
Robbery		
Mean	6.6	13.7
Median	1.0	2.5
Cases	9.0	90.0
Assault		
Mean	10.8	18.3
Median	1.0	2.0
Cases	26.0	216.0
Theft		
Mean	119.9	76.7
Median	24.0	11.0
Cases	30.0	162.0
Car Theft		
Mean	9.1	23.7
Median	1.0	2.0
Cases	7.0	89.0
Forgery		
Mean	94.3	239.7
Median	48.0	80.0
Cases	7.0	113.0
Fraud		
Mean	94.3	271.6
Median	48.0	12.5
Cases	7.0	58.0
Drug dealing		
Mean	3,612.9	2,156.5
Median	270.0	309.0
Cases	31.0	233.0

type of offense and if they did, to recall how many of that type they had committed during the 12-month period immediately before their apprehension. Interestingly, 29 of the 128 women and 261 of the 872 men in the study reported no criminal activity during the 12-month period before their arrest. According to English, these ratios of inactive offenders are consistent with previous studies (English 1993: 364). Yet, a review of the prison data showed that "eight of the inactive women had been arrested for murder, six had been arrested for forgery, and four had been arrested for theft. Nearly 20% of the inactive men had been arrested for the crimes of burglary or robbery." English also notes that interviews with the inmates suggested that few appear to misreport arrests intentionally. Instead, they claimed "confusion about the behavior they described to us and the crimes defined in the questionnaire."

Three facts are striking about these results. First, the absolute numbers of reported offenses are extremely high, showing that "professional criminals" (or at least those found in prison) are very active. Second, even among this select group, the means are higher than the medians, suggesting the existence of outliers or "high performers." Third, the selectivity of female inmates is clearly exemplified by the close similarity of their behavior with that of their male counterparts. In her original study, English reported only marginal differences between men and women concerning the frequency of offending within similar offense categories. That is, among those who committed assault and forgery, the reported frequency for men was higher than for women while among those reported having committed theft, the expected frequencies were higher for women than men. Within the remaining offense categories, there are no significant differences by sex.

One might question the accuracy of some of these estimates, particularly for events with high frequencies. Drug dealing, for example, is clearly a routinized activity for many offenders and is simply part of their daily lives. This is reinforced by the fact that the mean number of self-reported drug deals for women is more than 3,600 per woman per year and for men, more than 2,100 per man per year. The volume of such common, high-frequency events is difficult to estimate with a high degree of accuracy. An intuitive feel for this difficulty is soon gained when one is asked to report the frequency of routine activities in one's own life. Try, for example, to estimate how often you went shopping last year, or how often you ate in a restaurant.

Implications

For Research Methodology

The repeated finding of a skewed distribution of criminal activity in large populations has relevance for research that would compare categories of people for their differential propensity to offend. If almost everyone commits minor offenses occasionally, there is no point in searching for differences among people with respect to such peccadilloes. However, if a few people commit more serious crimes, and do so more frequently, then it is possible that this minority differs from the majority in some discernible ways.

In brief, restricting the range of criminal activity that one studies reduces the associations that can be found between crimes and kinds of people and their situations. Moreover, range can be restricted in quality and quantity. It can be restricted by inquiring about a limited set of crimes and by failure to notice how many crimes, of which sort, have been committed by whom. Early research employing the self-report technique suffered from restrictions of both sorts.

For Policy

In a major study by the Rand Corporation in 1982, Greenwood argued that it might be possible to increase the efficiency of the criminal justice system by taking advantage of the fact that criminal activity is highly skewed (Greenwood 1982; also see Greenwood and Turner 1987). Specifically, Greenwood argued that robbery could be reduced by 20%, without increasing the prison population, by selectively incapacitating offenders. That is, robbery rates could be reduced if it were possible to identify the small group of high-volume offenders and remove them from the general population.

Greenwood's suggestion has caught the interest of both researchers and policy makers. Clearly, the ability to identify those offenders who contribute disproportionately to the crime rate makes sense for increasing the cost-efficiency of the criminal justice system. The unfortunate difficulty is that, while identifying high-rate offenders after the fact is easy, predicting who will become a high-rate offender is not so easy. To date, most of the schemes developed to predict individual criminality often lead to overpredictions. That is, we tend to predict too many offenders and to predict more than the number of offenses they will commit. Still, acknowledging that there is an unequal distribution of offending among offenders serves as a focus for research.

Areas of Disagreement: Correlates of Criminality

Early research with confessional data provided mixed results concerning the correlates of criminal conduct. (These correlates are summarized in Chapters 8, 9, and 10.) The presumed value of asking people about their offensive behavior is that it gives a clearer picture of the social location of crime, a picture undistorted by the alleged biases of a judicial system. It is not at all certain, however, that self-report measures provide a more accurate description. Pictures of criminal conduct drawn from admissions vary with who is drawing them, with which instruments, and for which samples of people.

Self-report instruments have ranged from questionnaires with only six items to questionnaires with nearly 50 items. In addition, those who use these instruments have interrogated, in large, "captive" samples of youths in schools and detention facilities and have neglected confessional inquiries among adults. For example, when it comes to correlating self-reports of adult crime with socioeconomic position among noninstitutionalized samples, Braithwaite (1981: 38) states that he can find only one such study. Over a decade later, the situation has not changed.

Interpretation of findings based on self-report instruments requires recognition of these limitations, and others to be described later. Meanwhile, it is of methodological, as well as substantive, interest to note that a debate exists among criminologists with respect to the relationship between two major markers of social position—ethnicity and family income—and juvenile crime.

Ethnicity, Family Income, and Juvenile Crime

It is commonplace for sociologists to use, in varying mixtures, eight "social locators" as presumed correlates, and possible causes, of conduct: sex, age, socioeconomic status (SES), ethnicity, religiosity, rural or urban residence, school performance, and some indicators of familial relationships. To these social locators, psychologists add such personal indicators as IQ, measures of motivation, interests, and dimensions of personality. Of these locators, SES and family income have been of primary concern in self-report studies.

SES: An Issue

The various measures of juvenile delinquency—official and unofficial—tend to agree about the associations of youthful criminality with differences in age, sex, school performance, rural or urban residence, and some measures of religiosity and domestic relations—an agreement that runs in the popularly expected direction. However, early research with self-report instruments led to disagreement as to the connection of delinquency with ethnicity and socioeconomic status. The disagreement was more notable in American research than in European studies. Thus, McDonald wrote:

> from the American studies . . . evidence . . . both supports and denigrates the theory that the working class is more delinquent than the middle class . . . [whereas] almost all of the literature on delinquency in Britain is in favor of the view that the working class is more delinquent. (McDonald 1969: 19)

Disagreement among American criminologists on this subject continues. It reached a high point with a publication that called the correlation between social class and delinquency a "myth" (Tittle et al. 1978). This allegation was met by an expanded review of the research literature (Braithwaite 1981) and by the first of a series of national surveys of youthful crime (Elliott and Ageton 1980). Both of these more recent investigations returned myth to reality, but not with peace among criminologists as a recent work by Tittle and Meier (1991) shows.

Braithwaite's Review

John Braithwaite (1981) improved upon Tittle et al.'s (1978) inquiry by enlarging the number of reports reviewed. Where Tittle et al. found only 35 works relating official and self-report tallies of juvenile and adult crime, Braithwaite found 53 studies using official statistics on the relationship between juvenile crime and socioeconomic status and 46 studies correlating such data between adult crime and SES.

Braithwaite also reviewed 47 studies using self-reports of the association between juvenile delinquency and SES but, as indicated, could find only one self-report study relating adult crime to SES. In addition, Braithwaite examined 57 documents correlating the social status of areas in which juveniles live and their crime rates as recorded officially plus eight studies correlating residential areas by status with self-reports of delinquencies. To these inquiries, Braithwaite added 13 studies of the social status of areas and official tallies of adult crimes in several countries (Braithwaite 1981: 38–48). His findings follow.

1. Of the 53 studies correlating police data on social status and juvenile delinquency, "44 showed lower-class juveniles to have substantially higher offense rates than middle-class juveniles. Among adults, all 46 studies found lower-class people to have higher crime rates."
2. Studies correlating the social status of areas with juvenile and adult crime found lower-class zones to have higher crime rates—without exception. Such consistency, Braithwaite notes, is rare in social science.
3. Among the 47 studies examining the relation between youthful admissions of delinquencies and SES, "18 found lower-class adolescents to report significantly higher levels of involvement in delinquent behavior than middle-class youth. Seven studies provided qualified support for this hypothesis, and 22 found no significant differences in reported delinquent involvement among classes."
4. The eight self-report studies correlating residential areas and delinquency also yielded mixed results. "Four studies supported the hypothesis, one provided qualified support, and three found no significant difference."
5. The one study examining the connection between a sample of adult crimes and SES found no relationship between social status and admissions of some kinds of theft, gambling, tax cheating, assault, and marijuana use (Tittle and Villemez 1977). However, with the exception of males' reporting of income tax fraud, the nonwhites in this sample (both male and female) admitted to higher levels of criminal activity than did whites.
6. Braithwaite concludes, "the present review covers 90 investigations (both official records and self-reports) of the class-crime relationship published since 1970. Only 21 of the 90 failed outright to support the hypothesis, while two provided only qualified support."

BRAITHWAITE ON CLASS AND CRIME

The conclusion is . . . inescapable from the voluminous, though not always satisfactory, evidence available at this time that lower-class people do commit those direct interpersonal types of crime which are normally handled by the police at a higher rate than middle-class people. If, however, we are talking about those less directly interpersonal forms of crime which involve the abuse of the power inherent in occupational roles (and which are normally policed by special regulators of commerce), then, of course, the reverse is true. (Braithwaite, 1981: 49)

Braithwaite correctly adds that the distribution of crimes in a stratified jurisdiction depends on the kind of crime for which an investigator tests.

National Youth Survey

The first national survey of juvenile crime yields a picture that conforms with Braithwaite's conclusion, official data, and other unofficial measures of crime. Elliott and Ageton (1980) report findings from an American study that interviewed a representative sample of 1,726 adolescents, aged 11–17 years, in 1977. The interviewers asked 47 items that addressed all Uniform Crime Report (UCR) Part I (more serious) offenses except homicide, 60% of Part II crimes, and a range of additional misdemeanors and status offenses. For purpose of analysis these 47 items were grouped in six categories (Elliott and Ageton 1980: 101):

1. Predatory crimes against persons (sexual assault, aggravated assault, simple assault, and robbery)
2. Predatory crimes against property (vandalism, burglary, auto theft, larceny, stolen goods, fraud, and joyriding)
3. Illegal service crimes (prostitution, selling drugs, and buying/providing liquor for minors)
4. Public disorder crimes (carrying a concealed weapon, hitchhiking, disorderly conduct, drunkenness, panhandling, making obscene phone calls, and marijuana use)
5. Status crimes (runaway, sexual intercourse, alcohol use, and truancy)
6. Hard drug use (amphetamines, barbiturates, hallucinogens, heroin, and cocaine)

Admissions to these offenses were then compared with self-reported race and social status. The number of Latinos in this sample was small, and this ethnic category was dropped from analysis. The resulting ethnic comparisons are thus limited to diffuse aggregates called whites (Anglos) and blacks.

Social status was measured with an index derived from a young person's report of the occupation of the "principal wage earner" in his or her family. From this report, respondents were grouped in five "social classes," ranked from I (professional and managerial) to V (unskilled.) The principal findings follow:

1. Youthful admissions reveal significant race differences in criminal conduct. African Americans, compared with whites, admit to all offenses in the order of 3:2 and to predatory crimes against property in the order of more than 2:1. Small ethnic differences are reported for other categories of crime.
2. Lower-class youths admit to more total criminality than working-class or middle-class youths. They admit to nearly four times as many attacks on persons as middle-class youths and $1\frac{1}{2}$ times as many as working-class youths. Other class differences by category of admitted crime are not significant.
3. Race and class differences are produced principally by relative differences in criminal conduct at the high end of the frequency continuum. In other words, when one compares kinds of people who infrequently commit crimes, differences in conduct by race and SES are small. Nevertheless, as one looks at higher frequencies of violating the law, greater differences between groups become apparent.

Elliott and Ageton (1980: 104) write that

> not only are the relative proportions of blacks and lower-class youth higher at the high end of the frequency continuum but also, within the high category, blacks and lower-class youth report substantially higher frequencies than do whites and middle-class youth.

In Conclusion: Interpreting Findings on Ethnicity, Income, and Crime

It deserves mention that differences in behavior between groups of individuals are seldom absolute, but are usually relative. They are matters of degree, and this means that there is overlap in the distributions of amounts and kinds of crime committed by kinds of people.

Furthermore, one gets different results depending on definitions of "kinds of people" and their situations. Thus, findings of the National Youth Survey would be more informative if they told us about race differences holding SES constant and class differences holding race constant.

With these qualifications, the National Youth Survey reveals more status differences in criminality than did some earlier research, in part because of the broader range of individuals studied and in part because of the greater range of crimes assessed. This means that self-reports yield results in parallel with official statistics when two measures count more of the same kinds of activities.

Still, some ambiguity remains in the empirical literature. Tittle and Meier (1991) conducted a follow-up to the Tittle et al. (1978) review that asserted that the delinquency-SES relationship was a myth. While they move away from the extreme position of the earlier article, they are clearly concerned with the many contrary and inconclusive findings that appear in the literature supporting the SES-delinquency relationship. In an attempt to break the "yes it does—no it doesn't" conundrum, they propose that three approaches might be pursued (Elliott and Ageton 1980: 101). First, they suggest that researchers "continue to try to find the conditions under which SES predicts delinquency." As they note, much remains to be investigated within this framework and not all of the existing research is of high quality. Second, they suggest that researchers "reconceptualize the problem in terms of interactions among SES and other variables that ultimately have import for delinquency." Third, they note that SES is a complex indicator that acts as a proxy for other, more specific factors. As they say, "if SES supposedly predicts youthful misbehavior because more lower status than higher status youths are deprived, it would make more sense to measure deprivation directly than to measure SES, which is a step removed from the real variable at issue."

Advantages of Self-Report Surveys

Self-report surveys of criminal and delinquent activity have certain advantages over official measures. First, they may obtain an estimate of the incidence of crimes not known to the police. Official statistics only reflect the number of offenses known to the police and the number of offenders who have been apprehended by the police. It is likely that those "fortunate" enough not to be caught by the police are different from those who are apprehended. They may, for example, be more intelligent, more professional, less active, commit fewer serious offenses, or simply be luckier than those who are caught.

Unfortunately, such distinctions cannot be determined from official statistics. Some evidence suggests that more than 80% of serious violent offenders are not recorded as official delinquents or are known to police only as minor offenders (Huizinga and Elliott 1987).

A second advantage of these surveys is that they provide an opportunity to collect ancillary information about offenders. At best, official statistics provide a limited description of characteristics of offenders from a few demographic variables—usually age and sex, and occasionally race or ethnicity. When individuals are quizzed about their criminal behavior, we can ask them questions about their socioeconomic background and subject them to social-psychological testing.

A third advantage of self-report surveys is that a wider range of behaviors can be examined than those officially recognized as delinquent or criminal. For instance, in testing the *progression hypothesis*, which assumes progress from mildly deviant to more offensive behaviors, it is possible to ask respondents about noncriminal forms of antisocial behavior.

Problems with Self-Report Surveys

As with any data collection procedure, self-report surveys have not only strengths but some weaknesses as well. Some shortcomings with self-report surveys are a consequence of how researchers have chosen to carry out the procedure; some are intrinsic to the procedure itself. One long-standing difficulty with many self-report studies is that they are often only conducted with young people, usually convenience samples of school children or reformatory inmates. This limits the generalizability of their findings to the broader population. Similarly, many early self-report studies of delinquency included a variety of behaviors beyond those that were strictly criminal or delinquent. Thus, many surveys included behaviors that we might consider deviant, noxious, or mildly offensive, but clearly not criminal. The measurement of nondelinquent along with delinquent behavior often leads people to overestimate the amount of delinquent or criminal behavior.

Other difficulties with some self-report studies include matters such as small sample sizes and the use of convenience samples. Small samples are problematic because many behaviors we wish to study are rare events and may not be captured in a small sample. Samples made up of respondents who are chosen because they are conveniently available, as opposed to random samples, are prone to selection bias and the attendant problem of low generalizability.

Some problems are intrinsic to the self-report method itself, and to the general modes of implementation—questionnaires and interviews. One difficulty with such research is that it is the respondent who decides what forms an offense. As noted in the discussion of definitions of crime, the mere commission of an unsanctioned act does not necessarily mean that it is a crime. From some per-spectives, what makes a crime is not just the behavior, but the states adjudication of that behavior as criminal. Thus, not all homicides are murders, and not all appropriations of property are theft. It is only when the judiciary defines the behavior as criminal that it becomes so.

The other side of this definitional issue is also problematic. Individuals may not be aware that their behavior is criminal. While this problem can be reduced through the careful wording of questions to specify particular acts or actions, people still infuse words with both connotative meanings and denotative mean-ings. For example, abusive parents might not admit to hitting or assaulting their children. Instead, they might define the behavior as the socially acceptable "roughhousing" or "discipline."

The same subjective processes that allow some individuals to misdefine behaviors as criminal when they are not, or vice versa, also lead to problems of timing. Imposing time boundaries on the target behavior is crucial for the estimating rates of incidence. Thus, self-report questionnaires usually phrase their questions with statements such as: "Have you ever . . ." or "In the past year have you . . . ?" Unfortunately, human beings are notorious for their mis-judgment of time. Often, we engage in a process known as *telescoping* where we recall events as having happened more recently than in actuality. One's grandparents, for example, are often guilty of telescoping when they start dis-cussions with the exclamation, "Can it be that long ago? Why it only seems like yesterday when we. . . . "

In surveys where recall of past events is essential, the telescoping of events is not inconsequential. Of course, the opposite is also true although it appears less frequently, and that is the recollection of events as having taken place in a far more distant past than their actual occurrence. Perhaps the ultimate expression of telescoping backward is to place events in the infinite past—that is, to forget their occurrence.

Such compression and expansion of events in time can lead to biases in the estimates of rates of occurrence. Telescoping or compressing the timing of events often leads to an overestimation of rates of occurrence; the expansion of events over time usually leads to an underestimation of rates. Unfortunately, while this issue is generally recognized by researchers as a problem, little methodological research exists to give us an estimate of its extent. The issue of recall, on the other hand, has been studied extensively by psychologists and many key findings have become well integrated into the methodological litera-ture (see Groves 1989; Bradburn and Sudman 1991: 34). As a result, research-ers have incorporated cues and other devices into their instruments to increase the amount and accuracy of recall.

Because of the vagaries of recall and the deliberate attempts of some respon-dents to falsify reports, many researchers have called into question the value of self-report studies as a tool for investigating criminal behavior. These questions concern the reliability and validity of self-report instruments, namely, do self-report procedures produce stable, consistent results, and do they reflect what we want to measure?

Reliability and Validity of Self-Report Surveys
Reliability

As noted in Chapter 3, reliable indicators are those with little or no measurement error. Reliable measures are those that are stable and accurate. Unfortunately, investigators get mixed results when they test the reliability of people's answers to questions about their crimes. The mixture varies with what is asked, of whom, and how.

Studies of the reliability of self-reports have considered reliability to mean the stability of an instrument over a series of similar measurements or on the same measures on separate occasions. Examining a limited number of studies using the latter approach—the test-retest procedure—Huizinga and Elliott (1986) report typical reliability coefficients at +.85 and above, with some in the high +.95–.98 range. (Recall that reliability coefficients have a possible range from 0.0 to 1.0, where 0.0 reflects a completely unreliable instrument and 1.0 reflects total reliability.) Such associations are evidence of good measurement reliability. A similarly positive assessment was made Singh (1979).

Reliability is influenced by many methodological factors such as the number of items in the instruments, the length of time between subsequent tests, and the commitment of those being questioned. Thus, as Huizinga and Elliott report, even well-designed studies conducted by experienced researchers, such as that by Michael Hindelang and his coauthors, can produce reliability coefficients in the barely acceptable +.50–.70 range (Hindelang, Hirschi, and Weis 1981).

Validity

Validity is the degree to which an instrument measures what it is intended to measure. In an insightful review of self-report studies, Cernkovich, Giordano, and Pugh (1985) note that most self-report-based studies consistently underreport the incidence of serious offenses. Similarly, Glanz (1990) reports response rates for self-report studies as low as 50%. It is findings such as these that lead critics to question the validity of self-report research.

The issue of the validity of studies based on self-reports has been a major concern ever since the earliest studies were conducted. The validity of self-report measures is crucial if these indicators are to be used in place of police statistics and other records. However, results of validation studies are not reassuring.

Validation of criminal confessions has been attempted in three ways: (1) by checking admissions of crime against self-reports given in different settings; (2) by comparing the self-reports of known groups; and (3) by comparing confessions with official records. None of these procedures is completely satisfactory, and some of them assume what was questioned by using self-reports, namely, that official records are true ones.

Self-Reports Validated by Self-Reports

Confessions of delinquency have been checked against admissions of other misconduct such as truancy or behavior resulting in school suspension or contacts with police. This is, of course, a redundant form of validation—self-report against self-report. One would expect a high degree of association among such measures. The reported correlations are, however, modest.

Hirschi (1969: 57) found that individual items in his self-report index correlated between +.24 and +.33 with truancy, between +.18 and +.28 with admitted school suspensions, and between +.28 and +.39 with admitted contacts with police. An index of confessed delinquencies among these Bay Area youths correlated variously with their answers to the single question, "Have you ever been picked up by the police?" The correlations varied by age, sex, and race, and ranged from a high of +.79 for white females aged less than 13 to lows of +.05 and +.06 for African-American females aged less than 17 and 18 years (Hindelang et al. 1981: 102). Most of the associations were modest—below +.50—and higher among white youths and males than among African-American youths and females.

Validation can be difficult when the wording of questions varies across surveys. Thus, the National Institute of Education survey described earlier found that interviews produced different reports of victimization from anonymous questionnaires. Overall, twice as many victimizations were admitted to questionnaires as were told to interviewers, and four times as many robberies were reported on questionnaires as were told to interviewers.

One intriguing approach to this problem is to use a form of internal validity checking. In a wonderful example of invalid responses, Schuman and Presser (1981) summarize a study where respondents reported having firm opinions on a fictitious Agricultural Reform Act. Using a similar approach in a self-report drug survey among high school students, Adlaf et al. (1995) included a fictitious drug among the list of substances. It is believed that high response rates to this item would suggest how much over reporting occurs. Of the 3,870 students who participated in the survey, only 36 (0.93%) responded positively to the use of the fictitious drug (Adlaf et al. 1995: 11). While not a definitive indicator, the low rate of outright falsification adds credence to the validity of that instrument with respect to over-reporting. Under-reporting is a different matter. It is well established that when it comes to behaviors such as use of alcoholic beverages (and especially the heavy use of alcoholic beverages) that considerable under-reporting occurs (Embree and Whitehead 1993; Popham and Schmidt).

Known-Group Validation

Known-group validation looks at patterns of scores from confessions of criminality made by segments of the population "known" to have behaved differently. For example, the self-report scores of "official" delinquents, such as boys in training schools, are compared with the scores of a sample of nondelinquents. When this has been done, significant differences are usually reported on the confessional instruments between known delinquents and less offense-prone populations (Nye and Short 1957a, 1957b; Hindelang, Hirschi, and Weis 1981).

This form of validation assumes, of course, what the self-report technique was to have tested, namely, that official delinquents really do behave differently. Such convergent validation gives some assurance that both official statistics and unofficial confessions are measuring the same thing. This convergence does not permit a conclusion about the greater validity of one measure over another, however. This can be said, too, about the third procedure for validating self-report instruments: checking admissions of crime against police or court records.

Self-Reports and Official Records

The more typical procedure used to cross-validate self-report studies is to attempt a cross-referencing with official statistics. It is paradoxical that critics of official records of criminal activity should revert to them as validators of data from questionnaires and interviews. It is difficult to know what kind of finding would constitute a validation and yet justify the preferred use of confessions. Without an informed hypothesis, framed in advance, as to the expected relation between what people say they have done and what they get arrested for, investigators have no way of deciding how strong a correlation is required to validate the confessions they collect. If the association between admitted crime and official records approaches zero, presumably the self-reports are invalid. If the association approaches unity, then one measure may be substituted for the other. Between these poles, however, one cannot tell whether a modest correlation signifies the validity, or invalidity, of either instrument.

Huizinga and Elliott (1987), for example, correlated the results of the American National Youth Survey with a search of police records within a ten-mile radius of every location where each respondent lived between 1979 and 1983. Typical of such results, Huizinga and Elliott note that only a minority of self-reported offenses appears in the official police records. In a Dutch study, Junger (1989) noted striking differences across young people of different ethnic backgrounds in the Netherlands. As she states,

> overall, Moroccans and Turks are much less likely to mention offenses than Surinamese or indigenous Dutch boys are. For example, with "delinquency ever," the discrepancy for Moroccans and Turks is respectively 63% and 56%, while for the indigenous Dutch and the Surinamese it is 87%. Differences are found on all discrepancy scales except "police contacts last year." This suggests that self-report police contacts might be a better measure of differences in involvement in delinquent activities among the four ethnic groups than self-report delinquency measures. (Junger 1989)

Clearly, self-report studies vary greatly in their validity. A study by Poulain et al. (1991), for example, shows that even a 90+% correspondence between self-report measures and population register data can pose an ongoing challenge to researchers. Consequently, researchers seek evermore creative solutions to the problem (Poulain, Riandey, and Firdion 1991).

One ingenious approach to the problem is Clark and Tiffts (1966) use of polygraph (so-called lie detector) results to validate the self-reported deviant behavior of a small group of male university students. While results varied considerably across items, Clark and Tifft noted an overall 81.5% agreement in the results of both instruments. Such forms of validation are rare, however, because of the expense involved in conducting polygraph tests.

It has been argued that one factor that differentiates how well self-report studies perform is the sensitivity of the questions being asked. Conventional wisdom suggests and research results confirm that questions relating to less socially acceptable or desirable behavior produce lower response rates and fewer valid responses than questions relating to more acceptable behaviors. Being aware of this issue, researchers have attempted to devise less threatening or intrusive approaches to measuring sensitive behaviors. These include such things as phrasing the question in a way that makes the deviant behavior appear customary or normal. With respect to asking about the frequency with which certain acts have been committed, having categories of extremely high frequency make it easier (more likely) that respondents will admit to lower, but objectively deviant, levels of activity (Embree and Whitehead 1993; see also, Tracy and Fox; Miller, Fox, and Tracy).

In conclusion: unreliability and invalidity. It is neither true that everyone tells the truth nor that no one tells the truth. Telling the truth and deceiving oneself and others are activities that are contingent on several factors. They depend on kinds of people, settings and the perceived rewards or penalties that may result from one's admissions or concealments. Some people believe that the truth will set you free while others agree with Mark Twain that confession may be good for the soul, but bad for the reputation.

As we have seen, even in circumstances where people want to answer truthfully, their responses may be affected by other sources of error including forgetting. The problem for those who study crime is that we frequently do not know which—if any—of the potential sources of unreliability or invalidity are operating. Thus, it's difficult to forecast their impact on the estimates we derive from their use.

Conclusion

Considerable attention has been paid to the utility of self-report measures of criminality because they have been devised and employed as correctives of the apparent deficiencies in official statistics. An evaluation of these unofficial ways of counting crime reveals that they do not fulfill the promise of providing a better enumeration of offensive activity. Instead, they provide a different enumeration. We know best where certain kinds of crime are generated when the major measures of criminality converge. Fortunately, the different measures point to similar social sites of kinds of crime. Confessions of criminality, surveys of victims, test situations, direct observations, unobtrusive measures, and official records draw similar maps of the social locations that produce more murderers, muggers, rapists, robbers, burglars, and thieves than others. We also know something—although with less certainty—about the social locations of less visible crime such as shoplifting, fraud, and embezzlement.

These social sites form the major correlates of crime to be explained by theories of crime causation. Chapters 8 and 9 describe these correlates in greater detail. However, in thinking about these correlates of crime, we should bear in mind that our defined scope concerns principally the more serious predatory crimes, the crimes *mala in se* that are the objects of most citizens' concern. It bears repeating, too, that these correlates are not necessarily the causes of offenses, but simply the material with which the sociologist looking for explanations of crime works.

Part III
Social Location of Serious Crime

8. Age, Sex, and Crime

Age and Sex As Correlates of Crime

Two of the most striking and persistent conditions associated with the risk of committing crimes are being young and being male. If one groups people by age and sex and then looks at their proportional contributions to rates of arrest or conviction, the worldwide experience is that young men, compared with older persons and women, are more likely to commit serious crimes.

Violence, for example, is almost a monopoly of men in their late teens and early twenties. In Canada and the United States, about 90% of all arrests for violent crimes are arrests of men (FBI 1996, table 41; Statistics Canada 1994). The violent crimes index, we are reminded, includes murder and nonnegligent manslaughter, forcible rape, robbery, and aggravated assault. Disproportionately, these are activities of young men.

American men aged 15–19 contributed approximately 23% of the arrests for such crimes in 1995, while men aged 20–24 accounted for another 18% of such arrests (FBI 1996, table 39: 220–221). Thus, about half the arrests for these violent crimes occur among a class of the citizenry that forms approximately 10% of the population (U.S. Bureau of the Census 1996). Canadian figures run in parallel. Males aged 14–18—who make up about 7% of the 1996 population—account for 11% of arrests for violent crimes (Statistics Canada 1994).

Property crimes correlate less strongly with age and sex—a function, in part, of the greater variety of ways in which people steal that are not dependent on youthful vigor. Nevertheless, the Uniform Crime Reports (UCR) for 1995 count 75% of arrests for the more serious (Part I) property crimes among males (FBI 1992, table 42: 230). These crimes, to repeat, include burglary, larceny-theft, motor vehicle theft, and arson.

It is notable that this sex differential narrows a bit as arrests are tallied for the less popular, but more profitable, thefts by forgery and counterfeiting, embezzlement, and fraud. American males in 1991 constituted 65% of arrests for forgery and counterfeiting, 61% of arrests for embezzlement, and 57% of arrests for fraud. In fraud, sexual equality is approached.

Age differentials also vary with kinds of theft, as we should expect. About 80% of all arrests for burglary and motor vehicle theft are of persons aged less than 25, as are about 70% of arrests for larceny-theft (FBI 1992, table 38: 223). However, the more "intelligent" and less common larcenies such as forgery, counterfeiting, fraud, and embezzlement peak during the prime of life, ages 25–35. While such crimes peak at these ages, they continue to be practiced by persons of older age. Both ability and opportunity to commit these styles of theft decline less rapidly with age than do chances to commit the more "muscular" thefts and violent attacks.

The "Age Effect"

The impact of variations in age structure on crime rates has been studied often during the past three decades. Research in the United States (Sagi and Wellford 1968; Chilton and Spielberger 1971; Ferdinand 1970), Australia (Biles 1976), Canada (Hartnagel 1978; Maxim and Jocklin 1980), Scandinavia (Jepsen and Pal 1969; The European Committee on Crime Problems 1970), and Great Britain (Maxim 1985) has shown a substantial relationship between fluctuations in the age pyramid and rates of crime, (There are also some contrary findings. For example, Steffensmeier et al. [1992] find no support for the Easterlin hypothesis that crime rates vary by the size of the age cohort.)

The primary reason for this relationship is that crime rates are not evenly distributed over the age range. Age-specific rates are highest among adolescents and young adults. Thus, all things being equal, small increases or decreases in the proportion of young people can often lead to sizable swings in both the overall volume of crime and in the gross rate of crime. An example of the pattern of the age gradient in crime rates is presented in Table 8.1. Taken from the UCR, the table illustrates age- and sex-specific patterns of arrests for 1995.

Table 8.1   Age- and Sex-Specific Rates and Age Ratios to Overall Rates for U.S. Arrest Statistics.

	Males		Females	
Age	*Rate per 100,000*	*Ratio to total*	*Rate per 100,000*	*Ratio to total*
10–12	1199.7	0.58	418.4	0.67
13–14	4651.8	2.23	1855.8	2.98
15	6900.6	3.31	2367.2	3.80
16	7752.3	3.72	2443.7	3.93
17	7650.1	3.67	2215.7	3.56
18	7360.1	3.53	1947.0	3.13
19	5635.4	2.70	1567.1	2.52
20	4489.5	2.15	1348.3	2.17
21	4041.2	1.94	1228.8	1.97
22	3676.4	1.76	1159.8	1.86
23	3374.3	1.62	1109.0	1.78
24	3143.2	1.51	1026.0	1.65
25–29	2870.1	1.38	961.6	1.54
30–34	2455.9	1.18	829.1	1.33
35–39	1896.6	0.91	615.7	0.99
40–44	1285.0	0.62	390.8	0.63
45–49	774.0	0.37	234.8	0.38
50–54	469.4	0.23	154.0	0.25
55–59	302.3	0.15	99.1	0.16
60–64	198.6	0.10	70.1	0.11
65+	95.8	0.05	31.3	0.05
Total	2083.5	1.00	622.2	1.00

Sources: Federal Bureau of Investigation (1996, tables 39 and 40); U.S. Bureau of the Census (1996, table 16).

These data show a peaking of age-specific rates in the 16–18 age groupings for males and in the 15–17 age groupings for females. The pattern for the United States follows that generally found elsewhere. In the high-risk age groups, the absolute rate for males is roughly 3.8 times the overall average for males; for females, the highest risk group has a rate 4.7 times that of the overall rate for females. The lowest absolute rates and the relative age-specific ratios are to be found among the very young and the very old.

An analysis of the relationship between crime and age by Wilson and Herrnstein (1985: 133–135) also shows that this overall pattern holds whether we use police statistics or self-report data. Self-report studies mirror this curvilinear pattern of self-reported crime, but also suggest that the absolute frequency of offending is higher than that indicated by official statistics.

The distribution typified by Table 8.1 can be modified if age-specific rates do not stay constant. From the late 1960s and through the 1970s significant increases in absolute age-specific rates appeared among those groups that already had the highest crime rates. This led to increases in overall or gross rates that were significantly out of proportion to the population base. In the mid-1990s, however, lower rates of violent crime have been observed in the United States and Canada.

While detailed annual studies have shown considerable year-to-year variations, the overall consensus in the literature is that up to one half the fluctuation in the overall volume of crime, and 25–20% of the fluctuation in crude rates can be attributed to variations in age structure alone.

Having noted that age-specific rates vary considerably, the next step is to define that shape of the relationship. Overall, age-specific rates appear to increase consistently until they peak, somewhere in either late adolescence or early adulthood and then decrease, until the limits of human life expectancy are reached. Data presented by Hirschi and Gottfredson (1983) and Farrington (1986) support the notion that the age-crime relationship is essentially curvilinear (an inverted U-shape) across all time and all societies for which we have data. What is also obvious from these data is that slopes and the peak of this curve vary over time and location. In Britain, for example, there has been a gradual decline in the peak age of criminal involvement from around 20 to 25 years in the 1840s to about 14 to 17 years in recent times (Gattrell and Hadden 1972; Maxim 1989).

As noted previously, age is not only related to how much crime is committed but also to the type of crime committed. Wilson and Hernstein have analyzed American UCR data for 1980 based on the rank order of crimes among those arrested before the age of 18 and among those arrested after age 40 (Wilson and Herrnstein 1985: 130). Among the younger population, the most common offenses are (in rank order): larceny theft; all other offenses, except traffic, (this is a residual category after 29 specific offenses have been taken into account); burglary; liquor law infractions; and disorderly conduct. Among those more than 40 years of age, the most common offenses are: drunkenness, driving under the influence, all other offenses, larceny theft, and disorderly conduct.

Perhaps more interesting than the simple rank orders, however, are those offenses that show the greatest differences among the rank orders. The offenses young people are far more likely to commit than their older counterparts are motor vehicle theft, burglary, robbery, vandalism, and arson. Among the offenses most likely to involve older offenders as opposed to younger offenders are the crimes of gambling, driving under the influence, fraud, drunkenness, and offenses against the family. In comparison then, it may be the case that younger people are more likely to be arrested for crimes involving physical prowess, while older people are more likely to be arrested for vice and nonphysically demanding property offenses. Interestingly, there is little difference in the rank order of murder although it has a higher relative ranking among the older than the younger offenders.

TRENDS IN JUVENILE HOMICIDE

The shift toward lower ages in homicide . . . poses new challenges to prevention efforts and to the criminal justice system. An increasing proportion of the defendants charged with homicide are not juveniles. Although juvenile homicide cases are still a very small proportion of the juvenile offender cases coming into the courts, and are a minority among homicide cases, they are cases that are given exceptional publicity in the mass media. Public perceptions of juvenile delinquency are being shaped by highly publicized instances of homicides committed by juveniles. (Greenberg, 1994: 372)

Because the absolute volume of crime is so much higher among juveniles than the rest of the population, little attention is focused on the elderly offender. Still, as Wilson and Herrnstein note, there are some interesting generalizations. Specifically:

A substantial portion of the arrests of the elderly . . . are for relatively passive offenses committed by hard-core, lifelong criminals engaging in such crimes as fraud, receiving stolen property, and illegal gambling, which typically require little physical activity but some contact with a criminal network. There are, of course, first-time older offenders, and their crimes tend to be more violent than those of the recidivists. They commit most of the murders, assaults, rapes, and other sex crimes of the elderly, often in association with drunkenness and other forms of substance abuse. (Wilson and Herrnstein 1985: 132)

Significance

The crucial determining issue in research focusing on age is the exact causal components behind this variation in age-specific rates. According to Hirschi and Gottfredson, the significance of the constancy of the distribution of criminality by age is that no current theory of criminogenesis accounts for it. This is ironic since the relationship is so strong that Hirschi and Gottfredson[1] describe it as the closest the social sciences come to discovering a "law."

From a methodological perspective, the primary problem with the concept of age (and gender for that matter) is that it is a variable that stands for other vari-

---

[1.] The age-invariance thesis is outlined in Hirschi and Gottfredson (1983). The most cited critique of this position is presented in Greenberg (1985) with a subsequent response by Hirschi and Gottfredson (1985) in the same issue. Other responses can be found in the commentaries section of the *American Journal of Sociology*, 1984, vol. 90. Tittle (1988: 78) best illustrates the stridency of the advocates when he notes that Hirschi and Gottfredson are: ". . . two leading scholars, one of whom might rightly claim title as the most frequently cited criminological theorist in the world today, conclude that no theory can explain the age-crime relationship and that a specific idea (and research) that appears contrary to the presumed invariant pattern is without theoretical import."

ables involved in underlying socio-cultural and biological processes. Such variables that stand for others are called *proxy* variables. Both the strength and weakness of age as a variable stems from its high correlation with such factors as physical maturation, cognitive development, moral development, acculturation, and earned and ascribed positions within the social structure. The task of any theory, therefore, is to identify which among those causal factors age is a proxy. From one perspective, the inability to identify the specific causal referent that age represents dooms the production of adequate explanations of criminal behavior, and, supposedly, a wide range of intervention strategies.

Fortunately, for many purposes, our inability to identify age's underlying causal factor does not invalidate its use in research and policy development. Examples abound of empirical relationships that are useful despite a lack of understanding of the generating process.

As Greenberg's critique of Hirschi and Gottfredson rightly notes, the invariance of the age-crime relationship may have been overstated (1985). However, the relationship *does* appear to be a stable one, and if it does change, it does so only slowly or under extreme circumstances. As even a cursory review of the delinquency literature will show, there is a variety of plausible explanatory factors that may be related to chronological age. In fact, it is conceivable that there is some substitutability of factors such that as one loses its impact another takes its place to maintain a certain level of empirical regularity.

Our inability to identify what it is that age represents in the age-crime equation does not diminish its importance as a factor to be considered in planning exercises or crime prevention schemes. The knowledge that longer-term changes in both the volume and relative mix of crime can be indexed by variations in age structure is of significant worth both at the micro and the macro level. One would, for example, be very suspicious of any evaluation of a neighborhood watch program that gave credit to the program for a five-year decline in residential burglaries, if it were known that the area in which the program was evaluated had also experienced a considerable out-migration of teenagers during that same period.

Despite the theoretical confusion in this area, a great deal of attention remains focused on the issue. If Hirschi and Gottfredson are correct, this line of research may lead to a breakthrough in our understanding of the origins of crime (Tittle 1988; Hirschi and Gottfredson 1990).

Note: On Interpreting the "Age Effect"

Age and sex correlates of crime represent crude estimates. They are crude, in the first place, because the categories of crime called "assault," "robbery," or "larceny-theft" are broad. Such legal titles do not describe homogeneous kinds of events. There may be, then, degrees of seriousness within each category. With respect to age differentials in particular, Greenwood et al. (1980) suggest that the picture of disproportionate crime among youths may be distorted by the lesser seriousness of their offenses.

Other sources of roughness in the data include the observation that thefts by younger offenders are often group crimes, while older predators more frequently operate alone. To the extent that this is so, arrest figures exaggerate youthful crime. In brief, the privacy accorded juvenile records means that we have only approximate tallies of offenses by their frequency and gravity as youths move into and out of careers in crime (see Figure 8.1).

Age, Sex, and Repetition

Some interesting interactions exist between sex, repetition of crime, and the age at which one begins criminal activity. For example, women are arrested disproportionately for the "chemical offenses"—drunkenness, violation of liquor laws, and driving while intoxicated—at earlier ages than men (FBI 1992, table 42). There is also evidence that, in Western cultures at least, females who become addicted to the "comforting chemicals" do so at earlier ages than males, with graver consequences, and with less probability of reform (Blane 1968; Curlee 1970; Schuckit 1972; Sclare 1970).

Figure 8.1 Young males make up the most criminogenic part of the population in all known societies. Photo courtesy of Corbis.

Despite this possible sex difference, the younger a person of either sex is when first arrested, the greater the likelihood of a second arrest and, usually, the shorter the time span between offenses (Mannheim and Wilkins 1955; Sellin 1958). Commitment to a career in crime, like success in lawful occupations, is frequently characterized by early devotion to preferred activities. Blumstein et al. (1986) and Farrington et al. (1990) have concluded that age at first arrest is among the best predictors of later legal involvement. The earlier the first arrest, the more likely a criminal career. Patterson et al. find that childhood aggression is "a significant predictor for age of onset" (1992: 353) and that "early onset may simply be an extension of a pattern of high rates of antisocial acts already in place in late childhood" (1992: 350).

Sex and Kinds of Crime

The types of crime that men and women commit also differ. Until recently only men have been charged with forcible rape. In some jurisdictions (Canada, for example), only women could be victims of this crime by legal definition. Female offender–male victim "rape" is rare and usually where it does take place, it is a case of "statutory rape" where the victim may not be a complainant, but the act is considered criminal because the victim is underage. An example of such an instance is illustrated in Figure 8.2. In this case the offender is a 35-year-old elementary school teacher who bore a child by a former student who turned 14 years old a month after their daughter was born. The two met in his second grade class.

Furthermore, it has been principally, but not entirely, women who have been arrested for prostitution and infanticide. Indeed, under Canadian criminal law only females can be guilty of "infanticide."

Legal definitions are subject to change, of course, and such change will have some impact on the quality of charges laid without changing the behaviors. Furthermore, men do "rape" men, particularly in prisons (Carroll 1974, 1977; Davis n.d.),

Figure 8.2   This 35-year-old Seattle elementary school teacher pleaded guilty to a charge of raping one of her former pupils. The boy turned 14 one month after his daughter was born. Photo courtesy of Associated Press.

but the crime in such cases is usually called something else—like buggery, sodomy, or assault. Because of the difficulties in proving heterosexual rape, it is now suggested that such attacks by men on women also be charged as something other than rape—that is, as assault. Legislation to this effect was passed in Canada in 1982.

Despite changes in legal nomenclature, the male is universally the more physically violent of the sexes. This does not mean that females of one culture cannot be more violent than males of another culture. In fact, as we will see, this is the case even within one society. Biology is channeled by culture, but this does not eliminate biological facts or differential physiological propensities.

Thus, not only are men more frequently rapists than are females, but they are also disproportionately arrested for and convicted of the other violent crimes—kidnapping, aggravated assault, robbery, manslaughter, and murder.

Sex differences rest, of course, on a biological foundation, a foundation that is itself multidimensional. Thus physiologists recognize "chromosomal sex, endocrinologic sex, genetic sex, gonadal sex, morphologic sex, nuclear sex, psychologic sex, and . . . social sex" (Money 1982: 54). Nevertheless, the masculinizing hormone, testosterone, secreted by the testes, is associated with physical aggressiveness. It is notable that among male prison inmates, in one very good study, the higher the adult testosterone level, the earlier the age of the first arrest. That is, the men who had the highest levels had been arrested youngest, in early adolescence. In another study, the level of testosterone in male juvenile delinquents was correlated with their level of observed aggressive behavior (Konner 1982: 59).

Such physical realities do not deny that biochemical variations are shaped into conduct through social channels. These facts show, however, that physiology differentially provides vulnerabilities and immunities to lessons the environment carries.

Sex differences are also apparent in arrests and convictions for the lucrative thefts by fraud and embezzlement. These rewarding crimes have been largely a male activity. Difference here may be, in great part, a matter of opportunity. One cannot be an embezzler unless one is in a position of financial trust, and anyone who is "stuck in the house" has limited opportunity for fraud, although some frauds are perpetrated by telephone and via computer terminals. We have records of female embezzlers, of course (Nettler 1974); but a sex differential in commission of this crime persists despite the increasing entry of women into managerial positions. The various frauds also remain disproportionately male crimes, although women are represented in arrests for credit card theft, "check passing," the small "cons," and welfare cheating.

Cultures and Sex Differences in Crime

Although males have consistently higher rates of arrest and conviction than females and although they have exhibited this proclivity over the years in a variety of cultures, *the disparity between the sexes fluctuates with the kind of crime, with time, and with the social setting.* For example, the rate for males of *crimes against persons* exceeds the rate for females in Canada and the United States by more than 8:1, but the rate for males of *crimes against property* exceeds the rate for females by about half that, something on the order of 4:1 in recent years.

The influence of culture is strong here and affects the sex ratio of crimes exhibited at different times and in different places. For instance, it must not be concluded that any men, anywhere, are always more murderous than any women. As an illustration, Wolfgang's detailed study of homicide in Philadelphia (1958) reports that white males were convicted of criminal homicide eight times as frequently as white females. By contrast, the sex ratio for this offense among blacks was half that. However, the disparity in cultures is such that African American females in Philadelphia had a recorded homicide rate three times that of white males (Wolfgang 1958: 55).

It is true that men generally produce higher rates of crime than women. However, the sex ratios for criminal activity are not constants. The styles of crime differentially practiced by men and women are in flux. The changes are themselves conditioned by the cultures in which they are embedded. For example, in an early study of the criminality of women, Pollak observes that where poisoning has been recorded as a specific homicidal method, as in Italy, it has appeared as a specialty of women (Pollak 1951). During the late nineteenth century, 123 women were convicted of the "Borgia practice" for every 100 men. What is important is the conclusion Pollak draws from data obtained in Canada and the United States and in Europe: that if one looks at all the serious crimes for which men and women are convicted, homicide makes up a larger proportion of all crimes committed by females than of all crimes committed by males.

Equality and Changing Sex Ratios in Crime

The most interesting hypothesis advanced to explain cultural differences in the sex ratios of criminal activities, and changes in these ratios over time, is the suggestion that as women become the equals of men in terms of rights and privileges, they also become their equals in terms of crime (see Figure 8.3).

Cross-culturally, the more distinct and different the roles of the sexes, the wider the reported disparity between their rates of crime. As societies become less stratified based on sex, the disparity between the rates of crime for the two sexes narrows. For example, Houchon calculated sex ratios in crime for nine regions of Africa and found that the crime rates for men exceeded the rates for women by differences ranging from 900:1 to more than 20,000:1 (1967). The cultures he studied draw distinct lines between the work and privileges of women and men. Findings of the same order are reported for Sri Lanka (Ceylon 1957), where most (98%) juveniles on probation are male; and for prewar Algiers and Tunis, where the number of men convicted of crime exceeded the number of women by almost 3,000:1 (Hacker 1941).

Such disparities contrast with the figures for North America and western Europe, where women more closely approach equality with men. For example, Wolf studied a representative sample of Danes and found that 18.8% of the men and 2.3% of the women had criminal records, a ratio of about 8:1 (Wolf 1965). Similarly, British criminal statistics report that for England and Wales in 1995,

Figure 8.3   What makes "Bonnie and Clyde" more provocative than Bob and Clyde? Photo courtesy of Corbis.

the ratio of convictions of males to convictions of females for all indictable offenses was 4.5:1 (UK Home Office, 1996, calculated from table 5B).

Convergence Hypothesis

Cross-cultural comparisons such as these can be taken as some evidence in favor of a *convergence hypothesis*, the idea that as the social roles of the sexes move toward equality, the difference between the sexes in criminal activity is diminished. Fox and Hartnagel (1979) provide an interesting test of the hypothesis by analyzing fluctuations in Canadian rates of criminal convictions from 1931 through 1968 for their association with three measures of varying sex roles.

A *total fertility rate* is used as a measure of women's adherence to the familial role, and it is hypothesized that this would be negatively correlated with female rates of conviction. Women's participation in the labor force and the proportion of postsecondary educational degrees awarded to women are used as measures of sex role inequality, and it is hypothesized that these signs would be positively associated with rates of convictions among females. Overall, these data affirm the convergence hypothesis. The familial role is negatively associated with criminality among women, while the work-education factor is positively associated with women's involvement in crime. These effects are particularly striking in convictions for theft.

The convergence hypothesis receives added support from G. Won Lee's (1982) analysis of changes in sex- and age-specific conviction rates for indictable crimes in Canada between 1949 and 1968. With age controlled, Lee finds that females nearly tripled their criminal activity, as measured by conviction rates, during that 20-year period, while males did not experience much change in their age-specific conviction rates.

On the other hand, Steffensmeier (1993) finds that much less change has taken place in the patterns of arrest of males and females (Table 8.2) than has been suggested by those who argue that the changes that have occurred in the labor force participation of women will be mirrored in their criminal involvement (see for example, Austin 1982; Simon and Landis 1989). As Steffensmeier notes,

> three general conclusions can be drawn about recent trends in female arrests. First, the distribution of offenses for which both males and females are arrested has changed, but relative to males, the profile of the female offender has not changed. Second, females made arrest gains (mostly small gains) in many UCR offense categories but the most significant change in the female percentage of arrests involves the overall rise in property crime, especially minor thefts and frauds. Third, female-to-male involvement in serious or violent crime has held steady since 1960. . . . [It] dropped for homicide, was constant for aggravated assault, and increased slightly for robbery. Evidence from other sources on crime trends also shows more stability than change in female crime relative to male crime over the past several decades. (1993: 433)

In a twist on the convergence hypothesis, Maxim and Keane (1992) suggest that any convergence in gender roles ought to be reflected in rates of victimization and also offending. Their study of patterns in violent death in Canada since 1950 suggests that such a convergence has not taken place regarding homicide.

Smith and Krichton (1993: 42) examined data from the National Crime Victimization Survey (NCUS) in the United States, and find that from 1973 to 1989 that women did not experience increased rates of victimization with respect to violent crime (robbery, aggravated assault, simple assault, and homicide).

Interpreting Trends

In industrialized countries, the "sexual revolution" of the past three decades and political pressure for sexual equality have encouraged extension of the convergence hypothesis and have led to forecasts of sexually equal crime rates within this decade. For example, in 1975, Simon (1975: 42) predicted equality

Table 8.2 Incidence of Arrests of Males and Females/100,000 Population; Percentage of Persons Arrested Who Are Female, and Arrest Profiles of Males and Females (1960–1990 Uniform Crime Reports)[a]

| | Incidence | | | | | | Percentage of arrests | | | Offender-profile percentage[b] | | | |
| | Male | | | Female | | | Female | | | Male | | Female | |
Offense	1960	1975	1990	1960	1975	1990	1960	1975	1990	1960	1990	1960	1990
Against persons													
Homicide	9	16	16	2	3	2	17	14	11	0.1	0.2	0.2	0.1
Aggravated assault	101	200	317	16	28	50	14	13	13	1	3.0	2	2.0
Weapons	69	137	165	4	11	14	4	8	7	1	2.0	0.5	0.7
Simple assault	265	354	662	29	54	129	10	13	15	4	6.0	4	5.0
Major property													
Robbery	65	131	124	4	10	12	5	7	8	1	1.0	0.5	0.5
Burglary	274	477	319	9	27	32	3	5	8	4	3.0	1.0	1.0
Stolen property	21	103	121	2	12	17	8	10	11	0.3	1.0	0.2	0.5
Minor property													
Larceny–theft	391	749	859	74	321	402	17	30	30	6	10.0	9	20.0
Fraud	70	114	157	12	59	133	15	34	43	1	2.0	2	7.0
Forgery	44	46	51	8	18	28	16	28	34	0.5	0.5	1	1.0
Embezzlement	–	7	8	–	3	5	–	28	37	–	0.2	–	0.1
Malicious mischief													
Auto theft	391	128	158	5	9	18	4	7	9	2	1.0	1	1.0
Vandalism	–	187	224	–	16	28	–	8	10	–	2.0	–	1.0
Arson	–	15	13	15	2	2	–	11	14		0.3		0.1

Offense	1960	1975	1990	1960	1975	1990	1960	1975	1990	1960	1990	1960	1990
Drinking/drugs													
Public drunkenness	2573	1201	624	212	87	71	8	7	9	36	8.0	25	4
DUI	344	971	1193	21	81	176	6	5	11	5	15.0	3	9
Liquor laws	183	276	428	28	43	102	13	14	17	3	5.0	4	5
Drug abuse	49	523	815	8	79	166	15	13	14	1	7.0	1	6
Sex/sex related													
Prostitution	15	18	30	37	45	62	73	73	65	0.2	0.4	4	3
Sex offenses	81	55	78	17	5	7	17	8	8	1	1.0	2	0.3
Disorderly conduct	749	597	499	115	116	119	13	17	18	11	5.0	14	6
Vagrancy	265	45	26	23	7	4	8	14	12	4	0.3	3	0.2
Suspicion	222	31	13	28	5	3	11	13	15	3	0.1	3	0.1
Miscellaneous													
Against family	90	57	51	8	7	12	8	10	16	1	0.5	1	0.5
Gambling	202	60	14	19	6	2	8	9	15	3	0.2	2	0.2
Other except traffic	871	1139	2109	150	197	430	15	15	19	13	23.0	19	20.0
Total	7070	7850	9211	831	1383	2122							

[a] Adapted from Steffensmeier (1993: 416–417).

[b] "The profile represents the percentage of all arrests within each sex that are arrests for that particular offense. The homicide figures for 1990 of 0.2 for men and 0.1 for women indicate that only 0.2% of all male arrests were for homicide, and only 0.1% of all female arrests were for homicide" (Steffensmeier 1993: 418).

between American men and women by 1990 in arrests for larceny, fraud, and embezzlement.

Crystal balls are never clear, however, and they are clouded by variations in police practices, by differences in cultural contexts, and by unforeseen fluctuations in moral fashions. Thus, patterns of recent changes in sex ratios of crime are mixed.

In Canada, for example, overall rates of crime increased slowly during the 1960s and leveled during the 1970s and early 1980s, but the pattern of arrests among men and women did not appear to change appreciably. However, as we saw, patterns of *convictions* for serious crimes did change, with young women making a disproportionate contribution to crime thus measured.

In Japan, arrests of women increased 22% during the early 1970s, while overall rates of crime were declining (*U.S. News and World Report* 1975a). Britain also experienced increases in female criminality, qualified by age and type of crime. Between 1968 and 1974 the number of women convicted of serious offenses rose by 54%, more than twice the rate of increase in convictions of men (*U.S. News and World Report* 1975b).

In England and Wales, as in Canada, narrowing of sex ratios in crime has been most striking among young people. Convictions of teenage girls in Britain rose three times as fast as convictions of boys over the past two decades. The increase has been most apparent in convictions for violent crimes. During a 30-year period when overall conviction rates for assault and murder remained constant, convictions of girls younger than 17 years of age rose from around 1% of all persons found guilty of violence in 1950 to almost 3% in 1995 (United Kingdom, Home Office 1996).

In the United States, by contrast, stability of sex ratios in crime seems to be the recent rule. Contrary to expectations that the women's movement would be linked to increased female criminality, several studies using a variety of measures find little narrowing of the gap between rates of crimes for males and females. For example, Steffensmeier and his colleagues have analyzed official arrest records, juvenile court data, imprisonment statistics, self-report findings, observations in the field, and autobiographies of thieves to assess change in the sex ratios of crime (Steffensmeier 1978; 1980; 1993; Steffensmeier and Jordan 1978; Steffensmeier and Steffensmeier 1980). Their principal findings can be summarized thus:

1. The rank order of kinds of crime committed by American men and women remained quite stable between 1960 and 1990.
2. Men continue to contribute disproportionately to the violent crimes: murder and manslaughter, assault, and robbery. Men are also disproportionately the predators in forcible rape, whether the act is given that legal title or another.
3. Burglars are disproportionately male.
4. American women have made some gains in arrests for property crimes of a petty nature. As mentioned earlier, their arrests for fraud and embezzlement usually occur at the lower echelons of these crimes in terms of take.
5. Younger American women have been increasingly arrested for violation of drug and liquor laws. This does not mean that they have caught up with men in these offenses, but that there has been some diminution of the sex ratio for

such arrests. However, despite the apparent increase in women's use of alcohol and the "soft" drugs, the proportion of females classified upon arrest as "active users" of heroin has remained a constant 15% in recent years.

These findings challenge expectations of some feminist advocates of two decades ago. Writing in 1975, Adler found it curious that there should be a continuing disparity between the sexes in their violence (1975: 16). Adler noted exceptional cases of women becoming leaders in "violent, revolutionary" crimes such as "ravaging banks, robbing commercial establishments, and assassinating victims with cyanide-tipped bullets" (1975: 20–21). Such a conception of change in women's contribution to crime was helped by Ruth Eisenmann-Schier's having become the first female to make the FBI's list of Ten Most Wanted Fugitives (FBI 1968). During the late 1960s and early 1970s, as many as 3 of the 10 most-sought fugitives were women. However, interpreting exceptional cases as signifying general trends is a popular error, and one to be resisted. For most of the 1980s and 1990s, it has been rare for a woman to appear on the Ten Most Wanted Fugitives list.

Significance of Sex Ratios

Steffensmeier assumes that the relative stability of a sex difference in crime indicates continuity of traditional male-female roles and is bolstered by widespread preference for this division of labor (Steffensmeier 1980; 1993). Moreover, Steffensmeier suggests that the kinds of occupations into which women have moved may be those with fewer temptations to crime, that women's work provides an income that reduces temptation, and, last, that women continue to be excluded from the "male buddy network" in which some kinds of crime are generated. Male professional thieves still look upon females as untrustworthy colleagues in crime (Steffensmeier and Kokenda 1979).

Ann Bartel (1979) tested some of these assumptions with an analysis of the characteristics of women arrested in 33 states during 1970. She found that married women with husbands in their households were *more* likely than single women to be arrested for property crimes, a fact that challenges "economic need" as a uniform cause of theft. Furthermore, she found that, when controls were applied for other relevant factors, female participation in the labor force bore a slightly negative relationship to rates of crime for females, a finding that challenges the popular assumption that crime is principally a matter of opportunity.

Last, Bartel discovered two significant determinants of women's resistance to crime: having young children to care for and fear of arrest. The average number of preschool children in husband-wife families correlates negatively with the criminality of women, a finding that accords with the Fox-Hartnagel thesis described earlier. Bartel also noted that probability of arrest and conviction bore a negative relationship to female property crimes, an indication of a general deterrent effect. The principal lesson may be that it is important that we not over-generalize about the changes in gender roles that have taken place.

Conclusions

Age and sex have been and are significant correlates of serious crime. We hope that we have made clear that two things are important about each of these variables: first, they are social variables not biological ones; and second, they represent or stand for complex clusters of other social variables. For instance, with respect to the age of the organism, chronological age matters—perhaps most at the extremes—but it is the psycho-social maturity of the organism and the socialization influences to which it has been exposed that correlate with age and, in turn, with rates of crime. In comparable ways the same is true of sex because it is the cultural elaborations on the biological fact of sex that produces gendered notions of masculinity and femininity, social facts that can be part of the explanations of crime. Specifically, the social roles of women with respect to education and labor force participation have changed considerably, but their roles in other aspects of life have changed far less. During the same period, the social roles of men have changed little. It is not surprising, therefore, that rates of criminality have displayed so little convergence.

9. Ethnic Differences in Rates of Crime

Understanding Ethnicity

The distinctive assumption of a social science, and particularly sociology and anthropology, is that the interesting aspects of human action are learned. When what is learned has some discernible pattern for some people, and when such a pattern is distinguishable from that of other groups, the scholar speaks of the style of life as a "culture." Although the boundaries of a culture are never mapped exactly, it is assumed that they are roughly discriminable and that cultures are both products of human interaction and generators of it. Cultures are thought to be both the causes and the effects of human beings teaching one another how to behave.

Whether one studies cultures professionally or observes them as a citizen, it is apparent that human beings group themselves by categories of preferences. Not only do we group ourselves, but our cultural identity is, in turn, recognized by others. Such "consciousness of kind," or "sense of peoplehood" (Gordon 1964: 28), acknowledged by insiders and outsiders alike, has been conveniently considered a hallmark of ethnicity. The word "ethnic" (from the Greek *ethnos*, "nations") designates aggregates of individuals who share a sense of being alike, who regard themselves as a people with bonds of kinship, a shared history, and a relatively distinct pattern of doing things. The term "ethnic" points to a subjective reality—to how people think and feel about their affiliations. Feelings of identification are correlated, in turn, with objective indicators of ethnic difference such as language, race, religion, citizenship, costume, dietary, and artistic preferences. Correlations are not perfect, however. Not all who are of the same race or who share citizenship, language, or religion, regard themselves as "the same people." Language, particularly dialect, is probably the strongest external indicator of ethnic identity. Dialect strengthens identification when it is combined with distinctive dress, hairdressing, gestures, cosmetics, and ideas about how women and men should behave.

Ethnic criteria are a principal set of markers by which people affiliate and segregate. They are not the only criteria of identity, of course. Other differentiations cut across ethnic distinctions, such as those between sexes, generations, and groups bound by different interests in the arts, sports, and sexual preferences. Nevertheless, ethnic differences persist as important sources of affection and antagonism. Against the prophecy and the hope that Asians, Africans, Europeans, and aboriginal groups would "melt" into one kind of person in the new world, recent decades have witnessed a rising "fever of ethnicity," as Alpert (1972) terms it. Differences persist among groups that claim a distinctive identity. Differences in patterns of living are observable in family structure, residential clustering, income and occupation, consumption habits, communicative styles, and calendars (Chapman et al. 1981; Kochman 1981; Novak 1981; Sowell 1981a; Staples 1976; Thernstrom 1981; Zerubavel 1982).

However much one deplores differences within the species, human beings continue to claim the right to be different; in extremity, they kill one another in favor of their "self-determination."

The Issue

There is a lack of agreement over the value of studying the relationship between ethnicity and crime and the disagreement is greatest on the matter of race as one aspect of ethnicity. Heated debate exists over whether and how such studies should be conducted in the first place. A special controversy arises over whether official statistics on crime should include ethnic variables. The principal arguments on the two sides of the issue follow.

Against: No Study of Ethnicity

Four principal arguments are used against collecting and using information on ethnicity in the study of crime.

1. Ethnic categories, generally, and race specifically, are somewhat arbitrary and nonspecific to such an extent that measuring them involves so much error as to make any subsequent findings unreliable or just plain wrong (Gabor and Roberts 1990a: 295, 1990b: 336; Johnston 1994:171; Hatt 1994: 164; Doob 1991; Sweet 1991).
2. In each of its parts and as a whole, the system of the administration of justice discriminates among members of certain ethnic groups to such an extent that it is inevitable that official statistics will find certain ethnic groups overrepresented in criminal statistics (Gabor and Roberts 1990a: 299, 1990b: 336; Gale and Wurindersitz 1989: 1–2; Harding 1991: 364; Hatt 1994: 164).
3. Results of studies on the relationship of ethnicity and crime will be used *against* certain groups such as forming the basis for receiving closer attention from the police or being feared by the public and that the groups most adversely affected are the very ones that are already least favorably treated by the criminal justice system (Johnston 1994: 171; Fergusson et al. 1993: 193–194).
4. Since race is an ascribed characteristic, one with which we are born and is not changeable, it has no policy relevance and therefore should not be collected (Hatt 1994: 165; Johnston 1994: 170–171).

For: Study Ethnicity

The other side of the argument is a mirror image of the first one.

1. Ethnic differences including racial ones are distinctions that are real and made daily with a high level of accuracy. The test of their utility is not whether every person can be correctly categorized by every other person, but whether it is successfully done most of the time. When it comes to trying to identify suspects, even those against studying ethnicity proponents do not disagree that race is a useful identifier.

2. Whether the system of the administration of justice at any of its levels (police, prosecutors, courts) discriminates against members of any groups is an empirical question that can only be answered if data on ethnicity are available. Without the information to support or refute such claims all that we can have is argument without a basis for resolving the issue. Kruttschnitt and Gartner (1993: 326) make a point about the need for quantitative information about sex and crime that can be applied to race and crime: those who "want to redress social injustices . . . need to be able to document the existence of such injustices."

3. Perceptions—even stereotypical ones—about the relative involvement of different minority groups already exist in the minds of the public and the police (Gabor 1994: 158–159). Gabor (1994: 157) has argued that it is by publishing such information that one can rectify certain incorrect impressions that involve translating true overrepresentation into a notion that nearly all violent crimes belong to certain groups. The findings from studies of ethnicity and crime have the potential of finding some groups overrepresented in criminal statistics and also of finding other groups to be underrepresented. Such findings may be used to highlight those groups that have received too little attention. It can also lead to findings that are potentially helpful in reducing stereotypes, such as similarities in rates of recidivism between African Americans and whites (Votey 1991: 123) or when collecting ethnic information on both victims and aggressors reveal that whites are the prime aggressors relative to certain minorities (see, for example, Bowling 1993: 232) or where well-established patterns of violence occurring within groups appear not to apply (Jang et al. 1991: 14; Salts et al. 1995: 392). It is precisely because of their *willingness* and *ability* to study the relationship between race and delinquency that Huizinga and Elliott (1987: 219; see also Krisberg et al. 1987) can conclude that "there are no social differences in this measure of offending . . ." and that "it does not appear that differences in delinquent behavior can provide an explanation for the observed differences in incarceration rates." Of course, it is the same set of conditions that allowed Grogger (1992: 105) to find that much of the difference in white and African-American rates of youth unemployment are a result of differences in rates of arrest for the two groups and that "past arrests . . . affect current employment possibilities."

4. Information on other ascribed characteristics, age and sex, is routinely collected without apparent objections. On the policy question, Rushton (1994: 80) has addressed it through relevance to individuals: "It is, therefore, quite rational for members of the public to attempt to reduce their chance of being victimized by avoiding individuals with predator characteristics (age, sex, socioeconomic, and other variables such as race . . .)."

Parker et al. show that fear of crime is not restricted to women, older people, and whites but is very much alive among African Americans and Hispanics (1993: 729–730).

Conclusion

It is important to note that those who argue most strongly against the reliability and validity of crime statistics oppose most strongly the collection of information on ethnicity. Leaving aside the policy question of whether information on ethnicity should be routinely collected or only collected as part of special studies (Roberts 1994), it is our view that important scientific questions remain to be answered by the study of ethnicity and crime. These include evaluations of whether the administration of justice is evenhanded, or discriminatory and in what directions. In addition, as Hill and Crawford (1990) have shown, being able to examine differences between the rates of crime for African-American women and white women can be revealing about their differences in experiences. The same is true of natives and non-natives.

DISCOURSE ON RACE AND ETHNICITY

". . . public and scholarly discourse on the subject of ethnicity, race, and crime itself can be used to justify ethnocentricism, bigotry, and discriminatory policies and practices. Such discourse can also lead to the eradication of myth, pseudo-science, and stereotypes. . . ." (Hawkins 1995: 8)

Without arguing that the ends justify the means, it is nevertheless true that several valuable tests of theories of crime have been successfully conducted with data that include race as an important variable: opportunity theory (Messner and South 1992); differential association and control theory (Matsueda and Heimer 1987), and rational (economic) theory (Myers 1992), to name a few.

This reminder is offered in apology for looking at ethnic differences in criminal activity. All tribes are proud of their differences when they are deemed commendable and resentful of differences that suggest their misbehavior. Reporting ethnic differences in crime rates is uncomfortable, and, in fact, some countries, such as Canada and Germany, prohibit official publication of crime statistics with tabulations by ethnicity of offenders. The topic is a sensitive one in multicultural countries.

A Sample of Ethnic Differentials in Crime Rates

Difference can be found only when there is variation, of course. Research has been directed, therefore, toward countries that have culturally heterogeneous populations.

Israel

Israel, in its short history since 1948, not only has experienced a rise in crime and delinquency, but has also noted differences in rates among Jews from different lands and between Jews and other residents. About 89% of the Israeli population is Jewish, with the balance divided among three principal groups: Muslims, Christians, and Druses. Jews themselves recognize cultural differences between Israelis of Western, African, and Asian origin.

Shoham reports differential rates of arrest for serious offenses among Jews of African origin at 13 per 1,000 persons, compared with rates of 10 per 1,000 among Jews from Asia, and 5 per 1,000 among those from Europe and the Americas (Shoham 1966: 80–83). Amir and Hovav (1976) found such differentials continuing among juveniles a decade later.

Differences are even more apparent as one limits attention to violent crimes. Israeli Jews from Africa and Asia are convicted of homicide at a rate twice that of Jews from Western countries (Landau and Drapkin 1968: 11). In addition, the non-Jewish minority in Israel has rates of homicide conviction and victimization six times that of the Jewish population.

Europe

Given the large movement of workers from poorer to richer sections of Europe, attention has been paid to their possible differential contribution to crime. Thus Franchini and Introna (1961) find that migration of rural workers from southern Italy to the "industrial triangle" of northern Italy is accompanied by increases in their rates of juvenile delinquency and adult crime. In addition, Italians who migrate to Switzerland exhibit higher rates of violent offenses than the Swiss nationals, although many of these attacks are not reported to police (Ferracuti 1968; Gillioz 1967).

Differentials in violent crimes are particularly notable. Hungarians and Yugoslavs living in Sweden are differentially arrested for personal attacks (Klemming 1967; Sveri 1966), as are Italians in Germany (Nann 1967), and Belgium, (Liben 1963), Algerians in France (Hirsch 1953), and African and Mediterranean migrants in Germany (Wenzky 1965).

Some of these investigations have not controlled for age and sex differentials between host and guest populations. Nevertheless, differentials persist when such controls are applied. Zimmerman compared the conviction rates of males aged 18–50 years, from four migratory ethnic groups in the Federal Republic of Germany with rates for German men of the same age during 1965 (Zimmerman 1966). He omitted from his tabulation tourists, members of foreign armed forces (principally Americans), and internationally mobile professional criminals.

Overall, Zimmerman confirms other research reporting ethnic differentials in rates of physical attack, such as Turkish men committing a disproportionate number of violent crimes, including murder and attempted murder, minor and serious wounding, robbery, forcible rape, and sexual abuse of children. Italian men in Germany are also disproportionately violent, except for their lesser contribution to robbery. Greek men, too, are overrepresented in convictions for violent crimes, excepting robbery and murder. By contrast, Spanish migrants in Germany are relatively immune to crime and to violent crime in particular.

It is notable that native Germans are more frequently found guilty of styles of stealing—the more common crimes—and less frequently found guilty of the violent crimes. The differential in fraud between guests and hosts undoubtedly depends on occupational opportunities.

No explanation has been advanced for the lesser criminality of Spanish migrants, but the greater violence of other foreigners has received two interpretations: (1) that it represents loss of social control as men move from their homelands to strange lands where their ties with significant others, particularly women, are loosened; and (2) that it represents cultural continuity, men exhibiting in new lands behaviors that are habitual.

Both processes may be at work. We note, for example, that Finns who at home are more violent than other Scandinavians, exhibit their difference when they move to Sweden. Much of their violence, like that of other people, is stimulated by heavy drinking (Kaironen 1966).

New Zealand

New Zealand is one of many countries in which people of diverse ethnicity live under one set of laws and in which cultural groups differentially break those laws. However, a persistent question is whether differences in propensity to crime and delinquency represent cultural differences or differences in the economic status of ethnic groups.

Fergusson et al. (1975) sought an answer to this question by taking a random sample of all boys born in New Zealand in 1957 and observing the frequency of their appearances in children's court to the end of their sixteenth year. The sample of 5,472 boys was grouped into six socioeconomic classes by occupations of their fathers and into 11 ethnic categories later grouped as "European" and "non-European." The "non-European" class refers principally to Maori (11.5%), part Maori (3.5%), other Pacific Islanders (1.0%), and small numbers of Asians—a total comprising 17.6% of the sample.

Application of a technique for standardizing risks of delinquency among socioeconomic (SES) and ethnic categories revealed that "even after the SES distribution has been adjusted, the risk of offending for non-European boys is still over twice that for European boys " (Fergusson et al. 1975:13).

In sum, both ethnicity and SES affect the risk of a youth's offending, but "ethnic effects" do not reduce to economic effects. "There are substantial differences in the offending rates which cannot be attributed to SES or conditions related to SES" (Fergusson et al. 1975:19).

In a subsequent study, Fergusson et al. (1993) used data from two different sources to examine whether young people of Maori/Pacific Island descent had higher rates of offending behavior than European children. The two sources of data were reports of children and their parents (self/parentally reported rates) on the one hand and officially kept statistics on the other. They found that based on self/parental reports that children of Maori/Pacific Island descent had rates of offending that were 1–2 times those of children of European descent. When official statistics were used, they were 2–9 times more likely to come to police attention.

Interestingly, both techniques of measurement produced a result in the same direction, but the authors chose to interpret the results as suggesting that the official police "statistics contain a bias which exaggerates the differences in the rate of offending of children . . ." from the two categories of descent (Fergusson et al. 1993: 193); rather than attributing some or all of the difference to underreporting by parents or adolescents.

North America

Canada and the United States have a long record of ethnic differentials among the nations that have met in the new world. The native peoples of Canada, for example, are convicted of indictable offenses (felonies) at rates disproportionate to their representation in the population. Throughout Canada, but in western Canada in particular, Indian, Inuit, and métis adults are in jails and prisons far more than their proportions in the general population.

Persons of aboriginal ancestry comprise about 3% of Canada's population (Statistics Canada 1993). Even if one counts persons of multiple origin the aboriginals comprise less than 4% (3.7%) of the population (Synnott 1996: 195). Yet, aboriginal people make up 8–10% of the population in federal correctional facilities and much more in provincial and territorial institutions, particularly in northwest Ontario and the western provinces (LaPrairie 1990: 429).

Moreover, "native" women are more highly represented in the female prison population than "native" men are in the male convict population. Compared with other offenders, Canada's "original peoples" are more likely to have a record, and one of crimes against persons. They have higher rates of recidivism than other convicts and they serve shorter sentences (Schmeiser et al. 1974: 81; La Prairie 1992; Moyer 1992).

Blacks and Ukrainians in Canada also contribute disproportionately to capital murder convictions. Blacks are 0.2% of the population and 2.4% of capital murder convictions, while Ukrainians represent 2.6% of the population and 5.8% of capital murder convictions (Chandler et al. 1976; Pearson 1978).

Many the offenses for which native people are convicted are alcohol-related. No one knows why some ethnic groups have difficulty with alcohol, although evidence of genetic differences in the metabolism of ethanol accumulates (Fenna et al. 1971; Gilbert 1976; Rosenfeld 1981). This might explain differential response to alcohol once it is ingested, but it does not explain the initial differential preference for alcohol. Indeed, the "flushing" response to the metabolism process in Mongoloid populations includes mild nausea and is more likely to be a deterrent to consumption rather than promoting it. Alcoholism is not a unitary disorder, of course, and dispute about its etiology continues (Frankel and Whitehead 1981). Nevertheless, alcohol is clearly implicated in the high rates of a wide array of social problems including violent crime among First Nations peoples (Whitehead and Hayes 1998).

The United States also records wide differences in the amount and style of crime committed by its numerous ethnic residents. At the extremes, it is immediately notable that the Asian and Jewish populations have low rates of arrest and conviction for the serious predatory crimes, while African Americans and Latinos have high rates. American Indians have rates of homicide that are double those of whites (Bachman 1991: 456–457). This type of differential persists even where Asians are a plurality of the population, as in Hawaii. Voss (1963) reports that Hawaiians, who make up about one-fourth of Honolulu's population, account for 40% of the delinquency among males and half the arrests of females.

Box 9.1 PATTERNS IN OFFICIAL STATISTICS FOR INDIGENOUS PEOPLE

Summary of the findings of research on patterns of criminal behavior for indigenous people recorded in official statistics (Smandych et al. 1993: 7).

- Indigenous peoples tend to commit less serious crimes and are generally imprisoned for offenses against good order, including motor vehicle offenses, petty theft, resisting arrest, and drunk and disorderly charges.

- In Canada aboriginal peoples compose respectively 7% and up to 70% of federal and provincial corrections institutions, and in Australia the nationwide proportion is around 17%.

- Aboriginal peoples are arrested at a greater rate than others in the population—up to 29 times as great—and overall there is less likelihood that noncustodial dispositions will be invoked.

- There is a considerably higher rate of recidivism among aboriginal groups, which is estimated at up to 80% in some regions.

- Indigenous women are overrepresented in police and prison statistics and can constitute up to 70% of admissions in some states and provinces, and this disproportion appears to be increasing.

- The age of incarceration of aboriginal youths appears to be declining, and they are also overrepresented in the juvenile justice system.

- In comparison to their nonindigenous counterparts, indigenous offenders are first identified by the criminal justice system at an earlier age, and in many jurisdictions indigenous youths evidence rates of arrest between 3 and 90 times those of their nonindigenous counterparts.

- Alcohol use is present in a high percentage of crimes committed by indigenous peoples, up to 90% in some jurisdictions.

- A high proportion of aboriginal violent crimes are usually directed against family or community members.

- There has been a trend toward more serious violence, especially rape and domestic assault, within communities and groups in recent years.

Japanese and Chinese, who make up about 40% of the population, account for less than one-fifth of male delinquency and about 6% of violations by females.

Other deviations from a criminal norm are apparent among Dutch, German, and Scandinavian migrants to America and their children, who have experienced low degrees of contact with the police. The lawful behavior of these people is equaled or bettered by that of ethnic religious enclaves such as the Mennonites and Amish.

Facts such as these raise doubts that differences in criminality can be explained as due only to racial prejudice and economic disadvantage. On the contrary, low crime rates are found among some minorities that are physically visible and that have suffered discrimination and persecution. For example, Jews have one of the longest histories of any people as objects of hatred and oppression. They have, however, notably low rates of crime in both the new world and the old world as suggested by records of the past 100 years. Von Mayr (1917) reports conviction rates of Jews in Germany from 1881 to 1901 and finds their rates lower than the general population for all crimes except those of "insult" and "fraud." Segall (1924) confirms von Mayr for the period 1909–1916 in Germany. Herz (1908) provides a similar picture of Jewish immunity to crime in Austria, 1885–1900; as does Thon (1907) for Hungary, 1904–1909; Hersch (1938) for Jews in Poland, 1924–1925; and Bonger (1913) for the Netherlands, 1901–1919. Both self-report and official statistics show similarly low crime rates for Jews in more recent times in Great Britain, Canada, and the United States (Koenig 1942). Criminal conviction of Jewish women in these countries is rare.

Given the anti-Semitism common in Europe throughout the nineteenth and much of the twentieth centuries and prevalent in various forms in North America, it becomes difficult to explain criminal conduct as principally a product of prejudice and reduced opportunity.

A similar challenge to popular theorizing lies in the low crime rates of Chinese and Japanese in the new world, where both visible minorities have been objects of violent treatment. Chinese have been victims of lynchings and riots in western American cities, while Japanese are the only Canadian-American ethnic group to have been selected for exclusion and containment in military camps, euphemistically called "relocation centers."

It bears repeating that these immunities to crime are not reported to make invidious comparisons, but as part of the effort to "locate" differential criminality in pursuit of its explanation. It must also be remembered that, besides the hardships of discriminatory treatment, Asians and Jews have suffered economic disadvantages. Like most migrants to America, their original settlers were often poor people seeking a better way of life, rather than rich wanderers seeking more wealth.

The experience of African American people in the new world has been sadly different from that of groups who migrated voluntarily, and it may be expected that their struggle from slavery toward autonomy may have consequences different from those of voluntary migration.

African Americans have much higher rates of arrest and conviction for Part I crimes, with notably higher arrests for murder and nonnegligent manslaughter, forcible rape, and robbery. Although African Americans represent 12% of the American population, they make up about one-third of all persons arrested for "index crimes" (Maguire and Pastore 1995, table 4.11). Discrepancies of this size have persisted for some years. They appear in the United States census of 1910 and in more recent tabulations (Wolfgang 1966: 46; Maguire and Pastore 1995, table 4.11).

At any one time, more than 40% of all prisoners in the United States are African American (Maguire and Pastore 1995, tables 6.14, 6.30, and 6.36). Compared with other offenders, smaller proportions of African-American criminals are first offenders. In other words, African Americans have higher rates of recidivism than whites. They are charged with, and convicted of, more serious crimes; and the population of African-American offenders is, crime for crime, younger than the population of white offenders (Johnson 1970).

Over two decades, African Americans have accounted for about 60% of all arrests for murder (FBI 1981, table 35; Graham 1970). Wolfgang's study of criminal homicide in Philadelphia reports that nonwhite men aged 20–24 had a conviction rate more than 25 times that of white men of the same age (Wolfgang 1958). Ethnic differences in homicide are of such magnitude that murder rates among African-American women are two to four times as great as those among white men (Wolfgang and Ferracuti 1967: 154). In Chicago between 1965 and 1973, Richard Block found that African-American men aged 15–24 were 20 times as likely to be murdered as white men of similar ages.

During 1993, African Americans accounted for 62% of arrests for robbery and 41% of arrests for forcible rape. They are disproportionately represented in all Part I crimes, with a low representation of 24% for arson (Maguire and Pastore 1995, table 4.11). They are also disproportionately represented in arrests for all 21 of the Part II crimes, except "driving under the influence" (11%) and liquor law violations (13%). Such differentials are so great that some criminologists have suggested that the caste-like position of the African American in American society calls for "constructing a theory of Negro delinquency and criminality which would be quite different from a possible model of criminal behavior among whites" (Savitz 1967: 61).

Some scholars continue to claim that " black and white crime rates become very similar when people of the same age and socioeconomic condition are compared" (Sowell 1981a: 8). This is not so. Reported differences in rates of crime do not disappear when comparisons are made holding constant the sex, age, and socioeconomic distributions of African-American and white groups (Blue 1948; Forslund 1970; Moses 1970; Silberman 1978; Stephenson and Scarpitti 1968; Wolfgang et al. 1972: 300–308).

Differences of such size cannot be attributed solely to prejudice in law enforcement (Black and Reiss 1967, 1970; Green 1970; Kephart 1957; Terry 1967). As we have seen, studies of victimization yield the same orders of difference as official statistics. For example, Hindelang assesses parallels between official tallies (UCR data) and information from the National Crime Survey (NCS) for "the common law personal crimes of forcible rape, robbery, and assault" and finds that "both data sources show that this disproportionality [between African Americans and others] is greatest for robbery, followed by rape, aggravated assault, and simple assault" (1978: 103).

Finding differences in rates of arrest or rates of conviction or rates of incarceration between ethnic groups does not necessarily mean that either they have different rates of crimes or that there is discrimination operating to affect the group with the higher rate adversely. Studies of ethnicity and crime need to take into account (control for) at least three variables: the quantity of crime, the severity of crime, and previous record of crime. It is to be expected that persons or categories (ethnic categories) of persons who commit increasingly more serious crime and who have been apprehended for it will have a greater likelihood of apprehension, conviction, and severe sentencing than persons who have committed fewer offenses that are less serious and who have not previously come to the attention of the authorities.

As we saw in the review of official statistics on crime in Chapter 4, there is some discretion as to how some items are categorized and processed. However, as we also saw, the more serious the matter, the less discretion there is; the more likely matters are to be handled "by the book."

Being intoxicated in a public place may lead to formal processing in some cities but not in some towns. Being apprehended with a knife in one's hand and a bleeding victim nearby gets one formally processed in both.

When it comes to sentencing much has been done to supply decision rules and reduce the variation from judge to judge that is independent of case to case differences. Some crimes have sentencing minimums as well maximums. Some jurisdictions have sentencing guidelines and many others make information readily available to judges via personal computers—the range of sentences and average sentences that prevail in a given area for certain types of crimes with an array of aggravating features. All these measures are designed to make sentencing more rational and to remove (more or less) the predilections of individual judges. What discretion is left, therefore, is supposed to manifest itself within narrow boundaries. This is designed to achieve equity in sentencing and remove (reduce) the impact of extralegal factors and allow differences in sentences to reflect the legal factors of quantity and seriousness of crime.

Walsh (1991) examined the impact of race in an Ohio jurisdiction during the period 1978–1985. The data are based on 712 convicted male offenders in 20 different crimes from murder to receiving stolen property. For each case a composite index of the severity of the sentence was calculated. Measures of the seriousness of the crime and of the prior criminal record were also obtained. Walsh's (1991: 14) results showed that, contrary to the presumed effect on sentencing, "white offenders were punished more severely than black offenders. . . ." The sentences imposed were very close to what the sentencing guidelines suggested and nine of the ten judges in this jurisdiction are white so Walsh (1991: 15) concluded that the social differences in sentencing "seem to be more a function of leniency extended to black defendants."

It can be argued that such results document a form of discrimination against African-American communities in that they are not being provided the same protection from criminals as white communities, but the results do not support the notion that the sentences of African Americans are more severe because of race.

GENDER AND RACE DISCRIMINATION

"Our findings indicate that gender and race differences exist in juvenile justice handling of serious crime involved youths, even when controlling for criminal behavior level, seriousness of offense type, and juvenile record. [T]he most obvious gender and race differences . . . [are] a function of differential offense visibility . . . this dynamic does not appear to indicate direct gender or race bias in the justice system. . . ." (Horowitz and Pottieger 1991: 96)

Note: On Interpreting Ethnic Differentials

A schizoid tension exists in democracies between denying ethnic differences—since admitting them opens the door to "prejudice"—and defending ethnic differences as valuable. It would be curious if cultural difference, maintained as distinctive and valuable, had no relevance to behavior.

Prudence is required, however, in interpreting differentials in crime rates between ethnic groups. Considering the history of ethnic relations, it is difficult today to compare the relative importance of the alleged causes of any differences in observed behaviors of large groups. Subjective factors, of an unmeasurable sort, may intrude where objective measures reveal no differences in condition or treatment. Legally enforced segregation is only now ending, and the marks of oppression trivialize the scientist's attempts to hold socioeconomic status or schooling constant while examining crime and delinquency differentials between races. The possible operation of such subjective factors can be acknowledged, although it cannot be assessed.

None of this denies, however, that ethnic differences are real differences. They have a bearing upon crime rates, and the explanation of this impact is a task for theories of criminogenesis.

Summary

Ethnic differentials research on the differential criminality of ethnic groups can be summarized by saying that

1. Ethnic groups do exhibit different patterns of criminal behavior within the states in which they reside. These patterns differ both in the kinds of crime committed and in the relative amounts of specific crimes.
2. Ethnic differentials in criminality cannot be explained away as due only to the length of residence of a minority in a country, its age and sex distribution, or its socioeconomic position, or to prejudice in the judicial system.
3. Migrants often exhibit in their adopted lands the kinds of crime familiar to their homelands.
4. Ethnic styles of life represent preferences that have a surprising durability—surprising, that is, if one assumes that behavior is nothing but response to an environment. Contrary to an economic determinism which assumes that all people respond the same way to similar conditions, to be "ethnic" is to exhibit a difference in taste and talent that affects how the acculturated organism reacts to its environment.

Culture Contact and Crime

Cultural Continuity

Cultural persistence and change are mysteries. This is to say that no law of cultural development exists that allows one to predict which cultures will break and which will endure, and how and when.

Social psychology provides one explanation of resistance to change when it recognizes the intimate connection between culture and personality. Such recognition acknowledges the value of cultural immersion for personal health. Conversely, it notes the hazards to personal identity produced by cultural fragmentation. This thesis has been well put by an anonymous scholar in explaining the durability of Jewish culture in a people dispersed for centuries. This writer concludes that "almost every planned change has brought about results different from those anticipated. The student of culture is therefore highly skeptical of too optimistic plans for controlled culture change" (Anonymous 1942: 260).

Those who would correct the conduct of ethnic groups are repeatedly frustrated by the durability of habits. Communists, for example, deny the causal role of ethnic teaching and assume the greater power of economic conditions. Thus, the former communist regime in Hungary was embarrassed by the persistence of poverty, criminality, and self-segregation among gypsies. The government therefore instituted programs of "affirmative action" and "reverse discrimination" that were ineffective in changing gypsy life, but that increased Hungarian hostility toward gypsies (Spivak 1979a). Ossowska details similar failures to "reeducate" Polish gypsies and to move them into legitimate jobs and government housing. "At one meeting," Ossowska reports, "a gypsy woman declared that life is too short to work, a statement that was very much applauded by the whole Tzigany audience " (Ossowska 1971: 40).

It will be argued later (Chapter 17) that sociologists use the notion of "culture" in convenient, but contradictory, ways to claim that, since cultural habits have been learned and are therefore not "innate," they can be changed, and yet also they claim that cultural practices resist guided change. Our conclusion, again, should be that there are no laws of social change or social engineering that permit secure prediction.

The impact of time upon a culture includes the possibility that a way of life may disintegrate and also the happier possibility that a new culture may grow out of the mixture of old ones. The metaphor of the "melting pot" is just that—a figure of speech. It more often expresses hope rather than fact (Glazer and Moynihan 1963; Novak 1972).

Meanwhile, while old cultures are dying and new ones evolving, there is little surprise in finding that the process of "assimilation" may mean the substitution of new styles of crime for old. After a generation or two in the United States, for example, southern Europeans gradually abandon their traditionally prescribed code of vendetta for the more American property offenses.

It is also not surprising to find that, as an ethnic enclave breaks down, its crime rates, particularly rates of its juvenile offenses, may go up. So-called ghettos, areas of ethnic concentration, may be sites of remarkably low, and also high, crime rates. The popular notion of a ghetto as necessarily a slum and necessarily crime-ridden is false.

Ghettos and Slums

The popular use, and abuse, of the word *ghetto* should not seduce students of sociology into confusing a ghetto with a slum. Originally a ghetto was an area inside or outside the walls of early medieval European cities, where Jews lived. The first ghettos were voluntary congregations of Jews and only later became areas of legally enforced isolation (Wirth 1929). Such ghettos first appeared in Spain and Portugal toward the end of the fourteenth century and were, justified as a protection of the "true faith." These compulsory ghettos were usually closed off by gates, and their residents were subject to curfew restrictions. Within the ghettos, autonomous institutions operated, such as schools, churches, welfare associations, and courts.

Today, the term "ghetto" has been expanded from its original meaning to refer to any area of ethnic concentration. In the cities of Western countries, ghettos are now less independent of the greater societies in which they are situated (see Figure 9.1). They are, at the same time, more voluntary. Except for laws concerning the status of reserve Indians in Canada and the United States, the legally enforced segregation of cultural groups is now nonexistent in western Europe, Canada, and the United States. It is debatable, of course, to what extent the laws of such states are used to protect or to break down modern ghettos.

By contrast with a ghetto, a *slum* need not be a zone of ethnic concentration. The defining characteristics of a slum are vice, dirt, density, and poverty. Fairchild's *Dictionary of Sociology* calls it "an area of physical and social decadence" (1944), while the *Oxford English Dictionary* speaks of "a crowded district . . . inhabited by people of a low class or by the very poor . . . where the houses and the conditions of life are of a squalid and wretched character."

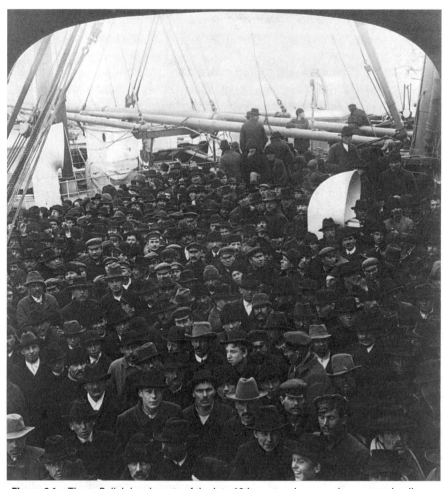

Figure 9.1   These Polish immigrants of the late 19th century became the newest dwellers in existing ghettos. Photo courtesy of Corbis.

"Squalid," in turn, means "foul through neglect or want of cleanliness; repulsively mean and filthy."

It follows that slums and ghettos are two different things—despite journalistic confusion of the terms. Some ghettos may be slums, but many are not. Conversely, some slums may be ghettos; others are not. It is conceivable that, with time, all slums become ghettos, while not all ghettos become slums. What is of interest to sociologists, and to other students who would understand freedom of choice, is the extent to which, in any particular cultural setting and epoch, ghettos or slums are voluntary. This is meat for debate. In this debate, clarity requires that slums and ghettos be regarded as distinct.

Ghettos and Crime

Holding this distinction, it is possible to ask whether ghettos are more or less criminogenic than "melting pots." Are ghettos the distinctive locations of high crime rates? Do rates of offenses in ghettos change with a weakening of their boundaries?

North American studies are particularly rich in reporting the effects of the meeting of cultures upon rates of crime. These investigations suggest that migrants, and more specifically their children, are relatively immune to the crime about them if a ghetto is intact.

This phenomenon has been well documented, for example, among Asian residents in the United States and their children (Crook 1934; Kitano 1967; Lind 1930a, 1930b; McGill 1938; Petersen 1967). A similar pattern of ethnic protection is reported by Beynon (1935) for Hungarian immigrants to America and by Vislick-Young (1930) for Russian immigrants.

The low crime and delinquency rates among descendants of Chinese and Japanese immigrants to North America have already been noted. These rates usually remain low, however, if ethnic identity is maintained, but to rise with assimilation into the host culture. For example, Kitano found some interesting signs of this when he compared Japanese-American delinquents and their parents with Japanese-American nondelinquents (1967). The delinquents and their families were much less "Japanese" than the nondelinquents. Moreover, the delinquent children exhibited their greater identification with the American culture in their speech, dress, hair styles, and patterns of friendship. Similar observations have been made of the Chinese ghettos that have defended their children against delinquency in the United States. Sollenberger lived among the residents of the New York City enclave and observed family life and behavior of children in this densely populated ghetto. In this area of near-zero delinquency, Sollenberger (1968: 17) found children to be remarkably well behaved—to be able, for example, to go on an all-day outing with "no crying, no scolding, no scuffling, or quarreling of any kind." He considered that the sources of this were to be found in family solidarity. There were no divorced or separated parents in this community. Mothers held their husbands in high regard, and authority was shared. The Chinese children spent much time in the company of their parents. Sollenberger reports that, as compared with a sample of Caucasian mothers, the Chinese women were stricter in their control of children's aggression, but more permissive regarding weaning, toilet training, and bedtime routines.

This kind of community is, of course, subject to disruption. Chinese ghettos have reportedly felt the winds of change and that, under the impact of new immigrants—mostly young, unskilled men from south China—the delinquent warfare reminiscent of other enclaves has been reenacted in some Chinatowns where youths have organized themselves as "Red Guard" and "Wah Ching" gangs (Harvey 1970; Peterson 1972).

As noted earlier, the experience of African Americans has been made different by the fact of their involuntary migration to, and enslavement in, the new world. The lively question, however, is whether, today, their "ghettoization" proceeds differently from that of any other ethnic group and whether, therefore, the consequences may differ.

No definitive answer is available to this question, but opinion about it has changed. During the 1940s and 1950s, the popular liberal attitude toward this subject was assimilationist. Its ideal was, again, the "melting pot." The ideal often minimized or denied cultural differences between African Americans and whites and to reduce such alleged differences to class distinctions. The contrary suggestion, that behavior of African Americans and whites might differ culturally and not merely as a function of socioeconomic status, was resisted. An illustration of this resistance was the professional response to an anthropologist's study in 1941 showing that it was "a myth of the Negro's past" to believe that no cultural elements had been borne by the slaves from west Africa to the Americas (Herskovits 1941). Reviews of this book in professional journals have been characterized as "a furor."

Times Change

With demands by African Americans for identity, it now becomes more comfortable for white students to agree that African Americans, like other migrants, brought a culture with them and that a distinctive black culture has evolved (Jones 1972; Metzger 1971). To the extent to which African-American culture is observable, it should be expected that ghetto experience would have the same relationship to crime and delinquency among African Americans that it has had among other minorities. The evidence is not at all clear, however. A few attempts have been made to study the effects of ethnic congregation upon crime rates among African Americans by examining variations in known violations as the races live apart or together. Findings vary with the time and place of investigation. William Julius Wilson (1978) has shown that race is becoming less important with respect to many phenomena, including crime, and that it is socioeconomic status that is the more relevant variable.

An early study conducted by the research bureau of the Houston Council of Social Agencies found that for zones in Houston "the higher the proportion of Negro population, the lower is the rate of Negro delinquency; . . . conversely, the higher the proportion of white population, the higher is the rate of Negro delinquency" (Hooker 1945: 23).

A later study in Baltimore reported similar results Lander (1954). Willie and Gershenovitz (1964) tested for this distribution of delinquency among mixed and separated tracts in Washington, DC. They also found that ethnic concentration reduced youthful violations, with one qualification:

1. In higher socioeconomic areas, no differences in juvenile delinquency rates appear between neighborhoods of homogeneous and heterogeneous racial composition.
2. In lower socioeconomic areas, juvenile delinquency rates are often higher in racially heterogeneous than in racially homogeneous neighborhoods (1964: 743).

The National Crime Victimization Survey of victims reports a different relationship between neighborhood ethnic composition and crime. Sampson et al. (1981) evaluate data from 1973 to 1978 and find that whites are more likely to be victimized as the proportion of African Americans in their neighborhoods increases. This relationship holds more strongly for property crimes than for personal attacks. By contrast, African Americans are more likely to be victimized in predominantly white as well as predominantly black neighborhoods. African Americans experience the least reported victimization in neighborhoods of intermediate composition.

Conflict among these findings has been attributed to differences in police activity, to regional differences in the willingness of victims to call the police, and to inadequate description of the quality of neighborhoods. Consequently, the question remains open whether residential segregation of the races is more or less criminogenic than residential mixing.

An interesting interpretation of the varied findings on this issue holds that the peculiarities of African-American history do not allow an easy equation of residential segregation with ghetto life, in the classic sense, any more than residential mixing signifies ethnic integration. For example, Molotch (1969) concludes from a study of a changing community that *biracial propinquity*—the physical closeness of the races residentially—does not mean "racial integration." In short, when peoples meet, they do not necessarily become one. It is incorrect to equate ethnic congregation—coerced or voluntary, casual or durable—with ethnic integration.

Contrary to the assumption that equates these two processes, ethnic identity is frequently stimulated by ethnic contact, so that claims of difference and pleas for a separate life become stronger after one has tested assimilation than they were before such an experience. Borhek (1970) found this to be true of ethnic groups in Canada, and a similar pattern of ethnic cohesion is being displayed by African-Americans in the United States (Harris 1972). Research on attitudes of African-American students, for instance, finds that African-American students in white colleges are more militant and more separatist than African-American students in African-American colleges (Kilson 1971).

When peoples meet, they may assimilate, or separate, or accommodate by maintaining "social distance" while living within close physical proximity. The last pattern has been visible in old southern cities where residential blocks were "marble-caked," with African-American and white houses alternating on the alleys and avenues, respectively.

There are contexts in which diverse peoples meet, and these contexts make a difference in the meaning of the meeting Patterson (1975). In these various settings, "group boundaries can become wider or narrower" (Horowitz 1975: 115). We need not spell out these contexts; our purposes here require only the recognition that residential and educational mixing may not suggest integration. Conversely, the simple fact of segregation may not be a strong sign of "ghettoization." Some "ghetto effects" may become stronger as ethnic groups meet one another. Research on this issue awaits development of better measures of ethnic identification and cultural difference than mere patterns of propinquity.

Slums and Crime
Ghettos and Crime Represent One Issue; Slums and Crime, Another

We have seen that ghettos may immunize residents against crime and delinquency. By contrast, slums have a relationship with crime that seems built-in by definition. Zones of squalor tend also to be zones of common larceny, rape, robbery, assault, and homicide. Observing this association, some students have inferred a causal connection, and a connection with the causal arrow pointing in only one direction: not that crime produces slums, but that slums produce crime.

We have already commented on the appealing fallacy of deducing causation from correlation without tests for direction of influence or power of the nominated causes (see Chapter 3). Caution against this error applies here as well, but it is a caution that is difficult to heed because of compassion. Sympathy encourages the assumption that slums are imposed upon people rather than made by them. Drawing policy from such sympathy is easy and to predict that government provision of "decent housing" will reduce the vice and crime associated with slums. This is a questionable assumption. The economist Thomas Sowell puts the point well (1981b: 1,011):

> That criminality and slums have gone together down through history is demonstrable, but the direction of causation is by no means clear. The same attitudes that create crime may also create slums. It is not a question of which theory sounds more plausible a priori, but (1) what different consequences follow from the two different theories, and (2) which set of consequences is found in factual data. To make such an empirical test possible, "slums" must be defined as neighborhoods with structures of given physical characteristics, independently of the amount of crime taking place there.

> As the proportion of physically substandard housing units declined in the 1960s, crime rates soared. New York's Chinatown once had one of the lowest crime rates in the city, despite having older and more run-down buildings than Harlem. The later crime increase in New York's Chinatown—and Chinatowns in other cities— was not associated with housing deterioration but with the arrival of new Chinese immigrants from a different culture in Hong Kong.

> The central role of people and their values—rather than physical surroundings— raises the question of whether much of the physical deterioration is not itself a result of the same set of values, or lack of values. Brand-new government housing projects around the country have become instant slums as former slum-dwellers moved in. All the characteristics of old-fashioned slums—filth, noise, violence, and physical destruction of property—have reappeared in government housing projects.

In summary, crime and slums are both human products, a statement that is obvious and yet one that requires utterance, since it is popular to assume that slums are somehow generated by impersonal, even nonhuman, forces. Noting that people make slums and the crime within them does not deny compassion to those who would escape their slums, but cannot. However, the observed correlation does raise the possibility that slums and their crimes may be simultaneously produced, rather than one causing the other. The association of slums and crime raises further questions whether some people may not prefer slum life and, if so, how such preference comes to be. Differential taste for vice and crime and, in slums, the associated preferences for noise over quiet, dirt over cleanliness, and public exposure over privacy are matters for theories of criminogenesis to explain.

Conclusions

Ethnicity, including race, has a place in the study of crime. Its place is social and not biological. As with the case of age and sex, in the previous chapter, it stands for a diverse bundle of experiences, conditions and ideas that impact on criminality. Ethnicity generally and now specifically has had strong correlates with socioeconomic status as one of their more important features.

Explanations of crime, therefore, can only start with the social location of serious crime and its links to these variables. The best explanations will be those that can make sense of these correlations as well as unpack the complicated social phenomena that are contained within the realities of age, sex, and ethnicity.

10. Urbanism and Wealth

Urbanism and Crime

The earliest systematic attempt to collect crime statistics is believed to be the compilation of the *Compte Générale* by the French government in 1825 (Morris 1957: 44). In 1833, the French statistician, Guerry, published a monograph that illustrated the relationship between crime and such factors as poverty, population density, and level of education by displaying their geographical concordance. Guerry's work and subsequent publications by the Belgian statistician Quetelet and the English researcher Rawson, demonstrated that crimes and other "social pathologies" were not distributed randomly, but were spatially coincidental. Areas of high rates of crime were also areas of high relative poverty and areas of high density (Morris 1957: 44–53).

Thus started a long tradition in criminology of conducting what has become known as *cartographic, social geography,* or *social area* studies. With refinements in the level of aggregation at which the statistics were collected, such area studies allowed researchers to focus on "crime zones." With the attempt by the human ecology movement in the 1920s to introduce the theoretical principles of biological ecology to the explanation of crime, this general type of research adopted the generic term of *ecological* studies.

These area or ecological studies have repeatedly focused on two primary correlates of crime: urbanism or population density, and variations in the distribution of wealth.

The city has long been considered a greater producer of crime than the countryside, and there is a popular explanation for this: that the crowding, impersonality, and anonymity of urban relations generate crime. As with many popular theories, this one contains some truth, but it also deserves some qualification. The truth resides in the fact that official statistics for Canada and the United States and for Europe report a tendency, with some inversions, for serious crimes to increase with size of the city (Clinard 1942, 1960; Harries 1976; Lottier 1938; Ogburn 1935; Wolf 1965; Wolfgang 1968). The FBI Uniform Crime Reports (UCR), for example, note that rates of violent crime are about three and a half times as high in large cities (Metropolitan Statistical Areas or MSAs) as in rural areas, and over twice as high in the non-MSA cities as in rural areas. Similar, although not quite as dramatic, ratios are reported for property crimes.

Bachman reports on American victimization data that show a similar pattern to police statistics. As Bachman points out, "central city residents had significantly higher rates of household victimizations; those in other metro areas were in the intermediate position. . . individuals residing in nonmetro areas experienced the lowest household victimization rates; indeed, such rates were an average of 70% lower than those for central cities and 30% lower than what occurred in other metro areas" (Bachman 1992: 551). Other studies consistently show that crimes of violence, such as homicide and assault, are a particularly urban phenomenon in the United States (Bursik 1984; Stark 1987).

The tendency for urban centers to have higher crime rates than rural areas should not be overstated, however. The crime rates of such cities as Tokyo, Singapore, Geneva, and London, England, are below those of many midsized American cities. Since the time of Rousseau, it has been all too easy to view the country as a pristine refuge from the evils of urban life.

A study by Land et al. (1991) addressed the question of what distinguishes those cities with the highest crime rates from those with the lowest. Using police data for all U.S. cities with more than 25,000 population for 1960, 1970, and 1980, these researchers examined rates of crimes known to the police for the seven index crimes (homicide, rape, robbery, assault, burglary, larceny-theft, and motor vehicle theft). Despite tremendous variations in overall crimes rates over these years, they noted that several factors related to the index offenses showed a "substantial level of invariance" over time. Among the factors most strongly related to rates of urban crime was population size.

Other factors related to rates of crime included several that are themselves confounded with urbanization. Thus, the percentage of the population divorced and the percentage of children not living with both parents were related to all offense categories. The Gini Index of income inequality and the percentage of parents living below the poverty line were both related to all crimes except for motor vehicle theft. Median family income was strongly (and, of course, negatively) related to homicide, assault and burglary, and to a lesser extent, rape.

The confounding impact of poverty, urbanization, and crime is not totally surprising. In a review essay, James Short (1991: 501) notes that "once largely a rural problem, poverty is now primarily urban in the United States. Cities long viewed as 'the promised land' by generations of European immigrants have become centers of poverty for many, particularly for racial and ethnic minorities. 'Natural' ecological processes that once promised assimilation, or at least accommodation, are increasingly influenced by human interventions that destroy functioning communities and/or isolate those who are left behind, mired in poverty or confronted with institutional decline and community degradation."

The fact that population size is not correlated with rates of crime alone leads to the question of determining the exact process by which population is related to crime. Two variables that have received a great deal of attention from social scientists throughout this century are crowding (or population density) and the *process* of urbanization.

Density and Crowding

Findings such as these strongly qualify the idea that the quantity of human aggregation is a major producer of crime. Borrowing from laboratory and field studies of animals that become "pathological" when densely packed, criminologists have tested for a similar possibility among humans. Results have been inconsistent and debate persists about the degree to which "people packing" generates a "behavioral sink" in which civility is lost and predation stimulated (Calhoun 1962a, 1962b). Debate is complicated by two major considerations and their "spinoffs." One issue concerns measurement of density; the other concerns the difference between density and crowding and causes of the difference.

What is density? To begin with, density is different from city size or crowding. Density refers to some indicator of animal concentration in space. Human density has been measured as the following:

- Number of people per acre or square mile
- Number of residential structures per acre
- Number of housing units per structure
- Number of rooms per housing unit
- Number of persons per room

Number of persons per room is sometimes called *crowding,* but this is not its psychological definition. An urbanologist's rule of thumb considers 1.01 to 1.49 persons per room "crowded" and 1.50 or more persons per room "extremely crowded" or "overcrowded." Still, this usage differs from the psychological conception of crowding. Psychologically, crowding refers to the experience of discomfort associated with the presence of others. Thus, as Baum and Paulus (1987: 534) note, "density is probably necessary but insufficient by itself to elicit the experience of crowding."

Two issues become apparent: different results can be expected from different measures of density, and density becomes crowding under varying contingencies.

On the first issue, different results can clearly be expected with different conceptions of physical density and by combining measures in different ways. For example, persons per room and rooms per structure are not uniform measures of available space. The second issue concerns the conditions under which density produces crowding.

When does density become crowding? The distinction between density and crowding is important because it is the experience of discomfort that is supposed to translate density into action. The connection, however, between any quantity of human aggregation or any degree of "people packing" and feelings of being crowded is loose. The loose connection is briefly summarized by noting that conversion of density into crowding varies with physical features of the spacing, with temperature and air circulation, with cultural preferences, and with such psychological traits as temperamentally "sensation seeking" or "sensation reducing" (Baum and Paulus 1987: 546).

In addition, much depends on whether one is congregated with strangers or intimates. For example, Mitchell's (1971) study of high-density housing in Hong Kong shows that "what hurts" is involuntary contact with people who are not members of one's family.

Effects vary, too, with the sexual composition of the aggregate—whether it consists only of women or men, or of some mixture (Freedman 1975: 148–151). Women often have a pacifying effect on men. This is a principal argument used by university officials for having coed residences rather than single-sex residences.

Furthermore, novelty or familiarity of the aggregation makes a difference to human response to density, as does the pleasantness or unpleasantness of the activity of the aggregate.

Mobility and insularity also affect the relation between density and crowding. Mobility refers to time spent in a residential area and to circulation in and out of that zone. Some people are more "trapped" than others, although their domiciles may be in equally dense areas. Insularity refers to ability to maintain privacy. For example, some areas that pack many people into a small space by stacking them vertically nevertheless allow a high degree of insulation from neighbors, including freedom from their noises. Conversely, some loosely packed residential areas permit more intrusion of neighbors upon one another through thin walls and adjacent patios.

To this dimension of insularity, Hawley (1972) adds a factor that he calls *social density,* by which he refers to "the number of interactions or messages exchanged per unit of time." Hawley's aspect of density reminds us that even people who live in the same domicile may "exchange messages" frequently or hardly at all, and such social density may affect the experience of being crowded.

After reviewing the literature on crowding, Baum and Paulus (1987: 560) conclude, "there is evidence that . . . crowding can have physical, psychological, and social consequences for humans and animals. However, the severity and range of these effects appear to depend on a wide variety of individual, environmental, and social factors." Among the factors identified by these authors as mediating the impact of density are the following: the level of social stimulation; the level of intimacy; the behavioral constraints placed on the actors; threats to personal control; one's personal characteristics and coping assets; and the social and physical characteristics of the setting.

Effects of Density

Saying that people need both privacy and human connection is trite. Nevertheless, what balances these needs and, when "out of balance," translates contact with others into crowding, is a psychological variable. This variable is a compound of taste for external stimulation and a sense of control, or its lack, over one's living space (Proshansky et al. 1970a, 1970b).

Given these many contingencies that affect how human congregation influences behavior, it is no surprise to find disagreement among investigators concerning effects of density. Their findings refer to zones in Chicago and apply with ethnicity and socioeconomic status held constant. For example, they record a correlation of +0.50 between density and delinquency with ethnicity and "social class" controlled. Schmitt reports comparable results from research in Honolulu: high density is associated with high crime rates even when income and educational levels are held constant (1957, 1966).

By contrast, Freedman et al. (1975) find no significant relation between two measures of density and delinquency in New York City when income and ethnicity are controlled.

We can conclude that density is a complex variable, the effects of which are contingent upon a multiplicity of conditions. In this vein, Roncek argues that the effects of dense concentrations of people vary with their "social integration," and that anonymity, rather than density as such, is the significant correlate of crime (Roncek 1975).

While density may or may not be a factor influencing levels of civility, it does produce situations that are more or less conducive to criminal activity. Dense urban areas result in greater opportunities for locating suitable targets than rural areas for a given amount of search effort. Dense urban areas also tend to be more heterogeneous than rural areas.

Some of this is reflected in a study by Rountree, Land, and Miethe (1994). The researchers sampled 5,090 residents of Seattle, Washington. They constructed a hierarchical model that allowed for examination of both structural (largely neighborhood) effects as well as individual effects. Although they drew several conclusions from their study, two exemplify the points being made here. First, they note that "a clear implication of our analyses is that the effects of individual-level crime opportunity risk factors may be overwhelmed by the powerful effects of the social-disorganization neighborhood-contextual variables in our models. Specifically, the presence of neighborhood incivilities, population density, and ethnic heterogeneity in a neighborhood dramatically affects the residents' risk of violent crime and burglary" (Rountree et al. 1994: 411).

Second, the issue of opportunity clearly comes to the forefront. Most crimes are a consequence of the convergence of a motivated offender, an available target and a minimal amount of guardianship (Brantingham and Brantingham 1981; Cohen and Felson 1979). Thus, "in the case of burglary . . . higher levels of target attractiveness (higher family income, more expensive goods present) increase burglary risk; more guardianship (home unoccupied less frequently) decreases this likelihood" (Rountree et al. 1994: 410).

The Process of Urbanization
Rural-Urban Migration

Studies such as these tell us about the correlates of crime within metropolitan areas. The connection between urbanization and crime is further illuminated by studies of the urbanizing process—the conditions under which people move from countrysides to cities.

We should expect that the effects of urbanization will vary with the rapidity of the process and with the ability of cities to absorb migrants economically and culturally. In this regard, urbanization in the twentieth century differs from that in the nineteenth century. It differs in its rapidity, in its volume, and in the economic assimilability of migrants.

The rich countries of North America were urbanized during the nineteenth century at a much slower rate than that which the poor countries of Africa, Asia, and Latin America have experienced in the latter half of this century. The movement of people from rural areas to cities in some of these third world states is novel and disturbing.

This movement is seen, of course, against a backdrop of increasing world population, at a rate that means a doubling of the number of people on this globe in 35 years. Moreover, in countries that are now poor, it is expected that the number of people will triple during the next century (Gwatkin and Brandel 1982). The proliferation of people in poor locations has been accompanied by the migration of landless peasants into cities, where most of them become squatters in shanty towns. Among all the so-called developing countries 30 years ago, there were only 16 cities with one million people or more. By 1990 there were 174 such cities, and by 2015 it is expected that there will be more than 400. In Latin America, there were only nine cities with more than one million people in 1960. It is estimated that there are close to 30 such congregations in the Americas now and about three-quarters of all people are living an urban life in this region (United Nations 1995: 3)

The level of urban growth is currently such that urbanologists now speak of *mega-cities*, urban agglomerations with populations in excess of eight million residents. In 1994, there were 22 megacities worldwide, with 16 being located in less developed regions of the world. The largest of these megacities is Tokyo, with a population of 26.5 million. It is expected that by 2015, the threshold to be included in the top 15 megacities will be a population of 14.7 million (United Nations 1995: 3).

In contrast to the rapid urbanization of the developing world, many parts of the developed world are experiencing *counter-urbanization* (United Nations 1995: 8). At its core, counter-urbanization is a process of decreasing size and decreasing density. Major cities such as Copenhagen, Marseilles, Düsseldorf, Milan, and Madrid have all recently experienced a decrease in population. The trend to counter-urbanization was first noticed in the United States in the 1970s and is now common throughout much of western Europe.

The urbanizing process is now marked by some signs of technological change and increasing affluence for some portion of the population, but it is also characterized by increasing demands on governments to provide a variety of services, ranging from the provision of food, shelter, and energy to the removal of garbage and the control of crime. Figure 10.1 (A and B) shows this marked contrast in Detroit.

Harman (1982: 37) provides a more detailed description of life in Africa's most populous country, Nigeria, where an estimated one-third of all Africans live:

> Gangs of 30 or more armed men have held up streams of traffic, systematically looting every vehicle. Entire neighborhoods have been savaged in a single night. . . . No one can count on being safe. A month ago, the chief justice of Nigeria was robbed. Two weeks ago, the wife of a permanent secretary was raped in an appalling mass assault by 40 armed men on all the women in a government residence. . . . At least 13 cars a day have been stolen in Lagos for a good many years now.

The people off the land have gone on producing babies as though they were still on it—more mouths to feed, scarcer and dearer food.

In contrast to many other developing countries, Nigeria is not poor. It is one of the world's great oil producers, but "oil money," Harman writes, "is paid not to people but to the government. Its immediate result is a growth of government jobs, and of offices for government servants." Given such growth of government, Harman (1982: 37) asks,

A

B

Figure 10.1 Two faces of Detroit, (A) Urban density, (B) Now-vacant lots awaiting renewal. Photos courtesy of Corbis.

How can so much money and such high hopes engender such chaos? Why won't the telephones, or the bureaucrats, work? Why can't you turn on a switch, or a tap, or turn up for a scheduled flight, with any confidence that light, or a wash, or a journey, will result? Why, at almost every level of public and private administration, do people expect bribes? Why is almost everyone so infernally aggressive, and why, when aggressive driving kills people, can't they at least clear the corpses off the streets? (1982: 37)

In the differing contexts of changing nations, and therefore in differing degree, both formal and informal observers report increasing criminal activity with movement of people from hinterlands to cities in Africa, Asia, the Caribbean islands, and Latin America (Jones 1981). For example, in Sao Paulo, Brazil, there were an estimated 6,710 murders in 1995, which is an average of about 18 per day. In 1996, there were 7,171 recorded murders during the first 10 months alone (*Folha de Sao Paulo* 1996). Many killings in Brazilian cities stem from competition in the illicit drug trade, numbers games, and extortion rackets.

Jeff Builta (1997) reports that in Rio de Janeiro, with a population of almost 12 million,

> kidnappings of wealthy businessmen have become an almost daily occurrence. The last full year for which statistics have been released is 1994. In that year, 110 kidnappings were reported in Rio state alone. And the actual number of unreported kidnappings is thought to be around three times that. . . . And Rio's problems seem to be mounting. Police say an average of 20 people a day are killed with firearms, although some officials say the actual murder rate is at least twice that. In many slums, teenagers, and often even children, can be seen toting rifles and handguns, mostly to protect drug-dealers.

The situation is not much different in Caracas.

> Venezuela also has many homeless youngsters in the vast Caracas slums, home to one-third of the city's residents. In fact, sociologists estimate that 25 percent of the entire Venezuelan population is today made up of homeless or semi-homeless youngsters, left to somehow make a living in the streets. The potentiality for crime is painfully obvious.

Developing countries provide extreme examples of the crime-producing effects of population movement from agricultural areas to commercial zones, but similar effects can be seen in industrialized countries that experience large-scale, rapid immigration. For example, such effects are reported for Los Angeles, where murder rates increased 50% between 1975 and 1979 in parallel with mass immigration (Leff 1980).

Criminogenic effects are also visible when once "sleepy hamlets" are invaded by migrants and "enjoy" a sudden increase in population. Thus when Grants, New Mexico, doubled its numbers it found that its crime rates doubled as well (Blundell 1980).

Residential Mobility

It is not only the uprooting of rural people and their transfer to cities that is associated with criminality, but also residential mobility within cities. For example, when African-American neighborhoods in the San Francisco Bay area are compared by their rates of ethnic change, both official records and self-reports suggest higher delinquency rates among the less stable neighborhoods (Kapsis 1976, 1978).

English research comparing the mobility of families also finds a relationship between residential change and a collection of "behavior disorders," including delinquency (Osborn 1980; Rutter 1976). American research agrees (Kantor 1965).

With aggregate data from 65 large American MSAs, Crutchfield et al. (1982) find that three measures of geographic mobility correlate significantly with both property and violent crime. Their measures of population movement include (1) "mover rate," a measure of local residential change; (2) "immigration rate," the proportion of people that had moved into the MSA during the study period; and (3) a "total mobility" measure that sums the first two indicators. These investigators do not interpret the association of mobility with crime to mean that migrants themselves are necessarily more criminal than more permanent residents. They believe that the movement of people is a sign of lack of "social integration" and that such "loosening" is criminogenic. It may be true that much movement signifies a state that may be called "lack of social integration"; but it is also true that studies of individual families locate seeds of crime and delinquency among the more transient people.

In a review of recent studies on family violence (particularly spouse abuse), Fagan and Brown conclude that for some elements of domestic assault, there is a strong relationship with urbanism and geographical mobility. Regarding murder, Fagan and Brown (1994: 176) note that "there is some evidence that marital homicide is an urban phenomenon, more often located in social areas that typify the problems of urban areas: poverty, residential mobility, weak family structures, and concentrations of minority populations." Regarding less lethal dimensions of violence, they note a continuity with other forms of violence. Thus,

> the convergence of risk factors that implicate social class and social status for assaultive males suggests that there are social structural correlates of wife assault similar to stranger assaults. What is unknown is whether the assault of female partners is concentrated in areas marked by social disorganization, poverty, and other ecological risk factors of stranger violence. The correlation among men of social class and social structural variables with participation in both wife assault and stranger violence suggests that for wife assaults, there are some risk factors that reflect social area effects and social disorganization. These include the salience of formal and informal social controls, and anonymity of urban areas with high residential mobility, limited economic mobility, and patterns of family disintegration. (Fagan and Brown 1994: 205)

High levels of mobility result in a lack of attachment—of people to places and people to other people. Therefore, it is not surprising that the primary conclusions reached by Land et al. (1991: 228) are that, "those cities with extremely high (low) crime rates tend to be the largest (smallest), most (least) socially disintegrated, and most (least) deprived. Moreover, the association with the latter two city characteristics has grown stronger over the past three census periods."

Note: On Urbanization

We can conclude from these many studies that what makes a significant difference in criminal conduct is not being urbanized—especially not for a long time—but getting that way. The *process* is criminogenic; the *condition* need not be.

Wealth and Crime

Criminologists have employed the ecological method to investigate the association of social position and criminal activity by comparing areas of a country or zones within a city. Such area studies have been widely conducted since the nineteenth century and have repeatedly found an association between low status and rates of crime and delinquency. As early as 1861, Mayhew reported a connection between "low neighborhoods" and the presence of many juvenile thieves.

Starting in the 1920s, Shaw and McKay (1942) constructed indexes of the economic status of residential zones in 20 American cities and correlated these measures with official rates of crime. The usual correlation of poverty and criminality was found, an association that held true for delinquency among males and females and for crime committed by young people and adults. Other accompaniments of poverty were associated with the higher crime rates—such as high rates of infant mortality, families dependent upon state aid, tuberculosis, and mental disorder.

Sarah Boggs (1965) started an interesting line of research that focused on the distinction between the kinds of crime committed where the offender lives and the kinds of crime that attract offenders from other areas. Businesses that are "crime targets" are those located in high-status neighborhoods close to neighborhoods in which high proportions of offenders live. The neighborhoods in which high proportions of offenders live, however, are characterized differently. These are areas of higher rates of homicide, assault, residential (as opposed to business) burglary, "highway robbery" (as opposed to business robbery), high proportions of African Americans, more urbanization, and lower social rank.

Simon (1980) reported a similar pattern among New Jersey suburbs where some of the highest rates of victimization were to be found in high status suburbs that bordered on central cities.

Stanley Turner's (1969) study of Philadelphia supports many of Boggs' findings for St. Louis. Turner, too, suggests that a particular type of crime area be distinguished—one in which few criminals reside, but in which most thefts occur. These target areas have a high *effective population*—"effective," that is, for thieves. Many transients move through these target zones which lie close to neighborhoods with high proportions of offenders (see Figure 10.2). When Turner describes the areas high in resident offenders, he also finds them characterized by low income and low occupational status, high density, high proportions of blacks, and high proportions of unrelated persons living in the household and contributing to its income.

Distributions from Victimization Studies

Some findings from area studies are modified when victimization rates are used rather than official statistics. For example, Sampson et al. (1981) analyze results from the American National Crime Survey (NCS) for 1973 to 1978 aggregated by *neighborhood*. The Census Bureau defines "neighborhoods" as "usually contiguous, computer aggregate enumeration districts (EDs) or block groups with a population minimum of 4,000" (Shenk and McInerney 1978: 22). These investigators limit inquiry to "personal crimes," defined as rape, robbery, assault, and personal larceny (purse snatching and pocket picking). They then look at these offenses committed by and inflicted upon persons in three age categories: juvenile (12–17 years), young (18–20 years), and adult (21 years and older). They also assess differences that may occur in urban, suburban, and rural contexts. Their principal findings of relevance here are these:

Figure 10.2 Homelessness is a fact of life in North American cities as well as in developing countries. The homeless live in the core areas of cities. Photo courtesy of Corbis.

1. "Neighborhood economic status has a negative relationship with victimization rates in urban areas. . . . In contrast, rural juveniles have higher rates of victimization in high economic status neighborhoods than in low economic neighborhoods" (Shenk and McInerney 1978: 1–2).
2. Thieves of all ages (for the kinds of theft considered) are disproportionately found in urban neighborhoods of low economic status. Violent urban adults are similarly distributed, but the pattern is weaker than that for theft.
3. "Juvenile and adult offending were found to have a moderate negative relationship with neighborhood economic status in suburban areas but a weak and inconsistent relationship in rural areas" (Shenk and McInerney 1978: 3).

In interpreting these results, we should remember the limitations of surveys (Chapters 6 and 7) and of aggregated data (Chapter 4).

Continuity of Ecological Correlations

Many of these ecological studies confirm each other, with, of course, some variations across cities and methods. What is striking about this kind of research is not merely the parallels in the observations, but also the continuity—the persistence—of the correlations reported. The "things that go together" in the neighborhoods tend to cluster in like fashion over the years.

Schmid and Schmid, reporting in 1972, found strong similarities in the distribution of the serious offenses recorded since 1945 in the state of Washington and within its major city, Seattle. Similarly, Galle et al. (1972) confirm for Chicago what Shaw and McKay discovered decades before: a negative relation between social status and such "social pathologies" as the public-assistance rate, mortality and fertility rates, rate of admission to mental hospitals, and officially recorded juvenile delinquency. Similar findings have been found for Racine, Wisconsin (Shannon 1984; Schuerman and Korbin 1986), and Los Angeles.

Cross-cultural comparisons support the findings for Canada and the United States. For example, in London, Ontario, Jarvis and Messinger used both court appearances and unofficial delinquencies known to the police to compute delinquency rates by census tracts (1974). Delinquency rates correlated with a cluster of variables including "social status," which in turn was a compound of poverty, little schooling, and old dwellings.

British area studies also reveal the usual inverse association between social class and crime rates. Burt found this pattern in London as early as 1925, and Wallis and Maliphant note that, even after 40 years, the social class characteristics of high-delinquency areas persist in that city (1967).

Similar reports are given by Bagot (1941) for Liverpool, Morris (1957) for Croydon, Baldwin et al. for Sheffield (1976), and Giggs (1970) for Barry in Wales. Giggs tested the relation between 43 "intraurban" characteristics, including physical features of areas, plus thirteen other measures indicative of what Giggs calls "social defects." Again, social troubles generally go together. Thus, in Wales, as elsewhere, zones characterized by higher crime and delinquency rates also have higher shares of divorce, tuberculosis, and people with financial problems.

A study by M. J. Brown et al. (1972) also employed a cluster analysis plotted for electoral wards in a northern English industrial town, These investigators found areas with higher proportions of subsidized houses, and with more unemployment and poverty, to be the more violent zones. Offenses against property were negatively associated with owner-occupied houses, but they were positively correlated with government housing, unemployment, poverty, and high proportions of Irish immigrants.

Summary: American, Canadian, and British Studies

Studies conducted in Britain, Canada, and the United States show certain conditions to be correlated so that goods and evils appear in bunches. A pattern appears in ecological research that associates high rates of crime and delinquency with indicators of physical illness and disability, mental disorder, low standards of hygiene, parental disharmony, and inconsistent, brutal, or lax discipline of children.

Ecological Studies Around the World

A similar map of the social location of crime is drawn, with some variation, by area studies around the world. For example, Hayner (1946) plotted such criminogenic zones for Mexico City; Grillo (1970) for Caracas, Venezuela; Mangin (1967) for Lima, Peru; and Ferracuti et al. (1975) for Puerto Rico. In San Juan, Puerto Rico, certain districts have a long-standing criminal repute, but high crime rates are also reported for new areas of housing projects for the resettled poor (Caplow et al. 1964; Kupperstein and Toro-Calder 1969; Lewis 1966).

In Conclusion: What Area Studies Do and Do Not Tell

Social geography is valuable as one means of finding out what goes with what. Social maps of correlated events describe life patterns and therefore may give us an "appreciation," in Matza's (1969) sense, of the way others live.

As far as the findings of such studies overlap, we have confidence that something causal is at work. However, what is causal and what is only correlative has to be tested, not assumed. For this test, area studies are not enough.

As we will see, competing explanations of crime quarrel about facts, accepting some and denying others. They also provide different interpretations of the same facts. The soundness of both fact and interpretation is bolstered as we locate criminality by additional procedures. This is particularly required if we are to avoid the aggregative fallacy into which area studies might lead us. Area studies tell us about the macro dimensions of crime; however, they are limited in what they can tell us about individuals (King 1997). Identifying the relationship between wealth and crime at the individual level requires the study of individuals, and it is to that unit of analysis that we now turn our attention.

Individual Case Studies

Studies of individuals of varied social status essentially confirm the associations revealed by ecological research. The consistency between findings from aggregate level studies and individual studies is not complete, however, for two major reasons. First, there are differences in how processes work at the macro and the micro levels. Thus, while wealth and crime are strongly correlated at the macro level, that relationship appears to be of lesser magnitude at the micro level. Second, while macro-level studies almost invariably use police or court data to measure the dependent variable, micro-level or individual case studies generally use self-report data. Thus, many of the controversies surrounding self-report data (particularly as they relate to SES) that are addressed in Chapter 7 resurface here.

Summarizing a number of cross-sectional, longitudinal, and cohort studies, the primary findings may be stated as follows:

1. Although the prevalence of police contact is high among boys of all SES backgrounds (about one-third of all boys in the Philadelphia cohort studies experienced at least one contact), more frequent and serious delinquency occurs in the lower strata. Furthermore, persistent or career-oriented offenders are generally found only among lower-class boys (Tracy and Kempf-Leonard 1996; Tracy et al. 1990; Wolfgang et al. 1972).

2. The relation between social status and delinquency varies with the status structure of the residential community and the extent to which delinquency is part of a cultural tradition in these residential areas. "The largest proportion of delinquents for any status group comes from the more homogeneous status areas for that group, while the delinquency life-chances of boys in any status group tend to be greatest in the lower status areas and in high delinquency rate areas" (Reiss and Rhodes 1961: 720).

3. Overall, SES seems to have a complex effect on delinquency. Sampson and Laub (1993: 247) note "that the strongest and most consistent effects on both official and unofficial delinquency flow from the social processes of family, school, and peers." Specifically, SES appeared to proxy patterns of discipline, supervision and parent-child attachment that are more proximal or direct correlates of delinquent behavior. This pattern seems to hold

regardless of how one measures delinquency—using official data, self-reports or first-hand reports of teachers and parents.

4. "Negative structural conditions (such as poverty or family disruption) also affect delinquency, but largely through family and school process variables" (Sampson and Laub 1993: 247). Thus, a significant correlate of delinquency is poor schoolwork, a relationship that holds true regardless of race.

5. There is an interaction between delinquency rate, social status, and intelligence. Holding IQ constant, "the probability of being classified a serious, petty, or truancy offender is greater for the blue-collar than white-collar boys" (Reiss and Rhodes 1961: 723). Turning the relation around and holding social status constant, there is also a substantial association between higher IQ and nondelinquency. Generally, the data show an interaction between a boy's social status, his IQ, and level of delinquency.

In Conclusion: "Street Crime" and "White-Collar Crime"

The many correlations found by individual case studies pertain to the kinds of crime that are publicly visible, that have "street nuisance value" that more frequently result in complaints by citizens, and that are more likely to reflect the options, and also the tastes, of poorer people. Such offenses are often the crimes *mala in se* (wrong in themselves) rather than the newer forms of crimes *mala prohibita* (wrong because prohibited).

Nevertheless, there is a built-in bias in looking at the first order of crimes and neglecting to look at the less visible crimes of middle-class entrepreneurs and upper-class persons of power in government, business, labor unions, and the information industry.

The late, great American criminologist Edwin Sutherland (1949: 9) coined the term *white-collar crime* and used it to refer to "a crime committed by a person of respectability and high social status in the course of his occupation." The *Dictionary of Criminology* later changed the reference slightly when it defined a white-collar criminal as "a person with high socioeconomic status who violates the laws designed to regulate his occupational activities" (Nice 1965).

A trouble with the concept of white-collar crime is that at its boundaries, it shades off into violations of regulations that may not be crimes, although they may be wrongs, and that involve us, again, in disputes about "social harms." There is little question that white-collar crime constitutes crime when the concept refers to such offenses *mala in se* as treason and theft. Nevertheless, there is question about the criminality of violations of laws that would regulate employees, unions, professions, commerce, and industry. Such laws define crimes *mala prohibita*—relatively new offenses, the wrongness of which is disputed. For example, one need not take sides in the debate to note that some legislators who believe monopoly in industry to be evil also believe monopoly in public service to be good.

Monopolies are therefore both condemned and protected—by law—and it is a sore issue whether, and when, violations of such laws constitute real crimes.

The notion of white-collar crime refers to a core content of illegal activity, the dark figure of which is poorly illuminated. We have only partial studies of bribery, perjury, libel, embezzlement, fraud, criminal negligence, and treason committed by persons of power. Such research as bears on this topic suggests, commonsensically, that the more power one has, the more damage one can do (Braithwaite 1979, chapter 10; Carson 1970; Pearce 1976).

It is reasonable to conclude that maps locating all crimes by social status of offenders are incomplete. A large unknown territory of middle-class and upper-class crime remains to be charted, and the correlations we have noted are quali-fied, then, by their reference to particular kinds of more visible attack upon per-son and property.

This qualification does not challenge maps of juvenile crime as much as it does maps of adult crime, nor does it challenge depictions of the social locations of direct physical attack.

Studies of Styles of Violence
Studies Around the World

In all countries for which we have records, beatings and killings are distributed inversely with wealth. Within the context of each jurisdiction, poorer people fight one another, and wound and kill one another, at higher rates than richer people do.

This correlation has been observed historically, on several continents, and in countries with diverse economies and governments—capitalist, commu-nist, and in-between. The story can be read for Italy (Morselli 1879; Ferri 1895; Franchini and Introna 1961) and France for both the nineteenth and the twentieth centuries (Amiot et al. 1968; Aron 1973; Fregier 1840; Tarde 1890). The English picture in modern times is provided by T. P. Morris and Blom-Cooper (1964) and for the thirteenth century by Given (1977). Connor finds the usual negative correlation of social status and homicide in the former Soviet Union (1972). Svalastoga reports similarly for Denmark (1956), Verkko for Finland (1951), Bustamente and Bravo for Mexico (1957), Lamont for South Africa (1961), Jayewardene and Ranasinghe (1963), Wood for Sri Lanka (1961), and many sources for the United States in recent and distant decades (Bensing and Schroeder 1960; Brearley 1932; Monahan 1975).

A Grand Correlation: Violence and Disadvantages

If one takes a still picture of people who live in any one period under the laws of one state, the negative association between their wealth and their violence becomes part of a bigger correlation—a correlation that suggests that good things go together, and bad things too.

Most correlations are not perfect. They describe tendencies, and the tendency for advantages and disadvantages to cumulate is just that—a probability. It is a probability that seems to increase at extremities of wealth, and with particular force at the bottom of the hierarchy. It is a probability that decreases among most of us who are in the middle—neither poor nor rich.

For our present interest, we note that physical brutality is part of a life marked by other disadvantages—"disadvantages," at least, as these are conceived by most sociologists. For example, Loftin (1980) is but one among many who have calculated relationships between poor circumstances and violence. Using American homicide rates for states, Loftin finds these to be associated with several indicators of disadvantages—with percentage of children living with one parent (+0.88), with proportion of persons failing the U.S. armed forces' mental test (+0.84), with infant death rates (+0.83), with percentage of the population that is illiterate (+0.77), and with percentage of families with less than $1,000 income (+0.71). These correlations among aggregates are often confirmed by studies of individuals (Gilder 1974; Lewis 1959, 1966; Robins 1966; Robins and O'Neal 1958; Rutter and Madge 1976).

Quantity and Quality of Violence

The status location of violence within societies says nothing about the social status of those who do violence, or order it, when groups called "states" or "nations" fight. The quantity of mortality in such encounters exceeds that of ordinary fighting, of course.

In addition, there are qualities of group violence, variously legitimated; and the inverse social class correlate of person-to-person brawling, maiming, and killing need not hold when people organize for homicide in those large-scale fights called "revolutions" and "wars" of varied scale. In fact, in Europe, Japan, Canada, and the United States, most of those killers called "terrorists" come from middle- and upper-class families; and their killing differs from traditional lower-class violence in that it is "impersonal"—directed against innocents and people who have given no personal affront but who are symbols of a hated authority. Timothy McVeigh's role in the Oklahoma City bombing of a federal building causing the death of 167 persons comes immediately to mind. By contrast, lower-class attack is directly personal—to settle a dispute or take something from the victim.

However, even within the context of person-to-person brutality, qualities of attack differ by the status of offenders and victims. For example, Green and Wakefield (1979) studied characteristics of 119 American cases of criminal homicide from 1955 to 1975 in which offenders met their criteria of "middle- or upper-class" status. They then compared some details of these killings with lower-class homicides. They report differences such as these:

1. The richer killer tends to be a white male, aged 30 years or more. The poorer killer tends to be an African-American male younger than 30.
2. Victim-precipitation (homicides in which the victim was the first to use force or display a weapon) seems to be a lower-class phenomenon. At least, Green and Wakefield find no such provocation in their sample of upper-class homicides, while between one-fifth and one-third of lower-class killings have this feature.
3. Richer people, compared with poorer ones, kill members of their own family more frequently. Put another way, poorer people are more likely than rich ones to kill persons outside their families. This means that upper-class homicides more frequently occur in the victim's home. By contrast, more lower-class homicides occur outside the victim's home.
4. The domestic arena in which upper-class homicides occurs is also associated with suicide of the killer. About one-fourth or more of upper-class homicides

are followed by the killer's suicide. Among the lower class, this pattern occurs in fewer than 10% of homicides.

5. The sex ratio of offenders does not differ by social status: men are disproportionately the killers. However, upper-class male murderers kill women more frequently than lower-class male murderers do—in the ratio of more than 2:1. By contrast, female offenders of whatever status kill five times as many males as females.

6. Richer people, compared with poorer ones, seldom kill by stabbing.

7. More than half of the lower-class killings are fueled with alcohol. By contrast, upper-class homicide is relatively alcohol-free, a fact associated with the greater premeditation of high-status murders (see 9 below).

8. Given the relationship between drinking and homicide among lower-class persons, their killings peak on weekends—"party time." Upper-class homicides show no daily pattern. However, murders on all social levels often occur during evening hours—from 8 P.M. to 2 P.M.

9. More than three-fourths of the upper-class homicides appear to be premeditated. Most of the lower-class killings appear a consequence of "trivial altercations."

Regarding point 9, Green and Wakefield comment:

> The wish for pecuniary gain motivates the upper-class killer more than any other single desire; while in studies of lower-class cases, it appears only in connection with murders committed during robberies. Mental depression, the next most frequently ascribed motive in upper-class homicide, does not even appear as a category of analysis in the lower-class studies. (1979: 180)

Clusters of Injury

An additional fact describes differences in the violence of persons up and down the status ladder: violence in the lower echelons is associated with a range of other physical injuries.

People who more frequently attack one another physically also have more accidents, which include a range of wounds from car crashes, fires, falls, and fights at public places of entertainments (Braucht et al. 1980; Reinhart 1978; Trivizias 1980). Children who become delinquent tend to have had more "hospital contacts" before age 4; they continue to have an excess of hospital attention between the ages of 14 and 16; and their debilities include not just illnesses and psychiatric disorders, but injuries to face and head, many of which are deemed to have been accidental (Gibbens 1963; Lewis and Shanok 1977).

Among persons, and within areas, there is a clustering of physical damage, and it runs on a continuum from injuries that are apparently intended to those which seem to be unintended and therefore, are called "accidents."

In Conclusion: Violence and Status
Status and Money

Some students who read these many correlations have difficulty resisting the temptation to translate dollars into conduct and income into "class." However, money means more than one thing.

There are many ways of being rich, poor, or middling. The effects of income upon behavior vary with how one becomes more or less wealthy, with the duration of one's wealth or poverty, with the rapidity of changes in status up or down the income ladder, and with interests and expectations that define how one should live. In short, the meaning of money varies with the social context in which any level of income is embedded.

Social class that makes a difference in behavior depends on more than money. A sum of money earned does not have the same effect as the same sum given. Reward divorced from effort produces syndromes of *learned laziness*—the "spoiled brat" phenomenon—and it does so in laboratories and also in real life (Seligman 1975). What one does makes a difference to what one is, whatever the wealth one has.

Culture, a word that refers to a spectrum of habits and tastes, is only loosely connected to income, however the money is gained. Today, many families that are "middle-income" are not "middle-class," and many families with high incomes are not "high-class"—in the cultural meaning of those terms. A rock star who "makes it big" does not have the same tastes as the equally rich corporation executive. A middle-income drug dealer does not behave like a middle-income schoolteacher. A poor peasant does not act like an urban parent on welfare.

In brief, the effects of some indicators of social status, such as money, are less strong and less direct than popular theorizing assumes. It is questionable to what extent being in a certain income bracket causes any particular kind of behavior (Brown 1970–1971). Or, as the Las Vegas showgirl commented, "Money can't buy class."

There are, to be sure, accompaniments of wealth and poverty that are part of the definition of being rich or poor. These correlates of income are the kinds of things money allows one to do, like taking holidays abroad or owning expensive cars, but such things are not the causes of any particular patterns of behavior such as being criminal or lawful, disciplined or dissipated. Popular observation has long noted that, just as there are the deserving poor and the depraved poor, there are also the productive rich and the "filthy" rich—by which one means "lazy and dissolute."

Status and Class

Criminologists continue to dispute the shape of the distribution of crime and delinquency by social status (or socioeconomic status, SES). Still, wealth is only one marker of status, and the results one finds will vary with the indicators used. As the preceding pages suggest, confusion is generated when scholars broaden conceptions of material well-being into the concepts of "social status" and "social class."

A *class* of anything—people, objects, or events—refers to a presumably discrete grouping. Class refers to a category that can be distinguished from other clusters. So, when sociologists speak of "social classes," they often use categorical labels such as "proletarian," "bourgeois," and other names of purportedly distinct kinds of people.

By contrast, "social status," as measured, is a continuous attribute. Thus, one measures degree of prestige accorded to occupations, or amounts of income, or years of schooling completed.

In clarification of the criminological debate, Thornberry and Farnworth (1982) note the distinction between social class and social status and point out that, within each of these markers of difference, sociologists have counted different things. For example, social status has been measured by single, or combined, indicators such as race, occupational prestige, job stability, education, income, and place of residence.

Confusion has also been sowed by sometimes assessing the impact of parents' SES, as in studies of juvenile delinquency, and sometimes studying the impact of offenders' own SES. In addition, criminologists have disputed the relationship between SES, criminality, and delinquency using different measures—in particular, official statistics and self-reports.

Thornberry and Farnworth tested the independent effect of these many indicators of social position with data from a cohort of males in Philadelphia who were followed to age 26. They found the following:

1. "When self-reported and official criminality are measured in parallel fashion, the results appear to be concordant rather than discordant."
2. Among juveniles, SES is measured as background variables such as place of residence during high school and fathers' reported occupation (on the latter, see Chapter 7). In the Philadelphia cohort, neither of these is highly correlated with the less serious delinquencies as self-reported.
3. However, when analysis shifts to the individual's own social status as an adult then the usual significant, negative association appears between SES and criminal activity.
4. Among the indicators of adult SES, job instability and low educational attainment loom large as correlates of criminality in this sample. Income and occupation play a lesser role. In other words, people who drop out of school and who have trouble working steadily engage more frequently in crime. One interpretation of this repeated finding regards personality as determinant of all three outcomes (see Chapter 12).
5. The degree to which measures of SES correlate with adult criminality varies with race. Therefore, Thornberry and Farnworth conducted separate analyses for African Americans and whites. These reveal that social status indicators have a stronger correlation with black than with white criminality.

The investigators conclude that

> previous studies may have underestimated the effects of status and criminality, since many studies focused exclusively on whites while others did not present results separately for whites and blacks. Thus, the subpopulation in which the relationship between social status and criminal behavior is strongest, adult blacks, has been the group least likely to be studied in the past. (Thornberry and Farnworth 1982: 22)

Income, a person's cash flow, has been used as an alleged determinant of need which, in turn, is supposed to affect inclination to steal and perhaps to fight and kill. Therefore, the effects of income should be studied separately from those of other markers of social status.

Comparative and Historical Studies:
Rich Nations, Poor Nations; Good Times and Bad

Money means more than one thing; wealth has more than one consequence. This means that the effects of wealth and poverty vary with the social context—with where one is, as opposed to where one has been, and with how wealth is gained. Given this lack of uniform relation between the money one has and the life one leads, we should expect no single relation between the economic status of a society as a whole and its crime level. Furthermore, the link between prosperous times, or poor ones, and criminal behavior should also be loose. This is, in fact, what we find when we study the connections between wealth and criminality comparatively, among many countries, and historically over time.

It is apparent by now that affluence in itself provides no cure for crime. In fact, for many industrialized countries in recent times, crime rates and prosperity have moved in tandem. Some criminologists believe this to be true because prosperity means that there are more things to steal and more opportunities for theft. Prosperity also elevates crime statistics, it is said, because affluence is associated with better recording of offenses and because property insurance encourages the reporting of crime. Furthermore, it is maintained that since some people have more than others, there is both motivation and justification for theft.

Whether or not one agrees with these explanations and justifications of affluent crime, attempts to link criminality to the business cycle or to unemployment figures have not produced any clear conclusion except that the relationship between material "need" and criminal behavior is not direct.

Difficulties of Economic Studies

Students of criminology get a liberal education in the sense that they learn how difficult it is to gather and to transform information into that coherent form called "knowledge." One hundred fifty years of research have produced volumes on the impact of economic conditions on conduct, with particular attention to the effects of unemployment on crime. Nevertheless, extracting sturdy conclusions from these tons of documents remains difficult. Before considering some recent studies, we should note the nature of their difficulties. These are both theoretical and methodological.

Troubles with Theories

Scholars study economic conditions because significant features of behavior are presumably shaped by material needs. Thus stealing is obviously one way to get what one needs, although we have trouble distinguishing "what one needs" from "what one wants" as a criminal motive. In addition, explaining much fighting, killing, raping, and vandalism in this economic manner remains difficult.

An inference is that researchers should specify kinds of offenders and kinds of crimes supposed to be affected by the business cycle. Yet even with such specification, contradictory hypotheses abound concerning the effects to be expected by changes in the production and distribution of wealth. Thus it has been simultaneously proposed that prosperity should increase crime and so should depression.

Prosperity ought to increase theft, in the first place, because there are more things to steal and more things left unguarded by people at work (Cohen and Felson 1979; Cohen et al. 1980). It has also been suggested that prosperity generates adult crime because stealing is an extension of legitimate business activity (Vold and Bernard 1986), and that prosperity generates juvenile crime because parents are more preoccupied and therefore neglect children.

Such positive association of good times and crime contends with the opposite hypothesis: that property crimes, at least, should increase during poor times and decrease with an upturn in business activity. Unemployment, in particular, is expected to increase theft.

These contending assumptions are difficult to harmonize, and tension between them leads to the possibility that any change in crime rates can be explained by any change in economic conditions—after the fact. In their summary of theories of crime Hughes and Carter (1981: 21) conclude that

> Marxian criminology predicts an increase in criminal activity in a declining economy, for all classes of potential offenders and for all kinds of crimes. . . . Anomie theory predicts an increase for all crimes with abrupt changes in the economy, either up or down [and] labeling theory's predictions are all contingent on the reaction of social control institutions to the threat of crime in a declining economy.

Troubles with Measures

A contest between hypotheses is no problem if one can generate facts with which to test them. Nevertheless, facts require tallies and, better than mere counting, measurement.

Measuring economic conditions is as difficult as measuring crime. *Unemployment,* for example, is difficult to define because in modern countries the "unemployed" category includes persons with various degrees of motivation to work, various dispositions to accept certain kinds of jobs, and various states of need.

In most Western countries, unemployment is counted by asking samples of citizens, representative of the civilian, noninstitutionalized population, about the work status of every member of their households aged 16 or older. In the United States and Canada such surveys are conducted monthly.

Unemployed persons are those who did not work during the survey week, although they were available, and who had tried to find work during the preceding four weeks. In addition, people are termed "unemployed" if they were idle while waiting to report to a new job within 30 days or were waiting to be called back to a job from which they had been laid off (United States Department of Labor 1976). The unemployment rate is then calculated by dividing the number of unemployed persons by the number in the civilian labor force.

Critics contend that such a measure of unemployment is not a sound measure of hardship or of labor market conditions (Bregger 1971; Shiskin 1976). Some argue that unemployment statistics underestimate the true rate because they omit the *hidden unemployed* who wish to work but who have abandoned the search for a job (sometimes called the *discouraged*). Other critics argue that these statistics overestimate the true rate of unemployment because of the size of the *underground economy* in which people work "off the books" to evade taxes (Ball 1982; Henry 1980; Malabre 1980, 1981; Martino 1981; Mirus and Smith 1981). Additional observers complement the picture of an underground, and sometimes criminal, economy by counting job vacancy rates and noting the contradiction between unfilled jobs and unemployment statistics (Ginzberg 1980; Lublin 1980; Seligman 1981). Recognition of facts such as these has moved scholars to urge changes in the definition, measurement, and interpretation of unemployment (Levitan 1975; O'Neill 1975; Wetzel 1975).

Difficulties in measuring economic conditions do not end here, of course, because unemployment is only one of many indicators of the state of an economy. Other indicators, whose tallies vary with what is counted and how, include the money supply, inflation rates, income per person, the consumer price index (CPI), and gross national product (GNP).

Correlations of economic conditions with crime rates will vary, therefore, with the economic indicators employed and with the period covered. In addition, there is the question of time lag to be allowed between a change in the economy and its presumed effect on criminality. This can be assessed, as we will see, but one confronts an additional problem: that of distinguishing between trend effects and causal effects. Since many of these economic indicators and social behaviors are moving together, it becomes important to be able to separate changes that reflect patterned trends from changes that represent causal impact.

Unfortunately for our satisfaction with research on this topic, the overwhelming bulk of it has used aggregate numbers. There has been little adequate research counting change in the lawful and criminal conduct of individuals as they move in and out of the work force. What is to be counted in such investigation is, of course, movement in and out of lawful employment that is involuntary, rather than that which is a matter of choice. Research using individual data is important because we should expect differences in conduct if a person has been chronically outside the labor force—that is, unconnected to lawful work—as opposed to being temporarily out of work.

Given these difficulties in assessing economic conditions and correlating them with crime rates, it is no surprise to find contradictions in the research literature (Brenner 1976, 1977; Danser and Laub 1981; Paez 1981).

In Conclusion: Historical and Comparative Studies

While a great deal of political reliance has been placed on the value of rational explanations of crime, the empirical evidence is less than overwhelming. Most research has used aggregate or macro level data; few studies have focused on the behavior of individual offenders. This is unfortunate, because even if we could draw conclusions with macro analyses, we would be limited in what we could say about individual offenders.

The aggregation fallacy informs us that it is difficult to relate patterns across levels of analysis. For example, it is not inconsistent to report that crime rates are related to unemployment rates at the macro level but not at the micro level. Specifically, high unemployment rates may raise levels of criminal activity among those employed in marginal jobs (thus increasing the overall crime rate) while having no effect on the crime rate among those who are unemployed.

Part of the cost is visible in programs that assume the accuracy of the prediction, "Reduce unemployment and you will reduce crime." Most interventions that would reduce crime—recidivism in particular—by providing jobs, vocational training, and unemployment benefits do not produce strong effects. Effects vary, of course, with older and younger offenders; with efforts before trial, in prison, and after release; with quality of offender's community; and with "class" of offender. Still, a review of these many efforts does not confirm an optimistic prediction. Orsagh (1980: 183) summarizes his review by saying, "Unemployment may affect the crime rate; but even if it does, its general effect is too slight to be measured. Therefore, the proper inference is that the effect of unemployment on crime rates is minimal at best."

Future investigations can provide more sensitive tests of an economic hypothesis if they use individual data; distinguish between young, middling, and old candidates for crime; examine the social contexts in which economic opportunities are presented; and note possible differences between those chronically out of legitimate work and those temporarily displaced.

Meanwhile, a reasonable conclusion from research to date, and from comparative observations around the world and through history, is that crime may increase with both good times and bad, and that neither the poverty nor the wealth of nations is a major determinant of their levels of criminal conduct. The best that can be said is that crimes *mala in se* are associated ecologically (in social and physical space within a society) with relative economic deprivation. This "ecological connection" allows the inference that one way to guarantee greater amounts of ordinary crime is to have many poor people live in proximity to small numbers of rich people. Otherwise, crimes of direct predation are not associated historically (in time) or comparatively (across cultures) with relative impoverishment.

Part IV
Explaining Crime

11. The Search for Causes: Explanations and Other Answers

Explaining crime requires that one be able to describe criminal acts and actors and the social settings of different crimes. The search is for things that make a difference. This search is an attempt to find the causes of crime. It proceeds, however, by identifying the correlates of crime, that is, the conditions or events that go with the criminal activity. When these conditions or events are of an interpersonal nature, they constitute, as we have seen, the social location of crime.

Causality

Criteria for Causality

Statements that only describe events or only state continuities between events usually do not qualify as explanations. When we ask for an explanation of something, particularly of social action, we want to know what causes it.

The idea of causation is a tangled one. It is so complex a notion that some observers have urged us to try to ameliorate social problems without thinking of their causes (Horton 1973; Wilkins 1968). It is possible to do this. When we respond to our environment as individuals, we adjust well to a variety of conditions without first having to analyze their causes. Thus, we can sidestep abusive people without having to know what "made" them that way.

When we wish to do more than "merely adjust"—when we wish to explain occurrences and, more important, to shape events according to plan—we argue for a preferred policy by referring to the alleged causes of the happenings that concern us. Even criminologists who explicitly advise us to avoid thinking about causes and trying to explain them (Hartjen 1974; Quinney 1974a), are nonetheless constrained to think in terms of causes (Nettler 1975, 1982a; Scriven 1971). What is explicitly denied is implicitly assumed.

Although there is considerable debate around the edges of the social sciences over whether the concept of causality is a necessary component, there is general agreement among those who work within causal theoretical frameworks over what the necessary conditions are for identifying a causal relationship.

For a relationship to be causal, it must satisfy three criteria: there must be a statistically significant correlation between the cause and the effect (the independent and the dependent variables); the cause must precede the effect; and, the relationship must be nonspurious.

The first issue (correlation) is reasonably straightforward to determine, at least in principle. It usually involves collecting empirical data and applying one or more standard statistical techniques to determine whether two or more items appear together, or move in tandem. If the items are related beyond some level expected by chance alone, we say that they are correlated. Often the determination of correlation is clouded by methodological problems. For example, if we assume that the tendency to commit juvenile crime is related to peer pressure, it may not always be possible to observe that precipitating peer pressure; thus, we may conclude that the two items are not related when, in fact, they are.

The second issue (temporal precedence) is also an empirical question. It is easy to say that the cause ought to precede the effect, but often the time delay between cause and effect may be so small as to preclude their disentanglement. Thus, cause and effect may appear simultaneous, or we may even mistake one for another. Much official data relating to crime is gathered over a long interval (often a year or more), making it very difficult to separate out the time sequencing. Furthermore, many social relationships feed back on one another leaving us with the proverbial "chicken and egg" conundrum. Does, for example, relative neighborhood poverty lead to crime or vice versa? Likely, the relationship is reciprocal, with some aspects of poverty influencing crime, and high crime rates further undermining the financial integrity of the neighborhood.

The third issue (nonspuriousness) is far more difficult to disentangle at the empirical level. Spurious relationships occur when a nondetermining third variable is merely associated with both the cause and the effect. For example, poor labor force participation may be related to criminal activity leading us to conclude that rates of crime might be reduced by decreasing rates of unemployment. In fact, it may be that poor self-concept influences both labor force participation and propensity to crime, and the relationship between labor force participation and crime is nonexistent once self-concept is taken into account.

The best solution to the problem of spuriousness is to randomly assign individuals to experimental and control conditions. Clearly, this is difficult to do in the study of crime. Since a methodological solution to the problem is often not available, we rely on the next best approach. When we cannot achieve *physical* control over the conditions to which people are assigned, we use *statistical* controls based on theoretical considerations as to what may or may not be a reasonable variable to control in our model.

How Causes Are Assigned

Explanations of crime emphasize different causes of conduct. The differing emphases arise from more than our imperfect knowledge of the causes of social events. These competing theories are also stimulated by the different questions we ask and by the fact that the very concept of causation is vague. "To cause" means more than one thing, and there are varied criteria by which we identify causes. Furthermore, the events nominated as the "causes" of crime come in assorted packages (densely and sparsely packed), in assorted shapes (rectilinear, curvilinear, and interacting), and with differing content. These variations need not be discussed here, but their descriptions can be read in a number of standard sources (Cartwright 1989; Mackie 1980; Holland 1988; Hoover 1990; among others). For our purposes, it is sufficient to be reminded of two facts and to be informed of an interesting hypothesis.

The first fact is that, despite the variety of causal models available, social scientists always think causally with correlations. The second fact is that neither high nor low correlations between things proposed as causes and their supposed effects tell us what generating power these causes may have. Our estimates are based on judgments, and our judgments are a based on a melding of facts and preferences.

The mixing of preference with fact in the judgment of causation suggests a hypothesis to explain the differential attribution of causation and responsibility (Nettler 1970: 35). This hypothesis has received experimental support and deserves description in preparation for our evaluation of explanations of crime. The hypothesis says that *we tend to move the location of causation according to our approval or disapproval of actors and their acts.* When people whom we like, or with whom we sympathize, do things we approve of, we locate the causes of their conduct within them, and we speak of their dispositions or their purposes as sources of their action. Similarly, when people we dislike do things we disapprove of, the "moral balancing act" locates causes within the actors.

For example, if Millicent Innocent (whom we like) is marrying John Goodfellow (whom we also like), and we approve of their marriage, then the question, "Why are they marrying?" is answered by reference to their dispositions ("They are in love") or to their purposes ("They want to share a life and have a family"). However, when our preferences are thrown out of balance, as when "good guys" do bad deeds or when bad actors perform good deeds, then we tend to move causation outside the actors, and we refer to circumstance, pressure, accident, or luck.

"Temperaments select philosophies," the psychologist William James (1907) believed. Temperaments and views of the world underlie the moral balancing act by which we assign causation—blame and responsibility—to actors or their circumstances. In turn, these sentiments affect our politics.

Brickman et al. (1982) propose four models that describe how we assign causation to human action:

1. According to the *moral model*, actors are deemed to be the causes of their problems and responsible for solving them. The prescription for such actors is proper motivation.
2. According to the *compensatory model*, people are deemed not to be responsible for their actions or situations, but are believed to be responsible for their own improvement. The prescription here is for people to get, or to receive, power.
3. According to the *medical model*, people are deemed not to be responsible either for their bad actions and unpleasant situations or for remedies of their lives. The prescription that this model gives is for treatment.
4. According to the *enlightenment model*, actors are deemed to be responsible for their problems, but are considered to be unable or unwilling to solve them. The prescription for such people is discipline.

As we will see, these models intrude upon the many theories of crime causation discussed in the remaining chapters. They are difficult to analyze objectively because they are aspects of our temperaments, world views, and political preferences.

Political Preference and Causal Location

Preferences that move the location of causes are embedded in our morals and our politics. (See Figure 11.1.) The things we want to see done get elevated from values in themselves to general cures for a variety of miseries. If poverty offends us, while affluence does not, and if we consider relieving poverty as an end in itself, it becomes tempting to justify our political preference by expanding its suggested causal power. Our prescribed program for alleviating poverty then becomes a program with a promise to reduce crime, alienation, and unhappiness.

Conversely, our assessment of explanations of crime is influenced by more than the factual soundness of the explanations. There is a tendency to be influenced by what an explanation suggests we can and cannot do about crime. If the explanation points to evil sources of wrong acts—sources that we would just as

Figure 11.1   "How do I feel about being mugged? Well naturally I didn't enjoy it and certainly don't condone violence or threats of violence as a means toward social change. However, I can empathize with my assailant and realize that in his terms this is a valid response to the deteriorating socio-economic situation in which we find ourselves." Lee Lorenz © 1972 from *The New Yorker* Collection. All rights reserved. [1972 09 021 LLO . HG Mugged].

soon liquidate anyway—it is easier for us to accept it. On the other hand, if the explanation does not point to what can readily be changed or if it does not point to things we are prepared to change, then it tends to be devalued, and this devaluation is produced more by our morals than by the state of our science.

This is particularly true when a science is thin; however, the tendency has been illustrated even in sciences more firmly grounded than the behavioral studies. The tug of ethicopolitical preference on knowledge occurs in many scientific arenas. Historians of science have been particularly energetic in showing how frequently scientific hypotheses are accepted or rejected, not just because of the evidence available, but also because of a moral pressure to interpret the evidence in a congenial way. For example, Provine (1973) studied the inferences drawn by biologists from their research on the genetics of racial mixture. In Provine's demonstration, the morals of scientists changed their beliefs without there having been any change in their knowledge.

Levels of Explanation

What is to be explained about human behavior can be conceived as referring to different levels of action. *Level* refers to the unit of analysis. Units of analysis commonly employed in discussions of human conduct are individual and aggregate, and the kinds of questions asked on these different levels are recognized as psychological and sociological, respectively.

Thus, in talking about criminal activity, a frequent question is the psychological one, "Why did he do it?" By contrast, the sociological question asks about the behavior of aggregates, "Why does this society have more crime of type *y* than another society" or "Why have crime rates for our society risen?"

We ordinarily expect answers to these two levels of question to be consistent, and we often explain the behavior of groups by referring to the motives or intentions of their members. In short, many sociological explanations *may* refer to the psychology of individuals taken collectively.

This need not be the case, however. It is possible to explain the actions of aggregates without reference to the actions of their individual components. For example, one can explain and foretell the movement of a cloud without accounting for the behavior of the droplets of water within it. Such is also the case with human action. We are able, for example, to predict mortality rates for persons between the ages of 30–39 years for the coming year. It is much more difficult to predict with any degree of certainty which specific individuals within that age category will die. It is also possible to explain group behavior without describing the motives of individuals within the group. There may be an implicit psychology underlying certain sociological explanations, of course, but the behavior of aggregates can be studied without making statements about individuals within the collectivity.

It is an open question whether the behavior of human populations is better explained on the sociological or the psychological level. Sociological explanations that omit reference to individuals do not always satisfy; individual level explanations often omit an evaluation of the serious structural constraints that mold or restrict people's behavior. Intellectual satisfaction depends, again, on the question that is asked and on what one wants to do with the explanation.

The Aggregative Fallacy

Criminologists often use data that describe aggregates—collections of people. They do so because they are interested in populations and because much public information is reported in this manner. Thus, correlations may be calculated between rates of crime in areas (aggregates of individuals) and features of those areas such as their average income.

It is usually the case, however, that the degree of association and sometimes even its direction changes when we correlate the actions of *individuals* with their circumstances as opposed to correlating a rate of criminal activity in a population with an average of some measure of its situation.

The *aggregative fallacy* is the error of assuming that associations found among events when we describe aggregates with single figures—an average, proportion, or rate—will also be found, to the same degree and in the same direction, when we study the association between actions and situations person-by-person. It is the mistake of believing that what-goes-with-what when we compare an average or proportion of activity in an area will be found when we compare what-goes-with-what among individuals in that area.

The "aggregative fallacy" (Riley 1963) was originally titled the "ecological fallacy" (Alker 1969; Robinson 1950) and is still referred to in that manner (e.g., Visser 1994). The original label is misleading, however, because of its connection with the study of social ecology.

In his early study, William Robinson (1950) demonstrated *that* this error occurs, and he explained *why* it happens. He calculated the degree of association between the proportion of African Americans in *regions* of the United States and rates of illiteracy in those areas, and discovered a strong correlation (+.95). When he recalculated the association with information about individuals in those regions, it dropped by almost 80% to +.20.

In a parallel computation, Robinson found that the degree of association revealed by single numbers, such as averages or proportions, assumed to be adequately descriptive of behaviors in populations, changed with size of the population, and was *reversed* when the tallies were made with information about individuals.

It is popular among some users of the results of social science research (e.g., government officials and journalists) to take correlational results, report the nature of the association and illustrate it with an individual case. This is done so often that many readers have difficulty understanding how the aggregating error can occur.

It occurs because an average, proportion or rate is a *summarizing statistic*, a single number that is supposed to describe the behavior of individuals in a population. It abstracts from everything that is going on in a collection of people and presents the events as one figure. Such a statistic *loses* information. The loss of information is greater the larger variation in the population it tries to describe. The more varied the people for whom a summarizing statistic is abstracted, the greater the aggregating error.

For social scientists who use the aggregate as the basic unit of observation or unit of analysis—such as many sociologists and macro economists—the aggregation fallacy is a nonissue. This is not the case, however, for many psychologists and some criminologists whose interests lie with the individual. What they want to know, of course, is the probability of individuals within populations, characterized by certain attributes and circumstances, behaving in particular ways. In theory it is possible to approximate this by looking at averages, proportions or rates; in practice, it seldom happens (King 1997).

Note: On Causes and Predictions

To be of practical value, an explanation should be *distinctive* in the sense that it improves our ability to forecast events, or to predict them, more accurately than we could if we employed just common sense. Explanations that are vague or that do not suggest distinctive courses of action with warranted results are not scientific explanations. They do not increase knowledge, although they may provide other comforts such as being congenial to our morals.

Improving predictive power means something different from increasing the ability to forecast. It has been argued earlier that forecasts can be made without knowledge of causes. A forecast is a statement about the probable course of events, made on the basis of public evidence, where the forecaster has no control over those events. The forecaster may adapt to them, naturally, but cannot alter their course. This is why we say that we forecast the weather, not that we predict it. By contrast, to be able to predict means to be able to say that if one does *x*, then with such-and-such probability, *y* will result.

We look for the causes of conduct when we want to increase our predictive power. We remain content with statements about the correlates of conduct, and with descriptions of continuities between situations and behaviors, when we are satisfied to forecast events.

Four Important Conclusions

Our three points about questions and answers lead to four conclusions:

1. An answer to one person's question may not be an answer to another's. The adequacy of an explanation depends on the question it attempts to answer.
2. Some questions and their answers may be so vaguely phrased that one can never tell whether an answer is correct or not. The advice is to be clear about one's concepts.
3. All scholarly explanations of complex social events may have some truth in them. Since ethicopolitical preferences look in different places for the causes of our troubles, it is likely that they will attend to some true things while ignoring others.
4. Explanations are to be tested by what they *distinctively predict*. Both italicized words are important.

Nominated Causes

Some of the explanations of crime to be discussed contribute to our ability to forecast; few contribute to predictive power. Nevertheless, the explanations of crime emphasize different causal locations, and it is both useful and convenient to classify them by the causes they nominate.

Distinctive Explanations

Theories of crime differ from one another in a number of ways, including what they emphasize and their implications for public policy. The *fundamental* difference, however, among explanations of crime is that each distinctly identifies the "place" where crime is caused (i.e., its locus of causation) and just what it is that causes crime.

Explanations of crime can be grouped by the locus of causation and just what it is that is crimogenic about that locus. We have classified theories of crime in terms of three loci that are sociological and social psychological in character.

The sociological and psychosocial explanations identify the locus of causation of crime to be in one of three "places": socialization, the social structure, or interpretations of the world. There are, of course, important variations within each of the three. In each case these variations constitute a different explanation because each emphasizes a different cause as implicated in the genesis of criminal behavior.

Each of these types of explanations is distinctive in that it identifies different conditions as the cause of crime (Table 11.1). In the chapters that follow, each is developed and examined in the light of relevant studies.

Table 11.1   Explanations of Crime Classified by Their Emphasized Causes.

Locus of Causation	Emphasis	Theme	Chapter
Socialization; nurturing	Training regimes	Method of training and content of lesson taught	12
Social-structure	Choice	Rationality	13
	Power	Injustice in the production and administration of criminal law	14
	Opportunity	Inequality in chance to earn a legitimate living	15
	Inequality	Relative deprivation leads to resentment, which leads to crime	16
Interpretations of the world	Cultures as learned patterns of thinking, valuing, doing	Subcultures as distinctive ways of appreciating and responding to the world	17
	Actors' ideas	Differential definitions of situations	18
	Reactors' ideas	Labeling, stigmatization	19

Socialization

The first major locus of causation that has been identified is the manner and content of the training (socialization or nurturing) to which one has been exposed. Some regimens of socialization are seen as more likely to result in conforming behavior while other regimens are less likely to be effective and crime is a result.

Social Structure

Social structure comprises the complex interrelationships of roles and statuses in a society. It comprises the social arrangements that connect persons to persons, persons to groups, and groups to groups. In different ways, some explanations of crime identify the causes of crime as rooted in these arrangements. Four of these types of explanations are discussed and each has a different emphasis: choice, power, opportunity, and inequality.

1. *Choice.* Explanations that emphasize choice see crime as a rational, that is efficient, way of achieving desired goals. Crime is seen as the result of social arrangements that make it less costly and more rewarding than lawful means of achieving the same objective.
2. *Power.* Some explanations of crime are rooted in the idea that if social arrangements allow some persons to hold and exercise power (control) over others, they will do so to the detriment of those others and that the underdogs will rise up and break the rules (commit crime) to remove the source of their oppression.
3. *Opportunity.* Other explanations contend that the social structure is crimogenic if the arrangements are such that opportunities are unevenly accessible to persons who occupy positions in different parts of the social structure. When opportunities to earn a legitimate living are differentially available, a way of dealing with the disparity between one's goals and the opportunity to achieve them is by breaking the rules and employing unlawful means in order to achieve cultural ideals.
4. *Inequality.* The fourth type of explanation contends that social arrangements that produce or allow inequality will lead to persons identifying the inadequacy of their position to be not a matter of individual failure, but rather as a failure of the system. They feel deprived relative to other persons, develop resentments against the system (the social arrangements), and express their displeasure and preference for change by breaking the law.

Interpretations of the World

There are three different emphases in explanations that identify as the locus of crime causation interpretations of what the world is and how it works: those that focus on culture; those that focus on the ideas that actors have; and those that emphasize the ideas of those who react to the behavior of others.

1. *Culture.* Cultures have several components including learned patterns of thinking, valuing, and doing. All societies have cultures and they also have subcultures that have distinctive ways of appreciating and responding to the world. Their distinctiveness is in their departure from the culture of the

larger society. To the extent that subcultures exist and have different inter-pretations of the world and different ideas of what should be valued and done, there will be deviation from the norms valued by the culture. Some of that deviation involves legal norms and this we call crime.

2. *Actor's ideas.* The way in which individuals define situations and the mean-ings that these ideas have for them will influence how they will behave. Those who hold ideas about the correctness (appropriateness) of law are likely to behave accordingly, but those who harbor negative ideas about the law are more likely to break it. In other words, it is the *content* of the ideas we acquire that is crimogenic.

3. *Reactor's ideas.* Some explanations of crime identify the cause of crime as being in the social processing that occurs when there is a reaction to some other act that person may have committed. Societies cause crime by reacting to classes of acts or classes of actors that have been singled out for attention. Social labeling and stigmatization are identified as the causes of crime.

Implications for Social Action

Explanations differ from one another in that each specifies what would have to change (the cause) if there were to be a difference in the rate of crime (the effect). Each explanation, therefore, contains the basis for a different prescrip-tion for public policy and social action.

Not all social action is equally congenial to all people. Our preferences may favor certain types of intervention over others regardless of their actual or dem-onstrated connection to the rates of crime. Therefore, two things follow. First, explanations may be accepted or rejected on other than empirical grounds. Sec-ond, the acceptance of certain explanations implies a commitment to certain forms of social action over others.

12. Control: Socialization and Training

The French philosopher Rousseau asserted that the mind of the human infant is a *tabula rasa*—a blank slate. All human behavior, both good and bad, is therefore learned behavior. The newborn infant is predisposed to be neither criminal nor noncriminal. It is how one is socialized that largely determines whether one will engage in illicit or lawful behavior.

Rousseau's assertion provides one of the underlying assumptions of the psychological theory of behaviorism. While not totally rejecting the role of genetic or constituent predispositions, behaviorists argue that it is our experiences (that is, what we learn) that determines who and what we are. Beyond its supportive empirical evidence, behaviorism is also consistent with the social constructivist concept of crime. If, as is argued in Chapter 1, there is no natural essence of crime or criminality, then it makes little sense to search for innate predispositions to criminality. It does make sense, however, to focus on the learning of social norms and values, and how attitudes and orientations toward those norms and values develop within the individual.

Other psychologists maintain, however, that while most aspects of behavior are learned, the role of genetic or constitutive predispositions should not be minimized. Some researchers propose that evolution has provided us with certain survival mechanisms that when left unchecked, naturally lead us into conflict with one another (Dawkins 1989; Wonderly 1996).

This view of humanity is also fundamental to that of Freud and his followers. According to Freud, the unsocialized individual is inherently criminal. From birth, people are self-centered, acquisitive, and hedonistic. This tragic fact can be countered, to some degree, only by training the human organism *not* to do what comes naturally—*not* to take, grab, kick, bite, and walk over other people if they get in the way. When those who must live together lack this training, the only remaining defense is force. If we will not control ourselves *internally*—out of conscience—we will attempt to control one another *externally*, through force. If we are not regulated by our will, we shall be controlled against our will.

Unfortunately for society, unrestrained self-centeredness beyond infancy inevitably leads to interpersonal conflict as unsocialized individuals pursue their own interests. Therefore, it is the role of society to socialize its young by training them to restrain their baser instincts. For Freud this process leads to the development of the conscience, or in his terminology, the *superego*.

It is not the purpose of this chapter to resolve the issue of how much of our behavior is determined by nature and how much by nurture (see Figure 12.1). What is important for our purpose is that much of our behavior can be understood by focusing on the issue of socialization: the processes by which we are

Figure 12.1   Mike Tyson biting the ear of Evander Holyfield: doing what comes naturally? Photo courtesy of Wide World Photos, Inc.

taught society's rules—its norms, mores, and values. With this as a starting point, some explanations of crime assert that variation in the propensity to commit criminal acts is related to deficiencies in the socialization process.

Those explanations that focus on one aspect of socialization—the importance of learning self-restraint and all that it entails—are generally called *control theories*. It is the goal of control theorists to identify and quantify those aspects of our personality that insulate us from carrying out acts of crime. Control theorists also examine the societal mechanisms by which socialization takes place. Particular attention has been drawn to the family and how varying family structures and "dysfunctionalities" affect our socialization.

In the next section, we will briefly review the major theories used to explain how people learn. After that, the major variations on control theory will be presented. Finally, our attention will be directed toward how the social contexts within which socialization takes place affect criminal behavior.

Learning Theories

Human learning involves three sets of processes. In ascending order of importance, these are classical conditioning, operant conditioning, and social learning. Every human being experiences these processes to some extent, but for each person the blend, consistency, timing, and content are unique.

Classical Conditioning

Classical conditioning processes, first described by the Russian psychologist Pavlov, build on the natural relationships between certain stimuli and responses (Bower and Hilgard 1981: 49–73). For example, when meat powder is placed on a dog's tongue (the *unconditioned stimulus*), the dog salivates (the *response*)—as humans would, too. In his experiments, Pavlov rang a bell (a *neutral stimulus*) while he put meat powder on the dog's tongue. After several repetitions of this procedure, the dog began to salivate when it heard the bell, even when there was no meat.

As psychologists would say today, the initially neutral stimulus (e.g., the sound of a bell) becomes a conditioned stimulus that automatically produces the original response (e.g., salivation). In this experiment, the bell becomes associated with the food, but there is no implication that the organism is aware of this process. The same thing happens to human beings: when the host of a sumptuous dinner party rings the bell, our mouth begins to water as we make our way into the dining room. People's reactions to the same stimuli vary, depending on their conditioning experiences. For example, as we drive past a familiar fast-food restaurant on our way home, we may automatically think of our favorite sandwich, our child's birthday party, or greasy unhealthy food. A visitor from the planet Mars, on the other hand, would not be affected by the dinner bell, and the "golden arches" would mean nothing.

Emotions and attitudes are learned through classical conditioning as well as new behaviors. For example, Staats and Staats (1957) produced emotional significance in nonsense syllables by presenting meaningless letter combinations (e.g., "igk") in association with pleasant or unpleasant words (e.g., "wonderful"). In this manner, what began as nonsense ended with emotional meaning. Later studies show that positive and negative attitudes regarding foods, events, and people can be created by associating them with positive or negative words (e.g., Petty and Cacioppo, 1981). In this way, we become prejudiced without realizing what is happening. When delinquents see a policeman or hear a siren, both their emotions and their behaviors are likely to be quite different from the reactions of nondelinquent youths.

Operant Conditioning

A more important way in which humans learn is through *operant conditioning*, first described by the psychologist B. F. Skinner (Bower and Hilgard 1981: 169–211). These processes build upon the physiological fact that the consequences of a behavior affect that behavior by strengthening or weakening it in the future. When a behavior is followed by a positive consequence (i.e., a reward), it is more likely to be repeated in the future; conversely, when an action is followed by negative consequences (i.e., punishment), it is less likely to be repeated in the future.

Through numerous experiences of daily life, which especially in childhood are largely a matter of trial and error, human beings (and animals, too) learn a great number of activities. Behavior is established and maintained through differential reinforcement. Actions that are reinforced, or followed by positive consequences, are learned and maintained; actions that are punished, or followed by negative (or aversive) consequences, are not learned and not maintained. It is important to understand that the consequences of past activities affect present activities; future events cannot influence present behavior.

Psychologists sometimes speak of consequences as "guiding" future behavior along socially and culturally approved channels. That guiding function requires a combination of both positive and negative consequences: aversive events that follow our actions in effect tell us what *not* to do, while positive consequences tell us *what* to do. A society or subculture that emphasizes only one side will find it difficult to adequately socialize its members (e.g., Skinner 1974). Sociologists would point out that a society's class system skews the proportion of positive and negative events in citizens' lives, and thus is likely to produce some interesting behavioral variations. Some of these will be investigated later in the chapter. Among human beings, these processes are considerably more complex than they appear at first glance; in order to understand crime, we have to mention a few additional features.

A person's definitions of positive and negative consequences, and thus perceptions of reinforcement and punishment, are a matter of individual experience and expectation. For example, when one is given an ice cream cone, that can be positive (when not having had ice cream for a week), or neutral (after having had some for lunch), or negative (when faced with another cone after having eaten a gallon). When a child takes out the garbage out for a sick neighbor, a friendly "thank you" is a reward if nothing is expected, or quite aversive if a dollar's compensation was anticipated. A raise of $2,000 is viewed as sufficient, and thus rewarding, if a lower amount is expected; but it will be deficient, and thus aversive, if much more is expected. Making a few dollars by dealing drugs may be rewarding if there are no other opportunities, but a mere pittance if one can make more through legal activities.

It is important to distinguish between learning a behavior and maintaining it. All of us know how to suck our thumbs or wet our bed, for example, but these behaviors are not maintained because they would be followed by negative consequences. Most people have a large behavioral repertoire, but use only a small portion of it in daily life. However, one cannot assume that everyone has learned the thousands of complicated activities that are part of normal life in our complex, dynamic society, or has had the opportunity to "practice" these behaviors to the same extent. For example, a shy person may have a psychological problem, or may not have learned *how* to interact with other people, or not *well* enough, or not *often* enough, to be comfortable with small talk. Typically, the "smooth operator" has a larger behavioral repertoire than the "wallflower." Similarly, a playground bully or an aggressive gang member probably has not learned how to be popular or gain status in other, more culturally acceptable, ways. Finally, it might be suggested that members of the middle class have a larger, and often quite different and more effective, behavioral repertoire than do lower-class people; hence, they feel less pressure to try illegal activities (even if they know them).

Behavior that has been learned and maintained can be eliminated in two major ways. One procedure is *punishment*, where an activity is followed by aversive consequences. As a result, the activity is less likely to occur later on, and after several repetitions it will disappear. However, the behavior is likely to reappear when the threat of punishment diminishes. A more efficient way of eliminating behavior is through *extinction*. In this procedure, an activity is no longer rewarded, but there are no aversive consequences either. The length of time required for successful extinction depends on the training regimen that encouraged the behavior in the first place. If reinforcers were previously provided on a frequent and consistent basis (i.e., each time the target behavior was performed), a relatively short period of time of not providing the reinforcer will lead to extinction. In contrast, if the schedule of reinforcers was intermittent (i.e., irregular, as in after five successful performances now and after twelve successful performances other times), then a longer period of time without reinforcers would have to elapse before extinction was achieved.

Ethnological research into gangs that deal in drugs suggests that some members may drift into legitimate activities as they get older because the rewards assumed to be associated with street-level dealing are simply not there (Sullivan 1989). According to Padilla (1992), these gang members become disillusioned and shift their aspirations to finding a legitimate job.

Punishment is least effective when it is delayed. The threat, "Wait until your father gets home!" has little power to change future behavior among young children, and prisons have similarly weak effects. On the one hand, time dissolves the linkage between the disapproved act and the eventual aversive consequence, in part because so many other events intervene. On the other hand, an immediate aversive consequence that follows an initial behavior, or even attempt, is more likely to eliminate future attempts. Moderate punishment given consistently and in an otherwise supportive environment, will have the most enduring effects, especially when people learn alternative behaviors that are more effective in producing positive events. When we examine our society in the light of these learning principles, the implications for criminal activities are clear.

Social Learning

Through differential reinforcement (or trial and error) we can learn simple activities easily and well. But what about complex activities that are chained together, such as driving a car? Numerous activities, especially in complex, urban-industrial societies, are likely to involve errors that can be deadly. As the psychologist Albert Bandura has pointed out, if people learned how to drive by means of differential reinforcement alone, most of us would not live to get a license.

Social learning principles, elucidated primarily by Bandura (1969, 1986) build upon three major aspects of human beings: (1) people observe what others are doing; (2) people have a tremendous capacity to remember; and (3) people can anticipate and assess future events. These three aspects are combined in the process of modeling, the crucial component of learning new behaviors. These aspects are also involved in maintaining behavior: we select activities on the basis of our evaluation of the consequences we anticipate on the basis of our own and other people's experiences. It is this emphasis on cognitive processes that distinguishes the social learning perspective of behavior from the operant conditioning perspective.

According to Bandura (1986), most human activities are learned through direct and indirect modeling. That is, we observe—and remember—what other people are doing in specific situations, and what happens to them afterward. Those consequences, of course, could be positive or negative (in the observer's opinion). Later, when we find ourselves in a similar situation, we try out the observed activity (if the consequences were positive), because we anticipate that the same good things will happen to us. If negative consequences are observed, we will *not* perform that action; thus we learn to avoid certain actions. For example, when children watch aggressive acts against another person (or even a play doll), they become more aggressive, or less, depending on what happens to the aggressor. Modeling can also occur through *instruction* (see Figure 12.2), as when we tell someone: "if you push on this pedal, the car will accelerate." Most potentially lethal consequences of trial-and-error learning (operant conditioning) can be avoided by modeling through instruction, as when we tell a young driver: "if you take this curve too fast, the car will roll over."

Modeling refers to the processes involved in trying out, or avoiding, an observed action, in terms of its anticipated consequences. Whether or not the new behavior is repeated later depends on what actually happens to the observer, not the model. Thus, we can learn a new behavior from a model, but that new behavior will not be maintained if we are not rewarded. We are likely to try the new behavior a couple of times, but if the positive consequences we anticipated (on the basis of observation or instruction) do not occur, we are likely to drop the new behavior. However, the newly learned action will remain in our repertoire.

Modeling can be *direct*, as when we observe what another person does and what happens later, in real life or on TV; modeling is *indirect* when someone tells us about an individual's experiences or gives us instructions, or when we read about somebody's actions in a book or newspaper.

Given the abundant evidence of modeling effects, it is not surprising to learn that dramatic and well-publicized crimes are contagious. This seems true of the assassination of public figures (Berkowitz and Macaulay 1971) and of skyjacking, campus vandalism, and urban guerrilla warfare (Moss 1972).

Figure 12.2   Lessons in life are not all taught; many are learned by observing role models. Photo courtesy of Corbis.

In a series of fascinating studies, D. P. Phillips (1974, 1977, 1978, 1979, 1980a, 1980b, 1982) shows that highly publicized suicides, murders, and fatal accidents stimulate short-term increases in the same and parallel modes of aggression. His findings suggest, again, that some fatalities that seem accidental may be imitative. Thus well-advertised suicides are followed by a short-term increase in single-car, driver-only fatal "accidents," confirming insurance adjusters' long-standing hunch that some portion of such crashes is "autocide."

These are rare events, and the amount of such contagion should not be exaggerated. What the evidence says, however, is that "out there" are some number of persons who are sufficiently disordered, depressed, or sick of their lives that they can be moved into copying the dramatically destructive acts they hear and see in the mass media. Anecdotal evidence of criminal contagion, especially of the contagion of violence, is abundant (Nettler 1982b, chapter 12).

Most of us come into daily contact with hundreds of people, all of them potential models; and if we like to read we get information about thousands of other people's experiences. On what basis do we select models from among the many possibilities? This is clearly an important question, especially in a heterogeneous society, because in the course of a week—not to mention a year—we observe or find out about such a great variety of people and activities.

People tend to select models from those who are most like themselves. Perceived similarity may be actual, as when a young woman selects an older woman as a model for new behaviors; or it may be imagined, as when a poor boy who wishes to improve his lot selects a middle-class man as a model for the activities he deems necessary for upward mobility. Whether or not the selected model is appropriate depends, in part, on the cultural definitions of subsequent activities. A girl who selects a model from a fashion magazine may end up anorexic, and a boy who selects the neighborhood bully as a model may end up a delinquent.

According to Bandura, *self-reinforcement* is probably the most important factor that maintains human behavior. This process is learned in childhood and begins when parents praise us ("What a good girl!") and what we do ("What a good job!"). When this is done frequently enough—an important aspect of a nurturing family setting—children begin to say these things to themselves. Eventually, self-reinforcement comes to be a significant positive consequence that can be overtly verbal ("I wrote a good paper"), or behavioral ("I deserve a beer for finishing this paper"), or simply feeling good about oneself. The process of *self-punishment* is equally significant and involves similar procedures. It is important to note that self-reinforcement is problematic when parents do not pay much attention to their children, or do not praise them enough. When there is little or no self-reinforcement, a person will have to rely on external consequences to learn new or maintain old behaviors. Persons we call "self-starters," and people admired for their "willpower," are essentially individuals whose activities are regulated primarily by reinforcers that they provide for themselves.

In recent years, social psychologists have added another important variable: an individual's self-concept (e.g., Fiske and Taylor 1991: 180–242). When parents react positively to their children and their actions, a positive self-concept is the probable result. Conversely, incessant and erratic criticism, especially when it is directed toward the child ("You are a liar") rather than toward the behavior ("Lying is not a good thing"), is likely to produce a poor or negative self-concept. A person's self-concept is important for behavior, because it affects self-reinforcement. A negative or poor self-concept (e.g., "I'm no good") makes self-reinforcement problematic and often impossible. Social psychologists have also discovered that people defend their self-concept against contrary evidence. In fact, people tend to search for information that supports the self-concept they already have—regardless of whether it is positive or negative. Furthermore, individuals consider such information more important and more reliable—and they remember it better and for a longer time—than contrary evidence. Self-concepts can be changed, but the procedures are complex and require much time.

This research has interesting implications for the study of crime. Some delinquents, for example, have a poor self-concept, as indicated by measures of low self-esteem. Consequently, self-reinforcement is rather difficult and even unlikely, and leads to a greater reliance on external, and usually immediate, reinforcers—which typically come only from the delinquent subculture. When well-meaning outsiders try to appeal to a delinquent by saying "I know you're basically a good person," such words are not likely to be effective.

Constitutions and Environments

Constitution refers to the materials of which we are composed. In psychological studies, the human constitution is considered to be a product of genetic material that has interacted with environments both before birth and since birth. Constitutions affect the impact of environments. What we can learn and how well we learn depend on constitutions. Psychologists measure the varying ways in which different human material meets environments along dimensions called "intelligence," "motivation," "temperament," and "cognitive style," to mention only four of the major attributes by which we distinguish personalities.

We do not respond equally to similar environments, and these differences are apparent even among newborn human beings (Clarke 1975; Freedman 1971, 1974; Post 1962a, 1962b, 1964; Salmon and Blakeslee 1935; Seligman and Hager, 1972; Vandenberg 1966; Williams 1979). Thomas Jefferson's famous statement, inscribed in the American Declaration of Independence, that "all men are created equal" is factually incorrect. We think Jefferson meant that "all persons are hereby *defined* as equal before the law," says Garrett Hardin (1982: 40). Yet as for the facts of our individuality, it is more accurate to say that we are born *dependent and unequal*, rather than "free and equal."

This issue is relevant to criminology as far as one is interested in explaining individual differences in propensity to crime. It is relevant to understanding why not all children in "bad environments" become equally criminal, and it is relevant to understanding how "good families" can produce "bad eggs." The social environment does not operate like a giant cookie cutter stamping us all into the same mold. Human material reacts differentially to environments; it learns *selectively* from the many lessons available, and this includes selecting, from among the many ideas presented, those few that become our *beliefs*.

In the study of careers, criminal and lawful, our powers of prediction work asymmetrically, so that we can more surely state what a person of 50 IQ cannot do than what a person of 150 IQ will do. It is, again, a matter of disabilities fore-closing use of opportunities, while having abilities themselves do not ensure their use (see Chapter 13).

Individual Differences in Learning

It was indicated earlier that people do not respond equally to similar situations, that one person's pain may be another's pleasure, and that what is stress for this person may be a challenge for that one. In short, the effects of conditioning and modeling vary with personality.

In contrast to other theories of crime production, learning theories acknowledge individual differences and recognize that some of us need more training than others. It has long been noted that this is true of "lower" species, but we have been reluctant to admit that it is true of *Homo sapiens*.

Eysenck (1977) emphasizes the introversion-extroversion dimension as affecting the way in which we learn. There are data showing that introverts condition more readily than extroverts. Franks (1956) reports that both the eyeblink and the psychogalvanic reflexes can be conditioned to an auditory stimulus "significantly more easily" for introverts than for extroverts. Furthermore, loss of these conditional responses, their "extinction," is reported to be much greater for extroverts than for introverts. Michael Eysenck's (1976) review of research suggests that differences in the way in which extroverts and introverts learn and remember varies with differences in their states of arousal. Introverts seem "more chronically aroused than extroverts."

It is assumed, then, that extroverts need more training than introverts. They may also require a different style of training. Praise and blame seem to affect them differently (Thompson and Hunicutt 1944). "While praise motivates intro-verted children," Eysenck (1966: 23) writes, "blame motivates extroverted children." Of interest to this point is Kennedy and Willcutt's (1964) report that, while praise *generally improves* the performance of schoolchildren, it *lowers* the performance of "underachievers."

It is a well-established fact that people respond differently to sensations. Styles of perception vary among us and are enduring features of our personalities (Witkin 1965; Witkin et al. 1962, 1974, 1979). These styles have cross-cultural validity (Witkin and Berry 1975) and affect how we appreciate our environments. In a series of clever experiments, Petrie (1967) and others have shown that people can be ranked along a continuum in the way in which they "handle sensation." While some people are fairly accurate in their perceptions, others markedly "reduce" what they perceive, and still others "increase" what they perceive. Petrie had subjects estimate the width of blocks of wood felt with the thumb and forefinger of one hand by running the fingers of the other hand along a tapered block until the subject found a place on the tapered bar that seemed to be the same width as the measuring block. Petrie observed that some people consistently overestimated the width of the measuring block, in some cases by as much as 50%. These persons are *augmenters*. Others consistently underestimated the size of the stimulus, and to as great a degree. They are *reducers*.

Whatever may have caused these differences in the handling of sensation, they affect how we learn. Compared with the augmenter, the reducer needs more stimulation before getting the message. Whether male or female, this type of person is less responsive to pain (Ryan and Foster 1967; Ryan and Kovacic 1966). Among males, the reducer tends to be more athletic (mesomorphic) in body build (Wertheimer 1955) and to prefer contact sports. He has a quicker reaction time and, like the persistent delinquent, estimates moments of time to be longer than they are (Ryan and Foster 1967). Reducers cannot stand isolation, silence, or monotony as well as augmenters can. They need to do things and to have things happen. In the poet Wordsworth's terms, extreme reducers have "a raging thirst for outrageous stimulation."

It is notable that serious juvenile offenders, male and female, disproportionately perceive their worlds as reducers do (Petrie 1967, chap. 5). Petrie believes that, as reducers, such delinquents have a greater immunity to pain, which explains, in part, their inability to sympathize with the pain of others. This might underlie reducers' greater involvement in accidents, their noisiness, and even the preference of both male and female reducers for tattooing themselves, an ornamentation rather painful to acquire and one that is a self-imposed stigma among young offenders and prison populations (Measey 1972; West and Farrington 1977).

Petrie's findings, along with those of the Gluecks, Sheldon, and others, tell us that some people need greater stimulation before they can be trained (Gluecks 1950, 1956; Sheldon 1949). These findings fit the repeated descriptions of serious young offenders as bored with school, conscience-free, and difficult to condition (Franks 1961).

Some evidence shows that introversion-extroversion and perceptual style have constitutional and, probably, genetic roots (Rosenthal 1970; Sontag 1963). Assuming this to be so, the fact that there are personality differences that affect the way people respond to reward and punishment and the fact that the more persistent offenders score differently on these traits do not mean that criminality is inborn. They mean only that, in learning to conduct ourselves, some of us need more lessons than others. This is one way of saying that some people are "brighter" than others.

Intelligence

The word "intelligence" is used to describe individual differences in ability to learn. It is conceived as a constitutional attribute. Again, this does not mean that it is fixed for life, but it is, nevertheless, a relatively stable characteristic of persons (Bloom 1964; Cattell 1979; Jensen 1969, 1971, 1972, 1979). As with every other constitutional feature of personality, ability to learn can be nourished or starved. Within normal ranges of intellectual nourishment, individual differences in intelligence hold quite constant (Brody and Brody 1976; Butcher 1968; Jencks et al. 1972; Vernon 1979; Wohlwill 1980). Moreover, as measured, intelligence is multidimensional. The concept denotes abilities, plural, rather than a singular kind of performance. However, correlations among "mental abilities" are moderate to high (Anastasi 1954; Cattell 1979; Horn and Donaldson 1980; Vernon 1979). What is correlated as "ability to learn" is an amalgam of powers of conceptualization with features of temperament.

The role of intelligence in criminal careers varies, of course, with the kind of career one has in mind. Con artists and embezzlers need, and have, more intelligence than muggers and rapists. We should expect the relationship between intelligence and crime to parallel that between intelligence and the kind of lawful work one does. That is, some crimes, like some jobs, require more intelligence than others. What researchers find, then, depends on where they look, and much of the looking has been at adolescents rather than adults.

Early investigations of the relations between intelligence and criminality suffered from the use of different samples of offenders and noncriminal comparison groups. They were deficient, too, in that they tended to group offenders as though they were all of one type despite the kinds of crime for which they had been convicted or the transient or durable character of their criminal careers. These investigations were also deficient in their manner of measuring intelligence. The range of measured ability was usually constricted, and group tests were frequently used rather than individual tests.

Studies suggest that, within similar environments, intelligence works as one defense against criminality. West and Farrington (1977) found this influence during a 14-year longitudinal study of 411 British boys from a working-class district in London. Kirkegaard-Sorensen and Mednick (1977) report a similar relationship between low IQ and later criminality in a 10-year follow-up of 311 Danish youths. In their longitudinal study in Philadelphia, Wolfgang et al. (1972: 93) also found a relationship between low IQ and chronic, as opposed to one-time, offending.

The so-called textbook crooks who are the largest membership in jails and prisons, and who are convicted of the less skillful crimes such as assault, burglary, petty larceny, rape, robbery, and vandalism, are not, to put it conservatively, gifted with high intelligence. Depending on the sample and the measurement procedure, these "common criminals" exhibit below-average IQs with associated learning disabilities. For example, in Alabama Smykla and Willis (1981) report that two-thirds of the youngsters under the jurisdiction of juvenile court suffer learning disabilities or are mentally retarded. One study, in Texas, found that the average IQ of adult prison inmates is 80—more than one standard deviation below normal. Almost one-fifth of these convicts are illiterate (Beto 1980).

The concept of intelligence in criminology has had its own career. Hirschi and Hindelang have reviewed this history and, for studies of juvenile offenders, they conclude the following:

- The relation between intelligence and delinquency is "at least as strong" as the relationship of either class or race to official delinquency.
- The relation is stronger than the relation of either class or race to self-reported delinquency.
- IQ has an effect on delinquency independent of class and race.
- The effect of intelligence on delinquency "is mediated through a host of school variables" (Hirschi and Hindelang 1977: 571).

Consequences of Training: Inhibition, Guilt, Conscience

An organism trained through some history of classical conditioning, operant conditioning, and modeling is a different organism from an untrained one. What has been learned is not merely stored in some nonphysical space called the "mind." The learning is in the physiology: the trained organism's neurochemical response system has been changed. That is why we commonly say things like, "I know I shouldn't be afraid of the snake. It's harmless, but I can't help myself." In a case like this, involuntary alarms are going off in the "internal environment" of the organism. Such alarms are largely a result of training, and they *literally* affect us in gut and gland and heart (Di Cara 1970; Gaito and Zavala 1964; Miller 1969).

Eysenck and Trasler hold that, in the morally conditioned person, these internal alarms constitute an anxiety triggered by the cues preceding a bad deed and that the anxiety is inhibiting. There is evidence that such inhibition of the forbidden act in the well-trained organism results from a different pattern of conditioning from that which produces guilt. Punishment that is administered early in a response sequence leading to an unwanted act is more likely to produce immunity to temptation; punishment given late in the sequence is more likely to generate "self-punitive" behavior (Aronfreed 1963).

Resistance to temptation is learned by a different process from that which teaches guilt. Bandura and Walters believe that resistance to temptation is learned largely by classical conditioning, while the self-punitive habit (guilt) is learned through operant conditioning (Bandura and Walters 1963: 203). However this may be, the important point is that the person trained to feel guilty need have little resistance to temptation. Both resistance and guilt, however, are acquired by human beings who have been *reared*. These activities do not come "naturally"—that is, without training.

Conscience, measurable either as immunity to temptation or as vulnerability to guilt, is built by means of conditioning and modeling. The result of this training is not merely inhibition, as our examples may have suggested. Another result is the development of new drives. An "honest" person is not merely one who refrains from stealing under opportunity. The honest person also does things in conformity with the acquired code. The story of Abe Lincoln walking many miles to return his customer's forgotten change is a paradigm. Similarly, the moral aversion to cruelty or to sexual license is not "in the genes," as far as we know, yet the person who has been trained in these values will engage in prolonged behavior to defend them.

Training not only changes physiologies; it also builds motivation. Once constructed, the acquired motives operate without memory of their origins. They are autonomous.

In Conclusion: Training Hypotheses

How we are today, then, is a result of several classes of causes. These determinants lie in our neurophysiological constitutions and environments; in how and in what we were taught.

In assessing the career of one person or in explaining the varieties of conduct within a group, behavioral scientists do not have measuring instruments that allow a definitive assignment of relative importance to these three determinants. An impact of each of these sets of causes can be separately detected, but the interaction of these causes cannot be accurately gauged, because the causal web in which they achieve their effects is dense. Each set of determinants has variations within it, and the numerous causes are closely intertwined. These determinants of our lives can be assumed, and they can be observed, but they cannot be accurately weighed.

In considering the first determinant, we acknowledge that there are individual differences in amenability to training, including persistent differences in temperament, tempo, and cognitive capacity. It need not be debated here how much of our different neural "wiring" and chemical construction is genetic, how much is constitutional, and how much has been affected by the environment. The fact of difference in learning ability and ways of becoming conditioned is indisputable. Nevertheless, how malleable we are remains an open question. An inherited constitution is not a fixed one.

The second set of determinants relates to how we were brought up. The quality of training we have received has been studied in terms of at least these dimensions of learning: respondent (classical) conditioning; operant (instrumental) conditioning; and modeling (social learning).

Each of these dimensions is itself a variable, as we have seen. For example, operant conditioning theory holds that a principal determinant of how we are is what has happened when we have acted. What happened when we acted may, in turn, be analyzed as reward and punishment, although these nouns are themselves without clear boundaries. However, the effects of reward and punishment are known to vary with at least their intensity, frequency, consistency, balance, temporality (their placement in time), and setting (which includes who gave the reward or punishment and in what social context).

The third determinant of how we are is what we were taught. The content of the lessons we have learned can be assessed as: rules, preferences, tastes, values; skills (which may range from solitary manual performances to interpersonal abilities); and information and ideas.

In considering this third determinant, we recognize that the same quality of training can impart different lesson content. "Good" training can teach "bad" lessons. It is possible for wicked lessons to be well taught and for good lessons to be poorly taught. If we can learn to be lawful, we can learn to be criminal. If we can learn how to earn money, we can learn how to take it.

Among these three sets of the causes of our careers, sociologists tend to ignore the first, to slight the second, and to emphasize the third. Subcultural, rational, and symbolic interactionist explanations of crime attend to what has been learned. It is only the control variety of sociopsychological explanation that stresses *how* we were trained. Both sets of determinants are important.

Control Theory

Basic Assumptions

What needs to be explained, then, is not so much why we behave badly as how we can be induced to behave well. The sociopsychological accounts that try to answer this question are called *control theories,* which start from the assumption that the higher organisms require training if they are to behave socially. The psychologists Margaret and Harry Harlow say:

> One of the most important functions of social learning in primates—and perhaps in all mammals and many other classes of animals as well—is the development of social

patterns that will *restrain* and check potentially asocial behavior. These positive, learned social patterns must be established *before* negative, unlearned patterns emerge. (1967: 47, emphasis added)

So too with *Homo sapiens*, a creature born only *potentially* human. If the potentiality is to be realized, if the infant is to develop into a recognizable human being, nurturing must take place. Without adequate training, the human animal grows up wild. It behaves violently. It destroys what it has not been trained to appreciate. It does not understand "right and wrong" except as greater and lesser might. Consequently, what offends the conscience of socialized persons cannot offend the conscience of the unsocialized. There is nothing to offend.

To speak of the "originality" of theft and assault is not to deny that these kinds of behavior may also be learned, channeled by a culture, and justified by its philosophy. To say that the feral person expresses violence does not deny that the socialized person may learn it. There *are* patterned urges toward larceny and aggression as well as unlearned sources of such self-interest. The subcultural and structural theories of criminogenesis address the patterning of these antisocial behaviors; the control theories account for their expression in the absence of discipline.

There is general agreement among students of human behavior as to the validity of the basic assumption of control theory: that *social* behavior requires socialization. Ethnological, developmental, and experimental studies repeatedly show that human egoism is reduced, and balanced with altruism, only as the organism is reared by parents or their substitutes and as it identifies with them and the moral codes they represent (Ainesworth 1967; Bowlby 1969; Goldschmidt 1959; Harlow et al. 1966; Spitz 1965).

Like other attempted explanations of crime, control theory is not a theory in the rigorous, scientific sense. It is, rather, a point of view with its own preferred locus of causation. Control theorists share some assumptions that are also shared by the public at large:

1. That the human animal requires nurturing.
2. That differences in nurturing account for variations in attachment to others and commitment to an ordered way of living.
3. That attachment and commitment may be described as *internal controls,* commonly called "conscience" and recognized in guilt, and *external controls,* usually tested by the production of shame.
4. That evidence from experimental studies, longitudinal research, comparative studies, and cross-cultural investigation tells us how attachment and commitment are developed. Conversely, such evidence describes the situations that loosen the moral bond with others and that, therefore, produce crime.

Varieties of Control Theory

Criminologists have advanced these assumptions with a medley of propositions: (1) Reckless (1967) and his associates call their ideas "containment theory"; (2) Hirschi (1969) speaks directly of "control theory," with emphases that differ somewhat from those of containment hypotheses, but that also overlap some of them; (3) psychologists have also contributed to control theory without giving their ideas this title. The British psychologists Eysenck and Trasler, working independently of each other, noted how training interacts with individually different constitutions to affect law abiding conduct (Eysenck 1977; Trasler 1962). These three families of ideas will be described as the following: containment theory; Hirschi's propositions about attachment and commitment; and training hypotheses.

Containment Theory

Containment theory recognizes that not everyone in the same environment catches the same disease. There are differences in immunity. So, too, is the case with criminality. Individuals are differentially immunized against the temptation to be criminal. Reckless and his colleagues conceive of immunity to criminality as a matter of control, of one's being "contained," or restrained, against the excitement of some crime and its conceivably rational benefits. The controls that contain a person are considered to be of two orders: *outer* and *inner*.

Outer Containment, or Social Pressure

One source of restraint consists of social pressures to obey the norms of one's group. In containment theory, attention is to groups whose norms are lawful, for social pressures can apparently also produce conformity to criminal norms.

Pressures to conform to lawful codes are exerted through training in roles, through affiliation with a community and a tradition, and hence through the development of a sense of "identity and belonging." Exercise of these external pressures can be seen in such relatively crime-free groups as the Hutterites of Alberta and Manitoba and the Mennonites of Pennsylvania and Ohio.

Pressures to conform to community expectations are a defense against crime if the religious community remains segregated from the host society. Again, there can be a beneficent "ghetto effect." Outer containment works because there are community standards condemning antisocial conduct, there is training in obedience to those standards, and there is little competition from codes that deny those standards.

Inner Containment, or Self-Control

No community can depend completely on the constant control of individuals through social pressure. All socialization aims implicitly, if not explicitly, at the development of self-control. The agent of such control is commonly called "conscience." In Reckless's schema this inner control is the result of a moral training that produces five indicators of its presence: a healthy self-concept, goal directedness, a realistic level of aspiration, the ability to tolerate frustration, and an identification with lawful norms.

Self-Concept   Reckless and his associates have conducted several studies that show the generally poorer self-concept of young boys who get into serious trouble with the law. Their measure of feeling about oneself is verbal—answers to questions—and their definitions of "good" and "bad" refer to being convention-ally law-abiding. It seems, then, that self-concept as measured here, is much like "respect for the law." Consequently, some criminologists have criticized the use of such an indicator of self-concept as redundant in the explanation of crime and delinquency (Jensen 1973; Tangri and Schwartz 1967).

Not all the containment theorists' items are so contaminated, however, and their verbal measure does discriminate between more and less delinquent young people. Reckless and Dinitz's questions (1967: 516) are a mixture of items con-cerning one's associates and one's present and future difficulty with law and authority such as the following:

- Will you probably go to jail sometime?
- If you found that a friend was leading you into trouble, would you continue to run around with him or her?
- Are grown-ups usually against you?
- Are you a big shot with your pals?
- Have most of your friends been in trouble with the law?
- Do you confide in your father?
- Do your parents punish you?
- Do you think you are quiet—average—active?

The original justification for including items of such varied reference as a measure of one attribute, "self-concept," was the ability of such questions to dis-criminate between boys considered by their teachers to be good and bad. How-ever, such items work outside school as well. At an early age, boys from the same neighborhood and economic background show differences in how they feel about themselves, their families, their fate, and persons in positions of authority. The more delinquent boys are more likely to believe that they will break the law and go to jail and that their friends will too. They are more likely to believe that they will not finish school, that their families are "no good," and that teachers, ministers, judges, and police officers are not worthy of respect (Dinitz et al. 1962; Rothstein 1961).

These differences are interesting in themselves, and some of them are objective. That is, such differences do not depend on our believing what boys say. However, a difficulty with verbal reports as indicators of something "inside" the person that causes conduct is, that we do not know how much independence, if any, the verbal-ization (nominated cause) has from its effect: more and less criminality.

There is evidence that people who talk bad about themselves also admit to more bad acts (Kaplan 1976). People who put themselves down verbally also confess to more delinquency. We do not know whether these are two similar ways of telling the truth or two similar ways of saying the same thing or whether something causal is at work. If something causal is at work, we still do not know in which direction causation runs—from bad acts to bad feelings about oneself or from bad feelings to bad acts. Of course, an additional possibility is the likely one: being good, doing good, feeling good, and saying good things about oneself are a package with a similar set of causes.

In an attempt to clarify Reckless and Dinitz's notion of self-concept, Jensen (1973) "purified" their scale and produced three dimensions of *inner contain-*

ment: feelings of self-esteem, ability to control oneself, and acceptance of conventional morality. These measures, with their narrower focus, were administered to more than 4,000 students in junior and senior high schools in the San Francisco Bay area. Tabulated results from 1,000 African-American and 1,588 white males suggest that, when race, class, family, and peer-group situations are held constant, all three dimensions of feeling toward oneself make a difference. The association is not a strong one, but it is contributory. This is to say that, when one looks at young men from (1) similar socioeconomic conditions, (2) similar family situations, and (3) "similar categories in terms of number of friends picked up by the police," there yet remains an element in "attitude toward oneself" that contributes to immunity or vulnerability to delinquency (Jensen 1973: 470). An exact weight cannot be given this factor, but this variable is a vindicated aspect of the containment thesis.

Goal-Directedness   An element of inner containment, according to Reckless, is orientation to goals. It is claimed that people who commit themselves to long-range, legitimate goals are thereby insulated against criminality. Critics see circularity here, since a commitment to a legitimate career is, by definition, a defense against crime and therefore part of what theories of criminogenesis seek to explain. However, Reckless and his colleagues use signs of such commitment as *indicators* of self-control rather than as the causes of it.

Realistic Objectives   A related sign of effective inner control is the "realism" of a person's goals. Reckless and his colleagues judge some goals of young people to be extravagant. Such unrealistic aspiration, such striving beyond one's means, indicates to Reckless the possibility of a "collapse" of inner containment.

Tolerance of Frustration   Living is frustrating. We call a grown person who has not yet adapted to this fact a "baby." An indicator of the self-control expected of adults is tolerance of frustration, the ability to avoid the extremes of rage and despair when we do not get what we want when we want it. Some varieties of adult offenders and the more committed juvenile delinquents exhibit *less* tolerance of frustration ("blocking") than their more lawful counterparts.

Being tolerant of frustration is, of course, related to having realistic goals and to *being oriented toward a future*. A person whose goals are out of reach is bound to be frustrated, and one who is easily frustrated is not apt to pursue long-range objectives. Conversely, when one has a dedication to some distant and achievable goal, present obstacles are less frustrating ("feelings") than they are to the person who lives for nothing but the present.

In support of Reckless's hypothesis on this point, there is evidence that urban delinquents are more hedonistic, impulsive, and impatient than nondelinquents. Time seems longer to them. That is, when youngsters are asked to "guess a minute"—to tell when a minute has passed—the delinquent guesses sooner. This impatience is compounded because the persistent delinquent has a less rich fantasy life. It is recognized that fantasy is one of our mechanisms (an "inner resource") for filling up time. Being impatient and being deficient in imaginative self-stimulation mean being easily bored. These attitudes toward time are related, in turn, to less realistic views of the past, present, and future. Differences in temperament and time perspective of this sort have been reported between offenders and their more lawful neighbors, juvenile and adult (Barndt and Johnson 1955; Bixenstine and Buterbaugh 1957; Black and Gregson 1973; Davids et al. 1962; Landau 1976; Mischel 1961; Siegman 1966; Stein et al. 1968).

This sociopsychological evidence fits findings from studies of moral development. Research on the moral judgment of children and on the correlates of their judgments indicates that *concepts of time* and *concepts of morality* develop together. The evidence is abundant (Kohlberg 1964; Kohlberg and Turiel 1971; Seltzer and Beller 1969).

Our attitude toward time is part of our attitude toward ourselves, others, and our situations. Moral judgment develops along with ways in which we estimate time and use it. These attitudes, in turn, are connected to how we act, including how we act when frustrated ("blocking"). The package looks like this: Happy people, productive people, and morally principled people make more long-range commitments, are more punctual and efficient, and overestimate the time needed to do their work (Jones 1976; Seltzer and Beller 1969; Wessman and Ricks 1966). There are good grounds for suggesting, as control theorists do, that tolerance of frustration and time-orientation build immunity against criminal proclivities. This hypothesis fits some assumptions advanced by subcultural theorists (see Chapter 16).

Identification with Lawfulness   A fifth aspect of the self which, according to containment theory, immunizes a person against criminality is attitudinal. It is a set of beliefs in support of the law and its agents. The beliefs acknowledge the legitimacy of the criminal law and identify the actor with lawful standards of conduct. Again, there is abundant evidence that this feature of the self, this attitude toward the law, does distinguish more lawful people from the more serious lawbreakers. The distinction is discernible *before* a criminal career is developed, although, as labeling theory argues, official handling of offenders in response to their crimes may confirm them in their hostility toward the law.

It is no surprise to learn that people who break the law dislike the law. A host of studies reports that convicted offenders have more unfavorable conceptions of the law, the court system, and the police than nonoffenders who live in the same environment. Toro-Calder et al. (1968) found this to be true in Puerto Rico, and similar findings have been reported in Ohio, Ontario, Quebec, Rome, Athens, Pakistan, and South Korea (Cho 1967; Mylonas and Reckless 1963; Toro-Calder et al. 1968).

In Conclusion: Containment Theory

Containment theory, like other explanations of crime, describes some true things. At the same time, it is quite general. It points to a set of interlocking conditions that move people toward or away from criminal careers.

For some critics, the theory is too broad to inform public policy, and its concepts are too vague for explanatory precision. For other critics, this generality is "good enough" to illuminate the causes of crime. Travis Hirschi has attempted to clarify some of the propositions of control theory, and to test them, with cleaner measures of its concepts.

Hirschi on Attachment, Commitment, Involvement, and Belief

The Four Controls

Hirschi (1969) conceives of the "controls" that allow us to live together pacifically as "attachment, commitment, involvement, and belief." According to Hirschi, these are separable, but interrelated, strands tying us to one another and defining our sense of obligation and duty.

Attachment refers to a person's sensitivity to the opinion of others. It is measured as a feeling of obligation to others and of consideration of one's relations with others as guides to conduct. The person who lacks such attachment is called psychiatric names like "psychopath." The psychopath appears sane and can mouth a morality for which there is no feeling. The psychopath, we say, lacks conscience—which, in Hirschi's terms, is the same as saying that he or she lacks empathy, the ability to identify with the experience of another person.

Commitment is expressed in the investment of time and energy in a chosen way of living. The commitment may be, of course, to essentially lawful careers, and we judge the strength of our ties, one to the other, through signs of this differential investment. Commitment, for Hirschi (1969: 20), "is the rational component in conformity." It refers to how one has decided to live as signified by the use of time and the direction of energy.

Involvement is a consequence of commitment. If one chooses a patterned existence, some lines of action are opened, while others are closed. Every distinctive mode of living exposes us to different possibilities. For example, being committed to the life of a scholar involves one in a routine that reduces the opportunity to sample the full range of experience. We cannot do everything. Involvement describes the constriction of our actions demanded by a chosen way of living. The relevance to crime production is that involvement in many lawful activities reduces exposure to many illegal opportunities. Conversely, the lack of commitment to a conventional life and the lack of involvement in conventional activities unavoidably provide an opportunity for accepting the costs and benefits of rational or expressive crime.

Belief is Hirschi's term for acceptance of the "moral validity" of conventional rules. In opposition to views of the left, the control theorist "assumes the existence of a common value system within the society . . . whose norms are being violated" (1969: 23). What varies, then, between more and less lawful people is the degree to which they agree with the rightness of legal rules. This element in Hirschi's hypothesis is measured as an idea and is similar to the ordinary conception of "respect for the law.

Findings

Hirschi tested these four elements by using a self-report measure of juvenile delinquency with a sample of California youths. His data are largely verbal—

responses to a questionnaire—and they support the assumptions of control theory. Others have also tested elements with data from different sources.

1. Hirschi (1969: 23) found that attachment to parents is strongly associated with lawful conduct among youths, and this relationship holds regardless of social class. Rankin and Kern (1994) find that children who are strongly attached to both parents have a lower probability of self-reported delinquency than children who are strongly attached to only one parent.

2. According to Hirschi, attachment to school—liking schoolwork and being concerned about the opinions of one's teachers—is also associated with resistance to delinquency. Academic ability and school performance are among the important predictors of lawful behavior, and these factors operate quite apart from any reported "social disability" such as being shy, less than popular, or unathletic (1969: 23). Zingraff et al. (1994) find that good school performance is associated with substantially reduced delinquent involvement for young people who are neglected or physically abused.

3. Attachment to peers is also important says Hirschi, but not in the direct way commonly assumed. Birds of a feather do flock together, but the birds that so congregate acquired their feathers *before* they flocked. Boys who have been otherwise immunized against delinquency are rarely attracted to juvenile gangs. Young men choose friends who have similar interests, and the corrupting influence of the adventurous gang is limited to boys with little attachment to a conventional career (1969: 23). The quality of parenting is a good predictor of affiliation with deviant peers for adolescents who experience a late onset of delinquency. Quality of parenting is also a good predictor where most of the delinquency is early, but here it predicts oppositional/deviant behavior and this behavior predicted affiliation with deviant peers. Multiple studies have found that it is the behavior of peers rather than their attitudes that is criminogenic (Agnew 1993; Warr and Stratford 1991).

4. Hirschi (1969: 23) found that involvement in conventional activities, such as doing one's homework, reduces involvement in self-reported delinquency. Conversely, the more time one spends "cruising" or "hanging around with friends," the more likely delinquent activity is.

5. Hirschi measured "belief" by asking questions about respect for the police, the rightness of evading the law, the innocence of delinquents, and the harmlessness of criminality. These and similar questions point in the direction predicted by control theory. That is, more delinquent boys, compared with less delinquent boys, agree that

> "Most criminals shouldn't really be blamed for the things they have done."
> "I can't seem to stay out of trouble no matter how hard I try."
> "Most things that people call 'delinquency' don't really hurt anyone."
> "Policemen [do not] try to give all kids an even break."
> "It is alright [sic] to get around the law if you can get away with it."
> (Hirschi 1969: 203–211)

Gottfredson and Hirschi on Self-Control

Gottfredson and Hirschi (1990) propose what they call "a general theory of crime." They contend that crime results primarily from inadequate self-control, although they allow that environmental contingencies may have some role to play. The key, however, is the concept of self-control, which appears similar to Reckless' notion of "inner containment." They argue that the propensity to commit criminal acts is "reasonably stable" and is not very much affected by "changes in the social location of individuals" or by "changes in their knowledge of the operation of the sanction systems" (Gottfredson and Hirschi 1990: 87). Their point is that self-control is developed, or not, in childhood and remains fairly stable throughout life. The source of low self-control is seen to be inadequate (incomplete or ineffective) socialization by parents.

Gottfredson and Hirschi allow that there may be circumstances that keep a person with low self-control, and therefore a propensity to commit crime, from doing so. Nevertheless, they argue that such circumstances are far less important than having developed the propensity that has a higher likelihood of manifesting itself in a wide range of nonviolating activities, including the search for excitement and the use of drugs as well as crime. Within this framework, therefore, opportunity simply makes more likely the actual expression of a propensity, which is reasonably stable and criminogenic—that is, self-control.

Box 12.1   Gottfredson and Hirschi on Crime Control

According to Gottfredson and Hirschi, many theories give the burden of crime control to the state. . . . "We offer an alternative view, a view in which the state is neither the cause nor the solution to crime. In our view, the origins of criminality of low self-control are to be found in the first six or eight years of life, during which time the child remains under the control and supervision of the family or a familial institution. Apart from the limited benefits that can be achieved by making specific criminal acts more difficult, policies directed toward enhancement of the ability of familial institutions to socialize children are the only realistic long-term state policies with potential for substantial crime reduction." (1990: 272–273)

Application of Control Theory: Child Rearing and the Correlates of Criminality

Training and Social Location of Crime

There is a neat fit between the control thesis and the social location of serious crime. This is particularly so as one adds to Eysenck and Trasler's emphasis on classical conditioning the possibilities of other modes of learning such as operant conditioning and modeling.

Both ethnic and class correlates of the graver offenses fit with what is known about the training routines, the content of the socializing lessons, and the nature of the models available for children reared in different status and ethnic situations. Sociopsychological attention to individual differences in training susceptibility is a way of allowing for variations in the effects of these social climates on individual behavior. At the same time, sociopsychological attention to patterns of child rearing brings this schema into harmony with subcultural explanations of criminality. Both modes of explanation have emphasized the impact of human nurturing on human development.

Modeling Deficiency and Delinquency

The control hypothesis holds that serious juvenile offenders, and continuing criminals, have been defectively reared. In particular, it is claimed that such persons have lacked adequate models of lawful conduct. This fact can be documented in two ways. One procedure is to observe children from different socializing environments and to record how they grow up. Another procedure is to compare the childhood backgrounds of serious offenders with those of less criminal people from an otherwise comparable environment. The two methods of study yield similar conclusions.

Developmental Studies

Observations of children in orphanages, hospitals, foster homes, and intact families uniformly indicate that there is some physical, mental, and social damage to the child who lacks nurturing (Spitz 1946). The damage to physical functioning is least serious; that to cognitive functioning is most serious; and that to social conduct is midway between these extremities (Bowlby 1952). Children who have been reared in institutions or concentration camps tend to be more aggressive and to have difficulties in interpersonal relations, including difficulty in behaving honestly (Freud and Dann 1951; Goldfarb 1943c; Trasler 1962).

Longitudinal research confirms these findings. Goldfarb (1943a, 1943b, 1943c, 1944a, 1944b, 1945a, 1945b) reports a series of studies of adolescents who had spent the first three years of their lives in institutions. Beyond the learning deficits frequently associated with such rearing, Goldfarb found the institutionalized children to have trouble controlling their impulses. Either they were overcontrolled, rigid, and submissive, or they were aggressive. Furthermore, the children who were aggressive did not exhibit normal anxiety about, or guilty reactions to, their aggressiveness.

An earlier follow-up study by Theis (1924) yields similar results. Theis studied more than 200 adults who had been orphaned in infancy and compared the careers of those who had been institutionalized for at least five years with those who had lived in foster homes. The proportion of institutionalized children with records of persistent criminality was three times that of the foster children, and there were corresponding, but smaller, differences in their records of less serious misconduct.

Warr and Stratford (1991) analyzed data from a five-year panel study of the National Youth Survey. It comprises a national probability sample of 1,726 persons between the ages of 11 and 17 years (see Elliot and Ageton 1980). The study contains items that deal with both the attitudes and behavior of peers. They found that behavior of peers plays a greater role than the attitudes of those peers and they conclude that delinquency is "more likely to stem from . . . social learning mechanisms, such as imitation or vicarious reinforcement . . ." (Warr and Stratford 1991: 851). In brief, their results tend to support one of the major tenets of control theory.

Rohrer, Edmonson, and a team of behavioral scientists (1960) observed African Americans in the southern United States 20 years after these same persons had been described by other investigators (Davis and Dollard 1941). Rohrer and

Edmonson's research is a clinically oriented study concerned with the development of individual careers. Although this longitudinal research did not use a control group for comparison, it confirmed the image of the male gang-running criminal as a person who denies the legitimacy of religion, schools, law, and morals, and who considers occupational striving worthless. The descriptions of each career are well drawn and illustrate a central theme of control theory, namely, the harmful impact of fatherless households on the emotional development of boys. In the authors' words:

> Our data reaffirm, often dramatically, the great importance of significant adults to the shaping of the individual's personality. The presence or absence of such figures and the nature of the model they present are intimately linked to the individual's development of ego ideals: vague or vivid images of what he would like to become. (Rohrer and Edmonson 1960: 299–300)

A similar conclusion was reached by Bacon et al., (1963) who brought together ethnographic data from 48 societies and examined them for correlates of crime. These societies, most of them preliterate, were distributed across Africa, Asia, Oceania, and North and South America. They represent a range of family settings, child-rearing practices, degrees of social stratification, and levels of political integration.

Bacon et al. (1963: 294) concluded that "the frequency of both Theft and Personal Crime increases as the opportunity for contact with the father decreases." Crimes against the person, in particular, were significantly associated with a mother-child household in which there was "inadequate opportunity in early life for identification with the father," in which the sleeping arrangements for the mother and child fostered "a strong dependent relationship between the child and the mother," and in which the training for independence was abrupt and punishing (1963: 298).

The authors of this study incline toward a psychoanalytic interpretation of their findings. In the present context, however, this cross-cultural analysis corroborates the repeatedly reported relationship between hostility and dishonesty in males and the lack of a loving and lawful father figure with whom to identify.

Comparative Studies

Comparing the early training of criminals and more lawful persons is made difficult by the obstacles to direct observation of familial practices. The usual research procedure involves asking parents how they treated their children and asking parents, peers, and teachers how the children behave. Investigators have a problem in coding these reports; in addition, defects of memory, inaccuracies in parents' observation of themselves and their children, and defensiveness of parents in responding to interviewers have guaranteed that there can be only a slight relation between how parents *say* they trained their children and what actually went on (Yarrow et al. 1968).

Furthermore, training is subtle. It is composed of many lessons taught and learned of which both trainer and learner may be unaware. Parents, even highly educated ones, are not necessarily accurate recorders of their own behavior toward their children.

Sociologists have tried to compensate for these obstacles to observation by analyzing the effects of broad categories of childhood environment, such as illegitimacy and broken homes. In addition, self-report instruments have been used to compare ratings of family climates given by young offenders, nonoffenders, and their parents.

Births Outside Marriage and Criminality

One measure of the quality of models available to youngsters is the presence or absence of a parent. *Ratios* of marital to nonmarital births have been used as one such index with which to correlate crime rates: *proportions* of all births that are outside of marriage is a second, and different, measure; and the *rate* at which women of selected ages and races reproduce without marriage is a third such index. (On proportions, ratios, and rates, refer to Chapter 3.)

Nonmarital births, or illegitimacy as it was once called, as with the "broken home," is a crude category. It is crude because the social meaning of illegitimacy varies with the culture. There are societies in which being born out of wedlock carries less stigma and may betoken less lack of fathering than it has in Western industrialized states (Goode 1960). However, even where "consensual unions" are common, as in some South American and Caribbean countries, they do not carry the commitment to parenthood of formal marriage (Stycos and Back 1964). Judith Blake's survey in Jamaica revealed that half of the unmarried women she studied reported three or more "unions" by an average age of 31 years, while 35% of her male subjects said they had had 15 or more such alliances (1961). Hartley's survey of cohabitation in Jamaica concludes:

> Men seem generally unwilling to take responsibility for the physical and financial support of their own offspring by miscellaneous alliances and are even more reluctant to care for the children of the wife or concubine from previous unions. So the child is shuttled from person to person and has to fend for himself. (1980: 369)

A similar situation is apparent in Western countries, many of which have experienced an increase in both the numbers and the ratios of nonmarital births since World War II. In the United States and much of western Europe, rates of childbearing outside formal marriage increased two to three times during the period 1970–1989 (Belle and McQuillan 1994). In 1970, approximately 11% of all births occurred to unmarried women; by 1989, 27% of all births took place outside of marriage. By 1996, 30% of births nationwide are out of wedlock and in some urban areas the rate is 60% (*Cincinnati Inquirer* 1997). Similar trends occurred in Canada, where the percentage of births outside marriage increased from 10% to 23%; in the United Kingdom where the increase was from 8% to 26% and in France where the increase was from 7% to 28%.

Attributing such increases to urbanization and industrialization has been popular; but the impact of cultural factors is apparent in the contrary experience of Japan, where the ratio of marital to nonmarital births *declined* as the country became industrialized and urbanized. The rate there is now less than 1%.

Undoubtedly, many nonmarital births are taking place in relatively stable and long-term common-law marital arrangements (Bumpass, Sweet, and Cherlin 1991; Prinz 1995); many, however, are not. Sonenstein, for example, reports that paternity was identified in less that a third of American babies born to unmarried women in 1989. Perhaps an even more disconcerting trend is the increase in teenage pregnancy in the United States. When compared to other industrialized nations, America has inordinately high rates of pregnancy among those in their early teens. Among U.S. teens aged 15–19, the pregnancy rate is more than twice that of Canada, France, and Great Britain, and over seven times as high as that of the Netherlands (Alan Guttmacher Institute 1993).

In much of Europe and North America, birth outside of marriage is but one facet of a complex of disadvantages. In these settings, being born outside of marriage means being functionally fatherless. Lack of a father shows itself in deficits in almost every measurable aspect to socially important behavior. Functionally fatherless children, "are more likely to die at birth or in the first year, to do poorly in school, to become juvenile delinquents, and to land eventually in unskilled jobs" (Goode 1966: 491).

Research by Frank Furstenburg confirms the devastating effects of being a child of a young mother (Furstenburg et al. 1992). Furstenburg conducted a 20-year follow-up study of a sample of teenage mothers in Baltimore where he compared the outcomes of children born to mothers aged 18–21 with those born to mothers under the age of 17. Children of young mothers were significantly more likely to drop out or be expelled from school; more likely to be on welfare; over seven times as likely to become pregnant under the age of 17; and about four times as likely to have a criminal record.

This description also appears in an extensive survey of "bastardy and its comparative history" over the past four centuries in Britain, France, Germany, Sweden, North America, Jamaica, and Japan (Laslett et al. 1980). Laslett et al. report that

1. American ratios of illegitimate to legitimate births remained relatively stable between colonial times and 1940.
2. Illegitimate reproduction occurs disproportionately among persons "of low social status."
3. Regional differences persist, so that one may speak of a "bastardy-prone sub-society" and "bastard-producing women" who pass on their values and practices to their children.

For individual children, the damage of "fatherlessness" may be lessened by early adoption and the compensatory training given by substitutes for the biological parents. However, control theory receives confirmation from the fact that the social location of high rates of illegitimacy is identical with the class and ethnic locations that produce high rates of serious crimes. Similar indirect "proof" of the control hypothesis has been attempted, with modest results, from the many studies of broken homes and their behavioral effects.

Households without Fathers

According to control theory, crime—particularly violent crime—may be expected to remain high in the United States in parallel with recent increases in the proportions of children that are being reared without fathers. Part of this increase is a consequence of the increase in childbearing outside of marriage, but part of the increase is a consequence of divorce and separation.

It is estimated that "about half of the children in one-parent households formed by marital disruption will spend five years in this type of family before their mother remarries or they turn 18" (Cherlin 1992: 14).

Single-parent households arise as a consequence of divorce as well as out-of-marriage births. Thus, the question may be posed as to how well children fare when their parents separate through divorce. At first glance, it would appear that paternal involvement is greater among those men who marry their child's mother as opposed to those who do not. In a study of American women, Nord and Sill (1996: 34) report that, "40.6 percent of never married mothers and 46.7 percent of mothers who are currently in their first marriage report that the non-resident father did not visit their children at all in the previous year, compared to 35 percent of remarried mothers and 26.7 percent of currently divorced mothers."

Unfortunately, for many children, divorce results in a situation not very dissimilar to that found among unmarried mothers. In their study of the participation of non-custodial parents in their children's lives, Nord and Zill report that among divorces where there is a visitation agreement, over 26% of the noncustodial parents had no contact with their children in the previous year, and in instances where there is *no* custodial agreement, over 45% of the noncustodial parents had no contact with their children in the previous year. Even where non-custodial parent-child contact did take place, the total amount of contact is often minimal.

> Among those reporting that some contact took place, parents with sole custody with no visitation report less contact than those with sole custody with visitation or with joint custody arrangements. The mean days of contact reported by parents with sole custody arrangements with no visitation provisions was 27.8 days compared to 32.4 days for those with sole custody with visitation provision, and 47.3 days for those with joint custody arrangements. The median days of contact tell a similar story: one day of contact for those with sole custody and no visitation, 12 days for those with sole custody with visitation provisions, and 30 days for those with joint custody.
> (Nord and Zill 1996: 32)

Broken Homes and Youthful Offenders

The trouble with attempting to test control hypotheses, or any other explanations of criminality, by looking at "broken homes" is that the concept of the broken home is not a clear one. As for effects on child rearing, there may be as many styles of "broken homes" as there are of "intact" ones. There is, in fact, evidence that some ruptured families may be healthier nurturing environments than some whole ones (Burchinal 1964; Goode 1956; Nye 1957). Much depends on how the home was broken, when in the child's life the break occurred, and what kind of modeling relationship succeeded the disruption of the household. A household broken by divorce after years of wrangling provides a different psychic climate from one disrupted by sudden death. A family that changes early in an infant's life has a different impact from one broken during a child's middle years. There are differences in effect, too, depending on the sex, and the age of the child and on the sex of the parent with whom the child remains. For example, Toby (1957) presents data showing that the "broken home" has a different effect on girls and preadolescent boys from that which it has on older boys. The impact is greater (worse) for girls and for younger boys.

Despite these weaknesses in the notion of the "broken home" as a measure of a child's nurturing, research on delinquency has produced a mass of data on the comparative incidence of broken families among more and less lawful young people (see, for example, Wells and Rankin 1991).

An early study by Shaw and McKay (1931) compared 1,675 African-American and white delinquent males aged 10–17 years in Cook County, Illinois, with a sample of 7,278 less delinquent schoolboys of similar age. Shaw and McKay report that 42.5% of their offenders came from broken homes, as compared with 36.1% of the nonoffenders, and this small spread is interpreted as insignificant.

Others have quarreled with this finding and, as might be expected, have challenged the kinds of controls employed, the lack of females in the sample, the lumping together of all styles of disrupted households as "broken" ones, and even the interpretation of the statistical spread.

Maller (1932), for example, argued that, given the shape of the distributions of delinquency among broken and intact families, a difference of 6.4% between them is statistically significant. Hodgkiss (1933) conducted a replication of Shaw and McKay's investigation in Cook County using female subjects. Here a wide discrepancy was found between delinquents and lesser offenders in the experience of broken homes. Of the delinquent girls, 67% came from broken homes, as compared with just less than 45% of the nondelinquent sample.

Investigations in England and the United States tend toward findings that juvenile offenders are the products of broken homes $1\frac{1}{2}$ times to 2 times more frequently than nonoffenders. An illustrative result derives from the Gluecks' research, which compared the familial experiences of 500 delinquent boys with a matched control group of 500 nondelinquents (Glueck and Glueck 1956). More than 60% of the delinquents were from broken homes, as compared with 32.4% of the nondelinquents. Merrill (1947) found comparable differences in a study of 300 consecutive arraignments in juvenile courts in the United States in which the offenders were matched by age, sex, and ethnicity with a sample of nondelinquents. Some 50% of these young offenders were from disrupted families, as compared with 26.7% of the control group.

Monahan (1957) studied all delinquency charges brought over a six-year period in Philadelphia. He analyzed the family status of more than 44,000 cases, holding constant the sex and race of the offenders. His findings are in essential agreement with those of Merrill and the Gluecks, with the additional observation that the broken home had a more harmful effect on the girls and the African Americans in his sample than on the boys and the whites. The proportions of delinquent girls and African Americans from broken homes exceeded those found for delinquent boys and whites. In addition, Monahan reports that repetitive offenders were disproportionately from broken homes and that the highest recidivism rate was among children who had been reared in institutions.

A replication of this type of research yields parallel conclusions. Chilton and Markle (1972) compared the family situations of 5,376 delinquent children in Florida with the family situations of children in the general United States population. As expected, they observed that children from disrupted families were more likely to be charged with delinquency and that this association was closer for the more serious offenses.

Studies conducted in England produce comparable findings. Burt's (1925) early research contrasted domestic experience of young delinquents and nondelinquents, holding constant their cultural background, social class, age, place of residence, and school attendance. Burt reports that 61.3% of the delinquents came from broken homes, as compared with 25.1% of the nondelinquents.

These are retrospective studies. They look backward from the age of offense to discover whether the young person's family was disrupted. As noted, these studies seldom control for when the family was broken, for *how much* decay the family experienced before its rupture, or for the *quality of control* exercised after the break. Longitudinal studies that begin *before* the domestic breach or *before* the commission of a crime are rare. In one such investigation, however, Gregory (1965) followed the careers of boys who had lost parents during childhood and found that the children of divorced and separated parents were disproportionately represented among delinquents. Boys who had lost parents through death were slightly more likely to be involved in delinquencies than boys from intact families, but their rates of offense did not approach those of boys from homes disrupted by divorce or separation.

In Conclusion: Developmental and Comparative Studies

Wells and Rankin (1991) analyzed the results of 50 studies of the relationship between families (broken homes) and delinquency. They found that most of the variation in findings across studies is attributable to methodological differences in the studies, but they also produced some substantive findings. These findings are the following (1991: 87–88).

1. No clear historical shift is apparent such that incomplete families have less impact now than in earlier decades (when the family was ostensibly more important). Rather, any impact of family structure on juvenile delinquency appears stable.
2. The effect of intact versus "broken" families is a consistent and real pattern of association . . . this means that the prevalence of delinquency in broken homes is 10–15% higher than in intact homes.
3. The correlation between broken homes and juvenile delinquency is stronger for minor forms of juvenile misconduct . . . and weakest for serious forms of criminal behavior.
4. The type of family break does seem to affect juvenile delinquency. The association with delinquency is slightly (albeit not significantly) stronger for families broken by divorce or separation than by death of a parent.
5. There are no consistent or appreciable differences in the impact of broken homes between girls and boys or between African-American youths and white youths.
6. There is little consistent evidence to show that the impact of marital separation varies with that age of the child.
7. There is no consistent evidence of the often cited negative impact of stepparents on juvenile delinquency. Apparently, stepparents do not make a problematic family situation worse, at least in terms of controlling the children.

It must be cautioned, however, that research on the association of "broken homes" with criminality provides a weak test of the control hypothesis. The test is poor for all the reasons mentioned, reasons that can themselves be summarized by saying that a "broken home" is not the only kind of broken family. Families can be divided, and are divided, while they continue to share a legal status and domicile. For a measure of the possible extent of such riven households among prominent Americans, read the report by Cuber and Harroff (1966).

It is the *quality of training* and the *content of the lessons* taught that are the important determinants of lawful behavior, according to control theory. Neither of these dimensions of nurturing is well described by statistics on divorce, and both are only suggested by statistics on desertion and illegitimacy.

Meanwhile, times change. Divorce is now the expectation of about one-fourth of all people who marry in Canada and the United States, and remarriage is the expectation of more than 20% of all those who marry for a first time. With these and other changes in the structure of the family, family ties may probably loosen so that "intact" households in various social settings may come to have no more modeling effect for the youngsters involved than some kinds of single-parent households.

These changes may be expected, too, with changes in socioeconomic stratification, with a blurring of differences in child-rearing practices among families of high and low occupational status, with a decline of neighborhoods and neighborhood schools, and with the intrusion of other models of behavior for youngsters as replacements for defaulting parents.

BURTON ET AL. ON CONTROL THEORY
Burton et al. describe as their "most noteworthy" finding support for control theory:
". . . the measure of low self-control was the most powerful predictor of criminal involvement. This finding is consistent with the emerging literature, which suggests that low self-control increases criminal, delinquent, and 'imprudent', behaviors. . . ." (1994: 232)

Advantages of Control Theory

Both developmental and comparative studies yield the same description of what makes us the way we are. If we grow up "naturally," without cultivation, like weeds, we grow up like weeds—rank. If our nurturing is defective—unappreciative, inconsistent, lax, harsh, and careless—we grow up hostile, and the hostility seems as much turned inward as turned outward. The nurturing environments that produce this denigration of self and others are the same ones that breed criminality.

Control theories have an advantage over the more strictly sociological explanations of crime causation in that they allow for individual differences in reaction to an environment. It is not assumed that "culture" or "class" or "the family" is a huge stamping mill producing stereotyped images on the human material. The material varies. Some is tough alloy; some is more malleable. Furthermore, the production process itself varies. Being taught and being trained are not just one kind of procedure. The *Oxford English Dictionary* tells us that education is "the process of 'bringing up' [young people]." The "bringing up" is not accomplished on only one escalator. We have been brought up, in some part, by parents or by substitutes for parents. We have been trained, too, by everything that happened when we acted. This means that we have learned from friends and strangers, from lovers and enemies, and even from the jumbled lessons available in books and paintings, in newspapers, and on film. This means, further, that we are still learning, that there are lessons in adulthood as there are in childhood, and that, therefore, even "well-brought-up" children may be moved by their later lessons into rational or impetuous crime.

For a theory of criminogenesis, giving exact weights to the many determinants of our destinies is not necessary. It is particularly unnecessary if we are interested in the sociological questions. To answer these questions, it is enough to know the kinds of causes that make a difference so that the consequences of broad changes in any of them may be estimated.

The subcultural and the control orientation point to the same requirements if we are to reduce the injuries we inflict on one another. One requirement is that young people be nurtured so that they grow up as adults whose lives are explicable and purposeful. Another requirement is that, as adults, we live in some pattern of accord with others, an accord that allows us individuality bounded by the legally defined rights of those with whom we live and limited by the reasonably probable possibilities open to each of us.

The theme of this theory is that human beings may be domestic animals, but they need domestication. Human creatures may be civic organisms, but they need civilization, and this means steeping in a culture.

Disadvantages of Control Theory

The trouble with this theme is that it gives no political handle for planned change. Explanations, particularly correct ones, need not promise cures. Knowing the causes of earthquakes does not prevent them, although such knowledge may promote better defense against them.

A difficulty with control theory is that it gives politicians and others who would "solve social problems" no lever with which to manipulate change according to plan. For people who want promising answers, control theory is unsatisfactory.

No one has polled social scientists on this matter, but it seems likely that the control orientation, despite its empirical grounding, is less popular among sociologists than its more fact-free explanatory competitors. By contrast, it has been noted that the public at large accepts the propositions of control theory and places the "blame" for crime where control hypotheses do—in the nurturing process.

Accurate explanations are not adequate for those who demand more of an explanation than that it describe things truthfully. What is often demanded, beyond truth, is utility—that the explanation show us what to do to get us what we want.

Those who seek such "illumination" will receive it, but because an explanatory promise is less than factual, it will get its believers less than what was promised. The truth sometimes tells us more clearly what we can*not* have and what will *not* work. The truth about the human condition also tells us that everything of value has its cost. Some of the "trade-offs" that constitute the price of reducing crime are described in the Epilogue.

We turn now from explanations that are psychosociological to explanations that are sociological in character. The first set of these, Chapters 13 through 16, identifies the social structure as the locus of causation of crime.

13. Rational Crime

Rationality

Many of the wrongs we do each other serve our purposes. They get us what we want. There are other causes of the damage we produce, of course—accidents and impulses, for example. Yet, some ill-defined, but important amount of damage is intentional. It is decided upon; it is chosen in satisfaction of some objective. This is true of both offenses against persons and offenses against property. When a criminal act achieves one's purpose economically, it is rational.

Being Rational Versus Being Moral

At first blush, it sounds paradoxical to call crime "rational." "Rational" is a good word with favorable connotations. Most of us claim to be rational, and we generally consider it better to be rational than to be nonrational or irrational.

Nevertheless, being rational is not the same as being good or doing good. One can be rational without being moral, and moral without being rational, and the terms should be disentangled. Philosophers distinguish among a "rational belief," a "rational person," and a "rational act." Our concern is with the last idea. To act *rationally* is to employ one's reason to select the most appropriate means for the attainment of one's goals (Cousineau 1967). All terms in this definition are important. This definition states, first, that a rational act is a purposive act. It is done consciously to obtain an objective. Acts that attain objectives incidentally or accidentally do not count as rational, nor do acts that are purely expressive.

Purely expressive behavior, behavior that is its own end, is not rational in this sense. For example, dancing out of joy is an expressive act. It is fun and it may be deemed "good," but it is something other than instrumental and, hence, different from a rational act. The proof is that when we convert an expressive act into an instrumental one, we destroy its pleasure. Skiing, surfing, or making love in order to experience pleasure is less pleasurable than doing these things in fun, as ends in themselves. Conversely, the attempt to produce the pleasure of an expressive act intentionally—by thinking about it—fails to capture the joy of doing that thing for its own sake.

The distinction between expressive and instrumental acts is artificial, but useful. It is artificial because in "real life" many acts are mixtures of the instrumental and expressive. Thus robbing a bank may be an "intrinsic good"—pleasurable in itself—and at the same time it may be instrumental, a way to get money, as Willie Sutton (1976) (pictured in Figure 13.1) assured us. However, we reserve the notion of a "rational act" for those done to achieve something

Figure 13.1   Willie Sutton in custody (1952). Q: "Why do you rob banks, Willie?" A: "Because that's where the money is." Photo courtesy of Corbis.

other than the pleasure of its activity. This distinction is useful when we come to debate whether people "know what they are doing."

Second, our definition limits the objectives of a rational act to those that are empirical, to those that can be experienced. The ends of rational actions must be ascertainable. Utopian goals whose attainment can never be achieved, such as the creation of heaven on earth, are not rational goals.

Finally, a rational act is one based on a reasoned—that is, informed—choice of the most economical means for the actor. "Economical means" are not only those that are efficient in obtaining a particular objective. They are also those that do not carry a cost in the reduction of other goals that the actor values. This definition of rational action, we note, says nothing about the goodness of the ends toward which persons are using their reason efficiently. Neither does it say anything about the goodness of the means. The idea of moral behavior is quite another matter. It has its own difficulties, which need not concern us here. The present point is simply that many categories of crime, however they may be judged morally, are nonetheless rational.

Implications of Rational Crime

An immediate implication of the conception of some crime as rational is a challenge to the popular psychiatric assumption, readily adopted by many schools of social work, that crime is a symptom of social and personal sickness. In this medical model of criminogenesis, criminals are considered to be sick people, but never rational ones.

"Symptom" is, of course, another emotionalized term that special-pleads. Its use signifies that the behavior called a "symptom" is regarded as an effect that is itself not to be controlled. Calling an activity a "symptom" recommends, and sometimes demands, that something other than the behavior itself is to be treated. In the social studies, "symptom" operates as "a transfer term . . . [It] shifts the burden of blame from the actor to his social setting" (Nettler 1976: 3).

The medical image of crime causation rests on a common belief expressed by a former attorney general of the United States who told us that "healthy, rational people will not injure others. . . . Rehabilitated, an individual will not have the capacity . . . to injure another or to take or destroy property" (Clark 1970: 220). Such a statement is either a tautology or an unsupported hope. Carried to its logical extremity, this therapeutic recommendation leads to such futilities as doing social work among the Mafia.

Utility Theory: Jeremy Bentham

It is perhaps a testament to the value of his ideas that the person who has had the greatest impact on the conventional wisdom on criminal justice is currently one of the lesser recognized names among social philosophers. Jeremy Bentham's (1748–1832) intellectual legacy forms the cornerstone of the deterrence model of criminal justice as well as basis of the "utility" framework of modern economics. We will focus our attention on this utility framework, where humans are assumed to make decisions based on a hedonistic calculus.

Bentham believed, as did many eighteenth-century thinkers, that people are rational creatures who exercise free will. While widely accepted today, this view of humans as autonomous, rational beings constituted a final break with the medieval concept of possession. It was widely held in medieval Europe that human affairs are often influenced and occasionally guided by demons, spirits, and the hand of God. Under such a system of beliefs, people's abilities to make choices are constrained and if their behavior is controlled by outside forces, they cannot be held accountable for their actions. In fact, such a belief system leads us to expend much energy on the purging or exorcism of demons rather than on the determination of human culpability. It is difficult today to appreciate that medieval legacy against which the Reformists of the eighteenth century railed. While demonological beliefs were on the wane, most criminal justice systems of the time still contained a legacy of practices that were often capricious and excessive when viewed from a rationalist perspective.

Bentham's views were much influenced by Cesare Beccaria, who attacked such practices in his monograph *Essays of Crime and Punishment,* published in 1764. While not the originator of the notions, Beccaria impressed Bentham with the ideas of a proportionality between pain and pleasure and the goal of achieving the greatest happiness for the greatest number.

When the assumption is made that people are rational and possess a degree of free will, then the question of how people exercise that free will arises. The exercise of choice is the exercise of will, and the utility theory espoused by Bentham attempts to explain how people make choices.

Box 13.1   Jeremy Bentham

In his day, Bentham had a profound impact on both social philosophy and practical matters of state. As Barnes (1948: 56) notes, "Bentham produced epoch-making contributions to criminal-law reform, prison reform, the reconstruction of the system of poor relief, the establishment of a public health system, the encouragement of public education, the recommendation of general thrift and savings banks, the reform of local government, colonial self-government, and the like. He is said to have carried in his pockets model constitutions for the leading countries of his time."

Bentham's model is simplicity itself. It starts with the fundamental assumptions that people seek pleasure over pain and that all social action has elements of pleasure and pain associated with it. People are induced to act if the pleasure associated with a particular element outweighs the pain; they are deterred if the pain outweighs the pleasure.

The rationality component of Bentham's model is brought to bear on two issues: first, people must be capable of objectively perceiving and weighing the amount of pleasure and pain associated with some behavior; second, they must be capable of making the judgment as to which component outweighs the other (the exercise of what Bentham called the "hedonistic" calculus).

It is no longer popular to use the terms "pain" and "pleasure" when speaking of Bentham's model. Instead, we identify pain factors as "costs" and the pleasure components as "utilities" or benefits. It is possible to present the basic elements of the utility model in a simple diagram. In Figure 13.2 we see a two-dimensional graph where the axes are defined as "utility" and "cost." Line i defines the boundary at which an individual perceives the utility of a given behavior to be equal to cost. This line is referred to as an "indifference curve"—the set of points where there is neither an incentive to act nor to not act. The area to the right of the curve constitutes the region where the costs of a particular behavior outweigh the utility; hence, rational individuals ought to choose not to engage in the behavior. We refer to this state-space as that of *deterrence*.

The area to the left of the curve, on the other hand, is the region where the utility of a given behavior outweighs its costs. When this is the situation, rational individuals ought to choose to act. This state-space is usually referred to as that of *incentive*. From the point of view of social policy, society attempts to deter behaviors decided as criminal by increasing the cost component while reducing the utility so that it falls to the right of the indifference curve. When societies fail to do this, the utilities outweigh the costs and there is an incentive to commit crime.

The principle is illustrated in Figure 13.2. For a behavior that has a utility at level y and a cost at level x, the ratio of utility to cost is defined by the point a. Since a is to the left of the curve, a rational individual is urged to act. If the cost is increased from x to x', the resulting ratio is defined by point B. Since B lies on the indifference curve, the person is indifferent or undecided as to acting or not acting. By moving the cost to x'', however, the ratio defined by point C clearly results in the cost being greater than the utility associated with the behavior, so a rational person ought to be deterred.

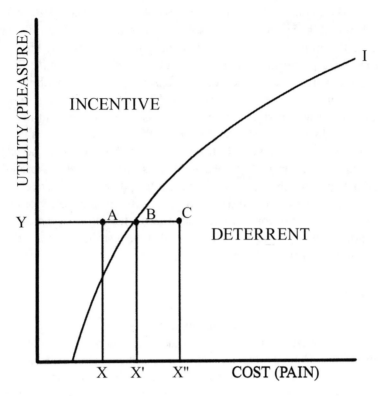

Figure 13.2   Hedonistic calculus.

Crime as Utilitarian Behavior

Our conventional thinking about criminal justice follows this model. We assume that deterrence occurs when we increase the pain (the penalty) associated with a particular act. Furthermore, we assume that as the amount of utility associated with an act increases, the cost required to deter that act will also need to increase. The key for society, however, is to identify the actual distribution of the indifference curve. Logically, it ought to be possible to deter all criminal behaviors by attaching extremely high costs to them (e.g., capital punishment for relatively minor offenses). *Efficient deterrence*, however, is defined as those points just to the right of the curve. From Bentham's perspective, too high a cost associated with a behavior is inefficient. It is unjustified in a rational society because excessive punishment imposes too high a cost on society. That is to say, by increasing the cost (punishment) to the individual, society incurs increasing costs associated with implementation. Such excessive use of resources is wasteful and irrational.

Assumptions Underlying Utility Theory

There are three primary assumptions underlying the utility framework. The first assumption is that people are rational. That is to say, it is assumed that people act consciously and logically when they make a choice. This view of rationality has a number of supporting implications. Among these are the following assumptions: people are goal-oriented; people seek to maximize their utility (i.e., they seek as much pleasure as possible); people are fully informed with regard to the utility and cost associated with particular acts; and finally, people are capable of performing the calculation of the utility-cost ratio. The second assumption is that there is a reasonable consensus in society with regard to the perception of the relative utility (pleasure, benefit) and cost (pain, loss, disutility) associated with certain classes of actions. Contemporary utility theorists admit that individual differences do exist in the perceptions of utility and cost. These differences, however, are usually dismissed as minor in the aggregate. The third assumption is that behavior that is *instrumental* has preference to behavior that is purely *expressive*. That is, "I will choose to dance for money and recognition before I will dance for joy." Instrumental behavior achieves a desired outcome for people. In its naked form, the logical conclusion of this assumption is that people are selfish and that altruism is either a facade or an error in judgment (i.e., a miscalculation).

Contextual Effects

Rational choice theory assumes human beings, both individually and in groups, are free to make decisions. However, human decision making is not completely unconstrained. There are factors that limit both the decisions we can make, and our decision-making ability. Among the constraints often incorporated into rational choice theories are (1) our tastes and preferences, (2) our level of human capital, and (3) variations in structural opportunities.

Tastes and Preferences

Individuals and societies have preferences for certain kinds of commodities and certain kinds of behaviors. This is clear in the marketplace where different people express different brand preferences for the same commodity. Some of those differences in taste and preference are idiosyncratic; some are culturally determined. Morals and ethical values, for example, are primarily culturally defined. It is a culturally defined value to which most people adhere most of the time, that behaviors considered criminal have a low level of social acceptability. From the perspective of utility theory, these differences in preference determine the location of the indifference curve. Thus, referring to Figure 13.3, a behavior for which people have little preference might be defined by line I' whereas a preferred behavior would be defined by I. From a societal point of view, the advantage of an indifference curve at I' as opposed to I is that it takes less cost (pain) to deter the behavior.

All other things being equal, it is to society's advantage to generate indifference curves relating to criminal behaviors that are as far to the left as possible. If this can be done, then the social resources required to deter the behavior will be minimized. That is to say, engendering feelings of guilt is less costly than increasing the number of constables on the beat.

Human Capital

Human capital consists of a person's skills and abilities and it is those factors that determine one's value in the labor force. Highly skilled and talented people

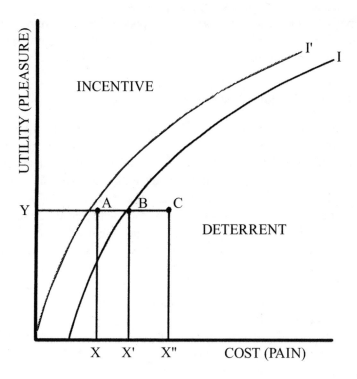

Figure 13.3   Changes in preference reflected in different indifference curves.

generally earn more in the marketplace than do less skilled and less talented people. Beyond innate talent, however, human capital is generally acquired through education. The more one learns, the more human capital one acquires. The same is true whether one considers licit or illicit activities. Repeat and career offenders generally become more successful the more they learn about their trade and the criminal justice system.

The fact that many criminals learn the trade has been well documented since the time of Edwin Sutherland's interviews with "Chic Conwell" in the 1930s. As offenders learn more about the trade, they increase their potential returns and decrease their costs by minimizing the risk of capture, and if captured, the risk of a severe sentence. Learning how the system operates and how to negotiate with the police and the courts are valuable skills. It might be expected that as individual criminals become more skilled, the incentives to engage in criminal activity increase, and the relative rewards from that activity increase.

Opportunities

Contrary to the popular adage, while America may be the land of opportunity, not everyone has the opportunity to become President, no matter how hard they work. Social reality is that we all face constraints or limitations on our choices. Some choices are simply not open to some categories of people. Utility theory accepts those constraints as given. It is evident, though, that variations in opportunities influence the likelihood of choosing to engage in legal or illegal activities. For some individuals, the opportunity to pursue rewarding legal activities is severely limited. For others, the opportunity to pursue illegal activities is similarly constrained. For yet others, the seemingly perverse situation arises where the successful pursuit of legal activities generates opportunities to commit rewarding illegal activities. Indeed, much of the truly rewarding white-collar crime we see—fraud, insider trading, receiving bribes—results from this situation.

Contributions of the Utility Framework

For a model to stand the test of time it must have both empirical veracity and social benefits over competing frameworks. It also helps that it is consistent with prevailing ideologies. The empirical aspects of utility theory will be examined later. At this point, it is sufficient to examine the theoretical advantages that distinguish utility theory from other explanatory frameworks.

Perhaps the prime feature is that utility theory makes the assumption of human beings being rational. It does not rely upon the medieval notions of possession, nor does it require us to assume that criminals are "sick" or deviant. Unlike many explanations of crime, utility theory is universalistic. It is not simply an explanation of why some women or some men or juveniles or old people behave in a criminal fashion. It is a nondiscriminating theory that attempts to explain the behavior of all people.

A second benefit of utility theory is that it allows us to step back from a purely moral view of crime. That is, one need not deal with the problem of why seemingly "good" people commit crimes. In fact, the terms "good" and "bad" do not appear in the utilitarian vocabulary.

A third benefit of this framework is that the issue of knowledge is raised. In order for people to make rational choices, they must have full and "objective" knowledge of the options before them, and of the utilities and costs associated with those options. For example, misjudgments regarding the costs associated with a behavior, either in terms of over- or underestimating the costs, are used to account for some seemingly irrational behaviors. Post-Benthamite developments in utility theory have also been successful in incorporating a time dimension into the framework. Depending upon the circumstances, the delayed implementation of punishment (cost) can lead to a subjective depreciation of that cost.

Limitations of the Utility Model

As with all social theories, the utility framework has its limitations. Some are by design; some are a consequence of inadequate development. The most noticeable limitation is that utility theory does not explicitly address "irrational" behavior. Many economists address apparent "irrationalities" or deviations as differences in preferences. The model does accommodate this problem to some degree. For example, distinct groups of individuals may not share a common curve of indifference. Looking back at Figure 13.2, it will be noted that there are two indifference curves, I and I'. Clearly, one's cultural background and life circumstances can modify the subjective perception of costs and utilities. A week in prison in the middle of winter for a street person might be perceived as beneficial; for a business person, it is generally not so.

As indicated above, utility theory does not address the problem of structural constraints. It is an explanation of how people make choices, but what if there are no choices to make? Choices can be constrained by objective realities (e.g., it is difficult to get a job when none is available) and by normative or preference factors. Utility theory accepts that preferences are determined by morality and cultural values. It cannot, however, explain the sources and the adoption of those normative constraints.

Rational choice theories got a boost in the late 1960s with the work of the economist Gary Becker.

BOX 13.2   ECONOMIC MODELS

"... economic models of criminal behavior take as given those influences in the personal and social backgrounds of individuals that determine 'respect for law,' proclivities to violence, preferences for risk, and other behavioral characteristics held to be determinants of criminality. These models are based upon characteristics of individuals which are alleged to be common not only to large classes of offenders, but to large classes of economic agents in general. In a sentence, the models of economic choice theory, of which the criminal choice is a special case, hypothesize that all individuals, criminal and noncriminal alike, respond to incentives; and if the costs and benefits associated with an action change, the agent's choices are also likely to change." (Heineke 1978: 1–2)

Becker's prime contribution to criminology was to reawaken the discipline's Benthamite tradition. For Becker, the contribution of economic perspectives to crime "is to demonstrate that optimal policies to combat illegal behavior are part of an optimal allocation of resources" (Becker 1968: 209). Becker's initial writings improved upon Bentham's very simple utilitarian approach by emphasizing the uncertainty associated with the decision to engage in criminal activity. In order for economic choice models to work, the assumption must be made that all costs and benefits translate into a common measurement. For economists, the common measurement is a monetary one. Thus, all proceeds of criminal activity, both monetary and nonmonetary, must be seen as having monetary equivalents, and all costs associated with crime—fines, periods of incarceration, social condemnation, etc.—must also have monetary equivalents. While some may find this difficult to accept, it is also true that we make such equivalences in our day-to-day lives. For instance, we place a value on our time when we decide that we will or will not accept wage labor for a given dollar amount. We value pleasure and excitement when we are willing to pay the price of admission to a theme park or to go bungee jumping or skydiving. Courts regularly equate fines and periods of incarceration when offenders are offered the option of a $300 fine or three days in jail.

In its simplest form, Becker's model considers two outcomes for criminal activity: one is either caught or not caught. When not caught, the utility associated with the crime is simply the gain, both monetary and psychic—there is no cost with which to be concerned. When caught, on the other hand, the utility of the activity is the difference between the gains associated with the activity and the costs associated with apprehension, processing, and punishment. In a situation where one is caught, the traditional elements of utility theory hold: an incentive appears when the gain from the crime outweighs the punishment while a deterrent appears when the punishment outweighs the gain. Becker, however, reminds us that a crucial factor in the decision process to commit or not commit a crime is the *likelihood* of being caught. Thus, a low probability of being caught combined with a relatively low net cost (i.e., the difference between the income and the penalty) may make the criminal enterprise appealing.

The key advantage of the economic perspective is the acknowledgment that all enterprise (either legitimate or illegitimate) involves some element of risk (both the perceived and/or the actual likelihood of apprehension). To understand the incentive or disincentive to crime, one must combine the risk factor with the potential income or loss (again, both monetary and psychic). If the risk of apprehension is high, the potential gain will be discounted thus making the crime less attractive. On the other hand, if the risk of apprehension is low, the potential loss will be discounted making it less of a deterrent. While current implementations have elaborated on this model (primarily by focusing on how offenders attempt to control risk), it is still possible to formulate a number of insights that are not incorporated into the more traditional positivistic approaches to crime.

In his review of Becker's work, Taylor outlines the following (1978: 37–40):

1. There is the intuitive notion that criminal activity is influenced by not just the severity of punishment (cost) but also by the likelihood of punishment. Thus, "almost all empirical studies [within this framework] have included measures of certainty and severity."
2. "Criminal behavior can be described in much the same way as conventional economic behavior, without particular reference to psychological theories."
3. There is an interaction between criminals and their behavior and the criminal justice system. "Criminals are not the only expected utility maximizers; society, in its operation of the criminal justice system, also maximizes utility by weighing the costs of operating the system against the costs to society of criminal behavior."

Macro Versus Micro Rationality

Rational choice theories, particularly those that focus on the economic determinants of crime, tend to come in two variants. There are those that focus on macro-level or aggregate rationality; and there are those that focus on individual choice behavior. While similar models may be applied at both levels of analysis, the interpretation and implications of those models are often very different from each other. In macro level studies, where the unit of analysis is the society or the social institution, the appeal to rationality is that of a metaphor. At the aggregate level, rational choice models are applied on an "as if" basis; that is, we analyze social processes as if they were the calculations made by an individual who was acting rationally. Thus, as Taylor (1978) states, "the hypothesis is that criminals (as a social category) act *as if* they are responding rationally to incentives and deterrents presented by their socio-economic environment, including the criminal justice system." It is not necessary to assume that societies or institutions are rational actors. In fact, to do so is to engage in *reification*—the fallacy of treating an abstraction or theoretical concept as if it were real.

Often the question is raised as to whether or not rational choice models that are based on supposed characteristics of individuals can explain the behavior of aggregates. While the ultimate answer is an empirical one, there is no necessary philosophical reason why such modes of explanation cannot be fruitful. In fact, our ability to form empirically valid predictions (one of the criteria of successful explanation) is often better at the aggregate than the individual level.

At the individual level, we are probably more willing to believe that actors behave in a rational manner, at least some of the time. It is still not necessary, however, for individual actors to be "truly rational" as long as they behave in a manner that is consistent with some theoretical model that we choose to define as a rational choice model. By keeping these factors in mind, it is possible to exploit rational choice models as a form of explanation without having to view human beings as omnipotent supercomputers, instantaneously weighing several variables to generate an optimal decision.

Models of Macrorationality

Not long after Becker's theoretical work appeared in print, a number of aggregate level econometric studies were published that attempted to operationalize the framework and assess the impact that certainty and severity of punishment had on deterring crime. All of these studies are cross-sectional in nature—Ehrlich's (1973, 1975, 1977) is based on U.S. state data, Phillips and Votey (1975) use counties in California, Carr-Hill and Stern (1973) use police districts in England and Wales, and Sjoquist (1973) uses American cities—and all use official statistics to operationalize their models.

Typically, the dependent or outcome variable is crimes known to the police. Deterrence is operationalized by rates of arrest, imprisonment rates, or mean length of prison sentences and economic variables are taken into account by such indicators as median family income or proportions of working- or middle-class families in an area.

Findings and Cautions

Despite these studies being drawn from different jurisdictions, the results tend to be reasonably consistent with one another. If we focus on Ehrlich's study, which precedes the others, the primary finding may be outlined as follows:

1. Economic variables have a greater impact on property crime than personal crime.
2. Deterrence is more effective in reducing crimes against the person than crimes against property.
3. Except for some property crimes, more certain punishment is a greater deterrent than more severe punishment.

While these findings appear to be reasonably robust, we should be aware of their limitations. First, the data are cross-sectional and not longitudinal. As methodologists have long known, causal inferences cannot be drawn from cross-sectional data without some extremely restrictive assumptions regarding the historical invariance of the relationships. Second, the statistical models typically used in econometrics (and much other social research for that matter) are very sensitive to measurement error in the independent or explanatory variables. As indicated, the dependent variable in such studies is often the ratio of crimes known to police to total population. Deterrence is often operationalized by taking the ratio of arrests to crime known to police. Under this circumstance, any measurement error in the crimes known to police will result in a spurious relationship between the crime rate and the arrest rate. Because economists have traditionally been far more aware of this and other statistically based problems than most other social scientists, a great deal of the econometric literature is devoted to getting around these difficulties.

Designing Economic Models

Economists have attempted to test the rationality of criminal activity by constructing mathematical models that might weigh costs and benefits of criminal work. These models are constructed from available data and therefore do not include the actors' subjective appreciations of risks and profits that constitute job satisfaction. Economists call such preferences "tastes" and regard them as givens, while social psychologists ask how differential tastes are produced.

An inventory of possible costs and benefits of criminal work is set out in Table 13.1. This inventory does not assign weights to the advantages and disadvantages of living by the rackets or theft. Our inability to assign values to these costs and benefits makes economists' models of crime causation suggestive rather than definitive. Tests of the rationality of larceny, smuggling, terrorism, and gangsterism must therefore be interpreted as estimates rather than as certainties. This becomes clearer as we note that economists who attempt to measure the profit-loss balance from illegal work must disregard the psychic costs and benefits and concentrate on the more material values of crime. If these qualifications are allowed, the results of some provisional studies indicate that much crime does pay.

In a material sense, many careers in crime are rewarding. However, the economist's scales do not weight the variability that must exist among burglars, robbers, embezzlers, smugglers, and peddlers of illegal sex, drugs, and games. Just as there are differences in the rewards of successful and unsuccessful lawyers, accountants, and teachers, so too there must be differences in the net payoffs of skillful thieves when compared with the gains of bungling burglars.

Models of Microeconomic Rationality

More recent investigations based on rational choice models have tended to focus on individual decision makers. Thus, the question is: how do individual criminals decide to commit a crime, select a target, and evaluate the accompanying risks? The issue of risk assessment has been of particular interest to researchers. As Carroll and Weaver note (1986: 26),

> interviews with experienced criminals suggest that certainty and severity of punishment are not static properties of a crime . . . but are under partial control of the crimi-

Table 13.1   Cost-Benefit Schedule for Illicit Money-making.

Costs	*Benefits*
Probability of being caught; probability of being punished if caught *times* dollar value of punishment (fine or time); lost earnings.	Market value of stolen property when fenced plus money stolen; earnings from rackets.
Loss of legal income; time out from lawful occupation.	Use value of stolen property retained by thief; accumulation of capital from rackets for investment in legal enterprise.
Loss of peripheral benefits of lawful occupation: paid vacation, medical insurance.	Freedom from taxes.
Job costs: learning skills and acquiring tools; payoffs to inside confederates and others; fencing.	Job satisfaction: Pleasure in one's work, satisfaction of self-employment; excitement; pleasure in being a skilful thief, heavy muscle, or racket boss.
Job risks: accident, being wounded or killed.	Security: freedom from risk of unemployment.
Work involved in theft—casing and doing; work involved in smuggling, loansharking, or extortion; bird-dogging, enforcing.	Leisure: e.g., a burglar's work week versus work week of legal job available to thief.
Subjective cost: anxiety about getting caught and punished.	Security: free room and board, free health care, aid to dependents, wages earned *if* imprisoned.
Subjective costs of punishment: shame, guilt. How much does a specific fine hurt? How much are time and freedom worth, subjectively?	Repute: as successful thief, smuggler, loan shark, heavy muscle, mafioso.
Damaged repute: as thief, or as unsuccessful thief if caught.	

Note: Costs and benefits are *possible* ones. They need not all pertain to a particular actor, and they may, of course, differ in actuality from an actor's *judgment* of them.

nal. Criminals are experts at controlling or minimizing risks. The criminal's skill in leaving no evidence that will stand up in court, in manipulating the legal system through bargains and bribes, and in setting up and carrying out crimes and disposing of the gains is indicative that an experienced criminal faces different opportunities and sanctions than does an amateur.

In their research on shoplifters, Carroll and Weaver discovered that successful shoplifters develop and employ their "human capital," which includes intelligence and effort (as do individuals in the "legitimate" labor market), to maximize their gains and minimize their risks. Among their findings, Carroll and Weaver (1986: 27–32) note that "experts were far more efficient in analyzing shoplifting possibilities [than amateurs]." Furthermore, "the decision process for expert shoplifters seemed to involve the selection of strategies to overcome deterrents and minimize risks" (1986: 32). For all shoplifters, the major deterrents were the presence of security devices, item accessibility, the likelihood of being observed (especially by store personnel), and feelings of guilt. Professionals tended to focus on the first two items, while amateurs tended to be preoccupied with the latter two. For the professionals, the issue of what might happen if caught (i.e., the penal sanction) was a nonissue once they had decided to go to work. Carroll and Weaver (1986: 32) suggest then, that shoplifters may be operating at two levels of rationality. The *distal* (more remote) consequences of capture "are considered when deciding to become a shoplifter, that is, to become the sort of person who looks for shoplifting opportunities in stores." When on the job, however, "distal consequences are vague, usually not experienced, and generally uncontrollable."

Walsh (1986) reports that similar rational behavior and accumulation of knowledge takes place in his study of commercial burglars and robbers. The offenders in Walsh's study focused, once again, on the matter of minimizing risk while simultaneously realizing that it cannot be avoided totally. Offenses committed by the burglars tended to be well planned with a previously worked out scheme. Once a job is planned, the strategy is consciously reviewed and examined. As Walsh states, the scheme is

> scrutinized and assessed with free-ranging negative thinking, in which a catalogue of objections are itemized and considered. There is then a phase of flaw hunting, searching for chinks in the "impregnable" security system that protects the target . . . and looking for what might in the broadest sense be termed "the window of vulnerability"—the one feature the target custodians have neglected to provide for. (1986: 45)

Despite the care and effort that often go into planning a job, burglars—even experienced burglars—consider the many factors to be considered as infinite rather than finite. All of the factors can neither be controlled nor considered. Yet, "a trip-up on any . . . might be (wrongly) considered to be evidence of irrationality by outside armchair assessors, especially if the error was allegedly foreseeable " (Walsh 1986: 44).

What is clear from these studies, and similar ones on robbers (Feeny 1986) and opiate abusers (Bennett 1986) is that risk assessment is a crucial consideration for most experienced criminals and the consequences of failure are simply part of the price of doing business.

Crime-Producing Situations

The economist's assumption of human rationality admits that there are crazy people and irrational ones. It recognizes, too, that we operate with imperfect knowledge and that, even when we try to act rationally, we may be less than efficient because we are ignorant of the full range of consequences of our acts. Our ignorance, in turn, is a function not only of lack of information but also of our difficulties in handling much information and in processing it. In addition, rationality is limited by the fact that we usually have mixed motives; thus, we often want more than one thing at the same time, and some of these desires conflict and befuddle choice of means. Since we act with such limitations, H. A. Simon (1958) has termed rational action under such contingencies *bounded rationality*.

With the qualification that our efforts to be rational are thus constrained, economic analysis starts with the premise that most of us, most of the time, know what we are doing. The idea of "knowing what we are doing" assumes that we have preferences—however they were caused—and that we select means of achieving these values in terms of their estimated costs and rewards.

The assumption that criminal activity is rational is considered a form of structural explanation because economists regard situations as determining how one achieves one's purposes. Situations are viewed as constraints, or opportunities, that affect how a person's objectives can be achieved. Circumstances impose costs upon the satisfaction of desires, and the economist is interested in how people weigh costs against satisfactions (McKenzie and Tullock 1981: 9–13).

It should be noted here, however, that the same action can be differently interpreted. It is possible to move the cause of conduct from what the situation allows and the costs it imposes to the preferences that are to be satisfied, to the ideas one has about expected costs and benefits, or to the learning process by which one has acquired both preferences and ideas. Attention to learning-training processes is the explanatory task of control theory (Chapter 12). Emphasis on differential preferences ("values") is part of the subcultural explanatory style (Chapter 17). And emphasis on ideas is the preferred explanatory mode of symbolic interactionists (Chapter 19).

Crime and Unemployment

One of the longest, ongoing debates in criminology has been over whether unemployment has an impact on the tendency to commit crime, and if so, how are the two related? The literature goes back well into the nineteenth century (Sellin 1937) and as Vold (1958: 165) notes, "almost from the first studies . . . there has been disagreement in findings and a good deal of wrangling about whether the conclusions drawn are justified." The research literature on the issue can be broken down into two broad categories: crime as a consequence of structural unemployment, and crime as a function of fluctuations in the business cycle. Structuralist arguments generally posit that it is the fundamental organization of the economy (e.g., class relations) that explain most of the variance in crime, and that short-term variations in the business cycle are inconsequential in comparison to those structural determinants. Little research based on structuralist principles is to be found within the rational choice domain. Instead, it tends to be incorporated in the explanatory frameworks outlined in this chapter and the two that follow, where this discussion is further pursued. On the other hand, the crime and unemployment/business cycle literature has a natural affinity to rational choice explanations.

To date, a clear and unambiguous empirical link between crime and cycles of unemployment has not been confirmed. While much of the literature shows a negative relationship between unemployment and crime, other studies show either a positive or no statistically significant relationship. In that respect, the situation is not much different from that of the earlier part of this century when contrary to much conventional wisdom, Paul Weirs' (1945) study showed that delinquency increased as economic conditions improved, while the much respected study of Dorothy Swaine Thomas (1925) showed either no relationship or at best, a small negative relationship.

There have been several detailed reviews of this literature in the past 20 years including those by Tarling (1982), Field (1990), and Timbrell (1990). The overall conclusion on the topic is perhaps best summarized by Box (1987: 96) who notes the following:

1. Income inequality is strongly related to criminal activity—with the exception of homicide. It should be emphasized that no existing research has produced results which contradict this.
2. The relationship between overall unemployment and crime is inconsistent, even when victimization survey data are used as the measure of crime. . . . On balance the weight of existing research supports there being a weak but nonetheless significant causal relationship.

The more recent research does tend, however, to suggest reasonably strong and statistically significant relationship between crime and the business cycle (Pyle and Deadman 1994). Part of the reason for this may be, as Chiricos (1987) suggests, that structural unemployment has been much higher in Western countries since the 1970s. This allows for greater variation in the independent variable. On the other hand, Tarling (1983) raises two important issues. First, much crime is conducted by young people who are likely to engage in crime before they participate in the labor market. Second, the impact of unemployment on crime seems to decrease as one puts more control variables into one's equations. This would suggest that many of the key variables in which we are interested fluctuate together over time. Under this circumstance, it is difficult to determine empirically which is the crucial determinant.

Another part of the empirical literature shows ambiguity on this second point is that the structure or form of the relationship has not been well specified. Theoretically, if economically rational actors decide to engage in illicit activities, they are assumed to weigh the risks and consequences of that decision. Risks, costs, opportunities, and rewards differ for individuals according to whether they make short-term or long-term commitments to work activities. For example, in the licit labor force, many workers decide that it is in their long-term best interest to select a career. Choosing to be a physician or priest, for example, involves a commitment to that vocation that allows one to maximize returns in that field. At the same time, that commitment reduces one's mobility across other sectors of the labor force. As many middle-aged professionals have discovered, midlife changes in career are not easy—one's options are reduced and one becomes "locked in." The same is true of many who "choose" illicit career options. Thus, for some hard-core career criminals, it is unlikely that there is a great deal of movement across licit and illicit sectors.

The level of commitment to licit or illicit sectors, however, is likely a consequence of both long- and short- term prospects in each sector. Most studies of unemployment and crime have not focused on the long-term issue. Britt's (1994) longitudinal analysis of crime and unemployment among young people, however, does suggest that unemployment has a dual impact on crime rates. The first effect is consistent with the availability of short-term opportunity and the second is through a frustration motivation that is consistent with the prospects of long-term unemployment. Britt suggests that part of the reason that some studies show either no relationship or a positive relationship between crime and unemployment is that overall increases in unemployment may serve to decrease opportunity to crime, especially for property crime. That is to say, unemployment hits both potential victims and offenders, and that as unemployment increases among potential victims, there are simply more "guardians" around to supervise their property.

Britt's research shows that,

> the effect of youth unemployment is consistent with the expectation of a current decline in property crime in response to a high level of unemployment, and therefore lower levels of person-property circulation. Similarly, the . . . effect of youth unemployment is largely consistent with the expectation of an increase in property crime in response to prolonged and increasing unemployment, vanishing public assistance monies, and an increase in the proportion of the population motivated to commit criminal acts. (1994: 105)

Costs of Engaging in Crime

What, we might ask, is the opportunity cost to committing crime? Grogger (1995) studied a sample of offenders in California who had been arrested at least once between 1973 and 1987. Merging the arrest records with unemployment insurance records, Grogger managed to obtain an estimate of the impact of arrest on the employment and earnings of young men. Grogger finds the following: (1) in the first quarter, arrest led to a decrease in mean earnings of about 4%. (2) In the second to sixth quarters following the arrest, mean earnings fell slightly less—in the 2–3% range. (3) After the sixth quarter, the decrease in earnings was statistically nonsignificant. He concludes that "the effects of arrests on employment and earnings are moderate in magnitude and rather short-lived."

In a separate analysis of the impact of arrest on joblessness, Grogger (1992) also reports that the effect of an additional arrest is to lower the likelihood of employment in the next quarter by approximately 2 percentage points. Grogger's results also show that anywhere from one-third to two-thirds of the difference in employment between African Americans and whites in his sample is a consequence of arrest record.

In a fairly sophisticated analysis of drug dealing, Myer (1992) argues that some criminal activities are not simply substitutable with legal activities (i.e., illicit work taking the place of licit work) but may also be complementary. In the instance of drug dealing, Myer (1992: 83) points out that there are "two reasons for thinking of drug dealing as a complement to work and not a substitute. First, working helps to conceal transactions and thereby helps to reduce the risk of apprehension. Second, working provides a natural base for matching buyers and sellers."

In his analysis, Myer notes that patterns of drug dealing are different for African Americans and whites in the United States. Among white drug dealers, their illegal activity appears to coincide with legal work suggesting that for this group, the relationship is complementary. Among African-American drug dealers, however, the process appears to be one of substitution. Myer argues that this racial difference is a consequence of restricted wage labor opportunities for many African Americans and is reinforced by the fact that, in comparison to whites, African Americans "can expect to receive lower legal wages relative to their illegal earnings." One of the truly astounding interpretations that can be drawn from Myer's data is that, with all other things being equal,

> if blacks had white relative wages, blacks would experience a huge upward adjustment in their relative earnings and would reduce their participation in drug dealing by nearly 90 percent. The black drug dealing probability would drop from 13 percent to not much more than 1 percent." (1992: 91)

Markets for Crime

Some criminal activity involving offenses against both person and property is an enterprise engaged to fulfill the demands of a market. There are always people ready to make their living supplying any public "needs" that are made illegal. Whenever a relatively inelastic demand, like that for gambling, sex, and the habituating chemicals, meets a short supply, the price of the service goes up and with it the opportunity to make money illegally.

ESTIMATES OF UNREPORTED INCOME
Greenfield (1993: ch. 4) estimates that unreported income from a variety of illegal activities, including drugs; gambling; prostitution; pornography; illegal abortion; audio, video, and software piracy; cigarette smuggling and loan sharking, to be approximately $69.2 billion. Of this total, drugs are estimated to account for about $45 billion. Greenfield estimates this amount to be approximately 6.2% of the GNP for the U.S. in 1990.

Some of the largest incomes ever gained have been made by criminal merchants supplying the public with illegal merchandise. Thus the gangster Al Capone is reported to have earned the highest gross income (in constant dollars) ever achieved by a private citizen in a single year, something on the order of $105 million for 1927 (McWhirter and McWhirter 1966: 230). This money came principally from the illegal manufacture and marketing of liquor, but also from gambling, prostitution, extortion, and some legitimate businesses. In his time, Capone was very popular. If he and others like him killed their rivals, it was only assassins murdering assassins, and good riddance. Meanwhile, a public "need" was being met. As Capone himself said, "Public service is my motto. I've always regarded it as a public benefaction if people were given decent liquor and square games" (Kobler 1972: 210).

There is a criminal gradient, again, from organized crime serving an illicit market to people "doing the best they can" when government regulations promote black markets. Working the black market, although punished as a crime, is not regarded by its traders as criminal.

Most traditional criminological research focuses on offenders and victims. One of the advantages of viewing crime from a rational economic perspective is that our focus is shifted onto other significant actors who might otherwise be ignored. One such group is receivers of stolen goods. While it is the case that much of the property appropriated by offenders is for their own consumption, it is also true that a great deal of stolen property has little intrinsic worth for the offender. A great deal of stolen property is "retailed" on the black market either through a professional fence or by the offender directly. The literature on professional fences suggests that for most of these people, marketing illicit commodities is

---

Box 13.3 THE UNDERGROUND ECONOMY

The underground economy is defined as the trade in licit goods and services that are beyond the purview of tax collectors. Drawing on data from a number of sources, Greenfield (1993: 40–41) estimates that individual U.S. tax filers underreported somewhere around $197.2 billion in income in 1987. He concludes that tax evasion on individual income taxes is around $41.6 billion, and is a further $10.4 billion on corporate income taxes. A number of studies have attempted to estimate the size of the underground economies in various countries. Dallago (1990: 21–23) summarizes several studies focusing primarily on the late 1970s and early 1980s. For the United States, estimates of the size of the underground economy range from a low of about 2% of GNP to a high of 27% of GNP with a median being in the neighborhood of about 15%. Estimates for Italy range from a low around 10% to a high of about 30% with most studies generating an estimate in the mid-20% range. Estimates in the mid teens and low twenties are also provided for Hungary, Poland, and the former Soviet Union while they still retained Soviet-type economies.

---

complementary to their legitimate entrepreneurial activities (Klockars 1974; Steffensmeier 1986; Dallago 1990). For professional fences, stolen goods are simply another category of marketable commodities. The markup on these goods is higher than for normal, or licit goods, but the indirect costs associated with these goods are also higher. That is, while there is a risk of the goods being confiscated by the authorities, one can also be charged for having received stolen property, and in the extreme case, one's legitimate enterprise might also be shut down.

Professional fences are not the only point of distribution for illicit goods. Cromwell and McElrath (1994), for example, focus on the amateur buyer of stolen property. Their self-report survey in Texas suggested that 17% of their sample had knowingly bought stolen goods in the past and a further 12% indicated that they would do so given the opportunity. As these authors point out, "the marketplace for stolen goods is diverse and ubiquitous, and that ordinary, otherwise honest, citizens constitute a significant market for stolen property." For many people, knowingly receiving stolen property is just another routine activity.

Governments are forever torn between attempting to control people through police power and allowing them to do what they want. The justification of control is that a people's unbridled economic activity is harmful or that their appetites are vices. Making people better than they are is a continuing motive for making the satisfaction of some desires criminal. The idea was clearly expressed by Vladimir Ilyich Ulyanov (Lenin), who told us that "the people themselves do not know what is good or bad for them."

Laws that prohibit constant impulses—to trade, to think and speak freely, and to satisfy hungers for sex, food, and the comforting chemicals—create markets for crime. Such laws are usually justified by calling the activities they forbid "vice." However, vice is durable. With the exception of cases in which heavy majorities control slim minorities through the application of severe and probable sanctions, attempts to suppress vice create black markets and their criminal suppliers (Schelling 1967), such as the case in Grozny, Chechnya (see Figure 13.4).

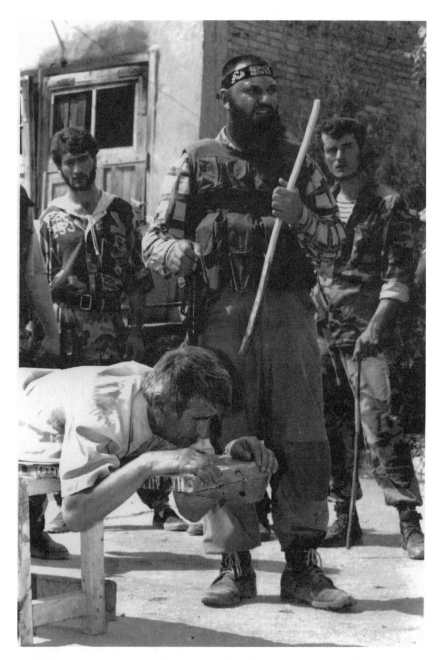

Figure 13.4   Certain and probable? A man caught selling alcohol in Grozny, Chechnya, braces for a penalty of 40 lashes from a cane, consistent with Muslim law. Photo courtesy of *Ottawa Citizen*, September 5, 1996.

Problems and Limitations with the Research Literature

Economic theories of crime provide clear and insightful explanations of a great deal of property crime and some crimes against persons. Crimes of acquisition and most crimes of vice respond readily to economic incentives and disincentives. As with all explanations of human behavior, however, research based on rational-economic models has limitations.

1. Some variants of utility theory come close to being circular or *tautological*. For example, it is argued that if people are rational, they should select *a* over *b*. The empirical evidence shows, however, that *b* is selected. Often, the explanation for the selection of *b* is that people have different tastes or preferences. The selection of *b* must be a consequence of different preferences since people are logical and it would be illogical to select *a* unless they had preferences for *b*.

2. It is often assumed that the utilities of crime received by offenders and the disutilities incurred by victims are static. In a theoretic analysis of this issue, van Dijk (1994) suggests that this is not the case because both offenders and victims alter their strategies in response to each others' behaviors in a complex fashion.

3. While most economic models since Becker have included an indicator for the likelihood of apprehension as well as an indicator for the severity of punishment, few (if any) include an indicator of celerity. Yet the swiftness with which punishment is administered is assumed to be a major factor in the deterrence literature. Some research also suggests that this applies to the trial stage (Corman 1981). Where punishment is not dealt out expeditiously, we would expect offenders to further depreciate the costs involved.

4. Most economic theories have not addressed the fact that, in most jurisdictions, women have both lower rates of crime and lower rates of labor force participation than men. This might be dismissed by arguing that women have a greater preference for leisure or child rearing over both licit and illicit "work," but the argument once again becomes tautological.

5. Most econometric models are highly sensitive to problems of measurement error. Unfortunately, most crime data are not error-free, thereby leading to some problems of bias and inaccuracy in the estimates.

6. Except for a few core items, there is neither consensus as to what variables ought to be included in economic models of utility, nor is it always clear what the functional form of the models ought to be. This is important since, as Tarling (1982) shows, key theoretical relationships (such as that between crime and unemployment) are often reduced when control variables are added. That many studies employ similar measures is more a consequence of what data happen to be available than a consensus in the discipline. Thus, current economic choice theory might best be described as a framework as opposed to a well-defined theory.

Lessons Learned from Economic Models of Crime Production

1. David Hume (1957) was correct. Wealth available for the taking will be "transferred." Gold left unguarded will disappear. Therefore, the first line of defense against theft is "target hardening," that is, any tactic of wealth protection that adds costs to thievery.

2. Every preventive and protective measure, including use of police and courts, carries its own cost. Therefore, there will always be some quantity of crime that a society will tolerate because the costs of defense exceed the value of property stolen. An optimum enforcement of the criminal law is never known in advance of policy creation (Stigler 1970). It is only approximated by the tugs of competing interests for private and public funds (Benson et al. 1994).

3. Insofar as criminals are rational, they may not be "sick." A popular assumption (the "medical model") holds that there must be "something wrong" with thieves and racketeers. The second consequence is the development of therapeutic industries to "straighten crooked actors." However, these efforts are not so uniform, happy, and assured as the medical model suggests (Nettler 1982c). If impulsive actors are tough to change, rational actors may be still more difficult to alter, depending, of course, on the relative values of their costs and benefits from crime.

4. No one is perfectly rational. Since we act out of mixed motives, we do not behave merely to maximize financial gain and minimize monetary loss. This is true of corporate enterprise where "business is supposed to be business" (Leibenstein 1981), and there is no reason to doubt the intrusion of nonfinancial motives in the choice of a criminal career.

   Humans are not just *Homo sapiens* and *Homo ratio* (wise and reasoning), but also *Homo ludens*—playful. There are aesthetic pleasures in work—in "work," at least, as compared with "labor"—and robbers and racketeers have described for us their satisfactions in "the caper," and in their autonomy and domination.

5. The general policy prescriptions that flow from economists are to increase the value of legal work and the costs of criminal work.

   An optimum balance of these prescriptions is not known, because the relationship between any means used toward either of these ends and their long-term "prices" is unknown. This is a way of saying that we do not always know how to translate these prescriptions into efficient policies. Nevertheless, economists attempt to calculate some costs. Thus Ribich (1968) estimates that the trade-off between reducing poverty and providing police protection in the "war on crime" is such that it would require income gains of $300,000 per family in high-crime zones to equal a reduction of $1,300 in police costs.

   In this vein, economists regard minimum wage laws as criminogenic because they drive unskilled youths out of the legal labor market (Reynolds 1973; Williams 1982). Governments cannot decree a minimum wage for all work without producing some unforeseen, and usually unpleasant, consequences.

6. Varying the severity of punishment is not enough. Rational choice theories suggest that punishment does work in deterring crime. However, severe punishments with a low probability of implementation have a low deterrent effect. As Myers (1992: 87) points out, some types of offenses, such as drug dealing, carry a low absolute risk. "The calculation of the ratio of drug arrests to admitted drug sales . . . confirms this. The ratio is an astonishingly low 0.005 [5 out of 1,000] for those with drug sales. If this ratio is to be

regarded as a measure of the riskiness of illegal drug activity, then one must conclude that this is as risk-free a criminal enterprise as one can find."

Conclusion

If crime is made rational by a social structure that creates needs for theft and illicit services and provides chances to steal, the defender of that social structure calls for reformation or punishment of those who feel those needs and take advantage of such chances.

If, on the other hand, the social structure itself is deemed unworthy, corrupt and corrupting, then the recommendation is for overthrow of the entire structure in the hope of a new start. This remedy is the preferred course of sociologists who identify themselves by many titles—such as "new," "Marxian," "radical," "critical," or "conflict" criminologists. Their explanation of crime is the subject of Chapter 14.

14. Power and Conflict

Conflict Theory and Radical Theory

Every explanation of crime production rests on a notion of conflict. Unfortunately for theories of criminogenesis, the idea of conflict is a broad one and its boundaries are seldom specified. For example, boundaries can be drawn along dimensions of time and numbers. Thus there can be conflict that prevails over a lifetime between groups, as in ethnic warfare; or conflict of some years' duration among a few people, as in domestic battling; or conflict of a moment between individuals, as in a barroom brawl. However, the conflict that is emphasized by theorists who have appropriated the title "conflict criminology" is moral and material, relatively enduring, and between segments of populations rather than between individuals. It is dispute over what is right and wrong and whose ethics should be codified in criminal law, but it is also dispute over who should have the "right" to which freedom, which privilege, and which wealth.

Economists who look at theft as rational are conflict theorists in the sense that they observe some people wanting, and taking, what others have. Subculture theorists who look at crime as produced by people of different tastes living together under one law are also resting their explanation on conflict. Similarly, from their different points of emphasis, social psychologists who stress the causal importance of opportunities, interpretations of situations, or training regimes all rest their explanations of crime on some sort of conflict. For all these many theorists, conflict resides in differences—whether the differences be in opportunities, in ideas, or in nurturing.

At issue, then, is the *kind* of conflict that a theory emphasizes, the *source* of that conflict, and the *prescriptions* that follow. Criminologists split into competing camps on these matters. Some, who have appropriated the title *conflict theorists,* stress "culture conflict" (Sellin 1938), "group conflict" (Vold and Bernard 1979), and, more generally, conflicts among "interest groups" with differential powers (Turk 1969). Others, who term themselves *radical* or "Marxist" criminologists, regard conflict theory as vague and as reformist rather than revolutionary. By contrast, radical theorists, and particularly the Marxists among them, point to a particular source of crime and a particular remedy. Since a *conflict criminology* is implicit in *every* vision of crime production, and since a Marxist conception is one of the more popular among sociologists, attention here turns to views from the left.

Theses of Leftist Criminology

To be "radical" is "to get to the root of the matter," but how one does this varies. There are theorists who consider themselves radical but non-Marxist—anarchists and some conservatives, for example. However, some variety of Marxism holds a majority position among theorists of the left, and does so internationally. We should like, then, to understand Marxist theses, but this is made difficult because Marx and Engels had little to say about crime or criminal law. Therefore, Marxist criminologists translate essays on history into particular theses about current conditions and crime production, and such translation is always subject to dispute. Dispute is a result of the difficulties of reading all the works of Marx (Figure 14.1) and Engels and interpreting their voluminous writing. Thus a sympathetic critic has contested appropriation of

Figure 14.1   Karl Marx, the intellectual "father" of conflict criminology, wrote little about the causes of crime. Photo courtesy of Corbis.

the Marxist title by criminologists, and an early participant in leftist criminology concluded that "[we are] more agreed on what we are against than what we are for" (Cohen 1971: 16).

If we acknowledge, then, that Marxist criminologists differ among themselves on some issues, their major theses can be described and assessed. Since a central theme holds that "capitalist" societies are criminogenic, this school may be regarded as offering a structural explanation of crime.

The following assumptions characterize views from the left: ideas are socially situated; human nature is a social product; crime is politically defined; and crime is a form of protest.

Ideas Are Socially Situated

Marxists emphasize what seems indisputable—that ideas, including explanations of crime, are "socially situated." This means that ideas reflect our times and our places.

There is little novel in this proposition when it remains a broad generalization—that what we know depends on when and where we live. What fifteenth-century inhabitants of North America could know about their world is not what we know. The social world has changed, of course, but so too have our powers of observation and inference.

However, Marxists narrow this truism. Ideas, they contend, are differentially generated in times and places; but they also differ among people who, at any one time, occupy different "social niches." Many of our ideas—and we are not told exactly which ones—are said to justify our economic interests.

Marxists have developed a "relational" theory of knowledge that seeks to ascertain the connection between a mode of existence and a mode of thought (Mannheim 1936: 254). There is more than one way of thinking and that where a person is in time, place, and social structure limits what she or he can know and, more strongly, *determines* beliefs. Thought is deemed to be "situationally conditioned"; and therefore, says Karl Mannheim, "a group whose class position is more or less definitely fixed already has its political viewpoint *decided* for it" (1936: 143, emphasis added.)

In short, conceptions of social reality are *social constructions,* an idea with which non-Marxists can agree (Berger and Luckmann 1966). It follows that such constructions may be *ideologies*, serving to defend a power position while deluding ("mystifying") the powerless into acquiescence in their subjugation. If "sociologies" are made by people, however, they can be remade, and it is a function of critical criminology to "demystify" present social relations and to think of new possibilities. Critical thinking, it is said, removes "the myths—the false consciousness—created by official reality [and] will move us to a radical reconstruction of our lives—indeed, to revolution itself" (Quinney 1974a: 11, 13).

Given these premises, attempts to know the social world scientifically are presumptuous. What has been called "positivism" or "scientism" is said to be a defective way of finding out about social relations because this procedure selects topics "(1) simple enough to lend themselves to quantitative measurement or

(2) socially insignificant enough to permit the appearance of value-neutrality" (Flacks and Turkel 1978: 195).

SOCIOLOGY AS A HUMANISTIC ENDEAVOR
Sociology, it is said, is "inescapably humanistic [and] interpretive; any attempt to impose a scientific framework on social inquiry [is] both socially dangerous and intellectually fatuous." (Flacks and Turkel, 1978: 195)

In opposition to "scientism," Marxists believe that observers cannot separate themselves from that which they study and that the very fact of choosing a topic of inquiry and a method with which to pursue it is saturated in the values of the inquirer.

Human Nature as a Social Product

Christians and classical conservatives assume that there is a human nature, a mixture of good and evil propensities, that deters us from achieving heaven on earth. In opposition, Marxists believe that human nature is always a social product and that no "basic human nature" can be discerned independent of the social formation of character. Thus Venable, describing the Marxian view of human nature, writes:

> Slave to classes, slave to the conditions which precipitate from the conflict of classes, man is and has always been, as plebeian, patrician, serf, lord, journeyman, guildmaster, bourgeois or proletarian, no "truly human" animal, but merely a "class" animal, no creator of history, but history's creature. (Venable 1945: 150)

Given a Marxian "science of society" a different kind of human being can be produced through alteration of the social conditions that forge motives and channel conduct. In sum, Marxists stand in "that long line of social thought that assumes the 'infinite perfectibility' of humanity" (Flacks and Turkel 1978: 193).

Political Definition of Crime

In accord with other schools of criminology, conflict criminology emphasizes that crime is defined, not discovered. This means that there is no "essence" of criminality that is "merely perceived" by everyone; rather, calling an action "criminal" imposes a definition. This imposition is deemed by those on the left to be a political act, that is, an act reflecting the differential distribution of power. It is further argued by some radical theorists that, in capitalist societies, people do *not* agree on what is right and wrong and on what should be considered criminal (Chambliss and Ryther 1975: 349). On the contrary, it is held that it is a minority with economic privilege that has the power to enact laws defining as crimes those acts which threaten its economic interests.

"Criminal law," says Quinney, "is an instrument that the state and dominant ruling class use to maintain and perpetuate the social and economic order" (Quinney 1975: 291). And Chambliss adds, "In any complex, modern society there is no value-consensus that is relevant to the law" (1974: 37).

Recognizing that "crime" is defined, rather than objectively perceived, suggests the possibility that social harms other than those classically *mala in se*

Box 14.1 Economic Base of Social Institutions

Under the agrarian mode of production known as feudalism, the single most important means of producing was land. Under feudal economies, lords and kings owned nearly all the land, and they employed the labor of serfs to produce agricultural goods. Serfs, on the other hand, owned nothing. They related to the mode of production as nonowners, and as nonowners they were deprived of the primary sources of wealth, status, and power. Thus the economic relationship of lords and serfs to the feudal mode of production doubles as a political relationship of one class (lords) to another (serfs). Needless to say this political relationship, which in Marx's model must always be seen against its economic background, as one in which the dominant class was in a position to exploit and oppress the subordinate class, which again explains why Marx saw class conflict as an important and economically grounded concept.

- -

First and foremost, Marx is saying that any economic system will tend to be supported by "superstructural" factors such as law, politics, education, and consciousness. For example, in a capitalist mode of production (1) laws will be enacted to protect private property, (2) those holding economic power will tend to promote and defend their interests by purchasing political clout with campaign dollars, (3) education will reproduce the skills and techniques required to operate the machinery of production, and (4) consciousness will be shaped in a manner consistent with one's class position. (Lynth and Groves, 1989: 10, 13)

should be pursued as criminal. These include corporate damage to the environment, persistence of dangerous working conditions, and manufacture of unsafe consumer products. Herman and Julia Schwendinger (1975: 136–137) advocate also that "imperialistic war, racism, sexism, and poverty" be made criminal. Furthermore, *social systems*, as well as individuals, should be deemed criminal when they "cause the systematic abrogation of basic rights."

Social Order and Coercion

Marxism sees criminal law and its administrative apparatus as required by capitalism to discipline the workforce (Marx 1967: 899–900). This apparatus is a control mechanism of last resort, however.

Control of the populace is produced primarily through the rigors of the labor market. Marxists believe that workers are *forced* to sell their labor. This "silent compulsion of the market," as Young (1981: 296) terms it, is the major mode of social control in capitalist society. Secondarily, capitalists are believed to keep the masses quiet through indoctrination in schools and the media of mass communication which, allegedly, they control.

It is only against a marginal minority that defenders of capitalism resort to direct, extraeconomic force. Such a circumstance arises from capitalism's production of a "surplus population" of the unemployed, the underclass, and social critics.

According to Marxists, this explains the nature of prison populations among whom unskilled laborers, African Americans, and aboriginal people appear disproportionately. Bourgeois prisons are said to fulfill two vital functions: (1) they serve as deterrents, keeping the "lawful," working population in its place, and

(2) they are ideological instruments, transmitting the message that only the working class is criminal while concealing the crimes of the powerful (Young 1981: 298). It is also alleged that legal attention to the crimes of the underclass distracts attention from the exploitative (that is, immoral if not criminal) nature of capitalism itself.

Marxist explanation is, then, a variant of *functional explanation*. A functional explanation is one that tries to account for actions by showing that they have consequences that maintain a system. The consequences may be intended, as when they serve the actor's purposes, or they may be unintended results appreciated by some external observer. Intended effects are called *manifest* functions; unintended consequences are referred to as *latent* functions (Merton 1949). Marxism interprets the nature of criminal law and its administration as serving the interests of capitalists; it provides, therefore, a form of functional explanation.

Crime as Protest

Given the Marxist view of the definition and production of crime, it is congenial to see much criminality as protest against an unjust society (Krisberg 1975). And, on the assumption of exploitation—that is, of capitalist theft of the "surplus value" of workers' efforts—certain convicts are deemed to be "political criminals," prosecuted more for the ideological threat they pose to the ruling class than for the damage they have done. In this light, some radical criminologists suggest that "criminals, rather than the working class, might be the vanguard of the revolution" (Greenberg 1981: 28, n. 10).

If crime is protest against injustice, then such political criminals are rational. In turn, this means that we need not bother looking for something pathological in their characters. It is not biological difference or psychological difference that is the cause of crime, but the social system that keeps segments of the population poor, that chains them to miserable work, and that drives them to violence among themselves as well as to theft from members of their own class and others.

In this schema, the locus of responsibility for criminality is not individual, but social. And it is not social in some limited sense—as, for example, attributable to broken homes—but social in the Marxist sense of deriving from the productive relations of the capitalist system.

Policy

Prescription follows easily from these premises. If social inequalities are the result of private ownership of the instruments of production, and if these inequalities generate crime, then the solution is a classless society.

Since a classless society is not likely to evolve, it will have to be created. Creation of a classless society cannot occur through reform of capitalism and expansion of "opportunities," because "the unequal distribution of property and power in capitalism will always result in the privileged reproducing inequalities of opportunity areas" (Young 1981: 303). Therefore, consistent Marxists, but not all on the left, assume that the classless, crime-free society will have to be produced through revolution, through violent overthrow of the present social order.

Promises

In sum, the "end product" of Marxist revolution, Quinney (1974b) assures us, "will be a life released from the repressions of today." This promise is believed to be plausible because ultimately it is not law that makes people good. Individuals are basically good. It is the institutions which oppress them that make for any shortcomings. Let people be free. Let them control their own institutions rather than be controlled by them, and they will be good people by the nature of their being.

Advantages of Leftist Criminology

Conflict criminology has several advantages. Simply being radical, in the sense of being challenging, is refreshing. It suggests new ways of thinking about our lives.

Among these suggestions are questions raised about uses of the criminal law. Marxist criminology suggests studies in the sociology of law as tests of its functional explanation of the evolution of legal conceptions of crime. The leftist thesis that laws are created in capitalist countries by the powerful to dominate the powerless and that criminal justice systems function to maintain that dominance has been alleged, but not proved.

Marxist criminology can also be interpreted as supporting the more general structural theme—economic or opportunistic—which says that where one is in the social structure opens or closes opportunities to lawful and unlawful ways of getting what one wants. In this manner, the radical thesis emphasizes the parallel roots of the different kinds of theft committed by white-collar criminals and lower-class offenders. The different styles of stealing are seen as generated by a common structure of pressures and chances. Given the injustice it sees in bourgeois countries, socialist criminology regards some crime as rational. At the same time, it defends those "political" crimes it considers to have been caused by unjust social relations.

The greatest advantage of criminology on the left, however, lies in its popular appeal. It is popular because it criticizes and promises.

Criticism, we are reminded, is one of the vocational characteristics of intellectuals, the "professionally thoughtful people" (Furst 1952; Shils 1972; von Mises 1960). Criticism is pleasurable. It is part of our making discriminations in the world, part of our preferring this to that. Criticism becomes popular, however, when it is inspirational, when it promises a better world upon acceptance of its assumptions. Political movements, like religious ones, promise, at the minimum, improvement. At the maximum, they promise salvation, the end of human misery.

Promise is comforting, of course. For people who live in impoverished circumstances (this does *not* include most Western intellectuals) and for those whose lives are hollow (and this may include many intellectuals) promise gives one "something to live for." It becomes difficult, then, to say nay to the needy person's faith. Nevertheless, it is part of the scholar's job to be critical, and there is much to be critical about in Marxist criminology.

Deficiencies of Leftist Criminology

Deficiencies of Marxist criminology have to do with concepts, facts, and promises.

Quarrels about Concepts: Exploitation

Exploitation is an idea used to distinguish "agents" from "victims" and employed to justify rebellion and "social banditry." In its moral sense—and there are other meanings— exploitation refers to the unfair use of a person or thing.

Marxists develop their idea of exploitation out of the *labor theory of value*, also called the " theory of surplus value." This doctrine assumes that the value of a product or service is determined, or can be determined, by some uncertain evaluation of the cost of the maintenance or effort of the workers. Persons are "exploiters," therefore, if they can coerce workers, appropriate the product of their labor, sell the product for more than the cost of maintaining those employees, and retain for themselves the "surplus." Mandel (1968: 89) tells us that, "surplus value . . . represents . . . the difference between the product of labor and the cost of maintaining labor." Thus profit is considered to be exploitative.

Economists define exploitation from an idealized model of an efficient economy. According to this idealization, an economy is efficient if it achieves *Pareto optimality*. An economy is Pareto optimal if no change is possible that increases someone's welfare without decreasing someone else's. Economic efficiency, so defined, occurs when "every factor is paid its marginal contribution to the total supply of economic goods and services" under conditions of competitive supply and demand. "In Marxian terms, a factor that is paid less than its marginal product is being exploited; a factor that is paid more than its marginal product is an exploiter" (Thurow 1973: 70).

This assumption ignores the fact that value is never defined abstractly, independent of exchange. Value can be ascertained only as a function of what someone is willing to pay (in time, effort, money, or things) for a service or commodity.

In this view, value is something that results from a mixture of workers' efforts, capital, organization, and management. *Capital* refers to *surplus* saved from previous enterprise. It includes tools, but it also includes human capabilities expanded by education—by time out from productive work. *Organization* refers to ways in which individual efforts are coordinated. *Management* refers to leadership, the provision of direction to coordinated effort.

Capital makes a difference in the creation of wealth; so too do organization and management. Therefore, no one knows in advance of engaging in any collective enterprise how much a worker contributes to the value of a product. What the product is worth cannot be established by fiat, and it is not established by the fact that someone has "worked."

Some work is worth little; no one wants to buy it. Other work has a meager payoff. And some work is deemed to be valuable beyond any measure of the maintenance costs of the worker or the energy expended. In this last instance, people pay more for the product than is needed to maintain the laborer. Thus, people pay to witness extreme skill in ballplayers like Michael Jordan and other entertainers such as Michael Jackson, Madonna, or Garth Brooks. The value of these workers is not determined by their effort or by what is required to keep them alive.

In the everyday world, exploitation is discerned through a subjective appreciation of what someone's effort *should be* worth. This is an exchange-free, that is, moral, evaluation. In extreme cases, people tend to agree about such subjective evaluations. For example, in the modern world, there would be agreement that slaves are exploited. Similarly, at the other extreme where union power or bureaucracy has created job monopoly, there may be subjective agreement that such workers are "exploiting" employers and taxpayers. In short, a subjective appreciation of exploitation permits the possibility that workers may make too much money as well as too little. However, these evaluations are far removed from anything specified by a labor theory of value.

In summary, extreme cases lead to agreement in moral assessment of fairness, and unfairness, of reward—that is, of exploitation. But as a theoretical term, exploitation is defective. It is a stimulating idea and one that motivates by building resentment. But it is not a scientific concept; that is, it is not a concept with a clear referent and a demonstrable utility in constructing a theory of social action that can inform rational policy. Inspiration is not to be confused with illumination.

Factual Deficiencies

Concepts are tools with which we think. Unclear concepts produce unclear thought. Nevertheless, vague ideas can excite emotion, and they can move people to political action without providing accurate maps of reality.

An idea that is morally stimulating need not be clear or accurate. An idea that has political utility may have no factual validity. What is good for politics may be bad for science. In sum, obscure concepts promote errors in fact and errors in forecast.

All attempts to explain human behavior scientifically claim to rest upon facts and to make sense of those facts. Thus, the central theme of radical criminology is scientifically useful only if it is both factual and clarifying. The central theme says that criminal laws in bourgeois societies define crimes as interested minorities want them defined and not as a majority agree, they should be defined.

Tests from the Left

This hypothesis is empirical; it refers to facts. However, those who have advanced this assumption have not tested it adequately. The principal tests of this allegation advanced on the left have been anecdotal. That is, a few criminal laws have been studied in an attempt to show how interested minorities rather than consensual majorities have pushed for their passage. Laws studied in this way have been largely those regarding administrative offenses and crimes *mala prohibita* rather than the more universal crimes *mala in se*. For example, Chambliss studied the evolution of the laws of vagrancy in England to demonstrate that these laws changed to serve the needs of landowners for a supply of cheap labor (Chambliss 1964, 1973). Such a demonstration requires, of course, an accurate reading of the laws and an accurate representation of public support for their passage and enforcement. Both the reading of these English laws and their alleged causal link with particular economic interests have been challenged, and largely refuted, by Edwards (1977). However, the debate about the history of vagrancy laws need not be resolved here. The significant deficiency of radical criminology is its lack of evidence for its central allegation: that criminal law in capitalist countries is entirely, or mostly, produced by elites to defend their economic interests.

Burden of proof rests on the affirmative. Those who advance a hypothesis have the responsibility of proving it. However, radical criminologists have done little to test their major thesis. They are not even clear as to which criminal laws do not serve particular economic interests. It has been left to criminologists in the mainstream to test for class bias in production of criminal law.

Related Issues

Refutation of the radical thesis about lawmaking in bourgeois societies addresses one part of the Marxist claim. A related issue concerns whether crimes *mala in se* are considered worthy of state attention by majorities or only by an elite. Are treason, murder, manslaughter, kidnapping, wounding, forcible rape, robbery, burglary, and fraud considered criminal by the majority of citizens in capitalist countries, or are definitions of these wrongs only imposed upon the majority by powerful minorities? It is a significant defect of Marxist criminology that its advocates have not tried to answer this crucial question.

An approximate answer is found in studies of the judged *gravity* of crimes. These investigations compare the seriousness of kinds of crime as rated by a sample of citizens and as ranked by the penalties allowable under the criminal laws (Boydell and Grindstaff 1972; Gibbons 1969; Levi and Jones 1985; Parton et al. 1991; Rauma 1991; Rose and Prell 1955; Smith and Glans 1989; Smith and Hill 1991).

Such studies show both agreement and discrepancy between the popularly judged gravity of some offenses and the legal definition of their seriousness. They show, however, that people and their laws in capitalist states tend to rank gravity of offense in parallel fashion. Thus, attacks on persons are judged as more serious than attacks on property, and both these wrongs are felt to be more serious than some kinds of "victimless" crime. Nevertheless, this demonstration does not answer the central question about how much agreement there is among the citizenry and their laws in the *definition* of acts as crimes.

Answering such a question with the tools of social science is relatively simple. Failure of radical criminologists to perform empirical tests of their major assumption makes their schema suspect. The failure allows C. W. Thomas (1976: 15) to say that the assumptions of both consensus and conflict theses "lie more in the realm of self-evident truths than empirically validated facts." When Thomas and his associates tested the radical hypothesis in a limited way, they found no support for its central assumption. On the contrary, they found considerable support for a consensual model.

Consensus About Crime

Thomas's study: C. W. Thomas and his coworkers received questionnaires from 3,334 households in the Norfolk, Virginia, Standard Metropolitan Statistical

Area (1976). These questionnaires asked citizens what would be a "fair sentence" for each of 17 offenses committed by a hypothetical person who was guilty, adult, and a first offender.

Respondents were divided into 12 classes by their distribution on six indicators of their relative position in the social structure: age, sex, race, education, income, and occupational prestige. It was hypothesized that, if the radical perspective were correct, there would be considerable *disagreement* between people of low and high status in their evaluation of the 17 sample crimes.

Contrary to this hypothesis, rankings of the gravity of crimes were close to perfect among persons in different social positions:

> The average correlation was .977 for the six social background variables and .989 for the twelve comparisons involving the social background characteristics and the total sample ranking. The lowest correlation we obtained . . . was the .917 coefficient yielded by a comparison of the rankings of our black and white respondents. (Thomas 1976: 10)

The study by Thomas is not a direct test of a citizenry's agreement in its *definition* of acts as criminal. However, a subsequent study by Newman does directly assess the amount of agreement among people in defining crime.

Newman's research: Graeme Newman (1976), with the cooperation of students in six countries, tested the degree to which nine acts were considered to be more or less serious and worthy of control by the state or other agency.

Samples of residents in urban and rural districts were questioned in India, Indonesia, Iran, Italy (Sardinia), Yugoslavia, and the United States (New York). These people of diverse culture were asked to consider nine acts ranging from crimes *mala in se* and crimes *mala prohibita* to those that are morally ambiguous. The nine acts were described briefly:

- *Robbery:* A person forcefully takes $50 from another who, as a result, is injured and has to be hospitalized.
- *Incest:* A person has sexual relations with his adult daughter.
- *Not helping:* A person sees someone in a dangerous situation and does nothing.
- *Abortion:* A woman who is two months pregnant seeks and obtains an abortion.
- *Factory pollution:* A factory director continues to permit his factory to release poisonous gases into the air.
- *Homosexuality:* A person has homosexual relations in private with the consent of the partner.
- *Protest:* A person participates in a protest meeting against government policy in a public place. No violence occurs.
- *Appropriation:* A person puts government funds to his own use.
- *Taking drugs:* A person takes drugs (specified "heroin" in U.S., "soft" in Sardinia, "opium" in Iran, "gange" in India and Indonesia) (Newman 1976: 317).

Respondents were asked six questions about each of these acts:

1. Do you think this act should be prohibited by law?
2. Is this act prohibited by the law?
3. How active do you think the government is in trying to stop acts of this kind?

4. To whom (if anyone) would you report this act?
5. How serious do you think this act is?
6. What do you think should be done with a person who performs an act of this kind? (1976: 318–19)

Newman's findings contradict the radical criminologist's allegation that "crime" is only "political," a definition imposed by the powerful upon the powerless. To the contrary, Newman's (1976: 153) data demonstrate that

> there is a universal (i.e., cross-cultural) consensus concerning the disapproval of a number of crimes and deviances [*sic*]. This applies especially at the general level of opinion and intensity of reaction. A generally deep, probably emotional reaction, as measured by choice of sanctions, was also found cross-culturally.

Furthermore:

> Respondents in all cultures tended to classify the acts into similar groupings. . . . For traditional crimes, a high degree of consensus was found for their disapproval. . . . One might argue that these crimes have always been disapproved of. They are therefore not relative to particular periods or places, but are standards; one hesitates to say it, but they are, functionally speaking, absolute standards. (1976: 285–286)

Agreement among individuals in their conceptions of "traditional crimes" means, of course, that "class position" in a society does *not* affect the definition of criminality, as it is supposed to do according to radical criminology. Attitudes toward robbery, incest, drug use, and embezzlement are not class attitudes, but definitions of a more universal character. So, too, is disapproval of the new version of the old crime of poisoning the environment. It is only as one inquires about acts that have *not* always been considered wrongs in themselves—acts such as abortion, homosexuality, protest, and not helping—that wide differences are found in opinions. The fact of widespread disapproval of acts long considered to be inherently wrong means that other "background variables," in addition to social class, are also of minor significance in response to the "traditional crimes." Newman found low correlations between age, sex, schooling, literacy, occupation, rural-urban residence, and conceptions of crime (Kaupen 1973; Newman et al. 1974; Weil 1952).

The major point holds, however. Contrary to Marxist allegation, the classic crimes against person and property are widely condemned by people of diverse culture and social position.

Conclusion: Differences Between Crime and Deviance

Findings from Thomas's study and Newman's research suggest a difference between crime and deviance. The frontier between crime and deviance may be defined by the *degree of agreement* among a people about acts deserving social condemnation and control. There are wrongs generally conceived as crimes that stand in contrast to a range of morally ambiguous acts about which we disagree.

Other Issues

Neither the definition of crime nor the production of criminal law in bourgeois societies is the work of a capitalist class imposing its economic interest upon the majority of citizens. However, there are additional deficiencies of fact and theory that characterize the criminological view from the left. Briefly, these concern (1) unfair application of criminal law in capitalist countries, (2) the allegation of distinctively capitalist "crimes against humanity," and (3) the possibility of a crime-free society.

1. It is alleged that criminal justice administration in bourgeois societies is used as an instrument of class oppression and that the criminal law is applied to people less for their crimes than for the powerless position they occupy and by the necessity of "keeping them in their place."

The charge of such discriminatory application of the law has been investigated principally in capitalist countries and rarely in socialist states. Comparison of the justice of legal systems is therefore tentative. Such data as we have, however, do not support the claim that criminal justice in bourgeois societies is nothing but "class justice." To the contrary, it is precisely in capitalist lands that due-process protection of defendants is strongest (Gastil 1976). Freedoms *are* correlated.

BOX 14.2   SOVIET-STYLE LEGAL DEFENSE

As part of the Canadian Broadcasting Corporation's inside look at the [then] Soviet Union's criminal justice system in the fifth year of Mikhail Gorbachev's administration, a defense lawyer was quoted as saying "I cannot say anything flattering about my client. My deeply held personal opinion is that it would be immoral to defend this man. Fighting for his innocence would not reflect the morality of our society." (Cuff 1989)

---

2. Voices from the left claim that capitalist societies are peculiarly guilty of "crimes against humanity." Racism, sexism, and poverty are "crimes" allegedly more characteristic of market economies than of planned ones. War, too, is held to be a *distinctive* product of capitalism, at least when it is conceived as a certain kind of war called "imperialist" (Schwendinger and Schwendinger 1975: 136).

None of these activities is defined with that *specificity* required of criminal law in Western countries. Vagueness of the nominated crimes against "human rights" permits emotional charges to be made without proof, and it makes comparison of the protection of these rights in different societies difficult. It is apparent, however, that deprivation of these rights is *relative*. Violation is more readily seen where these privileges are most protected. Thus Hollander (1973: 334) notes:

> Paradoxically poverty is seen as a social problem in the United States, but not in the [former] Soviet Union. It is an American social problem to a large extent because the standard of living is high and consequently expectations are also higher. In the Soviet Union, against the background of generally low living standards, poverty is not a social problem, but rather a normal state of affairs.

The burden of proof rests, again, on those who lay a charge. Proof of the greater violation of "human rights" in capitalist than in communist countries has thus far not been given. To the contrary, such evidence as we have runs against the radical allegation. It is in modern states that purport to be Marxist that torture, expropriation, censorship, forced migration, concentration camps, internal

---

Box 14.3   AKERS ON MARXIST CRIMINOLOGY

In Marxist theory, capitalism itself is the major cause of crime. Ownership of the means of production by the capitalist ruling class produces a society which is inherently criminogenic. Some Marxists propose that all forms of crime simply reflect the crime-producing system of capitalism. The crimes of the working class are either "crimes of accommodation" or "crimes of domination and repression," which are committed to protect and promote the interest of the ruling class. Other Marxist theorists have departed from this oversimplified approach. However, the more complex models they offer essential rely on concepts and explanations from non-Marxist theories.

Whether the more simplified or complex Marxist theories are valid can be adequately judged only on the basis of direct comparisons of real capitalist with real socialist societies. Such comparisons have yet to substantiate the primary Marxist argument that crime is a problem in capitalism but not a problem in socialism. (Akers, 1994: 177–178)

---

passports, forced labor, and imprisonment without defense are most common. And it is in such lands that "the people" are prisoners, to be shot if they try to escape. This novel phenomenon of prohibiting citizens—more appropriately, "subjects"—from leaving the country is strikingly in evidence in Albania, Cuba, Kampuchea, North Korea, and the People's Republic of China to name a few of the communistically "liberated" lands. Paul Hollander (1982: 347) concludes a survey of Marxist societies by noting:

> No Marxist society, with the possible exception of Yugoslavia, has ever allowed its citizens to emigrate without punitive restrictions—e.g., the loss of employment or housing upon application for an exit visa, and the prohibition against taking anything but the most minimal personal property.

Factual errors in locating "crimes against humanity" are complemented by conceptual deficiencies.

3. Promises of better worlds depend on images of "society." No image of social relations developed by thoughtful persons is entirely true or false, although many such models are sufficiently vague as to be beyond test.

A theme of our discussions is that all explanations of crime point to something causal. Criticism of the major modes of explaining crime is based, then, on the *clarity* of the nominated causes, the *factual evidence* for each nomination, and the *predictive accuracy* of the many theories of criminogenesis.

With this qualification, a major sociological deficiency of radical criminology becomes apparent. It is the assumption that only property divides us. It is the assumption that if private ownership of the instruments of production were eliminated, there would be, by definition, no "social classes" and therefore no elite with the power to criminalize the deviance of anyone. Crime would wither away, as would the state, which is said to be required only as an instrument of class oppression.

In contradiction of this image of social relations, studies in anthropology, psychology, and sociology demonstrate repeatedly that struggles over material things are only one source of division among people. Deviation is a normal feature of our living together, and even moral communities find it necessary to define boundaries of acceptable behavior as a means of ensuring moral continuity. This thesis has been well expressed by one of the founders of sociology, Emile Durkheim (1858–1917), who urged us to

> imagine a society of saints, a perfect cloister of exemplary individuals. Crimes, properly so called, will there be unknown; but faults which appear venial to the layman will create there the same scandal that the ordinary offense does in ordinary consciousness. If, then, this society has the power to judge and punish, it will define these acts as criminal and will treat them as such. (1958: 68–69)

Promissory Deficiencies

The theory of society advanced by the left promises many good things, not all of which are well defined. Among these good things are liberation, justice, material abundance, and happiness. We are also promised a social network in which, as we have seen, there will be no need for criminal law or for a state to enforce it.

Unfortunately, radical theorists do not *know* how to achieve what they promise, and the real world casts doubt on their vision. The liberation and material well-being promised through socialist and communist revolutions have not been achieved. Their opposites, tyranny and "normal poverty," have been the most common consequence of destruction of freedom in the marketplace. Under socialism and communism, the state has grown, not withered away, and fewer people have more power over more aspects of the lives of their subjects.

There is a difference between nations that *evolve* toward equality and those that employ political action toward that objective. Political action, by definition, requires power. Applying power—coercing people—yields different results from cultural evolution. The Berlin wall was designed not so much to keep outsiders from entering what was then East Germany, but to keep East Germans in. Anti-immigration policies of the former Soviet Union were designed to prevent an exodus of "people voting with their feet." Philosophers have known this for centuries and have wrestled unsuccessfully with the question of how to use power to achieve beneficial results without inducing unpleasant byproducts like tyranny. No one has solved this riddle, because ends cannot be divorced from means.

Variations on the Theme

It is against this backdrop of the origins of conflict criminology that its more recent variations can be understood. They have in common the central idea that it is structural arrangements that allow and maintain differences in power that cause crime. As we shall see, these structural arrangements do not have to be fundamentally economic and the sources of differences in power are irrelevant. What is crucial is that differences in power exist and that there are structural arrangements that maintain them.

The general form of the explanation is that when differences in power exist, for whatever reason, power will be used for the purpose of being maintained and extended and that the power will be used, as well, to the advantage of those who have it and to the disadvantages of those who do not. Power means the ability to control the behavior of others. Crime is a consequence of differential access to power.

Three forms of explanation that parallel the Marxist one, but are not based on one's relationship to the means of production, are the following: feminist theories; power-control; and family violence theory.

Feminist Explanations

There is no feminist *theory* of crime. Feminist *perspectives* have been applied to a number of types of crime, particularly with respect to certain crimes that men perpetuate on women such as rape and domestic violence. Feminist perspective have also been applied to analyses of the criminal justice system. Empirical support for ideas that stem from the former has been stronger than support for the latter.

Feminist perspectives identify the basis for differences in power between men and women and indicate how these differences manifest themselves in different rates for certain type of behavior. Some of these feminist perspectives fall within the context of opportunity theory (Chapter 15) and others have a close relationship to cultural and subcultural perspectives (Chapter 17). There are others, however, that fall squarely within the tradition and perspective of radical criminology.

The actual forms of that perspective differ and these differences are at the heart of the distinctions among different types of feminism. What distinguishes types of feminism is that each system of ideas (-ism) identifies a different cause (basis) for the inequality that exists between men and women and, since the causes are different, also offers different prescriptions of what it is that would have to change in order to reduce or eliminate such inequity.

Liberal feminism accounts for differences in power between men and women as a function of unequal opportunity and the violation of individual rights.

Radical feminism accounts for differences in power between men and women as rooted in patriarchy and male control of female sexuality.

Socialist feminism accounts for differences in power between men and women as rooted in the structure of capitalism and its connection to patriarchy.

Regardless of the perceived cause of the difference in power and its implications for public policy, the feminist perspective identifies that differences in power manifest themselves in differences in rates of various behaviors. In some cases, the perspective has been used in attempts to account for lower rates of crime among women (Messerschmidt 1986). In other cases, it has been used to challenge the accuracy of official statistics on crime that "miss" and "underrecord" female criminality (Smart 1976). In still other cases, it has been used to account for the elevated rates of female representation in some forms of criminality such as prostitution (Chesney-Lind and Sheldon 1992).

There is, however, no feminist explanation of female criminality that is applicable over a broad range of criminal behaviors. The same explanations that see crime as a result of differences in power across social groups or socioeconomic groups would make forecasts about female criminality that are not supported by studies of crime whether they rely on official or unofficial statistics.

Specifically, explanatory frameworks that see crime to be a result of relative powerlessness would forecast—as happens for a variety of racial and socioeconomic minority groups—that women would display higher rates of crime, particularly serious crimes of violence and that they would be treated more harshly by the system of criminal justice (e.g., more severe sentences and longer incarceration than would be experienced by men who are found guilty of comparable crimes).

Power-Control Theory

Hagan and his collaborators (1987) have offered "power-control theory" as an explanation of some delinquency among young women. The essence of power-control theory is this: Mothers in traditional roles exercise control over their daughters to an extent that it reduces their likelihood of engaging in law-violating behavior. This control is greater than that exercised over sons. In contrast, mothers who have occupational roles that are nontraditional and involve the exercise of control over others are less controlling of the behavior of their daughters. Young women with such mothers are at higher risk of delinquency, a risk that is said to be more like that of their brothers (Hagan et al. 1987; Hagan 1990; Grasmick et al. 1996).

The explanation has two features that are of interest. First, the social position of fathers is considered to be irrelevant. Second, the social position of women is considered to be irrelevant with respect to the behavior of boys. The empirical evidence with respect to power-control theory has been mixed.

Domestic Violence

The last set of explanations of rates of crime that emphasize power and see criminogenic forces as rooted in the social structure have, at their focus, the differences in rates of physically violent acts between men and women, particularly in the area of domestic violence. There is no question that in some spheres, women are disproportionately victims of violence. For example, in the United States, the ratio of men to women charged with murder is approximately 7.9:1 while the ratio of men to women victims is about 3.4:1 (Calculated from Maguire and Pastore 1995: Table 3.123). Furthermore, if our attention is focused upon victim-offender relationships, we note that there are 2.8 times as many "wife" murder victims as there are "husband" victims and 2.4 "girlfriend" victims for every "boyfriend" victim (calculated from Maguire and Pastore 1995: Table 3.111).

The relationship between gender and homicide is even more pronounced in low homicide-rate countries such as Canada. As DeKeseredy and Hinch (1991: 15) report, "most (39%) of the Canadian homicides solved by the police between 1974 and 1987 were classified as domestic homicides, and men who killed their wives or cohabiting partners were the largest cohort of perpetrators (37%)."

Survey data on nonfatal violence in the home further support the contention that substantial "wife abuse" takes place. Based on the 1985 National Family Violence Resurvey, Strauss and Gelles (1990: 96–97) report that the estimated rate of "any" violence by husbands against their wives is 116 per 1,000 couples.

The rate of "severe" violence by husbands against their wives is estimated to be 34 per 1,000 couples. These researchers report that these figures must be seen as an estimate of the "lower bound" since it is "virtually certain that not every respondent was completely frank in describing violent incidents."

Straus and others, however, have explored the dynamics of domestic violence beyond husbands' abusiveness toward their partners. The feature of this literature that is particularly intriguing has less to do with women as victims of violence than the need to account for women as perpetrators of violence. In the same National Family Violence Resurvey, Straus and Gelles (1990) also report that women might be even *more* violent that men in domestic situations. Their estimates are that the rate of "any" violence directed toward a husband by a wife is 124 per 1,000 couples and the rate of "severe" violence perpetrated by wives is 48 per 1,000 couples. These figures do not include violence directed toward children in the household—much of which is also committed by women. As Straus and Gelles (1990: 96) report, "the fact that women are so violent within the family is inconsistent with the extremely low rate of assault by women outside the family, but consistent with our 1975 national survey . . . and with a number of other studies. . . ."

While not all researchers who agree with these results (Dobash et al. 1992) call the supposed "symmetry" in marital violence a "myth," there is increasing evidence to support the notion that domestic violence is not the sole domain of men (see Farrell 1986; McNeely and Mann 1990; and Shupe et al. 1987). In a review of the experimental literature, Frodi, Macaulay, and Thome (1977: 634) report "that women are often as openly hostile and as directly aggressive as men, and occasionally more so."

While this intriguing line of research clearly goes against the conventional wisdom of the stereotype of the aggressive male and the passive female, it does not mitigate the negative consequences of male aggression. As Anne Campbell, whose research tends to support sexual symmetry in domestic violence notes, "women's injuries evidently make wife beating by far the most serious form of spousal abuse." Yet, it clearly creates theoretical complications for simplistic approaches to the understanding of gender and aggression.

One potential solution to the issue might be found in the work by Campbell and her co-authors who suggest that men and women both view and direct aggressiveness in different channels (Campbell, Muncer, and Coyle 1992; Campbell, Muncer, and Gorman 1993). These researchers suggest that men's violence may be much more instrumental in its origin and perception. Thus, it is directed toward social control and coercion in the service of self-esteem or sexual or material gain. Women's violence, they hypothesize, may be seen as more expressive—a consequence of a temporary failure of self-control. Within this framework, women's violence is seen more often as stemming from stressful life-events such as monetary problems or an abusive spouse and is more often cathartic rather than goal-directed.

Conclusion

Criminology on the left has been assessed as one version of a structural story about crime causation. The exciting element in this criminology is its condemnation of the total structure of contemporary Western societies and its abandonment of reform in favor of a revolution that will eliminate the power of one group over another.

Against the enthusiasm of such promise, competing theories of criminogenesis seem pallid. For many scholars they are boring because they suggest tedious reforms and little hope. This lack of promise does not make such explanations of crime untrue, of course, but it does make them less interesting. Nevertheless, students who wish to expand their experience will examine other ideas about crime production.

Chapter 15 describes a peculiarly North American version of structural explanation of crime—the notion that crime is generated by the balance of lawful and criminal opportunities.

15. Structures of Opportunity

Circumstances and Structural Explanations

The circumstances in which we find ourselves influence our conduct. That seems obvious, and yet such a statement is vague. The important question is, "How much do situations affect behavior?" If circumstances were powerful causes of conduct, a social science might be constructed. Such a science would tell us that, whenever people are in situation *x*, they do *y*, with such-and-such probability. Hope for such a science rests on assumptions that people are "all pretty much the same," that their different histories don't matter much, and that "situation *x*" can be identified.

The last assumption requires that similarity and difference in circumstance be specified. This, however, is a difficult task. We do make judgments about people being in similar, or different, situations, but we make these estimates with crude tools that omit much and do not draw clean boundaries between similar and different events.

These comments on the circumstantial conditioning of action are relevant to the underlying, but often tacit, assumption of structural explanations of crime. By definition, a structural explanation refers conduct to some element of the situation we are in. This assumption, again, is both obvious and open. Its openness is apparent in the variety of situational elements that are deemed to be important, as the following chapters indicate. In general, structural explanations of crime consider ways in which rewards and punishments are handed out. Notice that these explanations are immediately bilateral; one "side" of the explanation looks at the generation of desires, the other "side" looks at their satisfaction. One can stress rewards and punishments, "carrots or sticks," or mixtures of situational pleasures and pains.

Economists emphasize human striving as rational, as mediated by costs and benefits that are judged, imperfectly of course, by actors in particular situations. Radical criminology moves attention from the rationality of criminality—which it does not deny—to differentials in power that allow minorities to exploit majorities and to define threats to their power as crimes.

Another form of structural explanation parallels the views of economists and leftist criminologists in that it conceives of actors as struggling in webs of circumstance to achieve their ends. However, a structural story that emphasizes the causal role of *opportunities* stresses choice less and "pressure" more than economists do. In comparison with the radical school, those who speak of opportunities as generating criminality emphasize power less and economic chances more.

Those who conceive of opportunities as moving people toward more and less lawful activity assume that "people everywhere are pretty much the same" and that there are no significant differences in abilities or desires that might account for lawful and criminal careers. Attention is paid to the organization of social relations that affects the differential exercise of talents and interests, which are assumed to be roughly equal for all persons.

Opportunity-Structure Explanations of Crime

It is emphasis upon *equality* that marks boundaries between an "opportunity-structure" thesis of crime and delinquency and other hypotheses such as those advanced by subcultural theorists (see Chapter 17). The boundaries are drawn by the causes nominated as sources of crime.

This point is important because some authors who stress opportunities also write about subcultures. For example, A. K. Cohen gave his book *Delinquent Boys* the subtitle "The Culture of the Gang" (1955), and the famous study by Cloward and Ohlin (1960), *Delinquency and Opportunity*, also speaks of "delinquent subcultures."

Present assessment of varying ideas about criminogenesis is based on what is *emphasized as causing criminal conduct*. It is apparent, and will be more obvious, that there is overlap among the attempted explanations of crime. However, we can distinguish these explanations by what they stress as causal, rather than by the incidental language they use. And what is stressed as causal is best recognized by the policy prescriptions, if any, that these many authors offer.

The classification presented here of explanations as structural, rather than subcultural, is based on the political advocacy provided by the respective themes. Thus, some authors who speak of delinquent subcultures recommend change *not* in individuals or cultures, but in "the social setting that," in the words of Cloward and Ohlin, "gives rise to delinquency" (1960: 211).

Opportunity-structure theories, then, are those that see all members of a society as wanting much the same things. Such explanations do not emphasize difference, as subcultural or control hypotheses do. Rather, people are conceived to be "pressured" into different courses of action by the structure of life chances available to them. This is a thesis that has appropriately been named "strain theory" (Agnew 1985, 1989, 1992; Burton et al. 1994; Bernard 1987; Farnworth and Leiber 1989).

There is another variation that is sometimes called life style theory (Hindelang et al. 1978) or routine activities theory (Miethe et al. 1987; Messner and Blau 1987) that asserts that it is the styles of life and routine activities of victims that provide the opportunities for crime. Thus, according to Liska and Warner (1991), when members of communities perceive rates of crime as high, they change their comportment (e.g., staying home more) and thereby reduce the opportunity for their goods and their person being the targets of crime.

The focus here, however, will be on the "strain" version that is also known as anomie theory.

Anomie

Concept of Anomie: Durkheim

The conception of social relations as opportunities that push and pull people into different courses of action borrows heavily from the ideas of the French sociologist Emile Durkheim. Durkheim viewed human beings as social animals as well as physical organisms. To say that we are *social* animals means more than the obvious fact that we live for a long time as helpless children, depending on others for our survival. For Durkheim, the significant social aspect of human nature is that human physical survival also depends upon *moral* connections.

Moral connections are, of course, social. They represent a bond with, and hence a bondage to, others. "It is not true," Durkheim (1951: 252) writes, "that human activity can be released from all restraint." The restraint that is required if social life is to ensue is a restraint necessary also for the psychic health of the human individual.

The notion of *pressure* is implied by Durkheim and his followers. Human beings are depicted as requiring a social environment to keep them sound. The pressure of that environment must be neither too little nor too great. Just as we can be crushed by the excessive demands of others upon our lives, so too we fall apart when we live without restraint. The metaphor is that of a denizen of the deep sea that requires just so much pressure to survive and that explodes when brought to the surface.

Absolute freedom, the escape from all moral bonds, would, for Durkheim, be a precursor of suicide. The suicide might be the act of a moment—"taking one's own life"—or it might be the piecemeal and prolonged suicide of those bored with life who kill themselves with vice.

Social conditions may strengthen or weaken the moral ties that Durkheim saw as a condition of happiness and healthy survival. Rapid changes in one's possibilities, swings from riches to rags and, just as disturbing, from rags to riches, may constitute, in Durkheim's (1951: 246) words, "an impulse to voluntary death." Excessive hopes and unlimited desires are avenues to misery. Durkheim's conception of the human being is similar to that found among the ancient Greeks: the idea that men and women require a balance, a proportion, between their appetites and their satisfactions, between their wants and their abilities. Social conditions that allow a "deregulation" of social life Durkheim called states of "anomie." The French word *anomie* derives from Greek roots meaning "lacking in rule or law." Contemporary sociologists frequently refer to anomie as "normlessness," but this seems to lack meaning for many students of social life. It is recommended that the term be used to *refer to the social conditions* characterized by a lack of congruence between the distribution of goals and the socially approved means of achieving goals (Nettler 1957: 671).

DURKHEIM ON ANOMIE

"No living being can be happy or even exist unless his needs are sufficiently proportioned to his means." (1951: 246)

When the concept of anomie is employed by structuralists to explain behavior, attention is directed toward the "strains" produced in the individual by the conflicting, confusing, or impossible demands of the social environment. It is this tension between ends and means to which many social problems are attributed, including the undesirable conditions of hatred of oneself and hatred of one's social connections. There is truth in Durkheim's vision, and many writers have incorporated it into their political attitudes. The rub comes, however, in deciding whether the gap between desires and abilities is to be narrowed by modifying the desires or by changing the world that frustrates their fulfillment. Eastern philosophies and conservative thinkers emphasize the first path; Western philosophies and radical thinkers, the second.

Application of Anomie: Merton

The American sociologist R. K. Merton (1949) applied Durkheim's ideas to the explanation of deviant behavior with particular reference to modern Western societies. According to Merton (1949: 118), there are two aspects of society that are of consideration here. "The first consists of culturally defined goals, purposes, and intents, held out as legitimate objectives for all or for diversely located members of the society." He then goes on to note that "a second element of the cultural structure defines, regulates, and controls the acceptable modes of reaching out for these goals."

Merton's hypothesis is that a state of anomie is produced whenever there is a discrepancy between the goals of human action and the socially structured legitimate means of achieving them. The hypothesis is, simply, that crime breeds in the gaps between aspirations and possibilities. The emphasis given to this idea by the structuralists is that both the goals and the means are provided by the pattern of social arrangements. As Merton (1949: 186) states, the "aim is to discover how some *social structures exert a definite pressure upon certain persons in the society to engage in nonconforming rather than conforming conduct*." It is, therefore, the "structure" of a society, which includes some elements of its culture, that builds desires and assigns opportunities for their satisfaction. This structural explanation sees illegal behavior as resulting from goals, particularly materialistic goals, held to be desirable and possible for all, that motivate behavior in a social context which provides only limited legal channels of achievement.

Merton suggests individuals faced with this disjunction or strain between cultural goals and the institutionally acceptable means of achieving those goals may adapt in one of five ways. These modes of adaptation comprise a typology based on whether the individual either accepts the prevailing cultural goals and means of achieving those goals (+); rejects them (−), or attempts to substitute a new set (±).

While little used to guide current research, Merton's typology has provided the starting point for a number of adaptations of opportunity and strain theory; thus, it is worth examining in some detail (see Table 15.1).

Conformity: According to Merton, this is the modal form of adaptation in most societies. If this were not the case, society would devolve to anarchy. Thus, despite limited access to success, most members of society "troop on." Since the focus of Merton's analysis is on deviance, conformists are not of particular interest within the present context.

Table 15.1   A Typology of Modes of Individual Adaptation.

Modes of adaptation	Culture goals	Institutionalized means
I. Conformity	+	+
II. Innovation	+	–
III. Ritualism	–	+
IV. Retreatism	–	–
V. Rebellion	±	±

Innovation: Both Merton and subsequent researchers have noted that most "normal" criminals accept conventional social goals. Most criminal activity, therefore, is directed toward finding alternate avenues to success. Creative fraud (such as pyramid or Ponzi schemes), organized crime, and white-collar crime are all attempts to adapt to limitations to achieving culturally sanctioned goals. As Merton (1949: 193) notes, "the history of great American fortunes is threaded with strains toward institutionally dubious innovation as is attested by many tributes to the Robber Barons."

Ritualism: Ritualists may be defined as social deviants but are rarely criminals. To accommodate to the dissonance between cultural goals and institutionally acceptable means, ritualists reject the prevailing goals but conform to normative standards of behavior. Thus, their compliance is hollow or ritualistic. Typically, ritualists are assumed to permanently lower their aspirations. They "play it safe" or adopt an "I'm satisfied with what I've got" attitude. It is, to quote Merton, "the mode of adaptation of individually seeking a *private* escape from the dangers and frustrations which seem to them inherent in the competition for major cultural goals by abandoning these goals and clinging all the more closely to the safe routines and the institutional norms."

Retreatism: According to Merton, retreatists are those who are "*in* the society but not *of* it." They reject the culturally prescribed goals and the societal approved means for achieving them. Typical retreatists are skid row alcoholics, drug addicts, and vagrants. Retreatists neither adhere to the productive values of society nor do they conform to institutional practices. Often, retreatists are simply viewed as eccentrics; in less benign circumstances, they are viewed as pariahs and criminals.

Rebellion: Rebels are those who seek to replace the social and cultural structure with a "new order." Rebels are often found in religious orders or radical political movements. As with retreatists, how society reacts to them depends upon their perceived threat to the existing order. If seen as nonthreatening (as is the case with many religious orders), rebels may be tolerated. If perceived as a threat to mainstream society and dominant cultural values (as is the case with Marxists and some religious zealots such as the Branch Davidians), rebels may be identified as criminal.

Opportunity-Structure Theory: Cloward and Ohlin's Delinquency and Opportunity

The most prominent application of Merton's ideas has been to the explanation of juvenile delinquency and, in particular, to that of urban gangs. One formulation is given by Cloward and Ohlin's work, aptly titled *Delinquency and Opportunity*. The central hypothesis is this:

> The disparity between what lower-class youth are led to want and what is actually available to them is the source of a major problem of adjustment. Adolescents who form delinquent subcultures . . . have internalized an emphasis upon conventional goals. Faced with limitation of legitimate avenues of access to these goals, and unable to revise their aspirations downward, they experience intense frustrations; the exploration of nonconformist alternatives may be the result. (1960: 86)

This type of explanation sees delinquency as *adaptive*—as instrumental in the achievement of "the same kinds of things" everyone wants. It sees crime, also as partly *reactive*—generated by a sense of injustice on the part of delinquents at having been deprived of the good life that they had been led to expect would be theirs. Finally, this hypothesis, which may with accuracy be described as the social worker's favorite, looks to the satisfaction of desires, rather than the lowering of expectations, as the cure for crime. To be sure, it approaches the satisfaction of desires not directly but indirectly, through the provision of expanded opportunities for legitimate achievement.

Since this explanatory schema has been so popular, and since it has provided the theoretical justification of government programs for the reduction of delinquency, its key ideas deserve special note.

It is apparent, first, that, in common with other sociological explanations, this hypothesis is *socially deterministic*. Cloward and Ohlin's statement does not talk about "what lower-class youths want." It talks about "what lower-class youths are led to want." The causal agent that does things to people is "in the society," rather than in individuals themselves.

Second, it is assumed that the gap between the desires of lower-class people and their legitimate opportunities is *greater* than the gap between the aspirations of middle-class persons and their legitimate opportunities. This can be believed, but it is not known and it may not be true. Research lends credence to the opposite possibility. At least, there is evidence that middle-class persons suffer *more strain* than lower-class persons do when their occupational aspirations are unfulfilled (Green 1946; Mizruchi 1964).

It is argued, third, that gang-running delinquents have "internalized conventional goals," and, fourth, that legitimate avenues to these goals are structurally limited.

Fifth, the hypothesis holds that lower-class youths do not, and *cannot*, "revise their aspirations downward." Finally, it is said that the breach between promise and fulfillment generates intense frustration and that this frustration *may* lead to criminal conduct.

While the opportunity-structure thesis as a whole sounds plausible, closer attention to its assumptions lessens confidence in its explanatory power.

Recent Developments: Agnew's General Theory of Strain

Because of the many difficulties encountered in the early opportunity structure theories of, for example Merton, Cohen, and Cloward and Ohlin, these theories fell out of favor in the 1970s to the degree that some argued for their complete abolishment (Hirshi 1969).

However, this tradition has experienced a resurgence of late in the form of "strain theory" which, again, focuses on the gap between aspirations and accomplishment. The shift in focus is away from the strictly structural-opportunity sources of strain to include many social-psychological sources of strain. Although several researchers are directing their attention to the problem (Bernard 1987; Farnworth and Leiber 1989; Mawson 1987), the strongest proponent of a strain theory is Robert Agnew (1985, 1989, 1992). Agnew terms his a "general" theory of strain, but his practical focus parallels that of Cohen and Cloward and Ohlin and emphasizes the strains experienced by adolescents.

Agnew draws from the broader psychological literature and includes many components currently found in the research on stress. Unlike the criminological tradition, the stress tradition in psychology has tended to address issues more directly related to the life course rather than disjunctions and contradictions among broader cultural norms. Consequently, Agnew's (1992: 50) theory is not a pure "structuralist" theory; instead, it blends across several levels of analysis. The primary implication is that the causal locus of the strain-producing elements may be found outside the structural-cultural aspects of society. Thus, as Agnew notes, "more recent versions of strain theory have argued that adolescents are not only concerned about the future of goals of monetary success/middle-class status, but are also concerned about the achievement of more immediate goals—such as good grades, popularity with the opposite sex, and doing well in athletics."

Accordingly, Agnew identifies three major types of strain faced by young people. All are consequences of negative relationships with other individuals. Thus, others may do the following: prevent one from achieving positively valued goals; remove or threaten to remove positively valued stimuli that one possesses; or, present or threaten to present one with noxious or negatively valued stimuli. Within each of these major types of strain, resides a number of specific causal factors.

1. Strain as the failure to achieve positively valued goals.

This type of strain is akin to that outlined by Merton, and Cloward and Ohlin. It is elaborated, however, by three other subtypes that Agnew draws from the justice/equity literature.

2. Strain as the disjunction between aspirations and expectations/actual achievements.

This is the classical type of strain most closely associated with Merton. Strain results from disjunction between aspirations or ideal goals and expectations or anticipated levels of goal achievement. This approach recognizes that many young people are influenced by a youth subculture that places a heavy emphasis on immediate goals. Often, those subcultural goals are in conflict with higher order social goals.

3. Strain as the disjunction between expectations and actual achievement.

It is suggested that this form of strain leads to such emotive responses as anger, resentment, and general unhappiness. Delinquency is one option for dealing with the gap. The gap between expectations and achievement is considered by Agnew to be more emotionally distressing since expectations, unlike aspirations, are more immediate. Aspirations, as ideal goals, are far more distant, or "existential" in Agnew's words.

4. Strain as the disjunction between just/fair outcomes and actual outcomes.

This aspect of strain is concerned with the broader notion of equity or fairness. Thus, individuals are concerned with the broader issues of "Are equals treated equally?" and "Is the system just?" Inequality that is attributed to an unjust system leads to resentment and is the subject of Chapter 15.

The two remaining broad categories of strain (the removal of positively valued stimuli and the presentation of negatively valued stimuli) are social psychological extensions of anomic theory. They deal with the training to which persons are exposed, a type of explanation outlined in Chapter 12.

By broadening the concept of strain beyond the classical Merton-Cohen-Cloward and Ohlin approach, however, Agnew has added new impetus to an ailing concept. Beyond fleshing out a typology of strain-producing situations, Agnew also points out that strain "is likely to have a cumulative effect on delinquency after a certain threshold level is reached." According to this view, we would not necessarily expect to see delinquent events result from exposure to a single situation or element of strain; their criminogenic impact is expected to be greater when they occur in (unspecified) combinations.

Opportunity and Human Ecology

Human ecology deals with the relationship between persons and physical space. Robert Park and other members of the now legendary "Chicago School" (such as Burgess, Shaw, and McKay) studied the ways in which spatial relationships influence social processes and impact on human behavior.

Park and his colleagues developed a theory of urban ecology (1928). They viewed the city as analogous to communities of animals and plants in natural ecological settings. According to this way of explaining deviant behavior (e.g., crime, delinquency, mental illness), it is the characteristics of the area (areal features) that affect persons and account for the rates of deviant behavior displayed in these areas.

Park and his coworkers identified patterns of urban settlement that they described as a set of concentric zones that spread from the center or core of the city, to the outskirts (Figure 15.1). The zone directly adjacent to the commercial and business core of the city is an area characterized by transition including the change from residential to commercial and a high level of turnover among residents. There are other factors beside distance from the core that delineate the zones of transition, such as railroad tracks. It is in the zones of transition that one finds the highest incidence of delinquency and crime. These areas are also characterized by poor housing, squalor, alcoholism and other forms of drug addition, prostitution, broken homes, high rates of single parenthood, and a population that is poor, transient, and heterogeneous.

Park's theoretical framework is one in which humans are seen to live in territorially organized communities in which everyone contributes to the well-being of everyone else. Within these arrangements operate "subsocial forces" including competition, dominance, invasion, and succession that govern the existence

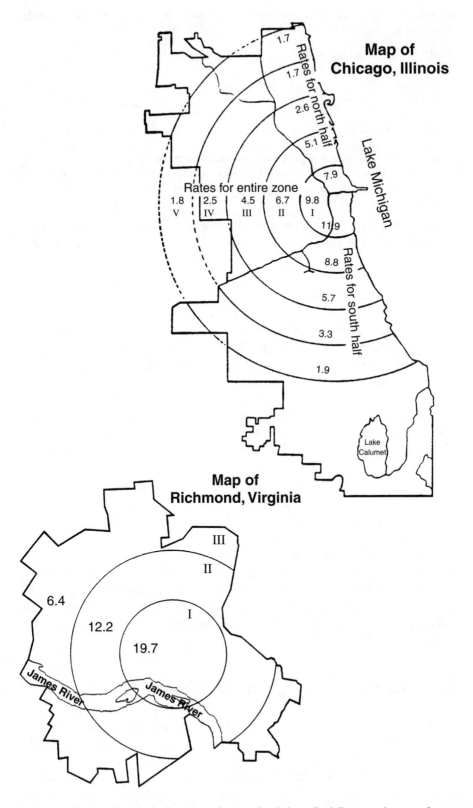

Figure 15.1   Display of ecological patterns of rates of male juvenile delinquents by zones for two cities. *Source:* Shaw and McKay (1972).

of spacial clusters called natural areas. As Michaelson (1970: 8–90) says of the Chicago School,

> they typically studied a phenomenon (usually a pathology such as crime or mental illness) at an aggregate level, having divided the city into a number of subareas corresponding as much as possible to natural areas. They explained the existence of the phenomenon by referring to the homogeneous social organization to be found within the subarea, which in turn was dependent on the spatial relations of that place to surrounding subareas. Since the people or use of an area often changed, the character of a natural area at any given point in time would be a function of the constant competition for space and a hierarchy of dominance. . . . Social pathologies were explained in this setting by social variables; but the ultimate explanation of both of them, inasmuch as they were found together in a local area, lay in subsocial forces.

Because of the forces that operate within them, areas provide the opportunities for crime and other pathologies to manifest themselves. They do so by, in some cases, restricting access to legitimate means (anomie) and in other cases by increasing access to illegitimate means ("delinquency and opportunity" as described by Cloward and Ohlin).

It is in this sense that areal/spatial characteristics constitute structures and that different arrangements define the structure of opportunities for criminal and law-abiding behavior. As the composition of the population moving through an area changes, the rates of deviant behavior exhibited remains remarkably stable. It is the contention of the ecological school that it is not the characteristics of the population but the characteristics of the area that matters. As human populations migrate from these areas and into spatial arrangements with other features their behavior is expected to change as well.

According to the Chicago school way of thinking about these matters, the residents of these transition areas are not abnormal. Rather, the deviance they display is seen as what Akers (1994:142) calls "normal responses of normal people to abnormal social conditions. Criminal and delinquent traditions develop under these conditions. . . [and are] culturally transmitted from one generation to the next."

There are two ideas of crimogenesis contained in this statement. The first has to do with structural features of areas producing opportunities or a lack of them that are conducive to crime, which is the focus of this chapter. The second is that crime and other deviation as a response to these structural features of areas becomes a part of the culture that is then transmitted to the next generation. This is the topic of Chapter 17.

Criticism of Opportunity-Structure Theory

Three principal charges are brought against the opportunity-structure thesis. Each criticism has numerous points to it, but the various doubts can be brought together under three questions: (1) Are the key concepts clear? (2) Does the theory accurately describe persistent offenders? and (3) Are the recommendations of opportunity-structure theory feasible and effective? The answers to all three questions seem more negative than affirmative.

Are the Key Concepts Clear?

Two words are central in thinking about crime in terms of the opportunity-structure hypothesis: "aspiration" and "opportunity." Neither concept is clear. Both words are borrowed from lay language, where the denotations of many useful concepts are embedded in emotionalized connotations so that common words, the principal currency of communication, become slippery. Such ambiguity is comforting in politics, where points can be proved by sliding from one respectable meaning of a term to its less reputable meanings. Ambiguity may be a social lubricant in this sense, but it is a defect in a social science that would guide rational social policy.

Aspirations

Like many other explanations of human behavior, opportunity-structure theory starts with what people want. The engine of action is desire. It is assumed that the desires called *aspirations* have been quite similar for all North Americans, if not for all Westerners, at some time in their careers. Opportunity-structure theory is silent, however, about the life histories of delinquents and hence takes for granted what needs to be known—the extent to which lawful careers and all they entail *are* preferred or derided.

"Saying" Versus "Wanting"

This neglect is both cause and effect of the structuralist's ready assumption that what people *say* they want out of life is an adequate measure of their aspiration. Such an easy equation of words with motives leaves out of the definition of aspiration. Most dictionaries and common usage minimally include the notions of: ambition, drive, and yearning. To accept words at face value as indicators of aspiration strips the concept of its motivating power and permits students to confuse daydreaming with the desire that fuels intent. In response to interviewers with their clipboards and questionnaires, it is easy for any of us to tell "what we'd like"—usually "money and repute." It is another matter, however, to equate this ready verbalization with aspiration—intention, direction, plan.

Values as Words and Deeds

The possibility of a difference between verbal aspiration and effective motivation is increased by evidence that the values of more persistent delinquents and career criminals differ from those of lesser offenders. *Values* here refers to what people want as noted in *both* their words and their deeds. The values that energize aspiration, and give it its proper meaning, do differ between committed violators and more lawful people.

    Evidence of such difference is found in a host of studies that draw us a portrait of the more serious offender as a hasty hedonist and jungle cat. The "philosophy" of persistent miscreants is cynical, hostile, and distrustful. Their morality denies the rules of the game. It avoids responsibility for fulfilling obligations to others except under fear of reprisal (Yochelson and Samenow 1976). It downgrades the victims of their crimes and categorizes them as "punks, chumps, pigeons, or fags" (Schwendinger and Schwendinger 1967: 98). Confirmed offenders employ a "jungle philosophy" that sees friends as fickle and "everybody as just out for himself" (Nettler 1961). According to the criminal ethic, you should "do unto others as they would do unto you . . . only do it first"; and, "If I don't cop [steal] it . . . somebody else will" (Schwendinger and Schwendinger 1967: 98).

It does not matter whether we agree or disagree with these offensive values. The point is that the difference in attitude is real. It is not just a difference in words; it is a difference that is acted out. Opportunity-structure theory neglects this difference, apparently as a result of its weak conception of aspiration.

Opportunities

The other term central to this explanation of crime, *opportunity,* is equally vague. As dictionaries define the word and as most people use it, it refers to a time or situation favorable to the attainment of a goal; it refers to a "chance."

Perceived and Real Opportunities

The perception of a chance is always a function of the perceiver and where he or she stands. Its assessment involves some notion, usually tacit, of what one could have done if one had had the chance or had seen it.

There is, then, a possible difference between perceived opportunities and real ones—between what was there and what we thought was there, between what we might actually have done and what we, or other observers, believe we might have done if we had thought differently or acted differently.

Opportunities Are by Their Nature Much Easier to See After They Have Passed Than Before They Are Grasped.

These many intangibles in the idea of an opportunity mean that sociologists who employ the term come to judge differences in opportunity from differences in result. If people do not end up equally happy, healthy, lawful, or rich, these differences are attributed principally to differences in "opportunity." This attribution is not necessarily incorrect; but as it is used, it does two questionable things (1) it assumes that all or most of the causes of a career are encompassed in something called "the chances" or "the breaks" (situations again) and (2) it performs a semantic cheat by substituting *how one is* for *the chances one had.* This is illegitimate because it first poses a cause of conduct called "opportunity" and then it uses the alleged effects of that "opportunity" as a measure of it. It is as if one were to argue that c causes e, and then prove the causal connection by using e as the measure of c.

For most of us, the proper attribution of a causal relationship requires that whatever is called a "cause" must be a *different set of circumstances* from that which is called its "effect." Otherwise we are trapped in a logical circle, an entrapment that may be comfortable for purposes of moral or political debate, but that is a hindrance to effective action. The scientific requirement of any hypothesis that proposes that opportunities may be the causes of careers is that the indicators of opportunity be defined before the signs of outcome are decided upon. The two sets of indicators must then be kept separate if any inference is to be derived as to the causal relation between them.

Tests of Opportunities

Attempts have been made to test for the power of "structured opportunities" to affect careers. Investigators have defined "life chances" before gathering data and have then tried to tally how much of people's lives correlate with differences in their beginnings. This is a difficult task, of course, because everything depends on how well one measures life chances and outcomes.

A popular conception of one's start in life is "family background." Many studies indicate that there is *some* force to the chances families provide, but the interesting question is, "How much?" A secondary question is, "When and where?"—implying that these matters may change with time and place.

American research on "social mobility"—principally that of male subjects—shows that the correlation between fathers' occupational statuses and that of their sons is modest. The correlation between fathers' vocational positions and sons' incomes is even lower.

One large-scale study reports a correlation of +.40 between fathers' and sons' occupational rankings, a correlation which means that 16% of the variation in sons' working status is "accounted for" by fathers' status (Blau and Duncan 1967: 402). In this study, fathers' "contribution" to sons' occupational careers is less than sons' own attainment in education ($r = +.60$) and status of sons' first job ($r = +.54$). Later research reports a correlation of +.35 between fathers' and sons' occupations in a national sample of "non-Negro men with nonfarm background" (Duncan et al. 1972: table 3.1). These data yield correlations between fathers' and sons' occupational rankings that are about of the same order as correlations between fathers' and sons' height, weight, size of head, IQ, and amount of schooling (Jencks 1968: 34; also see Jencks 1990). If one combines fathers' socioeconomic status (SES), fathers' education, and sons' education as possible determinants of sons' income in Western societies, the combined impact is still *less* than whatever else causes people to move up and down income ladders (Boudon 1974).

A detailed investigation of the determinants of status and earnings in the United States analyzed results from 11 surveys (Jencks et al. 1979). This summary assumed that "family background" referred to "the predictable consequences of having one set of parents rather than another" where such family background includes parents' characteristics plus the neighborhoods in which children are reared, the schools they attend, the economic opportunities in the parents' community, and "the genes the parents passed on to their sons" (1979: 50). Jencks et al. conclude that "all aspects of family background explained about 48% of the variance in mature men's occupational statuses" (1979: 213–214). However, when these investigators look at annual earnings, rather than occupational status, family background explains only about 22% of the variance in sons' incomes (1979: 292).

A more sensitive test of the impact of family background involves a comparison of the occupational statuses and incomes of brothers. Since brothers share similar family backgrounds—varying, of course, with the number of siblings and the age spread between brothers—the hypothesis that "situation" determines career would expect that brothers' adult occupational statuses and incomes would be similar. However, when cognitive test scores and the schooling of brothers are held constant, brothers still end up with differences in occupational status that, on the average, are as widespread as 70–76% of the status differences in random pairs of men (Jenks et al. 1979: 297). Differences in brothers' *incomes* are, on the average, as wide as 84–89% of those found between random pairs of men.

Jencks concludes that "no characteristic of a parent will ever explain more than a quarter of the variation in this same characteristic among the parent's children." In addition, Jencks notes that "more than 60 percent of variation in men's school attainment is completely unaccounted for by any background characteristic" (Jencks 1968: 34).

Jencks's conclusion is verified by White's (1982; 1983) analysis of the relation between SES and academic achievement (1982; also see White et al. 1993). White reviewed more than 200 studies that weighed the association between SES and school achievement. He found that, when SES is measured by the usual indicators such as parents' income, education, or occupational status, the correlation with the academic attainment of individual students is negligible. The median value of reported coefficients of correlation is +.22, which means that less than 5% of the variance in individuals' academic achievement is accounted for by these common measures of SES.

White did find a background variable that is moderately associated with individual achievement in school. It is a factor titled "home atmosphere," a measure that includes

- Amount of "cultural activities" in which family participates
- Quantity and quality of reading material in the house
- Aspirations of parents for child
- Family stability
- Family's attitude toward education
- Quality of language in the home
- Work habits and democracy in the home (1982: 473, table 9)

These are, of course, "cultural attributes" rather than indicators of economic condition. Thus, White's analysis runs against the grain of much of what has been reported in the educational literature.

A recent study by White et al. (1992) suggests that the overstatement of the socioeconomic status-achievement relationship in the literature may be a consequence of the aggregation fallacy. Much early research was based on aggregate level data and these authors indicate that as a consequence of the aggregation fallacy, there may be as much as a fourfold overstatement of the relationship in many studies.

In Conclusion: Opportunities

This brief excursion into studies of social mobility and career development has been required to demonstrate that the concept of "opportunity" is not simple and that, when we attempt to assign outcomes to life chances as measured by family background, we do not get strong results. At least this is the case in heterogeneous, changing, and "open" societies such as Australia, Canada, and the United States.

Finding weak effects of background suggests that, in open societies, careers depend more on how one uses opportunities than on whether opportunities are presented. This possibility shifts attention from the chances we had to the uses we made of them. It draws attention, in particular, to use of schools, which scholars and laypeople alike regard as a major legitimate opportunity. In turn, this direction of attention asks whether persistent offenders are well described by the opportunity-structure story.

Box 15.1   FRAUD AND OPPORTUNITY

Fraud is sometimes called the crime of opportunity. A prosecutor of fraud cases characterized the situation as "20 percent of people are never in trouble. Another 20 percent we see in court all the time. And the other 60 percent who can be tempted and succumb to committing fraud."

Much fraud, however, is not committed by people who lack economic opportunities, but rather by people who are experience the opportunity to commit the crime. Thus, "in January, 1996, KPMG, one [of Canada's] largest assurance, consulting and financial advisory and tax firms, sent a survey to 1,000 of Canada's largest public and private companies, including financial, manufacturing, energy, consumer, wholesale, insurance, and retail sectors. The following are some results from that survey:

- 52% of respondents from Canada's largest companies reported that fraud had taken place within their organization during the past 12 months.
- 73% of respondents believe computers have led to an increase in the level of fraud in society.
- Management fraud costs more per occurrence than employee fraud ($42,000 v. $20,600 respectively).
- Of the total fraud losses reported in the survey, 49% was external, 46% was from employees, and 5% was from management.
- The profile of the typical fraudster is: male, aged 26–40 years, with an annual income of less than $50,000 per year. (Roelofsen, 1997)

Does the Opportunity-Structure Thesis Accurately Describe Persistent Offenders?

Equality and Opportunity

The fundamental assumption of opportunity-structure theory is equality. Not equality of opportunity, of course, but equality of aspiration, interest, motivation, application, and ability.

Cloward and Ohlin, for example, attribute juvenile delinquency to the offender's sense of injustice. They argue that delinquents see unfairness in "the system," with people of the same ability as themselves, or less ability, getting a bigger slice of the pie. Furthermore, Cloward and Ohlin contend that the delinquents' perception is correct.

The first part of this allegation is hardly news. It has long been common for criminals to argue that "the system" is more crooked than they are, that "straight people" are just as dishonest as thieves, and that "it's not what you do, but who you know" that determines one's fate. What is surprising is that social scientists accept this rationalization and, in so doing, confuse a justification of criminality with its cause.

Cloward and Ohlin say:

> is our impression that a sense of being unjustly deprived of access to opportunities to which one is entitled is common among those who become participants in delinquent subcultures. Delinquents tend to be persons who have been led to expect opportunities *because of their potential ability* to meet the formal institutionally established criteria of evaluation. (1960: 117, emphasis added)

They then support this allegation of equal ability with a footnote:

> There is no evidence . . . that members of delinquent subcultures are objectively less capable of meeting formal standards of eligibility than are nondelinquent lower class youngsters. In fact, the available data support the contention that the basic endowments of delinquents, such as intelligence, physical strength, and agility, are the equal of or greater than those of their nondelinquent peers. (1960: 117, fn. 10)

Unless one is to earn one's keep as a professional athlete—and, in the age of televised sports, this is a good way to do so—the "basic endowments" of physical strength and agility are of slight relevance to occupational achievement. Intelligence, persistence, diligence, reliability, interest, emotional control—these traits are of greater relevance in climbing the legitimate class ladder. Contrary to the belief of opportunity-structure theorists, persistent offenders *do not* exhibit these abilities in the same proportions as more legitimately successful youths.

Traits and Opportunity

Such evidence as we have of how people legitimately climb upward in society indicates that those who successfully use lawful means exhibit differences in interests, motivation, and ability. These differences are apparent early in adolescence and sometimes even before puberty. Furthermore, achievers, when compared with their less successful counterparts, differ in these attributes even when social-class origins are held constant (Jayasuriya 1960; Straus 1962). The pattern of difference is found consistently in industrial countries of otherwise varied cultures.

People who are legitimately successful tend to be more interested in schoolwork, to score higher on tests of mental ability, and to be more emotionally stable and diligent than those who are less successful. They move toward their vocational objectives with greater persistence and defer other gratifications in favor of these longer-range goals. They demonstrate greater self-confidence and a greater need to achieve. They function more independently of their parents while respecting their parents more. They are described as being possessed of greater self-control, responsibility, and intellectual efficiency. Evidence of these differences is widespread (Crockett 1962; Douvan and Edelson 1958; Hibbett et al. 1990; Hirschi and Hindelang 1977; Lane 1980; Moffitt et al. 1981; Schippmann and Prien 1989; Sewell et al. 1969; Srole et al. 1962; Terman and Oden 1947, 1959; Thompson 1971; Turban and Dougherty 1994).

Schools and Opportunity

Until recently, at least, going to school has been the major legitimate ladder by which people have climbed in status and income. As Jones, Kojima, and Marks note:

> [T]here is persuasive evidence that schools do have destratifying effects across generations and that they moderate the effects of social background. Not only do schools select gifted pupils from the working classes and prepare them for social mobility into the professions and management, they also condition the less talented offspring of middle class parents to expect status maintenance as an acceptable outcome, while preparing others for downward mobility. (Jones et al. 1994: 778–779)

It is therefore important to examine the relationship of schools and opportunity.

On Students

A multiplicity of studies tell us that juvenile offenders, and particularly the more serious offenders, differ from their less delinquent counterparts in their greater resistance to schooling. They hate schoolwork and they hate their teachers. They more frequently "ditch" school and destroy school buildings and equipment. They do poorly in academic work, are more frequently retarded in grade, and score low on tests of mental performance. They are judged by both their teachers and their classmates to be troublemakers, and they are, in general, disliked by both. This dislike is, of course, reciprocated.

Differences in the ways in which individual students use their schools parallel differences in the ways in which ethnic groups use them. From his study of the history of "ethnic America," Sowell finds this to be "perhaps the most striking difference between ethnic groups . . . [even those] living and working under very similar conditions" (1981a: 280). In turn, ethnic differentials in use of schools are associated with economic success where schools are appreciated and criminality where schools are denigrated.

On Good Schools

It is part of the conventional wisdom that what separates "good" schools from "bad" ones is the amount of resources available. Macro-level evidence such as national expenditures per student, clearly indicate that this is not necessarily the case (*Economist* 1997; U.S. Dept. of Education 1997). Furthermore, micro-level indicators such as class size, also seem to have little to do with performance (Gilbert 1995). On the other hand, school order and structured teaching methods do appear to be significant contributors to student success (Gaddy 1988; *Economist* 1997: 23). Just as parental discipline style has an impact on adolescent behavior (Shaw and Scott 1991).

In what is now a classic study in education, James Coleman suggested that what students *bring* to their schools is more important than what schools do for them. Family background contributes little—no more than 10–25% of the variation in individual achievement (1966b: 299). But personalities of students enter here. The single, strongest correlate of educational outcome, according to this study, is *students' attitudes*.

Coleman et al. (1966a: 319) say, "Of all the variables measured in the survey, including all measures of family background and all school variables, these attitudes showed the strongest relation to achievement, at all three grade levels." Concerning "attitude," these investigators add, "for many disadvantaged children, a major obstacle to achievement may arise from the very way they confront the environment" (1966a: 321).

In short, we are returned to *use* of opportunity rather than to *presence* of opportunity. But this only raises the further question of why people use similar opportunities differently, which was a topic discussed in Chapter 12.

On Money and Schooling

It has been recognized for many years that North American educators now face the unpleasant fact that, allowing for inflation, increases in per student expenditure bear a significant *negative* correlation with students' performance (Brophy 1980; Copperman 1980; Jones 1981; Mitchell 1981; Seligman 1978). A recent international study of 13-year-olds in maths and sciences in 41 countries showed that the United States spends three times as much as South Korea on pupils but ranked 28th in math and 17th in science. South Korea, however, ranked 2nd and 4th respectively (*Economist* 1997). Other high-spending countries such as Switzerland, Germany, and Denmark also produced mediocre scores while relatively low-spending countries such as Hungary, the Czech Republic, and Japan ranked near the top on both components.

There is more to education than money alone can buy. An important variable, related to students' attitudes, is "order in the classroom." The Coleman researchers attempted to measure this, did so with an inadequate "student disorder" scale, and then failed to report the strength of association between classroom discipline and students' achievement. However, studies on both sides of the Atlantic indicate that orderly classrooms make a difference in school output (Postman 1979; Rutter 1979; Solomon and Kendall 1979). How to achieve an orderliness with which learning can proceed is beyond our present concern, but the necessity points to educational conflict in North America.

On Schools, Vocations, and Delinquency

Opportunity theory, like other explanations of crime production, tells some truths. A kernel of truth in all structural views of criminogenesis is that young people need apprenticeship to maturity. Human beings who are moving from protected childhood toward independent adulthood need to practice the activities that will be their acceptable ways of life as adults. The best that can be hoped is that adults' lives will include vocations that meet their interests and that, therefore, are satisfying. There can be no guarantee of this, of course, and aspirations that are constantly raised are bound to be disappointed. Structuralists have called attention to some of the grosser deficiencies in the ways in which present social arrangements use youth and produce crime: (1) uselessness of young people; (2) irrelevance of schools; (3) lack of meaningful work, and other components of "growing up absurd."

1. *Useless youth.* Rich societies pay prices for their affluence. One price is the uselessness of many young people (Côté and Allahar 1994). Multitudes of people in their teens are presumably not needed by the more successful Western industrial societies. They are, as a consequence, kept in an ambiguous state, half child and half adult. Since these industrialized countries have gained their wealth by employing products of education, science, and technology, it is concluded that more of the same education for everyone will increase the benefits. If academic schooling is good for some, up to some age, it is believed that such academic work is good for all, for as long as a quarter or even a third of their lives. Under compulsory attendance laws, the schools then become a giant holding operation. They are an "opportunity," of course, for those with academic interests, but they are a jail for those without such interests. For the numerous remainder, who reside somewhere between a modest academic interest and a boredom relieved by social life and sports, the schools are a huge repository.

If this picture of teenage life in industrial societies seems accurate, no complicated assumptions are required to propose that youthful inutility and protracted semichildhood will generate disturbance, some of it criminal. We need only assume, with Marx and Veblen as with many contemporary psychologists, that human beings are curious animals, makers and doers, who "do best" when they have a vocation that others appreciate and that is rewarding in itself.

Rich societies do not provide such meaningful work for everyone. Many jobs are dull but necessary, and not everyone has the talent for the exciting work of a criminal lawyer or a neurosurgeon. For the sake of domestic peace and psychic health, the social requirement is to employ the great middle ranges of aptitude and ineptitude (Goode 1967).

2. *Irrelevant schools.* Given such assumptions, several writers have suggested that secondary schools in the Western world are excessively committed to college preparation and insufficiently adjusted to the interests of future workers in trade, industry, and the paraprofessions. It is argued that the pressure to succeed academically and the built-in probability of failure ensured by lack of interest and ability produce hostility (McDonald 1969; Polk and Schafer 1972). If to this cauldron of discontent one adds poor teaching, resentment is brought to a boil.

Hostility is further stimulated by the irrelevance of academic work for what many young people want to do, and see themselves doing, as adults. Such a way of life for juveniles is a way of "growing up absurd," Paul Goodman says (1956). Similarly, the sociologists Polk and Schafer (1972), and Côté and Allahar (1994) see a source of rebellion in the disjunction between school life and the adult life toward which many young people, boys in particular, are moving. The thesis advanced by many critics of Western education is that compulsory schooling is itself criminogenic for those youngsters who find no immediate gratification in academic work and who can see, correctly, no future reward from their present training. Such critics claim that schools in many rich countries threaten the self-respect of those who don't achieve academically and that the reaction to such wounding is violent.

Stinchcombe and other sociologists hold that the violent reaction to failure in school is accompanied by the substitution of "ascriptive symbols" of personal worth for the achieved marks of academic success. These ascriptive symbols are signs of adulthood and a denial of the adolescent and submissive role in which schools place young people. Things like smoking, drinking, owning a car, freer dating, and financial independence are status symbols that take the place of the school symbols. By their very adoption, they challenge the legitimacy and authority of the school. They are more than mere challenges, however. They are also indicators of an alienation from the honors that schools value and can give.

3. *Growing up absurd.* Paul Goodman's description of "growing up absurd" is in accord with the pictures provided by sociologists, but his interpretation proposes a more radical rejection of industrialized Western societies. Goodman believes that there is not enough "man's work" in North America and that our absurd societies are "lacking in the opportunity [for young men] to be useful," that they "thwart aptitude and create stupidity," that they "corrupt the fine arts, . . . shackle science, . . . and dampen animal ardor" (1956: 12). Goodman believes that delinquent behavior

> speaks clearly enough. It asks for manly opportunities to work, make a little money, and have self-esteem; to have some space to bang around in, that is not always somebody's property; to have better schools to open for them horizons of interest; to have more and better sex without fear or shame, to share somehow in the symbolic goods (like the cars) that are made so much of; to have a community and a country to be loyal to; to claim attention and to have a voice. (1956: 50–51)

The extremity of Goodman's position is likely to obscure the validity of what he and other authors have pointed out—that Western schooling does *not* provide an adequate apprenticeship in adulthood for a sufficient number of young people and that this inadequacy may be criminogenic. The schools are changing, however, and some educators are experimenting with broader avenues on which adolescents may move as they grow up. There is criticism of compulsory schooling of the same kind for everyone. There is awareness among educators that, beyond establishing some minimum of literacy and calculating competence, schools may *not* be the best providers of vocational initiation.

Such experimentation is not assisted, however, by the stimulating comments Goodman offers. Goodman is essentially an anarchist. His vision is utopian and, consequently, disillusioning. The high ideals are in accord with neither present reality nor future possibility, and they do not generate useful recommendations. As always, it is one thing to decry the world we live in; it is quite another matter to know how to change it without making it worse.

It is debatable, for example, whether there is "not enough manly work" in our societies. Much depends on who is defining "manly." It is even more debatable whether the pastoral life Goodman proposes is an adequate substitute for the jobs, the organization, the "system" which Goodman despises but which, nevertheless, produce the wealth that makes possible his disaffection. Goodman's recommendation is for something no one can give and no group can create. No one can produce the "symbolic goods (like the cars)" without organizing the work. Some of that work will be dirty work, and calling it "unmanly" will not help us appreciate it. Similarly, in a world growing more crowded, space will always be allocated, whether it be "somebody's property" or the state's. As for the "more and better sex" that Goodman recommends "without fear or shame," delinquents are certainly less deprived in this regard than more conventional young people, and it is difficult to see how this "remedy" might be implemented or how it might reduce the rates of serious crimes.

A Gloomy Outlook: Schools and Opportunity

No radical vision is necessary to agree with Goodman and other critics that school systems in many Western countries provide poor apprenticeship in adulthood for many adolescents. A poor apprenticeship in growing up is criminogenic.

In this way, structures of modern states encourage crime and delinquency. They lack institutional procedures for moving people smoothly from protected childhood to autonomous adulthood. During adolescence, many young people in affluent societies are neither well guided by their parents nor happily engaged by their teachers. They are adults in body, but children in responsibility. Placed in such a gray area between irresponsible dependence and accountable independence, they are compelled to attend schools which do not thoroughly stimulate the interests of all of them and which, in too many cases, provide the uninterested child with the experience of failure and the mirror of denigration.

Educators wrestle with remedies. However, in democratic societies, they are torn between conflicting prescriptions. On the one hand, the democratic ethic is interpreted as demanding that everyone be given the *same* education with at least some minimum of *equal result*—such as an "adequate" competence in reading, writing, and arithmetic. On the other hand, beyond this undefined minimum level of literacy and basic skills, the reformer acknowledges that different schools or different curricula must be provided for children of varied talents and interests. Thus Schafer and Polk recommend "creating diversity within student bodies" through government-enforced racial and class mixing (1972: 254–255), while at the same time recommending "divergent, not uniform, teaching styles for different populations" (1972: 191–192).

Such openness in apprenticing institutions would *not* produce uniform results in academic skills, in knowledge, in know-how, or—what hurts most—in status. This is the dilemma of democratic educators. They want equality *and* individuality, objectives that thus far in history have eluded social engineers. Meanwhile, the metropolitan schools of industrialized countries make a probable, but unmeasurable, contribution to criminality.

In Conclusion: Schools and Opportunity

Discussion of the relationship between schools and modes of youthful apprenticeship points to one facet of social structures that may be criminogenic. However, it puts a different light on the structural story from that cast by opportunity theorists. Opportunity theorists, to repeat, assume that juvenile delinquents and adult criminals are persons who in adolescence are the *same* in ability and motivation as less offensive persons and that they differ only, or principally, in their lack of "legitimate chances." By contrast, a broader view sees *differences* in the ways in which people are equipped to use present "legitimate opportunities." The distinction here is a disagreement about how people are. Criticism of the opportunity story claims that it does not accurately portray the talents, preferences, desires, and views of the world that reliably distinguish serious career offenders from their more lawful counterparts.

This descriptive failure has been attributed to the possibility that the inventors of the opportunity-structure hypothesis are middle-class persons who are imposing their conceptions upon others who, in fact, reject them. However this may be, the hypothesis does slight the fact that tastes differ and that criminal ways of life may have a rationale and a definition of "how things ought to be" that have their own validity. This structural explanation is blind, therefore, to the *fun* that is involved in being delinquent—fun like skipping school, rolling drunks, snatching purses, being chased by the police, staying out till all hours, going where one wants, and doing what one wants without adult supervision. The descriptive failure of the opportunity-structure thesis leads to doubts about its prescriptions.

Are Recommendations of Opportunity-Structure Theory Feasible and Effective?

A fair test of a hypothesis is whether it works. The work of a theory is to guide a distinctive course of action that will reliably get us more of what we want at known and lower costs.

The opportunity-structure explanation of criminogenesis has been interpreted as saying that if people had more legitimate opportunities to satisfy their aspirations, they would resort less frequently to crime. In the United States several large-scale projects have attempted to expand opportunities and thereby reduce adult crime, juvenile delinquency, and recidivism. These projects have included varied mixtures of individual and family counseling, psychotherapy and behavior therapy, social work with gangs, remedial reading classes, job training and employment subsidy, and attempts at community organization. Evaluations of these programs show that a few succeed, many fail, and some even produce "iatrogenic" effects—that is, they make people worse than they were (descriptions of these many efforts and summaries of research can be read in Auletta 1982; Braithwaite 1979: 222–227; Hackler 1966; Lipton et al. 1975; Martinson 1974; McCord 1978, 1980; Moynihan 1969; Taggart 1972; and Weissman 1969).

Program failure has moved theorists from emphasizing equality of opportunity to emphasizing equality of result. Thus Jencks et al. conclude their study of the determinants of economic success with the statement that, "if we want to redistribute income [i.e., achieve equality], the most effective strategy is probably still to redistribute income" (1979: 311).

Failure of programs to fulfill theories has many explanations and, when failure follows upon kind efforts, many apologists. The impotence of programs to prevent criminality and to reform offenders can always be attributed to insufficient funding or to unforeseen resistance by evil others, rather than to errors in the theories underlying the programs.

If, however, failure stimulates questions about opportunity theory, and if one asks why people do not change as they are expected to, the answer, in capsule form, refers to (1) the delights of crime, (2) the pains of menial, lawful work, (3) the pleasures of booze and dope, and (4) deficiencies of talent and temperament.

Failure may also be attributed to selective attention to what a theory recommends. In fairness to Cloward and Ohlin, they have *not* said that the cure for crime is simply the expansion of legitimate opportunities. Their emphasis has given this impression, of course. However, Cloward and Ohlin argue that "extending services to delinquent individuals or groups cannot prevent the rise of delinquency among others" (1960: 211). They hold that "the major effort . . .

should be directed to the reorganization of slum communities" because "the old structures, which provided *social control* and avenues of social ascent, are breaking down" (1960: 211; emphasis added).

"Social control" has been emphasized in this quotation because the opportunity hypothesis finally reverts to an assumption that is common to all sociological and sociopsychological explanations of crimes *mala in se*. All these explanations see serious crime as the result of a weakening of social controls. The explanations differ only in how they believe this deregulation of social life has come about, in what they emphasize as the crucial regulator, and hence in where they specify effort ought to be applied to reduce the harm we do one another.

Attention to social control moves us from theories that talk mostly about circumstances to theories that talk more about how people *react* to situations. The latter group of explanations invoke cultural differences and psychological principles, and do so with varied emphases, of course. Chapter 16 describes a variation on the structural theme which holds that inequality of social status promotes criminality by provoking resentment.

16. Social Inequality and Crime

Three Questions

A continuation of the structural story adds resentment to the depiction of anomie. It claims that inequalities of social status signify choked channels of achievement and unjust social arrangements. As a consequence, comparison of one's lowly status with others' higher position fuels hostility, some of which is turned inward against oneself and some of which is turned outward against acquaintances and strangers.

Psychology and philosophy now step on the explanatory stage beside sociology. The sociological question asks *whether* inequalities in "social position" are correlated with criminality within jurisdictions. The psychological question asks *how* inequality causes crime—if, indeed, inequality is found to be associated with higher rates of crime. The philosophical question asks *whether* any association that is revealed is to be interpreted as causal or as only correlative. Answering the philosophical question involves anthropology and history.

The Sociological Question: Crime and Inequality

For many, the existence of high rates of poverty in American society is incontrovertible (see for e.g., Danziger and Gottschalk 1995 and various chapters in Papadimitriou and Wolff 1993). Indeed, the conventional wisdom, even among academics (see Box 16.1, Poverty on the Increase) is that rates of poverty are high, increasing, and related to crime. Danziger and Gottschalk, for example, maintain that "no matter how it is measured, inequality in income, earnings, and wealth has increased over the past twenty years, and poverty has remained high" (1995: 2). Unfortunately, while the existence of significant poverty is not in dispute, our ability to measure how much poverty exists and to determine where people stand on the distributional continuum is not as unproblematic as authors such as Danziger and Gottschalk would have us believe. Thus, before we can address the issue of whether and how inequities might be related to crime, it is necessary to examine how the independent variable is defined and measured.

Measurement Problems

As might be expected, a first difficulty in answering the sociological question concerns concepts and their measurement. "Social inequality" has been variously conceived, and two sets of difficulties intrude upon its meaning. One set concerns *what* is unequally distributed; the second concerns *which* measure of

---

Box 16.1   Poverty on the Increase

"Tax and welfare policies have changed remarkably in most if not all advanced capitalist countries. Tax revolts and reductions of welfare supports are common. These have combined with changes in the economy to increase levels of social, and more specifically, racial inequality. These inequalities are linked in the United States to pervasive patterns of residential segregation and to intense concentrations of poverty that have increased the distress of low-income communities and their crime problems." (Hagan 1994: 60)

---

difference is to be used. Here we look at the first set of difficulties; the second group of problems will be discussed later.

Social inequalities have been defined as differences in position in the processes of production and consumption, and as differences in wealth, income, status, power, and "life chances." There are correlations among these indicators, but they are far from perfect and, indeed, they are sometimes negative. Therefore, the six definitions yield different conceptions of social class.

Definition by *position* (or "location") in the mode of production looks at occupational categories and at whether people do or do not own instruments of production.

Definition by *wealth* estimates shares of resources on hand, sometimes calculated as net worth—what a person could "cash in" for (assets minus debits).

Income refers to a flow of wealth but counting incomes runs into the difficulty, we shall see, of how to record incomes "in kind" and earnings from crime and the "underground economy."

Definition by *status* analyzes the prestige some people accord to others, usually in terms of their occupations. This idea of "status" is sometimes used as though it were the equivalent of wealth and income, but it should not be. Prestige and pay are only modestly associated. They do not always go together; and their relation can even be negative, so that some jobs with high prestige receive low pay and some work with low prestige receives high pay.

Definition by *power* examines how readily, and how extensively, some categories of people can move others to do as they wish; that is, power has to do with the ability to control others.

Last, definition by *life chances* usually looks at differences in infant mortality and life expectancy, or at shares of such goods as health, schooling, travel, and leisure.

Most research on social inequality has analyzed differences in shares of national wealth that individuals or clusters of individuals receive as income. Necessarily, all such measurement is imperfect. The imperfections make comparisons between countries and comparisons within one country over time subject to an unknown amount of error. The flavor of the difficulty in counting shares of resources is given briefly by noting the following points.

1. Governments count the economic resources of their citizens in different ways (Herriot and Haines 1979). Differences include who counts as a recipient, what counts as income, and what period of time serves as the basis of measurement. Government bureaus sometimes tally only the money earned by "income recipients." Sometimes they count the income received by each household,

and sometimes they calculate income per person within households. This means that the distribution of reported income varies with definition of the "income unit."

Differences also occur as official tallies include, or exclude, "social security" income such as food stamps, aid to dependent children, pensions, medical insurance, and unemployment benefits. They also vary in the degree to which they count income received through barter, as fringe benefits like expense accounts, as capital gains on investments, and from "home production" and "living off the land" (Atkinson 1975: 61–62).

Furthermore, different income distributions are portrayed with different units of time. Thus "weekly income appears more unequal than . . . income . . . measured over a longer period, such as a year" (Atkinson 1975: 36). And neither monthly nor yearly income is a fair measure of lifetime income.

2. Unreported income varies among countries and among citizens within countries. For example, in Italy the "underground economy" may account for up to one-third of the gross national product (GNP) and may involve one-fourth of all persons in the labor force (Dallago 1990: 21–23). Estimates in the United States suggest that anywhere from 5 to 33% of its GNP lies in the subterranean economy (Frumkin 1992: 18; Greenfield 1993). The Internal Revenue Service estimates that taxes lost on underreported and unreported income in 1992 amounts to $110–$127 billion (Frumkin 1992: 20).

3. Asking people about their incomes produces a different picture from that gained by recording their receipts of wealth from all sources. Paglin demonstrates that by using a broader definition of income—including in-kind government transfers and employee fringe benefits—"reduces the poverty rate and indicates that the official poverty rate is overstated by 39% and the number of poor persons by 10.3 million (1992 figures)" (1994: 2,256).

   The United States and Canada count income on the basis of voluntary answers to questions. Varying with the time of survey, between 10 and 15% of citizens refuse to answer such questions (Atkinson 1975: 57; Paglin 1994: 2,246).

4. International comparisons of GDP and income variation are extremely difficult because costs of living vary considerably from one nation to another (Dowrick and Quiggin 1997). Furthermore, it is difficult to control income for expenditures because of different preferences for goods and services across cultures. For example, wheat, rice, and potatoes are three major carbohydrate staples that are readily substitutable yet differ greatly in price depending upon location. Controlling income based on the cost of wheat in societies that have a preference for rice would seriously overestimate the cost of living in those societies and potentially inflate estimates of poverty.

We recall from Chapter 6 that asking people about their *achieved* status, such as their schooling and income, yields more error than asking people about their *ascribed* status, such as age and sex, although there is error even with ascribed status. Worse still, asking people about their socially desirable and undesirable behaviors results in even more inaccurate replies.

Validity checks on people's reports of their salaries and other receipts show significant discrepancies between actual income and reported income (Hyman

1944; Schreiber 1976; Weaver and Swanson 1974; Withery 1954). Asking members of the same families the same questions about "nondemographic data" and about one another's behaviors reveals only low to moderate concordance among them (Booth and Welch 1978; Card 1978; Niemi 1974). Asking people how much they drink produces a rate of responses that is related to how the question is asked and how "socially desirable" higher levels of consumption appear in the categories of responses (Embree and Whitehead 1991).

Status and Crime Differentials

Despite these difficulties in arriving at an accurate estimate of the distribution of wealth within countries, several investigators have addressed the sociological question concerning the relation between unequal distribution of rewards and crime rates. Their inquiry is made sensible by the fact that crimes *mala in se*, and particularly violent crimes, tend to be distributed differentially by "social class," as we saw in Chapter 10. We qualified this correlation by noting that the distribution of crime changes as we consider "white-collar crimes," many of which escape prosecution. Nevertheless, it follows that a differential distribution of crime on the status ladder ought to be correlated with particular measures of inequalities in social structures. However, the questions are conceptually separate; that is, distributions in themselves do not tell whether expanding or contracting differentials in status affect crime rates. This question has been independently tackled by researchers who have used different units of analysis and different measures of inequality.

Units of Analysis

The hypothesis that inequality causes crime rests on an assumption that this occurs among people who "live together." That is, one does not compare crime rates "here" with inequalities of wealth among people "over there." But the phrase "living together" is vague, and what one discovers will depend on the social and physical distance covered by the researcher's unit of analysis.

Crime-recording jurisdictions vary in area and in numbers of people within them. Thus some studies compare inequalities and crime rates within cities, some within counties or (SMSAs), some within states or provinces, and some within countries and between countries. These are cross-sectional studies, and they differ from the rarer comparison made for a jurisdiction over time—a time-series analysis or longitudinal research.

We are reminded that the *level of aggregation* of things counted, the *number of units* (data points) counted, and the time span over which events are counted affect the size, and sometimes even the direction, of association (Hannan 1971; Schelling 1978; Tufte 1974). Results can vary with degree of aggregation and with how much has been tallied for how long. As we shall see, research on the relation between income inequality and crime gives inconsistent results. This is partly a function of using different units of analysis: different levels of aggregation, different numbers of those aggregates (cities, metropolitan areas, or states), and different *spans* of time.

One criticism is that research on this topic has been conducted with little theoretical foundation. That is, investigators have not thought out which unit of analysis is appropriate to test the mechanism—the *psychological process*—by which inequality allegedly generates crime. The psychological underpinning of the inequality thesis—about which more will be said later—should dissipate with physical and social distance between people. Researchers have not addressed this issue.

Measures of Inequality

Inequality of income has been gauged in several ways, and the different procedures yield different results. Thus, the rank order of countries on "income inequality" changes with the measure of difference that is used (Atkinson 1970; Intima 1933). Notice that this is a different problem from that previously addressed—*what* to count. Here the problem is how to decide which distribution is more unequal when one has two or more measures of inequality.

Present purposes require only a brief sketch of the measures of inequality commonly employed—with the reminder that one can get different results with each of them. Social inequality has been evaluated in the following ways:

1. By the range and by the dispersion (standard deviation) of the distribution of incomes.
2. As the proportion of income units within an area that are "poor" as defined by some monetary level such as that used by certain departments of government.
3. As the proportion of income units within an area that receive *x* percent of total or average income. Since research is usually concerned with the distribution of "poverty," a popular measure of this distribution is the proportion of income units that receive less than half the median income in a particular area.
4. As the *gap* between the average earnings of income units in an area and some stratum of poor people—usually defined as the poorest 20% of all units in that area.
5. As the relation between selected percentiles of an income distribution and the median income. For example, estimating income dispersion by counting incomes earned by the top 1st, 2nd, 5th, 10th, and 20th percentiles of a population and the bottom 75th, 85th, and 95th percentiles.
6. As the average difference in incomes between all pairs of individuals relative to the average income of the population. This is the *Gini coefficient.*

The choice of the measure of inequality depends on the hypothesis to be tested. With the hypothesis that it is relative deprivation, rather than absolute need, that causes crime, we seek a measure of inequality that most sensitively depicts degrees of difference between one segment of the population and all others. There is competition among candidates for "best measure" of inequality, and the candidates yield different results.

Correlations

Allowing for all these many defects in data, and for the ones discussed earlier in crime recording (Chapters 4–7), we remain curious about the correlations between measures of income inequality and rates of crime. To repeat, such relationships have been computed using countries as units, zones within countries (such as cities, SMSAs, and states), and employing both cross-sectional and time-series analyses.

International Comparisons

Lydall (1968) ranked 20 nations by order of their income inequality. Braithwaite computed the correlation between Lydall's estimates and each country's homicide rate for the closest year for which data were available and obtained a significant, but modest, coefficient of +.41 (1979: 205). That is, countries with greater dispersions of income also have higher homicide rates.

Braithwaite also calculated the correlation between the distribution of national wealth and homicide rates. He used the U.S. Social Security Administration's figures on the ratio of a country's expenditure on social security to its GNP and then related national rankings on this measure to homicide rates. He reports a negative correlation of −.50 between these indicators, meaning that countries that spend more of their national wealth on social security have lower rates of homicide. (Reminder: Correlation alone says nothing about causation. It says nothing about causal power or causal direction. One can, therefore, read this association the other way: that countries that have lower rates of homicide spend more on social security.)

Krohn (1976) compared the rankings of 27 countries by their Gini coefficients of income inequality with their Interpol crime rates. In keeping with earlier studies, Krohn reports a positive correlation between nations' rates of homicide and their ranking by income inequality. But, Krohn reports a negative correlation between inequalities in income and rates of property crime and total rates of crime. In other words, Krohn's findings say that lands with greater income inequalities have higher homicide rates and lower rates of property crimes and total crimes.

In addition, Krohn finds that both rates of property crime and rates of total crime *increase* with a country's affluence as measured by "level of industrial development," GNP per person, and consumption per person. Krohn attributes these increases with riches to anomie, the dissolution of social bonds that constrain criminality (1976: 311).

Messner compared the reported homicide rates in 39 noncommunist countries during the early 1960s with their Gini coefficients (1980). He then controlled for each nation's population size, population density, degree of urbanization, and gross domestic product per person. He found a moderate, positive association of +.59 between income inequality and rates of homicide. This correlation is higher than that between homicide rates and income per person, population size, and density.

Messner's later research expands the data base to 50 noncommunist countries and finds that countries with less unequal income distributions tend to have lower rates of homicide (1982). The negative relationship between equality and homicide is −.38, and this significant inverse relationship holds when certain other factors are held constant.

Avison and Loring examined the impact of income inequality on rates of homicide for a sample of 32 countries (1986). They found "strong support" for

Blau's proposition that "vertical differentiation, as measured by income inequality, is strongly correlated with homicide rates" (1986: 745).

If, for the moment, one ignores the inconsistencies among reported findings, these various studies suggest that income inequality may be a correlate of homicide levels among different countries. Possible explanations of this phenomenon will be considered later. But here it is important to caution against glib interpretation of these studies.

It is hazardous to draw inferences from comparisons of data of questionable validity gathered from countries that differ in many relevant ways: in their legal codes, policing practices, attitudes toward crimes, rates of citizen complaints, rates of unemployment, monetary inflation, modes of government compensation for these debilities, population movement, and degrees of cultural homogeneity.

As regards cultural unity, it is notable that most international and intranational research on the relationship between inequalities in wealth and crime rates have not controlled for degrees of cultural identity. Thus, when Hansmann and Quigley attempt to test the possibility that "interaction within a society of heterogeneous cultural groups tends to increase the rate of homicide," they find confirmation of such an effect, independent of factors such as economic inequality, GNP per person, urbanization, population density, and age composition (1982). They conclude that ethnic heterogeneity, but not necessarily linguistic or religious heterogeneity, is one factor conducive to higher rates of homicide.

These cautionary points apply as well to comparisons made between cities or regions within one country.

Comparisons within Countries

Much early research addressing the connection between economic conditions and crime used unemployment as a proxy for inequality. The results, we saw (Chapter 9), are less than clear and vary with community context. The same can be said of attempts to relate crime to unequal distributions of wealth.

For example, Danziger (1976) used the Gini coefficient to assess its relation to crime in 222 American cities. He found income inequality in cities to be positively correlated only with their burglary and robbery rates. Yet, Cho's (1974) research yields a contrary conclusion with a different measure of inequality. Cho calculated multiple regression coefficients for 35 socioeconomic indicators and seven index crimes in the 49 largest American cities. His measure of income inequality—percent below the poverty line—was not significantly associated with any of these crimes.

A number of studies were conducted similar to those of Danziger and Cho using different indicators of inequality and crime (e.g., Booth et al. 1976; Ehrlich 1974; Loftin and Hill 1974; McCarthy et al. 1975). The results varied with almost equal distributions of positive, negative, and ambiguous results.

Braithwaite improved upon these many studies by examining average annual index crime rates for 193 American SMSAs over a seven-year period (1979). In addition, he used more than one measure of inequality and controlled for other possible relevant variables in testing for associations between inequality and crime. He reports that the three measures of inequality described earlier are differently related to kinds of crime:

Percentage of families below the poverty line and percentage receiving half the median income or less are both significantly related only to homicide and aggravated assault out of the seven offenses. The income gap between the poor and the average-income family is significantly [and] positively associated with rape, robbery, burglary, grand larceny, and auto theft rates. (1979: 213)

Braithwaite then employed multiple regression analysis to test these associations with controls for population size of American SMSAs and whether or not they were in the American South, a region that has had a record of high rates of violent crime. With such controls, Braithwaite finds *no correlation* between the proportion of poor families in metropolitan areas, measured absolutely or relatively, and rates of index crime rates. The only significant correlation is a negative one between the proportion of poor people and robbery rates, a reversal of some earlier findings and common assumptions.

However, a *gap* indicator of inequalities in wealth yields positive associations with index crimes, with the exception of aggravated assault. When an additional control is employed for the proportions of SMSAs that are African American, the positive correlations remain for five of seven index crimes, the exceptions being aggravated assault and homicide.

Since the income gap between African Americans and whites has been held to be particularly criminogenic, Braithwaite tested this hypothesis and found that

after the income gap between the poor and the average-income earner is controlled, the effect of a large income gap between blacks and whites is to decrease crime rather than increase it. We must therefore totally reject the hypothesis that inequality between the races causes special crime problems over and above those caused by the general level of income inequality in the community. (1979: 219)

Braithwaite bolsters this unusual conclusion by citing Boven and O'Neill's (1975) study of juvenile delinquency in regions of New Zealand. These investigators report that in those areas where incomes of Maoris and whites approach equality, white delinquency rates are high. Put the other way about, in New Zealand racial *inequality* in income is *negatively* associated (r = −.52) with white delinquency rates.

In a similar vein, Morgan and Clark (1973) find that American race riots of the 1960s—one kind of violence—were more likely in cities with greater job equality between blacks and whites. Jiobu's (1974) research yields the same result.

Findings such as these are disputed by Blau and Blau (1982). They examined the relationship between inequality and violent crime among the 125 largest American SMSAs. They used three measures of inequality—Duncan's (1961) SEI score, a measure of social status that includes schooling, income, and occupational prestige; the Gini index of income inequality; and the percent poor as defined by the American "poverty index." They also weighed the contribution to metropolitan violent crime of geographic region, population size, proportion of each SMSA that is African American, and the proportion divorced—using domestic disruption as a proxy for anomie. These multiple indicators of inequality and anomie were then correlated with rates of four violent crimes—those for murder, rape, robbery, and assault—and with an index combining these four crimes.

Analyses show that the proportion of populations that is divorced bears the strongest relationship to violent crime when other variables are held constant. The second most consistent correlate of violence is inequalities on Duncan's SEI score. Population size, percent African American, and income inequality also make independent contributions, in that order, to rates of violent crime in metropolitan areas (Blau and Blau 1982: 124, table 4). The Blaus conclude that

> economic inequalities, between races and within them, are positively related to high rates of violent crime in SMSAs, and when they are controlled, poverty is not related to these rates. Thus, aggressive acts of violence seem to result not so much from lack of advantages as from being taken advantage of, not from absolute but from relative deprivation. Southern cities have higher rates of criminal violence not as the result of the historical experience of the South that produced a tradition of violence but owing to the greater economic inequality there. (1982: 126)

Blau and Blau (1982: 127) add that "intraracial inequality has a direct influence primarily on violence against persons one knows [while] interracial inequality also has a direct influence on violence against strangers."

On the impact of black-white differentials in income, Blau and Blau disagree with Braithwaite's conclusion. They suggest that Braithwaite's measure of racial income inequality—the difference between African Americans' and whites' median incomes in each SMSA—is "probably strongly correlated with the controlled measure of overall inequality—the 'difference between median income and average income of poorest 20% of families'" (1982: 119, n.4). In other words, the Blaus raise the possibility that a measure of racial inequality in incomes is contaminated by its inclusion within the general measure of income inequality.

To this possibility, Braithwaite (1982) replies that the correlation between black-white inequalities and overall inequality in SMSAs is low (+.33), "suggesting that where there are large black-white differences, there are not always large white-white differences. However, there is . . . some correlation."

Differences between Braithwaite's findings and the Blaus' results illustrate our introductory comments about measurement problems. These investigators have employed different measures of inequality, for different numbers of metropolitan areas, for different spans of time.

One of the major problems with resentment analyses is determining the appropriate reference group. That is, relative to whom does one feel deprived and against whom is the resentment directed? While Blau and Blau use black-white comparisons, there is some evidence to suggest this is not an appropriate comparison (Harer and Steffensmeier 1992). Shihadeh and Steffensmeier (1994) suggest that a within-group comparison is more relevant. Thus, one ought to relate crime rates to inequalities within a specific community rather than across communities. Shihadeh and Steffensmeier's research provides support for this contention with their analysis of homicide among African Americans.

Martinez (1996) adds further credibility to this proposition with his analysis of homicide within Latino communities. Martinez's unit of analysis is city-level data. He uses the percentage of families below the poverty line to measure poverty and the Gini Index to measure both Anglo-Latino and Latino-Latino income inequity. Overall, Martinez (1994: 142) concludes: (1) "that economic inequality, not poverty, has a strong effect on Latino homicide," and (2) "independent of other measures, the effect of Latino inequality, not poverty or inequality relative to Anglos, on homicide was strong and significant across the United States."

Time-Series Analyses

Thus far the many correlations point toward intertwined conditions associated with higher rates of violent crime, and less strongly with property offenses. These conditions most clearly are those descriptive of anomie. Controlling for such conditions, it remains unclear whether status differentials among people who live in some proximity to one another cause crime. Additional evidence comes from *longitudinal*, or *time-series*, research.

We have already seen that cross-sectional studies often yield different results from longitudinal studies and that rates of crime can increase with both good times and bad, depending on social contexts. However, studies of the impact of economic fluctuations on crime have rarely looked at the issue of concern here: whether changes in inequalities in the distribution of wealth are correlated with changes in criminal activity.

In a rare study that addresses this question, Danziger and Wheeler (1975) employed both absolute and relative measures of inequality and both time-series and cross-sectional analyses to assess the relative impact of income inequality and other factors on aggravated assault, burglary, and robbery for 57 SMSAs (1975). Their time-series analysis revealed both absolute and relative income inequality to be associated with rates of these three crimes. They also found significant deterrent effects upon crime of the probability of being charged, the probability of being convicted when charged, and the probability of being imprisoned if convicted. They conclude, however, that reductions in inequality have greater impact on crime than increases in punitive responses do. They also note that unemployment levels seem unrelated to the crimes evaluated and that, as noted earlier (Chapter 15), rising affluence can be accompanied by rising crime rates. "Increases in income," they say, "which result from economic growth with a constant distribution lead to higher crime rates" (1975: 125).

The Psychological Question: Process

Despite the low correlations and conflicting evidence about the connection between social inequality and crime, future research should be informed by theory about how such an association might come about. Provisional theory describes the contingencies under which we may expect the nominated cause inequality—to produce an effect. Theory tells us *where* to look, *what* to count, and *which* unit of analysis is, or is not, appropriate.

The principal interpretation, and perhaps the only interpretation, that investigators of this matter have given their correlations invokes a psychological process. The process names "relative deprivation" as the stimulant of hostility. This inference is clear in the quotation from the Blaus cited earlier, and it is apparent throughout most treatises on the criminogenic effects of status inequalities.

Relative deprivation is a psychological state. It is conceived as a *compound* of emotions and of ideas that justify them. This compound is a variable, fluctuating among persons and their situations. A description of this psychological variable employs three intertwined concepts: envy, frustration, and the sometimes separately investigated sense of relative deprivation itself.

Envy Definition

Historically, and perhaps universally, inequalities of any sort have been, and are, grounds for envy. *Envy*, we are told, is a persistent emotion that every society attempts to control. According to this view, envy of the superior and hatred of the different are drives lying "at the core of man's life as a social being [which occur] as soon as two individuals become capable of mutual comparison" (Schoeck 1966: 1). In short, *envy is disinterested resentment*. It is disinterested in that nothing accrues to the envious person who "brings down" an envied person—nothing, that is, other than the satisfaction of seeing the more privileged one "laid low."

Envy versus Jealousy

Most dictionaries do not differentiate between envy and jealousy, but psychologists note a useful distinction. Envy is *impersonal* in the sense that the envied person does not directly threaten the envious one. By contrast, jealousy is *personal*. It is anxiety that one could lose a loved object to a rival. The rival is a direct, personal threat; the envied person constitutes no such threat, except symbolically as a reminder that someone is happier, better-looking, or richer than oneself.

Frustration

Frustration is a second key concept in the structural explanation of some crimes. Unfortunately, "frustration" is another fuzzy word. Sometimes it refers to a blocking, a thwarting; it is signaled by the failure of action to achieve its goal. Let's call this "blocking." At other times it refers to emotions, to feelings of despair and anger, to a free-floating discontent. In our shorthand, this is "feelings." The first meaning is *objective*. Observers can watch animals strive for goals and can agree about their success or failure: whether the monkey gets the banana or the runner wins the race. The second meaning is *subjective*. It refers to feelings attributed to the striver who fails.

The objective failure (blocking) that is sometimes called frustration is not the same set of events as the angry feelings also called frustration (feelings). The relationship between the two meanings of frustration is far from perfect, and one should not be inferred from the other.

Frustration (blocking) is a condition of being alive. To act is to risk not getting what one wants, fully, when one wants it. Because it is so common, it would be surprising if all of its effects were poor ones. We note, then, the many conditions under which being thwarted provides a spur to action. We see this in sports, art, business, romance, and politics. Observing a motivational effect of frustration does not tell us, of course, who will experience it under which conditions. The present point is simply that *there is more than one response to frustration (blocking)*.

When structural theories of criminogenesis employ the concept of frustration, they suffer the weakness of assuming that differences in social status associated with differences in violence *indicate* anger (feelings) with thwarting (blocking) as its cause. They assume this *without* directly measuring either blocking or feelings.

Such an assumption is weak. It is weak because some violence occurs without there having been a high level of anger in its anticipation—as when "friendly drinking bouts" end in beatings and killings. It is weak also because anger can be otherwise stimulated than by frustration (blocking). For example, it can be a function of having been born unwanted. It can be learned from violent peers. And it can be "free-floating," a matter of temperament rather than a function of thwarted life.

Similarly, blocking cannot be measured by proxy. Social position in itself does *not* indicate frustration (blocking), because it yields no measure of striving where the striving fails in its objective. These comments are required because some versions of structural explanation assume what needs to be demonstrated. What needs to be shown is the *fact* of blocking and its *connection* to feelings. Merely observing hostility in offenders does not establish either the fact of thwarted aspiration or its linkage to rage.

Relative Deprivation

Relative deprivation (RA) is the third element in the "structure of resentment." As with the two meanings of frustration, relative deprivation differs from "absolute deprivation" in that the former is a subjective state, a matter of emotion, while the latter is presumably an objective state, a condition of deficiency that observers agree constitutes "need" or "poverty."

Without discounting the possibility that absolute deprivation may stimulate some crimes, especially property offenses, the structural stories that emphasize inequality as criminogenic base their case on the sense of relative deprivation.

Dimensions of Relative Deprivation

The idea of relative deprivation rests on an ancient observation: that how we feel about ourselves depends in great part on comparison. Comparison can be made between where we were and where we are now, between where we are and where we expected to be, and between our own careers and those of others.

The sense of relative deprivation depends, then, on a "frame of reference"; and frames of reference vary with personal histories, with the groups *from which* one has learned standards of how to be and what to expect, with the groups *to which* one wishes to belong, and with the groups *against which* one compares his or her present condition. Herbert Hyman (1942) invented the notion of a "reference group" to explain feelings of social status, and we are reminded that his idea contains the three possibilities of comparison mentioned: group of *origin*, group of *aspiration*, and group of *comparison*.

Comparison also occurs as a dimension of time. For example, Gurr (1970: chap. 2) describes three such kinds of RD: decremental, aspirational, and progressive. *Decremental RD* occurs as the conditions of our lives deteriorate from our customary expectations. *Aspirational RD* occurs when expectations rise faster than the capabilities of realizing them. And *progressive RD* occurs as matters improve but then suffer "a short period of sharp reversal," as J. C. Davies (1962: 6) puts it.

In addition, RD can be assessed along dimensions of intensity (degree), incidence in the population, and persistence (duration). It is important to note the contingencies of RD because they influence the way in which economic structures translate into a sense of RD that may, in turn, be criminogenic. Moreover, government policies that promise reduction of crime through relief of RD need to be cognizant of the conditions under which they may, or may not, do so.

Contingencies of Relative Deprivation

Research, historical and experimental, tells us about the conditions under which the sense of RD grows and diminishes, and notices the connection between appreciation of RD and feelings of envy and ideas of justice.

1. Objective condition is independent of subjective appreciation of that condition. This is hardly news, but, as people move from thinking about their own lives to theorizing about others' lives, they tend to forget that there is slippage between how people live and how they feel about it. George Orwell writes:

   > Talking once with a miner I asked him when the housing shortage first became acute in his district; he answered, "When we were told about it," meaning that till recently people's standards were so low that they took almost any degree of overcrowding for granted. (1937: 64)

   There is no one-to-one correspondence between condition and its interpretation. There is no necessary symmetry between the advantages or disadvantages one has, or the good or bad luck one has experienced, and how one feels about his or her fate.

2. We tend to compare ourselves with our equals or with those just a bit better off than we are, and our reference groups remain quite stable. Comparison does not travel great social distance to generate a sense of RD (Runciman 1966; Thurow 1973). "The happiest people," says Thurow, "seem to be those that do relatively well within their own reference group rather than those that do relatively well across the entire population" (1973: 67). Therefore, raising the incomes of everyone is not a sure means of increasing their happiness. Easterlin (1973) summarizes 30 surveys of people's reported happiness in 19 countries to assess the relation between happiness and income. He concludes that:

   > *In all societies, more money for the individual typically means more individual happiness. However, raising the incomes of all does not increase the happiness of all.* The happiness-income relation provides a classic example of the logical fallacy of composition—*what is true for the individual is not true for society as a whole.* (1973: 4)

3. Progressive RD allows that we can feel worse as things get better. The witty poet Oscar Wilde (1854–1900) expressed this possibility in one of his plays in which a character exclaims, "In this world there are only two tragedies. One is not getting what one wants, and the other is getting it. The last is the real tragedy" (1892, act III).

Anomie results from progress as well as from regress. Elevated expectation paves one major road to anger and despair through the possibility of frustration (blocking). It also charts a second course when expectations are fulfilled, because fulfillment often results in expansion of desire. In some political circumstances, entitlements multiply. Expectations feed on themselves and the appetite grows with the feeding. The politician de Tocqueville (1805–1859) gave this hypothesis classic expression in discussing the French Revolution:

> Thus it was precisely in those parts of France where there had been most improvement that popular discontent ran highest . . . Patiently endured so long as it seemed beyond redress, a grievance comes to appear intolerable once the possibility of removing it crosses men's minds . . . At the height of its power feudalism did not inspire so much hatred as it did on the eve of its eclipse. (1855: 176–177)

More recent studies of domestic turmoil and revolution support de Tocqueville's thesis without proposing that progress-induced relative deprivation is the only cause of popular discontent (Brinton 1938; Davies 1962; Geschwender 1968; Gurr 1970; Marx 1967; Moss 1972; Pahlavi 1980; Schumpeter 1947). The fourth point follows from this.

4. Ideologies of entitlement increase RD (Crosby 1976; Ortega y Gasset 1932).

5. Those who lack something they want feel more deprived if they can blame others ("society"), rather than themselves, for their lack (Crosby 1976).

6. Discontent with one's occupational position is greater where the probability of promotion is higher (Runciman 1966; Stouffer et al. 1949).

7. We feel more frustrated (feelings) and deprived when we act and fail than when we fail because we did not act (Kahneman and Tversky 1982).

8. Passion increases with perceived proximity to the goal (Gurr 1970).

9. People who deem themselves to have been treated unfairly feel better—more satisfied—when they rectify the situation through violent, rather than nonviolent, means (de Carufel and Schopler 1979).

10. There is *no symmetry* between "being provided for" and gratitude. This is a corollary of fact 1, that there is no symmetry between objective and subjective deprivation.

    Foa et al. (1976) show that gifts which are *not* "earned" and benefits that are bestowed *without* an expression of affection—that is, routine gifts as opposed to loving gifts—*lose their power* to allay the sense of RD.

11. RD rests, obviously, on a sense of fairness. It rests on a conception of equity, rather than on notions of equality.

Conceptions of fairness, in turn, are embedded in a people's history and culture. American and British research indicates that current ideas of equity want rewards to be somehow proportional to efforts and other costs.

In Conclusion: Relative Deprivation

These many contingencies tell us that, if anger is one consequence of RD (remembering that despair and apathy are other possible responses) and, if anger is a generator of crime, as many structural theorists claim, then the relation between *absolute* inequality and rage is *not* straightforward. In addition, the relation between *relative* inequalities and rage is also *not* straightforward, but it is filtered through the psychological sieves described above.

In sum, anger runs on a two-way street. It can be produced by not having and comparing oneself with those who have, but it can also be produced by another type of deprivation—that of having one's earned income confiscated. Resentful social movements have been built out of middle-class, as well as lower-class, senses of RD. The success of political parties of the right and the movement toward the right by centrist parties during the 1980s and 1990s in the United States, Britain, and Canada illustrate this point.

These possibilities bring us to the philosophical question.

The Philosophical Question: Interpretation

Studies that relate inequality to crime require interpretation, and they require more interpretation than the *ad hoc* invocation of a presumed resentment that transforms inequality into crime. Saying this does not deny that there are conditions under which inequality stimulates criminogenic hostility. This is admitted when we recognize the universal propensity to envy. It is admitted, too, in our earlier recognition that placing many poor people next to a few rich ones invites theft. But interpretation of the contingencies linking inequality to crime through resentment must do more than merely acknowledge that this is one way of generating criminality. It must do more because public policies are advocated, and sometimes instituted, on the basis of theories such as those that posit unequal opportunities and structures of resentment as crime producers.

The central question, then, is whether income inequality causes crime or whether it is only a correlate of crime, a correlate that varies by degree with other conditions that are fundamental. Differently translated, this question asks whether government action to reduce income inequalities will reduce crime and, if so, *how much* reduction in inequality will produce *how much* reduction in crime.

The thesis to be maintained here is that inequality paves one road to crime, but only under certain conditions. A corollary of this theme is that there are other routes to similar criminal ends. Since much of the research on this topic attends to violence as a principal consequence of inequality, the present argument will be similarly limited. The thesis will be advanced by showing the following:

1. There are zones of income equality with high rates of violent crime.
2. There are zones of great income inequality with low rates of violent crime.
3. There are, therefore, other causes of violence than resentment born of inequality.

4. The big mistake is to translate correlation into causation so that the effects of evolutionary processes are confused with the likely effects of planned intervention.

Violence with Equality

Inequality is said to have its effect on conduct through comparison. But, comparison is limited, not universal. People compare themselves with those "close" to them in physical and social space. The boundaries of that space have been poorly drawn by researchers.

A fair test of the inequality→resentment→crime hypothesis requires specification of the reference groups that stimulate resentment. Otherwise, one does not know which unit of analysis to use. Nevertheless, investigators seldom meet this test directly. Rather, they implicitly assume boundaries of reference by selecting some convenient unit that limits the physical and social region within which inequality is supposed to operate. Thus, as we have seen, comparison is not between inequality here and crime there. Still, the units employed have ranged widely in scope—from entire countries, to provinces and states, to large metropolitan areas, cities, and towns.

One can find challenging exceptions to the inequality thesis, then, by looking at small communities where reference groups are visible and close, where income differences are minimal, but where murder rates are high. The exceptions tell us that something other than class-based resentment can generate violent action.

Canada provides one example. As was noted in Chapter 10, homicide rates have been consistently higher in the Canadian hinterland, among people of relatively equal wealth, than in the metropolitan areas, characterized by greater income inequality (Doherty and Joyal 1979; Schloss and Giesbrecht 1972: 22). Homicide in the backwoods is largely fueled with alcohol and the battles are predominantly domestic.

Mexico yields other examples. During the 1950s and 1960s, Tarascan and Mayan villagers, living in relatively egalitarian pueblos, killed one another at annual rates in excess of 250 per 100,000 population (Friedrich 1962; Nash 1967). An appreciation of the elevation of such a rate is gained by comparison with rates in most northwestern European countries, except Northern Ireland, which typically run about 1.2 to 1.5 per 100,000 people per year. As indicated in Chapter 4, the incidence is about 2 per 100,000 per year in Canada, and about 9 per 100,000 per year in the United States. Murder is so common in the Mayan village Nash (1967) studied that she titled her report, "Death as a Way of Life."

Tarascans and Mayans kill one another in political quarrels and in fights over women and land, but "class resentment is not an operative motive."

Another route to murder is described in a mestizo pueblo where L. R. Schwartz (1972) tallied even higher rates of homicide than either Friedrich or Nash had estimated. Schwartz calculates that her villagers kill one another at rates ranging from 250 to 800 per 100,000 population per year. The typical occasion for murder is friendly drinking that escalates from joking to insult. One can be killed for refusing a drink or for trying to leave an all-night gambling party. As always, jealousy, as distinct from envy, is a partner in homicide.

Schwartz indicates that homicide in this rural setting is not the result of previous conflict among the actors and it does not produce conflict. The killing Schwartz describes does not flow from frustration—neither "blocking" nor "feelings"—and it is not an expression of latent hostility. Given such "violence without conflict," it is no surprise to learn that most murderers are not jailed and that in many cases charges are not pressed. "Some cases," Schwartz (1972: 155) says, "are heard only in the village where they are treated mildly."

Elwin (1950) illuminates the separation between economy, equality, and homicide with his study of tribes in India. The bands he studied have similar modes of making a living and similar distributions of wealth within them, yet they differ in the ways they rear their children and in their inclination to murder. Elwin (1950: 37) reports that "the Bison-horn Maria have long had a bad reputation for violence and drunkenness" and that they kill one another at a rate three to four times that of a neighboring tribe. According to Elwin's tally, the principal occasions for homicide are saturated in alcohol and involve fights over women and property and the usual range of disputes within families.

Illustrations such as these can be multiplied. The anthropological and sociological literature tells many tales of neighboring towns and cities, similar in size and the distribution of wealth, that have widely different patterns of violence (Shields and Duncan 1964 report such differences in Scotland; Shoham 1966 in Israel; and Christie 1960 in Norway). Such findings alert us to cultural differences, to the fact, repeatedly recorded by anthropologists and sociologists, that people do not behave similarly in similar situations with a uniformity that allows prediction of conduct from description of condition.

The sociological truism that follows is that economic circumstances set limits to behavior, but do not determine behavior within those limits. The way in which one earns a living and the wealth one has make a difference in what one *can* do, but these economic bases do not uniformly determine what people *will* do—how they will use their lives, whether they will be happy or sad, peaceful or violent.

On this point, we should also recognize a selection factor at work. Different kinds of people are "selected" by their talents and tastes for differential participation in economies. This becomes truer among large aggregations with diversified modes of production. The selection process, then, is one of the causes of the conduct that is differentially distributed up and down the income ladder.

Recognition of this factor reverses the causal order of the inequality→resentment→crime hypothesis. Rather than proposing that inequality is the necessary and sufficient stimulant of violence, the reverse ordering suggests that different kinds of people choose different kinds of work, legitimate and illegitimate, which place them on different levels of an income hierarchy with different styles of social relations. According to this model, behavior comes first and economic placement follows, rather than vice versa as structural hypotheses suppose.

The cultural theme is developed in Chapter 17, but it also affects the second aspect of the philosophical question.

Peace with Inequality

The obverse of violence with equality is peace with inequality. Since inequality has been the characteristic condition of societies above the size of tribes, life would be more precarious than it is if inequality inevitably stimulated hostility.

Pacification is one of the functions of civilization. This does not mean that the process works easily or perfectly. A civil life, which is an orderly life among strangers, is always under challenge, and it can never be assumed to persist regardless of effort.

A *cultivated* way of living together is, then, one of the mechanisms by which human beings accommodate one another with a minimum of violence despite inequalities in wealth and power. An extreme modern example is Saudi Arabia, an autocratic state in which homicide rates (and rates of other crimes) are low, religious control is strict, punishment is probable and severe, and distinctions of wealth and status are both obvious and legitimated.

A less extreme case is Japan, a country with remarkably low crime rates, but with distributions of status and income similar to those in other industrialized states (Brown 1977: 194–202). The difference in conduct between citizens of rich Japan and citizens of other affluent countries is summarized in one short-hand symbol: culture. And the strength of Japanese culture is, in turn, a consequence of that nation's ethnic homogeneity (Bruce-Biggs 1982).

Other Roads to Violence

These exceptions, and others, to the inequality resentment crime hypothesis suggest that there are other ways of producing violent people. One is to have children who are unwanted; the other is to prefer violent action and teach it.

Chapter 11 advanced the thesis that children tend to grow up violent if they are not adequately nurtured (Eron et al. 1971; Harlow and Harlow 1967). Adequate nurturing includes both *appreciating* children and *training* them to acknowledge the rights of others. From this theoretical stance, the savagery of the urban gang-ster represents merely the natural outcome of a failure in child rearing.

Similarly, on a simple level of explanation, many sociologists and anthropologists believe that hostile behavior can be learned as easily as pacific behavior. Once learned, the codes of violence and impatient egoism are their own "positive values." Fighting and hating then become both duties and pleasures, the more so where enemies are defined. There are tribes, and segments of modern populations, where being "b-a-a-a-d" is considered good. Chapter 18 elaborates on this road to violence. Here we conclude with a description of the Big Mistake.

The Big Mistake

The Big Mistake is to translate correlation into causation and to do so by neglecting the system within which the nominated causes may produce their effects. This neglect leads to a related error: that of confusing the consequences of a *process* with the consequences of a *plan*.

The discussion of causation in Chapter 3 mentioned that all notions of cause and effect are system-bound. Ideas of causation assume boundaries to what will be considered causal. Furthermore, they assume that, within those boundaries, a cause seldom has a uniform effect but, rather, that causal powers are contingent. This means that what a cause "does" depends on other things that are going on.

The thrust of research on inequality and crime is that if we created (legislated) less inequality, there would be less crime. But the correlations brought to bear on this hypothesis do not support this predictive inference. These imperfect correlations do not bear such a conclusion, because the data point to more powerful causes than income inequality and because the inequalities discovered are not impositions, but are themselves the result of processes that have significance for crime.

Inequality is a constant of life. Inequality has always been associated with large aggregations of human beings, but, as we have seen, crime does not bear a constant relation to degrees of inequality. Our many descriptions of structures and behaviors tell us that the relation between them is not uniform. If the relation is not uniform, something else makes a difference. The "something else" can make a difference by coming before the revealed correlations or by *intervening* between the nominated independent variables and the dependent one.

Stratification in Western societies is more achieved than imposed. The "economic structure" operates like a giant sieve, sifting people into occupational and income niches by their geographic locations, and tastes and talents. Therefore, it may not be the *fact* of inequality that causes crime so much as it is whatever goes along with the *process* through which differing degrees, and qualities, of inequality result. Some of these processes affect the legitimacy accorded to inequality and hence affect the sense of RD. Other aspects of the sifting process reflect a population's cultural homogeneity or heterogeneity.

In short, the social filter sorts people, not just by income, but also by a host of traits that go along with their incomes and may even produce them—traits such as ambition, intelligence, diligence, specific talents, and bonded connections with intimate others. If this is so, then it is this *complex* of dispositions and actions out of which crime is, or is not, spun.

To repeat, we are warned against confusing that which has evolved with that which has been intentionally created. Results of a *process* are seldom the same as results of a plan. Chapter 17 describes theories that take cultural—evolved—differences into account.

17. Subcultures and Crime

Cultures and Subcultures

A fundamental observation upon which the behavioral sciences rest, and a fact that they attempt to explain, is that people do *not* behave the same way in what appear to be similar situations. Chapters 13–16 have commented on the explanatory inadequacy of an environmental determinism, recognizing that circumstances set limits to behavior, but do not allow the prediction of behavior within those limits.

The fact that individuals, and groups of individuals, differ in their responses to similar circumstances has led students of human action to propose *mediators* between situation and action. When these mediators have some generality and continuity among a people that regards itself as distinct—among a people that has, in Gidding's phrase, a "consciousness of kind"—anthropologists and sociologists speak of these "intervening variables" as a *culture*. The concept of "culture" refers to a way of life of a people who have sense of a common history, a sense of being "we" as opposed to "them," and who, usually but not necessarily, live within a bounded territory.

T. S. Eliot (1948: 57) describes a culture as a "peculiar way of thinking, feeling, and behaving." Cultures are identified as distinctive patterns of actions that mark off one group of human beings from others. Such patterns, we noted, can be discerned in diet, dress, art, etiquette, religion, and ways of using a language.

The concept of a culture includes standards of behavior, observable in both words and deeds, that are learned, transmitted from generation to generation, and hence somewhat durable. To call such behavior "cultural" means not necessarily that it is "refined," but rather that it is "cultured"—that is, acquired, cultivated, and persistent.

When people of diverse nationalities live under the laws of one state, they come to share some aspects of a common culture; this has been particularly true since the spread of electronic communication. However, modern states that govern many nations do not become "melting pots," as early social reformers thought they would. On the contrary, ethnic differences persist. The break up of the old Soviet Union after 75 years of attempts by the communist regime to create social homogeneity, and the tragic internecine warfare in the former Yugoslavia are prime examples of the resilience of ethnic identities. In addition to ethnic cleavages, societies may be characterized by generation gaps and by sex and class differences in commitment to common culture.

The possibility, then, that groups will share some elements of a common culture while retaining different cultural tastes has led to the idea of *subcultures*.

Sociologists and criminologists have studied a variety of criminal and deviant subcultures including motorcycle gangs (Wolf 1991; Lavigne 1996), "metal-heads" (Arnett 1996), skinheads (Hamm and Chambliss 1993), religious sects (Zellner 1995), and rootless single men (Courtwright 1996).

It is part of the definition of a subculture, as of a culture, that it is relatively enduring. Its norms are termed a "style," rather than a "fashion," on the ground that the former has some persistence, while the latter is fleeting. The quarrel comes, of course, when we try to estimate how "real" a cultural pattern is and how enduring it may be.

Subcultures and Crime: Conflict of Norms

Standards by which behavior is guided vary among us and change with time. It is in this change and variety that norms of conduct may conflict, and it is out of this conflict that crime is defined.

An early application of this principle to criminology was given by Thorsten Sellin (1938), who found sources of crime in the fact that groups have developed different standards of appropriate behavior and that, in "complex cultures," each individual is subject to competing prescriptions for action. "A conflict of conduct norms is said to exist," Sellin (1938: 29) wrote, "when more or less divergent rules of conduct govern the specific life situation in which a person may find himself."

Sellin is interested in the conflict of *all* norms of conduct, not merely in those that are codified in the criminal law. He sees the concern with crime as flowing from the conflict of standards about how we should behave.

In criminology, two kinds of conflict have received particular attention: that between social classes and that between ethnic groups.

Conflict Between Social Classes

One version of subcultural explanation of crime derives from the fact that, as we have seen, "social classes" experience different rates of arrest and conviction for serious offenses. When strata within a society are marked off by categories of income, education, and occupational prestige, differences are discovered among them in the amount and style of crime. In addition, differences are usually found between these strata in their tastes, interests, and morals. It is easy, then, to describe these class-linked patterns as cultures. Thus the anthropologist Oscar Lewis (1959, 1961) speaks of the "culture of poverty," and the sociologist Walter B. Miller (1958) writes about "lower-class culture."

This "class" version of the subcultural explanation of crime holds that the very fact of learning the lessons of the subculture means that people acquire interests and preferences that place them at greater or lesser risk of breaking the law. Miller, for example, argues that being reared in the lower class means learning a different culture from that which creates the dominant social rules. The lower-class subculture is said to have its own values, many of which run counter to the majority interests that support the laws against the serious predatory crimes.

Miller's "Focal Concerns"

W. B. Miller describes these lower-class values as "focal concerns" that include "trouble, toughness, smartness, excitement, fate, and autonomy." He claims that the lower class differs from the strata called "middle class" and "upper class" in its greater subscription to these focal concerns.

The lower-class person believes that "life is trouble," that much in one's career is fated regardless of what one does, and that the proper response to "the way the world works" is to be tough, cunning, and independent. It is considered smart to be "hastily hedonistic," to enjoy what one can when one can and let tomorrow take care of itself.

According to Miller, some 40–60% of North American citizens may be "directly influenced" by these values, but about 15% are said to be "hard-core lower-class"—that is, people for whom the focal concerns constitute a style of life. These hard-core lower-class people are also described as being produced by households headed by women, in which "serial monogamy" is practiced—in which, that is, the mother has one "spouse" at a time but more than one in a lifetime.

By contrast with lower-class values, those of the middle class are usually described as emphasizing ambition, cultivation of talent, the ability to postpone gratification and to plan for the future, and the acceptance of individual responsibility and social duties (Davis and Havighurst 1947; Hyman 1953; Kohn 1959; Kohn and Schooler 1969; Le Shan 1952; Pearlin and Kohn 1966; Rosen 1956). A number of studies report a class-linked clustering of attitudes toward time with ability to work for long-term rewards, with "achievement motivation," and with success in lawful occupations and immunity to criminality. These attributes, in turn, are often found in association with feelings of "internal control," that is, with the belief that one is master of one's own fate (Barndt and Johnson 1955; Heckhausen 1967; Jessor et al. 1968; Lefcourt 1972; Lessing 1968, 1971; Mischel 1973; Teahan 1958).

It is also reported (Cohen 1955) that the middle class emphasizes being rational and reasonable, having good manners, and using leisure healthfully (*to dissipate*, we recall, means "to waste"). The middle class stresses respect for property and the control of violence.

Miller's thesis is that middle-class values are themselves lawful, whereas acquiring lower-class preferences automatically involves one in a greater risk of breaking the laws against the more serious crimes.

Banfield's "Propensity and Incentive"

A similar class-oriented thesis is advanced by the political scientist Banfield. He holds that

> crime, like poverty, depends upon two sets of variables. One set relates mainly to class culture and personality (but also to sex and age) and determines an individual's *propensity* to crime. The other relates to situated factors (such as the number of policemen on the scene and the size of the payroll) and determines his *incentive*. The probability that he will commit crimes—his proneness to crime—depends upon propensity *and* incentive. (1968: 159)

Banfield's description of the lower-class "propensity" to crime parallels Miller's description of its focal concerns. Banfield contends that lower-class culture develops a different type of morality, one that he calls "preconventional," in which conduct is guided by what succeeds and what can be gotten away with, and in which the only authority is power.

The propensity to crime is also encouraged, according to Banfield, by the shorter "time horizon" and lesser "ego strength," or ability to control impulses, of the lower class. The lower class is seen as placing a low value on the avoidance of risk. It is less prudent than the middle class and hence more prone to criminality. Furthermore, Banfield, like other reporters, describes the lower class as being encouraged to violence by its training, so that part of its greater propensity to crime lies in its greater willingness to inflict injury.

The "Deprived" and the "Privileged" in England

Similar portraits of subcultural differences have been drawn by a number of English researchers (Downes 1966; Morris 1957; Spinley 1964; and Willmott 1966).

Downes's and Willmott's studies, in particular, challenge the ideas of American structuralists. The English investigators do not find that young people of the working class engage in thievery out of lack of legitimate opportunity or that they resort to vandalism out of resentment of their lower social position. The findings of the English investigators agree with those of Miller, Banfield, and others that lower-class criminality is more a function of subcultural differences in taste than of compensatory reaction against failure. Working-class young people in urban England are described as reconciled to careers in unskilled labor. Contrary to the American structural picture, these young English people are said not to aspire to be middle class and are *not* motivated to achieve fame or fortune. Their focal concerns are doing what they want, avoiding responsibility, and having fun.

These differences in values are said to be culturally acquired responses to circumstance, rather than rational or resentful adaptations. Downes (1966: 111) writes that

> the encouragement of spontaneity and autonomy from an early age leads the working-class boy to resist the assertion of middle-class authority he is bound to encounter via school and the law. Working-class culture is at once rigorously defined and sufficiently at odds with the controlling middle-class culture to make a head-on clash almost inevitable.

This description of subcultural differences is supplemented by the research of Morris (1957) and Spinley (1964), who were interested in patterns of child rearing and in the nature of the values among families of different occupational status.

Again, the findings of the English investigators agree with the description of delinquent subcultures provided by Miller and Banfield for Americans. Among families of unskilled English workers, discipline of children is much more haphazard and inconsistently punitive than among middle-class families. Children tend to be ignored or rejected. Punishment is more a function of how the parents feel than of what the child does. Abstract moral lessons are not taught, and life is lived in the present rather than for the future. As a result of such rearing, pangs of guilt and anxiety about shame are noticeably absent.

Time and Class in Germany

Subcultural studies of criminality and other behaviors refer repeatedly to differences among people in their sense of time. They do so for good reason. As the psychologist Mari Riess Jones (1976: 353) demonstrates in a review of research: "Time is one of the defining properties of our world and so of ourselves." Perception of time and the uses of time are correlated, and both are important markers of differences in character.

The hypothesis of Miller and Banfield and its English equivalents propose class-linked orientations to time, and, as we have seen, research in Canada, the United States, and England lends support to this thesis. Additional support comes from Germany, where Lamm et al. (1976) found parallel class-correlated conceptions of time. These investigators asked youngsters of high-school age about their hopes and fears for the future. They then analyzed these sentiments as pertaining to private or public matters, as optimistic or pessimistic, and as being dependent principally on the respondents themselves or on luck and circumstance. Hopes and fears were also examined for their "extension," that is, for how far into the future they were projected.

As previous research suggested, middle-class youngsters have a longer time perspective than lower-class youngsters, and this holds true in their attitudes toward both public and private affairs. This finding is made doubly interesting because, although middle-class adolescents expressed more concern about *public* affairs than lower-class adolescents, they still had a longer time orientation than lower-class youths about matters of *private* concern.

Notes on Criteria of Social Class

1. Shifting Boundaries of Class Cultures

In reading these descriptions of class cultures, one should not assume that such ways of life are fixed. A "culture" has some stability, but stability is not permanence. Cultures move and mix. The quality of their markers changes, and with that, class boundaries change too. For example, given some social mobility and shifts in income distribution, Bohlke (1961) suggests that what has been called "middle-class delinquency" may more accurately represent "middle-*income*" crime rather than "middle-class-culture" crime. Bohlke means by this that the values taught and exhibited by some portion of the middle-income stratum are no longer the traditional middle-*class* values of prudence, personal responsibility, restraint, and achievement through disciplined effort.

It need not be expected, then, that merely increasing income will increase whatever *used to be* associated with income—absolutely or relatively. Everything depends on the tastes that are cultivated as one's standard of living is elevated. An economic determinism is misleading if it assumes that styles of life now associated with different income levels will automatically be generated by changes in income *however* such a change is effected. Being *given* money does not require, or produce, the same culture as *earning* it does.

2. Indicators Versus Descriptions of Class

Proponents of subcultural explanations of crime do not define a class culture by any assortment of the objective indicators of rank, such as annual income or years of schooling. The subcultural theorist is interested in *patterned ways of life* which may have evolved with a division of labor and which, then, are called "class" cultures. The pattern, however, is not described by reference to income alone, or by reference to years of schooling or level of occupational skill or prestige. The pattern includes these indicators, but it is not defined by them. The subcultural theorist is more intent upon the *varieties of human value*, as C. W. Morris has depicted and measured them (1956). These are preferred ways of living that are acted upon. In the economist's language, they are "tastes."

The thesis that is intimated, by a subcultural description of behaviors is that single or multiple signs of social position, such as occupation or education, will have a different significance for status, and for cultures, with changes in their distribution. Money and schooling do not mean the same things socially when they become more or less equally distributed. The change in meaning is not merely a change in the prestige value of these indexes; it also reflects changes in the boundaries between class cultures.

Conflict between Ethnic Groups

A more general subcultural explanation of crime, not necessarily in disagreement with the notion of class cultures, attributes differences in crime rates to differences in ethnic patterns to be found within a society. Explanations of this sort do not necessarily bear the title "ethnic," although they are so designated here because they include the general assumption that there are group differences in learned preferences—in what is rewarded and punished—and that these group differences have a persistence often called a "tradition."

Such explanations are of the same type whether they are advanced as descriptions of regional cultures, generational differences, or national characteristics. Their common theme is the differences in ways of life out of which differences in crime rates seem to flow. Ethnic explanations are proposed under an assortment of titles, but commonly they do not limit the notion of subculture to "class culture." They seem particularly justified where differences in social status are not as highly correlated with differences in conduct compared to other indicators of cultural difference.

A Regional Theory

Gastil (1971: 414) argues that in the United States "economic and status positions in the community cannot be shown to account for differences [in homicide rates] between whites and Negroes or between Southerners and Northerners." Gastil then constructs an "index of Southernness" that he finds to be highly correlated with homicide rates in the United States. He claims, therefore, that there is a measurable regional culture that promotes murder. Gastil's hypothesis has drawn significant empirical support (Blau and Golden 1986; Huff et al. 1986; Kposowa and Breault 1993; Rice and Goldman 1994).

Subculture of Violence

In a similar vein, but examining the world as a whole, Wolfgang and Ferracuti (1967) have tried to explain variations in the amounts and kind of violent behavior by describing the lessons that are transmitted from generation to generation within ethnic groups. Their study brings together an enormous bibliography on the psychology of killing, on the characteristics of aggressors, and on the cultures that facilitate violence. Wolfgang and Ferracuti's thesis is that we can discern clusters of individuals, identifiable by their "consciousness of kind," exhibit different propensities for violence. These indications are observable in actions such as carrying weapons, taking quick insult from a wide range of stimuli, and fighting more frequently. The subculture of violence is also recognizable in rituals and accompanying verbalizations that define the world as a jungle, that recommend violent response to the jungle as both efficient and proper, and that prefer violent "adjustments" to more peaceful means.

Recent studies have focused on the existence of subcultures of violence within a number of broader ethnic communities including the Chinese (Lipman and Harrell 1990), Sicilians (Catanzaro 1992), Basques (Llera 1989), and American Indians (Bachman and Straus 1992).

The subculture is recognized, then, by two families of activities: (1) violent acts and preparations for them; and (2) verbal justifications of such acts. Among those who use the subcultural explanation, there is a tendency to employ the verbal justifications ("values," they are called) as *causes* of the violent acts. As we shall see, this is a popular mode of causal attribution and one of questionable generality.

In Conclusion: Politics of Subcultural Explanation

The beauty of a subcultural explanation of group differences in conduct is that it is descriptive and it is true. Furthermore, it seems truer as it becomes more descriptive. Adding detail adds truth value.

Discomfort with a subcultural explanation arises because such an explanation gives no handle for reasoned remedy. If there are violent others who like the way they are and we wish to pacify them, how do we do it?

The notion that their violence is congenial—that it is generated and supported not just by circumstance, but also by a valued way of being and doing—rules out the easy ideas of social work. If there are cultures and subcultures, we know that they may break down, but we also are told that they may persist and that they may persist beyond facile cures such as a guaranteed income and improved housing.

It is political preference, again, that fuels debate about the validity and utility of subcultural explanation.

Criticism of Subcultural Explanation

Criticism of this style of explanation runs on two tracks: (1) it asks whether subcultural explanation may not be circular; and (2) it questions the degree to which subcultures are persistent or responsive to changed circumstances.

Is Subcultural Explanation Circular?

As we noted in Chapter 3, a circular explanation is one in which whatever is supposed to do the explaining (the *explanans*) is part of the event to be explained (the *explanandum*). A circular explanation is a *tautology*, a sentence whose predicate is contained within its subject. For example:

- "You won't get bald if you don't lose your hair."—*an American mother*
- "When many people are out of work, you have unemployment."
  —*a president of the United States*
- "You can observe an awful lot just by watching."—*a baseball philosopher*

Subcultural explanation is accused of being tautological. It is said to explain one kind of behavior by reference to attitudes and other behaviors that are of the substance of what is to be accounted for. It is as though one were to say, "People are murderous because they live violently" or "People like to fight because they are hostile."

An example of the difficulty posed by subcultural theory is found in the study of violence in U.S. public schools by Felson and his coworkers (1994). Initially attempting to test whether a subculture of violence explanation can account for variations in interpersonal violence in public schools, the authors conclude that the results reflect a subculture of delinquency more than a subculture of violence. The line is a fine one, but the authors come very close to defining a subculture of delinquency by the fact that there are high rates of delinquency among some students and then predicting delinquency as a consequence of a subculture of delinquency.

Reducing Circularity

Such redundant statements are true, of course, but they seem not to satisfy. There are, however, at least three ways to reduce the circularity: (1) to describe the subculture more completely; (2) to tell how it is learned; and (3) to mix subcultural explanation with other explanatory devices.

Detailed Description

A first way out of circularity is to describe the culture that generates the behavior of interest in such breadth that "the whole way of life" is seen as making a particular kind of conduct more probable. This description usually includes a history of how the people "got that way." It becomes more plausible as an explanation when details of the differences between one group and another are added. These details can be *directly* associated with the behavior to be explained—as when Gastil describes the tradition of carrying weapons as Southern and relates such

"Southernness" to higher homicide rates. When given such a larger picture of a culture, consumers of explanations are frequently satisfied. Their curiosity rests. Whether curiosity ought to rest here—whether this explanation, or any other, is adequate—depends, again, on what one wishes to do with explanations.

If we want only to "understand" variations in violence, our curiosity will be satisfied to the degree to which the "subculture of violence" has been thoroughly described so that its end product, assault and homicide, seems logically related to the description of everything else that is going on within the subculture. Similarly, if we want to know whether, and how, to protect ourselves, a subcultural description will suffice. It provides a basis for forecast, and its utility does not require further knowledge of what *makes* violent people as they are.

The rub comes, however, if we want to "cure" a subculture of violence.

A subcultural explanation, by itself, provides no informed instruction for remedy of the criminal conduct it explains. This does not make it untrue, of course; it just makes it unsatisfactory for some purposes. This is, again, a political reason for rejecting a subcultural thesis.

Insofar as a subculture of violence is a *patterned* way of life, there is no particular lever for reformers to use. One might as well attack one facet of the offending culture as another—child-rearing practices or religious beliefs, leisure pursuits or job satisfaction.

A hazard of accepting a subcultural explanation and, at the same time, wishing to be a doctor to the body politic is that the remedies advocated may as easily spread the disease as cure it. For example, among Wolfgang and Ferracuti's recommendations for reducing assault and homicide is "social action" to disperse the representatives of the subculture of violence. This alleged remedy is quite commonly advocated for a variety of social concerns (Polk and Schafer 1972).

Apart from the political and moral questions involved in such a coerced dispersion of people, the proposal assumes more knowledge than we have. We do not know, for example, what proportion of the violent persons would have to be mixed with what proportion of pacific people in order to break down the culture of violence. What is more important, we do not know to what extent the dispersed violent people may act as "culture carriers" and contaminate their hosts. In sum, reducing the circularity of subcultural explanation by adding descriptive detail will satisfy some purposes but not others.

Adding Social Psychology

A second way in which subcultural explanation can be made less circular is by adding a sociopsychological explanation to it. Sociopsychological explanations, particularly those of the "control" variety (see Chapter 12), tell *how* cultural prescriptions and preferences "get inside" actors. They therefore answer questions about the transmission and durability of subcultures.

Mixing Subcultures and Structures

A third way out of the tautology of subcultural explanation is to combine it with another presumed determinant of criminality: the situation. The situation that is most frequently nominated as a cause of conduct is the web of economic circumstance. One's economic situation, in turn, has been analyzed as the income one receives, the wealth one has, the income one expects or needs, the kind of work one does, and the opportunity available for improvement. These signs of economic circumstance are not the same, of course, and their interchangeable use contributes to confusion in isolating the sources of behavior.

Despite this confusion, students of human action continue to blame circumstances for conduct. A persistent debate, then, is whether ethnic differences reduce to differences in economic condition or whether ethnicity has an independent role in the determination of crime rates.

Toby (1950) has provided an interesting proposal that incorporates both ethnic values and economic structures as sources of criminality. Toby's proposal shows how ethnicity and opportunity structures meet to determine risks of illegal conduct.

"Ethnic tradition," Toby argues, "is an intermediate structure between class position and the personality of the individual." Ethnic traditions that foster the particular attitudes and skills required by legitimate careers within a society reduce culture conflict and crime. Yet, those ethnic traditions that are less congruent with the requirements of a "system" are likely to be associated with higher rates of crime.

Toby contends that ethnic traditions, opportunity structures, and personality traits are intertwined determinants of lawful and criminal careers. This brings us back on the general ground of culture conflict. A blending of variables, such as Toby proposes, however, makes the subcultural explanation of crime less tautological.

Does Culture Cause?

It seems reasonable to explain group differences in behavior by mixing the facts of cultural difference with sociopsychological data on how we learn the lessons of our tribe, along with a description of the situations we are in. This reasonable mixture, however, does not satisfy many students of conduct, because it does not specify the relative powers of the ingredients. We are not told how much of which behavior is caused by how we were trained, what we learned (our culture), and what chances we really had or thought we had.

Social scientists continue to quarrel, therefore, about differences between people. Perhaps no questions are more uncomfortable for modern intellectuals than questions of difference:

- How different are individuals and groups?
- What causes the difference, if there is any?
- How changeable are these differences, and by what techniques?

The quarrel becomes heated as the debate moves from a description of the different conditions under which people live to differences in their *conduct* that are sometimes alleged to be effects of their circumstances and sometimes alleged to be their *causes*.

Among scholars, as opposed to the people they study, equality is an ideal. This ideal seeks equality of condition as well as equality of opportunity. The ideal is therefore challenged by the possibility that people differ in talent and taste. The moral movement in favor of equality has made it "politically incorrect" today to recognize differences in conduct among groups, and subcultural explanations of crime have not escaped this condemnation. Thus common responses to the description of criminogenic subcultures include (1) denying the difference, (2) denying the durability of the difference, and, finally, whether or not these denials seem plausible, (3) calling the difference "rational," "adaptive," or in some other way "understandable," if not actually preferable.

In Defense of Subcultural Explanation

In defense of the significance culture holds for conduct and in refutation of the structural argument that behavior is nothing but response to circumstance, several questions can be posed, and their answers suggested.

Do Different Cultures Behave Differently?

A first question asks whether individuals, and culturally identifiable groups, do behave differently in similar circumstances. The answer is yes, and the evidence is written in the library of ethnography. As individuals, and as inbreeding groups, we do things differently in what seem to be parallel circumstances. This fact, we have seen, is the justification of those special studies called psychology and sociology. These studies attempt to explain the differences.

The differences have been counted in many ways, in many times and places, and among many categories of activity—sexual, recreational, economic. Particular attention has been paid to economics, the "material bases" of life, about which two broad questions are asked: "Do different ways of organizing the uses of labor and capital produce different quantities of wealth and qualities of life?" and "To what extent do economic circumstances, variously defined, cause conduct?"

Quarrels continue about the fine points in answers to these questions, but, for present purposes, the answers can be summarized as follows: First, there *are* better and worse ways of responding to material conditions in the production of wealth, and culturally distinct groups do *not* behave with equal efficiency.

Second, there is abundant evidence that, while our economic situation *sets limits* to what we can do, it does not *determine* what we must do. Thus, under apparently similar economic circumstances, some ethnic groups have much higher rates of assault and homicide than others (see Chapter 9). In similar economic conditions some ethnic groups have difficulty handling alcohol and dope, while others do not (Snyder 1958). In addition, ethnic groups in apparently similar material circumstances differ in their sexual practices, rates of illegitimate births, and family stability, and levels of post-secondary education.

Some poor people use their schools; others abuse them. Some poor people throw garbage out their windows, urinate in their streets, and defecate in their halls; others do not. At the other end of the financial spectrum, some rich people are idle and bored while others are productive and happy. There is no "necessity" in these material circumstances that requires one kind of behavior rather than another. Even at the subsistence level, when we are reduced to trying to survive, it cannot be said that any one mode of response is necessitated.

How we *are* determines what we *do* when faced with difficulty or opportunity. And how we are is a result of a distinctive genetic constitution upon which particular experiences have impressed different lessons (see Chapter 12). When these experiences have been roughly similar and when their lessons have a pattern, we speak of the process and the product as *cultural*.

How Durable Is Culture?

A second set of questions follows. It asks how durable these "historically created systems" may be and under what circumstances they change and how much. There is no easy answer to this set of questions. We do not know the determinants of cultural change except roughly, and we therefore cannot predict the effects of particular altered circumstances.

No culture is permanent, of course, but would-be social engineers are repeatedly surprised by the durability of cultural ways. Cultural persistence in changed environments has been noted for a wide variety of groups (Alpert 1972; Armor 1972; Glazer and Moynihan 1963, 1975; Glenn 1974–1975; Herskovits 1941; Howe 1976; Isaacs 1975; Jones 1972; Maas 1975; Metzger 1971; Novak 1972; Reed 1975; Sutherland 1975).

The mysteries of cultural persistence are well-summarized by a student of Jewish culture who concludes, "Almost every planned change has brought about results different from those anticipated. The student of culture is therefore highly skeptical of too optimistic plans for controlled culture change" (Anonymous 1942: 260).

Consequences of Cultural Differences

Arguments for the greater or lesser rationality of different ways of living involve matters of taste and morals, as the cultural relativist maintains. These preferences stand in some relation to the ways of life being evaluated. Preferences may be part of the cultures being studied, but the professional student of behavior has no special competence for choosing among these *preferences*.

Arguments about the comparative rationality of cultures also involve matters of truth and consequences. The boundary of cultural relativism is drawn by some public test of truth, as the statistician Kendall notes:

> A friend of mine once remarked . . . that if some people asserted that the earth rotated from East to West and others that it rotated from West to East, there would always be a few well-meaning citizens to suggest that perhaps there was something to be said for both sides and that maybe it did a little of one and a little of the other; or that the truth probably lay between the extremes and perhaps it did not rotate at all. (1949: 115)

In brief, we may admit the cultural relativism of morals and tastes while denying the cultural relativism of truth and consequences.

Rationality and Objectives

The fact that rationality is limited narrows the circumstances under which the idea of "acting rationally" applies. The very requirements of rationality put us in a trap. The trap is that rationality assumes that people know what they want and that their desires are not in conflict. The "catch" is in the assumption that the satisfaction of one desire does not exact "too much" of a price in the frustration of other desires. If these assumptions fail, as they probably do, the idea of rationality cannot be applied in the evaluation of different ways of life.

To act rationally, we are reminded (see Chapter 13), is to use means known to be efficient toward the attainment of empirical ends. The difficulty is that we are not always clear about what we want and that we often want many things "all together." We never want just one thing. "No one ever acts from a single motive," Dostoyevsky assures us. Motives are always mixed, and sometimes they are in conflict.

Conclusion

"Outside observers," such as anthropologists and sociologists, have no moral authority for imposing cultural objectives, but they can count the consequences of such objectives. Among the consequences of subcultural variations are differences in crime rates.

Culture makes a difference, but the question remains, "How?" Social psychologists attempt to answer this question in two broadly different ways: (1) by emphasizing what we *think;* and, (2) by emphasizing *how* we were trained and the *lessons* we learned.

Social psychologists of the symbolic-interactionist school stress the importance of thought. They work to build a bridge between structures of social relations and our *interpretations* of them, and in this manner they try to describe how crime is produced. Their ideas are the subject of Chapters 18 and 19.

18. Definitions of Situations: Differential Association

Social Psychology and the Interactionist Perspective

Social psychology is the study of human behavior based on the assumption that significant portions of conduct are the result, directly or indirectly, of what other human beings have done to us and for us. Social psychology is concerned with the alterations in behavior that seem to be influenced by both enduring and short-term relations with others. The influential others may be physically present or only symbolically so. Social psychology is interested in the behavioral effects of "immediately present" others, but it also includes as a "social effect" the influence of past human interactions such as may be represented by a printed page, a work of art, or a folktale.

With so wide a definition of its interest, social psychology becomes coterminous with the study of conduct. Its distinctive perspective, however, is *interactional*. It accepts the possibility that it may be difficult, if not impossible, to divide the sources of behavior between those "inside" the organism and those external to it. It assumes that human behavior is the result of some reciprocal connection between an organism and its environment. According to a popular sociopsychological saying, in the production of human behavior "there is no environment without a heredity, and no heredity without an environment."

The interactionist perspective is carried beyond the study of heredities and environments and is applied also to the study of the effects of different styles of relationship between individuals. The assumption, again, is that John's behavior toward Mary is influenced by Mary's conduct toward John and by John's memory of previous experiences with other Marys. The sociopsychological emphasis in studying such interaction tends to fall heavily on how Mary and John *interpret* each other's acts.

Working with such a set of assumptions, social psychology imputes less continuity to the behavior of individuals or groups than a cultural or a statistical explanation of behavior does. In contrast with these ways of describing action, the sociopsychological premise is more optimistic regarding the possibility of engineering behavioral changes. It looks for the ways in which behavior is conditioned by the social environment, and it is hopeful, then, that knowledge of the laws of such influence will permit the favorable control of behavior.

The interactionist assumption on which social psychology is based does not, and could not, function as an explanation without specifying particular variables to be attended to. It is easy to agree with the general idea that people somehow influence one another. The important question is, how? In attempting to answer this question, social psychologists have looked at different portions of reality.

For example, many scholars have attended to the patterns of rewards and punishments by which behaviors seem to be shaped. Others have studied the kinds of models and associates with whom the developing human is reared. Such investigators tend to emphasize the necessity of "control" if crime is to be reduced, and their ideas were discussed in Chapter 12.

There are other social psychologists, however, who are less concerned with training in self-control as one kind of interpersonal relationship. These scholars pay more attention to what they regard as a distinctively human product of interpersonal influence: thought.

The kind of thought that is assumed to be important in the guidance of conduct is thought that assigns meanings to actions. It is assumed that, before we act in social settings, we interpret our situation. Our interpretation includes an assessment of the physical world around us, but it also includes an assessment of what "significant others" intend and of how they are likely to respond to our actions.

Conduct, then, is generated in interaction with others, but the important aspect of interaction is the exchange of meanings. Since such interpretation requires thought, and since thinking is believed to depend heavily on the manipulation of symbols, the sociopsychological school that emphasizes the guiding function of thought, has become known as "symbolic interactionism."

Symbolic Interactionism

It is assumed that awareness of self is developed in a process that is characterized, largely but not entirely, by the development of symbols and their interpersonal exchange. It is believed also that this process teaches each person to take the role of another person, that is, to imagine one's "self" in the other person's situation. This empathy, this ability to generalize from one's self-awareness to that of others, is both a social bond and a means by which we continue to instruct one another. The descriptions and the explanations that are given by art, drama, poetry, and even psychology and sociology gain much of their plausibility through their appeal to empathy (Nettler 1970: chapter 3).

The interactionist's attention to symbolic activity has meant that this kind of social psychology is cognitive psychology. It looks for the explanations of social behavior in *learned dispositions identified through their expression in symbols.* These dispositions are variously called "attitudes," "beliefs," "meanings," "perceptions," "expectations," "values," and "definitions of the situation."

The distinctive professional task of social psychologists of the interactionist school has been to describe and measure these cognitive conditions, to assess how they vary with circumstance, and to determine how they affect feeling and action. The last point is crucial. Symbolic interactionism locates the *causes* of our behaviors in our *interpretations* of reality.

There have been two major applications of symbolic-interactionist assumptions to the explanation of crime. The earlier representation is that advanced by the late E. H. Sutherland and his students under the title *differential-association theory*. A more recent version of symbolic interactionism in criminology is known as the *labeling* hypothesis, to be discussed in Chapter 19. Both types of explanations are more prevalent in North America than in Europe or Asia.

In evaluating these explanations of criminality, it is worth remembering that they need not contradict other hypotheses. There is overlap among various accounts of crime; the difference is often one of emphasis. Differences in what is emphasized as causal, however, remain important as the emphases are translated into policies.

The Differential-Association Hypothesis

What Is "Differentially Associated"?

Differential association was, until recently, a popular explanatory style among Western criminologists. Like many other sociological theories, it is poorly titled. The title "differential association" sounds as though it refers to people in association, as in the "bad companions" theory of crime production. This, however, is explicitly denied (Sutherland and Cressey 1978: 84). What is differentially associated, according to this school, is *definitions of situations*. These are learned from others, it is assumed, but the people from whom one acquires criminal "definitions" need not themselves be criminal, but there is evidence that the behavior of others is highly relevant (Bruinsma 1992). This theory separates kinds of people from the kinds of meanings they impart, and it is the cognitive work of interpreting situations that, by this hypothesis, moves people into and out of crime.

The major assumptions underlying differential association are these:

1. Criminal behavior is learned.
2. Criminal behavior is learned in interaction with other persons in a process of communication.
3. The principal part of the learning of criminal behavior occurs within intimate personal groups.
4. When criminal behavior is learned, the learning includes (a) techniques of committing the crime . . . (b) the specific direction of motives, drives, rationalizations, and attitudes.
5. The specific direction of motives and drives is learned from definitions of the legal codes as favorable or unfavorable.
6. A person becomes delinquent because of an excess of definitions favorable to violation of law over definitions unfavorable to violation of law. This is the principle of differential association.
7. Differential associations may vary in frequency, duration, priority, and intensity (Sutherland and Cressey 1978: 80–81).

The heart of this explanation is a ratio. The ratio is between definitions unfavorable to following the criminal law to definitions favorable to following it. However, and unfortunately for clarity, revisions of the theory originally proposed by Sutherland in 1939 sometimes change *what* it is that is being associated. It is clear that it is *not* kinds of people, but it is the "meanings" assigned the "patterns" that are presented (Matsueda 1982; Sutherland and Cressey 1978: 90–91).

In sum, the differential-association hypothesis proposes that most members of complex societies are subject to a continuing competition among definitions of situations that justify breaking a particular law and definitions that legitimize that law in the actor's mind, and thereby provide immunization against the propensity to break it. This is what is meant by "differential association." To repeat, this hypothesis is not just a statement about the kind of people with whom one associates, or even a statement about the kind of behaviors with which one is familiar. The "differential association" refers to a changing balance, within each actor, among the *definitions* he or she has learned to associate with categories of conduct held by law to be legal or criminal.

These "definitions" are attitudes. They are evaluations. As such, they are presumed to be motivating. The central idea of the differential-association schema is that of all symbolic-interactionist explanations: *Cognition causes conduct.*

The evidence from recent studies points in a different direction. Warr and Stafford (1991) and Bruinsma (1992) have found that the strongest associations with law-violating behavior is the behavior of others, particularly peers, and this suggests the importance of social learning, which was taken up in Chapter 12. Nevertheless, Bruinsma (1992: 46) argues that there is considerable support for differential association because the deviance of others has the most substantial impact on definitions favorable to the violation of law.

How Is Differential Association Related to Culture Conflict?

While differential-association theory does not emphasize culture conflict, the assumption of conflict underlies it (Barlow and Ferdinand 1992). The existence of changing ratios between criminogenic and lawful definitions of situations requires, at bottom, culture conflict. Competing attitudes toward the law constitute a principal indicator of the conflict of norms of conduct. The differential-association hypothesis is thus similar to other interpretations of criminality in considering crime production to be a consequence of breaches in the moral bond. *Despite their different foci of attention, all explanations of crime that locate its source in the social web reduce to a description of conditions that weaken moral community.*

In this, theories of criminogenesis are in accord with the moral beliefs of the great religions. Thus, they say little that is new except as they specify processes characteristic of alienation among people. It is the description of these processes that lends substance and authority to theories of crime causation. It is what such theories specify as eroding moral unity that makes them interesting and of political importance. It is on this point that the differential-association theory has been called "both true and trivial," for it does not describe the learning process it assumes to be central to the manufacture of criminality. This deficiency has led critics to regard differential-association theory as plausible, probable, and logical (DeFleur and Quinney 1966), but at the same time as irrefutable and uninformative (Gibbons 1968: 204; Jeffrey 1959).

Criticism of the Differential-Association Hypothesis

Specific criticisms of differential-association theory are that it (1) neglects individual differences, (2) is so general and so loosely phrased as to be impossible to disprove, and (3) provides no sure guide to action. Each of these criticisms deserves attention.

Differential Association Neglects Individual Differences

It has been argued by Kornhauser and Hirschi among others that differential association theory only attempts to account for differences in rates of crime for groups and not for differences across individuals (1978; 1969). Neglect of individual differences is common to all sociological explanations of criminality. Such neglect may not be a disadvantage if one is interested in comparing crime rates among aggregates of people or in changes in crime rates within a population over time. However, Akers argues persuasively that this is not the case and that the "theory is explicitly designed to account for variations in criminal behavior by individuals . . . " (Akers 1996: 232).

The nondelinquent child who lives in a highly criminal neighborhood or the "bad actor" reared in a "good" environment does not necessarily pose a problem for the theory because it is not the properties of the environment that the theory identifies as criminogenic, but the *ideas* held by the individual. The theory allows that those ideas could have been acquired (learned) in a variety of settings under a wide range of circumstances. Other explanations that are also sociopsychologically based (e.g., control theory) also attempt to explain such anomalies.

Differential Association Is Impossible to Falsify

An explanatory account that holds true no matter what happens is ordinarily considered unsatisfactory by scientists, although it may satisfy other consumers of explanations. The proposals of differential-association theory, like many other explanations of human behavior, locate the causes of conduct in dispositions inside the actor, which are to be inferred by observers. Such inference is not necessarily false. It is built upon empathy, upon a projection of our own thoughts and feelings in similar situations, and it is therefore useful in developing an understanding of the other person, particularly when this person is similar to us.

The difficulty with explaining behavior by inferring dispositions is that an inference can always be constructed after the fact to fit every act. Dispositions, like instincts, can be multiplied endlessly. The ratio of definitions of the situation favorable and unfavorable to the law can too easily be changed to suit every crime. The risk of using dispositions as an explanation, then, is that one may construct a circular explanation in which the acts are said to be caused by the dispositions (beliefs, attitudes) and the dispositions are known from the acts. Such circularity may be comfortable and it may appease curiosity, but it may not point the way to prevent crime. Such difficulties and risks aside, however, it needs to be noted that a large number of tests of parts of differential association theory

Figure 18.1 Good versus evil?

have been conducted (Agnew 1993; Bruinsma 1992; Johnson 1988; Makkai and Braithwaite 1991; Warr 1993; Zhang and Messner 1994). In some cases, aspect of the theory have been affirmed (Bruinsma 1992); other instances offer refutation (Makki and Braithwaite 1991).

Differential Association Gives Poor Advice

An important test of the adequacy of an explanation is the efficacy of the distinctive prescription it proposes. A valuable explanation, as opposed to a merely congenial account, is one that organizes information in such a way that predictive accuracy is increased. The term "predictive accuracy" refers to an ability, provided by public evidence, to say that if one does *x, y* is likely to result.

We predict well when we can manipulate the particular causes specified by a theory so that we more often get the desired effect. The differential-association hypothesis does not give us this power. What is worse, believing the differential-association theory probably leads to poorer prediction than accepting some commonsense assumptions about conduct.

Example: Prevention of Embezzlement

A definitive test of the relative predictive power of differential-association explanation is difficult to conceive because its proposed distinctive cause—balance of definitions of the situation—is vague. However, a tentative test is provided by listening to what practitioners of symbolic interactionism tell us to do in response to certain kinds of crime. We have such a test in recommendations for the control of embezzlement made by a prominent exponent of the differential-association hypothesis. Donald Cressey studied hundreds of embezzlers and has interpreted their careers in the light of symbolic-interactionist theory (1953, 1971). He has, in addition, prescribed procedures for reducing embezzlement that follow from his explanation of this crime.

Embezzlement, as criminologists use the term, is a peculiar crime. It is peculiar in that, while it is more planned than impulsive, it is "out of character." An embezzler is a person who accepts a position of financial trust *without* the intention of abusing that trust. By contrast, a person who takes such a position with the intention of stealing is a con artist rather than an embezzler.

People who are given positions of financial responsibility are usually "noncriminal" types. They have ordinarily not been delinquent as young people, and they usually have no record of theft. They tend to be better educated than the "textbook thief," and they are often respected members of their communities before their arrest. These facts make explanation of the embezzler intriguing. How does such "out-of-character" theft develop?

Cressey proposes a few steps in this career. However, these steps are alleged to occur *without exception* as a lawful person is caused to steal. This exceptionless course includes the following elements, as described by Cressey:

1. The person is in a position of financial trust. The position was accepted without the intention to steal.
2. The trusted person develops what Cressey calls a "nonshareable problem." This is vaguely defined, and its illustrations run the gamut of difficulties in living. However, whatever the "problem" is considered to be, it is soluble with money, and, most important for Cressey, it is *not* shared. It is not discussed with others. A "shared problem," it is said, will not lead to crime.
3. The honest person being converted to a thief has technical skills for stealing. This is a minor step in the causal chain, since any person in a position of financial responsibility learns how to violate it.
4. Last, and most important in the symbolic-interactionist formulation of this career, the embezzler acquires a rationalization that justifies stealing. For symbolic interactionists, it is this justification that indicates the actor's "construction of reality" and constitutes the criminal motive.

The justification is a verbalization; it is recognized as words uttered by the actor to himself or herself and repeated, later, to others. "The process of verbalization," Cressey claims, "is the crux of the individual embezzlement problem. This means that the *words* that the potential embezzler uses in his conversation with himself actually are the most important elements in the process that gets him in trouble, or keeps him out of trouble. The rationalization is his *motive*" (1964: 19, 22). In a later publication, Cressey stresses that "rationalization is a motive *preceding* an act " (1971: iv).

From this set of assumptions about the career of the embezzler, particular recommendations follow. Cressey's prescription is twofold:

1. That companies start programs designed to reduce those "unshared problems" that Cressey believes create breaches of the employer's trust.
2. That companies institute "education programs emphasizing the nature of the verbalizations commonly used by trust violators." We must, Cressey advises, "make it increasingly difficult for trusted employees . . . to think of themselves as 'borrowers' rather than as 'thieves' when they take the boss's money" (1964: 25–26).

The soundness of this explanation of a crime and of the preventive measures it proposes rests on the clarity and power of the causes it nominates. The causes selected by the symbolic-interactionist explanation are *not* without exception, as stated, and they are neither clear nor powerful.

In a test of Cressey's hypothesis carried out in Canada among six large-scale embezzlers, only *one* instance was found that conformed with the differential-association interpretation of this kind of theft (Nettler 1974). The confirming case was that of "an attorney whose charm, confidence, and enterprise involved friends in a wide stream of undercapitalized investments. Out of concern for his own name and his friends' fortunes, money left in trust was 'borrowed' until it was beyond recovery and the theft was discovered" (Nettler 1974: 74).

However:

> The five other embezzlers . . . did not steal out of any similar set of circumstances. With one possible exception, none of the remaining offenders initiated his or her series of thefts because [of being] "in a crack," to use Cressey's phrase. The possible exception that might be described as a person "in a bind" was a man who had been renting a farm and its buildings and improving the property. When the farm was to be sold and our subject to be evicted, he converted funds left in his trust so that he could purchase the estate. In this case, however, the "problem," how to keep the beloved land, was not unshared. It was fully and repetitively discussed with the embezzler's wife. (Nettler 1974: 75)

Two traditional ways of explaining embezzlement compete with the theme of differential association and symbolic interactionism. They are the *detective's theory* and the *auditor's hypothesis*.

Detectives called to investigate embezzlement look for the "three B's—babes, booze, and bets." They assume that what turns a straight man, or woman, crooked is some variable combination of sex, the alcoholic "sweet life," and gambling. Their advice to employers and partners is always to be alert to signs of vice and to indications that a trusted person is living beyond his or her means. Detectives are not interested in rationalizations.

Auditors agree with detectives, but they go further. Auditors assume that theft is generated by some meeting of *desire* and *opportunity*. Vice is only one generator of desire, and the temptation to take money that is readily available is deemed to be a timeless possibility for all of us.

Intensity of desire and the perception of opportunity—determinants of the threshold of temptation—are personality variables, variables that "control" hypotheses take into account (see Chapter 12). "These criminal seeds," it has been argued, "are variously germinated" (Nettler 1974: 75).

One of the largest one-person embezzlements in North American history confirms the auditor's hypothesis. This "proper theft" of at least $4.7 million by a small-town banker is better explained by the conjunction of desire and opportunity than by the stress of an "unshared problem" (Maxwell 1972). However, what remains at issue in evaluating differential-association theory is the power of words—in which "definitions" are presumably embedded—as motors of action.

Differential Association Overemphasizes Words as Motors of Action

Words, Motives, and Reasons

Ideas—those images that are put into words, numbers, and other symbols—are important. The crucial question, which can only be touched on here, is, "How important are ideas for which actions, and when?"

In practice, as we have seen, differential-association theory puts thought, recognized by words, in the engine room of the causal train. "Words," says Cressey, "are the most important elements. . . . The rationalization is [the] motive" (1964: 19).

Ideas can be in the caboose as well as in the locomotive of the causal train. When one studies criminal careers, or other patterns of lives, one sees that much rationalization of these careers appears to develop rather late in the causal process. The reasons we give are not necessarily the causes of our actions, and we may not know the causes of the acts for which we give reasons. In addition, there are offenders who do not rationalize their crimes at all except as the official helper asks them, "Why did you do it?"

When we ask people, "Why did you . . . ?" and listen to their answers, we are collecting their reasons. These reasons can be given honestly or dishonestly, but the point is that reasons are not necessarily motives. A motive is that which *impels* action. Motives are sometimes intentions, in which case they can be verbalized, but motives are often conceived as causes, in which case the actor may not be aware of them.

It is apparent that it is more difficult to know motives—our own and others'—than it is to gather reasons. This difficulty tempts us to confuse reasons with causes, but this is a temptation to be resisted. There may be instances of behavior in which reasons and motives unite, but the person who confuses the two and who accepts reasons as the causes of action is apt to be a poor predictor of conduct. This is so because words are only loosely linked to deeds; attempts to predict what people will do from what they say have been disappointing (Acock and De Fleur 1972; Coopersmith 1969; Gross and Niman 1975; Pace 1949; Phillips 1971; Rose 1961; Smith 1958; Wicker 1969, 1971; Zunich 1962).

Words correlate with deeds only when the deeds are highly specific, near in time, and characteristic of the actor-talker (Crespi 1971). Words tend to agree with deeds when the behaviors are institutionalized, routinized, specific, and devoid of moral significance. In explaining action, and in foretelling it, it is wiser to count continuities in conduct than to assign motor power to reasons. Evidence for this is extensive (Fancher 1966, 1967; Goldberg 1968, 1970; Kleinmuntz 1967; Meehl 1954, 1959; Nettler 1982a; Owens 1968, 1971; Sawyer 1966; Wiggins and Kohen 1971).

In Summary: Problems with Thoughts, Expressed in Words, as Causes of Conduct

Differential-association theory attributes crime to a balance of ideas called "definitions of the situation." It has been argued that acting upon this assumption leads to poor prediction and poor protection. Since the symbolic-interactionist school is so strong among social psychologists in North America, and since it enters labeling theorists' explanation of crime as well (see Chapter 19), the difficulties in employing thoughts expressed in words as causes of conduct deserve outlining and some repetition.

1. A major difficulty is that the thought supposed to explain behavior is frequently not known *independently* of the action that is to be explained.

Symbolic interactionists cite the dictum of the great sociologist W. I. Thomas, who wrote, "If men define situations as real, they are real in their consequences" (Thomas and Thomas 1928: 572). This means that ideas are important—that if you believe the shadow is a ghost, you will respond to it as if it were one.

This sounds informative, but it is not. When we try to use the proposition, its explanatory power vanishes, and Thomas's famous statement reduces to one of the grandest tautologies in social science. It is a tautology because we know whether a person "defines a circumstance as real" only when she or he acts as if it were. The "definition" that was to have explained the action is known only by the action that was to have been explained.

In short, it is difficult to ascertain how others "define" their situations. It is difficult to know what others—and even what we ourselves—*believe*.

In trying to get out of this trap, symbolic interactionists turn their attention from acting to saying as a measure of "definition of the situation." As Lindesmith and Strauss put it, "In order to explain why people do what they do, we must know how they think. The chief source of information about how people think is what they say " (1956: 9). Such reliance upon talk as the best measure of thought entangles the inquirer in the deficiencies of words as indicators of motives. These deficiencies result from the fact that we do not do all that we think, nor do we say all that we think, nor do we always act as we say we want to, or should, or intend.

2. A second source of the poverty of thought as an explanation of action is that we do not know how much people think before they act.

Everything depends, of course, on which kinds of acts we are trying to explain. In our daily lives, fortunately, much social interaction is the result of habit rather than thought. This is fortunate because, as Thorngate reminds us, thinking is costly (1976). It is costly in time and energy. As a consequence, many skillful performances, including interpersonal ones, occur with little thought.

3. A third defect in assigning causal priority to ideas is that, for considerable segments of our conduct, our thoughts may not be independent sources of activity.

Social psychologists of a behaviorist inclination view human action as a closely woven fabric out of which the thread of "what we think" can be pulled for inspection. However, the color and texture of the whole cloth will be only imperfectly known from an examination of this thread. Application of this sociopsychological attitude to criminology is described in Chapter 12. For present purposes, the weakness of attributing independent causal power to words and ideas can be illustrated by an extreme example.

Consider a man who exhibits a syndrome called, for communicative convenience, "paranoia." Our subject differs in degree from the rest of us by

- Being more nervous, tense, and excitable.
- Being exquisitely sensitive and alert to interpersonal cues.
- Acting and talking *self-referentially*, by which we mean that more acts of others are seen by our subject as directed toward him than you and I can perceive.
- Being suspicious and jealous.
- Demanding much of loved ones at the same time that he is critical of them for their obvious lack of appreciation of him.
- Talking with hate and behaving aggressively.
- Saying that he is rejected unfairly.
- Believing that people and the fates are against him.
- Talking more dirty sex than is "normal" and seeing more perversion in others.
- Being unreasonable.
- And, of course, talking and acting as though the social world were a jungle.

Now, in looking at this package of actions—and we must bear in mind that talk is a form of action—we may, if we wish, isolate those actions to be called "attitudes" or "ideas." We can even measure those characteristic behaviors of our subject which we might wish to call his "definitions of the situation." Having done this, two questions remain. First, "Are the subject's peculiar ideas causal or only correlative?" Did thinking that way *make* him that way, or is thinking that way *part of his being* that way?

The answer to this first question lies in a test proposed by a second question, "If our subject's physician works on his paranoid notions, will that change the subject's behavior?" The best answer to this question is, "Not much." The curative record of the talking therapies is poor, and it is particularly poor for major features of conduct (Cross 1964; Eysenck 1966; Landman and Dawes 1982; Levitt 1957; Rachman and Wilson 1980; M. L. Smith et al. 1980).

After the fact of such evidence, we can ask why working on people's ideas is so weak an instrument for changing their conduct. The answer has already been given. "Temperaments select philosophies" (James 1907). We are not empty vessels into which any and all ideas may be poured and converted into action. Human beings process ideas selectively.

Ideas are not all that is in our minds. Our minds include sensing, feeling, willing, conceiving, and consciously doing (Langer 1967; Ryle 1949). All of this was acquired together.

It makes as much sense, therefore, to say that actions cause ideas as to say what is more conventional—that ideas cause actions. On the record, it seems easier to change thoughts by changing actions than it is to change actions by changing thoughts (Boardman 1962; Clement 1970; Lang and Lazovik 1963; Lang and Melamed 1969; Meyer and Levy 1970; Romanczyk and Goren 1975; Stolz et al. 1975; Youell and McCullough 1975).

Conclusion

Our conclusion must be that we do not say much when we say that "definitions of the situation" are causal. Explaining conduct by reference to such a symbol-laden cause is conventional and comforting, but it is not productive and it does not answer public questions about crime. After citizens hear explanations from balanced definitions of situations, they still ask, "Yes, but from where do these differing definitions come?" and "Why do some people accept some definitions but not others?" A brief answer to such questions was given in Chapter 12.

In Chapter 19 we consider a popular variation on the symbolic-interactionist theme—one that attributes the production of crime to modes of social response.

19. Definitions of Situations: Social Reaction

The Social-Reaction Perspective

There are fashions in ideas as there are in costume, and scholars are not immune to changing fads in the explanation of crime. Until recently the two most visible, and perhaps most popular, views of crime among its North American students have been the ideas of criminologists on the left and those of "labeling" theorists. However, neither of these conceptions is supported by citizens in general, and both are under challenge (Banks et al. 1975; Gove 1975; Hoo 1972; Wilson 1975).

As with all explanations of behavior, there are variations within each style, and the labeling orientation is also called by other names, such as the "social-reaction" or "social-definition" hypothesis (Schur 1975: 288) and the "interactionist theory of deviance" (Becker 1974: 6). The set of assumptions common to these variations emphasizes the *causal power of response*—verbal and nonverbal—to classes of people and classes of acts. The so-called "labels" with which social-reaction theorists are concerned are not merely titles; they also include differential responses to categories of persons and conduct. With this understanding, we can use the many names for this set of ideas interchangeably for variety's sake.

The central assumption of the labeling perspective is an old one. It is the notion that the poet Johann Wolfgang von Goethe (1749–1832) expressed when he wrote:

> When we treat a man as he is, we make him worse than he is;
> When we treat him as he could be, we make him better.

Criminals, then, are "made" by the way they are treated. Tannenbaum (1938: 19–20) called the process the "dramatization of evil." He said:

> The process of making the criminal is a process of tagging, defining, identifying, segregating, describing, emphasizing, making conscious and self-conscious; it becomes a way of stimulating, suggesting, emphasizing, and evoking the very traits that are complained of.
> The person becomes the thing he is described as being. . . . The way out is through a refusal to dramatize the evil. The less said about it the better.

The assumptions that *dramatized* evil is a major source of evil and that wrongdoers reform when the other cheek is turned are therapeutic notions and hopeful ones. They contain some truth, but not all the truth. These assumptions are in the vein of the symbolic-interactionist idea that what counts as a cause of behavior is the *exchange of interpretations* of ourselves and others.

Despite their interest in interaction, proponents of the labeling hypothesis come to stress one side of the exchange of meanings. They stress the causal impact of the response of significant others on the way we are. This shifts attention from what we did to how others reacted to it. It also moves causation from what we do to who we are as sources of others' response. In criminology, such an emphasis transfers responsibility for conduct from bad actors to powerful reactors.

This reversal of the commonly assumed causal chain makes the social-reaction perspective distinctive. It challenges "conventional wisdom," a phrase that is, of course, pejorative. Indeed, Murray Davis contends that social theories are "considered great, not because [they] are true, but because they are interesting" and that "all interesting . . . social theories . . . constitute an attack on the taken-for-granted world of their audience" (1971: 309, 311).

The social-reaction perspective is certainly interesting because it suggests that things may not be as they appear to be and that attempts to explain crime by its conventional causes and attempts to control crime by conventional means may be uneconomical. The assumptions of social-reaction theorists therefore deserve description and evaluation.

Labeling Theory and Criminology

Concern for the impact of labeling behavior has a long tradition within sociology. It is Edwin Lemert (1951) who was primarily responsible for the elaboration and popularization of the idea. Lemert's view is that two categories of causes underlie deviant and criminal behavior. The first cause is an unspecified variety of pressure that contributes to what Lemert terms *primary deviance;* that is, some initial act that offends those who define what is acceptable or unacceptable in society. The second cause consists of the *social reaction* to that initial act. Depending upon the form of this reaction, a person may be led into committing subsequent or *secondary deviance*. It is upon secondary deviance that labeling theorists focus.

Labeling theorists assume that repeat deviance requires a psychological commitment to the behavior, and that "primary deviation has only marginal implication for the status and physic structure of the person concerned" (Lemert 1967: 40). On the other hand, "the secondary deviant as opposed to his actions, is a person whose life and identity are organized around the facts of deviance" (1967: 41). Thus, labeling theory builds upon Tannenbaum's contention that often, the social reaction to a behavior can be more harmful than the initial action and that if ignored, primary deviance will generally not result in repeated offensive acts.

Essentially, labeling theory suggest that the consequences of applying a label to, or *stigmatizing*, a person is twofold. First, it argues that others react to the stigmatized individual based on the label. Second, it alters people's perception of themselves so that they become a reflection of how others perceive them. Together, these consequences result in a reinforcement of the initial deviance, or, as Lemert states (1967: 41), "secondary deviation concerns processes similar or related to that which originally initiated the stigmatization, which create, maintain, or intensify stigma; it presumes that stigma may. . . lead to repetition of deviance."

The reinforcement of deviance may come about for many reasons. For example, stigmatized individuals may find more limited life opportunities than their nonstigmatized counterparts. However, from the labeling theorist's perspective, most labeling "necessarily misrepresents" the person's behavior and calls their integrity into question. This results in profound feelings of justice, and it is this sense of injustice, labeling theorists argue, that sets many youthful offenders on the path to a career in crime. As the stigma is reinforced through successive labeling, offenders engage in a spiral of deviance amplification, where labeling begets deviance that begets further labeling. Throughout this process, the person's self-concept of being deviant is reinforced, thus allowing evermore outrageous acts of deviance to be committed.

One insight of labeling theory that has caught many people's imagination is the suggestion that the process of law enforcement may inadvertently produce more crime than it seeks to suppress. It is for this reason that some labeling theorists, such as Edwin Schur (1973), argue for a "radical nonintervention" into people's lives, particularly those of young people.

The interactionist approach to criminology repeats the idea that right and wrong are socially defined and that "crime" is a word, not an act. It questions, then, the validity and the utility of particular definitions of crime.

Characteristics of Labeling Theory

Sympathy with Deviance

Questioning the legitimacy of conventional definitions of crime is associated with sympathy for those accused of socially constructed, and maligned, categories of difference. The sympathy is expressed in the labeling theorist's preference for speaking of deviance rather than criminality.

Deviance is a sociological term, to be found only in recent editions of English dictionaries. It is a term invented from the notion of deviation, a "wandering from the way," which connotes sin or offense, a departure from a desirable course according to *Webster's Dictionary*.

As we have seen (Chapter 1), such ideas of wrong are less exact than the idea of crime, but adoption of the term allows sociologists to consider the general theme of "disvalued people and behavior" (Sagarin 1975). What concerns students of deviance, then, is not just crime, as legally defined, but difference that is disapproved.

This shift in terminology directs attention to the fact that, in the "crime game," majorities are reacting to minorities. Or it is sometimes held that powerful elites decide what is to be penalized as crime. In either case, the translation of crime into deviance suggests the possibility that it may not be what one does that occasions arrest, censure, and punishment, but, rather, that what counts is being different in the sense of being powerless because of small numbers or social disadvantage.

Such a viewpoint is obviously sympathetic to those who have been despised for their difference. The labeling perspective has consequently been termed an "underdog philosophy." Its proponents ask, "Whose side are we on?" (Becker 1967).

The side chosen by advocates of the "interactionist theory of deviance" favors particular minorities that get labeled by the law. Thus, social reaction is not deemed to be important in explaining much about the careers of corporation executives who break antitrust laws or government officials who take bribes or produce Watergates. Money presumably immunizes such offenders against the effects of broken reputations and criminal records. Money does provide solace, but students of deviance are not so much interested in the effects of stigmatizing once-rich or once-powerful people as they are in the effects of stigmatizing offenders thought to have been less fortunate.

Reversal of Causation

The ideology of the underdog turns the table on popular thinking. Instead of assuming that it is the deviant's difference that needs explanation, it asks why the majority responds to this difference as it does. Shifting the question reverses the normal conception of causation. It suggests that another's peculiarity has not caused us to regard this person as different; rather, it is our labeling (an interpretation) that has caused the peculiarity.

Noting a difference, and defining it, may then confirm it. Thus, as we noted, labeling theorists distinguish between "primary deviance"—that is, some norm-violating act—and "secondary deviance" (Lemert 1951). Secondary deviance is the product or result of the reaction of others to an initial act of norm-violating behaviors. The social processing is said to confirm the deviant in the stigmatized behavior. Being cast out means being outcast. This, in turn, makes it comfortable for stigmatized persons to band together in defense of their egos and in justification of their peculiar interests.

Transcendence of Roles Over Behaviors

According to symbolic interactionists, the exchange of meanings that occurs when we meet, and the differences in mutual treatment that result from this exchange, push us toward the attribution and acceptance of roles. Roles are "parts that we play." We may not have started out in this way, but they may become us as we act them.

Emphasis upon role construction calls attention, then, to the way behavior may be shaped by the expectations of those with whom we interact. It suggests a process in which our conceptions of one another are reinforced by the early assignment of labels to samples of our acts.

Once roles are defined and acted upon, clusters of attributes are inferred. Such inference stimulates a selective attribution of traits to the actor and permits a linking together of diverse acts under some meaningful label (Turner 1972: 310).

Stressing role formation means that less attention is paid to how people behave, and more to how we categorize one another on the basis of small segments of behavior. The tendency of labeling theorists is therefore to deny or ignore differences in the ways in which we act and to emphasize the consequences of having power to categorize others. Throughout the literature on labeling, the prevailing sentiment denies original difference and, in particular, denies the "badness" of original difference. This way of looking at crime and criminals doubts the validity and justice of popular images of deviants.

Implications for Methods

Given this orientation, a preferred method of study follows. The research method advocated by labeling theorists is intensive observation of labelers and their victims. Fieldwork is preferred to the collection of statistics. The result of such study is a description of how the labeler comes to recognize and define the deviant and of how the deviant reacts to and interprets his or her own world. The test of the adequacy of such a description is understanding and insight rather than prediction and control.

As compared with statistical and experimental studies, the reportorial fieldwork recommended by the labeling theorist is more fun for students. It is good sport to engage in "participant observation," particularly among people who are "different." To this element of pleasure, labeling theory has added advocacy of the "rights" of minorities. Its attractive methods and its political stance have combined to make it a fashionable way of thinking about undesirable behaviors and "social problems." The fashion has spread from its application to crime and has been extended, with variations, to attempts to understand blindness (Scott 1969), attitudes toward the mentally ill (Socall and Holtgraves 1992), illness (Lorber 1967), civil disturbances (Turner 1969), "welfarism" (Beck 1967), job promotions (Baker et al. 1988), referrals to drug- and alcohol-treatment programs (Downs and Robertson 1990), the acceptance of under-the-table payments by NCAA athletes (Sack 1991), and to death by sorcery (McPherson 1991). An evaluation of this popular mode of explanation enables us to recognize its advantages and its liabilities.

Examining and Evaluating Labeling Theory

Assessing explanations of crime, or any other kind of conduct, requires a standard. In studies of social behavior, evaluative standards move about. They are sometimes esthetic, more often moral, and only infrequently practical. We do evaluate from "the side we're on."

Against this tendency, we struggle to be objective, and the attitude underlying our evaluation of explanations of crime is skeptical. Skepticism asks of each explanation three questions:

- How clear are its concepts and hypotheses?
- What factual evidence tests these hypotheses and with what result?
- When one acts upon the distinctive prescriptions of an explanation, do the predicted consequences follow?

The subject matter of criminology makes it easier to answer the first two questions than the third one. Without the power to experiment with human beings, the third question can be only tentatively tested, and the burden of assessment falls on issues of clarity and evidence.

Even here, however, labeling theorists have not been helpful. They have been reluctant to phrase clear propositions, and they have defended their reluctance by saying that they are more concerned with producing "sensitizing observations" (Schur 1971: 27), than with promoting empirical tests. In company with radical criminologists, labeling proponents prefer to "jostle the imagination, to create a crisis of consciousness which will lead to new visions of reality" (Scheff 1974: 445).

Given its intention to be more provocative than empirical, the social-reaction perspective evades the confines of fact, and its propositions become elusive. Indeed, one of the early proponents of this perspective, Howard Becker (1974: 6), states that

> Labeling theory . . . is neither a theory, with all the achievements and obligations that go with the title, nor focused so exclusively on the act of labeling as some have thought. It is, rather, a way of looking at a general area of human activity; a perspective whose value will appear, if at all, in increased understanding of things formerly obscure.

Such a statement relieves the social-reaction perspective of the burden of being scientific, for it is one of the obligations of a scientific stance to be propositional and empirical. Relieved of this responsibility, labeling theorists can lay claim to "increased understanding." To this claim, the skeptic replies with two questions:

1. As used here, what does "understanding" mean?
2. Without a specified empirical test, how will we know when we have it?

Although labeling theorists shift their ground as we try to comprehend them, two major propositions, with some auxiliary assumptions, can be extracted from their writing. The major hypotheses are

1. That it is the definition of the deviant, rather than what the person has done, that determines social response.
2. That a "negative" social reaction, one that is hostile and demeaning, produces more of the stigmatized conduct.

The first hypothesis examines social response as a dependent variable. It asks what causes the application of a denigrating title and the punitive response? In the administration of justice, this proposition raises the possibility that arrest and sentence depend less on what the persons did than on their legally irrelevant social characteristics.

The second hypothesis examines labeling as an independent variable. It suggests that stigma—degraded difference—increases offensive behavior among the stigmatized.

Both hypotheses are causal. The first says that it is disadvantage on the part of a minority and incorrect conception (stereotyping) on the part of a majority or its powerful elite that nominate people differentially for the title of "criminal" when all other facts and acts are equal. The second hypothesis says that the criminal justice system creates crime by branding with the criminal label those with whom it deals.

Hypothesis 1 calls Western justice systems "unjust"; hypothesis 2 calls them "uneconomical." It is important, then, to test these hypotheses, but evidence is difficult to develop. The difficulty is compounded by the tacit assumptions and imprecise ideas that are interwoven with the major premises. We can disentangle these ideas by addressing four questions to labeling theory:

1. Are the conceptions we have of one another correct?
2. Is "stigma" one thing—or, whose label counts?

3. Is social response to crime produced more by the fact of the act or by the legally irrelevant social characteristics of the accused?
4. Does a "bad name" cause bad action?

Are the Definitions We Apply to One Another Correct?

The Labeling Hypothesis

The political appeal of the social-reaction school lies in its assumption that, at the outset, we are equal. We are particularly equal in goodness and badness, in obeying criminal laws or breaking them. A starting point of labeling theory is that everyone has offended, sometime, and that the dark figure of crime is so impressive as to challenge a glib division of people into lawful and criminal. It presupposes that "the seeds of every crime are in each of us."

There are degrees of criminal conduct, of course, as there are degrees of all other behavior, but labeling theorists are less interested in measuring these degrees of action than in rightly criticizing neat dichotomies—honest and dishonest, pacific and violent, good and bad. However, the attack on such absolute partitions is used by social-reaction theorists to foster an untenable notion: that, when it comes to committing crimes, everyone, at some youthful time, was equal.

In the labeling theorist's conception of reality, what matters is being caught—and, more than being caught, being officially handled. Arrest, conviction, and sentence are assumed to be the causes of careers. They are turning points that change identities.

Certainly such official response affects the course of lives, and there is no news in this idea. However, the labeling perspective suggests something more interesting than this fact. It implies that these turning points depend more on definitions of categories of people than on what they have done.

These deviant-defining labels are supposedly imposed by majorities upon minorities, and since they are presumably based on conceptions of others rather than on observations of them, these labels are held to be mostly incorrect. An assumption, then, that is coiled through the interactionist theory of deviance is the assumption that others are misunderstood (Icheiser 1949). This premise is embedded in the concept of the stereotype.

Examining the Hypothesis: Images and Stereotypes

Social scientists have long noted that the images one group has of others, and of itself, run toward rigidity and toward complimenting our group and demeaning strangers. This is the phenomenon that Sumner called "ethnocentrism " (1906: 13–14). However, it was a journalist, Walter Lippmann, who described the process by which such images are produced and maintained. Lippmann applied the printer's term "stereotype" to this process and its product. In his book *Public Opinion* (1922), Lippmann wrote about stereotypes at length (five chapters), but he did not define the concept. The idea Lippmann conveyed was that, while perceiving the world is difficult enough, conceiving it is even more difficult.

Lippmann believed that we often respond to others with "pictures in our heads" that are caricatures rather than portraits. These pictures are alleged to be partly true, partly false, and always exaggerated. "The perfect stereotype," according to Lippmann (1922: 98), "precedes the use of reason . . . [It stamps] the data of our senses before the data reach the intelligence."

It is true that we sample only a small slice of life and that we have to make judgments on the basis of such few experiences. The questions are whether our samples are biased and whether the inferences we draw from these samples are correct. These questions are as old as philosophy, and thoughtful people continue to wrestle with them. Neither Lippmann nor later scholars have shown us how to answer these questions with confidence. We are only cautioned to recognize these possibilities and to be careful in judging others.

Unfortunately, social psychologists have used the notion of stereotyped images of others uncritically. Those who employ this term have not defined it. They have not agreed on how consensual an image must be to constitute a "stereotype," how limited it is in terms of experience, how rigid and overgeneralized it may be, or to what degree it is correct or incorrect.

From this lack of clarity, unfortunate consequences follow and become increasingly important with popularization of the term. Thus it is assumed, without adequate evidence, that (1) ordinary citizens' conceptions of "different" kinds of people are mostly wrong and that (2) we can think without stereotypes.

In opposition to the first assumption, the few tests that have been conducted of the validity of stereotypes find them to be more accurate than inaccurate. This is true of popular conceptions of occupations (Beardslee and O'Dowd 1961; Rice 1928), of social classes (Horn 1974; Mercer 1965), of personalities (Christensen 1974; Haas 1979; Stricker et al. 1974), and of ethnic groups (Abate and Berrien 1967; Akers 1968; Erskine 1967–1968; Freedman 1974; LeVine 1966; Mackie 1973; McCauley and Stitt 1978; Reed 1980). Indeed, people would be even more irrational than demagogues think they are if their consensual images of others were nothing but mirages. Psychologists now agree with Tagiuri (1969: 422) that "stereotyping does not necessarily lead to inaccuracy; sometimes it leads to more 'accurate' inferences about others than does detailed information about each individual person."

An additional consequence of the loose use of the notion of stereotype is its implicit suggestion that we can dispense with generalization. There is, however, no escape. Every noun and adjective we use to describe people and events categorizes. McCauley et al. (1980: 195) point out that, if there is something defective in the stereotyping process, then it is "no more and no less than what is wrong with human conceptual behavior generally."

Despite the poor conceptual status of the idea of stereotypes, the notion is pertinent to the attitude taken by the interactional explanation of crime production. The labeling advocate assumes that stereotypes of offenders influence use of the law. It is assumed, furthermore, that these stereotypes are false and that the criminal law is therefore applied less against classes of acts and more against classes of people. It is contended that this unfair application will be stronger where there is more judicial discretion, as there is in response to misdeeds committed by juveniles. Thus the labeling theorist Schur (1973: 120–121) tells us that

We are likely to have specific ideas of what "criminals" and "delinquents" are like, even if we have never had any direct encounters with known law-violators. Reactions based on these stereotypes may significantly affect how individuals are treated throughout the various stages in the administration of juvenile justice. Indeed, the considerable discretion vested in officials at all levels of the juvenile justice system makes them vulnerable to the influence of stereotypical thinking . . . the philosophy of the juvenile court . . . virtually ensures that stereotypes will influence judicial dispositions.

These allegations stimulate two critical responses. The first is that labeling theorists only assume that there are stereotypes of offenders and that these images are incorrect. They advance no evidence in support of this assumption.

A second criticism, and a more important one, is that, again, it is only assumed that stereotypes influence judicial practice more than actual criminality does. This allegation is easily made but seldom proved.

Our discussion of stereotypes has been necessitated, therefore, by the uncritical adoption of the concept by the social-reaction perspective. If the assumptions of this perspective were correct—if stereotypes were mostly false and if such erroneous images actually did influence arrest or trial—then, of course, injustice would be done. Against this possibility, doubt cast on the assumed inaccuracy of popular judgmental categories, and on the alleged function of these incorrect images in judicial systems, weakens the charge of the labeling proponent. It does not answer the charge completely, and additional questions remain.

Whose Label Counts?

The Labeling Assumption

A major assumption of the social-reaction perspective is that the labels that matter in the creation of criminals are those that hurt. Hurting is, in fact, part of the definition of "deviance." So Ericson (1975: 134) writes, "The labeling analyst sees all imputations of deviance as punitive."

Examining the Assumption

If such a statement is to be more than a definition—if, that is, it is to be converted into a proposition—it will be necessary to separate the stigmatizing act from the experience of its intended pain. Such a proposition asks more than what "social reactors" intend when they "label." It also raises the question of what hurts whom.

It is true that legal labels applied to rule-breakers are intended to set them apart and to condemn them and their acts. The theater of the court is designed to produce this effect. The trial dramatizes the morality threatened by crime and defended by law. The procedures of a justice system constitute, then, a form of "degradation ceremony," as Garfinkel (1956) has so aptly titled it. The question raised by Garfinkel and others, but never answered in the context of the manufacture of deviant careers, is, "When do degradation ceremonies work?"

Children sing a classic taunt:

Sticks and stones
May break my bones
But names will never hurt me!

Not all labels stick, and not all labels hurt. Some attempts to condemn are futile. As with punishment, so with stigma—what hurts varies with a number of contingencies.

Stigma is not one thing; it is not one denigrating act with one effect (Shoham 1970). What stigmatizes varies with who applies which label to whom at what stage in a career. It varies also with the support given by "significant others" to the accused person. Social disapproval, even official disapproval, does not count with some categories of actors. Their reference groups are not made up of police officers and judges. There is a mass of evidence that rule-breakers who are supported by "their own kind" ignore some attempted degradation ceremonies and are honored by others (samples of this evidence can be found in such studies as those by Hobsbawm 1969; Keiser 1965; Maas 1975; Polsky 1967; Schwendinger and Schwendinger 1967; Sutherland 1975; Taft 1946; and Thompson 1966).

The unanswered question, crucial to the labeling perspective is, "When is a 'personal identity' changed, and how much, by whose stigmatizing effort?"

Are We Reacting More to What People Do or to Who They Are?

The Labeling Hypothesis

Labeling theory says that it is "disadvantage" that determines against whom the law is applied. Proponents of this view are never definite about what constitutes disadvantage, and they seem to arrive at their conception after the fact of differential arrest. Thus, males, young people, and members of some poor ethnic groups, but not others, are differentially arrested and convicted of serious crimes. Given this fact, it is alleged that it was not so much what such categories of people did as who they were that determined their being legally handled. Moreover, as we have seen in connection with the notion of stereotype, who people "are" is also held to be problematic and incorrectly defined by official judges of deviants.

Testing the Hypothesis

The central allegation—that response to offenders depends on their social status rather than their deeds—is itself not clear. As Tittle (1975) points out, labeling theorists do not tell us whether "being disadvantaged" is supposed to have *some* effect on social response or, what is more important, whether the effect of disadvantage is supposed to be *greater* than the effect of actual rule-breaking.

The first suggestion is neither novel nor precise. Justice is not totally blind, and some effect may occur, but we are not told how much would have to occur to validate the labeling hypothesis.

The challenging question, and one that would add importance to the social-reaction explanation if it were answered in its favor, is whether Western systems of justice are responding *more* to the legally irrelevant social characteristics of the accused than to the quality of their acts. Tittle (1975: 164) shows that a rigorous answer to this question would require data that allowed us.

1. To hold actual rule-breaking constant while observing the relation between social reaction and selected disadvantages
2. To *compare* the size of that relation with the association between actual rule-breaking and social reaction when disadvantages are held constant

In other words, confirmation of the labeling hypothesis requires not merely the demonstration of a positive correlation between disadvantage and social reaction, but also a demonstration that such a correlation is *stronger* than the correlation between rule-breaking and legal treatment.

Requirements for Tests   It is clear that, if we are to test the hypothesis that labels, more than deeds, cause social response, we shall have to examine the relation between being categorized and being differentially handled by the criminal justice system, while holding constant all legally relevant considerations.

For logical reasons, this test should be complemented by its converse: an examination of the relation between kinds of crime and social response, holding labels constant. The relation between labels and arrests or sentences, while holding constant all legally relevant considerations, is then to be compared with the relation between deeds and arrests or sentences, while holding labels constant. The point of the comparison is, again, to test which association is stronger.

1. Such a comparison requires the use of techniques that allow us to assess the relative degree of association between an effect, such as a sentence, and a number of possible causes considered together.

Many studies of the influence of extralegal factors have not done this but have looked at a relationship between, say, race and sentence, holding constant one or two variables at a time—usually seriousness of offense and previous record. A court's judgment, however, is more like a gestalt—a patterned decision that is not based on bits of information received and processed one at a time.

John Hagan's (1974b) survey of research on sentencing in the United States makes this point forcibly. Hagan selected 20 frequently cited investigations of the effects of offenders' social characteristics on their sentences. The selected studies were those that had been repeatedly quoted by criminologists, and some of them had been cited as evidence before United States congressional committees and courts (Wolfgang 1974).

Hagan notes, first, that such studies characteristically use large samples; thus we should expect to find "statistical significance" for even small degrees of association. He then observes that, of these 20 prominent investigations, 8 employed *only* tests of significance as possible signs of causal connection. Such tests are not measures of the power of association.

Another eight of these important early studies applied no test of association. Only four of these research efforts computed measures of correlation.

2. Controlling for legally relevant variables: Deficiencies in tests of the labeling perspective's charge of judicial discrimination do not end here. Weak measures of relations are but one defect of such research. Another defect is poor control for legally relevant factors in the interpretation of correlations. This defect marks much research concerning the treatment of juveniles and the differential arrest and sentencing of members of ethnic groups.

A fair test of the allegation that the law responds to people on the basis of their social categories rather than their deeds requires that outcomes—arrest, conviction, sentence—be assessed against all legally relevant considerations. This is seldom done. This requirement is neglected because of the inadequacy of the information with which researchers work, and because of the expense involved in conducting an adequate longitudinal study of offenders' behaviors. In addition to these sources of neglect in research, the underdog ideology of the interactionist perspective motivates researchers to look at law, rather than at actors, as a cause of crime. There is a tendency, then, to ignore the many factors in offenders' histories—other than the immediate crime—designed by law to affect social response.

Judicial response in Western countries is ideally to be individualized, to be tailored to the individual offender. Such tailoring can occur only if there is judicial discretion. Discretion, in turn, is to be guided by legal objectives. The charge of labeling theorists is that discretion, rather than being so guided, is more strongly influenced by legally irrelevant stereotypes of rule-breakers.

Controls are the burdens of adequate research. It is clear that offenders' histories, the number of charges laid along with the offense, and characteristics of the present crime of notice must be among the factors controlled in examining relations between the social status of accused persons and their treatment under the law. However, even these important legal considerations are slighted in much research on the effect of social characteristics on social response to crime. Hagan's (1974b) study is instructive on this issue also.

Four of the twenty major studies of sentencing that Hagan assessed applied no controls for legally relevant variables. Nine of these investigations considered only type of offense in measuring the association between social status and outcome. Seven controlled for type of offense and previous record; and four of these seven also included counts of number of charges associated with the current offense.

Even those studies that instituted some controls for legally relevant variables did so in a less than comprehensive manner. Information was lost in handling the data. For example, "previous record" is treated in some of the studies as "some or none." Such a dichotomy ignores the number of previous convictions and the weighted gravity of each.

Walsh (1991) studied the relationship between sentence and race in 666 cases involving 20 crimes ranging from receiving stolen property to murder in Ohio. The two legal variables of seriousness of the crime and criminal history are controlled. The principal conclusion reached by Walsh is in the opposite direction from what is commonly assumed by those who view higher rates of incarceration among minorities to be pure and simple results of discrimination. Walsh (1991: 15) found that "white offenders were punished more severely than black offenders . . ." and that this seemed "to be more a function of leniency extended toward black defendants."

Findings and Conclusions   It is apparent that testing the labeling hypothesis is difficult. Bearing in mind these difficulties, some reasonable inferences can be drawn from recent research.

The major conclusion is that legal considerations outweigh extralegal factors, such as "labels," in determining who gets reported, arrested, prosecuted, convicted, differentially sentenced, and differentially handled on probation and parole in North America. This conclusion probably holds also for other industrialized countries in western Europe, Oceania, and Japan, although research in those areas is skimpy.

Three minor conclusions are added: (1) discretion varies inversely with the gravity of the crime, so that less discretion occurs in response to more serious crimes; (2) time and place make a difference; and (3) extreme cases challenge the major conclusion, but do not disconfirm it.

Without describing each piece of research in detail, one can note that justification of the major conclusion derives from findings such as these:

1. The decision to prosecute for shoplifting is influenced more by the value of goods stolen than by age, sex, or race of thief (Hindelang 1974).

2. When the seriousness of a juvenile's first offense is held constant, neither race nor socioeconomic status affects judicial decisions in a Southern state (Meade 1973). Sex, race, and "family disruption" are associated with juvenile crime in that state, but they do not affect judicial response independently of the gravity of a youth's first offense.

3. Following 32,694 persons arrested for felonies through the criminal justice systems in 12 California counties revealed the greater impact of legal than of extralegal factors in determining sentences (Pope 1975a, 1975b, 1975c). "Prior record," an index weighing number and gravity of previous crimes, was the strongest correlate of disposition (Pope 1975c: 16).

    There are qualifications in this study: females tended to receive lighter sentences than males, particularly in urban areas; younger offenders received lighter sentences in higher courts, but not in lower courts; African Americans received heavier penalties than whites in rural courts, but not in urban courts.

4. Sentences in United States federal district courts for automobile theft, bank robbery, forgery, and interstate transportation of forged securities, from 1967 to 1968, correlate most strongly with gravity of the crime (Tiffany et al. 1975). Trial by jury results in a heavier sentence than trial by judge alone. Previous record also makes a difference, particularly in sentences for the less serious crimes. But defendant's age, race, and type of counsel are not related to outcome.

    Findings from an independent study of sentences in federal district courts accord, in general, with those from the Tiffany-Avichai-Peters research (Sutton 1978).

5. In New York City, sentences for felonies are principally a function of the gravity of the immediate charge and the defendant's history of criminality (Vera Institute 1977).

6. A study of males arrested in Indianapolis finds complex interactions between legal and extralegal factors affecting outcomes (Burke and Turk 1975). Some of the interactions are:

    • The lower the offender's social status, the more severe the disposition. However, this relationship disappears when offense is considered. It is behavior, rather than status, that accounts for judicial decision.

    • The relationship between occupational status and judicial decision is complicated by the fact that there is also an association between social position and the probability of previous imprisonment. And previous incarceration is itself a factor affecting judicial decision, even when the present offense is held constant. This complication is compounded, in turn, by the relation-ship between race and occupation.

- "When type of offense is controlled . . . race has no independent effect upon case disposition" (Burke and Turk 1975: 328). Interpretation of this lack of effect is complicated because race, occupational status, age, and previous incarceration are not independent of one another. The interactions are difficult to interpret, but they provide no confirmation of the labeling hypothesis.

7. With data from San Diego County Superior Court, 100 coders worked for two years classifying hundreds of items in about 1,200 cases (Konecni and Ebbesen 1982). Coders recorded demographic characteristics of the accused, their employment and social histories, previous records, medical, psycholog-ical, and psychiatric evaluations, charges on arrest, charges on conviction, whether or not there had been bail and plea negotiation, characteristics of the crime, quality of evidence from witnesses and physical circumstances, the content of defendants' statements, including expressions of remorse, admis-sions of guilt, and signs of premeditation. In addition, they recorded proba-tion officers' assessments and recommendations.

These factors served as independent variables to be tested for their impact on four possible outcomes: sentence to state prison; sentence to county jail; straight probation; and all other sentences, such as commitment to a mental hospital, fine without imprisonment, or probation.

Contrary to assumptions of the underdog theory, these investigators found that age, sex, race, education, marital status, religion, and even offenders' physical attractiveness bore no relation to sentence when severity of crime and previous record were held constant. In further contradiction of some previous assumptions and research, Konecni and Ebbesen (1982) found no "judge effects"—that is, if one allowed for the kinds of cases assigned to judges, their individual differences did not affect sentences.

Among the many possible determinants of sentence, only four—all legally relevant—were significantly associated with judgment: type of crime, offender's previous record, offender's status between arrest and conviction (released on own recognizance, released on bail, or held in jail throughout), and probation officer's sentence recommendation.

The process by which sentences are meted out is described by Konecni and Ebbesen (1982: 322) this way:

> Probation officers' recommendations—the key cause of judges' sentencing deci-sions—were influenced by severity of crime, prior record, jail bail status, and two interactions according to which the effect of prior record was substantially aug-mented by the higher levels of severity of the crime and jail/bail status.

8. In California, neither sex nor ethnicity affects judicial discretion in first-degree murder trials (Judson et al. 1969). This research tested for ethnic effects among three groups: African Americans, whites, and defendants of Mexican ancestry. No differential was found, nor was there any difference in disposition between African Americans who had killed whites and whites who had killed African Americans.

9. In Fulton County (principally Atlanta), Georgia, sentencing by 11 judges in 1,219 cases reveals no evidence of racial differentiation when previous felony convictions and gravity of instant charge are held constant. However, individual judges differ, so that "blacks are the victims of discrimination by some judges, but the beneficiaries of discrimination by others" (Gibson 1978: 470).
10. In Philadelphia, a study of the disposition of 118 robbery charges and 291 burglary indictments finds no evidence of extralegal influence when, again, criminal history and gravity of instant offense are held constant (Green 1964).
11. In Alberta, outcomes at three stages of the judicial process are found to be influenced principally by legal factors (Hagan 1974a). The three stages examined were (1) charging in the Crown Prosecutor's Office, (2) pre-sentence report preparation by the Adult Probation Department, and (3) sentencing.

Hagan (1974a: v) reports, "Differences in sentences are minimal. Legal variables—prior conviction and the number and types of charges—are found to be salient at all three stages of the sentencing process."

The only discrepancies found in legal treatment of offenders by their ethnicity were (1) a greater tendency of rural (as opposed to urban) probation officers to treat First Nations people severely and (2) a greater tendency for métis and First Nations persons to serve jail sentences instead of paying a fine.

Furthermore, this ethnic differential in serving jail sentences is stronger for minor violations—the summary offenses—than for the major, indictable crimes. Interpretation of this difference notes that aboriginal people are disproportionately arrested for alcohol-related infractions of the law. When aboriginal offenders are compared with white inmates in a prison classification as "temperate" or "intemperate" users of alcoholic beverages, two times as many aboriginals as whites are diagnosed as having drinking difficulties.

In looking at the amount of fine decreed in lieu of incarceration and controlling for race and gravity of offense, Hagan found no difference in this levy among ethnic groups. Interpretation of the greater tendency of First Nations persons and métis to be jailed instead of paying fines rests on the fact that payment of a fine is an option. It is not known, however, whether First Nations persons and métis choose jail rather than payment of a fine or whether they are less able to pay.

The case of social response to aboriginal people in Canada illustrates another difficulty in assessing justice. The difficulty occurs when labels and deeds are themselves associated, as they are in public stereotypes and official records of drinking among native people. In such cases, researchers are hard pressed to disentangle the causes of differential sentencing when it is found.

To complicate matters, the way in which drunkenness is exhibited may differ among ethnic groups and consequently make them differentially liable to arrest. Hagan (1977a: 609) puts it this way:

> Indians more frequently than whites drink and recover in public. There are differences in access to, and preferences for, privacy in drinking. Given the resulting group-linked differences in behavior, equal treatment of those who violate public drinking norms cannot produce an equality of legal outcomes.

A remedy for this particular differential in legal effects is to use detoxification centers rather than jails in response to alcohol abusers.

In summary, the general conclusion to be drawn from this extensive Canadian study, as from American research, contradicts the interactionist's allegation that "labels" determine social response more than do crimes.

This sample of research could be amplified, of course. However, Michael Gottfredson and Don Gottfredson have compiled a volume in summary of research on decision-making in American criminal justice systems, and their conclusions, with qualifications to be added, seem fair. The Gottfredsons surveyed research on decisions to (1) report a crime, (2) arrest a suspect, (3) release a suspect before trial, (4) prosecute and, if so, for which crime, (5) sentence, and (6) administer offenders on probation, in institutions, and on parole. They conclude that three factors "play a persistent and major role throughout the system—the 'seriousness of the offense,' the prior criminal conduct of the offender, and the personal relationship between the victim of the crime and the offender" (Gottfredson and Gottfredson 1980: 330).

Qualifications   Generalizations *without* exceptions are not interesting. Generalizations *with* exceptions do not thereby lose their significance; they only become qualified.

Three qualifications apply to our present conclusion and concerns: (1) gravity of crime affects discretion; (2) time and place also make a difference; and (3) extreme cases also make a difference.

1. The Gottfredsons demonstrate that American criminal justice systems distinguish between two broad families of crime by their judged gravity. Discretion comes into play among those offenses deemed to be less grave; discretion narrows as it is employed in responding to more serious crimes.

The same physical act is not judged to be the same criminal act, depending on circumstance. The circumstance that most consistently reduces the judged gravity of an injury is intimacy between offender and victim. Conversely, attacks by strangers are judged to be more serious. Therefore, the system of legal response works to rid itself of lesser crimes. "Effort is expended," say the Gottfredsons (1980: 333), "to rid the criminal justice system of these cases [minor ones] everywhere and any way that ingenuity can devise. Victims disproportionately fail to report them to the police; and police choose not to arrest, prosecutors not to charge, and judges to apply less severe sanctions.."

This is apparently a universal phenomenon. Thus Laura Nader and Harry Todd (1978) collect descriptions of the "disputing process" in ten societies and show that efforts are always made to keep "cases out of court" when they involve complaints among intimates—that is, among people who will have to continue "to know one another." Formal sanctions are more commonly invoked against "outsiders." An attack by a stranger always seems more threatening than a similar injury from an intimate.

2. Time and place make a difference in application of the law because the sense of justice varies with moral codes and with defined relations among people.

The most frequently cited instances of unfair administration of the criminal law in recent times refer to the death sentence given African Americans who kill whites or African American men who rape white women.

Bowers and Pierce (1980) hold that racial prejudice intrudes upon all stages of legal reaction to murder suspects—from prosecution to conviction to applying the death sentence. They calculate probabilities of receiving the death sentence for criminal homicide by racial pairing of offender and victim in four states: Florida, Georgia, Ohio, and Texas. Uniformly, they find a gradient such that probabilities of the death sentence are highest for African Americans who kill whites, second highest for whites who kill whites, low for African Americans who kill African Americans, and almost zero for whites who kill African Americans. The last probability is qualified by the fact that there were no such cases in Florida and Ohio during the research period, only one in Texas, and two in Georgia (Bowers and Pierce 1980: 594, table 2).

3. African-American–white victimization and sentencing for murder and rape in particular zones of the United States may be considered extreme cases; they seem best interpreted as what statisticians call *outliers*. That is, they lie at extremities of a scatterplot relating one thing to another. If one does not discount such outliers, they distort the more characteristic general conclusion.

This possibility occurs also when one looks at extreme cases in which power affects justice. Wealth and prestige do provide "clout." Prestige does so by definition. We are concerned, then, with cases in which power influences dispensation of justice. Such cases are difficult to discuss because powerful people have their factions. By virtue of their status, luminaries attract devotees and enemies. People align themselves for and against, and every allegation of an injustice is countered by partisan justification.

We note this process, for example, in the quarrel about former president Richard Nixon's absolution from trial for obstructing justice and Senator Edward Kennedy's light penalty (a two-month suspended jail sentence and a one-year revocation of his driver's license) for an accident that killed a woman under circumstances that would have made the ordinary citizen liable to prosecution for negligent manslaughter. In addition, two recent cases in Canada make the point, but in a different way. In 1997, Guy Paul Morin and David Milgaard were exonerated for separate murders of which they had been previously convicted.

Each has served a long period of time in prison, in Milgaard's case, 23 years (Roberts 1997). Their crimes took place 15 years and thousands of miles apart. Sophisticated DNA testing led to their exoneration. Both were white; Morin was considered to be an "odd" young man by his neighbors and the police. Milgaard had a record of juvenile offences. Their "labels" led to police and witnesses adjusting their evidence to fit their presumed guilt so that both were convicted.

In a third case, a young First Nations man, Donald Marshall, (in yet another part of the country) was wrongfully convicted of murder. The significance of labels is more difficult to discern because not only was he a Mic Mac Indian, but he also lied to the police early in the investigation.

The present point is that such extreme cases are just that—outliers. They qualify, but they do not refute, the generalization that our criminal justice systems respond principally to deeds and less frequently to the "labels" of defendants.

Does a "Bad Name" Cause Bad Action?

We have seen that the social-reaction perspective does not fare well with its assumptions that "labels" are mostly incorrect, that they necessarily hurt, and that they affect justice more than do deeds. The most likely assumption of this perspective is that stigma reinforces bad action.

The labeling hypothesis calls attention to the possibility that official reactions to some kinds of disapproved behavior may confirm actors in their deviant ways. This is probably the most valuable contribution of the perspective.

The Labeling Hypothesis

It is suggested that some "sick behaviors" improve more rapidly when they are untreated and that some cures are worse than the diseases they treat. Interactionist theory emphasizes how minor events in the stream of life may become major events as a result of official notice. The careers of different kinds of people are made even more different by the fact that a portion of their lives must be spent dodging the consequences of official response to their deviation. The model here is that of the marijuana user, whose life may be changed by the criminalization of this preference.

Examining the Hypothesis

Labeling theory gains credence as it develops biographies showing that being "officially handled" increases the chances of future official attention. There is reason to assume that this risk is increased by the stigma associated with a criminal label and the consequent reduction in lawful opportunities (Schwartz and Skolnick 1962). There is no denying that this happens, *but we do not know how much of repeated offense is so caused.*

Requirements for Tests   The answer to the question about the causal power of stigma depends on how the question is phrased. There is not much point in asking whether official handling has *some* effect on crime, because such a question is vague and its answer conceded.

A more interesting way of putting the question is to ask, as labeling theorists do, whether stigma may not be one link in a causal chain that proceeds from some initial offense through labeling to discriminatory reaction to changed self-concept to differential relations with other stigmatized persons to more crime than the actor would have exhibited if he or she had not been so handled.

There has been no test of this alleged linkage. In particular, there has been no study that would allow assignment of a *relative causal force* to official handling as crime-producing. We are left with anecdotes—selective biographies—and with the assumption that stigma is criminogenic. Lacking a crucial test of the interactionist hypothesis, we revert to studies that are suggestive, but not conclusive.

Provisional Tests   Attempts have been made to ascertain whether similar classes of offenders behave differently if they are treated differently. As is true of studies of the impact of nonlegal variables on social reaction, everything depends on the quality of controls employed to assure us that classes of offenders are actually homogeneous and that it is only difference in social response that affects their careers.

This shaky assumption underlies studies that have compared differences in later criminality among allegedly similar offenders who were granted probation, placed on parole, or released from prison after full time had been served. Follow-up studies of these differences disagree—some find probationers doing better than those sentenced to prison, and some find no differences (Babst and Mannering 1965; Beattie and Bridges 1970; Levin 1971; Wilkins 1969). Such studies do not answer our question, however, since probationers are *selected* because they are considered to be better risks. The groups being compared are not similar in all relevant respects.

More recently, Bartusch and Matsueda (1996) use data from the National Youth Survey to test a variety of propositions that are derived from the social interactionist perspective of labeling. Their principal concerns deal with whether the views that young people hold of how they are perceived by others and the views held by parents are related to delinquent behavior. In general, the answer is that they are and that boys are more affected than girls and negative labels have more impact than positive ones.

Other findings are less compatible with labeling theory. For instance, the label of "sociable," which is usually thought of as positive, works the other way.

1. Reflected appraisals as sociable have a significant positive effect on delinquency. . . . Those who see themselves from the standpoint of others as well-liked and getting along well with others are more likely to engage in delinquent behavior. This finding, perhaps reflecting the group nature of delinquency, contradicts depictions of delinquents as isolated sociopaths (Bartusch and Matsueda 1996: 160–161).
2. Reflected appraisals in some cases have less impact than the labels of parents on delinquency.

PARENTAL LABELING IS INFLUENCED BY PRIOR DELINQUENCY

". . . parental labels of youths as rule violators are more likely among delinquents, non-whites, and urban dwellers. Most of these effects operate [when youths have a record of] prior delinquency; thus we find only modest evidence of disadvantaged youths being falsely accused." (Matsueda 1992: 1,602)

Abonetti and Hepburn (1996) tested the tenet of labeling theory that members of minority groups are treated more harshly in the criminal justice system than those who are not members of minority groups. In their study, the dependent variable is whether prosecutors choose diversion programs for categories of offenders rather than criminalize them.

The findings of this sophisticated study are mixed. The principal finding is that minority group status does not lower the likelihood of diversion. With respect to another ascribed (nonlegal) variable, in this case age, they find that younger defendants are more likely to be diverted from prosecution into treatment programs. They also find that regardless of defendants' minority status, the effect of having a record of prior arrests significantly reduces the likelihood of diversion" (Abonetti and Hepburn 1996: 71–78). Thus, contrary to the labeling hypothesis, the extralegal variable of minority status does not make a difference while the legally relevant variable, record of arrests, does make a difference.

When minority status, record of prior arrests, and age are combined the results are mixed: (1) a record of prior arrests has a stronger effect on being diverted for nonminority defendants; but (2) ". . . for young defendants with a record of prior arrests, the effect of minority status significantly increases the likelihood of diversion from criminal procedure. . . ." (Abonetti and Hepburn 1996: 78).

In brief, minority status does not have a direct or main effect on diversion, but in combination with other legal and extralegal considerations does have some effect, not all in the same direction. The principal tenet of labeling theory are not supported.

Advantages of Labeling Theory

The major proposals of the interactionist perspective are not well grounded in fact. This does not mean that the labeling orientation is without value. The value is, as promised, more political than scientific and, like everything of worth, carries a price. The advantage of assuming the labeling perspective lies where most recent advocates place it—in alerting us to the possibility that official reaction may do more harm than good.

Acceptance of this possibility is entirely within the nineteenth-century liberal tradition of getting governments out of our lives. We would rather have the state do less to us, although we are unclear about what it should do for us. The challenge of social-reaction theorists is intended to be liberating, and, it is valuable on this score.

Advocates of interactionist theory recommend particular policies, and they believe that their policies follow directly from their assumptions. However, it is possible to agree with many of this theory's prescriptions without basing policy on its dubious assumptions.

For example, proponents of labeling theory want to decriminalize many offenses, particularly those "without victims." They would have more legal provisions for erasing criminal stigmata—for expunging a criminal record—and for protecting the privacy of personal files. They favor experiments with diversion programs, particularly for young people, and "radical nonintervention." "Leave the kids alone wherever possible," Schur (1973) advocates.

There is a strong concern with safeguards in protection of individual liberty against arbitrary power. As a consequence, there is opposition to the substitution of indeterminate "treatment" programs for legally circumscribed punishment. There is also a strong tendency to remove the "protective" functions of delinquency laws—those that define "status offenses"—and to return young people to full rights under law. In short, defense of due process, even for young people, moves advocates of the interactionist theory away from the idea that offenders must be ignorant or "sick" and toward the idea that they are rational persons. "This means that labeling analysts prefer to opt for a conservative 'crime-responsibility-punishment' framework, because it is less likely to infringe on individual liberties and more likely to maintain a sense of justice" (Ericson 1975: 133).

It has been noted earlier (Chapter 1) that it is easier to speak generally of decriminalizing different tastes than it is to be consistent about our advocacy. It is also easier to recommend leaving people alone "wherever possible" than it is to agree on the boundaries of "wherever possible." Nevertheless, we can accept the liberating prescriptions of the labeling perspective *without* subscribing to its unproved assumptions. The reasons for doubting its assumptions, while approving its prescriptions, lie in the disadvantages of this orientation.

Deficiencies of Labeling Theory

The social-reaction school has been criticized for (1) ignoring the differences in behavior described by labels. The labeling schema draws attention from deeds to public definitions of those deeds. Such diversion means that (2) labeling theory does not increase, and may well decrease, our ability to predict individual behavior. Its low predictive power is a result not only of its neglect of individual differences but also of the fact that (3) it contains a defective model of causation. This, in turn, means that (4) its relevance to social policy is lessened. Each of these points will be amplified.

Labeling Theory Does Not Explain the Behaviors That Lead to Application of Labels

Labeling theorists argue as if popular and legal categories were devoid of content, as if they were never "well earned." The labeling explanation pays little or no attention to the fact that people do *not* behave similarly. It slights the possibility that a label may *correctly* identify consistent differences in conduct, and it pays little attention to the reasons why "society" continues to apply a label once it has been used.

The prescription that follows from the labeling hypothesis is to change the attitudes of majorities toward misbehaving minorities. In reply, majorities tell us that they are not yet convinced that a more compassionate attitude toward robbers or burglars will change these offenders' behaviors and reduce the pain they cause.

Labeling Theory Is a Poor Predictor of Individual Conduct

Optimistic Beliefs versus Reasonable Beliefs

The low predictive power of labeling theory results from its denial of personality differences. The interactional bias of the labeling theorist encourages such optimistic, but risky, beliefs as these:

- He will be honest if I trust him.
- She will be reasonable if you are.
- He will be pacific if we are.
- Her psychosis is not "in her," but "in the interactional situation." When the interpersonal mirrors in which she sees herself are changed, she will change.

On the contrary, there are personality differences that are reliably associated with behavior differences and that are remarkably persistent. These persistent ways of feeling and acting are not readily changeable with changes in the labels attached to them. Regardless of what we have been called or how people respond to us, *most of us continue to be what we have been a long time becoming.*

This does not mean that we cease to learn. Learning is lifelong. But what we learn has little bearing upon those distinctive marks of personality that we recognize in temperament, intelligence, and motivation.

A vast library of research demonstrates this point with reference to different dimensions of conduct (a summary of the literature can be read in Nettler (1982a: chapter 3). The point is made in the autobiography of the playwright S. N. Behrman who, after years of failure and impoverished struggle, wrote a play that was a hit. Behrman (1972: 37) comments:

> With the production of a successful play . . . you acquire overnight a new identity
> —a public label. But this label is pasted on you. It doesn't obliterate what you
> are and have always been—doesn't erase the stigmata of temperament.

The statement that there are persistent temperamental and cognitive differences underlying our behaviors can be qualified by adding that such personality variables have more of an impact upon behavior as circumstances are equalized. Nevertheless, most of us can tell the difference between behavior—our own and others—that is only situationally reactive and behavior that is characteristic. All of us operate, implicitly or explicitly, with the idea of *character*—the idea that there *are* enduring personal predispositions relevant to moral behavior. This means that, unless there are tremendous changes in environments, people are likely to continue to behave as they have behaved. Thus far, this has proved to be the best bet. Against the optimistic recommendations of the interactionist, it seems more sensible to believe that

- Embezzlers may need to be arrested, and stigmatized, before they "will turn honest."
- Being reasonable with a fanatic is futile.
- A soft answer turns away the wrath of some people, but not of others, and there is no point in pleading for your life with the likes of a Charles Manson, Ted Bundy, or Paul Bernardo.
- Cures of psychoses are exceptional. Most people who are "peculiar" are not disordered in all ways, all the time.

Misbehavior may be episodic; but ordinarily, safety lies in the assumption of behavioral continuity. Indeed, the historic reason for being tried by a jury of one's peers was that they would be able to determine guilt or innocence based on their knowledge of the kind of person one is—one's character—and the behavior they observed in the past. This is still the case in small-scale, that is, less complex societies (Raybeck 1991).

As societies have become more complex and more people in the community do not *know* one another, we have developed a system of justice that does not depend on previously held definitions about what the accused is like. The emphasis has shifted to testimony from witnesses and the use of hired prosecutors and defense counsel.

How Small-Scale Societies Decide Deviance
". . . the members of small-scale social units will openly discuss and weigh the social standing of the offender before assessing the degree to which an actor may have manifested deviant behavior. Such dimensions often include topics such as the actor's prior offenses, the value of the actor in the social unit, the extent of the actor's support network including family, wider relatives, and friends . . ." (Raybeck 1991: 22)

Usefulness of Labels

Every way of knowing the world categorizes. There is no escape from classification, although there is dispute about which categories are more useful.

As professional thinkers we are helped by acknowledging that we shall continue to "define" and that to define means to draw boundaries around events. We are also aware that these boundaries may be incorrectly set for predictive purposes and that they are not fixed. We are careful, then, with words that establish rigid frontiers. We protect ourselves against the belief that words have some magical and immovable connection to the things they describe. Our defense against this error includes a skepticism about verbs like "is" that fix people in categories: "He *is* a criminal." "She *is* a lesbian." The defects of such "is-ness" are that (1) such reification infers what we are from what we do, which is all that can be observed (Sagarin 1976); (2) it ignores *degrees* of activity; and (3) it produces an inflexible categorization congenial to dogmatism and deaf to information.

The words with which we describe one another *diagnose*. And each diagnosis carries with it a *prognosis*. The names we call one another may therefore do us good as well as harm. Everything hinges on the validity of the diagnosis, and diagnosis is always less than certain.

The point is that, while there are risks in classification, the risks are always taken. They cannot be avoided. The risks are taken by omission or commission, by denying a description or by accepting it. We may appreciate one another with adjectives and verbs rather than with nouns, but the adjectives and verbs are still prophetic categories. They are forecasting tools—some better, some worse. But the fact that they are predictive instruments means that there are times when learning the name which describes what we, or others, have been doing yields an economy, a relief; and a forecasting advantage. The predictions that mark our daily doings rest on "labels."

The Model of Causation Implicit in the Labeling Hypothesis Is Questionable

Every explanation of human behavior makes assumptions about its causes. Labeling theory locates the causes of conduct in an unusual place—in the people who respond to it. It shifts the "responsibility" for my action from me to you. It stresses how much of what I do is a result of what you have done to me, and for me. All theories that would explain human behavior, including popular theories, assume that behavior is shaped, to some degree, by the actions of intimate others. Sociopsychological hypotheses of the "control" variety pay particular attention to the "how" of this socialization process.

It is not denied, then, that how people respond to us when we misbehave may affect our subsequent conduct. But only in recent years have psychologists corrected the mistaken assumption that socialization is a one-way street, with parents affecting children but not vice versa. We now know that there are *child effects*, that is, that children train their parents (Bell and Harper 1977).

Recognition of an interactional web of causes raises lively questions concerning the periods of our development at which, and the degrees to which, others mold us. What is at issue is *how much* of the particular behaviors to be explained varies with the responses of others to them.

The valuable contributions of the labeling hypothesis have tended to obscure its deficiencies. It is one thing to study the way in which a defining process affects our response to the behavior of others. It is another matter to study the causes of the events we are defining. Studying how we respond to deviant others may suggest to us a more economical mode of reacting. This suggestion should not be confused, however, with information about the causes of the crimes that concern us.

Such confusion is created when advocates of labeling theory tell us, for example, that "*social groups create deviance by making the rules whose infraction constitutes deviance*, and by applying those rules to particular people and labeling them as outsiders" (Becker 1963: 9).

Some readers translate statements like this as saying that "social groups create crime by making the laws whose infraction constitutes crime." This translation is slippery; it slides between the truth that social groups created the definition of "crime" and the falsehood that the injuries condemned by these definitions would disappear (or would not have been produced) if the definition had not been formulated.

To the layperson, it sounds as though the labeling theorist believed that people would not wish to defend themselves against burglary or murder if they had not learned a rule defining those acts as crimes. It sounds also as though the interactionist believed that there would be less "burglary" if we did not use that term. The nonprofessional consumer of criminological explanations recognizes this for the semantic trick it is—the trick of saying, "If a crime is a breach of a rule, you won't have the crime if you don't have the rule." The ordinary reaction to this semantic sleight of hand is to say, "A mugging by any other name hurts just as much."

Our question has to do with the location of causation. When the causation implied by the labeling hypothesis is tested, it fails. The causes specified by this schema do not account for the production of the behaviors that disturb us. "Mental hospitals" do not cause "mental illness" (Gove 1970); nor do the agencies of social control, or the labels they apply, cause crime (Ward 1971). Indeed, individuals and organizations can exercise some influence over being labeled (McBarnet 1991).

The assumption of labeling theory is that those who become "criminal" are mostly those who, while behaving much like everyone else, just happened to get tagged, or that those labeled criminals were more liable to the tagging because they fit some public's prejudiced stereotype of the criminal. Contrary to these assumptions, however, studies of the operation of Western systems of justice show that they work like a sieve. As we have seen, the people who get caught in the sieve tend to be the more serious and persistent lawbreakers (Black and Reiss 1970; Bordua 1967; Terry 1967).

In summary, labeling theorists do not think about causes and effects, about antecedents and consequents; they prefer to think about interactions. This preference does not eliminate the idea of causation; it only obscures it by shifting the locus of causes from actors to their judges. This shift has some moral and political value in the fight between outsiders and insiders. It justifies challenge of police and courts, or of any other mechanisms of social control, that would condemn the conduct of an aberrant few. However, when the labeling hypothesis is applied to the explanation of the serious crimes, its model of causation reduces its value for public policy.

Labeling Theory Does Not Address Perennial Social Concerns about Crime

We are reminded that explanatory theories are only as good as the questions they answer. The answers provided by labeling theorists are not addressed to the questions about crime that are asked by most people. These questions are, again, "What causes crime?" "What accounts for increases or decreases in crime rates?" "How can crime be reduced?"

To these questions, labeling theorists give no good reply. The policy recommendation comes down to "Avoid unnecessary labeling." (Schur 1971: 171). This may be helpful in decriminalizing some activities. It is a recommendation useful in suggesting diversion of some misbehavior from official handling, and it is provocative in suggesting that we leave people alone.

20. Epilogue

Locations of Crime

Criminal behavior is universal. Some crime takes place in every community and every identifiable social group. The amount of crime that takes place, however, is not uniform. Research indicates that different communities and social groupings have different rates of crime and different types of crime. Thus, it is not surprising that no single factor or explanation adequately addresses all crime and criminality. The term "crime" defines a complex agglomeration of behaviors. Different processes produce different amounts and mixes of those behaviors in different communities at different times. What may explain a fluctuation in the rate of crime in Birmingham, Alabama, this year may not explain a similar fluctuation in Birmingham, England, or in either city 20 years from now.

It is incumbent on us, therefore, to specify as precisely as possible what behaviors we wish to explain and what level of analysis we wish to address. Thus, for example, questions addressed at crime among individuals will necessarily exclude certain classes of explanations (e.g., sociological ones) while questions addressed at the societal level will exclude others (e.g., psychological ones). It is for this reason, among others, that we appear, at times, to have a multitude of valid and, at other times, invalid explanations.

Overall, the two variables that "explain" the greatest amount of variation in rates of crime are sex and age. Crime—particularly violent, "street" crime—is universally and disproportionately localized among young males. Beyond that, and depending upon the society one examines, rates of crime vary among different social groups and in different geographical locations. Specifically in the North American context, crime rates tend to be highest among disadvantaged minorities and in the inner cities.

It is for these reasons that most explanations of crime have focused on young men at the expense of others in society. Despite this exposition of theory, however, Hirschi and Gottfredson (1983) have maintained that the causal mechanism that explains *why* the age-sex dimension is such a strong predictor of criminal behavior has not been adequately identified. Indeed, it appears that a great deal of our mental energy has been directed toward explanations of socially more interesting, but statistically less significant, factors.

Explanations of crime imply policy options. Ideally, those factors that are most highly criminogenic ought to be the focus of our attention when we consider ameliorative actions. We have made the point, however, that some explanations are more congenial to our beliefs and sensibilities than others, regardless of their empirical validity. Thus, some policy options are ineligible regardless of their "effectiveness." For ethicopolitical and economic reasons we pick and choose the explanations we wish to accept, and the actions we wish to take. It is for such reasons that first-time drinking drivers are fined in North America, jailed in Norway, yet executed by firing squad in Singapore. It is also why many states refuse to deal with violent crime by implementing stringent gun controls while some countries, such as Great Britain and Canada do.

Having explored many of the explanations put forward by social scientists to account for crime, we may now ask ourselves what the implications of those explanations are for social action. The implied policy directives of some explanations are more extensive than for others. Briefly, we consider some of the more central ones.

Explanations of Crime and Policy Implications
Definitions of Law

In Chapters 1 and 2, it was pointed out that crime is not a "natural" phenomenon. Instead, it is a reflection of our values and mores. All else being equal, societies that exhibit a greater moral consensus will have less crime than societies reflecting greater heterogeneity in values. In traditional societies, heterogeneity in values is not a serious problem. Modern democratic societies, however, need to create social and political institutions that respect and accommodate differences in values. Societies that provide mechanisms and opportunities for consensus building are more likely to experience less conflict than those that do not. In modern societies, consensus formation is not inherent, it is something that needs to be fostered and developed through social policies that encourage public participation in political decisions. Policies that lead to marginality and alienation do not engender commitment to the social order.

Societies also differ in how they use the criminal law. In North America, the criminal law is used increasingly to regulate a widening range of undesirable behaviors. Thus, the criminal law no longer reflects only society's core values, those behaviors traditionally defined as behaviors *mala in se*. Increasingly, the criminal law is used to address regulatory issues. Those actions that are *mala prohibita* range from matters of esthetics to commercial to environmental concerns. When the scope of the criminal law widens, it is a virtual truism that the amount of crime will increase.

As the criminal law becomes broader and more complex, enforcement becomes more difficult and the proportion of unapprehended offenders increases. Unenforced laws lead to overall disrespect for the rule of law, and, as respect for the law decreases, it loses its moral imperative (Packer 1968). America's grand experiment with Prohibition is a prime example how laws that are difficult to enforce can create their own set of problems, even when they are having a desired impact, as in the case of reducing alcohol-related damage. Prohibition was eventually repealed because it lost its moral imperative when consensus could not be achieved.

What then is the solution? The crucial element is balance. Societies need to decide where the balance between freedom and constraint ought to be drawn.

Too much freedom leads to license; too little freedom reflects totalitarianism. Sociologists like to distinguish among behaviors that are criminal, and those that are deviant, and those that are merely reflections of bad manners. Many behaviors offend our sensibilities; few, however, require state intervention and sanction. Culturally heterogeneous societies, in particular, need to be tolerant and sensitive to differences in taste and preference. They also need to be aware that the state has many more options than the criminal law at its disposal for implementing social policy.

Socialization

It is through the process of socialization that we learn what is right and what is wrong; what are appropriate behaviors, and what are unacceptable reactions to life's situations. Learning theorists argue that there are two mechanisms of learning that have the greatest impact upon our behavior: modeling and operant conditioning. In practice, these two mechanisms are not independent of each other. They work in tandem.

The existing research suggests that while lifelong learning takes place, it is what we learn in the first few years of life—the "formative years"—that has the greatest impact on whether we are likely to be involved in serious offending. Most of this formative learning generally takes place within the family. Containment theorists suggest that such "crime-insulating" personality elements as self-concept, attachment, commitment, involvement, and belief in the moral validity of rules are learned early and primarily in the home. Certainly, home-based attitudes toward the validity of education are among the best indicators of success in school.

Unfortunately, problems with broken and "dysfunctional" homes are probably the most difficult to address through social intervention. How, for example, does one turn an inadequate parent into an adequate one? How does one ensure that a child is exposed to appropriate role models? Is it possible to make up in later life for deficiencies in youth? If so, how?

While it may not be possible to turn bad homes into good ones or inadequate parents into adequate ones, we can avoid social policies that undermine the integrity of the family. For example, welfare policies that encourage fathers *not* to participate in the upbringing of their children, or to live apart from their children and their children's mother should be avoided. Louis Farrakhan's "Million Man March" may have been viewed askance by many middle-class Americans, but it called nationwide attention to a fundamental problem in many of our communities of not enough men taking responsibility for the children they father.

We also need to address the problem of children bearing children. Teenage mothers who are barely beyond childhood themselves rarely have the social, emotional, or economic resources to raise a child in favorable circumstances. Sadly, most of these young women have children by men who abdicate any responsibility to either the woman or the child.

Modeling also tells us that it is not just the absence of role models that can have a negative impact on values and behavior, but inappropriate role models may even be worse. Increasingly, evidence suggests that the irresponsible use of comforting chemicals such as alcohol, patterns of spousal battering, and child abuse are behaviors that are passed from one generation to the next.

Rational Crime

The values and preferences we acquire through socialization are not sufficient to explain crime. Just as the criminal law asserts that there must be an *actus reas* (a guilty act) to complement a *mens rea* (a guilty mind), so too our explanations of crime must take into account *how* decisions are made to act upon our preferences. Clearly, some criminal acts are unintentional—accidents, unanticipated consequences of lawful actions, or acts of impulse or passion. Many more, however, involve purpose and intent.

It is economics—often called the science of decision making—that has contributed most to the literature on how people choose among alternate courses of action. The dominant model underlying economic explanation of crime is that of utility theory. Utility theory asserts that it is the relative ratio of cost to benefits associated with particular behaviors that determines whether an external stimulus acts as an incentive or a deterrent. Into this simple model, economists factor in the risks associated with detection and punishment, and the degree to which costs and benefits either appreciate or depreciate over time.

Historically, utility theory provided the intellectual roots of both classical economics and psychological behaviorism. Thus, it is not surprising that the two modes of explanation share much in common. Both explanations assert that rewards (benefits) provide an incentive to act in one way as opposed to another, and that punishments (costs) serve as a deterrent.

Economists have shown that increasing the cost of criminal behavior through such actions as "target hardening," or increasing the punishment associated with criminal acts reduces the commission of those acts. Particularly where the cost of our vices is increased (for example, in the consumption of alcohol, cigarettes, or pornography), the demand decreases. Paradoxically, increasing the cost of goods and services too much, can increase the "profits" of such activities to such a degree that black markets thrive and the supply of the restricted good or service can actually increase. Prostitution, the thriving trade in illicit drugs and the illegal trading in "gray market" commodities, from cars to computer software, are some instances.

Trying to deter crime by increasing the criminal sanction by legislating harsher punishment and mandatory minimum sentences has been a popular option among politicians. Both economists and operant psychologists tell us, however, that increasing the cost of illegal goods and services is not, in itself, a sufficient deterrent. Just as important (if not more so in some instances) are the risks associated with apprehension and punishment, and the swiftness of the punishment. Thus, deterrent theorists speak of a trinity of deterrent factors— certainty, severity, and celerity. A low risk of apprehension and punishment delayed, depreciates the perceived severity of the punishment.

Both economists and behaviorists, therefore, would argue that merely increasing criminal sanctions is not enough. The criminal justice system needs to become more efficient in terms of expediting apprehension and sanction, and the risk of sanction needs to be increased in order to affect rates of crime.

Economists, as with moralists, tell us that undesirable acts cannot be viewed in isolation. The social cost of enforcing the criminal law may impose an even greater burden on society than the costs associated with the criminal behavior. Thus, while we may not find certain behaviors to be palatable, it may be in the society's interest to allow constrained, if not unrestricted trade, in such goods and services. The decision by some societies to allow for regulated dealings in prostitution and in the sale of alcohol are examples of such strategies.

The economic view of crime, which underlies our present system of criminal justice, is not without flaws. It cannot explain nonrational crime, and consequently, does not provide us with policy prescriptions for expressive actions. Furthermore, it provides few solutions to problems where there is significant dissension over the values associated with various costs and benefits. Thus, an overnight jail term might be perceived as a costly risk to a middle-class individual, but as a reward to a street person faced with the harsh realities of a northern winter. Further, we are still undecided as a society whether we perceive street crime to be more serious than what some have called "suite crime." As a result, we continue to debate the relative costs of white-collar, consumer, and environmental crimes, while we put most of our law-enforcement resources on the street.

Structural Factors

Sociologists have put forward many structural explanations of crime, most of which are a variant on either anomie theory or opportunity theory. As originally proposed by Durkheim, *anomie* meant a lack of regulation. Thus, societies that do not impose constraints on people's wants and desires produce a disparity or gap between aspiration and the possible. This disparity breeds deviance that may be expressed in a variety of ways, including suicide and crime.

Several American sociologists followed the lead of Robert Merton and focused on anomie, but they perceived the role of society differently than did Durkheim. Durkheim viewed society as the only force that could regulate the wants, needs, and desires of human beings. The role of society was to keep peoples' needs and goals in proportion to the means available to them. Merton and his followers, however, viewed culturally defined goals (needs) as being more or less the same for everyone. They viewed the role of society as providing the means (opportunities) to achieve those goals in a similarly uniform manner.

Based on Merton's work, and that of his intellectual disciples, Cloward and Ohlin, the United States embarked on a multi-billion-dollar campaign in the 1960s to increase access to legitimate opportunities to disadvantaged young people (Moynihan 1969). With varying degrees of success, attempts were made to increase the level and relevance of education for America's socially disadvantaged. Job creation programs were developed in the name of opening up the structure of legitimate means of achieving culturally defined goals. Whether these interventions improved the situation over what it would have been had the programs not been put in place remains a largely unanswered question.

In all, theories of anomie, blocked opportunities, and explanations based on resentment do offer some sound, but difficult to implement, suggestions. Clearly, universal access to quality basic education is essential. Combined with that, however, is a need to alter students' perceptions of the value and utility of that education. For better or for worse, research suggests that parental attitudes toward education affect students' progress in school as much, if not more, than characteristics of the schools themselves. Governments have not been shown to be good creators of long-term employment opportunities; governments have, however, been successful in developing policies to increase their constituents' base of human capital through education and training programs.

A significant cluster of correlates of crime at the aggregate level is implicated with the mass movement of people, urbanization, and neighborhood instability. Proponents of the Chicago School often used the term "social disorganization" to describe the end result of these processes. These factors are related to high rates of crime throughout the world. While mass rural-urban migration is no longer a significant issue in North America and Europe, it is a major concern throughout much of Latin America, Africa, and Asia. High rates of international migration whether of legal immigrants, refugees, or illegal aliens creates situations in many areas that are reminiscent of America in the late nineteenth and early twentieth centuries. Of course, illegal immigration in some parts of the South and Southwestern United States continues to pose serious social, economic, and political problems.

The mass movement of people often overwhelms existing social institutions. Moreover, large numbers of people and high rates of transience slow the development of new social institutions. Selective migration means that it is usually groups such as the young and the single who move while the elderly are left behind. The consequence of this is that the external social constraints imposed on people when they live in extended family structures with familiar neighbors and supportive institutions such as churches and social clubs are no longer available to moderate their behavior. Furthermore, most migrants see themselves as sojourners, pausing only to acquire sufficient assets to move to a better location. Even though they may never leave their new homes, the sojourner mentality undermines any serious commitment to the neighborhood. Thus, little effort is put into developing the kinds of social arrangements that foster community spirit and attachment. Dwellings are not worth fixing up, graffiti is not worth cleaning, property is not worth protecting, taxes are inadequately levied or not collected. Poor, disorganized communities cannot afford the kinds of social institutions that support law, order, and good government.

Governments have struggled for generations to moderate migration at the source. Largely unsuccessful programs have been introduced in attempts to keep people in the countryside in third-world countries. Tremendous resources are spent in developed countries on trying to interdict illegal migrants. Success is mixed. The movement of people often remains inexorable, especially where both "push" and "pull" factors are strong.

The response to high rates of immigration by existing residents has been threefold. Many move out, some attempt to build walls to keep out intruders, and a small number seek to have existing services extended into those areas where the newcomers settle. It is only the latter that enhances the likelihood of building communities and reducing rates of crime.

"Critical" or Marxist criminologists have focused our attention on two structural aspects of crime. First, they have reinforced the notion that most definitions of what is criminal are relative to the values and interests of specific groups in society. In the debate over whose values become enshrined in the law, critical criminologists have argued that it is generally the interest of those with the most power in society that hold sway. Where there are substantial inequities in a society, there is a natural tendency for power to both maintain and extend itself.

Second, critical criminologists have drawn our attention to the fact that all social orders contain inherent contradictions. Thus, for example, a fundamental contradiction in modern capitalist societies is that labor produces surplus value or profits for capital, but also provides the market for the commodities it produces. To maximize profits, capitalists needs to minimize wage costs yet workers who have little discretionary spending power make poor consumers. Many adherents of this perspective have pointed out that young people—those in the years most prone to crime—are also the most economically marginal within our society. We pressure young people to consume through massive advertising campaigns yet provide them with few legitimate opportunities to satisfy the demand we create. These young people either turn to illegitimate avenues to satisfy the desire for new consumer goods or they assuage their feelings of marginality and alienation by retreating into the world of substance abuse.

Critical criminologists have done a good job of describing the objective conditions under which a significant proportion of the world's population lives. Yet Marxist explanations involve their own paradoxes. A primary assumption of Marxist explanations is that capitalism cannot solve its own problems. Thus, the only consistent policy suggestion from this perspective is to restructure society along socialist lines. However, capitalism has only flourished in open societies where one finds the greatest respect for due process and the rule of law. Furthermore, it can be argued that there are no purely capitalist societies; societies we identify as being capitalist are actually mixed economies that use the law to moderate social inequality. Furthermore, practical attempts to organize societies on alternate social orders, such as socialism, have not been very successful in either obliterating social inequality or maximizing the well-being of their citizens. In fact, some socialist experiments have left the majority of their citizens worse off than before they began.

Ideas

Most explanations of crime based on socialization make the assumption that crime is a consequence of being *asocial*. That is, those things that "come naturally" to humans are at the root of what we call crime. It is the lack of adequate socialization, therefore, that results in the inherently asocial person not becoming a social one.

We may, however, consider other variations on this theme. A number of explanations assume that socialization has taken place, but the ideas (norms, values, etc.) that are acquired may be *antisocial* or, in some cases, even *prosocial*. Thorsten Sellin's (1938) elaboration of culture conflict starts from the premise that many conduct norms are culturally specific, and what is acceptable in one culture may not be acceptable in another. Sellin asserts that in circumstances where different cultures come in contact with one another (i.e., through migration, warfare, or at contiguous border regions), there is a high likelihood that those cultures will contradict each other on some dimensions. The key point made by Sellin, however, is that there is nothing inherently antisocial about the values of either culture. They are just different on some dimensions: what may be acceptable in one culture is not acceptable in another. Examples of culture conflict abound and range from what some would define as minor issues relating to dress codes (as in fundamentalist Islamic cultures) or the use of comforting chemicals (alcohol, cocoa leaves, khat), to more serious matters relating to vendettas.

Crime resulting from culture conflict is rare since in those circumstances where it is most likely to take place (migration), people tend to consciously avoid offending their host or adoptive culture. Perhaps the greatest source of culture conflict is termed "generational conflict," where the values of parents are sometimes at odds with the values of youth. This may particularly be the case where first generation immigrants are involved and young people adapt to the host culture at a faster rate than their parents. Young people who accept the host culture's practices on such things as dress or dating behavior may be viewed a delinquent by their "old country" parents. The ensuing intergenerational conflict may even escalate to the point where common assault and other offenses take place.

Other idea-based explanations of crime focus on values that are clearly antisocial. Cohen's (1955) explanation of working-class delinquency has, at its core, the notion that young people who cannot compete in a world of middle-class values reject those values and replace them with a value system in which they can compete that is purposefully antisocial.

Subcultural explanations in general accept that some subcultural value systems are inherently antisocial, delinquent, or criminal. Few would argue, for example, that those immersed in the drug, biker, or organized crime subcultures, are unsocialized. To do so would require a similar perception of "positive" subcultures, such as those of the police or college students. The difference between those subcultures we consider acceptable as opposed to those considered unacceptable, is simply the degree to which the groups' values conform to dominant cultural norms.

Differential-association theory is another idea-based explanation that purports to explain how one decides between lawful and unlawful patterns of behavior. According to Sutherland, it is not that individuals are unaware of prosocial values; it is the relative weight of prosocial to antisocial definitions that one holds that determines one's behavior (Sutherland and Cressey 1980).

It is unfortunate that while idea-based explanations provide detailed descriptions of criminality, they provide few obvious proscriptions for ameliorating the problem. It is difficult to consider how subcultural values might be changed or extinguished short of the exile or death of those who hold them. Perhaps the best we can do is to reinforce mom's directive to "stay away from bad people," so that their ideas will not "rub off" on you.

A complement to idea-based explanations that focus on the values that "bad" people hold is that of labeling theory. Labeling explanations focus on how others perceive and evaluate us. Labeling theory attempts to explain crime by arguing that is how others view and react to us that determines whether on not we will become delinquent, criminal, or law-abiding.

Box 20.1   Criminogenic Conditions

Kennedy and Baron (1993: 109–110) make the point that a variety of explanations have something to contribute to our understanding of crime:

". . . we must examine more fully how choices [Rationality] . . . , routines [Opportunity], and cultural milieu [Subcultures] . . . , interact to affect one another. The evolution of events leading to assaults or robberies may depend on conflict styles that vary by individual personality [Control] and the social situation [Opportunity] that individuals confront . . . [some] assume that people develop patterned responses to conflict. Decisions about style are made on the basis of past experience and learning [Differential Association]. People learn conflict styles by observing others' behavior [Control] and trying different responses. These responses may be molded by the routine activities [Opportunity] that people are involved in during their daily living. However, we might add that these responses and experiences and even routines are influenced by culture [Culture]. Culture will impinge on the routines people adopt, the exposure to others' conflict styles [Differential Association], and the expectations about decisions in certain situations. . . . [S]ocial groups transmit rules specifying levels of aggression in certain situations [Culture] and support those rules with the awarding and withholding of status and prestige [Labeling]. The rules are acquired through vicarious learning [Control] and maintained through reinforcement an instrumental learning [Control]. Thus culture, routines, and choice may actually promote certain conflict styles. Routine activities theory [Opportunity] must include a choice [Rationality] component and draw on ideas from the subcultural [Culture] literature to determine how conflict styles mediate the impact of exposure [Opportunity] to high-risk situations.

Research on labeling, however, does not suggest that it is a formidable explanation of criminal behavior, and by the admission of its own proponents, does nothing to explain initial or primary criminal and deviant behavior. Thus, whether one calls a young criminal a "delinquent," "child criminal," or "person in need of supervision" is likely of little consequence. The development of diversion programs, however, may be beneficial since it often allows for greater community involvement in the process and broadens the range of social responses to criminal behavior.

Despite its limitations, the labeling perspective has made significant policy inroads. Particularly in the realm of juvenile justice, extensive effort has been made to neutralize offensive labels and the stigma associated with contact with the criminal justice system. Thus, in many professional circles, it has become politically incorrect to speak of juvenile delinquents; instead we refer to "young offenders" or "young persons in conflict with the law." The extensive use of diversion programs throughout the 1980s and 1990s has been in an attempt to alleviate the stigma of formal contact with formal institutions of criminal justice.

In this text, we have dealt with each explanation of crime separately in order to highlight their distinctive feature. No one explanation accounts for all of the variation in crime rates, but this ought not to be the sole basis for discarding an explanation. The search for perfection should not blind us to the insights explanations do provide. Furthermore, in any given circumstance, changes in rates of crime may result from changes in a variety of social conditions. Social life does not evolve in a simple, orderly manner with social changes taking place one at a time. Social life is dynamic and complex.

In our search for explanations of crime, therefore, we have sometimes disaggregated the impact of some explanations by considering them one-by-one. At other times, we have aggregated them by examining hybrid explanations that can be more or less complex. Testing the validity of an explanation is neither simple nor expeditious. Evidence for or against the credibility of a particular scientific explanation accumulates over time with empirical replication and theoretical refinement (Bernard 1990). The foregoing has been one attempt to lay out the state of the art and identify the raw materials that are available to the next generation of students of crime.

Bibliography

Abate, M., and Berrien, F.K. 1967. Validation of stereotypes: Japanese vs. American students. *Journal of Personality and Social Psychology*, 7: 435–438.

ABC Survey. 1982 June 22. *On the Hinckley trial and the insanity defense*.

Acers v. United States. 1896. *United States Reports*. 164, 388.

Acock, A. A., and De Fleur, M.L. 1972. A configurational approach to contingent consistency in the attitude-behavior relationship. *American Sociological Review*, 37: 714–726.

Addington v. United States. 1897. *United States Reports*, 165, 184.

Adlaf, E. M., Ivis, F. J., Smart, R. G., and Walsh, G. W. 1995. *The Ontario Student Drug Use Survey, 1977–1995*. Toronto: Addiction Research Foundation of Ontario.

Adler, F. 1975. *Sisters in crime: The rise of the new female criminal*. New York: McGraw-Hill.

Adler, P. A. 1993. *Wheeling and dealing: An ethnography of an upper-level drug dealing and smuggling community (2nd ed.)*. New York: Columbia University Press.

Agnew, R. 1985. A revised strain theory of delinquency. *Social Forces*, 64: 151–67.

Agnew, R. 1989. A longitudinal test of the revised strain theory. *Journal of Quantitative Criminology*, 5: 373–87.

Agnew, R. 1992. Foundation for a general strain theory of crime and delinquency. *Criminology*, 30: 47–87.

Agnew, R. 1993. Why do they do it? An examination of the intervening mechanisms between "social control" variables and delinquency. *Journal of Research in Crime and Delinquency*, 30: 245–66.

Aho, T. 1967. *Crimes which have caused the victim's death and aggravated assaults in Helsinki 1950–1965*. Unpublished paper. Helsinki: University of Helsinki.

Ainsworth, M. D. S. 1967. *Infancy in Uganda: Infant care and the growth of love*. Baltimore: Johns Hopkins University Press.

Akers, F. C. 1968. Negro and white automobile-buying behavior: New evidence. *Journal of Marketing Research*, 5: 283–289.

Akers, R. L. 1996. Is differential association/social learning cultural deviance theory? *Criminology*, 34: 229–245.

Akers, R. L. 1997. *Criminological Theories*. Los Angeles: Roxbury.

Alan Guttmacher Institute. 1993. *Facts in Brief: Teenage Sexual and Reproductive Behavior*. New York: The Alan Guttmacher Institute.

Alberta Reports'. 1981. The anti-Catholic comic war: Canada customs bans the Christian bookstores best-sellers. (October 30) 8: 46–47.

Albonetti, C. A., and Hepburn, J. R. 1996. Prosecutorial discretion to defer criminalization: The effects of defendant's ascribed and achieved status characteristics. *Journal of Quantitative Criminology*, 12: 63–81.

Alker, H. R., Jr. 1969. A typology of ecological fallacies. In M. Dogan and S. Rokkan (Eds.), *Quantitative ecological analysis in the social sciences*. Cambridge, Mass.: MIT Press.

Allport, F. H. 1934. The J-curve hypothesis of conforming behavior. *Journal of Social Psychology*, 5: 141–183.

Alpert, R. 1972. A fever of ethnicity. *Commentary*, 53: 68–73.

American Law Institute. 1953. *Model penal code*. Philadelphia: The Institute.

Amiot, M., et al. 1968. *La violence dans le monde actuel*. Paris, Desclée, De Brouwer.

Amir, M., and Hovav, M. 1976. Juvenile delinquency in Israel: Major trends in statistical data. *Israel Annals of Psychiatry*, 11: 161–172.

Anastasi, A. 1954. *Psychological testing*. New York: Macmillan.

Anastasi, A., and Foley, J. P. 1958. *Differential psychology: Individual and group differences in behavior*. New York: Macmillan.

Anonymous. 1942. An analysis of Jewish culture. In I. Graeber and S. H. Britt (Eds.), *Jews in a gentile world: The problem of anti-semitism*. New York: Macmillan.

Archer, D., and Gartner, R. 1984. *Violence and crime in cross-national perspective*. New Haven: Yale University Press.

Arkes, H. 1978. Marching through Skokie. *National Review*, (May 12) 30: 588–595.

Armor, D. J. 1972. The evidence on busing. *Public Interest*, 28: 90–126.

Arnett, J. J. 1996. *Metalheads: Heavy metal music and adolescent alienation*. Boulder, CO: Westview Press.

Aromaa, K. 1971. *Everyday violence in Finland*. Helsinki: Institute of Criminology. (Mimeograph).

Aromaa, K. 1973. Victimization to violence: A Gallup survey. *International Journal of Criminology and Penology*, 2: 333–346.

Aromaa, K. 1974. Our violence. In N. Christie (Ed.), *Scandinavian studies in criminology* (Vol. 5). Oslo: Universitetsforlaget.

Aron, R. 1973. *Histoire et dialectique de la violence*. Paris: Gallimard.

Aronfreed, J. 1963. The effects of experimental socialization paradigms upon moral responses to transgression. *Journal of Abnormal and Social Psychology*, 66: 437–448.

Ashford, J. B., and LeCroy, G. W. 1993. Juvenile parole policy in the United States: Determinate versus indeterminate models. *Justice Quarterly*, 10: 179–195.

Atkinson, A. B. 1970. On measuring inequality. *Review of Income and Wealth*, 13: 12–15.

Atkinson, A. B. 1975. *The economics of inequality*. Oxford: Clarendon Press.

Auletta, K. 1982. *The underclass*. New York: Random House.

Aultman, M. G., and Wright, K. N. 1985. The fairness paradigm: An evaluation of change in juvenile justice. *Canadian Journal of Criminology*, 24: 13–24.

Austin, R. L. 1982. Women's liberation and increases in minor, major, and occupational offenses. *Criminology*, 20: 407–430.

Avison, W. R., and Loring, P. L. 1986. Population diversity and cross-national homicide: The effects of inequality and heterogeneity. *Criminology*, 24: 733–749.

Babst, D. V., and Mannering, J. W. 1965. Probation versus imprisonment for similar types of offenders. *Journal of Research on Crime and Delinquency*, 2: 60–71.

Bachman, R. 1992. *Death and Violence on the Reservation*. Westport, CT: Auburn House.

Backman, R. 1991. An analysis of American Indian homicide: A test social disorganization and economic deprivation at the reservation county level. *Journal of Research in Crime and Delinquency*, 28: 456–471.

Bachman, R., and Straus, M. A. 1992. *Death and Violence on the Reservation: Homicide, Family Violence, and Suicide in American Indian Populations*. Washington, DC: Bureau of Justice Statistics.

Bacon, D. C. 1976. Ripoffs: New American Way of Life. *U.S. News and World Report*, (May 31) 80: 29–32.

Bacon, M. K., et al. 1963. A cross-cultural study of correlates of crime. *Journal of Abnormal and Social Psychology*, 66: 291–301.

Bagot, J. H. 1941. *Juvenile delinquency: A comparative study of the position in Liverpool and England and Wales*. London: Cape.

Bain, R. 1958. Our schizoid culture and sociopathy. *Sociology and Social Research*, 41: 263–266.

Baker, P. M., Markham, W. T., Bonjean, C. M., and Corder, J. 1988. Promotion interest and willingness to sacrifice for promotion in a government agency. *Journal of Applied Behavioral Science*, 24: 61–80.

Baldwin, J., et al. 1976. *The urban criminal*. London: Tavistock.

Ball, R. 1982. Europe's durable unemployment woes. *Fortune*, (January 11) 105: 66–74.

Bamfield, J. 1994. *National Survey of Retail Theft and Security*, Northampton, UK: Nene College.

Bandura, A. 1973. *Aggression: A social learning analysis*. Englewood Cliffs, N.J.: Prentice-Hall.

Bandura, A., and Walters, R. H. 1963. *Social learning and personality development*. New York: Holt.

Banfield, E. G. 1968. *The unheavenly city*. Revised 1974 as *The unheavenly city revisited*. Boston: Little Brown.

Banks, C., et al. 1975. Public attitudes to crime and the penal system. *British Journal of Criminology*, 15: 228–240.

Barlow, H. D., and Ferdinand, F. N. 1992. *Understanding Delinquency*. New York: Harper Collins.

Barndt, R. J., and Johnson, D. M. 1955. Time orientation in delinquents. *Journal of Abnormal and Social Psychology*, 51: 343–345.

Bartel, A. P. 1979. Women and crime: An economic analysis. *Economic Inquiry*, 4: 29–51.

Bartusch, D. J., and Matsueda, R. L. 1996. Gender, reflected appraisals and labeling: A cross-group test of an interactionist theory of delinquency. *Social Forces*, 75: 145–177.

Bassiouni, M. C. 1974. A survey of the major criminal justice systems in the world. In D. Glaser (Ed.), *Handbook of Criminology*. Chicago: Rand McNally.

Bateson, G. 1979. *Mind and nature*. New York: Dutton.

Beardslee, D. C., and O'Dowd, D. D. 1961. The college student image of the scientist. *Science*, (March 31) 133: 997–1001.

Beattie, R. H., and Bridges, C. K. 1970. *Superior court probation and/or jail sample*. Sacramento, Calif.: Department of Justice, Bureau of Crime Statistics.

Beck, B. 1967. Welfare as a moral category. *Social Problems*, 14: 258–277.

Becker, G. 1968. Crime and punishment: An economic approach. *Journal of Political Economy*, 76: 169–217.

Becker, H. S. 1963. *Outsiders: Studies in the sociology of deviance*. Glencoe, Ill.: Free Press.

Becker, H. S. 1974. Labelling theory reconsidered. In S. Messinger et al. (Eds.), *The Aldine crime and justice annual—1973*. Chicago: Aldine.

Behrman, S. N. 1972. People in a diary: I. *New Yorker*, (May 13) 48: 36–94.

Beilin, H. 1956. The pattern of postponability and its relation to social class mobility. *Journal of Social Psychology*, 44: 33–48.

Bell, R. Q., and Harper, L. V. (Eds.). 1977. *Child effects on adults*. Hillsdale, N.J.: Erlbaum.

Belle, M., and McQuillan, K. 1994. Births outside marriage: A growing alternative. *Canadian Social Trends*, Cat. 11-008E. Ottawa: Statistics Canada, Summer.

Bennett, T. 1986. A decision-making approach to opioid addiction. In Cornish, D. B., and Clarke, R. V., *The Reasoning Criminal: Rational Choice Perspectives on Offending*, New York: Springer-Verlag.

Bensing, R. C., and Schroeder, O. J. 1960. *Homicide in an urban community*. Springfield, Ill.: Thomas.

Benson, B. L., Kim, I., Rasmussen, D. W. 1994. Estimating deterrent effects: A public choice perspective on the economics of crime literature. *Southern Economic Journal*, 61: 161–168.

Bereiter, C. 1973. Education, socioeconomic status, IQ, and their effects. *Contemporary Psychology*, 18: 401–403.

Berger, P., and Luckmann, T. 1966. *The social construction of reality: A treatise in the sociology of knowledge*. Garden City, N.Y.: Doubleday.

Berkov, B., and Sklar, J. 1975. Methodological options in measuring illegitimacy and the difference they make. *Social Biology*, 22: 356–371.

Berkowitz, L. 1952. *Aggression: A social psychological analysis*. New York: McGraw-Hill.

Berkowitz, L. 1965. The concept of aggressive drive: Some additional considerations. In L. Berkowitz (Ed.), *Advances in experimental social psychology* (Vol. 2), New York: Academic.

Berkowitz, L. 1967. Readiness or necessity. *Contemporary Psychology*, 12: 580–582.

Berkowitz, L. 1968. Impulse, aggression, and the gun. *Psychology Today*, 2: 18–22.

Berkowitz, L. 1970. The contagion of violence: An S-R mediational analysis of some effects of observed aggression. In W.J. Arnold and M. M. Page (Eds.), *Nebraska Symposium on Motivation*. Lincoln: University of Nebraska Press.

Berkowitz, L. 1973. Words and symbols as stimuli to aggressive responses. In J. F. Knutson (Ed.), *The control of aggression: Implications from basic research*. Chicago: Aldine.

Berkowitz, L. 1974. Some determinants of impulsive aggression: Role of mediated associations with reinforcements for aggression. *Psychological Review*, 81: 165–176.

Berkowitz, L., and Macaulay, J. 1971. The contagion of criminal violence. *Sociometry*, 34: 238–260.

Berkowitz, L., and Rawlings, E. 1963. Effects of film violence on inhibitions against subsequent aggression. *Journal of Abnormal and Social Psychology*, 66: 405–412.

Bernard, T. J. 1987. Testing structural strain theories. *Journal of Research in Crime and Delinquency,* 24: 262–280.

Bernard, T. J. 1990. Twenty years of testing theories: What have we learned and why? *Journal of Research in Crime and Delinquency*, 27, 4: 325–347.

Beto, G. 1980. Commentary. In C. H. Foust and R. D. Webster (Eds.), *An anatomy of criminal justice*. Lexington, Mass.: Lexington Books.

Beynon, E. D. 1935. Crimes and customs of Hungarians in Detroit. *Journal of Criminal Law, Criminology, and Police Science*, 25: 755–774.

Biderman, A. D., et al. 1967. *Report on a pilot study in the District of Columbia on victimization and attitudes toward law enforcement. Field Survey I.* (President's Commission on Law Enforcement and Administrations of Justice) Washington, D.C.: U.S. Government Printing Office.

Bierce, A. 1958. *The devil's dictionary*. New York: Dover. (Originally published, 1911, by Neale Publishing Co.).

Biles, D. 1976. Population movements and crime. *Australian and New Zealand Journal of Criminology*, 9: 143–151.

Bixenstine, V. E., and Buterbaugh, R. L. 1957. Integrative behaviour in adolescent boys as a function of delinquency and race. *Journal of Consulting Psychology*, 31: 471–476.

Black, D. J. 1970. Production of crime rates. *American Sociological Review*, 35: 733–748.

Black, D. J., and Reiss, A. J., Jr. Patterns of behavior in police and citizen transactions. *Studies of crime and law enforcement in major metropolitan areas* (Sec. 1, Vol 2). Washington D.C.: U.S. Government Printing Office.

Black, D. J., and Reiss, A. J., Jr. 1970. Police control of juveniles. *American Sociological Review*, 35: 63–77.

Black, W. A. M., and Gregson, R. A. M. 1973. Time perspective, purpose in life, extraversion and neuroticism in New Zealand prisoners. *British Journal of Social and Clinical Psychology*, 12: 50–60.

Blake, J. 1961. *Family structure in Jamaica: The social context of reproduction*. New York: Free Press.

Blane, H. T. 1968. *The personality of the alcoholic*. New York: Harper and Row.

Blankenburg, E. 1976. The selectivity of legal sanctions: An empirical investigation of shoplifting. *Law and Society Review*, 11: 109–130.

Blau, J. R., and Blau, P. M. 1982. The cost of inequality: Metropolitan structure and violent crime. *American Sociological Review*, 47: 114–129.

Blau, P. M., and Duncan, O. D. 1967. *The American occupation structure*. New York: Wiley.

Blau, P. M., and Golden, R. M. 1986. Metropolitan structure and criminal violence. *Sociological Quarterly*, 27: 15–26.

Block, R. 1993. A crossnational comparison of victims of crime: Victim surveys of twelve countries. *International Review of Victimology*, 2: 183–207.

Block R., and Block, C. R. 1980. Decisions and data: the Transformation of robbery incidents into official robbery statistics. *Criminology*, 71: 622–636.

Bloom, B. A. 1964. *Stability and change in human characteristics*. New York: Wiley.

Blue, J. T., Jr. 1948. The relationship of juvenile delinquency, race, and economic status. *Journal of Negro Education*, 17: 469–477.

Blundell, W. E. 1980. Growing pains: New rural migration overburdens and alters once-sleepy hamlets. *Wall Street Journal*, (July 3) 103 1: 16.

Blumstein, A., Cohen, G., Roth, J. A., and Visher, C. A. (Eds.) 1986. *Criminal Careers and Career Criminals*. Vol. 2. Washington, D.C.: National Academy Press.

Boardman, W. K. 1962. Rusty: A brief behavior disorder. *Journal of Consulting Psychology*, 25: 293–297.

Boggs, S. L. 1965. Urban crime patterns. *American Sociological Review*, 30: 899–908.

Bohlke, T. 1961. Social mobility, stratification inconsistency, and middle-class delinquency. *Social Problems*, 8: 351–363.

Boland, B. 1976. Patterns of urban crime. In W. G. Skogan (Ed.), *Sample surveys of the victims of crime*. Cambridge, Mass.: Ballinger.

Bonger, A. 1913. *Geloof en Misdaad: Een Criminologische Studie*. Leiden: Brill.

Booth, A., and Welch, S. 1978. Spousal consensus and its correlates. *Journal of Marriage and Family*, 40: 23–34.

Booth, A., and Welch, S., and Johnson, D. R. 1976. Crowding and urban crime rates. *Urban Affairs Quarterly*, 11: 291–308.

Bordua, D. J. 1967. Recent trends: Deviant behavior and social control. *Annals of the American Academy of Political and Social Sciences*. 369: 149–163.

Borhek, J. T. 1970. Ethnic-group cohesion. *American Journal of Sociology*, 76: 33–46.

Boudon, R. 1974. *Education, opportunity, and social inequality*. New York: Wiley.

Boven, R., and O'Neill, D. P. 1975. *A regional analysis of juvenile offending in New Zealand* (Report No. 7). Wellington, New Zealand: Department of Social Welfare, Research Section.

Bowers, W. J., and Pierce, G. L. 1980. Arbitrariness and discrimination under post-Furman capital statutes. *Crime and Delinquency*, 26: 563–635.

Bowlby, J. 1952. *Maternal care and mental health*. Geneva: World Health Organization.

Bowlby, J. 1969. *Attachment and loss. Vol. 1. Attachment*. New York: Basic Books.

Bowling, B. 1993. Racial harassment and the process of victimization. *British Journal of Criminology*, 33: 231–250.

Boydell, C. L., and Grindstaff, C. F. 1972. Public opinion and criminal law: An empirical test of public attitudes toward legal sanctions. In C. L. Boydell, Grindstaff, C. F. and Whitehead, P. C. (Eds.), *Deviant Behavior and Societal Reaction*. Toronto: Holt.

Bradburn, N. M., and Sudman, S. 1991. The current status of questionnaire research. In Biemer, P., Groves, R. M., Lyberg, L. E., Mathiowetz, N. A. and Sudman, S. *Measurement Errors in Surveys*, New York: Wiley.

Braithwaite, J. 1979. *Inequality, Crime, and Public Policy*. London: Routledge and Kegan Paul.

Braithwaite, J. 1981. The myth of social class and criminality reconsidered. *American Sociological Review*, 46: 36–57.

Brantingham, P. J., and Brantingham, P. L. 1981. *Environmental Criminology*, Beverly Hills, CA: Sage Publications.

Braucht, G. N. et al. 1980. Victims of violent death: A critical review. *Psychology Bulletin*, 87: 309–333.

Brearley, H. C. 1932. *Homicide in the United States*. Chapel Hill: University of North Carolina Press.

Bregger, J. E. 1971. Unemployment statistics and what they mean. *Monthly Labor Review*, 94: 22–29.

Brenner, H. M. 1976. Effects of the economy on criminal behavior and the administration of criminal justice in the U.S., Canada, England and Wales. In *Economic Crisis and Crime: Correlations Between the State of the Economy, Deviance and the Control of Deviance*. Rome, Italy: U.N. Social Defense Research Institute.

Brenner, H. M. 1977. Does unemployment cause crime? *Criminal Justice Newsletter*, (October 24) 8: 5.

Brickman, P., et al. 1982. Models of helping and coping. *American Psychologist*, 37: 368–384.

Britt, C. 1994. Crime and unemployment among youths in the United States, 1958–1990. *American Journal of Economics and Sociology*, 53: 99–109.

Brock. D. 1960. The innocent mind: Or, my days as a juvenile delinquent. *Canadian Journal of Corrections*, 2: 25–35.

Brody, E. G., and Brody, N. 1976. *Intelligence: Nature, determinants, and consequences*. New York: Academic.

Brophy, B. 1980. Pay more, get less. *Forbes*, (April 14) 125: 34–36.

Brown, H. P. 1977. *The Inequality of Pay*. London: Oxford University Press.

Brown, J., and Gilmartin, B. G. 1969. Sociology today: Lacunae, emphases, and surfeits. *American Sociologist*, 4: 283–291.

Brown, M. J. et al. 1972. Criminal offences in an urban area and their associate social variables. *British Journal of Criminology*, 12: 250–268.

Brown, S. R. 1970–1971. Review of M. L. Kohn, *Class and conformity: A study in values*. *Public Opinion Quarterly*, 34: 654–655.

Bruce-Biggs, G. 1982. The dangerous folly called theory Z. *Fortune*, (May 17) 105: 41–54.

Bruinsma, G. J. N. 1992. Differential association theory reconsidered: a extension and its empirical test. *Journal of Quantitative Criminology*, 8: 29–49.

Builta, J. 1977. "Rio and Caracas experience violent crime increases." *CJ The Americas Online*. [www.ascp.uic.edu/oic/pubs/cja/090203.htm].

Bumpass, L. L., and Rindfuss, R. R. 1979. Children's experience of marital disruption. *American Journal of Sociology*, 85: 49–65.

Bumpass, L. L., Sweet, J. A., and Cherlin, A. 1991. The role of cohabitation in declining rates of marriage. *Journal of Marriage and the Family*, 53: 913–27.

Burchinal, L.G. 1964. Characteristics of adolescents from unbroken, broken, and reconstituted families. *Journal of Marriage and Family Living*, 26: 44–51.

Bureau of Justice Statistics. 1994. *Criminal victimization in the United States: 1972–1992 Trends*, Washington, D.C.: U.S. Department of Justice.

Burke, P. J., and Turk, A. T. 1975. Factors affecting post-arrest dispositions: A model for analysis. *Social Problems*, 22: 313–332.

Bursik, R. J. 1984. Urban dynamics and ecological studies of delinquency. *Social Forces*, 69: 393–413.

Burt, C. 1961. Intelligence and social mobility. *British Journal of Statistical Psychology*, 14: 3–24.

Burton R. V. 1963. Generality of honesty reconsidered. *Psychological Review*, 70: 481–499.

Burton, V. S., et al. 1994. Reconsidering strain theory: Operationalization, rival theories, and adult criminality. *Journal of Quantitative Criminology*, 10: 213–39.

Buss, A. H. 1961. *The psychology of aggression*. New York: Wiley.

Bustamente, M. E., and Bravo, M. A. 1957. Epidemiologia del homicido en Mexico. *Higiene*, 9: 21–33.

Butcher, H. J. 1968. *Human intelligence: Its nature and assessment. London: Methuen.*

Butts, J. A, et al. 1994. *Juvenile court statistics 1991*, U.S. Department of Justice, Office of Juvenile Justice and Delinquency Prevention, Washington, DC: USGPO.

Calhoun, J. B. 1962. Population density and social pathology. *Scientific American*, 206: 139–148.

Calhoun, J. B. 1962. A "behavioral sink." In E. L. Bliss (Ed.), *Roots of behavior*. New York: Harper.

Calonious, L. E. 1982. A new idea in the war on crime: Don't let the bad guys into town. *Wall Street Journal*, (January 14) 106: 25.

Cameron, M. O. 1953. *Department store shoplifting*. Doctoral Dissertation. Bloomington, Indiana University, Department of Sociology.

Cameron, M. O. 1964. *The booster and the snitch: Department store shoplifting*. Glenco, Ill.: Free Press.

Campbell, A., Muncer, S., and Coyle, E. 1992. Social representation of aggression as an explanation of gender differences. *Aggressive Behavior*, 18: 95–108.

Campbell, A., Muncer, S., and Gorman B. 1993. Sex and social representations of aggression: A communal-agentic analysis. *Aggressive Behavior*, 19: 125–35.

Canada. 1955. *Report of the Royal Commission on the law of insanity as a defence in criminal cases*. Ottawa: Queen's Printer and Controller of Stationery.

Canada. 1996. *Martin's Annual Criminal Code*. Toronto, Ont.: Canada Law Book.

Canadian Broadcasting Corporation. 1997. What does shoplifting cost? *StreetCents*, [www.halifax.cbc.ca/streetcents/crime/price.html].

Canadian Press. 1975a. Maloney due in court Dec. 4. (November 7).

Canadian Press. 1975b. Two charged over pamphlets. (June 30).

Canadian Press. 1975c. We can police NHL, Morrison says. (November 7).

Canadian Press. 1995. Constitutional right to incest rejected by court. *Toronto Star*, (August 17), p. A15.

Canadian Press. 1996. Executive shot by former wife plans to remarry. *Toronto Star*, (July 15), p. A10.

Caplan, P. J., et al. 1980. Sex differences in a delinquent clinic population. *British Journal of Criminology*, 20: 311–328.

Caplow, T., et al. 1964. *The Urban ambiance: A study of San Juan, Puerto Rico*. Totowa, N.J.: Bedminster.

Card, J. J. 1978. The correspondence of data gathered from husband and wife: Implications for family planning studies. *Social Biology*, 25: 196–204.

Carr-Hill, R. 1970. *The violent offender: Reality or illusion*? Oxford: Blackwell.

Carr-Hill, R. A., and Stern, N. H. 1973. An econometric model of supply and control of recorded offense in England and Wales. *Journal of Public Economics*, 2: 289–318.

Carroll, L. 1974. *Race and sexual assault in a prison*. Kingston, R.I.: University of Rhode Island, Department of Sociology. (Mimeograph).

Carroll, L. 1977. Humanitarian reform and biracial sexual assault in a maximum security prison. *Urban Life*, 5: 417–437.

Carroll, J. and Weaver, F. 1986. Shoplifters' perceptions of crime opportunities: a process-tracing study. In Cornish, D. B. and Clarke, R. V. *The reasoning criminal: Rational choice perspectives on offending*, New York: Springer-Verlag.

Carson, W. B. 1970. White-collar crime and the enforcement of factory legislation. *British Journal of Criminology*, 10: 383–398.

Cartwright, N. 1989. *Nature's capacities and their measurement*. Oxford: Clarendon Press.

Catanzaro, R. 1992. *Men of respect: A social history of the Sicilian mafia*. New York: Free Press.

Cattell, R. B. 1979. *Personality and learning theory. Vol. 1: The structure of personality in its environment*. New York: Springer.

Cernkovich, S. A., Giordano, P. C., and Pugh, M. D. 1985. Chronic offenders: the missing case in self-report delinquency research. *Journal of Criminal Law and Criminology*, 76: 705–732.

Ceylon Department of Census and Statistics. 1957. *Juvenile probations in Ceylon*. Ceylon: Government Press.

Chambliss, W. J. 1964. A sociological analysis of the law of vagrancy. *Social Problems*, 12: 67–77.

Chambliss, W. J. 1973. Elites and the creation of criminal law. In W.J. Chamblis (Ed.), *Sociological readings in the conflict perspective*. Reading, Mass.: Addison-Wesley.

Chambliss, W. J. 1974. The state, the law, and the definition of behavior as criminal or delinquent. In D. Glasser (Ed.), *Handbook of criminology*. Chicago: Rand McNally.

Chambliss, W. J., and Ryther, T. E. 1975. *Sociology: The discipline and its direction*. New York: McGraw-Hill.

Chandler, D. B., et al. 1976. *Ethnic bias in commuting mandatory death sentences. Canada 1945–1962*. Honolulu: University of Hawaii, Department of Sociology. (Mimeograph).

Chapman, B., Levine, D., and Easterliln, R. 1981. What does the 1980 census show? Looking ahead and looking back. *Public Opinion*, 4: 14–20.

Cherlin, A. J. 1992. *Marriage, Divorce, Remarriage*. Cambridge, Mass.: Harvard University Press.

Chesney-Lind, M. and Sheldon, R. 1992. *Girls: Delinquency and Juvenile Justice*. Pacific Grove, Calif.: Brooks/Cole.

Chilton, R. J., and Markle, G. E. 1972. Family disruption delinquent conduct, and the effect of subclassification. *American Sociological Review*, 37: 93–99.

Chilton, R. J., and Spielberger, A. 1971. Is crime increasing? Age structure and the crime rate. *Social Forces*, 49: 487–93.

Chiricos, T. G. 1987. Rates of crime and unemployment: An analysis of aggregate research evidence. *Social Problems*, 34: 187–212.

Cho, S. T. 1967. *A cross-cultural analysis of the criminality level index*. Doctoral dissertation. Columbus: Ohio State University Department of Sociology.

Cho, Y. H. 1974. *Public policy and urban crime*. Cambridge, Mass.: Ballinger.

Choldin, H. M. 1994. *Looking for the last percent: The controversy over census undercounts*. New Brunswick, NJ: Rutgers University Press.

Christensen L., 1974. Generality of personality assessment. *Journal of Consulting and Clinical Psychology*, 42: 59–64.

Cincinnati Inquirer, The Legal Intelligencer. 1997. *Burden of Proof*, (August 31).

Clarity, J. F. 1996. Police lift ban on march by Ulster Protestant group. *The New York Times*, 145, p. A2, (July 12).

Clark, J. P,. and Tifft, L. L. 1966. Polygraph and interview validation of self-reported deviant behavior. *American Sociological Review*, 31: 516–523.

Clark, R. 1970. *Crime in America*. New York: Simon and Schuster.

Clarke, B. 1975. The causes of biological diversity. *Scientific American*, 223: 50–60.

Clement, P. W. 1970. Elimination of sleepwalking in a seven-year-old boy. *Journal of Consulting and Clinical Psychology*, 34: 22–26.

Clinard, M. 1942. The process of urbanization and criminal behavior; A study of culture and conflicts. *American Journal of Sociology*, 48: 202–213.

Clinard, M. 1960. A cross-cultural replication of the relation of urbanism to criminal behavior. *American Sociological Review*, 25: 253–257.

Cloward, R. A., and Ohlin, L. E. 1960. *Delinquency and opportunity: A theory of delinquent gangs*. New York: Free Press.

Cocozza, J. J., and Steadman, H. J. 1976. The failure of psychiatric predictions of dangerousness: Clear and convincing evidence. *Rutgers Law Review*, 29: 1084–1101.

Coeffic, N. 1993. Le recensement de 1990: L'enquête de mesure d'exhaustivité. *Journal de la Société de Paris*, 134: 3–20.

Cohen, A. K. 1955. *Delinquent boys: The culture of the gang*. Glencoe, Ill.: Free Press.

Cohen, L. E. 1981. Modeling crime trends: A criminal opportunity perspective *Journal of Research in Crime and Delinquency*, 18: 138–162.

Cohen, L. E., and Felson, M. 1979. Social change and crime rate trends: A routine activity approach. *American Sociological Review*, 44: 488–608.

Cohen, L. E., Felson, M., and Land, K. D. 1980. Property crime rates in the United States: A macrodynamic analysis, 1947–1977; with ex ante forecasts for the mid-1980s. *American Journal of Sociology*, 66: 90–118.

Cohen, M. R., and Nagel E. 1931. *Reason and nature*. New York: Harcourt, Brace.

Cohen, S. (Ed.). 1971. *Images of deviance*. Middlesex, England: Penguin.

Coleman, J. S. 1974. Review essay: Inequality, sociology and more philosophy. *American Journal of Sociology*, 80: 39–764.

Coleman, J. S., et al. 1966. *Equality of educational opportunity, Section I: Summary*. Washington, D.C.: U.S. Government Printing Office.

Coleman, J. S., et al. 1966. *Equality of educational opportunity, Section II: Statistical summary*. Washington, D.C.: U.S. Government Printing Office.

Collingwood, R. G. 1940. *An essay on metaphysics*. Oxford: Clarendon.

Comstock, G. 1975. The effects of television on children and adolescents: The evidence so far. *Journal of Communication*, 25: 25–34.

Connor, W. D. 1972. *Deviance in Soviet society: Crime, delinquency, and alcoholism*. New York: Columbia University Press.

Coopersmith, S. 1969. Review of M. R. Yarrow et al., *Child rearing. Contemporary Psychology*, 14: 369–371.

Copperman, P. 1980. *The literacy hoax: The decline of reading, writing, and learning in the public schools and what we can do about it*. New York: Morrow, 1980.

Corman, H. 1981. Criminal deterrence in New York: The relationship between court activities and crime. *Economic Inquiry*, 19: 476–87.

Coté, J., and Allahar, A. 1994. *Generation on hold*. Toronto: Stoddart.

Courtwright, D. T. 1996. *Violent land: Single men and social disorder from the frontier to the inner city*. Cambridge, Mass.: Harvard University Press.

Cousineau, F. D. 1967. *Some current conceptions of rationality and the policy sciences.* Edmonton: University of Alberta, Department of Sociology, M.A. dissertation.

Cousineau, F. D., and Veevers, J. E. 1972. Juvenile justice: an analysis of the Canadian Young Offenders Act. In Boydell, C., Grindstaff, C. F. and Whitehead, P. C.(Eds.), *Deviant behavior and societal reaction.* Toronto: Holt.

Crespi, L. 1971. What kinds of attitude measures are predictive of behavior? *Public Opinion Quarterly*, 35: 327–334.

Cressey, D. R. 1953. *Other people's money: A study in the social psychology of embezzlement.* Belmont, Calif.: Wadsworth, (2nd ed., 1971).

Cressey, D. R. 1964. *Causes of employee dishonesty.* Paper presented at the Top Management Business Security Seminar. East Lansing, Mich., (April 15).

Crockett, H. J. 1962. The achievement motive and differential occupational mobility in the United States. *American Sociological Review*, 27: 191–204.

Cromwell, P. 1996. *In their own words: Criminals on crime.* Los Angeles: Roxbury Publishing Company.

Cromwell, P., and McElrath, K. 1994. Buying stolen property: an opportunity perspective. *Journal of Research in Crime and Delinquency*, 31: 295–310.

Crook, E. B. 1934. Cultural marginality in sexual delinquency. *American Journal of Sociology*, 39: 493–500.

Crosby, F. 1976. A model of egoistical relative deprivation. *Psychological Review*, 83: 85–113.

Cross, H. J. 1964. The outcome of psychotherapy: A selected analysis of research findings. *Journal of Consulting Psychology*, 28: 413–417.

Crutchfield, R. D., Geerken, M. R., and Gove, W. R. 1982. Crime rate and social integration: The impact of metropolitan mobility. *Criminology*, 20: 467–478.

CTV Eye-to-eye: On public apathy. Broadcast of January 28, 1974.

Cuber, J., and Harroff, P. 1966. *The significant Americans.* Garden City, N.Y.: Doubleday.

Culliton, B. J. 1975. Habitat: U.N. conference to face crises in human settlements. *Science*, (December 19) 190: 1181–1183.

Curlee, J. A. 1970. A comparison of male and female patients at an alcoholism treatment centre. *Journal of Psychology*, 74: 239–247.

Czaja, R. and Blair, J. 1990. Using network sampling in crime victimization surveys. *Journal of Quantitative Criminology*, 6: 185–206.

Dallago, B. 1990. *The irregular economy.* Aldershot, UK: Dartmouth.

Danser, K. R., and Laub, J. H. 1981. *Juvenile criminal behavior and its relation to economic conditions* (Monograph Four of Analysis of National Crime Victimization Survey Data to Study Serious Delinquent Behavior). Washington, D.C.: Department of Justice.

Danziger, S. 1976. Explaining urban crime rates. *Criminology*, 14: 291–295.

Danziger, S., and Wheeler, D. 1975. The economics of crime: Punishment or income redistribution? *Review of Sociology and Economics*, 33: 113–131.

Danzinger, S., and Gottschalk, P. 1995. *America unequal.* Cambridge, Mass.: Harvard University Press.

Davids, A., et al. 1962. Time orientation in male and female juvenile delinquents. *Journal of Abnormal and Social Psychology*, 64: 239–240.

Davies, J. C. 1962. Toward a theory of revolution. *American Sociological Review*, 27: 5–18.

Davis, A., and Dollard, J. 1941. *Children of bondage.* Washington, D.C.: American Council on Education.

Davis A., and Havighurst, R. 1947. *Father of the man: How your child gets his personality.* Boston: Houghton Mifflin.

Davis, A. J. 1969. *Report on sexual assaults in the Philadelphia prison system and sheriff's vans.* Philadelphia District Attorney's Office and Police Department, n.d.

Davis, M. S. 1971. That's interesting! *Philosophy of the Social Sciences.* 1: 309–344.

Dawkins, R. 1989. *The selfish gene.* New York: Oxford.

de Carufel, A., and Schopler, J. 1979. Evaluation of outcome improvement resulting from threats and appeals. *Journal of Personality and Social Psychology*, 37: 662–673.

de Charms, R. 1968. *Personal causation: The internal affective determinants of behavior.* New York: Academic Press.

De Fleur, M., and Quinney, R. 1966. A reformulation of Sutherland's differential association theory and a strategy for empirical verification. *Journal of Research on Crime and Delinquency*, 3: 1–22.

DeKeseredy, W. S., and Hinch, R. 1991. *Woman abuse.* Toronto: Thompson Educational Publishing.

Della Fave, L. R. 1974. On the structure of egalitarianism. *Social Problems*, 22: 199–213.

Dershowitz, A. 1994. *The abuse excuse.* Boston: Little-Brown.

Diamond, B. L. 1961. Criminal responsibility of the mentally ill. *Stanford Law Review*, 1961–1962, 14: 59–68.

Di Cara, L. V. 1970. Learning in the autonomic nervous system. *Scientific American*, 222: 31–39.

Dinitz, S., et al. 1962. Delinquency vulnerability: A cross-group and longitudinal analysis. *American Sociological Review*, 27: 515–517.

Dobash, R. P., Dobash, R. E., Wilson, M., and Daly, M. 1992. The myth of sexual symmetry in marital violence. *Social Problems*, 39: 71–91.

Doherty, P., and Joyal, R. 1979. *Some selected statistics on homicide and other violent crime in Canada.* Ottawa: Ministry of the Solicitor General.

Dollard, J., et al. 1939. *Frustration and aggression.* New Haven: Yale University Press.

Doob, A. 1991. Crime, race and politics. *Toronto Star*, (October 17).

dos Santos, A. T. 1969. 1959 Lampeao, king of the bandits. Cited by E. J. Hobsbawm in *Bandits*: London: Weidenfeld and Nicholson.

Douglas, J. D. 1967. *The social meanings of suicide.* Princeton: Princeton University Press.

Douvan, E. 1956. Social status and success strivings. *Journal of Abnormal and Social Psychology*, 52: 219–223.

Douvan E., and Edieson, J. 1958. The psychodynamics of social mobility in adolescent boys. *Journal of Abnormal and Social Psychology*, 56: 31–44.

Downs, W. R., and Robertson, J. F. 1990. Referral for treatment among adolescent alcohol and drug abusers. *Journal of Research in Crime and Delinquency*, 27: 190–209.

Downes, D. M. 1966. *The delinquent solution.* New York: Free Press.

Dowrick, S., and Quiggin, J. 1997. True measures of GDP and convergence. *The American Economic Review*, 87: 41–64.

Du Cette, J., and Wolk, S. 1972. Locus of control and extreme behavior. *Journal of Consulting and Clinical Psychology*, 39: 253–258.

Duncan, O. D. 1961. A socioeconomic index for all occupations. In A. J. Reiss, Jr. (Ed.), *Occupations and social status.* New York: Free Press.

Duncan, O. D., Featherman, D. L., and Duncan, B. 1972. *Socioeconomic background and achievement.* New York: Seminar Press.

Durkheim, E. 1951. *Suicide: A study in sociology* (G. Simpson, Ed.). Glencoe, Ill.: Free Press.

Durkheim, E. 1958. *The rules of sociological method* (S. A. Solovay and J. H. Mueller, trans.). Glencoe, Ill.: Free Press.

Easterlin, R. A. 1973. Does money buy happiness? *Public Interest*, 30: 3–10.

Economist. 1981. Down with deviance. (October 17) 281: 43–44.

Economist. 1981. A bridge to Ireland. (May 23) 179: 11–13.

Economist. 1996. War cancelled: American trade policy. (June 22) 339: 72.

Economist. 1997. World education league. Who's top? (March 29) 342: 21–23.

Edwards, T. A. 1977. *A test of vagrancy law research used by Chambliss in support of the conflict perspective in criminology.* Master of arts dissertation. Edmonton, University of Alberta, Department of Sociology.

European Committee on Crime Problems. 1970. *Methods of forecasting trends in criminality.* Strasbourg: Council of Europe.

Ehrlich, I. 1973. Participation in illegitimate activities: A theoretical and empirical investigation, *Journal of Political Economy*, 81: 521–565.

Ehrlich, I. 1974. Participation in illegitimate activities: An economic analysis. In G. S. Becker and W. M. Landes (Eds.), *Essays in the economics of crime and punishment.* New York: Columbia University Press.

Ehrlich, I. 1975. The deterrent effect of capital punishment: A question of life and death. *American Economic Review*, 65: 397–417.

Ehrlich, I. 1977. Capital Punishment and deterrence: Some further thoughts and additional evidence. *Journal of Political Economy*, 85: 741–788.

Eliot, T. S. 1948. *Notes towards a definition of culture*. London: Faber.

Elliott, D. S., and Ageton, S. S. 1980. Reconciling race and class differences in self-reported and official estimates of delinquency. *American Sociological Review*, 45: 95–110.

Elwin, V. 1950. *Maria murder and suicide*. (2d ed.). London: Oxford University Press.

Embree, B. G., and Whitehead, P. C. 1993. Validity and reliability of self reported drinking behavior: Dealing with the problem of response bias. *Journal of Studies on Alcohol*, 54: 334–344.

English, K. 1993. Self-reported crime rates of women prisoners. *Journal of Quantitative Criminology*, 9: 357–382.

Ennis, B. J., and Litwak, T. R. 1976. Psychiatry and the presumption of expertise: Flipping coins in the courtroom. *California Law Review*, 62: 693–752.

Ennis, P. H. 1967. *Criminal victimization in the United States: A report of a national survey*. Washington, D.C.: United States Government Printing Office.

Ericson, R. V. 1975. *Criminal reactions: The labelling perspective*. Lexington, Mass.: Lexington Books.

Ericson, R. V. 1981. *Making crime: A study of detective work*. Toronto: University of Toronto Press.

Ericson, R. V. 1982. *Reproducing order: A study of police patrol work*. Toronto: University of Toronto Press.

Eron, L. D., et al. 1971. *Learning of aggression in children*. Boston: Little, Brown.

Erskine, H. 1967. The polls: Demonstrations and race riots. *Public Opinion Quarterly*, 31: 655–677.

Evans, J. L., et al. 1982. *Victimization in Greater Vancouver*. Ottawa: Ministry of the Solicitor General, Research Division.

Eysenck, H. J. 1966. *The effects of psychotherapy*. New York: International Science Press.

Eysenck, H. J. 1977. *Crime and personality* (2d ed.). London: Paladin.

Eysenck, H. J., and Nias, D. K. B. 1978. *Sex, violence, and the media*. London: Temple Smith.

Eysenck, M. W. 1976. Extraversion, verbal learning, and memory. *Psychological Bulletin*, 93: 76–90.

Fagan, J., and Brown, A. 1994. Violence between spouses and intimates: Physical aggression between women and men in intimate relationships. In Reiss, A. J. and Roth, J. A. (Eds.) *Understanding and preventing violence, Vol. 3*, Washington, D.C.: National Academy Press.

Fairchild, H. P. (Ed.). 1944. *Dictionary of sociology*. New York: Philosophical Library.

Fancher, R. E., Jr. 1966. Explicit personality theories and accuracy in person perception. *Journal of Personality*, 34: 252–261.

Fancher, R. E., Jr. 1967. Accuracy vs. validity in person perception. *Journal of Consulting Psychology*, 31: 264–269.

Franchini, A. and Introna, F. 1961. *Delinquenze Minorile*. Padua: Cedam.

Farley, F. H., and Farley, S. V. 1972. Stimulus-seeking motivation and delinquent behavior among institutionalized delinquent girls. *Journal of Consulting and Clinical Psychology*, 39: 94–97.

Farnsworth, P. R. 1975. Note 64 in appendix to R. T. La Piere and P. R. Farnsworth. *Social psychology* (3rd ed.). New York: McGraw-Hill.

Farnworth, M., and Leiber, M. J. 1989. Strain theory revisited: Economic goals, educational means, and delinquency. *American Sociological Review*, 54: 263–274.

Farrell, W. 1986. *Why men are the way they are: The male-female dynamic*. New York: McGraw-Hill.

Farrington, D. P., and Knight, B. J. 1980. Four studies of stealing as a risky decision. In P. D. Lipsitt and B. D. Sales (Eds.), *New directions in psycholegal research*. New York: Van Nostrand Reinhold.

Farrington, D. P., et al. 1990. Advancing knowledge about the onset of delinquency and crime. In Lakey, B. B. and A. E. Kazdin (eds.) *Advances in clinical and child psychology*, Vol. 13: New York Plenum.

FBI. 1981. *Uniform crime reports for the United States: Crime in the United States: 1980.* Washington, D.C.: U.S. Government Printing Office.

FBI. 1992. *Uniform crime reports for the United States: Crime in the United States: 1991.* Washington, D.C.: U.S. Government Printing Office.

FBI. 1996. *Uniform crime reports for the United States: Crime in the United States: 1995.* Washington, D.C.: U.S. Government Printing Office.

Feather, N. T. 1967. Some personality correlates of external control. *Australian Journal of Psychology*, 19: 253–260.

Feeny, F. 1986. Robbers as decision makers. In Cornish, D. B. and Clarke, R. V. *The reasoning criminal: Rational choice perspectives on offending*, New York: Springer-Verlag.

Feldman, R. E. 1968. Response to compatriot and foreigner who seek assistance. *Journal of Personality and Social Psychology,* 10:202–214.

Felson, R.B., Liska, A.E., South, S.J. and McNulty, T.L. 1994. "The subculture of violence and delinquency: Individual vs. school context effects." *Social Forces*, 73: 155–173.

Fenna, D., et al. 1971. Ethanol metabolism in various racial groups. *Canadian Medical Association Journal*, (September 4), 105: 472–475.

Ferdinand, T. 1970. Demographic shifts and criminality: an inquiry. *British Journal of Criminology*, 10: 169–175.

Fergusson, D. M., Donnell, A. A., and Slater, S. W. 1975. *The effects of race and socio-economic status on juvenile offending statistics.* Wellington, N.Z.: Shearer Government Printer.

Fergusson, D. M., Harwood, L. J., and Lynskey, M. T. 1993. Ethnicity and bias in police contact statistics. *Australian and New Zealand Journal of Criminology*, 26: 193–206.

Ferracuti, F. 1968. European migration and crime. In M. E. Wolfgang (Ed.), *Crime and culture: Essays in honour of Thorsten Sellin*. New York: Wiley.

Ferracuti, F., Dinitz, S., and Acosta E. 1975. *Delinquents and nondelinquents in the Puerto Rican slum culture.* Columbus: Ohio State University Press.

Ferracuti, F., et al. 1962. A study of police errors in crime classification. *Journal of Criminal Law, Criminology and Police Science*, 53: 113–119.

Ferri, E. 1895. *L'omicidio nell'antropologia criminale*. Torino: Bocca.

Feshbach, S. 1961. The stimulating versus cathartic effects of vicarious aggressive activity. *Journal of Abnormal and Social Psychology*, 63: 382–385.

Field, S. 1990. Trends in crime and their interpretation: a study of recorded crime in post-war England and Wales. *Home Office Research Study*, No. 119. London: HMSO.

Fineman, H., Miller, S., Wingert, P., and Samuels, A. 1994. Marion Barry's revival act. *Newsweek*, (September 26).

Fiora-Gormally, N. 1978. Battered wives who kill: Double standard out of court, single standard in? *Law and Human Behaviour*, 2: 133–165.

Fishbein, M., and Ajzen, I. 1972. Attitudes and opinions. In P. H. Mussen and M. R. Rosenzweig (Eds.), *Annual Review of Psychology* (Vol. 23). Palo Alto: Annual Reviews.

Flacks, R., and Turkel, G. 1978. Radical sociology: the emergence of neo-Marxian perspectives in U.S. sociology. In R. H. Turner, J. Coleman, and R. C. Fox (Eds.), *Annual Review of Sociology* (Vol. 4), Palo Alto: Annual Reviews.

Foa, U. G., et al. 1976. Some evidence against the possibility of utopian societies. *Journal of Personality and Social Psychology,* 34: 1043–1048.

Folha de São Paulo. 1996. Grande SP registra queda em homicídos. (December 10).

Forest, M. L., Fisher, B. A., and Coates, R. B. 1985. Indeterminate and determinate sentencing of juvenile delinquents: A national survey of approaches to commitment and release decision making. *Juvenile and Family Court Journal*, 36: 1–11.

Forslund, M. A. 1970. A comparison of Negro and white crime rates. *Journal of Criminal Law, Criminology, and Police Science*, 61: 214–217.

Fox, J., and Hartnagel, T. F. 1979. Changing social roles and female crime in Canada. A time series analysis. *Canadian Review of Sociology and Anthropology*, 16: 96–104.

Franchini, A., and Introna, F. 1961. *Delinquenze minorile*. Padova: Decam.

Frankel, B. G., and Whitehead, P. C. 1981. *Drinking and damage: Theoretical advances and implications for prevention.* New Brunswick, N.J.: Rutgers Center of Alcohol Studies.

Franks, D. M. 1956. Conditioning and personality. *Journal of Abnormal and Social Psychology,* 52: 143–150.

Franks, D. M. 1961. Conditioning and abnormal behavior. In H. J. Eysenck (Ed.), *Handbook of abnormal psychology.* New York: Basic Books.

Freedman, D. G. 1971. Genetic influences on development of behavior. In G. B. A. Stoelinga and J. J. Van der Werff ten Bosch (Eds.), *Normal and abnormal development of brain and behavior.* Leiden: Leiden University Press.

Freedman, D. G. 1974. *Cradleboarding and temperament.* Paper presented at the annual meeting of the American Association for the Advancements of Science. San Francisco, (February 28).

Freedman, J. L. 1975. *Crowding and behavior.* San Francisco: Freeman.

Freedman, J. L., Heshka, S., and Levy, A. 1975. Population density and pathology in metropolitan areas. Appendix 1 in J. L. Freedman, *Crowding and behavior.* San Francisco: Freeman.

Fregier, H. A. 1840. *Des classes dangereuses de la population dans les grandes villes, et des moyens de les rendre meilleures.* Paris: Balliere.

Freud, A., and Dan, S. 1951. An experiment in group upbringing. In R. S. Eisler et al (Eds.), *The psychoanalytic study of the child* (Vol. 6). New York: International Universities Press.

Friedman, L. M. 1975. *The legal system: A social science perspective.* New York: Russell Sage Foundation.

Friedrich, P. 1962. Assumptions underlying Tarascan political homicide. *Psychiatry,* 25: 315–327.

Friedrich, R. 1977. *The impact of organizational, individual, and situational factors on police behavior.* Doctoral dissertation, Ann Arbor: University of Michigan.

Frodi, A., Macaulay, J., and Thome, P. R. 1977. Are women always less aggressive than men? A review of the experimental literature. *Psychological Bulletin,* 84: 634–660.

Frumkin, N. 1992. *Tracking America's economy.* Armonk, N.Y.: M. E. Sharp.

Furstenburg, F. F. et al. 1992. The next generation: The children of teenage mothers grow up. In Rosenheim, M. K. and Testa, M. F. (Eds.) *Early Parenthood and Coming of Age in the 1990s.* New Brunswick, N.J.: Rutgers University Press.

Gabor, T. 1994. The suppression of crime statistics on race and ethnicity: The price of political correctness. *Canadian Journal of Criminology,* 36: 153–163.

Gabor, T., and Roberts, J. 1990. Lombrosian wine in a new bottle: Research on crime and race. *Canadian Journal of Criminology,* 32: 291–313.

Gabor, T., and Roberts, J. 1990. Rushton on race and crime: The evidence remains unconvincing. *Canadian Journal of Criminology,* 32: 335–343.

Gaito, J., and Zavala, A. 1964. Neurochemistry and learning. *Psychological Bulletin,* 61: 45–62.

Gaddy, G. D. 1988. High school order and academic achievement. *American Journal of Education,* 96: 496–518.

Gale, F., and Wundersitz, J. 1989. The operation of hidden prejudice in pre-court procedures in the case of Australian aboriginal youth. *Australian and New Zealand Journal of Criminology,* 22: 1–21.

Galle, O. R., Gove, W. R., and McPherson, J. M. 1972. Population density and pathology: What are the relations for man? *Science,* (April 7) 176: 23–30.

Ganzer, V. J., and Sarason, I. G. 1973. Variables associated with recidivism among juvenile delinquents. *Journal of Consulting and Clinical Psychology,* 40: 1–5.

Gardiner, J. 1967. Public attitudes toward gambling and corruption. *Annals of the American Academy of Political and Social Science.* 374: 123–124.

Garfinkel, H. 1956. Conditions of successful degradation ceremonies. *American Journal of Sociology,* 61: 420–424.

Garofalo, J., and Hindelang, M. R. 1977. *An introduction to the National Crime Survey.* Washington, D.C.: U.S. Government Printing Office.

Gartner, R. 1991. Family structure, welfare spending, and child homicide in developed democracies. *Journal of Marriage and the Family,* 53: 231–240.

Gastil, R. D. 1971. Homicide and a regional culture of violence. *American Sociological Review,* 36: 412–417.

Gastil, R. D. 1976. The comparative survey of freedom: VI. *Freedom at Issue*. 34: 11–20.

Geen, R. G. 1975. The meaning of observed violence: Real vs. fictional violence and consequent effects of aggression and emotional arousal. *Journal of Research on Personality*, 9: 270–281.

Geen, R. G., et al. 1975. The facilitation of aggression by aggression: Evidence against the catharsis hypothesis. *Journal of Personality and Social Psychology*, 31: 721–726.

Geen, R. G., and Stonner, D. 1974. The meaning of observed violence: Effects on arousal and aggressive behavior. *Journal of Research on Personality*, 8: 55–63.

Geis, G. 1972. *"Not the law's business?": An examination of homosexuality, abortion, prostitution, narcotics, and gambling in the United States*. Rockville, Md.: Centre for Studies in Crime and Delinquency.

Geschwender, J. 1968. Explorations in the theory of social movements and revolutions. *Social Forces*, 47: 127–135.

Gibbens, T. C. N. 1963. The effects of physical ill-health in adolescent delinquents. *Proceedings of Research in Social Medicine*, 56: 1086–1088.

Gibbons, D. C. 1968. *Society, crime and criminal careers: An introduction to criminology*. Englewood Cliffs, N.J.: Prentice-Hall.

Gibbons, D. C. 1969. Crime and punishment: A study in social attitudes. *Social Forces*, 47: 391–397.

Gibson, J. L. 1978. Race as a determinant of criminal sentences: A methodological critique and a case study. *Law and Sociology Review*, 12: 455–478.

Giggs, J. A. 1970. The socially disorganised areas of Barry: A multivariate analysis. In M. Carter and W. K. Davies (Eds.), *Urban essays: Studies in the geography of Wales*. London: Longmans.

Gilbert, J. A. L. 1976. Royal Alexandra Hospital survey. *Edmonton Journal*, (September 17), A–17.

Gilbert, S. 1995. Quality education: Does class size matter? *Research File*, Association of Universities and Colleges of Canada, 1: 1–8.

Gilder, G. 1974. *Naked nomads: Unmarried men in America*. New York: Quadrangle.

Ginzberg, E. 1980. Youth unemployment. *Scientific American*, 242: 43–49.

Given, J. B. 1977. *Society and homicide in thirteenth century England*. Stanford: Stanford University Press.

Glanz, L. 1990. Status of the self-report procedure in criminological research. *South African Journal of Sociology*, 21: 96–103.

Glazer, N., and Moynihan, D. P. 1963. *Beyond the melting pot*. Cambridge Mass.: M.I.T. and Harvard University Press.

Glazer, N., and Moynihan, D. P. 1975. *Ethnicity: Theory and experience*. Cambridge, Mass.: Harvard University Press.

Glenn, N. D. 1974–1975. Recent trends in white-non-white attitudinal differences. *Public Opinion Quarterly*, 38: 596–604.

Glueck, S., and Glueck, E. 1956. *Unravelling juvenile delinquency*. Cambridge, Mass.: Harvard University Press.

Gold, T. 1969. Roles in sociological field observation. In G. J. McCall and J. L. Simmons (Eds.) *Issues in participant observation*. Reading, Mass.: Addison-Wesley.

Goldberg, L. R. 1968. Simple models or simple processes? Some research on clinical judgements. *American Psychologist*, 23: 483–496.

Goldberg, L. R. 1970. Man versus model of man: A rationale, plus some evidence for a method of improving on clinical inference. *Psychological Bulletin*, 73: 422–432.

Goldfarb, W. 1943. Effects of early institutional care on adolescent personality. *Child Development*, 14: 213–223.

Goldfarb, W. 1943. Effects of early institutional care on adolescent personality. *Journal of Experimental Education*, 12: 106–129.

Goldfarb, W. 1943. Infant rearing and problem behavior. *American Journal of Orthopsychiatry*, 13: 249–265.

Goldfarb, W. 1944a. Effects of early institutional care on adolescent personality: Rorscharch data. *American Journal of Orthopsychiatry*, 14: 441–447.

Goldfarb, W. 1944b. Infant rearing as a factor in foster home replacement. *American Journal of Orthopsychiatry*, 14: 162–173.

Goldfarb, W. 1945a. Effects of psychological deprivation in infancy and subsequent stimulation. *American Journal of Psychiatry*, 102: 18–33.

Goldfarb, W. 1945b. Psychological privation in infancy and subsequent adjustment. *American Journal of Orthopsychiatry*, 15: 247–255.

Goldman, M. 1963. *The differential selection of juvenile offenders for court appearance.* New York: National Council on Crime and Delinquency.

Goldschmidt, W. 1959. *Man's way: An introduction to the understanding of human society.* New York: Holt.

Goldstein, A. S. 1967. *The insanity defense.* New Haven: Yale University Press.

Goldstein, J. H., and Arms, R. L. 1971. Effects of observing athletic contests on hostility. *Sociometry*, 34: 83–90.

Goode, W. J. 1936. *After divorce.* Glencoe, Ill.: Free Press.

Goode, W. J. 1960. Illegitimacy in the Caribbean social structure. *American Sociological Review*, 25: 21–30.

Goode, W.J . 1966. Family disorganization. In R. K. Merton and R. A. Nisbet (Eds.), *Contemporary social problems* (2nd ed.). New York: Harcourt, Brace.

Goode, W. J. 1967. The protection of the inept. *American Sociological Review*, 32: 5–19.

Goodman, P. 1956. *Growing up absurd.* New York: Random House.

Goranson, R. E. 1969. The catharsis effect: Two opposing views. In R. K. Baker and S. J. Ball (Eds.), *Violence and the media. A staff report to the National Commission on the Causes and Prevention of Violence.* Washington, D.C.: U.S. Government Printing Office.

Gordon, M. M. 1964. *Assimilation in American life.* New York: Oxford University Press.

Gottfredson, M. R. 1981. On the etiology of criminal victimization. *Journal of Criminal Law and Criminology*, 72: 714–726.

Gottfredson, M. R., and Gottfredson, D. M. 1980. *Decisionmaking in criminal justice: Toward the rational exercise of discretion.* Cambridge, Mass.: Ballinger.

Gottfredson, M. R., and Hindelang, M. J. 1979. A study of the behavior of law. *American Sociological Review*, 44: 3–18.

Gottfredson, M. R. and Hirschi, T. 1990. *A general theory of crime.* Palo Alto, CA: Stanford University Press.

Gove, W. R. 1970. Societal reaction as an explanation of mental illness: An evaluation. *American Sociological Review*, 35: 873–884.

Gove, W. R. (Ed.). 1975. *The labelling of deviance: Evaluating a perspective.* New York: Wiley.

Graham, F. P. 1970. Black crime: The lawless image. *Harper's*, 241: 64–78.

Grasmick, H. G., Hagan, J., Blackwell, B. S., and Arneklev, B. J. 1996. Risk preferences and patriarchy: Extending power-control theory. *Social Forces*, 75: 77–199.

Green, A. W. 1946. The middle-class male child and neurosis. *American Journal of Sociology*, 51: 523–530.

Green, E. 1964. Inter- and intra-racial crime relative to sentencing. *Journal of Criminal Law, Criminology, and Police Science*, 55: 348–358.

Green, E. 1970. Race, social status, and criminal arrest. *American Sociological Review*, 35: 476–490.

Green, E., and Wakefield, R. P. 1979. Patterns of middle and upper class homicide. *Journal of Criminal Law and Criminology*, 70: 172–181.

Greenberg, B. S., and Dervin, B. 1970. *Uses of the mass media by the urban poor.* New York: Praeger.

Greenberg, D. F. (Ed.). 1981. *Crime and capitalism: Readings in Marxist criminology.* Palo Alto: Mayfield.

Greenberg, D. F., and Stender, F. 1972. The prison as a lawless agency. *Buffalo Law Review*, 21: 799–838.

Greenberg, D. F. 1994. The historical variability of the age-crime relationship. *Journal of Quantitative Criminology*, 10: 361–373.

Greenfield, H. I. 1993. *Invisible, outlawed, and untaxed.* Westport, Conn.: Praeger.

Greenhouse, S. 1995. Veto threatened on U.S. bill to ease property claims against Cuba, *New York Times*, (August 20), 144: 4(N).

Greenwood, P. W. 1982. *Selective incapacitation*. Santa Monica, Calif.: Rand Corp.

Greenwood, P. W., and Turner, S. 1987. *Selective incapacitation revisited: Why the high-rate offenders are hard to predict*. Santa Monica, Calif.: Rand Corp.

Greenwood, P. W., Petersillia, J., and Zimring, F. E. 1980. *Age, crime, and sanctions: The transition from juvenile to adult court*. Santa Monica, Calif.: Rand Corporation.

Gregory, I. 1965. Anterospective data following childhood loss of a parent: Delinquency and high school dropout. *Archives of General Psychiatry*, 13: 99–109.

Grillo, E. G. 1970. *Delincuencia en Caracas*. Caracas: Universidad del Zulia.

Grogger, J. 1992. Arrests, persistent youth joblessness, and black/white employment differentials. *Review of Economics and Statistics*, 74: 100–106.

Gross, S. J., and Niman, D. M. 1975. Attitude-behavior consistency: A review. *Public Opinion Quarterly*, 39: 358–368.

Groves, R. M. 1989. *Survey errors and survey costs*, New York: Wiley.

Gurr, T. R. 1970. *Why men rebel*. Princeton: Princeton University Press.

Gwatkin, D. R., and Brandel, S. K. 1982. Life expectancy and population growth in the Third World. *Scientific American*, 246: 57–65.

Haan, N. 1964. The relationship of ego functioning and intelligence to social status and social mobility. *Journal of Abnormal and Social Psychology*, 69: 594–605.

Haas, A. 1979. Male and female spoken language differences: Stereotypes and evidence. *Psychological Bulletin*, 86: 616–626.

Hacker, E. 1941. *Kriminalstatische und kriminalaetiologische berichte*. Miskolc, Hungary: Ludwig.

Hackler, J. C. 1966. Boys, blisters, and behavior: The impact of a work program in an urban central area. *Journal of Research on Crime and Delinquency*, 3: 155–164.

Hagan, J. 1972. The labeling perspective, the delinquent, and the police: A review of the literature. *Canadian Journal of Criminology and Corrections*, 14: 150–165.

Hagan, J. 1974. *Criminal justice in a Canadian province: A study of the sentencing process*. Doctoral dissertation, Edmonton, University of Alberta, Department of Sociology.

Hagan, J. 1974. Extra-legal attributes and criminal sentencing: An assessment of a sociological viewpoint. *Law and Sociology Review*, 8: 357–383.

Hagan, J. 1977. Criminal justice in rural and urban communities: A study of the bureaucratization of justice. *Social Forces*, 55: 597–612.

Hagan, J. 1977. Finding "discrimination." A question of meaning. *Ethnicity*, 4: 167–176.

Hagan, J. 1990. The structuration of gender and deviance: A power-control theory of vulnerability to crime and the search for deviant role exits. *Canadian Review of Sociology and Anthropology*, 27: 137–156.

Hagan, J. 1994. *Crime and disrepute*. Thousand Oaks, CA: Pine Forge Press.

Hagan, J., and Leon, J. 1977. Rediscovering delinquency: Social history, political ideology, and the sociology of law. *American Sociological Review*, 42: 587–598.

Hagan, J., Simpson, J., and Gillis, A. R. 1987. Class in the household: a power-control theory of gender and delinquency. *American Journal of Sociology*, 92: 788–816.

Hagerdorn, J. 1988. *People and folks: Gangs, crime and the underclass in the rustbelt city*. Chicago: Lakeview Press.

Hall, A. C. 1902. *Crime in its relation to social progress*. New York: Columbia University Press.

Hamm, M. S., and Chambliss, W. J. 1993. *American skinheads: The criminology and control of hate crime*. Westport, Conn.: Praeger.

Hann, R. G., et al. 1973. Decision making in the Canadian criminal court system: A systems analysis (2 vols). Toronto: University of Toronto, Centre of Criminology.

Hannan, M. T. 1971. *Aggregation and disaggregation in sociology*. Lexington, Mass.: Lexington Books.

Hansmann, H. B., and Quigley, J. M. 1982. Population heterogeneity and the sociogenesis of homicide. *Social Forces*, 61: 206–224.

Harbin, G. 1979. Hands off. *Sports Illustrated*, (January 8), 50: 8.

Hardin, G. 1982. Grounded reason vs. received formulas. *Free Inquiry*, 2: 38–41.

Harding, J. 1991. Policing and aboriginal justice. *Canadian Journal of Criminology*, 33: 363–383.

Harer, M. D., and Steffensmeier, D. 1992. The differencing effects of economic inequality on Black and white rates of homicide. *Social Forces*, 70: 1035–1054.

Harlow, H. F., et al. 1966. Maternal behavior of rhesus monkeys deprived of mothering and peer associations in infancy. *Proceedings of the American Philosophical Society*, 110: 58–66.

Harlow, H. F., and Harlow, M. 1967. The young monkeys. *Psychology Today*, 1: 40–47.

Harman, N. 1982. The most African country: A survey of Nigeria. *Economist*, (January 23), 282, Special supplement.

Harries, K. D. 1976. A crime-based analysis and classification of 729 American cities. *Social Indicators Research*, 2: 467–487.

Harris, W. J. 1972. The militant separatists in the white academy. *American Scholar*, 41: 366–376.

Hartjen, C. A. 1974. *Crime and criminalization*. New York: Praeger.

Hartley, S. F. 1980. Illegitimacy in Jamaica. In P. Laslett et al. (Eds.), *Bastardy and its comparative history*. London: Edward Arnold.

Hartmann, D. P. 1969. Influence of symbolically modeled instrumental aggression and pain cues on aggressive behavior. *Journal of Personality and Social Psychology*, 11: 280–288.

Hartnagel, T. F. 1978. The effect of age and sex compositions of provincial populations on provincial crime rates. *Canadian Journal of Criminology and Corrections*, 20: 28–33.

Hartshorne, H., and May M. A. 1928–1930. *Studies in the nature of character (3 vols.)*. New York: Macmillan.

Harvey, P. 1970. Problems in Chinatown. *Human Events*, (May 15), 30: 21.

Hatt, K. 1994. Reservations about race and crime statistics. *Canadian Journal of Criminology*, 36: 164–165.

Hauge, R., and Wolf, P. 1974. Criminal violence in three Scandinavian countries. In N. Christie et al. (Eds.), *Scandinavian studies in criminology* (Vol. 5). Oslo: Universitetsforlaget.

Hawkins, D. F. 1995. *Ethnicity, race, and crime*. Albany: State University of New York Press.

Hawley, A. H. 1972. Population density and the city. *Demography*, 9: 521–529.

Hayner, N. S. 1946. Criminogenic zones in Mexico City. *American Sociological Review*, 11: 428–438.

Heckhausen, H. 1967. *The anatomy of achievement motivation*. New York: Academic Press.

Henry, S. 1980. *The hidden economy*. London: Martin Robertson.

Herriot, R., and Haines, A. 1979. Are we making more but enjoying it less? Apparently. *Public Opinion*, 2: 2–5.

Hersch, L. 1938. *Le Juif delinquant*. Paris: F. Alcan.

Herskovits, M. J. 1941. *The myth of the Negro past*. Boston: Beacon Press.

Hertzberg, L. 1975. Blame and causality. *Mind*, 84: 500–515.

Herz, F. O. 1908. Verbrechen und verbrechertum in Oesterreich. Tubingen: Mohr.

Hibbett, A., Fogelman, K. and Manor, O. 1990. "Occupational outcomes of truancy." *British Journal of Educational Psychology*, 60:23–36.

Hill, G. D., and Crawford, E. M. 1990. Women, race, and crime. *Criminology*, 28: 601–626.

Hindelang, M. J. 1973. Time perceptions of the self-reported delinquents. *British Journal of Criminology*, 13: 178–183.

Hindelang, M. J. 1974. Decisions of shoplifting victims to invoke the criminal justice process. *Social Problems*, 21: 580–593.

Hindelang, M. J. 1978. Race and involvement in common-law personal crimes: A comparison of three techniques. *American Sociological Review*, 43: 93–109.

Hindelang, M. J., Gettfredson, M. R., and Garofalo, J. 1978. *Victims of personal crime: An empirical foundation for a theory of personal victimization*. Cambridge, Mass.: Ballinger.

Hindelang, M. J., Hirschi, T., Weis, J. G. 1981. *Measuring delinquency*. Beverly Hills: Sage.

Hirsch, C. A. 1953. La criminalité nord-africaine. *Revue International de Criminologie et de Police Technique*, 7: 298–302.

Hirschi, T. 1969. *Cause of delinquency*. Berkeley and Los Angeles: University of California Press.

Hirschi, T., and Gottfredson, M. R. 1983. Age and the explanation of crime. *American Journal of Sociology*, 89: 552–584.

Hirschi, T., and Hindelang, M. J. 1977. Intelligence and delinquency: A revisionist review. *American Sociological Review*, 42: 571–587.

Hobsbawm, E. J. 1969. *Bandits*. London: Weidenfield and Nicolson.

Hodgkiss, M. 1933. The influence of broken homes and working mothers. *Smith College Studies in Social Work*, 3: 259–274.

Hohenstein, W. H. 1969. Factors influencing the police disposition of juvenile offenders. In T. Sellin and M. E. Wolfgang (Eds.), *Delinquency: Selected studies*. Toronto: Wiley.

Holland, P. W. 1988. Causal inference, path analysis and recursive structural equation models. In C. C. Clogg (Ed.) *Sociological methodology*. San Francisco: Jossey-Bass.

Hollander, P. 1973. *Soviet and American society: A comparison*. New York: Oxford University Press.

Hollander, P. 1982. Research on Marxist societies: The relationship between theory and practice. In R. H. Turner and J. F. Short, Jr. (Eds.), *Annual Review of Sociology*, 8: 319–351.

Hollinger, R., and Dabney, D. A. 1996. *1994 National Retail Security Survey*. Gainesville, FL: Dept. of Sociology, University of Florida.

Hoo, S. 1972. The rights of the victims: Thoughts on crime and compassion. *Encounter*, 38: 11–15.

Hooker, E. L. 1945. *The Houston delinquent in his community setting*. Houston: Council of Social Agencies, Research Bureau.

Hoover, K. D. 1990. The logic of causal inference: Economics and the conditional analysis of causation. *Economics and Philosophy*, 6: 207–234.

Horn, J. L., and Donaldson, G. 1980. Cognitive development in adulthood. In Brim, O. G., Jr., and K. Kagan (Eds.)., *Constancy and change in human development*. Cambridge, Mass.: Harvard University Press.

Horn, P. 1974. Newsline. *Psychology Today*, (May) 7: 22–27.

Horowitz, D. L. 1975. Ethnic identity. In N. Glazer and D. P. Moynihan (Eds.), *Ethnicity: theory and experience*. Cambridge, Mass.: Harvard University Press.

Horton, P. B. 1973. Problems in understanding criminal motives. In S. Rottenberg (Ed.), *The economics of crime and punishment*. Washington, D. C.: American Enterprise Institute for Public Policy Research.

Houchon, G. 1967. Les méchanisms criminologènes dans une société urbaine africain. *Revue Internationale Criminologie et de Police Technique*, 21: 271–292.

Howe, I. 1976. *World of our fathers: The journey of the East European Jews to America, and the life they found and made*. New York: Harcourt, Brace.

Huff, C. L., Corzine, J., and Moore, D. C. 1986. Deciphering the South's influence on homicide rates. *Social Forces*, 64: 906–924.

Hughes, M. M. 1974. Shoplifting statistics. *Security World*, 11: 58–60.

Hughes, M., and Carter, T. J. 1981. A declining economy and sociological theories of crime: Predictions and explications. In K. N. Wright (Ed.), *Crime and criminal justice in a declining economy*. Cambridge, Mass.: Oelgechlager, Gunn, and Hain.

Huizinga, D., and Elliott, D. S. 1987. Juvenile offenders: prevalence, offender incidence, and arrest rates by race. *Crime and Delinquency*, 33: 206–223.

Hutchison, J. B. 1978. *Biological determinants of sexual behavior*. New York: Wiley.

Hutt, C. 1972. *Males and females*. Middlesex, England: Penguin.

Hyman, H. H. 1942. The psychology of status. *Archives of Psychology*, 260.

Hyman, H. H. 1944. Do they tell the truth? *Public Opinion Quarterly*, 8: 557–559.

Hyman, H. H. 1953. The value systems of different classes. In R. Bendix and S. M. Lipset (Eds.), *Class, status, and power*. New York: Free Press.

Icheiser, G. 1949. Misunderstandings in human relations. *American Journal of Sociology*, 55 (Whole Part 2).

Insurance Information Institute. 1997. *Insurance fraud*. [www.iii.org/media/fraud.htm].

Issacs, H. R. 1975. *Idols of the tribe: Group identity and political change*. New York: Harper and Row.

Isaacson, D. S., et al. 1982. Insane on all counts. *Time*, (July 5), 120: 22–24.

James, W. 1906. *Pragmatism*. New York: Longmans, Green.

Jang, S. J., Messner, S. F., and South, S. 1991. Predictors of interracial homicide and victimization for Asian Americans: A macrostructural opportunity perspective. *Sociological Perspectives*, 34: 1–19.

Jarvis, G. K., and Messinger, H. B. 1974. Social and economic correlates of juvenile delinquency rates: A Canadian case. *Canadian Journal of Criminology and Corrections*, 16: 361–372.

Jaspan, N. 1960. *The thief in the white collar*. Philadelphia: Lippincott.

Jaspan, N. 1970. Interview. *U. S. News and World Report*, (October 26) 69: 32–33.

Jayasuriya, D. L. 1960. *A study of adolescent ambition, level of aspiration and achievement motivation*. Doctoral dissertation, London, University of London.

Jayewardene, C. H. S., and Ranasinghe, H. 1963. *Criminal homicide in the southern province*. Colombo, Ceylon: The Colombo Apothecaries Company.

Jeffrey, C. R. 1959. An integrated theory of crime and criminal behavior. *Journal of Criminal Law, Criminology, and Police Science*, 49: 533–552.

Jencks, C. 1968. Review of P. M. Blau and O. D. Duncan, The American occupational structure. *New Republic*, (April 20) 158: 31–35.

Jencks, C., et al. 1972. *Inequality: A reassessment of the effects of family and schooling in America*. New York: Basic Books.

Jencks, C., et al. 1979. *Who gets ahead? The determinants of economic success in America*. New York: Basic Books.

Jencks, C. 1990. What Is the True Rate of Social Mobility? In Breiger, R. L. et al. *Social mobility and social structure*. Cambridge, Mass.: Harvard University Press.

Jennis, A. L. 1984. The census undercount: Issues of adjustment. *Columbia Journal of Law and Social Problems*, 18: 381–417.

Jensen, A. R. 1969. How much can we boost I. Q. and scholastic achievement? *Harvard Education Review*, 39: 1–123.

Jensen, A. R. 1971. Twin differences and race differences in I. Q.: A reply to Burgess and Jahoda. *Bulletin of the British Psychological Society*, 24: 95–198.

Jensen, A. R. 1972. *Genetics and education*. New York: Harper and Row.

Jensen, A. R. 1979. *Bias in mental testing*. Riverside, N. J.: Free Press.

Jensen, G. F. 1973. Inner containment and delinquency. *Journal of Criminal Law and Criminology*, 64: 464–470.

Jepsen, J., and Pal, L. 1969. Forecasting the volume and structure of future criminality. In European Committee on Crime Problems. *Collected Studies in Criminological Research*, Volume IV, Strasbourg: Council of Europe.

Jessor, R., et al. 1968. *Society, personality, and deviant behavior*. New York: Holt.

Jiobu, R. M. 1974. City characteristics and racial violence. *Social Science Quarterly*, 55: 52–64.

Johnson, G. B. 1970. The Negro and crime. In M. E. Wolfgang, L. Savitz, N. Johnston (Eds.), *The sociology of crime and delinquency* (2nd ed.). New York: Wiley.

Johnson, V. 1988. Adolescent alcohol and marijuana use: a longitudinal assessment of a social learning perspective. *American Journal of Drug and Alcohol Abuse*, 14: 419–439.

Johnston, J. P. 1994. Academic approaches to rare-crime statistics do not justify their collection. *Canadian Review of Criminology*, 36: 166–174.

Johnston, L. D., P.M. O'Malley, and J. G. Bachman. 1995. *National Survey Results on Drug Use from the Monitoring the Future Study, 1975–1994*, Washington, DC: USGPO.

Jones, F. L., H. Kojima and G. Marks. 1994. Comparative social fluidity: Trends over time in father-to-son mobility in Japan and Australia, 1965–1985. *Social Forces*, 72: 775–798.

Jones, H. 1981. *Crime, race, and culture: A study in a developing country*. New York: Wiley.

Jones, J. 1972. *Prejudice and racism*. Reading, Mass.: Addison-Wesley.

Jones, L. V. 1981. Achievement test scores in mathematics and science. *Science*, (July 24), 213: 412–416.

Jones, M. R. 1976. Time, our lost dimension: Toward a new theory of perception, attention, and memory. *Psychological Review*, 83: 323–355.

Judson, C. J., et al. 1969. A study of the California penalty jury in first-degree-murder cases. *Stanford Law Review*, 21: 1297–1497.

Junger, M. 1989. Discrepancies between police and self-report data for Dutch racial minorities. *British Journal of Criminology*, 29: 273–284.

Kahneman, D., and Tversky, A. 1982. The psychology of preferences. *Scientific American*, 246: 160–173.

Kaironen, K. A. 1966. *A study of the criminality of Finnish immigrants in Sweden*. Strasbourg: Council of Europe.

Kantor, M. B. 1965. Some consequences of residential and social mobility for the adjustment of children. In M. B. Kantor (Ed.), *Mobility and mental health*. Springfield, Ill.: Thomas.

Kaplan, H. B. 1976. Self-attitudes and deviant response. *Social Forces*, 54: 788–801.

Kapsis, R. E. 1976. Continuities in delinquency and riot patterns in black residential areas. *Social Problems*, 23: 567–580.

Kapsis, R. E. 1978. Residential succession and delinquency: A test of Shaw and McKay's theory of cultural transmission. *Criminology*, 15: 459–486.

Kaufmann, H. 1968. *The unconcerned bystander*. Paper read at the annual meeting of the American Psychological Association. San Francisco.

Kaupen, W. 1973. Public opinion of the law in a democratic society. In A. Podgorecki et al. (Eds.), *Knowledge and opinion about the law*. London: Martin Robertson.

Keiser, R. L. (Ed.). 1965. *Hustler! Henry Williamson*. Garden City, N.Y.: Doubleday.

Kelly, I. 1979. Astrology and science: A critical examination. *Psychological Reports*, 44: 1231–1240.

Kennedy, L. W., and Baron, S. W. 1993. Routine activities and a subculture of violence: A study of violence on the street. *Journal of Research in Crime and Delinquency*, 30: 88–112.

Kennedy, L. W., and Wilcutt, H. C. 1964. Praise and blame as incentives. *Psychological Bulletin*, 264: 13–19.

Kephart, W. M. 1957. *Racial factors and urban law enforcement*. Philadelphia: University of Pennsylvania Press.

Keyfitz, N. 1973. Can inequality be cured? *Public Interest*, 3: 91–101.

Kilson, M. 1971. An American profile: The black student militant. *Encounter*, 37: 83–90.

King, G. 1997. *A solution to the ecological inference problem,* Princeton, NJ: Princeton University Press

Kinsey, A. C., et al. 1948. *Sexual behavior in the human male*. Philadelphia: Saunders.

Kirkwood, I. 1977. Unpublished report. Los Angeles: Security Consultants.

Kitano, H. L. 1967. Japanese-American crime and delinquency. *Journal of Psychology*, 66: 253–263.

Kleinmuntz, B. 1967. Sign and seer: Another example. *Journal of Abnormal Psychology*, 72: 163–65.

Klemming, L. G. 1967. *Grekers och Jugoslavers krinminalitet*. Stockholm: Institute for Criminal Science.

Klockars, C. B. 1974. *The professional fence,* New York: Macmillan.

Koch, K. F. 1974. *War and peace in Jalemoi: The management of conflict in highland New Guinea*. Cambridge, Mass.: Harvard University Press.

Kochman, T. 1981. *Black and white styles in conflict*. Chicago: University of Chicago Press.

Koenig, S. 1942. The socioeconomic structure of an American Jewish community. In I. Graeber and S. H. Britt (Eds.), *Jews in a Gentile world: The problem of anti-Semitism*. New York: Macmillan.

Kohlberg, L. 1964. Development of moral character and moral ideology. In M. L. Hoffman and L. Hoffman (Eds.), *Child development research* (Vol. 1). New York: Russell Sage.

Kohlberg, L., and Turiel, E. 1971. *Recent research in moral development*. New York: Holt.

Kohn, M., and Schooler, C. 1969. Class, occupation, and orientation. *American Sociological Review*, 34: 659–678.

Konechi, V. J., and Ebesen, E. B. 1982. An analysis of the sentencing system. In V. J. Konechi and E. B. Ebbbesen (Eds.), *The criminal justice system: A social-psychological analysis*. San Francisco: Freeman.

Konner, M. 1982. She and he. *Science 82*, 3: 54–61.

Koppin, M. 1976. *A validation study of Steadman's legal dangerousness scale with reference to related data*. Pueblo, Col.: Colorado State Hospital, Department of Research and Program Analysis.

Kornhauser, R. R. 1978. Social Sources of Delinquency: An Appraisal of Analytic Models. Chicago: University of Chicago Press.

Kposowa, A. J., and Breault, K. D. 1993. Reassessing the structural covariates of U.S. homicide rates: A county level study. *Sociological Focus*, 26: 27–46.

Kramer, B. 1979. Braking births: China, in big effort to slow population growth, is likely to impose harsh economic punishment. *Wall Street Journal*, (October 3) 101: 40.

Kraut, R. E. 1976. Deterrent and definitional influences on shoplifting. *Social Problems*, 23: 58–368.

Krisberg, B. 1975. *Power and privilege: Toward a new criminology*. Englewood Cliffs, N.J.: Prentice-Hall.

Krisberg, B., Schwartz, I., Fishman, G., Eisikovits, Z., Luttman, E., and Joe, K. 1987. The incarceration of minority youth. *Crime and Delinquency*, 33: 173–205.

Krohn, M. D. 1976. Inequality, unemployment, and crime. *Sociology Quarterly*, 17: 303–333.

Kruttschnitt, C. and Gartner, R. 1993. Introduction. *Crime and Criminal Justice*, 9: 323–327.

Kupperstein, L. R., and Toro-Calder, J. 1969. *Juvenile delinquency in Puerto Rico: A socio-cultural and socio-legal analysis*. Rio Piedras: Social Science Research Center.

Lamm, M. R., et al. 1976. Sex and social class as determinant of future orientation (time perspective) in adolescents. *Journal of Personality and Social Psychology*, 34: 317–326.

Lamont, A. M. 1961. Forensic psychiatric practice in a South African mental hospital. *South African Medical Journal,* 35: 317–326.

Lancet, 1980. Editorial: Choosing when to die and how. (September 13), 8194: 571.

Land, K. C., McCall, P. L., and Cohen, L. E. 1991. Characteristics of U.S. cities with extreme (high or low) crime rates: Results of discriminant analyses of 1960, 1970, and 1980 data. *Social Indicators Research*, 24: 209–231.

Landau, S. F. 1976. Delinquency, institutionalization, and time orientation. *Journal of Consulting and Clinical Psychology*, 44: 745–759.

Landau, S. F. 1978. Do the legal variables predict police decisions regarding the prosecution of juvenile offenders? *Law and Human Behavior*, 2: 95–105.

Landau, S. F., and Drapkin. I. 1968. *Ethnic patterns of criminal homicide in Israel*. Jerusalem: Hebrew University, Institute of Criminology.

Lander, B. 1954. *Towards an understanding of juvenile delinquency*. New York: Columbia University Press.

Landman, J. T., and Dawes, R. M. 1982. Psychotherapy outcome: Smith and Glass's conclusions stand up under scrutiny. *American Psychologist*, 37: 504–516.

Lane, B. A. 1980. The relationship of learning disabilities to juvenile delinquency: Current status. *Journal of Learning Disabilities*, 13: 20–30.

Lang, P. G., and Lazovik, A. D. 1963. Experimental desensitization of a phobia. *Journal of Abnormal and Social Psychology*, 66: 519–525.

Lang, P. G., and Melamed, B. G. 1969. Case report: Avoidance therapy of an infant with chronic ruminative vomiting. *Journal of Abnormal Psychology*, 74: 1–8.

Langer, S. K. 1967. *Mind: An essay on human feeling*. Baltimore: Johns Hopkins University Press.

LaPrairie, C. 1990. The role of sentencing in the over-representation of Aboriginal people in correctional institutions. *Canadian Journal of Criminology*, 32: 429–440.

LaPrairie, C. 1992. Aboriginal crime and justice: Explaining the present, exploring the future. *Canadian Journal of Criminology*, 34: 281–298.

LaPrairie, R. T., and Farnsworth, P. R. 1949. *Social psychology* (3rd ed.) New York: McGraw-Hill.

Lasky, M. S. 1974. One in 3 hotel guests is a towel thief, Bible pincher, or worse. *New York Times*, (January 27), Sec. 10, p. 1.

Laslett, P., et al. (Eds.). 1980. *Bastardy and its comparative history*. London: Edward Arnold.

Lavigne, Y. 1996. Hells Angels: Into the Abyss. Toronto: Harper Collins Publishers.

Lee, G. W. 1982. *Are crime rates increasing? A study of the impact of demographic shifts on crime rates in Canada*. Unpublished paper. Edmonton: Centre for Criminological Research, University of Alberta.

Lefcourt, H. 1972. Recent developments in the study of locus of control. In B. A. Maher (Ed.), *Progress in experimental personality research*. New York: Academic Press.

Leff, L. 1980. The immigrants: A flood of newcomers is turning Los Angeles into tense melting pot. *Wall Street Journal*, (September 25), 103: 1–21.

Lefkowitz, M. M. et al. 1972. *Environmental variables as predictors of aggressive behavior*. Paper read at the annual meeting of the American Association for the Advancement of Science, Washington, D.C.

Leibenstein, H. 1981. Microeconomics and x-efficiency theory: If there is no crisis, there ought to be. In D. Bell and I. Kristol (Eds.), *The crisis in economic theory*. New York: Basic Books.

Lemert, E. M. 1951. *Social pathology: A systematic approach to the theory of sociopathic behavior*. New York: McGraw-Hill.

Lentzner, H. R. 1980. *Criminal victimization in the United States, 1978*. Washington, D.C.: U.S. Government Printing Office.

Le Shan, L. L. 1952. Time orientation and social class. *Journal of Abnormal and Social Psychology*, 47: 589–592.

Lessing, E. E. 1968. Demographic, developmental, and, personality correlates of length of future time perspective. *Journal of Personality*, 36: 193–201.

Lessing, E. E. 1971. Comparative extension of personal and social-political future time perspectives. *Perceptual and Motor Skills*, 33: 415–422.

Levi, M., and Jones, S. 1985. "Public and police perceptions of crime seriousness in England and Wales." *British Journal of Criminology*, 25: 234–250.

Levin, M. A. 1971. Policy evaluation and recidivism. *Law and Society Review*, 6: 17–46.

Le Vine, R. A. 1966. Outsiders' judgments: An ethnographic approach to group differences in personality. *Southwest Journal of Anthropology*, 22: 101–116.

Levine, S. 1971. Sexual differentiation: The development of maleness and femaleness. *California Medicine*, 114: 12–17.

Levitan, S. A. 1975. *The case for revising the definition of unemployment*. Paper read at the annual meeting of the American Association for Public Opinion Research. Itasca, Ill..

Levitt, E. E. 1957. The results of psychotherapy with children: An evaluation. *Journal of Consulting Psychology*, 21: 189–196.

Lewis, D. O., and Shanok, S. S. 1977. Medical histories of deiinquent and nondelinquent children: An epidemological study. *American Journal of Psychiatry*, 134: 1020–1025.

Lewis, I. A., and Scheider, W. 1982. Is the public lying to the pollsters? *Public Opinion*, 5: 42–47.

Lewis, O. 1959. *Five families: Mexican case studies in the culture of poverty*. New York: Basic Books.

Lewis, O. 1966. *La vida*. New York: Random House.

Li, D. 1995. Economic development, social control, and murder rates: a crossnational approach. *Cross Cultural Research*, 29, 361–382.

Liben, G. 1963. Un reflet de la criminalité italienne dans la region de Liege. *Revue De Droit Penal et de Criminologie*, 44: 205–245.

Lind, A. W. 1930. The ghetto and the slum. *Social Forces*, 9: 206–215.

Lind, A. W. 1930. Some ecological patterns of community disorganization in Honolulu. *American Journal of Sociology*, 36: 206–220.

Lindesmith, A. R., and Strauss, A. L. 1956. *Social Psychology*. New York: Holt.

Lipman, J. N., and Harrell, S. 1990. *Violence in China: Essays in culture and counterculture*. Albany: State University of New York Press.

Lipton, D., Martinson, R., and Wilks, J. 1975. *The effectiveness of correctional treatment: A survey of evaluation studies*. New York: Praeger.

Liska, A. E., and Warner, B. D. 1991. Functions of crime: A paradoxical process. *American Journal of Sociology*, 96: 1441–63.

Llera, F. J. 1989. Continuidad y cambio en la politica vasca. *Revisita Espanola de Investigaciones Sociologicas*, 47: 107–135.

Loftin, C. 1980. The deterrent effects of punishment. In S. E. Feinberg and A. J. Reiss, Jr. (Eds.), *Indicators of crime and criminal justice: Quantitative studies*. Washington, D.C.: U.S. Government Printing Office.

Loftin, C., and Hill, R. H. 1974. Regional subculture and homicide. *American Sociological Review*, 39: 714–724.

Loftus, E. F. 1976. Federal regulations: Make the punishment fit the crime. *Science*, (February 13), 191: 670.

Lorber, J. 1967. Deviance as performance: The case of illness. *Social Problems*, 14: 301–310.

Lottier, S. 1938. Distribution of criminal offences in metropolitan regions. *Journal of Criminal Law and Criminology*, 29: 37–50.

Lovaas, O. I. 1961. Effect of exposure to symbolic aggression on aggressive behavior. *Child Development*, 32: 37–44.

Lowe, G. R. 1966. Response inhibition and deviant social behavior in children. *British Journal of Psychiatry*, 112: 925–930.

Lublin, J. S. 1980. On idle: The unemployed shun much mundane work, at least for a while. *Wall Street Journal*, (December 5), 103: 1–21.

Ludwig, I. A. 1982. *Race relations and the law*. Theme paper read at the Symposium on Race Relations and the Law.Vancouver, (April 23).

Lundman, R., Sykes, R., and Clarke, J. 1978. Police control of juveniles: A replication. *Journal of Research on Crime and Delinquency*, 15: 74–91.

Lydall, H. 1968. *The structure of earnings*. Oxford: Clarendon.

Lyle, J., and Hoffman, H. R. 1972. Children's use of television and other media. In E. A. Rubinstein et al. (Eds.), *Television and social behavior. Vol. 4: Television in day-to-day life: Patterns of use*. Washington, D.C.: U.S. Government Printing Office.

Maas, P. 1975. *King of the gypsies*. New York: Viking.

Maccoby, E. E., and Jacklin, C. N. 1974. *The psychology of sex differences*. Stanford: Stanford University Press.

Mack, J. A. 1972. The able criminal. *British Journal of Criminology*, 12: 44–54.

Mack, J. A. and Kerner, H. J. 1975. *The crime industry*. Lexington, Mass.: Lexington Books.

Mackie, J. L. 1980. *The cement of the universe: A study in causation*. Oxford: Clarendon Press.

Mackie, M. M. 1973. Arriving at "truth" by definition: The case of stereotype accuracy. *Social Problems*, 20: 431–447.

Maguire, K., and Pastore, A. L (Eds.) 1995. *Sourcebook of criminal justice statistics* 1994. U.S. Department of Justice, Bureau of Justice Statistics. Washington, D.C.: USGPO.

Makkai, T., and Braithwaite, J. 1991. Criminological theories and regulatory compliance. *Criminology*, 29: 191–220.

Makela, K. 1967. Public sense of justice and judicial practice. *Acta Sociologica*, 10: 42–67.

Malabre, A. L., Jr. 1980. Underground economy grows and grows. *Wall Street Journal*, (October 20), 103: 1.

Malabre, A. L., Jr. 1932. Off the books business booms in Europe. *Wall Street Journal*, (August 24), 105: 1.

Maller, J. B. 1932. Are broken homes a causative factor in juvenile delinquency? *Social Forces*, 10: 531–533.

Mallick, S. K., and McCandless, B. R. 1966. A study of catharsis of aggression. *Journal of Personality and Social Psychology*, 4: 591–596.

Mandel, E. 1968. *Marxist economic theory (Vol. 1)* (B. Pearce, trans.). New York: Monthly Review Press.

Mangin, W. 1967. Latin American squatter settlements: A problem and a solution. *Latin American Research*, 2: 65–69.

Mannheim, K. 1936. *Ideology and utopia* (L. Wirth, intro. and trans.). New York: Harcourt, Brace.

Mannheim, K., and Wilkins, L. T. 1955. *Prediction methods in relation to Borstal training*. London: Her Majesty's Stationery Office.

Margolick, D. 1994. Lorena Bobbitt acquitted in mutilation of husband. *The New York Times*, (January 22), 143: 1.

Martin, J., and Taylor, L. 1996. Kevorkian picks up the pace. *Detroit Free Press*. (August 23), B2.

Martinez, R. 1996. Latinos and lethal violence: The impact of poverty and inequality. *Social Problems*, 43: 131–146.

Martino, A. 1981. Measuring Italy's underground economy. *Policy Review*, 16: 12–22.

Marx, G. T. 1967. *Protest and prejudice: A study of belief in the black community*. New York: Harper and Row.

Matheson, J. 1975. Baum recalls tough times. *Edmonton Journal*, (November 7), p.65.

Mathewson, W. 1980. A special background report on trends in industry and finance. *Wall Street Journal*, (July 24), 103: 1.

Mathiesen, T. 1974. *The politics of abolition*. New York: Halstead.

Matsueda, R. L. 1982. Testing control theory and differential association: a causal modeling approach. *American Sociological Review*, 47: 489–504.

Matsueda, R. L. 1992. Reflected appraisals, parental labeling, and delinquency: Specifying a symbolic interactionist theory. *American Journal of Sociology*, 97: 1577–1611.

Matsueda, R. L., and Heimer, K. 1987. Social control theories. *American Sociological Review*, 52: 826–840.

Matza, D. 1969. *Becoming deviant*. Englewood Cliffs, N.J.: Prentice-Hall.

Mawson, A. R. 1987. *Criminality: A model of stress-induced crime*. New York: Praeger.

Maxfield, M. G. 1987. Household composition, routine activity, and victimization: A comparative analysis. *Journal of Quantitative Criminology*, 3: 301–320.

Maxfield, M. G., and Babbie, C. 1995. *Research methods for criminal justice and criminology*. Belmont, California: Wadsworth.

Maxim, P. S. 1985. Cohort size and juvenile delinquency: A test of the Easterlin hypothesis. *Social Forces*, 63: 661–681.

Maxim, P. S., and Jocklin, A. 1980. Population size, age structure, and sex composition effects on official crime in Canada. *International Journal of Comparative and Applied Criminal Justice*, 4: 28–36.

Maxim, P.S., and Keane, C. 1992. Gender, age, and the risk of violent death in Canada, 1950–1986. *Canadian Review of Sociology and Anthropology*, 29: 329–45.

Maxwell, N. 1972. Passing judgment: How a little town reacts when banker is accused of taking $4.7 million. *Wall Street Journal*, (August 8), 82: 1–14.

Maxwell, N. 1973. Voice of experience: Lamar Hill, embezzler, says stealing is easy. *Wall Street Journal*, (January 26), 83: 1–14.

McBarnet, D. 1991. Whiter than white collar crime: Tax, fraud insurance and the management of stigma. *British Journal of Sociology*, 42: 323–344.

Mayhew, P., and Smith, L. J. F. 1985. Crime in England and Wales and Scotland: A British Crime Survey comparison. *British Journal of Criminology*, 25: 148–159.

McCarthy, E. D., et al. 1975. The effects of television on children and adolescents: Violence and behavior disorders. *Journal of Communication*, 25: 71–85.

McCarthy, J. D., Galle, O., and Zimmern, W. 1975. Population density, social structure and interpersonal violence. *American Behavioral Scientist*, 18: 771–789.

McCauley, C., and Stitt, C. L. 1978. An individual and quantitative measure of stereotypes. *Journal of Personality and Social Psychology*, 36: 929–940.

McCauley, C., and Stitt, C. L., and Segal, M. 1980. Stereotyping: From prejudice to prediction. *Psychological Bulletin*, 87: 95–208.

McColm, R. B. 1981. Cuban intellectual dissidents. *Freedom at Issue*, 63: 34–35.

McCord, J. 1978. A thirty-year follow-up of treatment effects. *American Psychologist*, 33: 284–289.

McCord, J. 1980. The treatment that did not help. *Social Action and Law*, 5: 85–87.

McCord, W., and McCord, J. 1959. *Origins of crime: A new evaluation of the Cambridge-Somerville Youth Study*. New York: Columbia University Press.

McCurdy, H. G. 1961. *The personal world: An introduction to the study of personality*. New York: Harcourt, Brace.

McDonald, L. 1969. *Social class and delinquency*. London: Faber.

McEachern, A. W., and Bauzer, R. 1967. Factors related to disposition in juvenile police contacts. In M. W. Klein (Ed.), *Juvenile gangs in context: Theory, research, and action*. Englewood Cliffs, N.J.: Prentice-Hall.

McGarvey, B., et al. 1981. Reading social class, education, and criminality: A multiple indicator model. *Journal of Abnormal Psychology*, 90: 354–364.

McGill, H. G. 1938. Oriental delinquents in Vancouver juvenile court. *Sociology and Social Research*, 22: 428–438.

McKenzie, R. B., and Tullock, G. 1981. *The new world of economics* (3rd ed.). Homewood, Ill.: Irwin.

McLeod, J. M., et al. 1972. Adolescents, parents, and television use: Adolescent self-report measures from Maryland and Wisconsin samples. In G. A. Comstock and E. A. Rubinstein (Eds.), *Television and social behavior. Vol. 3: Television and adolescent aggressiveness*. Washington, D.C.: U.S. Government Printing Office.

McPherson, N. M. 1991. A question of morality: Sorcery and concepts of deviance among the Kabana, West New Britain. *Anthropologica*, 33: 127–143.

McNeeley, R. L., and Mann, C. R. 1990. Domestic violence is a human issue. *Journal of Interpersonal Violence*, 5: 129–132.

McWhirter, N., and McWhirter, R. (Eds.). 1966. *The Guinness book of records*. London: Guinness.

Meade, A. 1973. Seriousness of delinquency, the adjudicative decision and recidivism: A longitudinal configuration analysis. *Journal of Criminal Law and Criminology*, 64: 478–485.

Measey, l. G. 1972. The psychiatric and social relevance of tattoos in Royal Navy detainees. *British Journal of Criminology*, 12: 182–186.

Meehl, P. E. 1954. *Clinical versus statistical prediction*. Minneapolis: University of Minnesota.

Meehl, P. E. 1959. Some ruminations on the validation of clinical procedures. *Canadian Journal of Psychology*, 13: 102–124.

Mercer, J. R. 1965. Social system perspective and clinical perspective: Frames of reference for understanding career patterns of persons labeled as mentally retarded. *Social Problems*, 13: 18–34.

Merton, R. K. 1949. *Social theory and social structure: Toward the codification of theory and research*. Glencoe, Ill.: Free Press. (Rev., 1957).

Messerschmidt, J. 1986. *Capitalism, patriarchy and crime*. Totowa, N.J.: Rowman and Littlefield.

Messner, S.F. 1980. Income and inequality and murder rates: Some cross-national findings. *Comparative Social Research*, 3: 185–198.

Messner, S. F. 1982. Societal development, social equality, and homicide: A cross-national test of a Durkheimian model. *Social Forces*, 61: 225–240.

Messner, S. F., and Blau, J. R. 1987. Routine leisure activities and rates of crime: A macro-level analysis. *Social Forces*, 65: 1035–1052.

Messner, S. F., and South, S. J. 1992. Interracial homicide: A macrostructural opportunity perspective. *Sociological Forum*, 7: 517– 536.

Metzger, L. P. 1971. American sociology and black assimilation: Conflicting perspectives. *American Journal of Sociology*, 76: 627–647.

Meyer, V., and Levy, R. 1970. Behavioral treatment of a homosexual with compulsive rituals. *British Journal of Medicine*, 43: 63–67.

Miethe, T. D., Stafford, M. C., and Long, J. S. 1987. Social differentiation in criminal victimization: A test of routine activities/lifestyle theories. *American Sociological Review*, 52: 184–194.

Milgram, S. 1963. Behavioral study of obedience. *Journal of Abnormal Psychology*, 67: 371–378.

Milgram, S. 1974. *Obedience to authority: An experimental view*. New York: Harper and Row.

Mill, J. S. 1859. *On Liberty*. Reprinted 1964. New York: Dutton.

Miller, J. D., Fox, J. A., and Tracy, P. E. Complexities of the randomized response solution. *American Sociological Review*, 46: 928–930.

Miller, N. E. 1969. Learning of visceral and glandular responses. *Science*, (January), 163: 434–445.

Miller, W. B. 1958. Lower class culture as a generating milieu of gang delinquency. *Journal of Social Issues*, 14: 5–19.

Miller, W. B. 1967. Theft behavior in city gangs. In M. W. Klein (Ed.), *Juvenile gangs in context: Theory, research, and action*. Englewood Cliffs, N.J.: Prentice-Hall.

Minsky, T. 1982. A broker's intrigues prove intriguing to fellow Iowans. *Wall Street Journal*, (April 26), 106: 1–12.

Mirrless-Black, C., and Ross, A. 1995. Crime against manufacturing premises in 1993. *Research Findings*, No. 27. London: Home Office Research and Statistics Department.

Mirus, R., and Smith, R. S. 1981. Canada's irregular economy. *Public Policy*, 3: 444–453.

Mischel, W. 1961. Preference for delayed reinforcement and social responsibility. *Journal of Abnormal and Social Psychology*, 62: 1–7.

Mischel, W. 1973. Toward a cognitive social learning reconceptualization of personality. *Psychological Review*, 80: 252–283.

Mitchell, R. 1981. *The graves of academe*. Boston: Little, Brown.

Mitchell, R. E. 1971. Some implications of high density housing. *American Sociological Review*, 36: 18–29.

Mizruchi, E. H. 1964. *Success and opportunity*. New York: Free Press.

Moffitt, T. E., et al. 1981. Socioeconomic status, IQ, and delinquency. *Journal of Abnormal Psychology*, 90: 152–156.

Molotch, H. 1969. Racial integration in a transition community. *American Sociological Review*, 34: 878–893.

Monahan, J. 1975. The social ecology of deviance. In T. Lickona (Ed.), *Man and morality*. New York: Holt, Rinehart and Winston.

Monahan, J. 1978. The prediction of violent criminal behavior: A methodological critique and prospectus. In A. Blumstein, J. Cohen, and D. Nagin (Eds.), *Deterrence and incapacitation: Estimating the effects of criminal sanctions on crime rates*. Washington, D. C.: National Academy of Sciences.

Monahan, T. 1957. Family status and the delinquent child. A reprisal and some new findings. *Social Forces*, 35: 250–258.

Money, J. 1982. Search for the causes of sexual preference. *Contemporary Psychology*, 27: 503–505.

Money, J., and Erharst, A. A. 1972. *Man and woman: Boy and girl*. Baltimore: Johns Hopkins University Press.

Morgan, W. R., and Clark, T. N. 1973. The causes of racial disorders: A grievance-level explanation. *American Sociological Review*, 38: 611–624.

Morlan, G. K. 1949. A note on the frustration-aggression theories of Dollard and his associates. *Psychological Review*, 56: 1–8.

Morris, C. W. 1956. *Varieties of human value*. Chicago: University of Chicago Press.

Morris, T. P. 1957. *The criminal area: A study in social ecology*. London: Routledge and Kegan Paul.

Morris, T. P. and Blom-Cooper, L. 1964. *A calendar of murder: Criminal homicide in England since 1957*. London: Michael Joseph.

Morselli, E. 1879. *Il Suicidio*. Milano: Dumolard.

Moses, E. R. 1970. Negro and white crime rates. In M. E. Wolfgang, L. Savitz, and N. Johnston (Eds.), *The Sociology of Crime and Delinquency* (2nd ed.). New York: Wiley.

Moss, R. 1972. *The war for the cities*. New York: Coward, McCann.

Moyer, S. 1992. Race, gender, and homicide: Comparisons between Aboriginal and other Canadians. *Canadian Journal of Criminology*, 34: 387–402.

Moynahan, B. 1978. *Airport international*. London: Macmillan.

Moynihan, D. P. 1969. *Maximum feasible misunderstanding: Community action in the war on poverty*. New York: Free Press.

Mudge, E. M. 1967. *Bank robbery in California: A 35-year comparison with the rest of the United States and an intensive study of 1965 offenses*. Sacramento: Criminal Statistics Bureau.

Muldoon, L. (Ed.). 1979. *Incest: Confronting the silent crime*. Minneapolis: Minnesota Programs for the Victims of Sexual Assault.

Mundt, R. J. 1990. Gun control and rates of firearms violence in Canada and the United States. *Canadian Journal of Criminology*, 32: 137–54.

Murphy, F. J., et al. 1946. The Incidence of hidden delinquency. *American Journal of Orthopsychiatry*, 16: 686–695.

Mussen, P. H., and Rutherford, E. 1961. Effects of aggressive cartoons on children's aggressive play. *Journal of Abnormal Social Psychology*, 62: 461–464.

Myers, S. L. 1992. Crime, entrepreneurship, and labor force withdrawal. *Contemporary Policy Issues*, 10: 84–97.

Mylonas, A. D., and Reckless, W. C. 1963. Prisoners' attitudes toward law and legal institutions. *Journal of Criminal Law, Criminology, and Police Science*, 54: 479–484.

Nader, L., and H. F. Todd, Jr. (Eds.). 1978. *The disputing process: Law in ten societies*. New York: Columbia University Press.

Nann, E. 1967. *Die Kriminalität der italienischen Gastärbeiter im Spiegel der Ausländer Kriminalität*. Hamburg: Kriminalitistik Verlag.

National Crime Panel. 1975. *Criminal victimization surveys in 13 American cities*. Washington, D.C.: U.S. Government Printing Office.

National Institute of Education. 1978. *Violent schools—safe schools: The safe school study report to Congress*. Washington, D.C.: U.S. Government Printing Office.

Nelson, J. F. 1980. Multiple victimization in American cities: A statistical analysis of rare events. *American Journal of Sociology*, 85: 870–891.

Nettler, G. 1957. A measure of alienation. *American Sociological Review*, 22: 670–677.

Nettler, G. 1961. Good men, bad men, and the perception of reality. *Sociometry*, 24: 279–294.

Nettler, G. 1970. *Explanations*. New York: McGraw-Hill.

Nettler, G. 1974. Embezzlement without problems. *British Journal of Criminology*, 14: 70–77.

Nettler, G. 1975. Review of C. Hartjen, *Crime and criminalization*, and R. Quinney, *Critique of legal order*. *Contemporary Sociology*, 4: 243–245.

Nettler, G. 1976. *Social concerns*. New York: McGraw-Hill.

Nettler, G. 1979. Criminal Justice. In A. Inkeles et al. (Eds.), *Annual review of sociology* (vol. 5). Palo Alto: Annual Reviews.

Nettler, G. 1982a. *Explaining criminals*. Vol. 1 of *Criminal careers*. Cincinnati: Anderson.

Nettler, G. 1982b. *Killing one another*. Vol. 2 of *Criminal careers*. Cincinnati: Anderson.

Nettler, G. 1982c. *Responding to crime*. Vol 4 of *Criminal careers*. Cincinnati: Anderson.

Newman, G. 1976. *Comparative deviance: Perception and law in six cultures*. New York: Elsevier.

Newman, G., et al. 1974. Authoritarianism, religiosity, and reactions to deviance. *Journal of Criminal Justice*, 2: 249–259.

Nice, R. (Ed.). 1965. *Dictionary of criminology*. London: Vision Press.

Nichols, R. C. 1966. Schools and the disadvantaged. *Science*, (December 9), 154: 1312–1314.

Niemi, R. G. 1974. *How family members perceive each other*. New Haven: Yale University Press.

Nisbet, R. A. 1974. The pursuit of equality: Review essay. *Public Interest*, 35: 103–120.

Nisbet, R. A. 1974. Rousseau and equality. *Encounter*, 63: 40–51.

Nord, C.W., and Zill, N. 1996. *Non-custodial parents' participation in their children's lives: Evidence from the Survey of Income and Program Participation*, Volume I. Washington, D.C.: U.S. Department of Health and Human Services.

Normandeau, A. 1971. Some data on shoplifting in Montreal department stores. *Canadian Journal of Criminology and Corrections*, 13: 251–265.

Novak, M. 1972. *The rise of the unmeltable ethnics*. New York: Macmillan.

Novak, M. 1981. Race and culture and economics. *Fortune*, (October 5), 102: 209–211.

Nye, F. I. 1957. Child adjustment in broken and unhappy unbroken homes. *Journal of Marriage and Family Living*, 19: 356–361.

Nye, F. I., and Short, J. F. 1957a. Scaling delinquent behavior. *American Sociological Review*, 22: 326–331.

Nye, F. I., and Short, J. F. 1957b. Reported behavior as a criterion of deviant behavior. *Social Problems*, 5: 224–237.

O'Carroll, T. 1980. *Paedophilia: The radical case*. London: Owen.

Ogburn, W. F. 1935. Factors in variation of crime among cities. *American Journal of Sociology*. 30: 12–20.

O'Neill, J. 1975. *Interpreting unemployment differentials*. Paper read at the 30th annual meeting of the American Association for Public Opinion Research. Itasca, Ill..

Orsagh, T. 1980. Unemployment and crime: An objection to Professor Brenner's view. *Journal of Criminal Law and Criminology*, 8: 181–183.

Orwell, G. 1937. *The road to Wigan Pier*. London: Gollanca.

Osborn, S. G. 1980. Moving home, leaving London, and delinquent trends. *British Journal of Criminology*, 20: 54–61.

Ossowska, M. 1971. *Social determinants of moral ideas*. London: Routledge and Kegan Paul.

Owens, W. A. 1968. Toward one discipline of scientific psychology. *American Psychologist*, 23: 782–785.

Owens, W. A. 1971. A quasi-actuarial basis for individual assessment. *American Psychologist*, 26: 992–999.

Pace, C. O. 1949. Opinion and action: A study of the validity of attitude measurement. *American Psychologist*, 4: 242.

Packer, H. L. 1968. *The limits of the criminal sanction*. Stanford: Stanford University Press.

Padilla, F. 1992. *The gang as an American enterprise*. New Brunswick, New Jersey: Rutgers University Press.

Paez, A. L. 1981. *Myths and realities about crime*. Washington, D.C.: U.S. Department of Justice.

Paglin, M. 1979. Poverty in the United States: A re-evaluation. *Policy Review*, 8: 7–24.

Paglin, M. 1979. *Poverty and transfers in kind*. Stanford: Hoover Institution Press.

Paglin, M. 1994. The underground economy: New estimates from household income and expenditure surveys. *The Yale Law Journal*, 103: 2239–2257.

Pahlavi, M. R. 1980. *Answer to history*. Toronto: Clarke, Irwin.

Pampel, F.C., and Gartner, R. 1995. Age structure, sociopolitical institutions, and national homicide rates. *European Sociological Review*, 11: 243–260.

Papadimitriou, D. B., and Wolff, E. N. 1993. *Poverty and prosperity in the USA in the late twentieth century*. New York: St. Martin's Press.

Parker, B. 1977. Business: Victims of crime. *Security Management*, 21: 28–31.

Parker, K. D., McMorris, B. J., Smith, E., and Murty, K. S. 1993. Fear of crime and the likelihood of victimization: A bi-ethnic comparison. *Journal of Social Psychology*, 133: 723–732.

Parton, D. A., Hansel, M., and Stratton, J.R. 1991. "Measuring crime seriousness: Lessons from the National Survey of Crime Severity." *British Journal of Criminology*, 31: 72–85.

Pascal, M. 1992. *Varieties of man/boy love*. New York: Wallace.

Patterson, G. R., Crosby, L., and Vuchinich, S. 1992. Predicting risk for early police arrest. *Journal of Quantative Criminology*, 8: 335–355.

Patterson, O. 1975. Context and choice in ethnic allegiance: A theoretical framework and Caribbean case study. In N. Glazer and D. P. Moynihan (Eds.), *Ethnicity: Theory and experience*. Cambridge, Mass.: Harvard University Press.

Pearce, F. 1976. *Crimes of the powerful: Marxism, crime and deviance*. London: Pluto Press.

Pearlin, L. J., and Kohn, M. L. 1966. Social class, occupation, and parental values: A cross-national study. *American Sociological Review*, 31: 466–479.

Pearson, B. E. (Ed.). 1978. *Canada yearbook*. Ottawa: Statistics Canada.

Penick, B. K. E., and Owens, M. E. B. III (Eds.), 1976. *Surveying crime: Final report of the panel for the evaluation of crime surveys*. Washington, D.C.: National Academy of Sciences.

People v. McGinnis. 1908. *Northeastern report*, 84: 687.

Petersen, W. 1967. Family structure and social mobility among Japanese Americans. *Abstracts*, American Sociological Association, 119–120.

Petersen, W. 1969. The classification of subnations in Hawaii: An essay in the sociology of knowledge. *American Sociological Review*, 34: 863–877.

Petersen, W. 1969. *Population*. New York: Macmillan.

Peterson, J. 1972. Thunder out of Chinatown. *National Observer*, (March 8), 11: 1–18.

Petrie, A. 1967. *Individuality in pain and suffering*. Chicago: University of Chicago Press.

Philips, D. L. 1971. Sociologists and their knowledge. *American Behavioral Scientist*, 14: 563–582.

Philips, D. L. 1974. The influence of suggestion on suicide: Substantive and theoretical implications of the Werther effect. *American Sociological Review*, 39: 340–354.

Philips, D. L. 1977. Motor vehicle fatalities increase just after publicized suicide stories. *Science*, (June 24), 196: 1464–1465.

Philips, D. L. 1978. Airplane accident fatalities increase just after newspaper stories about murder and suicide. *Science*, 201: 748–750.

Philips, D. L. 1979. Suicide, motor vehicle fatalities, and the mass media: Evidence toward a theory of suggestion. *American Journal of Sociology*, 84: 1150–1174.

Philips, D. L. 1980. Airplane accidents, murder, and the mass media: Toward a theory of imitation and suggestion. *Social Forces*, 58: 1001–1024.

Philips, D. L. 1980. The deterrent effect of capital punishment: New evidence on an old controversy. *American Journal of Sociology*, 86: 139–148.

Philips, D. L. 1982. The impact of fictional television stories on U.S. adult fatalities: New evidence on the effect of the mass media on violence. *American Journal of Sociology*, 87: 1340–1359.

Phillips, L., and Votey, H. L. 1975. Crime control in California. *Journal of Legal Studies*, 4: 327–50.

Piliavin, I., and Briar, S. 1964. Police encounters with juveniles. *American Journal of Sociology*, 70: 206–214.

Pilon, R. 1978. Criminal remedies: Restitution, punishment, or both? *Ethics*, 87: 348–357.

Polk, K., and Schafer, W. E. (Eds.). 1972. *Schools and delinquency*. Englewood Cliffs, N. J.: Prentice-Hall.

Pollak, O. 1951. *The criminality of women*. Philadelphia: University of Pennsyvania Press.

Polsky, N. 1967. *Hustlers, beats, and others*. Chicago: Aldine.

Pope, C. E. 1975. *The judicial processing of assault and burglary offenders in selected California counties*. Washington, D.C.: U.S. Department of Justice.

Pope, C. E. 1975. *Offender-based transaction statistics: New directions in data collecting and reporting*. Washington, D.C.: U.S. Department of Justice.

Pope, C.E. 1975. *Sentencing of California felony offenders*. Washington, D.C.: U.S. Department of Justice.

Popham, R.E., and Schmidt, W. 1981. Words and deeds: The validity of self-report data on alcohol consumption. *Journal of Studies on Alcohol*, 42: 355–58.

Porterfield, A. L. 1946. *Youth in trouble*. Austin, Tex.: Leo Potishman Foundation.

Post, R. H. 1962a. Population differences in red and green color vision deficiency: A review, and a query on selection relaxation. *Eugenics Quarterly*, 9: 131–146.

Post, R. H. 1962b. Population differences in vision acuity: a review, with speculative notes on selection relaxation. *Eugenics Quarterly*, 9: 189–212.

Post, R. H. 1964. Hearing acuity variation among Negroes and whites. *Eugenics Quarterly*, 11: 65–81.

Postman, N. 1979. Order in the classroom! *Atlantic Monthly*, 244: 35–58.

Poulain, M., Riandey, B., and Firdion, J-M. 1991. Enquête biographique et registre Belge de Population: Une confrontation des données, *Population*, 46: 65–88.

Prinz, C. 1995. *Cohabiting, married or single*. Aldershot, U.K.: Avebury.

Proshansky, H. M., Ittelson, W.H., and Rivlin, L. G. 1970. Freedom of choice and behavior in a physical setting. In Proshansky, H. M., Ittelson, W.H., and Rivlin, L. G. (Eds.), *Environmental psychology: Man and his physical setting*. New York: Holt, Rinehart and Winston.

Proshansky, H. M., Ittelson, W.H., and Rivlin, L. G. 1970. The influence of the physical environment on behavior: Some basic assumptions. In Proshansky, H. M., Ittelson, W.H., and Rivlin, L. G. (Eds.), *Environmental psychology: Man and his physical setting*. New York: Holt, Rinehart and Winston.

Provine, W. B. 1973. Genetics and the biology of race crossing. *Science*, (November 23), 182: 790–796.

Pyle, D.J., and Deadman, D. F. 1994. Crime and the business cycle in post-war Britain. *British Journal of Criminology*, 34: 339–357.

Quay, H. C., et al. 1960. The interpretation of three personality factors in juvenile delinquency. *Journal of Consulting Psychology*, 24: 555.

Quinney, R. 1974. *Critique of legal order: Crime control in capitalist society*. Boston, Little Brown.

Quinney, R. 1974. The ideology of law: Notes for a radical alternative to legal oppression. In J. Susman (Ed.), *Crime and justice: 1971–1972*. New York: AMS Press.

Quinney, R. 1975. *Criminology: Analysis and critique of crime in America*. Boston: Little Brown.

Rachman, S. J., and G. T. Wilson. 1980. *The effects of psychological therapy*. (2nd ed.) London: Pergamon Press.

Rahav, G. 1980. Ethnic origins and the disposition of delinquents in Israel. *International Journal of Comparative and Applied Criminal Justice*, 4: 63–74.

Rankin, J. H., and Kern, R. 1994. Parental attachment and delinquency. *Criminology*, 32: 495–515.

Rauma, D. 1991. "The context of normative consensus: An expression of the Rossi/Berk consensus model, with an application to crime seriousness. *Social Science Research,* 20: 1–28.

Raybeck, D. 1991. Deviance, labelling theory and the concept of scale. *Anthropologica*, 33: 17–38.

Reckless, W. C. 1967. *The crime problem* (4th ed.). New York: Appleton-Century-Crofts.

Reckless, W. C., and Dinitz, S. 1967. Pioneering with the self-concept as a vulnerability factor in delinquency. *Journal of Criminal Law, Criminology and Police Science*, 58: 515–523.

Reed, J. S. 1975. *The enduring South: Subcultural persistence in mass society*. Chapel Hill: University of North Carolina Press.

Reed, J. S. 1980. Getting to know you: The contact hypothesis applied to the sectional beliefs and attitudes of white Southerners. *Social Forces*, 59: 123–235.

Reinhart, G. R. 1978. *Social and environmental aspects of self-destruction and homicide*. Paper read at the annual meeting of the Southern Sociological Society, New Orleans, (April 1).

Reiss, A. J., Jr. 1981. Foreword: Towards a revitalization of theory and research on victimization by crime. *Journal of Criminal Law and Criminology*, 71: 704–713.

Reiss, A. J., Jr., and Rhodes, A. L. 1961. The distribution of juvenile delinquency in the social class structure. *American Sociological Review*, 25: 720–732.

Repetto, T. A. 1974. *Residential Crime*. Cambridge, Mass.: Ballinger.

Reynolds, M. O. 1973. *The economics of criminal activity*. Andover, Mass.: Warner Modular Publications.

Reynolds, P., et al. 1973. *Victimization in a metropolitan region: Comparison of a central city area and a suburban community*. Minneapolis: Minnesota Center for Sociological Research, (Mimeograph).

Ribich, T. I. 1968. *Education and poverty*. Washington D.C.: Brookings Institute.

Rice, S. A. 1928. *Quantitative methods in politics*. New York: Knopf.

Rice, T. W., and Goldman, C. R. 1994. Another look at the subculture of violence thesis: Who murders whom and under what circumstances? *Sociological Spectrum*, 14: 371–384.

Riis, R. W. 1941a. The radio repair man will gyp you if you don't watch out. *Reader's Digest*, 39: 6–13.

Riis, R. W. 1941b. The repair man will gyp you if you don't watch out. *Reader's Digest*, 39: 1–6.

Riis, R. W. 1941c. The watch repair man will gyp you if you don't watch out. *Reader's Digest*, 39: 10–12.

Riley, M.W. 1963. *Sociological research. I. A case approach*. New York: Harcourt, Brace.

Rindfuss, R. R., and Bumpass, L. L. 1977. Fertility during marital disruption. *Journal of Marriage and Family*, 39: 517–518.

Rittenmeyer, S. D. 1981. Of battered wives, self-defense, and double standard of justice. *Journal of Criminal Justice*, 9: 389–395.

Roberts, D. 1997. Milgaard case puts strain on police. *Globe and Mail*, A1, (July 21).

Roberts, J. V. 1994. Crime and face statistics: Toward a Canadian solution. *Canadian Journal of Criminology*, 36: 175–185.

Robins, L. N. 1966. *Deviant children grown up*. Baltimore: Williams and Wilkins.

Robins, L. N., and O'Neal, P. 1958. Morality, mobility, and crime: Problem children thirty years later. *American Sociological Review*, 23: 162–171.

Robinson, W. S. 1950. Ecological correlations and behavior of individuals. *American Sociological Review*, 15: 351–357.

Rohrer, J. H., and Edmonson, M. S. (Eds.). 1960. *Eighth generation: Cultures and personalities of New Orleans Negroes*. New York: Harper.

Romanczyk, R. G., and Goren, E. R. 1975. Severe self-injurious behavior: The problem of clinical control. *Journal of Consulting and Clinical Psychology*, 43: 730–739.

Roncek, D. W. 1975. Density and crime. *American Behavioral Science*, 18: 843–860.

Rooney, E., and Gibbons, D. C. 1966. Social reactions to "crimes without victims". *Social Problems*, 13: 400–410.

Rose, A. 1961. Inconsistencies in attitudes toward Negro housing. *Social Problems*, 8: 286–292.

Rose A., and Pell, A. 1955. Does the punishment fit the crime? *American Journal of Sociology*, 61: 247–259.

Rosen, B. C. 1956. The achievement syndrome: A psychocultural dimension of social stratification. *American Sociological Review*, 21: 203–211.

Rosenfeld, A. 1981. Tippling enzymes. *Science*, 81: 24–25.

Rosenthal, D. 1970. *Genetic theory and abnormal behavior*. New York: McGraw-Hill.

Rothstein, E. 1961. *An analysis of status images as perception variables between delinquent and non-delinquent boys*. Doctoral dissertation, New York, New York University.

Rotter, J. G. 1966. Generalized expectancies for internal versus external control of reinforcement. *Psychological Monographs*, 80 (Whole No. 69).

Rountree, P. W., Land, K.C., Miethe, T. D. 1994. Macro-micro integration in the study of victimization. A hierarchical logistic model analysis across Seattle neighborhoods. *Criminology*. 32: 387–414.

Runciman, W.G. 1966. *Relative deprivation and social justice; A study of attitudes to social inequality in twentieth-century England*. London: Routledge and Kegan Paul.

Rushton, J. P. 1994. Race and crime: a reply to Cernovsky and Litman. *Canadian Journal of Criminology*, 36: 79–82.

Rutter, M. L. 1976. *The child, his family, and the community*. New York: Wiley.

Rutter, M. L., and Madge, N. 1976. *Cycles of disadvantage*. London: Heinemann.

Ryan E. D., and Foster, R. 1967. Athletic participation and perceptual augmentation and reduction. *Journal of Personality and Social Psychology*, 6: 471–476.

Ryan, E. D., and Kovacic, C. R. 1966. Pain tolerance and athletic participation. *Perceptual and Motor Skills*. 22: 383–390.

Ryle, G. 1949. *Concept of mind*. London: Hutchinson.

Sack, A. L. 1991. The underground economy in college football. *Sociology of Sport Journal*, 8: 1–15.

Sagarin, E. 1975. *Deviants and deviance: An introduction to the study of disvalued people and behavior*. New York: Praeger.

Sagarin, E. 1976. The high personal cost of wearing a label. *Psychology Today*, 9: 25–29.

Sagi, P. C., and Wellford, C. 1968. Age composition and patterns of change in criminal statistics. *Journal of Criminal Law, Criminology, and Police Science*, 59: 29–36.

Salmon, T. N., and Blakeslee, A. F. 1935. Genetics of sensory thresholds: Variations within single individuals in taste sensitivity for PTC. *Proceedings of the National Academy of Science*, 21: 78–83.

Salts, C. J., Lindholm, B. W., Goddard, H. W., and Duncan, S. 1995. Predictive variables of violent behavior in adolescent males. *Youth and Society*, 26: 377–399.

Sampson, R. J., Castellano, T. C., and Laub, J. H. 1981. *Juvenile criminal behavior and its relation to neighborhood characteristics*. Monograph five of analysis of national crime victimization survey data to study serious delinquent behavior. Albany: Criminal Justice Research Center.

Sampson, R. J., and Laub, J. H. 1993. *Crime in the making.* Cambridge Mass: Harvard University Press.

Santiago, L. P. 1973. *The children of Oedipus: Brother-sister incest in psychiatry, literature, history, and mythology.* Roslyn Heights, N.Y.: Libra.

Savitz, L. 1967. *Dilemmas in criminology.* New York: McGraw-Hill.

Sawyer, J. 1966. Measurement and prediction: Clinical and statistical. *Psychological Bulletin,* 66: 178–200.

Scheff, T. J. 1974. The labeling theory of mental illness. *American Sociological Review,* 39: 444–452.

Schelling, T. C. 1967. Economics and criminal enterprise. *Public Interest,* 7: 61–78.

Schelling, T. C. 1978. *Micromotives and macrobehavior.* New York: Norton.

Schippmann, J. S. and Prien, E.P. 1989. "An assessment of the contributions of general mental ability and personality characteristics to management success." *Journal of Business Psychology,* 3: 423–437.

Schloss, B., and Giesbrecht, N. A. 1972. *Murder in Canada: A report on capital and non-capital murder statistics, 1961–1970.* Toronto: University of Toronto, Centre of Criminology.

Schmeiser, D. A., et al. 1974. *The native offender and the law.* Ottawa: Information Canada.

Schmitt, R. C. 1955. Density, health and social disorganization. *Journal of American Institute Planners,* 32: 38–40.

Schmitt, R. C. 1966. Density, delinquency and crime in Honolulu. *Sociology and Social Research,* 41: 274–276.

Schneider, A.L. 1975. *Crime and victimization in Portland: Analysis of trends, 1971–1974.* Eugene: Oregon Research Institute.

Schneider, A. L., and Sumi, D. 1981. Patterns of forgetting and telescoping: An analysis of LEAA survey victimization data. *Criminology,* 19: 400–410.

Schoeck, H. 1966. *Envy: A theory of social behavior.* New York: Harcourt, Brace.

Schreiber, E. M. 1976. Dirty data in Britain and the USA: The reliability of "invariant" characteristics reported in surveys. *Public Opinion Qurterly,* 39: 493–506.

Schuckit, M. 1972. The woman alcoholic: A literature review. *Psychiatric Medicine,* 3: 37–44.

Schuerman, L., and Korbin, S. 1986. Community careers in crime. In Reiss, A. J. and Tonry, M. (Eds.) *Communities and crime.* Chicago: University of Chicago Press.

Schultz, H. D. 1972. *Panics and crashes and how you can make money out of them.* New Rochelle, N.Y.: Arlington.

Schuman, H., and Presser, S. 1981. *Questions and answers in attitude surveys: experiments on question form, wording and context.* New York: Academic Press.

Schumpeter, J. 1947. *Capitalism, socialism, and democracy* (2nd ed.). New York: Harper and Row.

Schur, E. M. 1965. *Crimes without victims: Deviant behavior and public policy.* Englewood Cliffs, N.J.: Prentice-Hall.

Schur, E. M. 1971. *Labelling deviant behavior: Its sociological implications.* New York: Harper.

Schur, E. M. 1973. Radical non-intervention: Rethinking in the delinquency problem. Englewood Cliffs, N.J.: Prentice Hall.

Schur, E. M. 1975. Comments. In W. R. Gove (Ed.), *The labelling of deviance: Evaluating a perspective.* New York: Wiley.

Schwartz, L. R. 1972. Conflict without violence and violence without conflict in a Mexican mestizo village. In Short, J. F. Jr. and M. E. Wolfgang (Eds.), *Collective violence.* Chicago: Aldine.

Schwartz, R. D., and Skolnick, J. H. 1962. Two studies of legal stigma. *Social Problems,* 10: 133–142.

Schwendinger, H., and Schwendinger, J. 1967. Delinquent stereotypes of probable victims. In M.W. Klein (Ed.), *Juvenile gangs in context: Theory, research, and action.* Englewood Cliffs, N.J.: Prentice-Hall.

Schwendinger, H., and Schwendinger, J. 1975. Defenders of order or guardians of human rights? In I. Taylor et al (Eds.), *Critical criminology.* Boston: Routledge and Kegan Paul.

Sclare, A. B. 1970. The female alcoholic. *British Journal of Addictions*, 65: 99–107.

Scott, R. A. 1969. *The making of blind men*. New York: Russell Sage.

Scriven, M. 1971. The logic of cause. *Theory and Decision*, 2: 49–56.

Sears, R. R. 1961. Relation of early socialization experiences to aggression in middle childhood. *Journal of Abnormal and Social Psychology*, 63: 466–492.

Security Sales Magazine. 1996 (August).

Security Sales. 1996. *Fact Book*.

Segall, H. 1924. Die Kriminalität der Juden in Deutschland während der Jahr 1915 under 1915 in Vergleich mit der Vorkriegszeit. *Zeitschrift*, 1.

Seidman, D. 1975. *The urban arms race: A quantitative analysis of private arming*. Doctoral dissertation, New Haven, Yale University, Department of Political Science.

Seidman, D., and Couzens, M. 1974. Getting the crime rate down: Political pressure and crime reporting. *Law and Society Review*, 8: 457–493.

Seligman, D. 1978. The news about education: I. *Fortune*, (September 24), 98: 35.

Seligman, D. 1981. Glum and dum. *Fortune*, (May 18), 103: 33.

Seligman, M. E. P. 1975. *Helplessness: On depression, development and death*. San Francisco: Freeman.

Seligman, M. E. P., and Hager, J. L. 1972. *Biological boundaries of learning*. New York: Appleton-Century-Crofts.

Sellin, T. 1937. *Research memorandum on crime in the Depression*, New York: Social Science Research Council.

Sellin, T. 1938. *Culture conflict and crime*. New York: Social Science Research Council.

Sellin, T., and Wolfgang, M. E. 1964. *The measurement of delinquency*. New York: Wiley.

Seltzer, A. R., and Beller, E. 1969. *Perception of time related to moral judgement and moral conduct*. Paper read at the annual meeting of the Eastern Psychological Association. Philadelphia.

Sewell, W. H. et al. 1969. The educational and early occupational attainment process. *American Sociological Review*, 34: 82–92.

Shannon, L. W. 1963. Types and patterns of delinquency referral in a middle-sized city. *British Journal of Criminology*, 4: 24–36.

Shannon, L. W. 1984. *The relationship of juvenile delinquency and adult crime to the changing ecological structure of the city*. Iowa City: Iowa Urban Community Research Center.

Shaw, C.R., and McKay, H. D. 1931. *Social factors in juvenile delinquency* (National Commission on Law Observance and Enforcement. Report on the Causes of Crime, No. 13). Washington, D.C.: U.S. Government Printing Office.

Shaw, C. R., and McKay, H. D. 1942. *Juvenile delinquency and urban areas*. Chicago: University of Chicago Press.

Shaw, J. M., and Scott, W. A. 1991. Influence of parent discipline style on delinquent behaviour: The mediating role of control orientation. *Australian Journal of Psychology*, 43: 61–67.

Sheldon, W. H. 1949. *Varieties of delinquent youth: An introduction to constitutional psychiatry*. New York: Harper.

Shenk, J. F., and McInerney, W. 1978. *Issues arising from applications of the National Crime Survey*. Paper read at the annual meeting of the Southwestern Political Science Association, Austin, Texas.

Shields, J. V. M., and Duncan, J. A. 1964. The state of crime in Scotland. London: Tavistock.

Shihadeh, E. S., and Steffensmeier, D. J. 1994. Economic inequality, family disruption, and urban black violence: Cities as units of stratification and social control. *Social Forces*, 73: 729–751.

Shils, E. 1972. *The intellectuals and the powers*. Chicago: University of Chicago Press.

Shiskin, J. 1976. Employment and unemployment: The doughnut or the hole? *Monthly Labor Review*, 99: 3–120.

Shoham, S. 1966. *Crime and social deviation*. Chicago: Regnery.

Shoham, S. 1970. *The mark of Cain: The stigma theory of crime and social deviation*. New York: Oceana.

Shupe, A. Stacey, W.A. and Hazelwood, L.R. 1987. *Violent men, violent couples: The dynamics of domestic violence*. Lexington, Mass.: Lexington Books.

Short, J. F. 1991. Poverty, ethnicity, and crime: Change and continuity in U.S. cities. *Journal of Research in Crime and Delinquency*, 28: 501–518.

Siegel, A. E., and Kohn, L. G. 1959. Permissiveness, permission, and aggression: The effect of adult presence or absence on aggression in children's play. *Child Development*, 30: 131–141.

Siegman, A. W. 1966. Effects of auditory stimulation and intelligence on time estimation in delinquents and nondelinquents. *Journal of Consulting Psychology*, 30: 320–328.

Silberman, C. E. 1978. *Criminal violence, criminal justice*. New York: Random House.

Silverman, R. A. 1980. Measuring crime: More problems. *Journal of Police Science and Administration*, 8: 265–274.

Silverman, R. A., and Teevan, J. L. J. (Eds.). 1980. *Crime in Canadian society* (2nd ed.). Toronto: Butterworth.

Simon, H. 1980. The attraction of property crimes to suburban localities. A revised economic model. *Urban Studies*, 17: 265–276.

Simon, H. A. 1958. *Administrative behavior: A study of decision-making processes in administrative organizations*. New York: Macmillan.

Simon, R. J. 1975. *Women and crime*. Lexington, Mass.: Lexington Books.

Simon, R. J., and Landis, J. M. 1989. Women's and men's attitudes about a woman's place and role. *Public Opinion Quarterly*, 53: 265–276.

Simon and Schuster, Inc., v. New York Crime Victims Board, 112 S. Ct. 501.

Simpson, S. N. 1994. Coverage of the Great Britain census of population and housing. *Journal of the Royal Statistical Society,* Series A, 157: 313–316.

Singh, A. 1979. Reliability and validity of self-reported delinquency studies: a review. *Psychological Reports*, 44: 987–993.

Sjoquist, D. L. 1973. Property crime and economic behavior: Some empirical results. *American Economic Review*, 63: 439–446.

Skelly, W. 1974. *The role of private police and security forces in the law enforcement picture of Canada*. Paper read at the Crime and Industry Seminar, Toronto.

Skinner, B. F. 1974. *About behaviorism*. New York: Knopf.

Skogan, W. G. 1974. The validity of official crime statistics: An empirical investigation. *Social Science Quarterly*, 55: 25–38.

Skogan, W. G. 1976. Crime and crime rates. In W.G. Skogan (Ed.), *Sample surveys of the victims of crime*. Cambridge, Mass.: Ballinger.

Smart, C. 1976. *Women, crime and criminology: A feminist critique*. London: Routledge and Kegan Paul.

Smandych, R., Lincoln, R., and Wilson, P. 1993. Toward a cross-cultural theory of an original crime: A comparative study of the problem of aboriginal overrepresentation in the criminal justice systems of Canada and Australia. *International Criminal Justice Review*, 3: 1.

Smigel, E. O., and Ross, H. L. (Eds.). 1970. *Crimes against bureaucracy*. New York: Van Nostrand Reinhold.

Smith, D. S. 1980. The long cycle in American illegitimacy and prenuptial pregnancy. In P. Laslett et al. (Eds.), *Bastardy and its comparative history*. London: Edward Arnold.

Smith, H. L. 1958. A comparison of interview and observational measures of mother behavior. *Journal of Abnormal and Social Psychology*, 47: 278–282.

Smith, K., and Glanz, L. 1989. Fear of crime among the South African public, *South African Journal of Sociology,* 20: 53–60.

Smith, L. N., and Hill, G. D. 1991. Perceptions of crime seriousness and fear of crime. *Sociological Focus,* 24: 315–327.

Smith, M. D., and Krichton, E. S. 1993. Trends in violent crime against women, 1973–89. *Social Science Quarterly*, 74: 28–45.

Smith, M. L., Glass, G. V., and Miller, T. I. 1980. *The benefits of psychotherapy*. Baltimore; Johns Hopkins University Press.

Smykla, J. O., and Willis, T. W. 1981. The incidence of learning disabilities and mental retardation in youth under the jurisdiction of the juvenile court. *Journal of Criminal Justice*, 9: 219–225.

Snyder, C. R. 1958. *Alcohol and the Jew: A cultural study of drinking and society*. Glencoe, Ill.: Free Press.

Socall, D. W., and Holtgraves, T. 1992. Attitudes toward the mentally ill. *Sociological Quarterly*, 33: 435–445.

Solicitor General, Canada. 1981. *The Young Offenders Act*. Ottawa: Minister of Supply and Services Canada.

Sollenberger, R. T. 1968. Chinese-American child rearing practices and juvenile delinquency. *Journal of Social Psychology*, 74: 13–23.

Solomon, D., and Kendall, A. J. 1979. *Children in classrooms: An investigation of the person-environment interaction*. New York: Praeger.

Solzhenitsyn, A. I. 1973. *The Gulag Archipelago, 1918–1956. An experiment in literary investigations* (3 vols.). New York: Harper and Row.

Solzhenitsyn, A. I. 1975. Words or warning to America. *U.S. News and World Report*, (July 14), 79: 44–50.

Sontag, L. W. 1963. Somatopsychics of personality and body function. *Vita Humana*, 6: 1–10.

Sorel, G. 1908. *Reflections on violence*. (Reprinted, 1950.) Glenco, Ill.: Free Press.

Souhrada, P. 1996. Compuserve eases access to adult material online. *Associated Press*, (February 14). [www2.phillynews.com/online/cyber/comp14.htm]

Sowell, T. 1981. *Ethnic America: A history*. New York: Basic Books.

Sowell, T. 1981. The uses of government for racial equality. *National Review*, (September 4), 33: 1009–1016.

Sparks, R. F. 1976. Crimes and victims in London. In W.G. Skogan (Ed.), *Sample surveys of the victims of crime*. Cambridge, Mass.: Ballinger.

Sparks, R. F., Genn, H. G., and Dodd, D. J. 1977. *Surveying victims: A study of the measurement of criminal victimization, perceptions of crime, and attitudes to criminal justice*. New York: Wiley.

Spencer, J. 1993. Criminal justice expenditure: A global perspective. *The Howard Journal*, 32: 1–11.

Spinley, B. M. 1964. *The deprived and the privileged*. London: Routledge and Kegan Paul.

Spitz, R. A. 1946. Hospitalism: A follow-up report. In R.S. Eissler, et al. (Eds.), *The psychoanalytic study of the child* (Vol. 2) New York: International Universities Press.

Spitz, R. A. 1965. *The first year of life: A psychoanalytic study of normal and deviant development of object relations*. New York: International Universities Press.

Spivak, J. 1979. Hungary's Gypsies, poor and unpopular, embarrass regime. *Wall Street Journal*, (June 11), 100: 25.

Spivak, J. 1979. Italy booms despite "crisis." *Wall Street Journal*, (July 18), 101: 18.

Srole, L., et al. 1962. *Mental health in the metropolis: The midtown Manhattan study* (Vol. 1). New York: McGraw-Hill.

Staats, C. K., and Staats, A. W. 1957. Meaning established by classical conditioning. *Journal of Experimental Psychology*, 54: 74–80.

Stacey, B. G. 1965. Some psychological aspects of intergeneration occupational mobility. *British Journal of Social and Clinical Psychology*, 4: 275–286.

Staples, R. 1976. *Introduction to Black sociology*. New York: McGraw-Hill.

Stark, R. 1987. Deviant places: a theory of the ecology of crime. *Criminology*, 25: 893–911.

Statistics Canada. 1993. *Ethnic Origin: The nation*. (Cat. No. 93–315). Ottawa.

Statistics Canada. 1994. *CANSIM*, matrices #2198 and #2199.

Statistics Canada. 1994. *Trends in criminal victimization: 1988–1993*. Ottawa: Ministry of Supply and Services. Statistics Canada Cat. No. 85–002.

Statistics Canada. 1995. *Canadian crime statistics 1994*, Ottawa: Minister of Industry.

Steffensmeier, D.J . 1978. Crime and the contemporary woman: An analysis of changing levels of female property crime, 1950–1975. *Social Forces*, 57: 566–584.

Steffensmeier, D. J. 1980. Sex differences in patterns of adult crime, 1965–1977: A review and assessment. *Social Forces*, 58: 1080–1108.

Steffensmeier, D. 1986. *The fence: In the shadow of two worlds*. Totawa, NJ: Rowman and Littlefield.

Steffensmeier, D. J. and Jordan, C. 1978. Changing patterns of female crime in rural America, 1962 –1975. *Rural Sociology*, 43: 87–102.

Steffensmeier, D. J., and Kokenda, K. 1979. *The views of contemporary thieves concerning patterns of female criminality*. Paper read at the annual meeting of the American Society of Criminology, Philadelphia, Pa.

Steffensmeier, D. J. and Steffensmeier, R. H. 1980. Trends in female delinquency: An examination of arrest, juveile court, self-report, and field data. *Criminology*, 18: 62–85.

Steffensmeier, D. J. 1993. National trends in female arrests, 1960–1990: Assessment and recommendations for research. *Journal of Quantitative Criminology*, 9: 411–441.

Steffensmeier, D. J., Streifel, C., and Shihadeh, E. S. 1992. Cohort size and arrest rates over the life course: The Easterline hypothesis reconsidered. *American Sociological Review*, 57: 306–314.

Stein, K. B., et al. 1968. Future time perspective: Its relation to the socialization process and the delinquent role. *Journal of Consulting and Clinical Psychology*, 32: 257–264.

Stephenson, R. M., and Scarpitti, F. R. 1968. Negro-white differentials and delinquency. *Journal of Research on Criminology and Delinquency*, 4: 122–133.

Stigler, G. J. 1970. The optimum enforcement of laws. *Journal of Political Economics*. 78: 526–536.

Stolz, S. B., et al. 1975. Behavior modification: A perspective on critical issues. *American Psychologist*, 30: 1027–1048.

Stouffer, S., et al. 1949. *The American soldier* (3 vols.). New York: Harper.

Straus, M. A. 1962. Deferred gratification, social class, and the achievement syndrome. *American Sociological Review*, 27: 326–335.

Straus, M. A., and Gelles, R. J. 1990. How violent are American families? Estimates from the National Family Violence Resurvey and other studies. In Straus, M. A. and Gelles, R. A. (Eds.) *Physical violence in American families*. New Brunswick, N.J.: Transaction.

Stricker, J. J., Jacobs, P. I., and Kogan, N. 1974. Trait interrelations in implicit personality theories and questionnaire data. *Journal of Personality and Social Psychology*, 30: 198–207.

Stycos, J. M., and Back, K. W. 1964. *The control of human fertility in Jamaica*. Ithaca, N.Y.: Cornell University Press.

Sudnow, D. 1966. *Passing on*. Englewood Cliffs, N.J.: Prentice-Hall.

Sullivan M. 1989. *Getting paid: Youth crime and work in the inter city*. Ithaca, New York: Cornell University Press.

Sumner, W. G. 1906. *Folkways: A study of the sociological importance of usages, manners, customs, mores and morals*. Boston: Ginn.

Sussman, F. B. 1959. *Law of juvenile delinquency*. New York: Oceana.

Sutherland, A. 1975. *Gypsies: The hidden Americans*. New York: Free Press.

Sutherland, E. H. 1949. *White collar crime*. New York: Dryden.

Sutherland, E. H., and Cressey, D. R. 1970. *Criminology* (8th ed.). Philadelphia: Lippincott.

Sutherland, E. H., and Cressey, D. R. 1978. *Criminology* (9th ed.). Philadelphia: Lippincott.

Sutherland, E. H., and Cressey, D. R. 1980. *Criminology* (10th ed.). Philadelphia: Lippincott.

Sutton, L. 1978. *Federal sentencing patterns: A study of geographical variations*. Washington, D.C.: National Criminal Justice Information and Statistics Service.

Sutton, W. 1976. *Where the money was: The memoirs of a bank robber* (with E. Linn). New York: Viking.

Svalastoga, K. 1956. Homicide and social contact in Denmark. *American Journal of Sociology*, 62: 37–41.

Sveri, K. 1966. Culture conflict and crime. In D. Schwarz (Ed.), *Svenska minoriteter*. Stockholm: Aldus.

Sveri, K. 1982. Comparative analyses of crime by means of victim surveys: The Scandinavian experience. In Schneider, H. J. (Ed.) *The Victim in international perspective.* Berlin: De Gruyter.

Sweet, L. 1991. Crime and race: A question of statistics. *Toronto Star*: (October 19).

Sykes, R., and Clarke, J. 1975. A theory of deference exchange in police-citizen encounters. *American Journal of Sociology*, 81: 584–600.

Sykes, R., Fox, J., and Clarke, J. 1976. A socio-legal theory of police discretion. In A. Niederhoffer and A. Blumberg (Eds.), *The ambivalent force* (2d ed.), Hinsdale, Ill.: Dryden.

Synnott, A. 1996. *Shadows: Issues and social problems in Canada.* Scarborough, Ontario: Prentice Hall.

Szasz, T. S. 1961. *The myth of mental illness: Foundations of a theory of personal conduct.* New York: Hoeber-Harper.

Szasz, T. S. 1963. Our despotic laws destroy the right to self-control. *Psychology Today*, 8: 19–29, 127.

Taft, D. R. 1946. The punishment of war criminals. *American Sociological Review*, 11: 439–444.

Taggart, R. 1972. *The prison of unemployment: Manpower programs for offenders.* Baltimore: Johns Hopkins University Press.

Tagiuri, R. 1969. Person perception. In G. Lindzey and E. Aronson (Eds.), *Handbook of social psychology* (Vol. 3). Reading, Mass.: Addison-Wesley.

Tanay, E. 1979. The Baxtrom affair and psychiatry. *Journal of Forensic Sciences*, 24: 663–672.

Tangri, S. S., and Schwartz, M. 1967. Delinquency and the self-concept variable. *Journal of Criminal Law, Criminology, and Police Science*, 58: 182–190.

Tannenbaum, F. 1938. *Crime and the community.* Boston: Ginn.

Tanner, Julian. 1996. *Teenage troubles: Youth and deviance in Canada.* Toronto: Nelson Canada.

Tappan, P. W. 1947. Who is the criminal? *American Sociological Review*, 12: 96–102.

Tarde, G. 1890. *La criminalité comparée* (2nd ed.). Paris: Alcan.

Tarling, R. 1982. Unemployment and crime. *Home office Research Bulletin*, 14: 28–33.

Taylor, I., Walton, P., and Young, J. 1973. *The new criminology: For a social theory of deviance.* London: Routledge and Kegan Paul.

Taylor, J. B. 1978. Economic models of criminal behavior: An overview. In J. B. Taylor (Ed.) *Economic models of criminal behavior*, Amsterdam: North-Holland.

Taylor, S. J. 1982. Too much justice. *Harper's*, 265: 56–66.

Teahan, J. E. 1958. Future time perspective, optimism, and academic achievement. *Journal of Abnormal and Social Psychology*, 57: 379–380.

Terman, L. M., and Oden, M. H. 1947. *Genetic studies of genius. Vol. IV: The gifted child grows up. Twenty-five years' follow-up of a superior group.* Stanford: Stanford University Press.

Terman, L. M., and Oden, M. H. 1959. *Genetic studies of genius. Vol. V: The gifted group at mid-life: Thirty-five years' follow-up of the superior child.* Stanford: Stanford University Press.

Terry, R. M. 1967. Discrimination in the handling of juvenile offenders by social-control agencies. *Journal of Research on Criminology and Delinquency*, 4: 218–230.

Theis, S. van S. 1924. *How foster children turn out.* New York: State Charities Aid Association.

Thernstrom, S. (Ed.). 1981. *Harvard encyclopedia of American ethnic groups.* Cambridge, Mass.: Harvard University Press.

Thomas, A. E. 1972. Community power and student right. *Harvard Educational Review* 42: 173–216.

Thomas, C. W. 1976. Public opinion on criminal law and legal sanctions: An examination of two conceptual models. *Journal of Criminal Law and Criminology*, 67: 110–116.

Thomas, D. S. 1925. *Social aspects of the business cycle*, London: Routledge and Kegan Paul.

Thomas, W. I., and Thomas, D. S. 1928. *The child in America: Behavior problems and programs.* New York: Knopf.

Thompson, G. G., and Hunicutt, C. W. 1944. The effect of repeated praise or blame on the work achievement of "introverts" and "extroverts." *Journal of Educational Psychology*, 35: 257–266.

Thompson, H. S. 1966. *Hell's Angels: A strange and terrible saga.* New York: Random House.

Thompson, P. G. 1971. Some factors in upward social mobility in England. *Sociology and Social Research*, 55: 181–190.

Thon, J. 1907. Kriminalität der Christen und Juden in Ungarn im Jahre 1904. *Zeitschrift*, 2: 16–26.

Thornberry, T.P. 1973. Race, socioeconomic status, and sentencing in the juvenile justice system. *Journal of Criminal Law and Criminology*, 64: 90–98.

Thornberry, T. P., and Farnworth, M. 1982. Social correlates of criminal involvement: Further evidence on the relationship between social status and criminal behavior. *American Sociological Review*, 47: 505–518.

Thorngate, W. 1976. Must we always think before we act? *Personality and Social Psychology Bulletin*, 2: 31–35.

Thurow, L. 1973. Toward a definition of economic justice. *Public Interest*, 32: 56–80.

Tiffany, L., Avichai, Y., and Peters, G. 1975. A statistical analysis of sentencing in federal courts: Defendants convicted after trial, 1967–68. *Journal of Legal Studies*, 4: 369–390.

Timbrell, M. 1990. Does unemployment lead to crime? *Journal of Interdisciplinary Economics*, 3: 332–424.

Tittle, C. R. 1975. Labelling and crime: An empirical evaluation. In W. R. Gove (Ed.), *Labelling of deviance: Evaluating a perspective.* New York: Wiley.

Tittle, C. R., and Meier, R. F. 1991. Specifying the SES/delinquency relationship by social characteristics of contexts, *Journal of Research in Crime and Delinquency*, 28: 430–455.

Tittle, C. R., and Villemez, W. J. 1977. Social class and criminality. *Social Forces*, 56: 475–502.

Tittle, C. R., Villemez, W. J., and Smith, D. A. 1978. The myth of social class and criminality: An empirical assessment of the empirical evidence. *American Sociological Review*, 43: 643–656.

Toby, J. 1950. Comment on the Jonassen-Shaw and McKay controversy. *American Sociological Review*, 15: 107–108.

Toby, J. 1957. The differential impact of family disorganization. *American Sociological Review*, 22: 505–512.

Toby, J. 1980. Crime in American public schools. *Public Interest*, 58: 18–42.

de Tocqueville, A. 1955. *The old regime and the French revolution.* Garden City, N.Y.: Doubleday.

Toro-Calder, J., et al. 1968. A comparative study of Puerto Rican attitudes toward the legal system dealing with crime. *Journal of Criminal Law, Criminology and Police Science*, 59: 536–541.

Tracy, P. E., and Fox, J. A. The validity of randomized response for sensitive measurement. *American Sociological Review*, 46: 187–200.

Tracy, P. E., and Kempf-Leonard, K. 1996. *Continuity and discontinuity in criminal careers.* New York: Plenum Press.

Tracy, P. E., Wolfgang, M. E., and Figlio, R. M. 1990. *Delinquency careers in two birth cohorts,* New York: Plenum Press.

Trasler, G. 1962. *The explanation of criminality.* London: Routledge and Kegan Paul.

Trivizias, E. 1980. Offences and offenders in football crowd disorders. *British Journal of Criminology*, 20: 276–288.

Tuchman, B.W. 1972. *Notes from China.* New York: Collier.

Tufte, E. R. 1974. *Data analysis for politics and policy.* Englewood Cliffs, N.J.: Prentice-Hall.

Turban, D. B. and Dougherty, T. W., 1994. Role of protégé personality in receipt of mentoring and career success. *Academy of Management Journal,* 37: 688–702.

Turk, A. T. 1969. *Criminality and legal order.* Chicago: Rand-McNally.

Turner, R. H. 1969. The public perception of protest. *American Sociological Review*, 34: 815–831.

Turner, R. H. 1972. Deviance avowal as neutralization of commitment. *Social Problems*, 19: 308, 321.

Turner, S. 1969. The ecology of delinquency. In Sellin T., and Wolfgant M. E., (Eds.), *Delinquency: Selected studies.* New York: Wiley.

Ullerstam, L. 1966. *The erotic minorities*. New York: Grove.

United Kingdom, Home Office. 1996. *Criminal statistics England and Wales, 1995*. London, Command Paper 3421.

United Nations. 1953. *Comparative survey of juvenile delinquency. Part I: North America*. New York: United Nations.

United Nations. 1960. *Estudio conpardo sobre delincuencia juvenil. Parte III: America Latina*. New York: United Nations.

United Nations. 1965. *Comparative survey on juvenile delinquency. Part V: Middle East*. New York: United Nations.

United Nations. 1965. *Third United Nations Congress on the prevention of crime and the treatment of offenders. Report by the secretariat*. New York: United Nations.

United Nations. 1995. *World urbanization prospects: The 1994 Revision*. New York: Dept. For Economic and Social Information and Policy Analysis.

United Nations. 1996. *Human Development Report, 1996*. New York: Oxford University Press.

United Nations. 1997. *Demographic Yearbook, 1995*. New York: United Nations Publishing Division.

United States Bureau of the Census. 1996. *Statistical Abstract of the United States*. Washington, D.C.: U.S. Government Printing Office.

United States Department of Justice, Bureau of Justice Statistics. 1995. *Criminal Victimization in the United States*. Washington, D.C.: U.S. Department of Justice.

United States Department of Labor. 1976. *BLS handbook of methods for surveys and studies*. Washington, D.C.: U.S. Government Printing Office.

United States Department of Education. 1997. *Pursuing excellence: A study of U.S. eighth-grade mathematics and science teaching, learning, curriculum, and achievement in international context*. Washington, D.C.: National Center for Education Statistics.

U.S. News and World Report. 1973. Combatting crooks overseas. (December 10), 75: 108.

U.S. News and World Report. 1975. The American home under seige. (February 24), 78: 41–42.

U.S. News and World Report. 1975. Crimes by women are on the rise all over the world. (December 22), 79: 50–51.

Valentine, P. W. 1971. D.C. crime reports: What they mean. *Washington Post*, (October 26), p. 12.

Vandenberg, S. G. 1966. Contributions of twin research to psychology. *Psychological Bulletin*, 66: 327–352.

van Dijk, J. J. M. 1994. Understanding crime rates: On the interactions between rational choices of victims and offenders. *British Journal of Criminology*, 34: 105–121.

van Dijk, J. J. M., Mayhew, P., and Killias, M. 1990. *Experiences of crime across the world: Key findings from the 1989 International Crime Survey*. Boston: Kluwer.

van Stolk, M. 1972. *The battered child in Canada*. Toronto: McClelland and Stewart.

van Stolk, M. 1978. Testimony before Canadian Senate. *Canadian Press*, (July 1).

Venable, V. 1945. *Human nature: The Marxian view*. New York: Knopf.

Vera Institute of Justice. 1977. *Felony arrests: Their prosecution and disposition in New York City's courts*. New York: The Vera Institute.

Verkko, V. 1951. *Homicides and suicides in Finland and their dependence on national character*. Copenhagen: G.E.C. Gads Forlag.

Vernon, P. E. 1979. *Intelligence: Heredity and environment*. San Francisco: Freeman.

Vislick-Young, P. 1930. Urbanization as a factor in juvenile delinquency. *Publications of the American Sociological Society*, 24: 162–166.

Visser, M. 1994. Beyond the ecological fallacy: The Duncan-Davis technique of ecological inference. *Quality and Quantity*, 28: 435–444.

Vold, G. B. 1958. *Theoretical criminology*. New York: Oxford University Press.

Vold, G. B., and Bernard, T. J. 1979. *Theoretical criminology* (2nd. ed.). New York: Oxford University Press.

Vold, G. B., and Bernard, T. J. 1986. *Theoretical criminology* (3rd. ed.). New York: Oxford University Press.

von Mayr, G. 1917. *Statistik und Gesellschaftslehre*. Tubingen: Mohr.

von Mises, L. 1960. The resentment and the anti-capitalistic bias of American intellectuals. In G. B. Huszar (ed.), *The intellectual: A controversial portrait*. Glencoe, Ill.: Free Press.

Voss, H. L. 1963. Ethnic differentials in delinquency in Honolulu. *Journal of Criminal Law, Criminology, and Police Science*, 54: 322–327.

Votey, H. L. 1991. Employment, age, race, and crime: A labor theoretic investigation. *Journal of Quantitative Criminology*, 7: 123–153.

Wade v. United States. 1970. *Federal Reporter* (2d series), 426: 64–86.

Walker, N. 1971. *Crimes, courts, and figures: An introduction to criminal statistics*. Harmondsworth, England: Penguin.

Wall Street Journal. 1970. Rising crime rates make it harder for many employers to hire help. (February 10), 81: 1.

Wallace, J., and Mangan, M. 1996. *Sex laws and cyberspace*, New York: Henry Holt and Co.

Wallerstein, J. A., and Wyle, C. J. 1947. Our law-abiding law-breakers. *Federal Probation*, 25: 107–112.

Wallis, C. P., and Maliphant, R. 1967. Delinquent areas in the county of London: Ecological factors. *British Journal of Criminology*, 7: 250–284.

Walsh, A. 1991. Race and discretionary sentencing: An analysis of obvious and nonobvious cases. *International Journal of Offender Therapy and Comparative Criminology*, 35: 7–19.

Walsh, D. 1986. Victim selection procedures among economic criminals: The rational choice perspective. In Cornish, D. B. and Clarke, R. V. *The reasoning criminal: Rational choice perspectives on offending*, New York: Springer-Verlag.

Walters, R. H., et al. 1962. Enhancement of punitive behavior by audio-visual displays. *Science*, 136: 872–873.

Ward, R. H. 1971. Labeling theory: A critical analysis. *Criminology*, 9: 268–290.

Warner, N. M. 1979. *Shoplifters in bigstore*. Master of Arts dissertation, Edmonton, University of Alberta, Department of Sociology.

Warner, W. L. 1953. *American life: Dream and reality*. Chicago: University of Chicago Press.

Warner, W. L., and Abegglen, J. 1955. *Big business leaders in America*. New York: Harper and Row.

Warr, M. 1993. Age, peers, and delinquency. *Criminology*, 31: 17–40.

Warr, M., and Stafford, M. 1991. The influence of delinquent peers: What they think or what they do? *Criminology*, 29: 851–865.

Weaver, C. N., and Swanson, C. L. 1974. Validity of reported date of birth, salary, and seniority. *Public Opinion Quarterly*, 38: 69–80.

Weaver, P. H. 1975. The hazards of trying to make consumer products safer. *Fortune*, 92: 132–140.

Webb, E. J., et al. 1966. *Unobtrusive measures: Nonreative research in the social sciences*. Chicago: Rand McNally.

Weil, S. 1952. *The need for roots*. Boston: Beacon Press.

Weinberg, S. K. 1955. *Incest behavior*. New York: Citadel.

Weiner, N. L., and Willie, C. V. 1971. Decision by juvenile officers. *American Journal of Sociology*, 77: 199–210.

Weirs, P. 1945. Wartime increase in Michigan delinquency. *American Sociological Review*, 10: 515–523.

Weissman, H. H. (Ed.). 1969. *Justice and the law in the mobilization for youth experience*. New York: Association Press.

Wells, L. E., and Rankin, J. H. 1991. Families and delinquency. A meta-analysis of the impact of broken homes. *Social Problems*, 38: 71–93.

Wenzky, O. 1965. Analyse zur auslander Kriminalitat. *Kriminalistic*, 1: 1–5.

Wertheimer, M. 1955. Figural after-effect as a measure of metabolic deficiency. *Journal of Personality*, 24: 56–73.

Wessman, A. E., and Ricks, D. F. 1966. *Mood and personality*. New York: Holt.

West, D. J., and Farrington, D. P. 1977. *The delinquent way of life*. London: Heinemann.

Wetzel, J. 1975. *Unemployment measurement and meaning*. Paper read at the thirtieth annual meeting of the American Association for Public Opinion and Research. Itasca, Ill.

Wheeler, L., and Caggiula, A. R. 1966. The contagion of aggression. *Journal of Experimental Social Psychology*, 2: 1–10.

White, K. R. 1982. The relation between socioeconomic status and academic achievement. *Psychological Bulletin*, 91: 461–481.

White, S. B., Reynolds, P. D., Thomas, M. M., and Gitzlaff, N. J. 1993. *Socioeconomic status and achievement revisited*. Urban Education, 28: 328–343.

Whitehead, P. C., and Hayes, M. 1998. *The insanity of alcohol: Social problems in Canadian First Nations communities*. Toronto: Canadian Scholars' Press.

Whiting, J. M. W. 1944. The frustration complex in Kwoma society, *Man*, 44: 113–121.

Wicker, A. W. 1969. Attitudes versus actions. *Journal of Social Issues*, 25: 42–78.

Wicker, A. W. 1971. An examination of the "other variables" explanation of attitiude-behavior inconsistency. *Journal of Personality and Social Psychology*, 19: 18–30.

Wiggins, N., and Kohen, E. S. 1971. Man versus model of man revisited: The forecasting of graduate school success, *Journal of Personality and Social Psychology*, 19: 100–106.

Wilbanks, W., and Lewis, R. 1981. *Racial bias in the processing of complaints about excessive force by police officers: An empirical examination of data from two police departments in Dade Country, Florida, 1974–1980*. Paper presented at the annual meeting of the American Society of Criminology. Washington, D.C., (November 13).

Wilde, O. 1892. *Lady Windermere's fan*. London: Methuen. (Reprinted, 1966.)

Wilkins, J. L., et al. 1974. Personality type, reports of violence, and aggressive behavior. *Journal of Personality and Social Psychology*, 30: 243–247.

Wilkins, L. T. 1968. The concept of cause in criminology. *Issues in Criminology*, 3: 147–165.

Wilkins, L. T. 1969. *Evaluation of penal measures*. New York: Random House.

Williams, G. 1955. The definition of crime. *Current Legal Problems*, 8: 107–130.

Williams, R. J. 1979. *Free and unequal: The biological basis of individual liberty*. Indianapolis: Liberty Press.

Williams, R. L. 1974. Scientific racism and I.Q.: The silent mugging of the black community. *Psychology Today*, 7: 32–41.

Williams, W. 1982. The week (Cited by the editors). *National Review*, (March 5), 34: 205.

Willie, C. V., Gershenovitz, A. 1964. Juvenile delinquency in racially mixed areas. *American Sociological Review*, 29: 740–744.

Willing, M. K. 1971. *Beyond conception: Our children's children*. Boston: Gambit.

Willis, P. 1977. *Learning to labour: How working-class kids get working-class jobs*. Aldershot: Gower Publishing.

Willmott, P. 1966. *Adolescent boys in East London*. London: Routledge and Kegan Paul.

Wilson, B. 1997. The high cost of auto theft. *Consumer Information*, Insurors of Tennessee. [www.iiaa.iix.com/caretheft.htm].

Wilson, E. O. 1975. *Sociobiology: The new synthesis*. Cambridge, Mass.: Harvard University Press.

Wilson, J. Q., and Herrnstein, R. J. 1985. *Crime and human nature*, New York: Simon and Schuster.

Wilson, W. J. 1978. *The declining significance of race: Blacks and changing American institutions*. Chicago: University of Chicago Press.

Wirth, L. 1929. *The ghetto*. Chicago: University of Chicago Press.

Wisher, C. 1974. The teenage shoplifter. In Hughes, M. M., (Ed.), *Successful retail security*. Los Angeles: Security World.

Withery, S. B. 1954. Reliability of recall of income. *Public Opinion Quarterly*, 18: 197–204.

Witkin, H. A. 1965. Psychological differentiation and forms of pathology. *Journal of Abnormal Psychology*, 70: 317–336.

Witkin, H. A., and Berry, J. W. 1975. Psychological differentiation in cross-cultural perspective. *Journal of Cross-Cultural Psychology*, 6: 4–87.

Witkin, H. A., et al. 1962. *Psychological differentiation*. New York: Wiley.

Witkin, H. A., et al. 1974. *Psychological differentiation*. (Rev. of 1972 work.) Potomac, Md.: Erlbaum.

Witkin, H. A., et al. Psychological differentiation: Current status. *Journal of Personality and Social Psychology*, 37: 1127–1145.

Wohlwill, J. F. 1980. Cognitive development in childhood. In O. G. Brim, Jr., and J. Kagan (Eds.), *Constancy and change in human development*. Cambridge, Mass.: Harvard University Press.

Wolf, D.R. 1991. *The Rebels: A brotherhood of outlaw bikers*. Toronto: University of Toronto Press.

Wolf, P. 1965. A contribution to topology of crime in Denmark. In K. O. Christiansen et al. (Eds.), *Scandinavian studies in criminology* (Vol. 1). London: Tavistock.

Wolf, P. 1972. *Violence in Denmark and Finland 1970/1971: A comparison of victims of violence*. Copenhagen: Scandinavian Research Council for Criminology. (Mimeograph)

Wolfgang, M. E. 1958. *Patterns in criminal homicide*. Philadelphia: University of Pennsylvania Press.

Wolfgang, M. E. 1966. Race and crime. In H. J. Sklare (Ed.), *Changing concepts of crime and its treatment*. London: Pergamon.

Wolfgang, M. E. 1968. Urban crime. In J. Q. Wilson (Ed.), *The metropolitan enigma*. Cambridge, Mass.: Harvard University Press.

Wolfgang, M. E. 1974. The social scientist in court. *Journal of Criminal Law and Criminology*, 65: 239–247.

Wolfgang, M. E., and Ferracuti, F. 1967. *The subculture of violence: Towards an integrated theory of criminology*. London: Tavistock.

Wolfgang, M. E., Figlio, R. M., and Sellin, T. 1972. *Delinquency in a birth cohort*. Chicago: University of Chicago Press.

Won, G., and Yamamoto, G. 1968. Social structure and deviant behavior: A study of shoplifting. *Sociology and Social Research*, 53: 44–55.

Wonderly, D. M. 1996. *The selfish gene pool*. Lanham, MD: University Press of America.

Wood, A. A. 1961. Socio-structural analysis of murder, suicide, and economic crime in Ceylon. *American Sociological Review*, 26: 744–753.

Yarrow, M. R., et al. 1968. *Child rearing: An inquiry into research and methods*. San Francisco: Jossey-Bass.

Yochelson, S., and Samenow, S. E. *The criminal personality* (3 vols). New York: Jason Aronson.

Youell, K. J., and McCullough, J. P. 1975. Behavioral treatment of muscous colitis. *Journal of Consulting and Clinical Psychology*, 43: 740–745.

Young, J. 1981. Thinking seriously about crime: Some models of criminology. In M. Fizgerald et al. (Eds.), *Crime and society: Readings in history and theory*. London: Routledge and Kegan Paul.

Zellner, W. W. 1995. Counterfultures: A sociological analysis. New York: St. Martin's Press.

Zerubavel, E. 1982. Calendars and group identity. *American Sociological Review*, 47: 284–289.

Zhang, L., and Messner, S. F. 1994. The severity of official punishment for delinquency and change in interpersonal relations in Chinese society. *Journal of Research in Crime and Delinquency*, 32: 416–433.

Zimmerman, H. G. 1966. Die kriminalitat der auslandichern arbeiter. *Kriminalistik*, 2: 623–625.

Zingraff, M. T., Leiter, J., Johnsen, M. C., and Myers, K. A. 1994. The mediating effect of good school performance on the maltreatment-delinquency relationship. *Journal of Research in Crime and Delinquency*, 31: 62–91.

Zunich, M. 1962. Relationship between maternal behavior and attitudes toward children. *Journal of Genetic Psychology*, 100: 155–165.

Index

Deviance, sympathy for, 349–351
Dictionary of Criminology, 178
Differential-association hypothesis
    criticism of, 339–343
    culture conflict and, 338
    defined, 337–338
    individual differences and, 339
    overemphasis on words of, 343
    poor advice of, 340
    prevention of embezzlement
        example, 340–342
Differential-association theory, 381
Divorce, crime and, 308–309
Domestic violence, 17, 273–275
Duress, crime under, 29
Durkheim, Emile, 279

Ecological fallacy, 196
Ecological studies
    around the world, 176–177
    continuity of correlations in, 175–176
    social status and, 177–178
Economic models
    crime production and, 254–255
    designing, 244
    See also Macrorationality; Microeconomic
        rationality
Economic studies
    difficulties of, 184–185
    measures, troubles with and, 185–187
    theories, difficulties of, 185
Embezzlement, prevention of, example,
    340–342
England
    Commercial Victimization Survey, 1994,
        93
    juvenile delinquency, broken homes and,
        227
    social class in, 324–325
Equality
    changing sex ratios in crime and, 137–139
    convergence hypothesis and, 139–142
Essays of Crime and Punishment (Beccaria),
    235
Ethnic differentials
    European crime rates and, 149–150
    interpretation of, 155–156
    Israeli crime rates and, 148–149
    jail sentences and, 361
    New Zealand crime rates and, 150
    North American crime rates and, 151–155
Ethnic groups, conflict between, 326
Ethnicity
    stereotypes and, 147
    understanding, 145–146
    See also Cultural contact
Ethnicity and crime
    arguments against study of, 146

arguments for study of, 146–148
Ethnocentrism, 353
Europe, ethnic differentials in crime rates in,
    149–150
European studies of victims, 103

Farrakhan, Louis, 375
Feminist explanations of crime, 272–273
    domestic violence and, 273–275
    power-control theory and, 273
    focal concerns, 323
Free speech, 16
Freud, Sigmund, 201
Frustration, 88

Gangs, study of, 74–75
Germany, subcultures in, 325
Ghettos
    crime and, 159–160, 162
    defined, 157
    versus slum, 157–159

Hate literature, Canadian law and, 16
Hedonistic calculus, utility theory and,
    236–237
Helms-Burton Law, 18
Hinckley, Jr., John W., 35–36
Holmes, Jr., Oliver Wendell, 26
Homicide, vocabulary of, 4–5
Household victimizations
    urbanism and, 165–166
Human capital, 239
Human ecology, 284–286

Incidence, 43
Inequality, social. *See* Social inequality
Injured party. *See* Vice; Victimless vice
Insanity defense, 32–38
    debate on, 37–38
    McNaughton rules and, 33–35
    moral considerations for, 32
    substantial capacity test and, 35–36
    tests of insanity and, 33–34
Insularity, density, crowding and, 168
Insurance fraud example, 7–8
Intelligence
    learning and, 210–212
    role of in criminals and, 211–212
Intention
    crime and, 26–27
    defined, 27–28
    versus movers of action, 28
Interactionist perspective, 335–336
International comparisons
    social inequality, 306–307
    of victims, 103–105
International comparisons
    of crimes, 68–70

Other Criminal Justice Books from Butterworth-Heinemann

Contemporary Criminal Law
David T. Skelton
1997   400pp   pb   0-7506-9811-X

Crime and Justice in America: A Human Perspective, Fifth Edition
Leonard Territo, James B. Halsted and Max L. Bromley
1998   707pp   hc   0-7506-7011-8

Criminal Investigation: Law and Practice
Michael F. Brown
1997   368pp   pb   0-7506-9665-6

Criminal Justice Statistics: A Practical Approach
Arthur J. Lurigio, M.L. Dantzker, Magnus J. Seng, and James M. Sinacore
1996   296pp   hc   0-7506-9672-9

The Juvenile Justice System: Law and Process
Mary Clement
1996   345pp   hc   0-7506-9810-1

Detailed information on these and all other BH-Criminal Justice titles may be found in the our catalog (Item #800). To request a copy, call 1-800-366-2665. You can also visit our web site at: http://www.bh.com

These books are available from all good bookstores or in case of difficulty call: 1-800-366-2665 in the U.S. or +44-1865-310366 in Europe.

E-Mail Mailing List
An e-mail mailing list giving information on latest releases, special promotions/ offers and other news relating to Butterworth-Heinemann Criminal Justice titles is available. To subscribe, send an e-mail message to majordomo@world.std.com. Include in message body (not in subject line) subscribe bh-criminal-justice